A MANUAL ON METHODS FOR THE ASSESSMENT OF SECONDARY PRODUCTIVITY IN FRESH WATERS

A Manual on Methods for the Assessment of Secondary Productivity in Fresh Waters

EDITED BY

JOHN A. DOWNING

Departement de Sciences Biologique
Université de Montréal
and Biology Department
McGill University
Montréal, Québec, Canada

AND

FRANK H. RIGLER

Biology Department
McGill University
Montréal, Québec, Canada

SECOND EDITION

IBP
HAND
BOOK
17

BLACKWELL SCIENTIFIC PUBLICATIONS

OXFORD LONDON EDINBURGH
BOSTON MELBOURNE

© 1971, 1984 by
Blackwell Scientific Publications
Editorial offices:
Osney Mead, Oxford OX2 0EL
8 John Street, London, WC1N 2ES
9 Forrest Road, Edinburgh, EH1 2QH
52 Beacon Street, Boston
    Massachusetts 02108, USA
99 Barry Street, Carlton
    Victoria 3053, Australia

First published 1971
Second edition 1984

Printed in Great Britain by
Galliard (Printers) Ltd
Great Yarmouth, Norfolk

DISTRIBUTORS

USA
    Blackwell Mosby Book Distributors
    11830 Westline Industrial Drive
    St Louis, Missouri 63141

Canada
    Blackwell Mosby Book Distributors
    120 Melford Drive, Scarborough
    Ontario, M1B 2X4

Australia
    Blackwell Scientific Book
        Distributors
    31 Advantage Road, Highett
    Victoria 3190

British Library
Cataloguing in Publication Data
A Manual on methods for the assessment
    of secondary productivity in fresh
    waters.—2nd ed.
    1. Freshwater productivity—
    Measurement
    I. Downing, John A.   II. Rigler,
    Frank, H.
    574.5′2632   QH541.5.F7

ISBN 0-632-00616-1

To Frank

'The wrong view of science betrays itself in the craving to be right; for it is not his *possession* of knowledge, of irrefutable truth, that makes the man of science, but his persistent and recklessly critical *quest* for truth.'

Karl R. Popper
The Logic of Scientific Discovery
Harper & Row, New York

Contents

Chapter 7 continued

Ellie E. Prepas

Contributors

I. J. DAVIES *Freshwater Institute, 501 University Crescent, Winnipeg, Manitoba, Canada R3T 2N6*

R. DE BERNARDI *Istituto Italiano di Idrobiologia, Consiglio Nazionale delle Ricerche, 28048 Pallanza, Italy*

J. A. DOWNING *Université de Montréal, Departement de Sciences Biologiques, C.P. 6128, Succursale 'A', Montréal, Québec, Canada H3C 3J7; and McGill University, Department of Biology*

W. LAMPERT *Max-Planck-Institut für Limnologie, Postfach 165, D-2320 Plön, West Germany*

E. McCAULEY *Department of Biological Sciences, University of California, Santa Barbara, California 93106, USA*

B. L. PECKARSKY *Cornell University, Department of Entomology, Comstock Hall, Ithaca, New York 14853, USA*

R. H. PETERS *McGill University, Department of Biology, 1205 Avenue Docteur Penfield, Montréal, Québec, Canada H3A 1B1*

E. E. PREPAS *The University of Alberta, Department of Zoology, Biological Sciences Centre, Edmonton, Alberta, Canada T6G 2E9*

F. H. RIGLER *McGill University, Department of Biology, 1205 Avenue Docteur Penfield, Montréal, Québec, Canada H3A 1B1.*

CONTRIBUTORS TO FIRST EDITION

The following scientists contributed principal parts of the text, were chairmen of working groups, or both.

Blažka P.	Kajak Z.	Patalas K.
Brinkhurst R.	Klekowski R.	Pieczyńska E.
Cassie R.M.	Kořinek V.	Richman S.
Cooper W.E.	Ladle M.	Rigler F.H.
Edmondson W.T.	Lawton J.	Ruttner-Kolisko A.
Fischer Z.	Lellák J.	Sládecková A.
Hall D.J.	Löffler H.	Straškraba M.
Hrbáček J.	Mann K.H.	Teal J.M.
Hynes H.B.N.	Morgan N.C.	Winberg G.G.
Ilkowska A.	Mundie J.H.	Wright J.C.

Preface to Second Edition

The second edition of this handbook has resulted from a very different process to the first. In the following few paragraphs I will discuss the history of this book, its organization, and its strengths and weaknesses. In this way I will show the manner in which this edition differs from the original yet how it attempts to fulfill the same purpose. Finally I will give thanks to the many scientists and colleagues that have helped make this new edition possible.

First of all, it is obvious that few authors contributing to this book were involved in the first edition. To understand the reason for this, one must know something of the history of this handbook. In 1978, Frank Rigler agreed to edit a new edition of IBP Handbook No. 17. He felt that one could decrease the massive editorial effort and increase the continuity in the second edition by decreasing the number of authors. He also felt that one should continue to view science from new perspectives as well as learning from past experiences. For this reason he wanted to assemble a group of young scientists to write the requisite chapters. Most of the authors contributing to this manual are in some ways products of IBP, not original contributors to it. Because of this one can see in this edition the manner in which the often brilliant work of the authors in the original edition has been translated into scientific progress and education. We have the chance to view the problem of the assessment of secondary productivity in freshwaters from fresh perspectives.

My involvement as an editor of this manual was less philosophical and more practical. In early 1980, FHR decided that he would not have the time to fulfill all the editorial duties himself, and asked me to be a co-editor. I felt honoured to accept a chance to help organize this important manual. As a student I learned much from the original edition and have continued to use it in my research. I hope that this effort will be as useful to others as the original was to me.

The organization of the chapters in this edition has been an impossible choice and will appear haphazard to some. The conclusions of each of the chapters suggested that the book should start with an introduction to the general justification for and the hypotheses under examination by production ecology. Starting from this chapter, I have tried to organize chapters corresponding to the chronology of a research problem. After choice of the problem should come a comprehension of the calculation of production so that one can decide which variables must be estimated (Chapter 2). The sampling routine must be planned next and Chapters 3, 4, 5, and 6 explore these techniques. Once samples are taken they must be processed (Chapter 7) and the data analyzed (Chapter 8). Finally, one might re-examine the components of the variables under consideration (Chapters 9 and 10). One could convincingly argue, however, that Chapter 8 (Statistics and Experimental Design) should be Chapter 2, or that other chapters should be rearranged. All such choices would seem equally arbitrary. The reason for this is that research does not always advance linearly, unlike the chapters in a book or the words in a sentence, but moves as an advancing front like a wave washing a beach. It may be necessary, therefore, for readers to turn from chapter to chapter seeking the information they desire. To facilitate this, the authors and the editors of this manual have put considerable effort into both author and subject indices.

The strengths of this handbook lie in its summarization of current literature and the synthesis of our technical progress. The authors have each tried to present an even-handed review of the existing knowledge of relevant techniques, and they have tried to make clear recommendations wherever possible. This task is difficult because different recommendations are appropriate to different studies. Whether or not our coverage has been sufficient can only be judged by the scientific community. I have no doubt that we have missed important topics or references. Similarly, I have little doubt that this handbook improves our situation because 70 % of the 1300 references cited have been published since the first edition went to press. Because most of the authors are new to this sort of publication, I cannot help but agree with FHR that many of them have supplied a fresh look at the topics at hand.

It is easier to point out the weaknesses of a book than to list its strengths; one can simply look for topics that are not covered. There are some relevant topics that are not covered in depth here, including subsampling and treatment of benthos samples, feeding and assimilation in the benthos, prediction of sampling variance for zooplankton samples, etc. We felt that complete coverage of all subjects for each sort of taxonomic category was not feasible within the size constraints of this book. Where specific information is not included, one can consult chapters on the same topic for different taxa. For example, researchers interested in subsampling benthos samples should consult Chapters 7 and 8, those interested in feeding and assimilation in benthos should consult Chapter 9, and those interested in optimizing zooplankton sampling programs can draw general guidance from Chapters 4 and 8. Regardless of the length of the book, some information could always be found lacking. I only hope that few serious omissions have been made, that we have covered the most important subjects thoroughly and accurately, and that readers are sympathetic to the enormity of this task.

Finally I would like to thank those people who have contributed to the quality of this handbook, although the final responsibility for errors rests with FHR and me. First, we thank the institutions that have made this handbook possible, most notably the Natural Sciences and Engineering Research Council of Canada, the Quebec Minister of Education (FCAC), the McGill University Centre for Northern Studies, Environment Canada, Atomic Energy Canada Ltd., Indian and Northern Affairs Canada, The Canadian National Sportsman's Fund, the faculty of graduate studies and research of McGill University, and the McGill University Department of Biology. I would especially like to acknowledge the indulgence of the Université de Montréal Departement de Sciences Biologiques. All individuals who have helped are too numerous to mention. *En masse* we would like to thank the ecologists at McGill, the Limnological Research Group (i.e. Memphremagog and Schefferville projects) also at McGill, and the Groupe d'Ecologie des Eaux douces at l'Université de Montréal. Most valuable assistance has come from R.H.Peters, E.McCauley, P.Harper, B.Leggett, J.Kalff, L.Legendre, P.Legendre, A.Morin, P.André, and M.Pace. Many other scientists, colleagues, and friends have contributed, among them are J.H.Mundie, S.C.Mozley, A.C.Benke, K.Patalas, J.T.Lehman, R.J.Conover, R.Epp, J.J.Peterka, R.H.Green, B.Marcotte, N.C.Morgan, V.H.Resh, G.Milbrink, W.T.Edmondson, W.L.Downing, E.L.Schmidt, C.Hudon, D.Bird, L.Rath, D.Rosenberg, M.Downing, R.Anderson, J.-G.Pilon, H.Evans, D.Skraba, A.Marnik, and E.Gnaiger. We also thank Robert Campbell, John Robson and Blackwell Scientific Publications for being patient and helpful. Last, FHR and I thank our families for understanding the extra time a work such as this requires.

Montreal 1982   JOHN ASHLEY DOWNING

AUTHOR'S ACKNOWLEDGMENTS

Some of the authors have asked to include acknowledgments of their own. These are assembled below.

I.J.DAVIES. I would like to thank L.A.Davies, who illustrated this chapter and gave me immeasurable help and encouragement during its preparation. I also thank L.Wilson for typing the manuscript and P.Campbell, J.A.Downing, J.F.Flannagan, J.H.Mundie, D.J.Ramsey, D.W.Schindler, and H.E.Welch who reviewed various drafts of the work and offered many helpful criticisms. Special thanks go to D.M.Rosenberg and K.E.Marshall for their suggestions and additional assistance.

E.McCauley. I wish to thank M.Pace, R.Peters, J.Downing, and D.Laflamme for constructive criticism and assistance. R.Anderson, A.Vézina, and D.Currie made numerous suggestions and checked calculations. E.Bentzen generously helped to assemble the manuscript. Finally, I wish to thank J.Downing and F.H.Rigler, for inviting me to contribute to this handbook.

B.L.Peckarsky. I would like to acknowledge Stan Dodson's unfailing support and inspiration, and ability to devise simple yet elegant techniques to answer difficult questions. Dick Ganje constructed all cages and observation boxes, and was very instrumental in their design. I thank Steve Horn and Cheryl Hughes for drafting the illustrations, and Beth French and Susan Pohl for editing this manuscript. Reviews by Peter Harper, and the editors of this manual (Downing and Rigler) considerably improved an earlier draft of this chapter.

R.H.Peters. Conversations with many scientists added immeasurably to this review. I particularly thank J.A.Downing, B.M.Marcotte, F.H.Rigler, and P.Starkweather.

E.E.Prepas. I thank G.Hutchinson and J.Vickery for their assistance with data analysis and manuscript preparation, J.O.Murie, P.A.Murtaugh, T.Reynoldson, and C.J.Strobeck for reviewing the manuscript, J.A.Downing and F.H.Rigler for their patience and encouragement, D.O.Trew, E.McCauley, and P.A.Murtaugh for providing unpublished data, K.Baert, P.Miller, and J.Scheinas for typing the manuscript, and the National Science and Engineering Research Council of Canada for financial support in the form of an operating grant.

Preface to First Edition

This book took form at a working meeting held at Liblice, Czechoslovakia, 3–8 April 1967 under joint chairmanship of W.T.Edmondson and G.G.Winberg. The meeting had been preceded by much correspondence, and preliminary drafts of most of the book were written in advance. At the meeting the participants worked in groups to examine the material, and made recommendations of changes and additions. After the meeting, most of the manuscripts were revised in accordance with the recommendations of the working groups. Some material was requested from people who did not attend the working meeting. Inevitably, some duplication occurred, and some topics were not given adequate attention. It has been the task of the editor to put together all these pieces into what is hoped to be a useful whole. Because of overlap and decisions about scope and emphasis that had to be made after the initial work, no manuscript is printed here exactly as it was written, and some have been greatly changed to fit them to the purpose of the book as the editors see it. An attempt has been made to indicate the primary authorship of the various sections, but some of them have been put together from contributions by so many people that it is impracticable to give a very exact authorship. The editor regrets any errors or omissions of attribution that may have been made.

It should be understood that this book has a somewhat transitory and ephemeral character. During the process of production, a steady stream of pertinent contributions has appeared in the scientific literature, and as the book goes to press, papers are about to appear that will make some sections of this book obsolete. Further, there is disagreement about the merits of certain methods and apparatus. Readers are encouraged to use the book as a guide to the literature and to look out for new papers appearing in the journals cited. More important, some of the basic concepts and theories are imperfectly developed.

Many people are owed thanks for making this volume possible. Primarily, we express our gratitude to the authors who worked so hard to prepare manuscripts, and who have cheerfully agreed to having them extensively revised for the special purposes of the book. For the very effective meeting at Liblice, thanks are due the organizer, Dr Jaroslav Hrbáček. The persons who agreed to chair sessions of the working groups made a valuable contribution. While it is difficult to single out individuals for special mention from among so many who helped, the work of Dr K.H.Mann and Dr F.H.Rigler at the meeting and later was especially useful to the editorial work. The indefatigable Dr Julian Rzóska has contributed more to the production of this book than meets the eye or can ever be defined and expressed.

Finally, a special word of thanks goes to the late Professor Vittorio Tonolli who, as former Convenor of Section PF of the IBP, initiated the process that has resulted in this book. His last piece of scientific writing, the section on zooplankton sampling in the book, was written when the end of his life was in sight.

W.T.EDMONDSON, Editor
G.G.WINBERG, Co-editor

Abbreviations

Abbreviations are listed by chapter. Where a single abbreviation is used for more than one term, the meaning of the abbreviation is described in text.

CHAPTER 1

a, b, c: fitted constants.
B: mean biomass.
M: body-size (mass).
N: average population density.
P, P_s: secondary production.
P_p: primary production.

CHAPTER 2

A: area under curve of number plotted against time.
b: instantaneous birth rate.
β: finite birth rate.
B: biomass of population, size class, or development stage.
C1, C2, C3...etc.: first, second, third copepodite stage.
d: instantaneous death rate.
D: time that it takes to grow through a size class. Also referred to as duration of embryonic development, or development time.
g: instantaneous growth rate.
*m: $m_{max} - m_{min}$.
$\bar{m}_i$: mean body mass of an individual.
m_{max}: $m_{max\,i}$.
$m_{max\,i}$: upper size limit of stage i.
m_{min}: $m_{min\,i}$
$m_{min\,i}$: lower size limit of stage i.
N1, N2, N3...etc.: first, second and third naupliar stage.
N_{egg}: number of eggs in the population.
$N_{\bar{m}i}$: number of individuals in a size class with mean body mass of $\bar{m}$.
N_t: number of animals at time t.
N_{t1}, N_{t2}: number of individuals in population at times t_1 and t_2.

P: secondary production.

P_i: production in size class or developmental stage 'i'.

r: instantaneous rate of change of population size.

T_N, T_B: turnover time of numbers and biomass.

Chapter 3

d: distance through which a plankton net is towed.

r: radius of a plankton net.

s: standard deviation.

Chapter 4

A: area of a sampling device.

CV: coefficient of variation.

L: largest length of a stone.

M: mean density of benthic organisms.

n: number of replicate samples.

P: ratio of standard error to mean density, and the largest perimeter of a stone.

s^2: variance.

$\bar{x}$: mean of replicate samples.

Chapter 5

$\bar{x}$: mean density of benthic organisms.

Chapter 6

A: area covered by an emergence trap; or number of adults retained by an emergence trap.

A_j: area of the jth sample stratum.

$\bar{B}$: lake average dry biomass.

B_{95}: the depth above which 95% of biomass emerges.

B_{zi}: average integral biomass of emerging insects.

CV: coefficient of variation.

d: total number of sampling days in a season.

E: number of exuviae found in an emergence trap.

$\bar{E}$: lake average number of emergent insects.

E_j: mean seasonal emergence per unit in the jth sample stratum.

ELA: Experimental Lakes Area (Ontario, Canada).

E_{95}: the depth above which 95% of numbers emerge.

E_{zi}: average integral number of emerging insects.

h: height of an emergence trap.

$\bar{N}$: average number of insects emerging per gC of PP_{zi}.

$\overline{PP}$: lake average phytoplankton production.

PP_{zi}: average integral phytoplankton production in the ith depth interval.

R′: radius of the base of an emergence trap.

R.I.: refractive index.

S.G.: specific gravity.

T_i: mid-point time of the ith sampling period.

$\bar{W}$: mean dry weight of an individual insect.

X: mean emergence (m^{-2} $year^{-1}$).

X_i: emergence per unit area per day on the ith sampling day.

$\bar{Z}_c$: mean depth of 1 % surface irradiance.

α: pitch or angle of a cone.

θ: angle of a pie shaped cut out of a cone.

CHAPTER 7

B: biomass.

C: biomass of crustacean zooplankton determined by counting and weighing, or biomass as carbon content.

C.L.: 95 % confidence limits.

CV: coefficient of variation.

DM: dry weight determined by direct measurement.

DW: biomass as dry weight.

F: biomass of crustacean zooplankton determined using a filtering technique, or ratio of explained to residual variance.

FW: biomass as fresh weight.

$\overline{\ln L}$: geometric mean length of individuals.

LW: dry weight determined by length–weight regression.

$\bar{M}$: average mass of a size class, cohort, or species.

n: number of paired observations used to determine regression.

N: number of individuals in a size class, cohort, or species.

P: phytoplankton biomass.

R: correlation coefficient.

RMS: residual mean square.

s.d.: standard deviation.

s^2: variance.

t: constant from the Student's t distribution.

w: dry weight.

W: dry weight of a group of organisms.

$\bar{x}$: mean of a group of measurements.

CHAPTER 8

A: area under a normal curve.
C: correction factor for Bartlett's test.
CV: coefficient of variation.
D: ratio of standard error to mean.
df: degrees of freedom.
D_i: difference between the ith pair of observations.
F: ratio of two variances.
f_i: observed frequency.
F_i: expected frequency.
L: allowable error in the sample mean, or linear combination of means.
$\log_e$: natural logarithm.
$\log_{10}$: logarithm to the base 10.
M: test statistic for Bartlett's test.
n: number of observations.
N: size of the total population.
p: proportion of a population containing a particular attribute.
P: probability.
q: $1 - p$.
Q: studentized range.
r: correlation coefficient.
r^2: coefficient of determination.
s: standard deviation.
SE: standard error of the mean.
$s_{\bar{x}}$: standard error of the mean.
s^2: variance of a set of samples.
t: student's t value.
W_i: size of a stratum to be weighted.
X: arithmetic mean.
X_i: the ith observation.
X_i': transformed observation.
Z: standard deviation unit.
μ: true population mean.
σ^2: population variance.
χ^2: chi-square statistic.
λ_i: fixed numbers.

CHAPTER 9

A: the amount of food assimilated or assimilation rate.
A_a: radioactivity of animals.
A_{ap}: concentration of ^{32}P in animals.

A_{at}: concentration of ^3H in animals.

A.E.: assimilation efficiency.

A_s: radioactivity of suspension.

A_{sp}: concentration of ^{32}P in suspension.

A_{st}: concentration of ^3H in suspension.

A_2, A_3: radioactivity of animal at times 2 and 3.

b: growth rate constant.

B: number of beads in an animal's gut.

C: average food concentration.

C_c: cell carbon.

CO_o, CC_t: initial and final food concentration in control containers.

C_o: initial cell concentration.

C_t: final cell concentration.

f: feeding rate.

F.R.: forage ratio.

G: grazing rate.

G_p: gut passage time.

H: volume of water per animal in container.

I: amount of food ingested.

L: volume of container.

M: wet weight of food cells, or duration of feeding experiment.

N: number of animals in container.

N_{p_i}: amount of food type i in the environment.

N_{r_i}: amount of food type i eaten.

p_i: the proportion of food type i in the environment.

q: constant of proportionality.

r: instantaneous rate of increase.

R: electrical resistance of a suspension of food cells.

r_e: resistivity of electrolyte.

r_i: proportion of food type i eaten.

r_p: resistivity of particle.

S: concentration of particles in suspension.

t: length of time animals are allowed to feed.

T: temperature.

U: proportion of unassimilable material in diet.

U': proportion of unassimilable material in feces.

V: volume of container.

V_i: volume of individual cells.

CHAPTER 10

C: carbon content of animals.

C_i, C_a, C_c: oxygen concentration of the initials, bottles with animals, and controls.

DPM_a: radioactivity of animals.

DPM_w: radioactivity of CO_2 per ml water.

ETS: electron transport system.

J: system flushing characteristic time.

L_c: carbon loss.

LSC: liquid scintillation counter.

ΔP: change of equilibrium pressure.

P_a: barometric pressure.

pCO_2: partial pressure of CO_2.

Po: normal pressure.

pO_2: partial pressure of oxygen.

Q_{10}: ratio of rates resulting from a temperature increase of $10\,°C$.

r: gas constant.

R: respiratory rate.

RQ: respiratory quotient.

S: solubility of oxygen at a given temperature.

STP: standard temperature and pressure.

T: water temperature.

Δt: time interval between readings.

t_a, t_c: incubation periods of bottles.

U: velocity of water flow.

V: volume of container or respiration bottles.

V_g: diver constant.

VO_2; rate of oxygen consumption.

w: chamber volume.

W: body weight.

μ: activation energy.

Chapter 1. Assessment of Secondary Production: the First Step

JOHN A. DOWNING

1 Introduction

This manual is designed to help freshwater ecologists choose methods for use in the scientific study of secondary productivity. Secondary production has been defined many times in the literature (e.g. Clarke 1946; Ivlev 1966; Allen 1971; Winberg 1971a, b; Waters & Crawford 1973; Edmondson 1974; Cushman et al. 1978; Benke & Wallace 1980) and most definitions are in agreement. Waters & Crawford (1973) use the term in the sense of Clarke (1946) as 'that amount of tissue elaborated per unit time per unit area, regardless of its fate'. Other definitions stress that reproductive products and production lost to predators and other losses must be included. The tissue elaboration that is usually considered to be 'secondary production' is the production not only of herbivores but of all freshwater invertebrates (see Morgan et al. 1980). Therefore, the rate of secondary production can be defined more specifically for this manual as that amount of tissue elaborated by freshwater invertebrates per unit time per unit area, regardless of its fate (after Clarke 1946; Waters & Crawford 1973). Many techniques exist for the study of secondary production in freshwaters, and it is the goal of this book to help the researcher to choose the appropriate ones to use under different circumstances.

Although each author contributing to this handbook has dealt with a different set of techniques, one single conclusion has been reached independently by each. This common conclusion is that the choice of proper technique depends upon the question posed or the hypothesis under examination. Many of the authors have come to a worrying second conclusion. They believe that few production biologists to date have posed questions or tested hypotheses; most have simply concerned themselves with the estimation of single rates of production or its components. Because the choice of technique depends upon the hypothesis to be tested, it has been difficult for production ecologists to choose among the many techniques available. The gravity of this conclusion has been discussed by many philosophers of science. For example, F.S.C.Northrop (1947) has written that 'One may have the most rigorous of methods during the later stages of

1

investigation, but if a false or superficial beginning has been made, rigor later on will never retrieve the situation.' When questions are only posed *a posteriori*, we risk the frequent choice of inappropriate methods (cf. LeCren 1972).

Because of this problem, this first chapter will review the general reasons why ecologists estimate secondary production, and will then provide a summary of the many interesting hypotheses suggested by the rich literature in this field.

2 Theoretical Justification for Secondary Production Research

A field of study is usually judged useful if it has a potential for contributing to established disciplines or goals. It is the same for the field of secondary production in freshwaters. Although some production biologists have estimated productivity of a species in a certain area merely because no such data have been published, many others feel that their studies are important because they address one or more of four main conceptual subject areas. These are:

(1)   The elucidation of energy or material transfers within communities and ecosystems.
(2)   The rational management of aquatic resources.
(3)   The detection of the effects of pollution.
(4)   The formation of general theories of biological productivity.

Below, I present a brief discussion of the relationship between production biology and these general ecological goals.

2.1 *Energy or material transfer within ecosystems*

G.E.Hutchinson (1942) has written that when Lindeman published his famous paper 'The Trophic–Dynamic Aspect of Ecology' (1942), he hoped that it would serve as a program for future ecological research. This has certainly been true. Lindeman suggested that if one could reduce the interactions among components of a community to a common currency (e.g. energy), then one could quantify the interactions and learn to predict changes such as succession within ecosystems. Lindeman introduced the major concept that an organism's success in an environment might be a function of its ability to fix and retain energy.

This concept not only underlies much of current productivity research, but was part of the stimulus for the research undertaken in the International Biological Programme of which this handbook is a result. The elegance of this concept is demonstrated by the frequency with which it has been accepted as justification for research in secondary production (e.g. Kimerle & Anderson

1971; Czeczuga & Bobiatyńska-Ksok 1972; Burke & Mann 1974; Nichols 1975; Zwick 1975; Benke 1976; Hibbert 1976; Zytkowicz 1976; Waters 1977; Neves 1979; Benke & Wallace 1980; Tonolli 1980). I believe that Edmondson (1974) has expressed it best: 'I cannot think of secondary production as a distinct process by itself. Rather it is part of a larger scheme of the movement of material through the ecosystem, and this is based on the activities of individuals and populations of animals.' Much effort has gone into the quantification of the components of this larger scheme (e.g. Kajak & Hillbricht-Ilkowska 1972). The frustrating aspects are that even the simplest community has many components, there are many different types of possible interactions among components, almost all individual organisms are behaviorally plastic, and it is difficult to obtain accurate estimates of even one rate of transfer under one set of simple circumstances. The result is that fulfillment of the trophic–dynamic goal of production ecology is a formidable task.

2.2 *Management of aquatic resources*

The measurement of secondary production is thought essential to the management of aquatic resources, probably due to our trophic–dynamic view of ecology. The most concrete freshwater resource is, of course, fish. Because many fish depend to a high degree upon zooplankton and benthos for food (e.g. Zelinka 1977), a variety of authors have suggested that an understanding of the production processes of invertebrates will facilitate management of fish stocks (Zytkowicz 1976; Waters 1977; Williams *et al.* 1977; Priymachenko *et al.* 1978) or prediction of rates of fish production (Johnson & Brinkhurst 1971; Moskalenko 1971; Czeczuga & Bobiatyńska-Ksok 1972; Johnson 1974; Zytkowicz 1976). A recent paper by Hanson & Leggett (1982) shows that fish yield is related to the mean standing biomass of macrobenthos in a lake, and thus suggests that a general relationship probably exists between secondary productivity and fish production. This relationship has yet to be described empirically, however. The importance of secondary producers to the study of fish dynamics (Hamill *et al.* 1979) is underscored by their trophic intermediacy between fish populations and energy sources (Mathias 1971; Dermott *et al.* 1977). Johnson (1974) has also suggested that enhancement of secondary production may be important to the development of freshwater aquaculture.

2.3 *Detection of pollution*

Because secondary production is a complex process that can be altered by variations in many variables, it seems logical that variations in rates of secondary production could be used to detect pollution (Winberg 1971b; see review by Waters 1977). For example, Golterman (1972) found that the ratio of production to biomass (P/B) of zooplankton is higher in thermally polluted waters than in control areas. A similar effect is suggested by McNaught& Fenlon (1972). Many researchers have found that benthos production in lakes is highest near areas of human activity (e.g. Mikulski *et al.* 1975; Wolnomiejski *et al.* 1976; Dermott *et al.* 1977). Zelinka (1977), on the other hand, found that human activities (stream bed modification, toxic wastes, etc.) most often have a negative effect on mayfly production. Other authors suggest that secondary producers could be used in sewage treatment (e.g. Kimerle & Anderson 1971; Waters 1977), or in the self-purification of polluted ecosystems.

2.4 *Formation of general theories of biological production*

Winberg (1971a; Tonolli 1980) has stated that the 'development of a theory of biological productivity is one of the central aims of contemporary biology . . .'. Mann (1972) has made a similar statement and suggests that we must 'make every effort to improve the accuracy of the observations and the confidence limits of resulting estimates' in order to help produce a general ecological theory of biological budgets. If we take the term 'theory' in the usual sense, that is, a construct that makes predictions about nature, then one of the basic reasons for measuring secondary production is to learn how to predict it. Looking back to Sections 2.1 and 2.2, we can see why it is very important to be able to predict rates of productivity. The trophic–dynamic analysis of ecosystems requires the estimation of the secondary production of many populations of animals. If these values could be predicted accurately under a variety of conditions, then much effort could be saved in the trophic analysis of communities. In addition, general theories of secondary production would be very useful in the management of aquatic resources.

Brylinsky (1980) has written recently that productivity data should be analyzed 'with a view to identifying those factors most important in controlling biological production. Once identified, management efforts could be directed towards manipulation of those factors appearing most important'. Most of the balance of this introductory chapter will be devoted to an exploration of those specific factors which have been suggested as important in determining the rate of secondary production in fresh waters. It is my hope that presentation of these hypotheses will help production biologists to define specific questions for study, and thus indicate appropriate methods for analysis.

3 Factors Affecting Rates of Secondary Production

This section contains a summary of the hypotheses suggested most frequently by production biologists. Most of these hypotheses have arisen from isolated observations; only a few have been tested explicitly. It is not my intention to suggest that these are the only interesting hypotheses or even the hypotheses that will yield the most or quickest progress in production ecology. I only wish to demonstrate that we possess a large set of implicit theories. These, or other hypotheses, if tested explicitly, could not only yield progress in production biology, but could make the choice of methods a more tractable problem.

For the sake of organization, I have arranged these hypotheses into four categories. I will first discuss how rates of secondary production are affected by characteristics of the population under study, then I will examine hypotheses that relate to aspects of the environment in which they live. Thirdly, I will present the few hypotheses in the literature that address the manner in which secondary production is affected by interactions among populations in the same community. Lastly, I will discuss the possible effects of basin characteristics.

3.1 Effect of population characteristics

There are certain intrinsic characteristics of populations which dictate the manner in which they live. When one examines an animal population casually, certain elementary questions materialize. Four of these questions are: How many are there, and what is their biomass? What is their life history like; how long do they live, How big are they? What kind of animal are they? Production biologists feel that each of these questions has a bearing on the rate of secondary production that populations are able to attain.

3.1.1 Biomass

The literature contains a number of specific hypotheses regarding the relationship of production (P) to mean biomass (B). First, there are many (e.g. Laville 1971; Gak *et al.* 1972; Eckblad 1973; Waters & Crawford 1973; Johnson 1974; Lavandier 1975; Mikulski *et al.* 1975; Wolnomiejski *et al.* 1976; Waters 1977; Hamill *et al.* 1979; Makarewicz & Likens 1979; Benke & Wallace 1980; Short & Ward 1980) who have suggested that the ratio P/B is a constant (c) for a given type of organism. That is:

$$P/B = c \qquad (1.1)$$

If in fact P/B is constant, then production is an increasing linear function of biomass with slope c and intercept zero:

$$P = cB \qquad (1.2)$$

This relationship suggests that $P = 0$ at $B = 0$, and that $P = \infty c$ at $B = \infty$. If P/B is constant then production is not density dependent and is not subject to the normal constraints imposed by the carrying capacity of the environment. A mental Malthusian exercise tells us that this cannot be so. Even though the relationship between P and B may appear linear over a small range of B, the convenient but inaccurate notion that P/B is constant should be abandoned. Many have already done this for empirical reasons (e.g. McLaren 1969; Schindler 1972; Paterson & Walker 1974; Jónasson 1975; Pedersen *et al.* 1976; Janicki & DeCosta 1977; Momot 1978; Pinel-Alloul 1978; Adcock 1979; Banse & Mosher 1980; Nauwerck *et al.* 1980; Uye 1982). Jónasson (1975) has found that it is not even safe to use the same value of P/B for one species at one site in successive years. He found that P/B for *Chironomus anthacinus* was 4 in one year and 0·8 the next. Because the relation between production and biomass is not linear, there will be a necessary negative relationship between P/B and B. The danger is that variables correlated with B (e.g. temperature, body size, respiration) may account for statistically significant variation in P/B when they would not account for significant variation in P beyond the accurately fitted effect of B. This could lead to errors in both interpretation and predictive ability.

3.1.2 Age, lifespan, and voltinism

The length of life or relative age of individuals in a population also seems to affect production. The influence of age on production is not clear-cut. Some authors feel that P/B declines with age (Hibbert 1976; Waters 1977; Banse & Mosher 1980) but this could simply be due to the non-linear effect of B on P, if B and age are positively correlated. Others have examined the effect of age on growth rate. Johnson (1974) found that the growth rate of amphipods declined with the age of the population, while Coon *et al.* (1977) found that the growth rate of mussels increased with age. This contradiction is probably due in part to the sort of growth rate under discussion. Sutcliffe *et al.* (1981) suggest that specific growth rates ($\%$ wet wt. day^{-1}) decrease with increased age, while absolute growth rate (wet wt. day^{-1}) occurs when the animal's body size is about one-half of the maximum. Although age and biomass are sometimes confounded, Borkowski (1974) feels that, at least for marine snails, older populations tend to have higher rates of secondary production. The lifespan of animals has a similar effect, such that longer-lived animals have lower rates of production (Zaïka 1970; Waters 1977; review by Banse & Mosher 1980).

The effect of voltinism (number of generations per year) is consistent and continuous with the effect of lifespan. All authors who cite this effect (e.g. Johnson 1974; Zytkowicz 1976; Waters 1977; Jónasson 1978; Banse & Mosher 1980; Benke & Wallace 1980; Wildish & Peer 1981) suggest that secondary production and P/B increase with the number of generations produced per year. Populations that are multivoltine have higher rates of production than those that are univoltine. An analysis presented by Jónasson (1978) suggests that we may have erroneously ascribed causation in this apparent correlation. He suggests that faster growth in the littoral zone permits more generations per unit time. Thus, multivoltinism may be an effect of high production rates, not a cause of them.

3.1.3 Body-size

The effect of body-size on secondary production is one of the few relationships that have been tested explicitly. Unfortunately, much of this work has employed P/B as a dependent variable and is, therefore, difficult to interpret mechanistically. The conclusion has been that P/B decreases with increasing body-size (M) in the population (Janicki & DeCosta 1977; Waters 1977; Finlay 1978; Banse & Mosher 1980; Benke & Wallace 1980). Banse & Mosher (1980) have shown that P/B varies as a function of M:

$$P/B = aM^b \tag{1.3}$$

where a and b are fitted constants. Because $B = NM$ (N = average population density) then:

$$P = aN^c M^{1+b} \tag{1.4}$$

where $c = 1$. This equation suggests that the effect of body-size would be more accurately determined by a multiple regression employing both population density and mean body-size (see Chapter 8). There appears to be a real effect of body-size on secondary production, upheld by the experiments of Zelinka (1977) who found that benthos communities made up of larger species had lower overall rates of secondary production.

3.1.4 Taxonomy and trophic status

A variety of authors have suggested that physiological and ecological differences among taxonomic units account for differences in secondary productivity. Jónasson (1978) suggests that similar species have developed different tolerances and efficiencies for dealing with environmental problems, thus production rates must vary among species. Coon *et al.* (1977) suggest the same for mussels. Makarewicz & Likens (1979) suggest that differences in P/B for rotifers among lakes are probably due to taxonomic differences. A number of workers (Mikulski *et al.* 1975; Pederson *et al.* 1976; Waters 1977; Nauwerck *et al.* 1980) have suggested that cladocerans are more productive than copepods, which are, in turn, more productive than rotifers. Schindler (1972), however, suggests that P/B is higher for rotifers than for other plankton, thus the apparent low productivity of rotifers could be due to inaccurate biomass estimation. Herbivorous taxa are generally thought to be more productive than detritivores or carnivores (Waters 1977; Jónasson 1978).

3.2 *Effect of environmental factors*

It is one of the basic tenets of ecology that the success of organisms in a particular ecosystem is determined in part by the suitability of the environment. Among the most obvious aspects of the environment that might affect animal production are the average temperature, the ability of the ecosystem to produce sufficient food of acceptable quality, the character of the substrate, and the concentration of respirable oxygen.

3.2.1 Temperature

Temperature has long been known to influence rates of activity from a molecular to an organismal scale. It is not surprising, therefore, that many production ecologists have found that rates of secondary production increase with temperature (e.g. Neves 1979; Laville 1971; McNaught & Fenlon 1972; Edmondson 1974; Kititsyna & Pidgaiko 1974; Paterson & Walker 1974; Pederson *et al.* 1976; Zytkowicz 1976; Iverson & Jesson 1977; Finlay 1978; Selin & Hakkari 1982). P/B also is thought to rise with increased temperature, either as a linear (Winberg *et al.* 1973; Johnson 1974; Paterson & Walker 1974; Wildish & Peer 1981; Uye 1982) or a curvilinear (Johnson & Brinkhurst 1971; Janicki & DeCosta 1977; Waters 1977; Nauwerck *et al.* 1980) function. Banse & Mosher (1980), on the other hand, show that P/B is not correlated with temperature after regression on body-size.

The general positive effect of temperature on secondary production is a result of the reproductive biology of zooplankton and benthos. A variety of authors have suggested that growth rates increase (Johnson 1974; Jónasson 1978; Humpesch 1979; Vijverberg 1980; Marchant & Hynes 1981; Sutcliffe *et al.* 1981), egg development times decrease (Schindler 1972; Bottrell 1975; Makarewicz & Likens 1979; Vijverberg 1980), the rate of population increase rises (Armitage *et al.* 1973), and feeding rates increase (Zimmerman & Wissing 1978; see Chapter 9) with increased temperature. These factors tend to increase production at high temperature (see Chapter 2). On the other hand, O'Brien *et al.* (1973) suggest that average clutch size of *Diaptomus leptopus* decreases with temperature, and Aston (1973) suggests that egg production by oligochaetes declines at high temperature. Pidgaiko *et al.* (1972) conclude that temperature variation could have either a positive or negative effect on secondary production, depending upon geographic location and basin morphometry.

3.2.2 Food production, availability, and quality

A community of heterotrophs can fix no more energy than the amount made available to them by primary producers. Edmondson (1974) has reasoned that the rate of primary production must set the upper limit for secondary production. Using similar logic, many authors have suggested that rates of production of freshwater benthos and zooplankton are positively related to food availability (Miller *et al.* 1971; Ladle *et al.* 1972; George & Edwards 1974; Prikhod'ko 1975; Martien & Benke 1977; Jónasson 1978; Neves 1979; Benke & Wallace 1980; Nauwerck *et al.* 1980). Others have found that rates of zooplankton and benthos production are positively related to rates of primary production (Patalas 1970, cited by Schindler 1972; Hillbricht-Ilkowska 1972, cited by Pederson *et al.* 1976; Monokov & Sorokin 1972; Brylinsky & Mann 1973; Johnson 1974; Dermott *et al.* 1977; Makarewicz & Likens 1979; Smyly 1979; Brylinsky 1980; Strayer *et al.* 1981). Winberg (1971b) has been more specific, hypothesizing that secondary production (P_s) is about 10% of primary production (P_p), on the average. This suggests that:

$$P_s = a + bP_p \qquad (1.5)$$

where $a = 0$ and $b = 0.1$. A recent analysis by Brylinsky (1980) shows that phytoplankton primary production is a better predictor of zooplankton production than phytoplankton biomass, but the relationship may not be linear. Equation 1.5 probably overestimates zooplankton production at low phytoplankton production, and makes underestimates at high phytoplankton production. The relationship between phytoplankton production and secondary production is probably also responsible for apparent relationships between secondary production and nutrient conditions (e.g. Stross *et al.* 1961; Hall *et al.* 1970; Wattiez 1981) and alkalinity (Waters 1977; Pinel-Alloul 1978; Neves 1979). It should also be remembered that quality of food is important in determining the secondary production of both zooplankton (Pederson *et al.* 1976; Vijverberg 1976, 1980; Makarewicz & Likens 1979; Nauwerck *et al.* 1980), and benthos (Swiss & Johnson 1976; Willoughby & Sutcliffe 1976; Zimmerman & Wissing 1978; Sutcliffe *et al.* 1981).

3.2.3 Oxygen concentration

The availability of oxygen is thought to be critical, especially to the benthos because they often live in areas that are oxygen-poor. Brylinsky (1980), however, has found that carnivorous zooplankton production in a wide range of lakes is also influenced by oxygen concentration in the epilimnion. Jónasson (1978) suggests that sufficient oxygen is important to benthos production because food cannot be metabolized efficiently at low oxygen levels. This conclusion has also been reached by Dermott *et al.* (1977) and

Rosenberg (1977). Aston (1973) suggests that egg production in freshwater oligochaetes is constant with decreasing oxygen concentration until some critical low level is reached. Pond benthos seem to require $> 1\,mg\,l^{-1}$ of dissolved oxygen in order to maintain positive production (Martien & Benke 1977). Laville (1971) suggests that, at least for some benthos, secondary production and oxygen concentration are inversely related (see also regression analysis of Brylinsky 1980).

3.2.4 Substrate characteristics

Another aspect of the environment that has been hypothesized as important to lake and stream benthos is the character and composition of the substrate. Resh (1977), for example, found that the production of stream caddisflies was positively related to the average size of particle in the substrate. Hamill *et al.* (1979), working in a large river, found that the production of benthic snails was highest at intermediate substrate particle size. Similar suggestions have been made by Mecom (1972), Martien & Benke (1977), and Neves (1979). For lacustrine benthos, secondary production seems to rely more heavily on organic matter content than particle composition (e.g. Johnson 1974; Zytkowicz 1976; Marchant & Williams 1977; Jónasson 1978). In addition, Zytkowicz (1976) feels that benthos production in lakes is a positive function of the depth to which sediments can be penetrated by benthic organisms.

3.2.5 Miscellaneous environmental factors

Three hypotheses have been advanced which do not fit neatly into broader categories but which are, nonetheless, interesting. An important factor in streams and rivers seems to be the current velocity. Zelinka (1977), Hamill *et al.* (1979). and Neves (1979) all suggest that secondary production decreases with increasing water flow rate. With respect to lacustrine zooplankton production, Edmondson (1974), Makarewicz & Likens (1979), and Selin & Hakkari (1982) have suggested a positive relationship with intensity of solar radiation. Finally, Burgis (1971) and Paterson & Walker (1974) suggest that high zooplankton and benthos production rates should be found in the most stable ecosystems.

3.3 Predation, competition, and diversity

Predation, competition, and diversity are three topics that have generated much interest in ecology, yet production biologists have seldom considered them. Current thought regarding the effect of predation upon secondary production is contradictory. Hall *et al.* (1970), Zytkowicz (1976), Waters

(1977), and Banse & Mosher (1980) suggest that predation leads to increased production, presumably because the slow growing organisms are removed from the population. Zndanova & Tseyev (1970), Miller *et al.* (1971), Prikhod'ko (1975), and Momot (1978) suggest that predation decreases production perhaps due to a decline in growing biomass. Thoughts on competition are less contradictory but less well developed. The basic belief is that competition decreases the production of a population (see George 1975; Benke 1976; Lavandier 1981). Production ecologists have not considered the possible positive effects of competition on community production (cf. economic theory). The effect of diversity upon secondary production has only been considered (to my knowledge) by Paterson & Walker (1974). Their data suggest that the low benthos diversity in a saline lake allowed very high rates of secondary production.

3.4 *Lake morphometry, lateral zonation, and allochthonous input*

The morphological characteristics of the ecosystem or placement within it also seems to affect secondary production. The literature generally suggests that shallower lakes support higher rates of secondary production (Johnson 1974; Zytkowicz 1976; Matuszek 1978; Brylinsky 1980). Johnson (1974) also suggests that the surface area of a lake may be important, since in larger lakes the profundal zone is less enriched by the littoral zone or allochthonous sources. Other authors have suggested the importance of allochthonous materials to secondary production in both lakes and streams (Edmondson 1974; Willoughby & Sutcliffe 1976; Marchant & Williams 1977; Martien & Benke 1977; Waters 1977; Adcock 1979). Possibly due to high primary production in the littoral zone, it is generally believed that secondary production in near-shore areas and macrophyte beds is greater than in all other areas (Mathias 1971; Johnson 1974; Kajak & Dusoge 1975a, b, 1976; Mikulski *et al.* 1975; Jónasson 1978; Neveau & Lapchin 1979; Kajak *et al.* 1980). The only contradiction seems to be for some stream ecosystems where highest rates of productivity are seen in mid-stream (e.g. Neves 1979).

4 Concluding Comments

The preceding paragraphs indicate that many variables are involved in the rich variety of hypotheses regarding secondary productivity. In some cases, it is difficult to extricate real effects from artefacts. For this reason tests of hypotheses should take one of two courses. Either we should test for the effect of certain factors under conditions that control all other variables, or we must pose multivariate hypotheses that account for simultaneous covariation in more than two variables. I believe that the former approach is currently more popular because it is conceptually simple; while the latter approach is more useful, because it is difficult to control circumstances without altering them. What is really important, though, is that production ecologists define problems before seeking methods for their examination. To quote again from Northrop (1947): 'It is like a ship leaving port for a distant destination. A very slight erroneous deviation in taking one's bearings at the beginning may result in entirely missing one's mark at the end regardless of the sturdiness of one's craft or the excellence of one's subsequent seamanship.' This first chapter has examined the range of production hypotheses currently under consideration by production biologists. The chapters that follow strive to supply methods that can be used to test these and other production hypotheses.

5 References

Adcock J.A. (1979) Energetics of a population of the isopod *Asellus aquaticus*: life history and production. *Freshw. Biol.*, **9**, 343–355.

Allen K.R. (1971) Relation between production and biomass. *J. Fish. Res. Board Can.*, **28**, 1573–1581.

Armitage K.B., Saxena B. & Angino E.E. (1973) Population dynamics of pond zooplankton, I. *Diaptomus pallidus* Herrick. *Hydrobiologia*, **42**, 295–333.

Aston R.J. (1973) Field and experimental studies on the effects of a power station effluent on Tubificidae (Oligochaeta, Annelida). *Hydrobiologia*, **42**, 225–242.

Banse K. & Mosher S. (1980) Adult body mass and annual production/biomass relationships of field populations. *Ecol. Monogr.*, **50**, 355–379.

Benke A.C. (1976) Dragonfly production and prey turnover. *Ecology*, **57**, 915–927.

Benke A.C. & Wallace J.B. (1980) Trophic basis of production among net-spinning caddisflies in a southern Appalachian stream. *Ecology*, **61**, 108–118.

Borkowski T.V. (1974) Growth, mortality and productivity of south Floridian Littorinidae (Gastropoda: Prosobranchia). *Bull. Mar. Sci.*, **24**, 409–438.

Bottrell H.H. (1975) The relationship between temperature and duration of egg development in some epiphytic Cladocera and Copepoda from the River Thames, Reading, with a discussion of temperature functions. *Oecologia*, **18**, 63–84.

Brylinsky M. (1980) Estimating the productivity of lakes and reservoirs. In E.D.LeCren & R.H.Lowe-McConnell (eds.), *The Functioning of Freshwater Ecosystems*. IBP 22. Cambridge: Cambridge University Press.

Brylinsky M. & Mann K.H. (1973) An analysis of factors governing productivity in lakes and reservoirs. *Limnol. Oceanogr.*, **18**, 1–14.

Burgis M.J. (1971) The ecology and production of copepods, particularly *Thermocyclops hyalinus*, in the tropical Lake George, Uganda. *Freshw. Biol.*, **1**, 169–192.

Burke M.V. & Mann K.H. (1974) Productivity and production to biomass ratios of bivalve and gastropod populations in an eastern Canadian estuary. *J. Fish. Res. Board Can.*, **31**, 167–177.

Clarke G.L. (1946) Dynamics of production in a marine area. *Ecol. Monogr.*, **16**, 321–335.

Coon T.G., Eckblad J.W. & Trygstad P.M. (1977) Relative abundance and growth of mussels (Mollusca: Eulamellibranchia) in pools 8, 9 and 10 of the Mississippi. *Freshw. Biol.*, **7**, 279–285.

Cushman R.M., Shugart H.H., Jr., Hildebrand S.G. & Elwood J.W. (1978) The effect of growth curve and sampling regime on instantaneous-growth, removal-summation, and Hynes/Hamilton estimates of aquatic insect production: a computer simulation. *Limnol. Oceanogr.*, **23**, 184–189.

Czeczuga B. & Bobiatyńska-Ksok E. (1972) The extent of consumption of the energy contained in the food suspension by *Ceriodaphnia reticulata* (Jurine). In Z.Kajak & A.Hillbricht-Ilkowska (eds.), *Productivity Problems in Freshwaters*. Proceedings of the IBP-UNESCO Symposium on Productivity in Freshwaters. Krakow: Polish Scientific Publishers.

Dermott R.M., Kalff J., Leggett W.C. & Spence J. (1977) Production of *Chironomus*, *Procladius*, and *Chaoborus* at different levels of phytoplankton biomass in Lake Memphremagog, Quebec-Vermont. *J. Fish. Res. Board Can.*, **34**, 2001–2007.

Eckblad J.W. (1973) Population studies of three aquatic gastropods in an intermittent backwater. *Hydrobiologia*, **41**, 199–219.

Edmondson W.T. (1974) Secondary production. *Mitt. Int. Ver. Theor. Angew. Limnol.*, **20**, 229–272.

Finlay B.J. (1978) Community production and respiration by ciliated protozoa in the benthos of a small eutrophic loch. *Freshw. Biol.*, **8**, 327–341.

Gak D.Z., Gurvich V.V., Korelyakova I.L., Kastikova L.E., Konstantinova N.A., Olivari G.A., Priimachenko A.D., Tseeb Y.Y., Vladimirova K.S. & Zimbalevskaya L.N. (1972) Productivity of aquatic organism communities of different trophic levels in Kiev Reservoir. In Z.Kajak & A.Hillbricht-Ilkowska (eds.), *Productivity Problems in Freshwaters*. Proceedings of the IBP-UNESCO Symposium on Productivity in Freshwaters. Krakow: Polish Scientific Publishers.

George D.G. (1975) Life cycles and production of *Cyclops vicinus* in a shallow eutrophic reservoir. *Oikos*, **26**, 101–110.

George D.G. & Edwards R.W. (1974) Population dynamics and production of *Daphnia hyalina* in a eutrophic reservoir. *Freshw. Biol.*, **4**, 445–465.

Golterman H.L. (1972) Report of the working group 'Production studies as a help in dealing with man-made changes in waters (eutrophication, pollution, self-purification).' In Z. Kajak & A. Hillbricht-Ilkowska (eds.), *Productivity Problems in Freshwaters*. Proceedings of the IBP-UNESCO Symposium on Productivity in Freshwaters. Krakow: Polish Scientific Publishers.

Hall, D.J., Cooper W.E. & Werner E.E. (1970) An experimental approach to the production, dynamics, and structure of freshwater animal communities. *Limnol. Oceanogr.*, **15**, 839–928.

Hamill S.E., Qadri S.U. & Mackie G.L. (1979) Production and turnover ratio of *Pisidium casertanum* (Pelecypoda: Sphaeriidae) in the Ottawa River near Ottawa-Hull, Canada. *Hydrobiologia*, **62**, 225–230.

Hanson J.M. & Leggett W.C. (1982) Empirical prediction of fish biomass and yield. *Can. J. Fish Aquat. Sci.*, **39**, 257–263.

Hibbert C.J. (1976) Biomass and production of a bivalve community on an intertidal mud-flat. *J. Exp. Mar. Biol. Ecol.*, **25**, 249–261.

Humpesch U.H. (1979) Life cycles and growth rates of *Baetis* spp. (Ephemeroptera: Baetidae) in the laboratory and in two stony streams in Austria. *Freshw. Biol.*, **9**, 467–479.

Hutchinson G.E. (1942) Addendum to R.L.Lindeman's 'The trophic–dynamic aspect of ecology'. *Ecology*, **23**, 418.

Iverson T.M. & Jesson J. (1977) Life-cycle, drift, and production of *Gammarus pulex* L. (Amphipoda) in a Danish spring. *Freshw. Biol.*, **7**, 287–296.

Ivlev V.S. (1966) The biological productivity of waters. *J. Fish. Res. Board Can.*, **23**, 1727–1759.

Janicki A.J. & DeCosta J. (1977) The effect of temperature and age structure on P/B for *Bosmina longirostris* in a small impoundment. *Hydrobiologia*, **56**, 11–66.

Johnson M.G. (1974) Production and productivity. In R.O.Brinkhurst (ed.), *The Benthos of Lakes*. London: Macmillan Press.

Johnson M.G. & Brinkhurst R.O. (1971) Production of benthic macroinvertebrates of Bay of Quinte and Lake Ontario. *J. Fish Res. Board Can.*, **28**, 1699–1714.

Jónasson P.M. (1975) Population ecology and production of benthic detritivores. *Verh. Int. Verein. Limnol.*, **19**, 1066–1072.

Jónasson P.M. (1978) Zoobenthos of lakes. *Verh. Int. Verein. Limnol.*, **20**, 13–37.

Kajak Z. & Dusoge K. (1975a) Macrobenthos of Lake Taltowisko. *Ekol. Pol.*, **23**, 295–316.

Kajak Z. & Dusoge K. (1975b) Macrobenthos of Mikolajskie Lake. *Ekol. Pol.*, **23**, 437–457.

Kajak Z. & Dusoge K. (1976) Benthos of Lake Sniardwy as compared to benthos of Mikolajskie Lake and Lake Taltowisko. *Ekol. Pol.*, **24**, 77–101.

Kajak Z. & Hillbricht-Ilkowska A. (eds.) (1972) *Productivity Problems in Freshwaters*. Proceedings of the IBP–UNESCO Symposium on Productivity in Freshwaters. Krakow: Polish Scientific Publishers.

Kajak, Z., Bretschko G., Schiemer F. & Lévêque C. (1980) Secondary production: zoobenthos. In E.D.LeCren & R.H.Lowe-McConnell (eds.) *The Functioning of Freshwater Ecosystems*. IBP 22. Cambridge: Cambridge University Press.

Kimerle R.A. & Anderson N.H. (1971) Production and bioenergetic role of the midge *Glyptotendipes barbipes* (Staeger) in a waste stabilization lagoon. *Limnol. Oceanogr.*, **16**, 646–659.

Kititsyna L.A. & Pidgaiko M.L. (1974) Production of *Pontogammarus robustoides* in the cooling pond of the Kurakhovka thermal power plant. *Hydrobiol. J.*, **10**(4), 20–26.

Ladle M., Bass J.A.B. & Jenkins W.R. (1972) Studies on production and food consumption by the larval Simuliidae (Diptera) of a chalk stream. *Hydrobiologia*, **39**, 429–448.

Lavandier P. (1975) Cycle biologique et production de *Capnioneura brachyptera* D. (Plécoptères) dans un ruisseau d'altitude des Pyrénées centrales. *Ann. Limnol.*, **11**, 145–156.

Lavandier P. (1981) Cycle biologique, croissance et production de *Rhithrogena loyolaea* Navas (Ephemeroptera) dans un torrent Pyrénéen de haute montagne. *Ann. Limnol.*, **17**, 163–179.

Laville H. (1971) Recherche sur les chironomides lacustre du Massif de Neouville (Hautes-Pyrénées) 2. Communautés et production benthique. *Ann. Limnol.*, **7**, 335–414.

LeCren E.D. (1972) Report of working group on 'Secondary production and efficiency of its utilization including fish production'. In Z. Kajak & A. Hillbricht-Ilkowska (eds.), *Productivity Problems in Freshwaters*. Proceedings of the IBP–UNESCO Symposium on Productivity in Freshwaters. Krakow: Polish Scientific Publishers.

Lindeman R. L. (1942) The trophic–dynamic aspect of ecology. *Ecology*, **23**, 399–418.

Makarewicz J.C. & Likens G. E. (1979) Structure and function of the zooplankton community of Mirror Lake, New Hampshire. *Ecol. Monogr.*, **49**, 109–127.

Mann K.H. (1972) Report of working group on 'Biological budgets of water bodies'. In Z. Kajak & A. Hillbricht-Ilkowska (eds.), *Productivity Problems in Freshwaters*. Proceedings of the IBP–UNESCO Symposium on Productivity in Freshwaters. Krakow: Polish Scientific Publishers.

Marchant R. & Hynes H.B.N. (1981) The distribution and production of *Gammarus pseudolimnaeus* (Crustacea: Amphipoda) along a reach of the Credit River, Ontario. *Freshw. Biol.*, **11**, 169–182.

Marchant R. & Williams W.D. (1977) Population dynamics and production of a brine shrimp *Parartemia zietziana* Sayce (Crustacea: Anostraca) in two salt lakes in Western Victoria, Australia. *Austr. J. Mar. Freshwat. Res.*, **28**, 417–438.

Martien R.F. & Benke A.C. (1977) Distribution and production of two crustaceans in a wetland pond. *Am. Midl. Nat.*, **98**, 162–175.

Mathias J.A. (1971) Energy flow and secondary production of amphipods *Hyallela azteca* and *Crangonyx richmondensis occidentalis* in Marion Lake, British Columbia. *J. Fish. Res. Board Can.*, **28**, 711–726.

Matuszek J.E. (1978) Empirical predictions of fish yields of large North American lakes. *Trans. Am. Fish. Soc.*, **107**, 385–394.

McLaren I.A. (1969) Population and production ecology of zooplankton in Ogac Lake, a landlocked fiord on Baffin Island. *J. Fish. Res. Board Can.*, **26**, 1485–1559.

McNaught D.C. & Fenlon M.W. (1972) The effects of thermal effluents upon secondary production. *Verh. Int. Verein. Limnol.*, **18**, 204–212.

Mecom J.D. (1972) Productivity and distribution of Trichoptera larvae in a Colorado mountain stream. *Hydrobiologia*, **40**, 151–176.

Mikulski J.S., Adanczak B., Bittel L., Bohr R., Bronisz D., Donderski W., Giziński A., Luscinska M., Rejewski M., Strzelczyk E., Wolnomiejski N., Zawislak W. & Zytowicz R. (1975) Basic regularities of productive processes in the Ilawa lakes and the Golpo Lake from the point of view of utility values of the water. *Pol. Arch. Hydrobiol.*, **22**, 101–122.

Miller R.J., Mann K.H. & Scarrat D.J. (1971) Production potential of a seaweed-lobster community in eastern Canada. *J. Fish. Res. Board Can.*, **28**, 1733–1738.

Momot W.T. (1978) Annual production and production/biomass ratios of the crayfish, *Oronectes virilis*, in two northern Ontario lakes. *Trans. Am. Fish. Soc.*, **107**, 776–784.

Monokov A.V. & Sorokin Yu.I. (1972) Some results on investigations on nutrition of water animals. In Z.Kajak & A.Hillbricht-Ilkowska (eds.), *Productivity Problems in Freshwaters*. Proceedings of the IBP–UNESCO Symposium on Productivity in Freshwaters. Krakow: Polish Scientific Publishers.

Morgan N.C., Backiel T., Bretschko G., Duncan A., Hillbricht-Ilkowska A., Kajak Z., Kitchell J.F., Larsson P., Lévêque C., Nauwerck A., Schiemer F. & Thorpe J.E. (1980) Secondary production. In E.D.LeCren & R.H.Lowe-McConnell (eds.), *The Functioning of Freshwater Ecosystems*. IBP 22. Cambridge: Cambridge University Press.

Moskalenko B.K. (1971) The biological productivity of Lake Baykal. *Hydrobiol. J.*, 7(**5**), 1–8.

Nauwerck A., Duncan A., Hillbricht-Ilkowska A. & Larsson P. (1980) Secondary production: zooplankton. In E.D.LeCren & R.H.Lowe-McConnell (eds.), *The Functioning of Freshwater Ecosystems.* IBP 22. Cambridge: Cambridge University Press.

Neveau A. & Lapchin L. (1979) Ecologie des principaux invertébrés filtreurs de la basse nivelle (Pyrénés-Atlantiques) 1. Simuliidae (Diptera, Nematocera). *Ann. Limnol.*, **14**, 225–244.

Neves R.J. (1979) Secondary production of epilithic fauna in a woodland stream. *Am. Midl. Nat.*, **102**, 209–224.

Nichols F.H. (1975) Dynamics and energetics of three deposit-feeding benthic invertebrate populations in Puget Sound, Washington. *Ecol. Monogr.*, **45**, 57–82.

Northrop F.S.C. (1947) *The Logic of the Sciences and the Humanities.* New York: World Publishing.

O'Brien F.I., Winner J.M. & Krochak D.K. (1973) Ecology of *Diaptomus leptopus* s.a. Forbes 1882 (Copepoda: Calanoidea) under temporary pond conditions. *Hydrobiologia*, **43**, 137–155.

Paterson C.G. & Walker K.F. (1974) Seasonal dynamics and productivity of *Tanytarsus barbitarsis* Freeman (Diptera: Chironomidae) in the benthos of a shallow, saline lake. *Aust. J. mar. Freshwat. Res.*, **25**, 151–165.

Pederson G.L., Welch E.B. & Litt A.H. (1976) Plankton secondary productivity and biomass: their relation to lake trophic status. *Hydrobiologia*, **50**, 129–144.

Pidgaiko M.L., Grin V.G., Kititsina L.A., Lenchina L.G., Polivannaya M.F., Sergeva O.A. & Vinogradskaya T.A. (1972) Biological productivity of Kurakhov's power station cooling reservoir. In Z.Kajak & A.Hillbricht-Ilkowska (eds.), *Productivity Problems in Freshwaters.* Proceedings of the IBP–UNESCO Symposium on Productivity in Freshwaters. Krakow: Polish Scientific Publishers.

Pinel-Alloul B. (1978) Ecologie des populations de *Lymnaea catascopium* (Mollusques, Gastéropodes, Pulmonées) du Lac St-Louis, près de Montréal, Québec. *Verh. Int. Verein. Limnol.*, **20**, 2412–2426.

Prikhod'ko T.I. (1975) A mathematical model of the production of *Daphnia longiremis* Sars in Lake Dal'neye. *Hydrobiol. J.*, **11**(4), 20–26.

Priymachenko A.D., Mikhaylinko L.Y., Gusynskaya S.L. & Nebrat A.A. (1978) The productivity of plankton associations at differing trophic levels in Kremenchug Reservoir. *Hydrobiol. J.*, **14**(4), 1–9.

Resh V.H. (1977) Habitat and substrate influences on population and production dynamics of a stream caddisfly, *Ceraclea ancylus* (Leptoceridae). *Freshw. Biol.*, **7**, 261–277.

Rosenberg R. (1977) Benthic macrofaunal dynamics, production and dispersion in an oxygen-deficient estuary of west Sweden. *J. Exp. Mar. Biol. Ecol.*, **26**, 107–133.

Schindler D.W. (1972) Production of phytoplankton and zooplankton in Canadian Shield lakes. In Z.Kajak & A.Hillbricht-Ilkowska (eds.), *Productivity Problems in Freshwaters.* Proceedings of the IBP–UNESCO Symposium on Productivity in Freshwaters. Krakow: Polish Scientific Publishers.

Selin P. & Hakkari L. (1982) The diversity, biomass and production of zooplankton in Lake Inarijärvi. *Hydrobiologia*, **86**, 55–59.

Short R.A. & Ward J.V. (1980) Life cycle and production of *Skwala parallela* (Frison)

(Plecoptera: Perlodidae) in a Colorado montane stream. *Hydrobiologia*, **69**, 273–275.

Smyly W.J.P. (1979) Population dynamics of *Daphnia hyalina* Leydig (Crustacea: Cladocera) in a productive and an unproductive lake in the English Lake District. *Hydrobiologia*, **64**, 269–278.

Strayer D.L., Cole J.L., Likens G.E. & Buso D.C. (1981) Biomass and annual production of the freshwater mussel *Eliptio complanata* in an oligotrophic softwater lake. *Freshw. Biol.*, **11**, 435–440.

Stross R.G., Neess J.C. & Hasler A.D. (1961) Turnover time and production of planktonic Crustacea in limed and reference portion of a bog lake. *Ecology*, **42**, 237–245.

Sutcliffe D.W., Carrier T.R. & Willoughby L.G. (1981) Effects of diet, body size, age and temperature on growth rates in the amphipod *Gammarus pulex. Freshw. Biol.*, **11**, 183–214.

Swiss J.J. & Johnson M.G. (1976) Energy dynamics of two benthic crustaceans in relation to diet. *J. Fish. Res. Board Can.*, **33**, 2544–2550.

Tonolli, L. (1980) Introduction. In E.D.LeCren & R.H.Lowe-McConnell (eds.), *The Functioning of Freshwater Ecosystems*. IBP 22. Cambridge: Cambridge University Press.

Uye S.-I. (1982) Population dynamics and production of *Acartia clausi* Giesbrecht (Copepoda: Calanoida) in inlet waters. *J. Exp. Mar. Biol. Ecol.*, **57**, 55–83.

Vijverberg J. (1976) The effect of food quantity and quality on the growth, birth-rate and longevity of *Daphnia hyalina* Leydig. *Hydrobiologia*, **51**, 99–108.

Vijverberg J. (1980) Effect of temperature in laboratory studies on development and growth of Cladocera and Copepoda from Tjeukemeer, The Netherlands. *Freshw. Biol.*, **10**, 317–340.

Waters T.F. (1977) Secondary production in inland waters. *Adv. Ecol. Res.*, **10**, 91–164.

Waters T.F. & Crawford G.W. (1973) Annual production of a stream mayfly population: a comparison of methods. *Limnol. Oceanogr.*, **18**, 286–296.

Wattiez C. (1981) Biomasse du zooplancton et productivité des cladocères d'eaux de degré trophique différent. *Ann. Limnol.*, **17**, 219–236.

Wildish D.J. & Peer D. (1981) Methods for estimating secondary production in marine Amphipoda. *Can. J. Fish. Aquat. Sci.*, **38**, 1019–1026.

Williams D.D., Mundie J.H. & Mounce D.E. (1977) Some aspects of benthic production in a Salmonid rearing channel. *J. Fish. Res. Board Can.*, **34**, 2133–2141.

Willoughby L.G. & Sutcliffe D.W. (1976) Experiments on feeding and growth of the amphipod *Gammarus pulex* (L.) related to its distribution in the River Duddon. *Freshw. Biol.*, **6**, 577–586.

Winberg G.G. (ed.) (1971a) *Methods for the Estimation of Production of Aquatic Animals*. (Translated by A.Duncan) London: Academic Press.

Winberg G.G. (1971b) Some results of studies on lake productivity in the Soviet Union conducted as part of the International Biological Programme. *Hydrobiol. J.*, 7(1), 1–12.

Winberg G.G., Alimov A.F., Boullion V.V., Ivanova M.B., Korobtzova E.V., Kuzmitzkaya N.K., Nikulina V.N., Finogenova N.P. & Fursenko M.V. (1973) Biological productivity of two subarctic lakes. *Freshw. Biol.*, **3**, 177–197.

Wolnomiejski N., Giziński A. & Jermolowicz M. (1976) The production of the macrobenthos in the psammolittoral of Lake Jeziorak. *Acta Univ. Nicolai Copernici Nauk. Matem.-Przyrod.*, **38**, 17–26.

Zaïka V.E. (1970) Rapports entre la productivité des mollusques aquatiques et la durée de leur vie. *Cah. Biol. Mar.*, **11**, 99–108.

Zelinka M. (1977) The production of Ephemeroptera in running waters. *Hydrobiologia*, **56**, 121–125.

Zimmerman M.L. & Wissing T.E. (1978) Effects of temperature on gut-loading and gut-clearance times of the burrowing mayfly, *Hexagenia limbata. Freshw. Biol.*, **8**, 269–277.

Zndanova G.A. & Tseyev Y.Y. (1970) Biology and productivity of mass species of Cladocera in the Kiev Reservoir. *Hydrobiol. J.*, **6**(1), 33–38.

Zwick P. (1975) Critical notes on a proposed method to estimate production. *Freshw. Biol.*, **5**, 65–70.

Zytkowicz R. (1976) Production of macrobenthos in Lake Tynwald. *Acta Univ. Nicolai Copernici Nauk. Matem.-Przyrod.*, **38**, 75–97.

Chapter 2. The Calculation of Secondary Productivity

FRANK H. RIGLER AND JOHN A. DOWNING[1]

1 Introduction

The final calculation of production is the simplest job that the production biologist has to do; all of the real difficulties are associated with the collection of the data that go into the calculation. However, the literature on secondary production contains such a diversity of equations, some correct and some erroneous, that a newcomer to the field can easily be misled into believing that the calculations are conceptually very difficult. This chapter will attempt to show, as did Gillespie and Benke (1979) that there is only one, simple method of calculating production.

In this chapter, the rate of production by a heterotrophic population will be taken to mean the biomass accumulated by that population per unit time.[2] This definition is generally accepted and is particularly useful because it is conceptually simple and makes it easy to calculate production.

I will illustrate the principle of these calculations by imagining a small, simple population of 10 animals ($N_0 = 10$) hatching from eggs simultaneously. On hatching, all animals are the same size and each has a dry mass of m_0. The initial biomass of our imaginary cohort (B_0) is $N_0 m_0$. This initial biomass will not be included in the production of our cohort. In other words, the production of eggs or newborns is assigned to that of the parent cohort.

Now, imagine the animals all growing at the same rate until eventually one dies or is eaten by a predator. If this loss occurs when the mass is m_1, the total production up to that moment is $10(m_1 - m_0)$. Figure 2.1a shows that this product of number of animals multiplied by the biomass increment is simply

---

1. JAD prepared this manuscript from drafts written by FHR. The ideas presented are primarily those of the principal author and 'I' refers to him throughout unless otherwise noted. JAD accepts full responsibility for any errors or omissions.

2. Biomass can be expressed in many ways. During the IBP an attempt was made to impose a uniform method of expressing it as energy equivalent of mass. This attempt failed since biomass can be expressed easily as dry mass, ash-free dry mass, carbon, nitrogen, etc. (see Chapter 7). Since dry mass is usually the first measurement made by most workers, I will express biomass as dry mass. It is not intended to suggest that this is the most generally useful estimator of biomass.

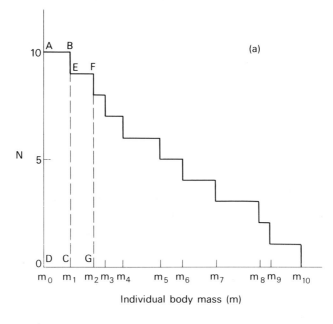

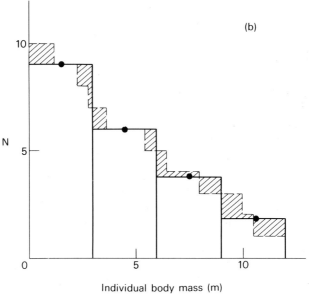

Individual body mass (m)

Fig. 2.1 The calculation of production for a cohort with initial population (N_0) of 10 organisms and a mass at birth of m_0. Panel (A) shows the calculation of production if the mass at death of each individual were known. The area enclosed in the rectangle ABCD is the production up to the death of the first individual, while the area in EFGC is the production between the death of the first animal

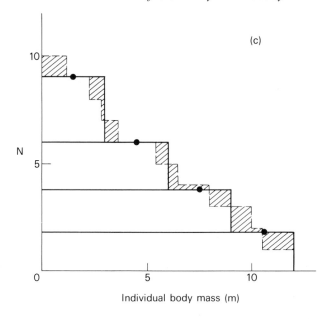

(c)

Individual body mass (m)

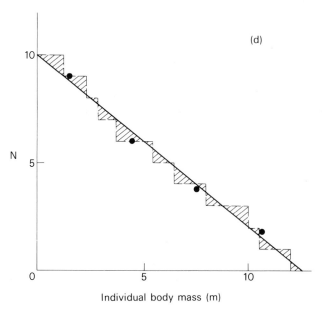

(d)

Individual body mass (m)

and the second. Other panels show the manner in which the production throughout the life of the cohort is estimated by: (B) the increment summation, (C) the mortality summation, and (D) the Allen curve methods of area integration. The bold points are observations made on the cohort and are means in a size class or during a time period. The shaded areas are errors in estimation.

the area enclosed within the rectangle ABCD on Fig. 2.1a. If the remaining nine animals continue growing at the same rate until a second dies, at a dry mass m_2, production during the interval between the death of the first and second individual is $9(m_2 - m_1)$. This increment of production is given by the area within the rectangle EFGC in Fig. 2.1a. Clearly, if we continue to record deaths and dry mass until the last individual dies with a dry mass of m_{10}, we will have the data necessary to calculate production by the cohort (P), which is merely the area under the curve of N plotted against m or:

$$P = N_0(m_1 - m_0) + N_1(m_2 - m_1) + \cdots + N_{i-1}(m_i - m_{i-1}) \qquad (2.1)$$

where N_0 is the number of animals living from hatching to the moment the first animal dies, N_1 is the number living from hatching until the moment the second animal dies, m_0 is the individual mass at birth, m_1 is the individual mass at the death of the first animal, and i is the total number of animals that hatched ($i = N_0$ in this case).

This example illustrates the basis of all calculations of secondary production. Considering its simplicity, one might wonder why the literature contains a multitude of different equations for calculating production. The answer is partially that real populations are not as simple as the one in Fig. 2.1a, nor can we always gather data on real populations comparable to data in Fig. 2.1a. For example, not all individuals in a cohort are born at the same time with the same dry mass, and we can rarely measure the mass at death of every individual in the cohort.

In the sections that follow, the 'different' methods of calculating production will be described and the essential similarity of these methods demonstrated. Then the diverse behavior of real populations and the types of data which we can gather about them will be described. Further, the ways in which production calculations have been modified for different types of population behavior or for inadequacies of data will be shown. Finally, we present real examples of the calculation of production for the two major categories of animals.

2 Four Methods of Calculating Production

The hypothetical cohort in Fig. 2.1a will be used again to illustrate the methods that have been used to estimate cohort production. In practice, because it would be virtually impossible to gather the data on the weight at death of every individual, we make do with less information. At best we have samples of the cohort taken at different times during its development or that we divide into different size classes. For each size class or time period we obtain a mean body mass of an individual ($\bar{m}_i$) and an estimate of the number of individuals in that size class ($N_{\bar{m}i}$). In most cases, $N_{\bar{m}i}$ is taken to be an estimate of the number of individuals that live long enough to attain a body mass of $\bar{m}_j$. This procedure does not give us a complete graph of cohort size against body mass as was seen in Fig. 2.1a, but (in this example) only four points. From here on, depending on our whim, we calculate production in one of four ways.

In the first two methods ('growth increment summation' and 'mortality summation'), we proceed as if we had a complete record and all mortality occurred at the boundaries between our size classes. The history of the cohort is reconstructed as a simplified histogram of numbers against individual mass. In the method of growth increment summation the histogram is divided into vertical slices, as in Fig. 2.1b, and their total area is calculated. To calculate production by mortality summation, we merely divide Fig. 2.1a into horizontal slices (e.g. Fig. 2.1c) and sum the areas of individual slices as in equation 2.2 (for actual calculations use equation 2.27):

$$P = (N_0 - N_1)(m_1 - m_0) + (N_1 - N_2)(m_2 - m_0) + \cdots + (N_{i-1} - N_i)(m_i - m_0)$$
$$(2.2)$$

where all variables are as in equation 2.1.

It should be clear from this comparison that the growth increment summation method and the mortality summation method are really identical. In particular, it is important to note that they require exactly the same population statistics and that there are no conditions under which either method is superior to the other. Example calculations are given in Section 7.

The remaining two methods differ from the first two only in the interpolation between the observed points. In the Allen curve method (named after K.R.Allen, 1951, who used it to calculate production of trout in a New Zealand stream) one merely draws a smooth curve by eye through the points and extrapolates the curve intuitively to its intercepts with m_0 and $N = 0$ (Fig. 2.1d). The area under the curve is easily measured by planimeter, square counting, weighing, or electronic digitizer. As Fig. 2.1d shows, the area under the smooth curve is similar to the area under the histogram and both give reasonable approximations of production.

The fourth method merely uses a least squares curve-fitting procedure to obtain an equation describing the Allen curve (see Chapter 8). The definite integral from the smallest to largest mass of the individual then gives production of the cohort. This formal method appears to yield the most accurate estimate of production, and it does have the advantage of eliminating subjectivity from the curve-fitting process. Usually, the only way of significantly improving the estimate of production is by obtaining more and better estimates of cohort size and body mass.

If natural populations behaved similarly to the hypothetical population in Fig. 2.1a, the only difficulty would be in obtaining accurate estimates of population size. However, no real population comprises individuals of all the same size and born at exactly the same time. Some do not even produce recognizable cohorts. Much of the remainder of this chapter will, therefore, deal with the problems posed by the differences between real populations and our hypothetical population.

3 The Simplest Case—A Population with Identifiable Cohorts

A few types of aquatic animals such as fish and lamelli-branch molluscs can be aged and have a reproductive period that is very short relative to their lifespan. Consequently, all members of a cohort can be recognized and analyzed in the same size class. In this case, the techniques in Section 2 can be applied easily. However, the more typical situation for small invertebrates is that of a reproductive period which is long relative to the lifespan, and cohorts, although they exist, are not clearly delineated. In this case individuals from one cohort will be of many sizes. The significant difference for the production biologist is that a sample taken at any point in time will catch members of the same cohort in many different size classes (Fig. 2.2). If animals can be aged there is no problem in determining the number of individuals in a cohort reaching any size, and since Ricker (1971) thoroughly covers this type of population it will be ignored here. Other invertebrates produce only a few cohorts per year and thus can be treated easily by the techniques in Section 2 (see example, Section 8).

In the population illustrated in Fig. 2.2, however, the number of members of a cohort reaching a given size must be estimated indirectly, because at any time during the growth of a cohort individuals will be spread throughout several size classes. One technique for estimating the production of this type of population is outlined below.

Southwood (1966) has developed a method to determine the total population of a cohort, where cohorts are not easily separable (Southwood & Jepson 1962; Southwood 1966). In this method, the abundance of animals in an arbitrary or developmental size class is plotted as a function of time (Fig. 2.3). If there is no mortality of animals as they grow through this size class, the number of animals growing from the lower size limit ($m_{min\,i}$) to the upper size limit ($m_{max\,i}$) of the stage can be calculated from the area (A) under the curve in Fig. 2.3. This area is equal to the number of animal-days m^{-2}, therefore, if we divide the area by the number of days which it takes an average individual to grow through the size class, we know the number of animals. In the example in Fig. 2.3, the area under the curve is 220 animal-days m^{-2}. If the average time spent in the size class (D) is 0·5 days, then the total number of animals that enter and leave the class will be $A/D = 220/0\cdot5 = 440$.

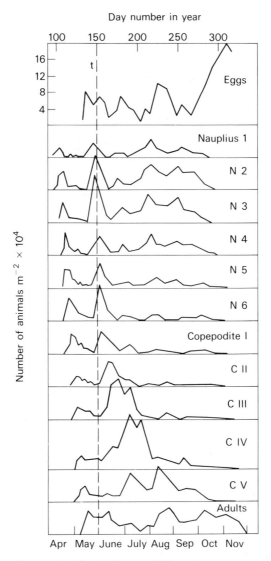

Fig. 2.2 The standing stock of each instar of *Skistodiaptomus oregonensis* in Teapot Lake during 1966 (from Rigler & Cooley 1974). The figure shows that lack of synchrony in the reproduction of small invertebrates often leads to the members of a cohort being dispersed throughout a variety of instars or size classes. A sample taken at time 't' would contain members of the cohort produced around day 140 that have attained developmental stages N1 to C2. The production of these sorts of organisms can be approximated using equation 2.3.

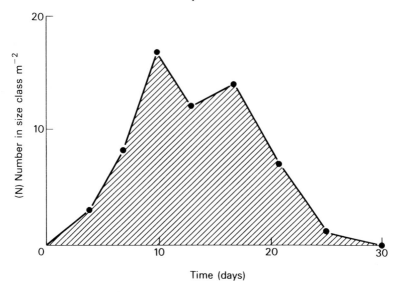

Fig. 2.3 Plot of hypothetical data for Southwood's technique for determining the number of organisms in a cohort. The data are concentration of organisms in an instar or size class plotted against time. The shaded area is integrated and divided by the average time required for an animal to pass through this stage or class which yields the average number of organisms in the cohort.

It follows that the production of this size class (P_i) is given by:

$$P_i = (A_i/D_i)(m_{max} - m_{min})_i \qquad (2.3)$$

If there is mortality within the size category, equation 2.3 may not be strictly correct. The error in the estimate of production that is produced by using equation 2.3 will depend on:

(1)   The pattern of mortality and growth.
(2)   The amount of growth.
(3)   The amount of mortality.

If growth and mortality are both constant with time there will be no error; if all mortality occurs at the beginning or the end of the period spent in the size category there will be no error. However, if growth and mortality are both exponential functions of time, then the application of equation 2.3 will overestimate production. Since exponential growth and mortality probably occur frequently, it is of interest to know the magnitude of the error. Table 2.1 shows that it increases with increased mortality and growth; an error from this source can, therefore, be decreased by increasing the number of size classes. This will decrease not only m_{max}/m_{min}, but also the percentage

Table 2.1 Percent by which production is overestimated when growth and mortality within a size class are exponential and P is calculated from equation 2.3.

Growth $[m_{max}/m_{min}]$	Mortality (%) $[100(N_0 - N_t)/N_0]$		
	25	50	75
2	1·7	4·1	8·2
4	3·3	8·2	16·8
8	4·8	12·2	26·2

mortality within each size class. Alternatively, the error could be estimated from Table 2.1 and an approximate correction applied to the calculated value of production.

Since information on the temporal distribution of mortality within each size category will almost certainly not be available, and will generally be impossible to collect, the recommended procedure is to divide the population into the largest number of size or developmental categories possible.

The methods for estimating the time spent in a size class (D) will be described in Section 4.4. If cohorts cannot be established with certainty by simple inspection of plots such as Fig. 2.3, probability paper can sometimes be used to determine their boundaries (Harding 1949; Cassie 1950; Southwood 1966). Methods described in Section 4 should be used if cohorts cannot be identified.

4 Populations in a Steady State

4.1 *General comments*

Not all populations of aquatic animals produce identifiable cohorts. In some populations the instantaneous birth rate (b) is very similar to the instantaneous death rate (d). For these populations:

$$b = d \gg r \qquad (2.4)$$

That is to say, the instantaneous rate of change of population size, although not necessarily zero, is very small, and cohorts cannot be recognized from analysis of a temporal series of samples taken from the population. In this situation, a slightly different method is used to calculate the required population statistics.

The method applied to steady-state populations has been called a time-specific analysis by Southwood (1966). In time-specific analysis, because we cannot identify real cohorts, we analyze the population at one point in time, or determine the average structure during a selected interval of time. Although the method of calculating production of a population in a steady state is essentially identical to the method applied to populations producing cohorts, the method of gathering the data that go into the calculation is different. This difference arises because the time in each size class cannot be inferred from a temporal series of quantitative samples of a population in steady state. In order to convert size classes into age classes one must obtain an independent estimate of growth rate. As will be shown later, this estimate is obtained by measuring the growth of identified individuals held under conditions that simulate natural conditions.

Because the embryo (developing egg) is often the easiest stage to maintain in culture, and because the development rate of the egg is exclusively a function of temperature (e.g. Fig. 2.4) (Eichhorn 1957; Bottrell 1975a, 1975b; Bottrell *et al.* 1976; Vijverberg 1980) more work has focused on the egg than on other stages. From this work, particularly through the ideas of Elster

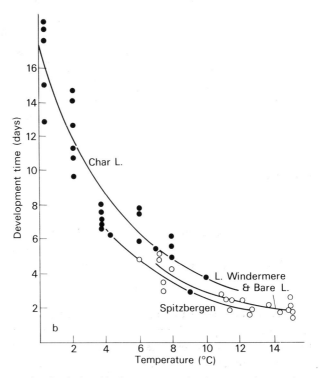

Fig. 2.4 Example of relationship between egg development time and water temperature. The development time of the rotifer *Keratella cochlearis* from Char Lake (Rigler *et al.* 1974) is compared with those measured by Amrén (1964) and Edmondson (1965).

(1954; Elster & Schwoerbel 1970) and Edmondson (1960, 1974), the egg ratio method of determining birth rate has become widely used. These birth rates are important in population statistics studies and have been used to examine the effect of various environmental factors and biological relationships on production (Edmondson 1974), and for the calculation of production from turnover in numbers (cf. Section 4.3.3). Because much confusion and dispute has surrounded this method I will describe it in detail and attempt to use it correctly. A later section (4.3) shows that similar population statistics can be used to calculate the productivity of populations for which cohorts are not identifiable.

4.2 The egg-ratio method of calculating birth rate

In the traditional method of estimating birth rate from egg ratio, quantitative samples of the number of eggs in the population (N_{egg}) are taken. The mean temperature to which the developing embryos are naturally exposed is estimated and the average D under natural conditions is estimated from an equation or graph relating duration of embryonic development (D) to temperature (Fig. 2.4). N_{egg}/D is then used as an estimator of birth rate. Some important questions remain, however: What is the relation between N_{egg}/D and birth rate? Is this a constant relation, and, if so, what is it? The confusion in the literature arose because many different answers have been given to these questions and almost all are both right and wrong. I'll now try to explain this apparent contradiction.

The literature makes a distinction between 'finite birth rate' and 'instantaneous birth rate'. The former is the average birth rate over some finite interval of time and the latter is the birth rate at some point in time. The latter can be thought of as the first derivative of births with respect to time.

Thus, there are two rates that can be calculated from the egg ratio. I will first discuss the calculation of finite birth rate and then the calculation of instantaneous birth rate.

4.2.1 Relation between N_{egg}/D and the finite birth rate

Traditionally, the finite birth rate (β) from t to t + D of a population sampled at time t has been considered to be equal to N_{egg}/D. Most papers dealing with production or population statistics of invertebrates have made this assumption, However, Paloheimo (1974) has shown that this assumption is valid only under certain conditions. Uncritical acceptance of this assumption can cause large errors in the calculation of birth rates.

The rationale for equating N_{egg}/D and β is that the eggs sampled at t will range in age from 0 to D. By t + D all of these eggs will have hatched and none of the eggs laid after t will have hatched. Problems arise if there is mortality of females carrying the eggs. If this is the case some eggs will die before they hatch and β from t to t + D will be less than N_{egg}/D. I will return to the calculation of finite birth rate after considering calculation of the instantaneous birth rate.

4.2.2 Relation between N_{egg}/D and instantaneous birth rate

Although production can be calculated without calculating the instantaneous birth rate (b). many workers have placed great importance on the calculation of b. This emphasis on b probably derives from the appeal and the apparent rigour of the exponential equations for population growth.

The point that needs stressing is that the analysis of population parameters by exponential equations is rigorous only when the population under study conforms to the assumptions implicit in these equations, that the birth rate and the death rate are both constant over the time interval between successive samples. Only if they are constant can the growth of the populations be described by:

$$N_{t2} = N_{t1}\, e^{(b-d)(t_2 - t_1)} \tag{2.5}$$

where N_{t1} and N_{t2} are the numbers of individuals in the population at times t_1 and t_2, b is the instantaneous birth rate, and d is the instantaneous death rate.

Since the instantaneous constant of population growth (r) is merely the difference between the instantaneous birth and death rates:

$$r = b - d \tag{2.6}$$

we can simplify equation (2.5) to:

$$N_{t2} = N_{t1}\, e^{r(t_2 - t_1)} \tag{2.7}$$

In practice, equations 2.6 and 2.7 are used as follows. First, the population under study is censused on two occasions, t_1 and t_2. The estimates of the population size on these dates (N_{t1} and N_{t2}) are then substituted in equation (2.7) and the equation is solved for r.

This is as far as we can go without an estimate of either b or d. Since d is usually impossible to measure (Prepas & Rigler 1978) it is necessary to obtain an estimate of b to substitute into (2.6).

Practical and conceptual difficulties arise at this stage because b can be measured directly only under exceptional circumstances. What we normally attempt to measure is the finite birth rate (β) over some specified interval. The finite birth rate is then converted to b.

Depending on the behaviour of the population, one of three equations is used to make this conversion (Table 2.2). These equations only apply when b and d are constant over the time interval $t_2 - t_1$. If the population is in a steady

Table 2.2 Equations used to calculate b from β and the conditions under which each applies.

Conditions		Applicable equation
b and d are	b = d	$b = \beta$
both constant	b > d = 0	$b = \ln(1 + \beta)$
from t_1 to t_2	b $\neq$ d > 0	$b = r\beta/(e^r - 1)$
b or d varies between t_1 and t_2		none of the above equations are valid

state because births equal deaths, then the instantaneous birth rate equals the finite birth rate. If there are no deaths from t_1 to t_2 then Edmondson's (1960) equation is valid. When b and d are not equal and d is greater than zero, the equation of Leslie (1948) and Caswell (1972) must be used.

The seductive appeal of the exponential growth equation and the rigorous conversion from finite to instantaneous birth rate probably convinces many field ecologists that one or another of the conversions in Table 2.2 must be used. However, real populations rarely conform to the assumptions of the mathematics. Usually b and d both vary such that none of the conversions is strictly correct. Therefore, it is not surprising that many field ecologists are confused and unsure about the appropriate conversion.

4.2.3 Usual measurement of finite birth rate

The method usually used to measure finite birth rate is as follows:

(1) The relation between the duration of embryonic development (D) and temperature for the species under study is measured in the laboratory.
(2) The mean temperature experienced by embryos in nature is estimated and D is calculated for the embryo population over finite intervals.
(3) From samples of the population, the number of developing eggs (N_{egg}) in the population is estimated for the sampling dates.
(4) If t_i is a sampling date then the finite birth rate over the period t_i to $t_i + D_i$ is calculated as $N_{egg\ i}/D_i$.

Since the absolute birth rate is usually of less interest than the birth rate relative to the number of animals in the population, the results are usually divided by the population size of free-swimming individuals (N_i) at t_i to give births over t_i to $t_i + D_i$ per animal on t_i.

Thus,

$$\beta \text{ (from } t_i \text{ to } t_i + D_i) = N_{egg\ i}/D_i N_i \tag{2.8}$$

This apparently simple computation is based on a most important, implicit assumption: that all of the developing eggs in the population at t_i will actually survive for the remainder of their development period and hatch. If there is predation on egg-bearing females this assumption is invalid and the real finite birth rate from t_i to $t_i + D_i$ will be lower than that calculated from the egg ratio. A mathematical demonstration of this source of error and an estimate of its magnitude was given by Paloheimo (1974). He showed that N_{egg}/D and β are approximately equal only when b, D and r are extremely small.

Again, we are faced with a situation in which the analysis of our data is only valid if the population we are studying conforms to the assumptions of the mathematical treatment. The best way of eliminating the uncertainty is to test our assumptions. Since all of these assumptions concern the age distribution of the embryo population, the simple solution is merely to measure this age distribution if possible (Threlkeld 1979).

Although measurement of the age distribution of embryos is easy, it has been done surprisingly rarely. Several examples show how useful this measurement can be. George & Edwards (1974) studied a population of *Daphnia hyalina* that was approximately in a steady state. Their results clearly showed that the frequency distribution of each morphologically identified group of embryos was indistinguishable from the relative duration of the group. In other words, the age distribution of embryos was uniform. Since the rate of production of eggs was constant, their study showed that embryo mortality was negligible. Consequently, they demonstrated that the egg ratio $= \beta = $ b.

Unfortunately, this paper also provides a good example of the confusion that surrounds the calculation of birth rates for, having demonstrated that in their population $\beta = $ b, they then made the mistake of applying Edmondson's (1974) formula to convert β to b.

In a paper strongly advocating the use of age distribution of embryos in population studies, Threlkeld (1979) showed that the age distribution of embryos varied diurnally, and inferred that this showed diurnal changes in mortality of *Daphnia galeata mendotae* females due to predation.

4.2.4 *Recommended method of measuring birth rate*

The method that is suggested here can be applied to any species that carries its eggs or for which an accurate sample of the egg population can be taken, and in which a series of development stages of the embryo can be identified. In principle this method is similar to the use of the Kolmogorov–Smirnov cumulative frequency distribution statistic recommended by Threlkeld (1979; Sokal & Rohlf 1981), but it is intuitively simpler.

First, measure the duration of as many morphologically identifiable stages of the embryo as is convenient (Obreshkove & Fraser 1940; Green 1956; Lei & Clifford 1974). Select females for observation that have well developed ovaries, maintain them in well-oxygenated water at a constant temperature and record when each lays its eggs. If the eggs can be separated from the female and develop normally one clutch of eggs can be observed repetitively. Otherwise it might be necessary to kill females at intervals to record developmental stages reached by eggs at different times after laying. Total development time (D) is recorded as is the fraction of D spent in each stage.

Although no observations exist to show that development rate of early or late embryonic stages is differently affected by temperature (Cooley 1971; Threlkeld 1979) it would be advisable to test this possibility by making measurements at several temperatures.

When planning the sampling program one must take great care to ensure that samples are representative. Eggs may not be distributed uniformly either horizontally or vertically. Additional care is needed in thermally stratified systems if egg-bearing females do not migrate freely through the temperature range occupied by the species. If this situation occurs, calculation of birth rate should be modified (Prepas & Rigler 1978).

It is also important to establish whether or not there is a diurnal change in age distribution of embryos. Either diurnal predation cycles (Threlkeld 1979) or cycles in egg production could cause temporal changes in age distribution. If such changes are found, it might be necessary to collect day and night samples routinely.

Methods of killing and fixing of specimens are also more important because differential loss of older or younger embryos will bias the results when loose embryos cannot be identified to species. Sometimes the sugar-formalin method of Haney & Hall (1973) is adequate to prevent loss of embryos (Threlkeld 1979) but occasionally this method causes a high loss of older embryos and must be modified. Prepas (1978) found that ice cold sugar-formalin prevented this loss in a population of *Daphnia rosea*. One must also consider the problems of distortion and weight loss if the same samples are to be used for determining taxon or biomass (see Chapters 3, 4 & 7). It is likely that no one technique will be adequate for all species. Consequently fixation methods should be investigated before sampling is started.

When samples are being counted, the number of embryos in each of the predetermined developmental stages is recorded. More embryos must be counted than in the traditional method. As a rule of thumb, one could increase the number counted by a factor equal to the number of stages identified. For statistical treatments of sampling and counting see Chapters 7 and 8.

If there are no diurnal changes in the age distribution of embryos, the instantaneous rate of egg production and the instantaneous birth rate can be calculated directly as shown in the following hypothetical example.

4.2.5 Example calculation of instantaneous birth rate

To illustrate the proposed method of calculating the instantaneous birth rate we will consider a hypothetical population of a species that has six easily identifiable stages of developing embryo. First, we measure in the laboratory the fraction of the total embryonic period spent in each stage (Column 2, Table 2.3). Then on two occasions at t_1 and t_2 we sample the population of animals (N) and the population of developing eggs (N_{egg}). The number in each stage on day t_1 and day t_2 is recorded in Column 4 and Column 5 of Table 2.3.

Table 2.3 Hypothetical data to illustrate the use of embryo age distributions to estimate the instantaneous birth rate. Total embryonic period is 2·5 days and the total egg population is 2500 m^{-2}.

(1)	(2)	(3)	(4)	(5)	(6)	(7)
Embryonic stage	Fraction of D in stage	D_i when $D = 2·5$ days	No. of eggs m^{-2}		Potential finite birth rate	
			at t_1	at t_2	at t_1	at t_2
1	0·20	0·50	500	750	1000	1500
2	0·30	0·75	750	925	1000	1233
3	0·15	0·375	375	325	1000	867
4	0·15	0·375	375	275	1000	733
5	0·12	0·30	300	150	1000	500
6	0·08	0·20	200	75	1000	375

The ratio of the number of eggs in the ith stage (N_i) to the time spent in that stage (D_i) gives the potential finite birth rate of the individuals in the ith stage (potential β_i) at the time of sampling, in animals per day, i.e. $N_i/D_i =$ potential β_i. Note that N_i/D_i is called the potential finite birth rate. This qualifier is to remind us that the actual finite birth rate of a stage will be lower than N_i/D_i if there is any embryo mortality.

Until now I have considered the potential finite birth rates of embryonic stages. However, we can also think of these rates as applying over finite intervals of time. For example, the stage 6 embryos will hatch over the period from t to $t + 0·2$ days. The stage 5 embryos will hatch over the period from $t + 0·2$ to $t + 0·5$ days. The results from Table 2.3 converted to time periods are shown in Fig. 2.5, where it can be seen that over the 2·5 days following t_1, the potential birth rate is constant. This is because the fraction of the population contributed by each stage on sampling date t_1 was equal to the fraction of the development time occupied by that stage. If a result such as this were obtained when the population was in steady state, it would tell us that egg

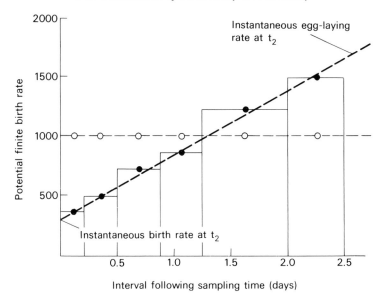

Fig. 2.5 Plot of hypothetical data from Table 2.3 used to illustrate the use of embryo age distribution to estimate the instantaneous birth rate. Potential finite birth rates are expressed in births m^{-2} day^{-1}. The total embryonic period is 2·5 days and the total egg population is 2500 m^{-2}. The data are for two sampling dates: open circles are t_1 and closed circles are t_2.

mortality was negligible. Under these conditions, the potential finite birth rate equals the real finite birth rate which in turn equals the instantaneous birth rate.

On sampling date t_2 the behavior of the population was quite different. The potential finite birth rate increased steadily over the 2·5 days following t_2. Provided the eggs were well sampled and diurnal fluctuations in age distribution did not occur, data such as these indicate one of two situations. Either egg mortality was very high or the population of females was increasing rapidly. Although the two situations are not mutually exclusive it is unlikely that they would coincide.

The situation at t_2 illustrates both the error of using N_{egg}/D as an estimator of the finite birth rate, and the value of a careful age analysis of embryos. To simplify the explanation, we will say that the population of adult females at t_2 was in a steady state. Consequently, the trend of decreasing potential finite birth rate with increasing age of embryo is due exclusively to mortality of embryos. If we had assumed that N_{egg}/D gave a measure of the finite birth rate from t_2 to $t_2 + D$, then we would have concluded that $\beta = 2500/2·5$ or 1000 births m^{-2} day^{-1}, whereas we know that the potential finite birth rate of stage 6, which still overestimates the finite birth rate of this stage, is $75/0·2 = 375$

births m^{-2} day^{-1}. The shorter the time period following t_2 included in the calculation, the lower and more accurate will be the estimate of finite birth rate at t_2.

This simple calculation merely illustrates what Paloheimo (1974) showed mathematically. All other things being equal, reducing D reduces the discrepancy between the finite birth rate and the potential finite birth rate. There are two consequences of this relation. First, the most accurate estimate of β is obtained by choosing late embryonic stages with short duration, provided, of course, that a good estimate of the population in these stages can be made. Second, as the duration of the oldest stage becomes infinitely short, the amount of unmeasured mortality between the sampling and hatching times approaches zero. With an infinitely short duration of the last stage, the potential finite birth rate equals the instantaneous birth rate at t_2. Consequently, to use these data to estimate the instantaneous birth rate we need only assume that the trend of decreasing potential birth rate with increasing age is continuous and extrapolates to t_2. This assumption is much less restrictive than those made by mathematical models. The population is not required to be in a steady state and we do not need to know r.

The simplest method of extrapolating is to apply the potential finite birth rate of a stage at the mid-time of hatching of that stage and fit a curve to the points as shown in Fig. 2.5. In the example given, the results were indistinguishable from a straight line. Therefore, a least squares linear fit was used to give an intercept at t_2 of 325. Other forms of curves could be fitted with other techniques (see Chapter 8). Thus, our estimate of the instantaneous birth rate by the method of embryo stage analysis is 325 births m^{-2} day^{-1}. The intercept of the line at $t_2 + D$ can be used as a measure of the instantaneous rate of egg production at t_2. It is important to note that these population statistics are valid only at the time when the population was sampled, unless the age structure of the population remains constant.

4.3 *Calculation of the production of populations in steady state*

Strictly speaking, this section is not concerned with populations in a steady state because this situation is encountered very rarely in nature. More appropriately, I will be describing the analysis of populations in which cohorts cannot be identified. Since species that produce this type of population are those which reproduce more or less continuously, their populations more closely approximate a steady state than do those that are suitable for cohort analysis. Therefore, it would be more accurate to say that this section will deal with the calculation of production of populations that are in an approximately steady state over discrete time intervals.

Ideally, we need exactly the same information to calculate production of steady-state populations as we do for those that produce identifiable cohorts. Simply stated, production is calculated as the summation of rates of production for each of a set of identifiable stages or size classes. The production rate of each of the different classes is inferred from measures of number of organisms and rate of growth in each of these classes. However, analysis of steady-state populations is invariably performed with inadequate data, just as cohort analysis is. In fact, we usually have less complete, or less reliable, data for steady-state populations, because growth rates cannot be calculated from samples of the real population but must be measured in the laboratory (e.g. Bottrell 1975b; Bottrell *et al.* 1976; Vijverberg 1980). Consequently, the methods of calculating production must make more assumptions about the behavior of the population. The different computational methods simply depend on different assumptions.

The two most frequently used methods are 'growth increment summation' and 'instantaneous growth rate'. The former is most accurate when individual growth within size classes is linear and the latter is most accurate when growth is exponential.

4.3.1 Growth increment summation

This calculation is based on the assumption that all individuals within a size class are growing at the same constant rate. Thus, the rate of production is proportional to the number of individuals within the class, and can be calculated from:

$$P = N(m_{max} - m_{min})/D \qquad (2.9)$$

where P is the average production in a particular size class per unit time, N is the average number of individuals in the class at t, and m_{max} and m_{min} are respectively the maximum amd minimum mass of individuals in the size class. D is the time taken by an average animal to grow from m_{min} to m_{max}. [*Note*: This technique has been applied to rotifer populations with the added assumption that production due to growth after hatching is negligible. In this case, the production of the population is assumed equal to egg production, $m_{min} = 0$, m_{max} = adult mass, $N = N_{egg}$, and D is equal to the egg development time. The technique is only valid if there is no egg mortality (see Section 4.2, and Fig. 2·7)].

4.3.2 Instantaneous growth method

This method is the one that is most frequently applied to steady-state populations. It assumes that all individuals in the size class are growing exponentially. Production will be proportional to the biomass of the size class and can be calculated from:

$$P = Bg \qquad (2.10)$$

where B is the mean biomass of the size class over t, and g is the constant of instantaneous growth in mass of individuals in the size class.

Since growth is described by $m_{max} = m_{min} e^{Dg}$,

$$g = (1/D) \ln (m_{max}/m_{min}) \qquad (2.11)$$

and we therefore calculate the production of the size class from:

$$P = (B/D) \ln (m_{max}/m_{min}) \qquad (2.12)$$

Provided there is no mortality within the size class, and the population is in an approximately steady-state, equations 2.9 and 2.12 are equally accurate regardless of the shape of the individual growth curve. When mortality is significant, however, it is important to use the equation appropriate to the type of growth characteristic of the size class. Choice of the wrong model can lead to large errors when mortality is high. For this reason, it is important to make growth measurements carefully and to attempt to simulate natural conditions as closely as possible.

4.3.3 A common error: computation of turnover of biomass from turnover of numbers

An apparently simple method of calculating production by steady-state populations has been used by many authors (Stross *et al.* 1961; Hall 1964; Wright 1965; Heinle 1966; Burgis 1971, 1974; George & Edwards 1974; etc.) and recommended in two reviews of methods of calculating production (G.A.Pecheń in Winberg 1971; Waters 1977). Winberg *et al.* in Edmondson and Winberg, eds. (1971) were non-committal, but clearly warned the reader that the method was valid only under certain conditions. However, they appear to have missed the critical condition.

I will attempt to clarify the problem with this method by comparing it with the increment summation, and the instantaneous growth methods, but will supplement explanation with a set of example calculations in an attempt to make my point more simply.

The comparison of methods will be made for the simplest case—the case in which there is no mortality of the individuals passing through the size class for which production is being calculated. I will first show that, in this case, the increment summation and instantaneous growth methods are identical. I will then compare the turnover of numbers method and show that only under one unlikely condition is it identical to the other two and thus correct.

To show the identity of the increment summation and instantaneous growth methods one can begin with equation 2.12. Because N is constant in the size class then:

$$B = N\bar{m} \qquad (2.13)$$

where $\bar{m}$ is the average weight of an individual passing through a size class. Therefore, equation 2.12 can be rewritten:

$$P = (N\bar{m}/D) \ln (m_{max}/m_{min}) \qquad (2.14)$$

Riggs (1963) demonstrates that the mean mass of an organism ($\bar{m}$) during a time period when its mass is changing exponentially would be calculated as the logarithmic mean:

$$\bar{m} = (m_{max} - m_{min})/\ln (m_{max}/m_{min}) \qquad (2.15)$$

Substituting 2.15 into 2.14 we find that:

$$P = N(m_{max} - m_{min})/D \qquad (2.16)$$

which is identical to equation 2.9 for the increment summation technique.

The rationale of the turnover method is difficult to explain because its development was intuitive rather than logical. The basis of the method is that, in a steady-state population, the number of new recruits entering a size class per unit time will be constant and exactly balanced by the number leaving the size class by death or by growing through it. Since finite and instantaneous birth rates are equal to each other and death rates the population is easily described by an input or output rate constant (b or d). Then, by analogy with the terminology of radioactive tracer kinetics or compartmental analysis, the reciprocal of this rate constant is called the turnover time in numbers of the size class. This is the time in which a number of individuals equal to the number in the class enters and leaves the class. So far, so good. Difficulties begin when we intuitively see a connection between the numbers passing through the size class (T_N), the amount of material (biomass) passing through the class (T_B), and production in the class. In general, it has been assumed that the three are related as in:

$$1/b = T_N = T_B \qquad (2.17)$$

If this relation were valid, then daily biomass production (P_B) would equal biomass divided by the turnover time of biomass (or numbers). Therefore production of a population is often calculated:

$$P = \bar{m}N/T_N \qquad (2.18)$$

where $\bar{m}$ is the mean weight of individuals in the size class, and N is the number of individuals in the size class. Because the turnover time in numbers of the population of organisms is the time it takes for the population to be replaced by new recruits, T_N is equal to the development time (D) of the population and thus equation 2.18 can be written:

$$P = \bar{m}N/D \qquad (2.19)$$

Although the set of relationships in (2.17) and (2.18) has been accepted uncritically by many experimentalists, several reviews have suggested that they are valid only under certain conditions. There is, however, no agreement about these conditions.

   For a class in which there is no mortality the condition can be defined unambiguously as the condition under which equation 2.16 predicts the same production as equation 2.19. That is:

$$\bar{m}N/D = N(m_{max} - m_{min})/D \qquad (2.20)$$

and because Riggs (1963) shows that:

$$\bar{m} = (m_{max} - m_{min})/\ln(m_{max}/m_{min}) \approx (m_{max} + m_{min})/2 \qquad (2.21)$$

the condition under which equation 2.18 yields an appropriate measure of

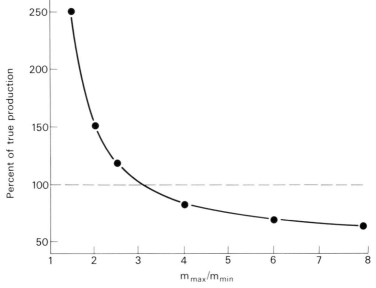

Fig. 2.6 The percent of true production, calculated by equating turnover of numbers with turnover of biomass, plotted against the ratio of maximum mass to minimum mass of animals in a population or size class. The calculations are simply the ratio of equation 2.19 (assuming equation 2.21) to equation 2.16. The figure shows that if m_{max}/m_{min} is low then production is overestimated by the turnover of numbers method, and if m_{max}/m_{min} is high then production is underestimated.

production is when:

$$3m_{min} = m_{max} \qquad (2.22)$$

that is, when the maximum size of an adult is three times the size at hatching.

The magnitude of errors produced by inappropriate calculations is shown in Figs. 2.6 and 2.7. Figure 2.6 shows that equating turnover of numbers and biomass produces large positive errors when $m_{max}/m_{min} < 3$ and negative errors when $m_{max}/m_{min} > 3$. Another factor that leads to errors in this sort of calculation is variability in age structure. This can be brought about not only by expansion and contraction of populations, but also through selective predation or mortality within a size class.

Figure 2.7 shows that when the increment summation method is applied to a size class in which individual growth is exponential the method overestimates

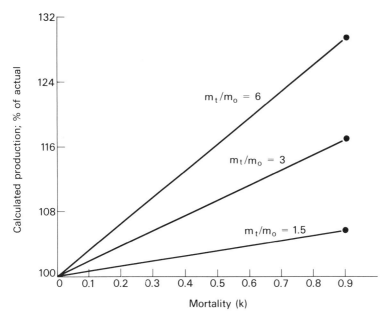

Fig. 2.7 Error of increment summation technique when applied to populations with exponential growth and varying mortality. The data are production, calculated by the increment summation technique, as a percentage of actual production plotted against mortality rate (k), where $N_t = N_0 e^{-kt}$, for size classes with differing ratios of maximum to initial mass (m_t/m_0). The rate of exponential growth was determined as in equation 2.11 using $m_t:m_0$ ratios and is expressed $m_t = m_0 e^{gt}$. Actual production from t_0 to t_D was determined as the area under a plot of N_t against m_t. The figure shows that the increment summation technique yields overestimates of production where there is mortality in the size class or where growth is not linear. Higher mortality and larger ratios of $m_{max}:m_{min}$ lead to larger overestimates of production.

production in all cases when mortality is not zero. This error increases with increasing mortality rate and increasing value of m_D/m_0.

From the above discussion it is clear that a key to the accurate calculation of production by populations in a steady state is a knowledge, for each age class, of m_{min}, m_{max}, and $\bar{m}$. Because $\bar{m}$ will depend on distribution of growth and mortality throughout each age class, these statistics are as important in the analysis of steady-state populations as in cohort analysis. Any method that appears to require less information, such as the turnover method, merely introduces new uncertainties or errors.

5 Two Apparently Simplified Methods

Occasionally a biologist wishes to calculate production from data that were not collected specifically for this purpose. Hence, several methods of approximating production from incomplete data have come into use. Two commonly used methods will be discussed here, although neither is recommended.

5.1 Size-frequency method ('average cohorts')

This method of estimating the production of species that do not produce cohorts, and for which the duration of each size class has not been measured, was first correctly described by Hamilton (1969). It was originally intended for application to a collection of species of stream insects that differ in maximum size and development time but are conveniently treated as one population because they are difficult, or as yet impossible, to separate into species. Those who still recommend using this method generally agree that if it is to be applied to a mixed group of species they should at least have a similar size and development time (Hynes & Coleman 1968; Hamilton 1969; Benke 1979; Waters 1977; Krueger & Martin 1980) and be of the same trophic level (Waters 1979; cf. Peters 1977). Several recent workers have also applied this method to single species (Eckblad 1973; Waters & Crawford 1973; Winterbourne 1974; Martien & Benke 1977; Benke 1979; Waters 1979; Benke & Wallace 1980; Menzie 1980; Waters & Hokenstrom 1980).

Since its first erroneous description by Hynes & Coleman in 1968, this method has generated confusion and conflict. Anyone wishing a history of the debate should consult Zwick (1975), Benke & Waide (1977), Waters (1977), and Menzie (1980). I will not repeat the arguments here, but will merely show that the method is derived from the increment summation method for populations that do not produce identifiable cohorts. Readers who would like a fuller, clear description of the method and its limitations, complete with many numerical examples, should consult Hamilton (1969).

The steps in applying this method are as follows:

(1) Collect representative samples of the population or group of populations on a number of occasions evenly spaced over a year. Some of the literature states that the method is only valid if samples are collected at equal intervals. This is not correct; all that is required is a good mean annual value for the number of individuals in each size class.

(2) Divide the population into (i) arbitrary size classes and count the number in each class ($N_1 \ldots N_i$). In the method generally described in the literature, length classes are measured and subsequently converted to volume units. This has the disadvantage of making the method appear more complex than it is. Dry mass or volume could be measured directly. If length is measured, it is wise to remember that the mean of a series of linear measurements is not necessarily equal to the mean of the cubes of those measurements. In addition, see Chapter 7 for a treatment of the important problem of error propagation in length: weight conversion.

(3) The total development time (D_{tot}) for the population is determined from the voltinism of the animals (e.g. univoltine: $D_{tot} = 1$ year). The development time of each class (D_i) is then assumed to be an equal fraction of D_{tot}. For example, if $D_{tot} = 365$ days and there are i size classes, then each size class is assumed to have a duration of 365/i days.

$$D_i = D_{tot}/i \qquad (2.23)$$

Thus, the rate of production by the ith size class, intead of being calculated by the normal method of increment summation (equation 2.9), is calculated from:

$$P_i = N_i(m_{max} - m_{min})/D_i \qquad (2.24)$$

where m_{max} and m_{min} are the maximum and minimum sizes of individuals in each size class. The total annual production is then calculated as the summation of the P_i. Recent work by Benke (1979; and *in press*) suggests that these production values must be corrected for the actual cohort production interval (CPI) and should therefore be multiplied by 365/CPI.

Before deciding to use this simplified method, the production biologist should consider two points. First, this method is no more than a simplification of the increment summation method. It might appear different because, as described in the literature, mortality increment, not growth increment, is summed. However, in Section 2 it was shown that the methods of increment and mortality summation are fundamentally identical (see also Gillespie & Benke 1976). Thus, the average cohort method is subject to the limitations of the increment summation method which, when there is mortality within a size class, gives the correct answer only when the individual growth curve within that size class is linear. It should be noted that this conclusion, which is derived from a consideration of the assumptions of the two mathematical models, and not from numerical examples, is inconsistent with the conclusion of Benke & Waide (1977; p. 63). The second point to note is that this method substitutes an assumption about D_i for the measurement of D_i. Where cohorts cannot be identified, it would be best to use the techniques outlined in Sections 4.3.1 and 4.3.2. See Benke (*in press*) for a more optimistic treatment.

5.2 *The use of production to biomass ratios (P/B)*

One simplification that has attracted some attention (e.g. Winberg 1971; Gak *et al.* 1972; Eckblad 1973; Johnson 1974; Kajak & Dusoge 1975; Mikulski *et al.* 1975; Waters 1977; Hamill *et al.* 1979; Makarewicz & Likens 1979; Banse & Mosher 1980; Benke & Wallace 1980; Nauwerck *et al.* 1980; Short & Ward 1980), is the use of production to biomass ratios (P/B). The expectation has been that species with similar physiology would have similar P/B ratios. If this were the case, given a knowledge of the production and biomass of one species (P_1 and B_1), and a knowledge of only the biomass of a second, similar species (B_2), we could calculate the production of the second species (P_2):

$$P_2 = B_2 P_1 / B_1 \qquad\qquad (2.25)$$

Used in this manner, P/B coefficients are anticipated as being a great labour saving device (Winberg 1971), and compilations of measured P/B ratios have been made (Waters 1977) in the hope that empirical rules relating P/B to lifespan or taxonomic group can be derived. Of more interest here is the theoretical work of Waters (1969) and Allen (1971) on the factors affecting P/B.

Allen's approach is more useful for the non-mathematical ecologist or for populations whose growth and mortality cannot be expressed in reasonably simple equations. He used families of Allen curves to investigate cohort P/B and produced several useful conclusions:

(1)   The growth curve (e.g. linear, exponential, or logarithmic) and mortality curve are not very important in affecting P/B.

(2)   P/B increases with increasing ratio of final weight to birth weight. However, this ratio has little effect above a final weight to birth weight ratio of 50, and since most invertebrates have a ratio > 50, this variable is unlikely to have much effect in real populations.

(3)   The most influential variable is the amount of mortality experienced by a population. The higher the mortality, the higher the P/B ratio.

Allen's conclusions summarized above refer to cohort production; it is generally desirable to perform a simple conversion to annual P/B. When individuals are present throughout the year, annual P/B equals cohort P/B regardless of lifespan (Allen 1971) or the number of cohorts maturing in one

Since Burgis could not infer growth rate from field data, she measured development times of eggs, nauplii and copepodites at various temperatures in the laboratory, and interpolated to obtain the rate at 26·4 °C. This is the most unsatisfactory aspect of the analysis of steady-state populations because we have no data to suggest that the development rate of the feeding stages in the natural environment is controlled entirely by temperature. We are, therefore, unsure whether laboratory growth experiments have duplicated the natural food supply. The findings of a number of workers (e.g. Kŏrinek 1966; Weglenska 1971; Ivanova, in Winberg 1971) have indicated that we could obtain more natural growth rates of zooplankton and benthos by raising animals in cages suspended in the lake water or placed in sediments. If these methods give better estimates of natural growth rates they should be used, despite their added difficulty, because growth rate is as important as N or m̄ in calculation of production and is the measurement most susceptible to error.

8.1.3 Weight increment within each size class

As is frequently true in studies of secondary production, the information on weight that we need is not provided by Burgis' raw data. To extract the data we need, we must make a series of approximations and assumptions.

(1) Egg weight. Since eggs were not weighed directly we must infer their weight from the difference between the weight of females with eggs (1.61 μg), females without eggs (1.19 μg), and the average clutch size (8). This gives an average egg weight of 0·05 μg.[1]

(2) Initial and final weight of nauplii. Since no nauplii were weighed, we must derive these figures as best we can. The initial weight of the first nauplius (N1) can be approximated from the egg weight. We will expect it to be less than the egg weight owing to losses by respiration and to the inclusion of egg membranes and egg sac in the egg weight. The data of Rigler & Cooley (1974) suggest that it would be reasonable to assign N1 an initial weight of 20 % less than the average egg weight, or 0·04 μg. To estimate the maximum weight of the sixth nauplius we can extrapolate the regression of logarithm of weight on instar (Fig. 2.11) to obtain the geometric mean between the mean weight of C1 and that of N6. As shown in Fig. 2.11 this is not likely to be the exact value of maximum nauplius weight, but will be a close approximation of it.

1. Burgis uses a weight of 0·02 μg obtained from measuring egg volume and consequently it is impossible to know what the real egg weight is from the data presented. The real weight is irrelevant here since our concern is with method rather than with production of copepods in Lake George. However, the descrepancy re-emphasizes the importance of obtaining data on the necessary population attributes as accurately as possible.

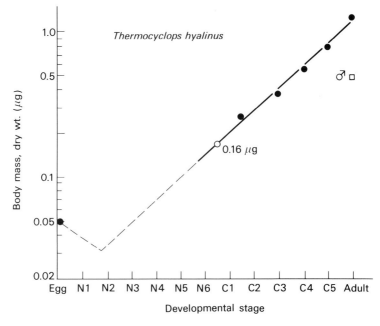

Fig. 2.11 Relationship of body mass to developmental stage of *Thermocyclops hyalinus* in Lake George, Uganda. Solid dots are observed mean weights, open dot is the estimate of mean body mass between the sixth naupliar and first copepodite stages. The open square indicates the mean body mass of adult males. The broken line indicates expected trends. Data are from Burgis (1970, 1971).

(3) Initial and final weight of copepodites. The value obtained (0·16 µg) can also be used as the minimum weight of C1. Of course, before setting m_{max} of N6 equal to m_{min} of C1 we will have made the conscious decision to ignore the contribution of exuviae to total production. If our data were detailed enough to allow analysis of production by each instar we might have decided to include exuviae in our estimate because exuviae can make up almost 15 % of total production by a copepod population (Rigler *et al.* 1974).

(4) Maximum Weight of C5. This can be estimated in several ways using the data given. We can simply take the geometric mean of the weight of females without eggs and of C5s, or we might take the weight of females without eggs to represent the maximum C5 weight. Our decision will be determined by the assumption which we decide to make about the biology of our animal. I will assume that the only weight gained by adult females is in the developing ovary and that the weight of a sample of eggless females is equal to the basic female weight plus one-half of the weight of a complete clutch of eggs. If we further assume that females

carrying eggs are laying down material in their ovaries for another batch of eggs, their average weight will represent the basic weight of a female plus one and one-half clutches of eggs. Consequently, the difference between the mean weight of females with and without eggs is equal to the weight of the clutch being carried ($1.61 - 1.19 = 0.42\,\mu g$), and the basic female weight (approximately equal to the maximum weight of C5) is equal to the average weight of females without eggs minus half the weight of a clutch of eggs ($1.19 - 0.42/2 = 0.98\,\mu g$). The maximum weight of C5 obtained in this way is almost identical to that obtained by taking the geometric mean of the weight of females without eggs and the weight of C5 (0.95).

I have laboured through the justification of my choice of maximum weight for C5 *T. hyalinus* not only to direct attention to the importance of the data we use in our calculation of production, but also to direct attention to another problem with our data set. Males weigh less than half as much as females (Fig. 2.11), but we have no data on the abundance of males. Are the copepodite weights applicable only to calculation of the production of females or to an average of female and male production? Simple inspection of Fig. 2.11 suggests that the copepodites weighed were almost all destined to become females. The above comparison of maximum weight of C5 determined by interpolation and that determined from female weights strengthens this conclusion. Therefore, I will assume that males are rare relative to females and that total copepodite production can be calculated from the regression line in Fig. 2.11. Obviously, this is, at best, a temporary expedient. For a more

Table 2.5 Production of *Thermocyclops hyalinus* in Lake George, Uganda, calculated from the data of Burgis (1970, 1971). The technique of growth increment summation is used here because the population has no identifiable cohorts (see Section 4.3.1). The symbol *m indicates the weight gain by individuals in each class which is calculated $m_{max} - m_{min}$. The derivations of all other data are explained in Section 8. All masses are expressed as μg dry weight.

Size class	Required data				Derived data		
	N	D	m_{min}	m_{max}	N/D	*m	P
Eggs	220	1.5	0.0	0.05	147	0.05	7.4
Nauplii	199	6.0	0.04	0.16	33	0.12	4.0
Copepodites	327	11.0	0.16	0.95	30	0.79	23.7

Total production, all stages: $35.1\,\mu g\ day^{-1}$
Annual production: $12.8\,mg\,l^{-1}\ year^{-1}$

accurate estimate of production we would have to recount enough samples to get a measure of the fraction of males in the adult population.

8.1.4 Actual production calculations

With the approximations and assumptions I have described we can generate the data required to calculate production and complete the calculation (Table 2.5). Note that once we have the necessary data, the calculation is extremely simple. The real problem in this example and in any other study of aquatic secondary production is in generating the required data from the raw data. Anyone about to embark on a production study should concentrate on the required data—the mean number in each size class, the average maximum and minimum weight of individuals in each size class and the duration of each size class—and the best methods of obtaining accurate estimates of them.

9 References

Adcock J.A. (1979) Energetics of a population of the isopod *Asellus aquaticus:* Life history and production. *Freshwat. Biol.*, **9**, 343–355.

Allen K.R. (1951) The Horowiki Stream. *N. Z. Mar. Dept., Fish. Bull.*, **10**, 238 pp.

Allen K.R. (1971) Relation between production and biomass. *J. Fish. Res. Board Can.*, **28**, 1573–1581.

Amrén H. (1964) Ecological studies on zooplankton populations in some ponds in Spitzbergen. *Zool. Bidr. Upps.*, **36**, 161–191.

Banse K. & Mosher S. (1980) Adult body mass and annual production/biomass relationships of field populations. *Ecol. Monogr.*, **50**, 355–379.

Baskerville G.L. (1972) Use of logarithmic regression in the estimation of plant biomass. *Can. J. For. Res.*, **2**, 49–53.

Benke A.C. (1976) Dragonfly production and prey turnover. *Ecology*, **57**, 915–927.

Benke A.C. (1979) A modification of the Hynes method for estimating secondary production with particular significance for multivoltine populations. *Limnol. Oceanogr.*, **24**, 168–171.

Benke A.C. (*in press*) Secondary Production of Aquatic Insects. In V.H.Resh & D.M.Rosenberg (eds.), *Ecology of Aquatic Insects.* New York: Praeger Publishers.

Benke A.C. & Benke S.S. (1975) Comparative dynamics and life histories of coexisting dragonfly populations. *Ecology*, **56**, 302–317.

Benke A.C. & Waide J.B. (1977) In defense of average cohorts. *Freshwat. Biol.*, **7**, 61–63.

Benke A.C. & Wallace J.B. (1980) Trophic basis of production among net-spinning caddisflies in a southern Appalachian stream. *Ecology*, **61**, 108–118.

Bottrell H.H. (1975a) The relationship between temperature and duration of egg development in some epiphytic Cladocera and Copepoda from the River Thames, Reading, with discussion of temperature functions. *Oecologia*, **18**, 63–84.

Bottrell H.H. (1975b) Generation time, length of life, instar duration and frequency of moulting, and their relationship to temperature in eight species of Cladocera from the River Thames, Reading. *Oecologia*, **19**, 129–140.

Bottrell H.H., Duncan A., Gliwicz Z., Grygierek E., Herzig A., Hillbricht-Illkowska A., Kurasawa H., Larsson P. & Węgleńska T. (1976) A review of some problems in zooplankton production studies. *Norw. J. Zool.*, **24**, 419–456.

Burgis M.J. (1970) The effect of temperature on the development time of eggs of *Thermocyclops* sp., a tropical cyclopoid copepod from Lake George, Uganda. *Limnol. Oceanogr.*, **15**, 742–747.

Burgis M.J. (1971) The ecology and production of copepods, particularly *Thermocyclops hyalinus*, in the tropical Lake George, Uganda. *Freshwat. Biol.*, **1**, 169–192.

Burgis M.J. (1974) Revised estimates for the biomass and production of zooplankton in Lake George, Uganda. *Freshwat. Biol.*, **4**, 535–541.

Cassie R.M. (1950) The analysis of polymodal frequency distributions by the probability paper method. *N. Z. Sci. Rev.*, **8**, 89–91.

Caswell H. (1972) On instantaneous and finite birth rates. *Limnol. Oceanogr.*, **17**, 787–791.

Cooley J.M. (1971) The effect of temperature on the development of resting eggs of *Diaptomus oregonensis* LILLJ. (Copepoda: Calanoidea). *Limnol. Oceanogr.*, **16**, 921–926.

Downing J.A. (1979) Aggregation, transformation and the design of benthos sampling programs. *J. Fish. Res. Board Can.*, **36**, 1454–1463.

Eckblad J.W. (1973) Population studies of three aquatic gastropods in an intermittent backwater. *Hydrobiologia*, **41**, 199–219.

Edmondson W.T. (1960) Reproductive rates of rotifers in natural populations. *Mem. Ist. Ital. Ibrobiol.*, **12**, 21–77.

Edmondson W.T. (1965) Reproductive rate of planktonic rotifers as related to food and temperature. *Ecol. Monogr.*, **35**, 61–111.

Edmondson W.T. (1974) Secondary production. *Mitt. Int. Ver. Theor. Angew. Limnol.*, **20**, 229–272.

Edmondson W.T. & Winberg G.G. (eds.) (1971) *A Manual for the Assessment of Secondary Productivity in Fresh Waters.* IBP Handbook No. 17, Oxford: Blackwell.

Eichhorn R. (1957 Zur Populationsdynamik der calanoiden Copepoden in Titisee und Feldsee. *Arch. Hydrobiol. Suppl.*, **24**, 186–246.

Elster H.J. (1954) Über die Populationsdynamik von *Eudiaptomus gracilis* Sars und *Heterocope borealis* Fischer im Bodensee-Obersee. *Arch. Hydrobiol. Suppl.*, **20**, 546–614.

Elster H.J. & Schwoerbel I. (1970) Beiträge zur Biologie und Populationsdynamik der Daphnien im Bodensee. *Arch. Hydrobiol. Suppl.*, **38**, 18–72.

Gak D.Z., Gurvich V.V., Korelyakova I.L., Kastikova L.E., Konstantinova N.A., Olivari G.A., Priimachenko A.D., Tseeb Y.Y., Vladimirova K.S. & Zimbalevskaya L.N. (1972) Productivity of aquatic organism communities of different trophic levels in Kiev Reservoir. In Z.Kajak & A.Hillbricht-Ilkowska (eds.), *Productivity Problems in Freshwaters*, Proc. IBP–UNESCO Symposium. Krakow: Polish Scientific Publishers.

George D.G. & Edwards R.W. (1974) Population dynamics and production of *Daphnia hyalina* in a eutrophic reservoir. *Freshwat. Biol.*, **4**, 445–465.

Gillespie D.M. & Benke A.C. (1979) Methods of calculating cohort production from field data—some relationships. *Limnol. Oceanogr.*, **24**, 171–176.

Green J. (1956) Growth, size and reproduction in *Daphnia* (Crustacea: Cladocera). *Proc. Zool. Soc. Lond.*, **126**, 173–204.

Hall D.J. (1964) An experimental approach to the dynamics of a natural population of *Daphnia galeata mendotae*. *Ecology*, **45**, 94–112.

Hamill S.E., Qadri S.U. & Mackie G.L. (1979) Production and turnover ratio of *Pisidium casertanum* (Pelecypoda: Sphaeriidae) in the Ottawa River near Ottawa-Hull, Canada. *Hydrobiologia*, **62**, 225–230.

Hamilton A.L. (1969) On estimating annual production. *Limnol. Oceanogr.*, **14**, 771–782.

Haney J.F. & Hall D.J. (1973) Sugar-coated *Daphnia*: a preservation technique for Cladocera. *Limnol. Oceanogr.*, **18**, 331–333.

Harding J.P. (1949) The use of probability paper for the graphical analysis of polymodal frequency distributions. *J. Mar. Biol. Ass. U.K.*, **28**, 141–153.

Heinle D.R. (1966) Production of a calanoid copepod, *Acartia tonsa*, in the Patuxent River estuary. *Chesapeake Sci.*, **7**, 59–74.

Hynes H.B.N. & Coleman M.J. (1968) A simple method of assessing the annual production of stream benthos. *Limnol. Oceanogr.*, **13**, 569–575.

Janicki A.J. & DeCosta J. (1977) The effect of temperature and age structure on P/B for *Bosmina longirostrus* in a small impoundment. *Hydrobiologia*, **56**, 11–16.

Johnson M.G. (1974) Production and productivity. In R.O. Brinkhurst (ed.), *The Benthos of Lakes*, London: Macmillan.

Kajak Z. & Dusoge K. (1975) Macrobenthos of Mikolajskie Lake. *Ekol. Pols.*, **23**, 437–457.

Kŏrinek V. (1966) The production of adult females of *Daphnia pulicaria* Forbes in a carp pond estimated by a direct method. *Verh. Internat. Verein. Limnol.*, **16**, 386–391.

Krueger C.C. & Martin F.B. (1980) Computation of confidence intervals for the size-frequency (Hynes) method of estimating secondary production. *Limnol. Oceanogr.*, **25**, 773–777.

Lei C. & Clifford H.F. (1974) Field and laboratory studies of *Daphnia schødleri* Sars from a winterkill lake in Alberta. *Nat. Mus. Can. Publ. Zool.*, **9**, 53 pp.

Leslie P.H. (1948) Some further notes on the use of matrices in population mathematics. *Biometrika*, **35**, 213–245.

Makarewicz J.C. & Likens G.E. (1979) Structure and function of the zooplankton community of Mirror Lake, New Hampshire. *Ecol. Monogr.*, **49**, 109–127.

Martien R.F. & Benke A.C. (1977) Distribution and production of two crustaceans in a wetland pond. *Am. Midl. Nat.*, **98**, 162–175.

Menzie C.A. (1980) A note on the Hynes method of estimating secondary production. *Limnol. Oceanogr.*, **25**, 770–773.

Mikulski J.S., Adanczak B., Bittel L., Bohr R., Bronisz D., Donderski W., Giziński A., Luscinska M., Rejewski M., Strzelczyk E., Wolnomiejski N., Zawislak W. & Zytkowicz R. (1975) Basic regularities of productive processes in the Ilawa lakes and the Golpo Lake from the point of view of utility values of the water. *Pol. Arch. Hydrobiol.*, **22**, 101–122.

Nauwerck, A., Duncan A., Hillbricht-Ilkowska A. & Larsson P. (1980) Secondary production: zooplankton. In E.D.LeCren & R.H.Lowe-McConnell (eds.), *The Functioning of Freshwater Ecosystems*, IBP publication No. 22. Cambridge: Cambridge University Press.

Obreshkove V. & Fraser A.W. (1940) Growth and differentiation of *Daphnia magna* eggs in vitro. *Biol. Bull.*, **78**, 428–436.

Paloheimo J.E. (1974) Calculation of instantaneous birth rate. *Limnol. Oceanogr.*, **19**, 692–694.

Peters R.H. (1977) The unpredictable problems of tropho-dynamics. *Env. Biol. Fish.*, **2**, 97–101.

Prepas E. (1978) Sugar-frosted *Daphnia*: an improved fixation technique for Cladocera. *Limnol. Oceanogr.*, **23**, 557–559.

Prepas E. & Rigler F.H. (1978) The enigma of *Daphnia* death rates. *Limnol. Oceanogr.*, **23**, 970–988.

Ricker W.E. (ed.) (1971) *Methods for Assessment of Fish Production in Fresh Waters.* IBP Handbook No. 3. Oxford: Blackwell.

Riggs D.S. (1963) *The Mathematical Approach to Physiological Problems.* Cambridge, Mass., USA: M.I.T. Press.

Rigler F.H. & Cooley J.M. (1974) The use of field data to derive population statistics of multivoltine copepods. *Limnol. Oceanogr.*, **19**, 636–655.

Rigler F.H., MacCallum M.E. & Roff J.C. (1974) Production of zooplankton in Char Lake. *J. Fish. Res. Board Can.*, **31**, 637–646.

Schindler D.W. (1972) Production of phytoplankton and zooplankton in Canadian Shield Lakes. In Z.Kajak & A.Hillbricht-Ilkowska (eds.), *Productivity Problems of Freshwaters.* Proc. IBP–UNESCO symposium. Krakow: Polish Scientific Publishers.

Short R.A. & Ward J.V. (1980) Life cycle and production of *Skwala parallela* (Frison) (Plecoptera: Perlodidae) in a Colorado montane stream. *Hydrobiologia*, **69**, 273–275.

Sokal R.R. & Rohlf F.J. (1981) *Biometry, The Principles and Practice of Statistics in Biological Research.* 2nd ed. San Francisco: Freeman.

Southwood T.R.E. (1966) *Ecological Methods with Particular Reference to the Study of Insect Populations.* London: Chapman & Hall.

Southwood T.R.E. & Jepson W.F. (1962) Studies on the populations of *Oscinella frit* L. (Dipt.: Chloropidae) in the oat crop. *J. Anim. Ecol.*, **31**, 481–495.

Stross R.G., Neess J.C. & Hasler A.D. (1961) Turnover time and production of planktonic crustacea in limed and reference portion of a bog lake. *Ecology*, **42**, 237–245.

Threlkeld S.T. (1979) Estimating cladoceran birth rates: the importance of egg mortality and the egg age distribution. *Limnol. Oceanogr.*, **24**, 601–612.

Vijverberg J. (1980) Effect of temperature in laboratory studies on development and growth of Cladocera and Copepoda from Tjeukemeer, The Netherlands. *Freshwat. Biol.*, **10**, 317–340.

Waters T.F. (1969) The turnover ratio in production ecology of freshwater invertebrates. *Am. Nat.*, **103**, 173–185.

Waters T.F. (1977) Secondary production in inland waters. *Adv. Ecol. Res.*, **10**, 91–164.

Waters T.F. (1979) Influence of benthos life history upon the estimation of secondary production. *J. Fish. Res. Board Can.*, **36**, 1425–1430.

Waters T.F. & Crawford G.W. (1973) Annual production of a stream mayfly population: a comparison of methods. *Limnol. Oceanogr.*, **18**, 286–296.

Waters T.F. & Hokenstrom J.C. (1980) Annual production and drift of the stream amphipod *Gammarus pseudolimnaeus* in Valley Creek, Minnesota. *Limnol. Oceanogr.*, **25**, 700–710.

Wegleńska T. (1971) The influence of various concentrations of natural food on the development, fecundity and production of planktonic crustacean filtrators. *Ekol. Pols.*, **19**, 427–473.

Winberg G.G. (ed.) (1971) *Methods for the Estimation of Production of Aquatic Animals.* (Transl. by A. Duncan). London: Academic Press.

Winterbourne M.J. (1974) The life histories, trophic relations and production of *Stenoperla prasina* (Plecoptera) and *Delatidium* sp. (Ephemeroptera) in a New Zealand river. *Freshwat. Biol.*, **4**, 507–524.

Wright J.C. (1965) The population dynamics and production of *Daphnia* in Canyon Ferry Reservoir, Montana. *Limnol. Oceanogr.*, **10**, 583–590.

Zwick P. (1975) Critical notes on a proposed method to estimate production. *Freshwat. Biol.*, **5**, 65–70.

Chapter 3. Methods for the Estimation of Zooplankton Abundance[1]

RICCARDO DE BERNARDI

1 Introduction

This chapter is intended to outline and compare some of the most commonly employed methods for determining abundance of zooplankton organisms in lakes. I will emphasize the practical aspects of use of each of the different devices with respect to the specific environments and research questions. To some extent, the choice of examples given to illustrate and corroborate the discussion has been rather arbitrary in that specific examples chosen to illustrate a particular technique are usually those commonly available in the literature.

The census problem is usually the first difficulty encountered in studying zooplankton production. We must determine the sizes of the various zooplankton populations in a lake (or in a study area of a lake) and the manner in which these populations vary with time. This is problematic because the plankton do not constitute a closed population with respect to sampling possibilities but must be considered an open population in which immigration and emigration processes may occur, even in small environments. Further problems in zooplankton census arise from the fact that, in general, the zooplankton do not present a uniform horizontal or vertical distribution, but tend to be patchy, with a strong vertical gradient of abundance which is continuously changing due to circadial vertical migrations.

In addition, the size of zooplankton organisms range from a few μm to about 15 mm. Their ability to avoid different collection devices varies among species, and with the age (stage), size, shape, consistency, and behavior of different organisms.

In order to solve or minimize these problems with regard to research purposes or the organisms investigated many kinds of devices and

1. This chapter mainly treats equipment for sampling the zooplankton. Readers interested in an explanation of sampling design should consult Chapters 7 and 8.

experimental designs have been employed by planktologists. As a consequence, different researchers have sampled the plankton using such a variety of methods that in many cases a direct comparison of results is practically impossible.

Because the population density of zooplankton represents the number of individuals in a given volume of water, one of the first essentials in quantitative plankton sampling is to know the volume of water sampled. In many cases this is simple but in some cases it is not easy to measure this accurately, and only a rough value can be estimated (e.g. when net hauls without current meters are used). Furthermore, no single device exists that can make quantitative collections of the complete spectrum of pelagic zooplanktonic organisms. The smallest animals may pass through the nets, while larger, more motile organisms may avoid being captured by volumetric samplers. Accordingly, different devices and sampling procedures must be employed when studying different organisms, lakes, and problems. Criteria for selection depends upon the volume of water to be sampled, the depths of strata, the kinds of organisms and whether integrated or point samples are needed.

A researcher usually uses only one of the available devices. There are circumstances, however, in which the complete census of a population that is changing rapidly in size-stage structure and/or habits can be obtained only by using two or more different devices. This fact, commonly accepted in sampling other kinds of organisms (e.g. insects), seems to have attracted little or no attention from planktologists.

A standardized method cannot be recommended, because at present no single sampler is practicable on a large scale which would cover all water bodies. However, comparability of results can be achieved if, as discussed by Bottrell *et al.* (1976), the relative efficiency of the sampling procedure utilized is determined with regard to the most efficient one. This assumes, as did Bottrell *et al.*, that 'the most efficient sampling (is) the one which catches the greatest number of individuals.'

The available devices for quantitative zooplankton collection can be conveniently divided into two basic categories:

(1) Devices based on collection of water samples.
(2) Devices based on the filtration of planktonic organisms from water directly in the field.

Gear of the first type includes bottles, pumps and tubes, while the second category includes plankton nets, towed plankton samplers, and plankton traps. Selection of one of the available devices will depend to a large extent upon the research purposes and characteristics of the environment. Some basic recommendations will be made in the following sections.

2 Descriptions of Sampling Gear

2.1 Sampling bottles

The most direct method for collecting plankton is to remove it from a known volume of water sample. Bottles can be used for collecting these samples. A variety of water-collection bottles can be used conveniently (Fig. 3.1), including those not designed specifically for this purpose.

A general characteristic of samples collected in this way is that a small amount of water is sampled. This implies that these methods, although generally efficient for small, less motile organisms, yield low collection efficiency when used to sample the larger, scarcer, and more active zooplankters. Furthermore, when a small amount of water is sampled, large

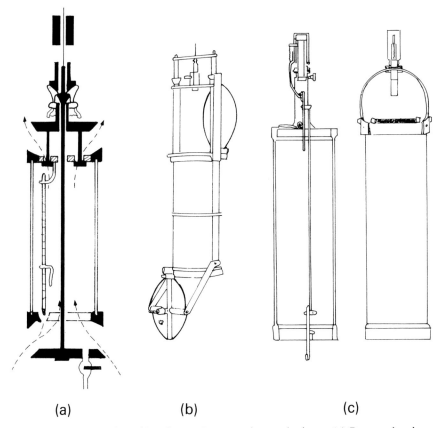

(a)   (b)   (c)

Fig. 3.1 Some examples of bottles used to sample zooplankton. (a) Ruttner bottle, (b) Friedinger bottle, and (c) Bernatowicz bottle (all redrawn from Chodorowski 1971).

numbers of replicates are needed in order to have a precise census of the organisms (including the rare forms) and to obtain representative figures. This is due to the spatial heterogeneity of plankton distribution both horizontally and vertically.[1]

When this method is selected, one must choose among the different bottles available according to the research purposes, after carefully considering the drawbacks and advantages of each. As Smyly (1968) demonstrated, one of the criteria for the choice of a given bottle is that it must close as quickly as possible at the desired depth so that the avoidance response of the organisms is minimal. According to Smyly, the opacity and the direction of approach of the bottle had little or no influence on the numbers of rotifers collected. For other zooplankters, however, avoidance can have a great effect on the evaluation of their density (Schindler 1969). For these reasons, Hodgkiss (1977) suggests the use of a transparent bottle instead of an opaque one. Although theoretically preferable in some circumstances, small bottles (i.e. 1–2 litre capacity) require more replicates than larger bottles (> 10 litre).

Several methods have been used to remove organisms from a water sample. The most common are sedimentation, centrifugation, and filtration of the animals onto a net or glass filter. Filtration seems the most convenient. Bottrell *et al.* (1976), however, suggest that sedimentation is the 'only satisfactory way to concentrate planktonic protozoans' and the best method for rotifers, even though it is practical only at high densities. It must be stressed, however, that with sedimentation it is always laborious and difficult to determine whether all the organisms have settled. The complete settling of suspended material can take several days. In addition, removal of the supernatant liquid by siphon requires much care to ensure that sedimented animals are not disturbed. Centrifugation, on the other hand, has the disadvantage that the volume of water that can be handled in this way is very small.

1. Editor's Note. The spatial variability of the zooplankton will affect sampling programs using any type of sampler, not just water bottles (see Wiebe 1971). The number of samples necessary for a given precision can be calculated if an estimate of the variance (s^2) is known (see Chapter 8, Section 2.1.3). Unfortunately, no single work has summarized the published data on sampling variance for zooplankton taken with various samplers. Langeland & Rognerud (1974) and Evans & Sell (1983) have presented interesting summaries. For the present, one might seek other estimates of s^2 from single publications (e.g. Tonolli 1949a; Ragotzkie & Bryson 1953; Siebeck 1960; Langford & Jermolajev 1966; Dumont 1967; Smyly 1968; Elster & Schwoerbel 1970; Burgis *et al.* 1973; Langeland & Rognerud 1974; Rey & Capblanq 1975; Wattiez 1978; Makarewicz & Likens 1979; Malone & McQueen 1983), bearing in mind that s^2 can vary markedly with population density and size of sampler (see e.g. Chapter 4, Sections 2.4.2 & 2.4.3).

Because it is rapid and easy to employ, filtration is the sorting method that is used most often. Some cautions are, however, necessary. The filtration must be done at low pressure and as gently as possible to avoid damage to the fragile organisms or their forced passage through the mesh. Rigid filters are preferable because their mesh size is invariable. Assuming that nets can theoretically select the lower size limit of organisms, but cannot discriminate for the upper size limit, which depends largely on the kind of plankton present, the mesh must be as small as the abundance of organisms permits without clogging. Likens & Gilbert (1970) suggest the use of nets with a mesh aperture of 35 μm which, according to the authors, permits an appropriate retention of even the smaller rotifers. Schindler (1969), however, indicates that nets with 28 or 10 μm mesh sizes are the most suitable for collecting the smallest forms from oligotrophic lakes. Similar results have been obtained by Ejsmont-Karabin (1978).

A very useful device that prevents high pressures and consequent damage to the organisms is described by Likens & Gilbert (1970). The device consists of a plexiglas funnel with three windows covered with nylon net (Fig. 3.2). The water sample is poured from the bottle into the funnel, which is partially submerged in a bucket of water. Lake water filtered through glass fiber filters is used to wash the plankton from funnels and screens. Special attention must be devoted to washing the net because, as shown by Ejsmont-Karabinova (cited by Bottrell *et al.* 1976), retention can greatly influence the estimation of

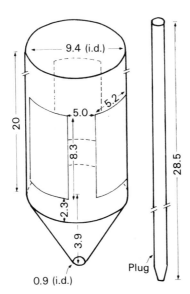

Fig. 3.2 Funnel for filtering water samples. All dimensions are in cm (after Likens & Gilbert 1970).

abundance, since it is directly affected by density of organisms and the adherance of certain species to the nylon net.

The use of bottle sampling to evaluate zooplankton density is not recommended in large, deep, oligotrophic lakes because too many samples would be necessary to obtain a realistic picture of population density and community composition. On the other hand, bottles can be usefully employed in shallow, eutrophic lakes, ponds, and pools, where the abundance of organisms and particulate matter might reduce the efficiency of other apparatus (e.g. clogging of nets), when spatial distribution on a fine scale must be estimated, or when littoral zone and interface layers between water and sediments must be sampled. Water collection bottles can also be employed to advantage for the study of small organisms, such as protozoans and rotifers, that do not usually exhibit significant avoidance reactions (Green 1977; Ruttner-Kolisko 1977).

Several authors have compared the efficiency of bottles with that of other devices in sampling different taxonomic groups of the zooplankton. There is no general agreement from these studies and no single picture emerges. Ferrari *et al.* (1973) have compared vertical net haul samples collected in a mountain lake with samples collected with a Ruttner bottle, and stated that the latter method seems to be much more effective in collecting *Eudiaptomus intermedius* and, in addition, yields information on its vertical distribution.[1] Opposite results have been obtained by Hodgkiss (1977), who found that nets collected a greater number of *Diaptomus gracilis* (20X), *Mesocyclops hyalinus* (3X), *Moina micrura* (30X), and *Diaphanosoma leuchtenbergianum* (30X) than a Friedinger bottle. On the other hand, he found that the Friedinger bottle collected 30 times more *Bosmina longirostris* and 1·5 times as many *Ceriodaphnia reticulata* than the plankton net. Langeland & Rognerud (1974) compared a Schindler trap, a Clarke–Bumpus plankton sampler, and a Friedinger bottle. They pointed out that, on a statistical basis, the Friedinger bottle yields lower precision and probably does not collect rare species efficiently. In addition, the population density of crustaceans is greatly underestimated with this last method, confirming the similar results of Patalas (1954) who tested a Ruttner bottle.

Hrbáček (1966) describes a special use of bottles for obtaining plankton samples representative of small water bodies, where extreme patterns of variation in horizontal and vertical distribution of plankton can occur (ponds and pools). The method consists of collecting a composite sample, obtained by pouring many samples together, with sample volumes determined on the basis of volume distribution of different strata of the water body. It is summarized

---

1. Editor's Note. This can be very important in production studies, because egg development times are temperature dependent (see Prepas & Rigler 1978).

by the author (Hrbáček 1971) as follows: 'If the water volumes below various depths are expressed as fractions of the total volume, we obtain a volume depth curve that can be used to compare different kinds of waters. The curve of the depth distribution of volumes can be used to estimate the proper volume of water to be sampled for the establishment of an average figure, or, if the same volume from different depths is sampled and evaluated (separately), for proper calculation of the average. The average of values at different depths should be weighted in proportion to the different volume of these layers.' A treatment of both weighted and stratified sampling is given in Chapter 8.

2.2 Plankton traps

Plankton traps can be regarded as a particular kind of bottle specifically designed for plankton collection (Fig. 3.3). These quantitative samplers usually present some advantages compared to common bottles. They have very rapid closing systems and large mouths, which reduces the possibility of avoidance reactions, and they allow the simultaneous collection and filtration of a large volume of water. They can usually be handled easily by a single person even in a small boat. Some have remote closing systems (messengers) (Juday 1916; Clarke 1942; Achefors 1971), while others such as those of Patalas (1954) and Schindler (1969) are immediately self-closing at the desired depth.

Because plankton traps combine the characteristics of both bottles and nets, the same cautions apply. Larsson (cited by Bottrell *et al.* 1976) concluded that, in general, all types of volume samplers (e.g. Schindler trap, Friedinger bottle, Ruttner bottle) are very similar in the level of their sampling efficiency (Table 3.1). Authors who have compared the efficiency of plankton traps to other sampling devices, however, have shown that traps usually present one of the highest degrees of efficiency. This is especially true with regard to the species which usually display the strongest avoidance reactions such as *Daphnia* sp., *Leptodora* sp., and adult copepods (Table 3.2) (Patalas 1954; Schindler 1969). Because of their characteristics, the use of plankton traps is recommended as a useful alternative to water bottles in all cases.

2.3 Pumps and tubes

The use of pumps and tubes to collect zooplankton was introduced many years ago (Hensen 1887). Tubes can be regarded as a sort of long bottle, are usually flexible, and they collect an integrated sample when lowered through the water column. Their length must be equal to the maximum depth to be sampled. The internal cross-section of tubes should be as large as possible in order to minimize the escape of zooplankters that are rapid swimmers. Tubes

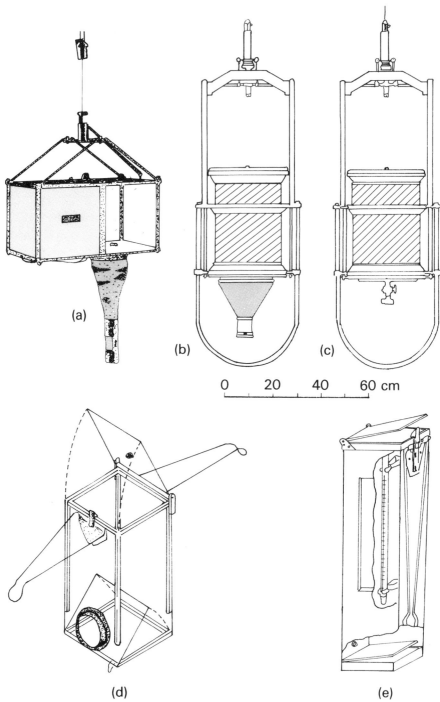

Fig. 3.3 Some plankton traps in common use for zooplankton collection. (a) Juday, (b & c) Akefors, (d) Schindler, and (e) Patalas.

0　　　20　　　40　　　60 cm

Table 3.1 A comparison of the efficiency of various volume samplers. Values are the mean number $l^{-1} \pm$ one standard deviation (Larsson in prep.). After Bottrell *et al.* (1976).

Species	Sampler			
	Schindler trap	Hand pump	Friedinger bottle	Ruttner bottle
Kellicottia longispina	$4\cdot33 \pm 1\cdot32$	$7\cdot40 \pm 2\cdot96$	$10\cdot23 \pm 3\cdot21$	$9\cdot67 \pm 4\cdot08$
Polyarthra vulgaris	$11\cdot30 \pm 3\cdot11$	$12\cdot75 \pm 5\cdot15$	$18\cdot29 \pm 3\cdot55$	$19\cdot33 \pm 4\cdot37$
Bosmina longispina	$1\cdot07 \pm 0\cdot50$	$3\cdot05 \pm 1\cdot12$	$2\cdot49 \pm 1\cdot26$	$2\cdot40 \pm 1\cdot51$
Holopedium gibberum	$0\cdot52 \pm 0\cdot26$	$0\cdot80 \pm 0\cdot59$	$0\cdot98 \pm 0\cdot59$	$0\cdot79 \pm 0\cdot68$
Cyclops nauplii	$4\cdot48 \pm 0\cdot71$	$2\cdot25 \pm 1\cdot53$	$2\cdot96 \pm 1\cdot13$	$3\cdot33 \pm 1\cdot51$
Cyclops copepodites	$11\cdot97 \pm 2\cdot50$	$6\cdot50 \pm 3\cdot54$	$11\cdot09 \pm 2\cdot28$	$9\cdot60 \pm 4\cdot12$

with a small diameter, however, can be closed more simply, and do not require special closing mechanisms. Flexible tubes are easily managed from small boats, but they must be weighted at the immersed end so that they remain vertical. If the weight is made of metal rings which are spaced at 10 cm intervals from one another (Tonolli 1971) and are connected to a small rope the same length as the tube, they can constitute an efficient system for closing the tube. The tube finds its greatest application in sampling an entire column of water in shallow environments or in littoral areas rich in vegetation (Pennak 1962). Transparent rigid tubes can also be employed for sample collection in

Table 3.2 Relative effectiveness of several zooplankton samplers. All figures are based upon an index of 100 for the transparent trap. Figures to the right of the '$\pm$' sign represent approximate 95 % confidence limits for 10 replicates (after Schindler 1969).

Species	Sampling device			
	28-l transparent trap	Opaque 9-l van Dorn	5-inch Clarke–Bumpus # 15 net	12-inch metered townet # 20 mesh
Holopedium gibberum	100 ± 18	65 ± 15	71 ± 18	65 ± 24
Daphnia sp.	100 ± 14	62 ± 18	74 ± 13	60 ± 30
Leptodora kindtii	100 ± 26	54 ± 41	35 ± 24	59 ± 33
Diaptomus leptopus	100 ± 21	60 ± 22	54 ± 23	49 ± 21
Diaptomus minutus	100 ± 18	105 ± 25	68 ± 12	86 ± 31
$\bar{X}$	100 ± 19	69 ± 24	60 ± 18	64 ± 28

plastic bag enclosures where a representative sample of a small volume is needed, or in shallow littoral waters, ponds, and pools. One should remember that integrated tube samplers weight all strata sampled as if they contribute equally to the lake volume. In addition, all information regarding the depth distribution of zooplankton is lost. This can introduce important errors to production calculations (see Chapters 2 & 8).

Tube samplers seem to yield samples comparable to other methods of sample collection. George & Owen (1978) have illustrated the efficiency of their own water corer that has a pneumatic closing mechanism, similar to that used on a 5-l Friedinger bottle. They have suggested that tube samplers can be used when a 'detailed bottle cast profile is not required'.[1]

Two types of pump samplers are presently used: hand pumps and motorized pumps. The latter are preferable because they guarantee a constant continuous water flow. Among volumetric samplers (bottles, tubes, pumps, and traps), pumps permit the collection of the largest volumes of water. In addition, they can be operated as a point or an integrating sampler. For this reason pumps can be employed as an alternative to bottles and tubes with some advantage if large water volumes are needed. When used as a point sampler, however, the definition of the sampling point is not very precise because the water currents that pumps produce can entrain waters from different layers.

The efficiency of pumps for plankton collection is, as yet, unclear. It must be stressed that some organisms seem to be negatively rheotactic. It must also be noted that different flow rates of pumps will select rheotactic organisms, with selectivity inversely related to the swimming abilities of the animals. More active zooplankters are usually captured less efficiently than with other methods (e.g. traps or nets). On the other hand, the collection of certain small organisms is favoured by the pump. Langford (1953) reported that pumps (both hand and motorized) collect more *Cyclops* and nauplii and less *Diaptomus*, *Daphnia*, and *Diaphanosoma* than a 45-l Juday trap. At present, however, a generalization of the efficiency of pumps with respect to the different zooplankton genera or species is still hazardous. The spatial patchiness of planktonic organisms probably contributes greatly to the confusion regarding the relative collection efficiency attained by pumps.

Patalas (1954) has compared different sampling devices (his own plankton trap, a Ruttner bottle, net, and pump), and found that the pump was more effective than the net and bottle, but less effective than the trap. For example, twice as many *Eudiaptomus graciloides* and *Leptodora kindtii* were caught

---

1. Editor's note. Tube samplers can rarely be used for production studies, since their valid use would require that all strata be at equal temperature, and contribute an equal proportion of the lake volume.

with the plankton trap as were obtained with the pump. Waite & O'Grady (1980) found that a filter pump collected an equal number of cladocerans but more rotifers and immature copepods and less adult copepods than a conventional plankton tow net. It should be noted, as Beers *et al.* (1967) and Ruttner-Kolisko (1977) have pointed out, that the results may vary greatly among seasons, even with regard to the sampling of a single species. Furthermore, Patalas (1954) has shown that the efficiency of various devices is different for day and night sampling. Pumps seem to have some advantages for sampling plankton in rivers (Bottrell *et al.* 1976; Waite & O'Grady 1980) even though the reason is not yet clear. They also seem to be the only practical method for the study of zooplankton entrained by the primary cooling water systems of power plants (Yocum *et al.* 1978; Waite & O'Grady 1980).

Tonolli (1971) has summarized some simple operational procedures and cautions that must be considered when using pumps to collect zooplankton samples: 'If the pumps are of the submersible type, the pump itself can serve to weight down the lower end of the tube. If the pump is in the boat, as is the upper end of the tube, the bottom end must be weighted. The choice of type of pump will be determined primarily by tests to ascertain that planktonic organisms will not be damaged by the moving parts of the pump.

Before collecting the sample of water, it is necessary to let flow a volume of water which is at least three times the internal volume of the entire length of the immersed tube; this is necessary to avoid introducing into the sample water that had already entered the tube from lesser depths . . .' '. . . For the regular flow of water it is best that the exit tube also be immersed in the water, rather than coiled in the boat, thus preventing stopping the flow by kinks.

One should determine once and for all the capacity of the pump per unit of time so that one need not collect the water each time in graduated vessels.

The tube should have a relatively large diameter because of the great velocity of the flow of water which may damage the delicate organisms. However, flow should not be so slow that flushing takes more than a few minutes . . .'

Pumps can also be used in connection with a set of instruments that make possible a record of some of the most important physical and chemical parameters relevant for plankton studies such as chlorophyll, temperature, oxygen, etc. This equipment, such as that described by George (1976), although simple, is usually quite costly, and requires specialized assembly of the different components and continuous routine maintenance. These aspects render it impractical for many laboratories.

2.4 *Plankton nets*

Plankton nets have been used for the collection of zooplankton since the

beginning of the nineteenth century. Although several important improvements have been introduced, many of the oldest net designs are still in use. At
present, we have at our disposal such a series of models that it is difficult to
choose only one (see for example Omaly 1966, Lamotte & Bourlière 1971).
Some were mainly designed for marine plankton collections, but they can be
employed to advantage in freshwaters (Fig. 3.4). The simplest, and perhaps
most widely used, is a simple conical net with a plankton bucket at its lower
end. Others, such as Hensen, Apstein, or Juday nets, have a reducing cone
forward of the mouth, and a simple closure system (see Fig. 3.4).

Shape and structure greatly affect the quantity of water that can pass

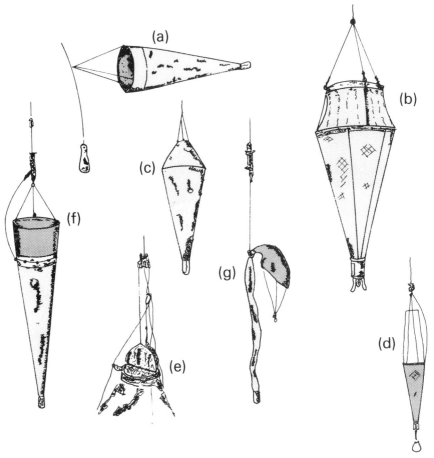

Fig. 3.4 Examples of different plankton nets. (a) simple conical tow net, (b)
Hensen net, (c) Apstein net, (d) Juday net, (e) Apstein net with semicircular
closing lids, (f) Nansen closing net in open position, and (g) Hansen net in closed
position (redrawn from Gehringer & Aron 1968).

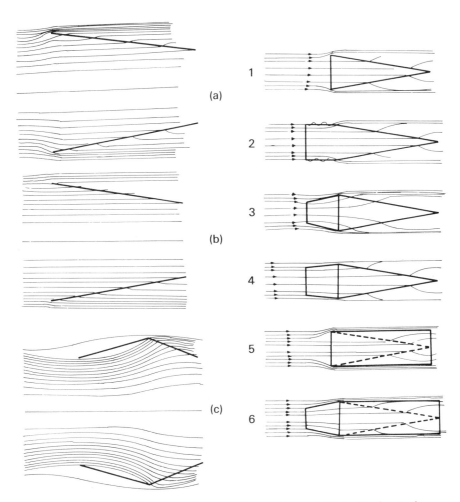

Fig. 3.5 The left panel indicates the water flow pattern established in front of plankton nets. Each line encloses 10% of the water entering a circular net. (a) illustrates a conical net which filters 75% of the water presented to it, (b) illustrates a conical net which filters 95%, and (c) represents a conical net with a mouth reducing cone that filters 125%. The right panel indicates the water flow pattern associated with some basic forms of plankton samplers. (1) a simple conical net, (2) a conical net with a porous collar, (3–4) conical nets with non-porous, mouth-reducing cones, (5) a conical net with a non-porous casing, (6) a conical net with non-porous casing and non-porous mouth-reducing cone (redrawn from Tranter & Smith 1968).

through the mouth of a net (Tranter & Smith 1968). Plankton nets with a reducing cone (Fig. 3.5) and with a filtering area three times larger than the area of the mouth (Tranter & Heron 1965, 1967) are the most efficient. Net efficiency, however, is affected by a series of factors including characteristics of the fabric used to construct the net (gauze), mesh sizes, porosity, speed of sampling, avoidance by target organisms, escape of sampled organisms, and clogging. Some of these are difficult to evaluate and require further study. Others are considered below.

2.4.1 Characteristics of the gauze

The type of fabric used for the construction of a net has a marked effect on the selectivity of the net, filtration efficiency (i.e. the ratio of the volume of water filtered by a plankton net to the volume swept by the mouth), and clogging. To ensure that the population sampled is well defined the gauze should consist of uniform meshes that will not distort during operation and which will resist deterioration. Among the various fabrics usually available the two that have been used most often for the construction of plankton nets are bolting silk and monofilament (or multifilament) nylon cloth (Fig. 3.6). Monofilament nylon fabrics are the best because they assure more uniform mesh size (Fig. 3.7), less distortion, and are efficient in self-cleaning. The use of monofilament gauze, in addition, prevents clogging, because strong nylon filaments break less often than those of other fabrics.

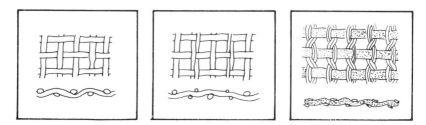

Fig. 3.6 Major types of weave used in plankton net fabrics (i.e. gauzes).

2.4.2 Mesh size

In theory, organisms smaller than the mesh aperture size pass through the net, while organisms greater than the mesh aperture size are retained. In practice, retention of small organisms can occur due to progressive clogging of the net and the presence of body appendages. Larger organisms can avoid capture. As a result, it is not possible to predict exactly what the mesh selection will be for a particular organism, and it must be determined experimentally. A practice

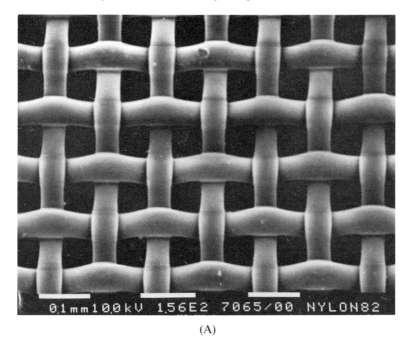

(A)

(B)

Fig. 3.7 Nets of the same mesh width: (A) nylon, and (B) silk.

which permits the collection of a large spectrum of zooplankters is the simultaneous use of two nets with different mesh sizes: one for smaller (e.g. 50 μm aperture or less) and one for larger (e.g. 126 μm aperture) species. As pointed out by Ejsmont-Karabin (1978), however, nets with apertures as small as 10 μm seem unable to collect rotifers quantitatively, so that nets should be avoided for rotifer sampling whenever possible.

The use of the terminology 'meshes per inch' or 'meshes per cm' must be avoided, because this does not usually give a real measure of mesh aperture, which depends upon the relative size of filament and the characteristics of the gauze. In order to permit comparison of results, the mesh aperture size, and when possible, the filtering area of the net should be specified since these are much more useful.

2.4.3 Volume of water filtered by plankton nets

The volume of water filtered should be determined indirectly as a rough value assuming that the net filters the volume of the column of water traversed by the net:

$$V = \pi r^2 d \tag{3.1}$$

where V is the volume of water filtered by the plankton net, r is the radius of the mouth of the net, and d is the distance through which the plankton net is towed. Clogging of the nets introduces an error in this calculation, however, and since clogging increases with the volume of water filtered the use of nets with flow meters is strongly recommended. As suggested by Gehringer & Aron (1968), the best position for the flow meter is not at the center of the mouth of the net, but in a position midway between the center and the net rim. A second flowmeter outside the net can give an estimate of net speed, and the two meters combined can yield an indication of filtration efficiency and clogging (Gehringer & Aron 1968).

2.5 *Towed plankton samplers*

Of the various instruments which have been devised for quantitative collection of zooplankton, the Clarke–Bumpus plankton sampler (Clarke & Bumpus 1940) is undoubtedly among the most versatile. Schematically, this instrument is simply a plankton net connected to a flowmeter which allows measurement of the volume of water filtered by the sampler. Its detailed structural characteristics are shown in Fig. 3.8.

The Clarke–Bumpus plankton sampler can be handled easily from a small craft, and can be equipped with nets of different mesh sizes to collect samples of organisms of very different body-size. It can be utilized advantageously for the collection of zooplankton samples along vertical, horizontal, or sinusoidal

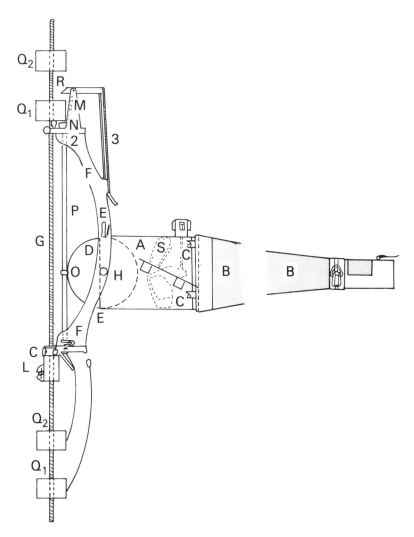

Fig. 3.8 Schematic representation of a Clarke–Bumpus plankton sampler: (A) tube, (B) net, (C) bayonet lock, (D) shutter, (E) pivot of shutter, (F) frame, (G) cable, (H) pivot for tube, (I) plane, (J) spring pin, (K) gate lock, (L) supporting clamp, (M) rod fixed to trigger, ($N_1 N_2$) arms in cap, (O_1) long finger lug, (O_2) short finger lug, (P) rod, ($Q_1 Q_2$) messengers, (R) trigger, (S) propeller, (T) counter, (U) semicircular bar, (V) escapement rod, (W) stop for messenger, and (1,2,3) are springs (after Tonolli 1971).

hauls within a selected layer of water. When it is used for vertical hauls it has the advantage over simple plankton nets of directly measuring the volume of water filtered, and consequently, has greater accuracy. Its most effective use, however, is for horizontal or sinusoidal hauls. Horizontal hauls make evaluation of the occurrence of irregularities and spatial discontinuities in the distribution of the planktonic organisms possible with precision and a high degree of resolution (Tonolli 1949a, b). Sinusoidal hauls, on the other hand, make possible the collection of representative samples from fairly extensive lacustrine areas (or water layers), and reduce the influence of the patchy distribution of plankton on the evaluation of its density.

The Clarke–Bumpus plankton sampler is equipped with a mechanism for opening and closing the mouth which can be operated at a distance by means of messengers. This means that even very deep layers can be sampled singly. In addition, a retaining device for a second pair of messengers makes possible the use and the simultaneous functioning of more than one sampler at different depths using a single cable. This has advantages when the vertical distribution of plankton in large and/or deep lakes is to be studied.

The basic model, conceived by Clarke & Bumpus in 1940, has, with the passage of time, undergone several improvements with regard to its efficiency and versatility. It has also been modified for the collection of plankton samples under specific conditions. Comita & Comita (1957) modifed the mechanism which controls the volume of filtered water; Paquette & Frolander (1957) improved the closing system. Other modifications have increased the size of the instrument in order to collect more organisms in a single haul, especially in water bodies characterized by low zooplankton densities (Paquette *et al.* 1961; Yentsch *et al.* 1962).

At present there are two kinds of Clarke–Bumpus samplers on the market, one with a mouth opening of 5 inches (12·7 cm) and the other with a mouth opening of 12 inches (30·5 cm). Experiments on the comparative accuracy of these two samplers, equipped with nets of the same mesh size (No. 20: 76 μm mesh aperture), in the collection of crustacean zooplankton in a large subalpine lake (Lago Maggiore), have demonstrated some significant differences. The samples obtained from three replicates of each sampler exhibit apparent community structures which are very similar within the replicates taken using a single instrument, but which are very different between the two instruments (de Bernardi, unpublished data). In particular, as shown in Table 3.3, the sampler with the larger mouth collects larger, more motile, and faster swimming crustaceans more efficiently, while smaller organisms dominate the samples collected by the smaller sampler.

Comparisons of the efficiency of the Clarke–Bumpus sampler relative to other techniques often disagree, although they all suggest that the Clarke–Bumpus is a good piece of sampling gear. According to Currie & Foxton

Table 3.3 Community structure as estimated by 3 replicate zooplankton samples collected with a 12 inch and a 5 inch Clarke–Bumpus sampler (net = No. 20: 76 μm pore size). Samples were taken in the upper 50 m of Lago Maggiore. [*Editor's Note:* A reviewer has suggested that percentage community structure figures may not reflect actual collection efficiencies well because the values for various species are not independent. Many researchers, however, use zooplankton samples for examining community composition using percentage composition measures. They should be warned that different samplers yield quite different pictures of the community.]

Species		net 76 μm			
		Sampler 12″		Sampler 5″	
		%	s	%	s
Diaphanosoma brachyurum		57·9 ± 4·3		51·4 ± 1·8	
Daphnia hyalina		4·4 ± 0·08		2·7 ± 0·6	
Bythotrephes longimanus		0·15 ± 0·04		0·03 ± 0·01	
Leptodora kindtii		0·72 ± 0·11		0·21 ± 0·17	
Bosmina coregoni		0·32 ± 0·14		0·74 ± 0·45	
Chydorus sphaericus		0·17 ± 2·7		11·4 ± 3·9	
Mesocyclops leuckarti	♀	0·38 ± 0·16		0·46 ± 0·08	
	♂	0·5 ± 0·26		0·26 ± 0·07	
Cyclops abyssorum	♀	5·3 ± 0·33		2·1 ± 0·9	
	♂	24·7 ± 5·6		8·8 ± 1·2	
Eudiaptomus vulgaris	♀	3·0 ± 1·4		9·2 ± 2·0	
	♂	1·1 ± 0·6		7·1 ± 1·5	
Mixodiaptomus laciniatus	♀	0·6 ± 0·3		0·8 ± 0·3	
	♂	0·3 ± 0·2		0·6 ± 0·2	
copepodites		0·4 ± 0·1		1·5 ± 0·3	

(1957), the Clarke–Bumpus is one of the samplers which yield the highest filtration coefficient.[1] Schindler (1969) reports that the sampling efficiency of the 5-inch Clarke–Bumpus plankton sampler is inferior to that of his own trap, but similar to that of other devices such as a 9-l Van Dorn bottle, and a simple plankton net with a 30 cm mouth. It must be emphasized, however, that the mesh size of the Clarke–Bumpus plankton sampler net was different from the mesh size of the sampler with the 12 inch mouth in this case, and this may have had a significant influence on the results. On the other hand, Langeland & Rognerud (1974) made a statistical comparison of the efficiency of three different devices for sample collection (the Clarke–Bumpus plankton

1. Editor's Note. 'Filtration coefficient' here means the ratio of the volume of water passed through the sampler to the volume of water through which the sampler would pass if there were no resistance to water flow. The implication is that the Clarke–Bumpus has little problem with clogging.

sampler, the Schindler trap, and the Friedinger bottle) in four lakes of different phytoplankton density. They found that the Clarke–Bumpus plankton sampler and the Schindler trap were of similar efficiency, while the Friedinger bottle was less efficient. Lewis & Saunders (1979) report that the efficiency of the Clarke–Bumpus sampler is very similar to that of a sampler of their own conception, which combines the features of the Van Dorn water bottle and the integrating tube sampler.

Because of its sampling characteristics, the Clarke–Bumpus plankton sampler is strongly recommended whenever the morphological features of the lake and the exigencies of the research allow it.[1] It is a particularly useful device for research on large lakes characterized by low zooplankton densities, or when the object of study is the large scale spatial distribution (both vertical and horizontal) of the zooplankton. An appendix (Section 5) reproduces some particularly detailed suggestions for the use of the Clarke–Bumpus plankton sampler, given by Tonolli (1971).

Other samplers for the quantitative collection of plankton have been designed, such as the various types of high-speed samplers, the Hardy continuous recording sampler (Hardy 1926), and the Motoda multiple sampler (Motoda 1962). Since the use of these samplers from small boats is quite difficult they have been used primarily for the collection of marine plankton and will not be discussed further here.

3 Sample Manipulation: Killing and Preservation

Once the samples have been collected, the organisms must be killed and treated at once so as to preserve them whole until analysis can be completed.

The simplest method of killing and preserving the animals uses a 5 % formaldehyde solution. It must be remembered in this connection that formalin is sold as a 40 % solution of formaldehyde. While useful for the treatment of routine samples, this method has a distinct disadvantage when the morphological structure or the population dynamics of the different species are the object of study. This is especially true when rotifers and cladocerans are the organisms concerned. Since 5 % formaldehyde solution takes a relatively long time to kill the animals distortion of the body structure often takes place in the case of soft-bodied organisms. Where cladocerans are concerned (e.g. *Daphnia*, *Bosmina*, *Diaphanosoma*), carapaces may balloon and the eggs and embryos contained in them may be lost (see also Chapters 2, 4 & 6). In this case, it is advisable to kill the organisms using more rapid and efficient methods or to utilize special solutions and techniques.

1. Editor's Note. K.Patalas suggests, however, that Clarke–Bumpus samplers should not be used with nets smaller than 70–80 μm because below this aperture, efficiency is very low.

A very quick and efficient method is to filter the collected material onto a nylon net of the appropriate mesh size which is then immersed in 95 % ethanol. The organisms are killed quickly, largely avoiding the negative effects mentioned above, and for this reason, this method has been employed with success in the study of the dynamics of *Daphnia* populations (e.g. Hall 1964; de Bernardi 1974). The use of alcohol also avoids carapace ballooning, a fact of fundamental importance when it is necessary to know the body-size in order to estimate the size structure of the populations in production studies. The organisms killed in this way must then be transferred to a 5 % formaldehyde solution in order to preserve them until analysis can be performed.

Recently, Haney & Hall (1973) have suggested using a solution of 40 g l^{-1} of sucrose and 4 % formaldehyde to kill and preserve zooplankton samples. This method has been modified by Prepas (1978) who found it to be somewhat inefficient, especially with regard to the problem of egg loss from the carapace. Prepas suggests a method of her own which consists of concentrating the samples on a nylon filter and treating them with a solution of 60 g l^{-1} sucrose and 2 % formaldehyde buffered with sodium borate and maintained at a low temperature (6 °C).

4 The Choice of a Sampler

As has been emphasized in Section 1, the problem of the choice of a sampler for quantitative plankton collection is not an easy one. There are many factors involved which cannot be ignored, particularly the characteristics of the environment, the zooplankton species to be studied, and the aims of the research. Each single device, in fact, has its own exclusive features which determine its relative utility according to the specific use for which it is intended. In addition, once a sampler has been selected its efficiency must be tested in comparison to other samplers, and this comparison should be repeated more than once in the course of the year. The efficiency of a particular instrument is often related to the composition, structure, and density of the population to be sampled, and the density of other populations (e.g. phytoplankton); thus, one can see how apparent sampler efficiency might vary with the seasons.

Some schematic suggestions for the choice of particular devices for plankton collection in different experimental situations are presented in Table 3.4. This table is certainly not to be considered definitive or exhaustive, but is intended only to indicate some basic solutions to the complex problem of quantitative plankton collection. Further useful information has been published by Omaly (1966), Schwoerbel (1966), Gehringer & Aron (1968), Tonolli (1971), Lamotte & Bourlière (1971), and Bottrell *et al.* (1976).

Table 3.4 Schematic recommendation for the choice of sampler to be used for the assessment of zooplankton population density under various conditions. [*Editor's Note*: K. Patalas suggests that the choice of sampling technique is not only reliant upon the nature of the water body and the spatial scale of the required data, but also upon the size of the target organisms. One should not, for example, use a small tube sampler for the collection of vertically integrated samples of mysids in deep, pelagic waters.]

	Deep and pelagic waters				Shallow and littoral waters			
	Point samples	Vertically integrated samples	Horizontally integrated samples	Sinusoidal samples	Point samples	Vertically integrated samples	Horizontally integrated samples	Samples within vegetation
Bottles	+	–	–	–	+	–	–	+
Traps	++	–	–	–	++	–	–	+
Tubes	–	++	–	–	–	++	–	++
Pumps	++	+	–	–	++	–	–	++
Nets	–	++	++	++	–	–	+	–
Plankton samplers (e.g. Clarke–Bumpus)	–	++	++	++	–	–	–	–

5 Appendix

Instructions for use of the Clarke–Bumpus plankton sampler given by Tonolli (1971).

The plankton sampler must be used from a moving boat, and it is therefore necessary to estimate the depth at which the instrument is towed. Knowing the angle which the cable coming off the winch forms from the vertical, measured with a clinometer, one can calculate the depth by applying the simple formula:

$$D = L \cdot \cos \alpha$$

where D is the depth in metres of the instrument,
L is the length in metres of the cable, and
α is the angle subtended by the cable to the vertical.

It is necessary that the angle not exceed a value greater than 50°, and it is therefore necessary to apply a weight to the lower end of the cable. This weight will be most efficient if it has the form of a cable depressor.

Actually the cable does not lie in the water in a straight line but rather as a reversed catenary, more or less pronounced according to the mass of the terminal weight, its more or less active hydrodynamic form, and the velocity with which the boat moves through the water.

When one is working in a small boat it may be inconvenient to measure the cable angle and calculate the true depth of the sampler. Advantage can be taken of the fact that an angle of 45° is rather easily estimated by eye and that the cosine is 0·7. Thus it is easy to calculate mentally the real depth under normal working conditions from a small boat when the cable will be nearly straight; one lets the cable out to a length 1·4 times the desired depth.

The collection of plankton should be carried out along as straight a course as possible, since each deviation from this involves a movement of the plankton sampler to a greater depth, but it may be convenient to move in the ark of a large circle to avoid towing the samples in the wake of the boat.

The velocity of the boat should not be less than 50 nor more than 125 m/min. Of course the velocity should remain constant over the whole collecting period. One may determine the velocity by measuring the distance travelled by the boat during a period of 60 seconds along a line of small floats placed at determined intervals, anchored to the bottom of a littoral zone, or by measuring the travel time between two points of known distance.

The plankton sampler may be used to collect horizontally, successively at different depths; this permits us quite exact knowledge of the populations of these depths, but requires interpolations that are not always acceptable, if from the data of horizontal collections we wish to obtain more general information about the total populations in a column of water.

One may sample a layer simply by raising the sampler from the bottom to the top of the layer. With a little experience, one may make zig-zag collections in a vertical plane, in general limited by the surface of the lake above and below by that depth to which one wishes to sample. Thus one may combine the two motions, the uniform motion of the boat, with a vertical motion, also of uniform velocity, but alternating its direction of motion. This operation may be repeated with the same plankton sampler many times in such a manner that the apparatus will describe in the layer of water a series of ascending and descending passages.

The Clarke–Bumpus plankton sampler is designed for use with more than one instrument attached to the same cable, so that the arrival of the first and then of the second messenger at the plankton sampler nearest the surface will liberate messengers attached to the base of the metal frame which, running down the cable, serves to perform the same function successively on plankton samplers at greater depths along the same cable. One has thus the great advantage of exploring with zig-zag collections adjacent and overlapping superimposed strata layers of the same water mass, permitting the evaluation of the planktonic population of a given stratum in relation to the populations of overlying strata. Obviously a powerful winch and heavy cable are needed for use of more than one sampler.

This possibility may also be exploited by having two samplers function simultaneously attached at a short distance (even 1 m) from one another, supplied with nets of different mesh. One has thus the advantage of being able to ascertain the real relations of the presence of organisms of rather different sizes in the same layer of water.

The calibration value (litres/revolution) varies somewhat with velocity but is relatively constant over a range of velocity (see below). The minimum velocity (50 m/min) is imposed by the characteristics of the impeller, of the transmission, and of the counters. Only with the attainment of this velocity does the relation between the amount of water admitted and the number of revolutions become constant.

It may happen that the plankton sampler, towed behind the boat at the indicated rate, will have the interior of the net clogged by a film of algae. In this case the number of revolutions is not reliable, since during a more or less long fraction of the course there may have been admitted to filtration a volume of water per unit of time insufficient for proper functioning of the counter (Yentsch & Duxbury 1956).

Each plankton sampler is provided with a certificate giving the value of the factor K, by which it is necessary to multiply the number of revolutions R registered by the counter, in order to obtain the volume of water filtered in litres. If the plankton sampler is used with care, and not too intensively, the value of K will not change with use. By simple means one may however easily recalibrate it, for example, by running the sampler without a net several times, in one direction and then the other, for the distance between two fixed buoys, making sure that the mouth remains normal to the direction of motion.

If the shutter fits imperfectly the capture of aliquots of small organisms may occur during the descent and recovery of the sampler through more highly populated layers. The remedy to this is very simple: apply to the shutter a disc of celluloid, or similar material, flexible, which conforms exactly to the interior dimensions of the tube: the disc of celluloid should be attached to the shutter by a single central screw, to keep the celluloid flexible and fitting accurately.

In reading the counter at the beginning and end of the collection, one must make sure that wind action does not add 'anemometric' revolutions to the count.

If the plankton sampler is not being used in horizontal tows or in oblique tows which terminate at the surface, it may become necessary to know the velocity of fall of the messenger along the cable. Because of the time it takes the messenger to fall to the depth of the sampler it may permit the sampler to rise above the desired level before it is closed.

One cannot furnish general information about the velocity of fall of the messengers, since it depends on the messenger itself (shape and weight), on the nature of the cable and of its angle of inclination, as also on the velocity with which the boat is moving. It is, however, not difficult to estimate the velocity of fall for small depths, since, holding one finger against the cable where it enters the water, one can feel the impact of the messenger when it strikes. Knowing the time of fall for a given depth, one can extrapolate arithmetically the times of fall for other depths, under the same conditions of those variables which can influence the velocity of fall.

The messengers may then be released far enough beforehand so that the plankton sampler in uniform motion can in the meantime reach the predetermined position.

The C-B sampler generally used has a mouth diameter of 25 cm but a larger model with 62 cm is now also available (Paquette *et al.* 1961). The use of this large model is recommended when one wishes to collect the planktonic predators which are large and fast-swimming, like *Heterocope*, *Ponteporeia*, *Leptodora*, *Bythotrephes*, etc.

6 References

Achefors H. (1971) A quantitative plankton sampler. *Oikos*, **22**, 114–118.
Beers J.R., Stewart G.L. & Strickland J.D.H. (1967) A pumping system for sampling small plankton. *J. Fish. Res. Board Can.*, **24**, 1811–1818.
Bottrell H.H., Duncan A., Gliwicz Z.M., Grygiereg E., Herzig A., Hillbricht-Ilkowska A., Kurasawa H., Larsson P. & Węgleńska T. (1976) A review of some problems in zooplankton production studies. *Norw. J. Zool.*, **24**, 419–456.

Burgis M.J., Darlington J.P.E.C., Dunn I.G., Gane G.G., Gwahaba J.J. & McGowan L.M. (1973) The biomass and distribution of organisms in Lake George, Uganda. *Proc. R. Soc. Lond. B.*, **184**, 271–298.

Chodorowski A. (1971) L'échantillonage des peuplements d'invertebrés des eaux continentales stagnantes. In M.Lamotte & F.Boulière (eds.), *Problemes d'écologie: l'échantillonage des peuplements animaux des milieu aquatiques.* Paris: Masson & Cie.

Clarke E.B. (1942) A modification of the Juday plankton trap. *Spec. Publ. No. 8, Limnol. Soc. Am.*

Clarke G.L. & Bumpus D.F. (1940) The plankton sampler. An instrument for quantitative plankton investigations. *Spec. Publ. No. 5, Limnol. Soc. Am.*

Comita G.W. & Comita J.J. (1957) The internal distribution patterns of a calanoid copepod population, and a description of a modified Clarke–Bumpus plankton sampler. *Limnol. Oceanogr.*, **2**, 321–332.

Currie R.I. & Foxton P. (1957) A new quantitative plankton net. *J. Mar. Biol. Ass. U.K.*, **36**, 17–32.

de Bernardi R. (1974) The dynamics of a population of *Daphnia hyalina* Leydig in Lago Maggiore, Northern Italy. *Mem. Ist. Ital. Idrobiol.*, **31**, 221–243.

Dumont H.J. (1967) A five day study of patchiness in *Bosmina coregoni* Baird in a shallow eutrophic lake. *Mem. Ist. Ital. Idrobiol.*, **22**, 81–103.

Ejsmont-Karabin J. (1978) Studies on the usefulness of different mesh-size plankton nets for thickening zooplankton. *Ekol. Pol.*, 479–490.

Elster H.J. & Schwoerbel I. (1970) Beiträge zur Biologie und Populationsdynamik der Daphnien in Bodensee. *Arch. Hydrobiol.* (Suppl.), **38**, 18–72.

Evans M.S. & Sell D.W. (1983) Zooplankton sampling strategies for environmental studies. *Hydrobiologia*, **99**, 215–223.

Ferrari I., Bellavere C. & Camurri L. (1973) Ricerche invernali al Lago Santo Parmense (Appennino Settentrionale). *L'Ateneo Parmense—Acta Naturalia*, **9**, 1–19.

Gehringer J.W. & Aron W. (1968) Field techniques. In *Zooplankton Sampling, UNESCO Monographs on Oceanographic Methodology*, **2**, 87–104.

George D.G. (1976) A pumping system for collecting horizontal plankton samples and recording continuously sampling depth, water temperature, turbidity and *in vivo* chlorophyll. *Freshw. Biol.*, **6**, 413–419.

George D.G. & Owen G.H. (1978) A new tube sampler for crustacean zooplankton. *Limnol. Oceanogr.*, **23**, 563–566.

Green J. (1977) Sampling rotifers. *Arch. Hydrobiol. Beih. Ergebn. Limnol.*, **8**, 9–12.

Hall D.J. (1964) An experimental approach to the dynamics of a natural population of *Daphnia galeata mendotae. Ecology*, **45**, 94–112.

Haney J.F. & Hall D.J. (1973) Sugar-coated *Daphnia*: a preservation technique for Cladocera. *Limnol. Oceanogr.*, **18**, 331–333.

Hardy A.C. (1926) The relationship of the Herring to its animate environment. II. Report on trial with the plankton indicator. *Fish. Invest. Lond. (Ser. II)*, **7**, 1–13.

Hensen V. (1887) Ueber die Bestimmung des Planktons oder des im Meere treibenden Materials an Pflanzen und Tieren. *Ber. Kom. Wissen. Untersuch. d. Deutsch. Meere*, **5**, 1–107.

Hodgkiss I.J. (1977) The use of simultaneous sampling bottle and vertical net collections to describe the dynamics of a zooplankton population. *Hydrobiologia*, **52**, 197–205.

Hrbáček J. (1966) A morphometrical study of some backwaters and fish ponds in relation to the representative plankton samples (with an appendix of C.O.Junge on depth distribution for quadratic surfaces and other configurations). *Hydrobiological Studies*, **1**, 221–265.

Hrbáček J. (1971) Special sampling systems. In W.T.Edmondson & G.G.Winberg (eds.), *A manual on Methods for the Assessment of Secondary Productivity in Fresh Waters*, IBP Handbook No. 17, Oxford: Blackwell.

Juday C. (1916) Limnological apparatus. *Trans. Wisc. Acad. Sci.*, **18**, 566–592.

Lamotte M. & Boulière F. (eds.) (1971) *Problemes d'écologie: l'échantillonage des peuplements animaux des milieux aquatiques.* Paris: Masson & Cie.

Langeland A. & Rognerud S. (1974) Statistical analyses used in the comparison of three methods of freshwater zooplankton sampling. *Arch. Hydrobiol.*, **73**, 403–410.

Langford R.R. (1953) Methods of plankton collection and a description of a new sampler. *J. Fish. Res. Board Can.*, **10**, 238–252.

Langford R.R. & Jermolajev E.G. (1966) Direct effect of wind on plankton distribution. *Verh. Internat. Verein. Limnol.*, **16**, 188–193.

Lewis W.M. & Saunders J.F. (1979) Two new integrating samplers for zooplankton, phytoplankton and water chemistry. *Arch. Hydrobiol.*, **85**, 244–249.

Likens G.E. & Gilbert J.J. (1970) Notes on quantitative sampling of natural populations of planktonic rotifers. *Limnol. Oceanogr.*, **15**, 816–820.

Makarewicz J.C. & Likens G.E. (1979) Structure and function of the zooplankton community of Mirror Lake, New Hampshire. *Ecol. Monogr.*, **49**, 109–127.

Malone B.J. & McQueen D.J. (1983) Horizontal patchiness in zooplankton populations in two Ontario kettle lakes. *Hydrobiologia*, **99**, 101–124.

Motoda S. (1962) Plankton sampler for collecting uncontaminated materials from several different zones by a simple vertical haul. *Rapp. P.V. Cons. Int. Expl. Mer.*, **153**, 55–58.

Omaly N. (1966) Moyens de prélevement du zooplancton. Essai historique et critique. *Pelagos*, **5**, 169 pp.

Paquette R.G. & Frolander H.F. (1957) Improvements in the Clarke–Bumpus plankton sampler. *J. Cons. Int. Expl. Mer.*, **22**, 284–288.

Paquette R.G., Scott E.L. & Sund P.N. (1961) An enlarged Clarke–Bumpus plankton sampler. *Limnol. Oceanogr.*, **6**, 230–233.

Patalas K. (1954) Comparative studies on a new type of self acting water sampler for plankton and hydrochemical investigations. *Ekol. Pol.*, **2**, 231–242.

Pennak R.W. (1962) Quantitative zooplankton sampling in littoral vegetation areas. *Limnol. Oceanogr.*, **7**, 487–489.

Prepas E. (1978) Sugar-frosted *Daphnia*: an improved fixation technique for Cladocera. *Limnol. Oceanogr.*, **23**, 557–559.

Prepas E. & Rigler F.H. (1978) The enigma of *Daphnia* death rates. *Limnol. Oceanogr.*, **23**, 970–988.

Ragotzkie R.A. & Bryson R.A. (1953) Correlation of currents with the distribution of adult *Daphnia* in Lake Mendota. *J. Mar. Res.*, **12**, 157–172.

Rey J. & Capblanq J. (1975) Dynamique des populations et production du zooplancton du lac de Port-Bielh (Pyrénées Centrales). *Ann. Limnol.*, **11**, 1–45.

Ruttner-Kolisko A. (1977) Comparison of various sampling techniques, and results of repeated sampling of planktonic rotifers. *Arch. Hydrobiol. Beih. Ergebn. Limnol.*, **8**, 13–18.

Schindler D.W. (1969) Two useful devices for vertical plankton and water sampling. *J. Fish. Res. Board Can.*, **26**, 1948–1955.

Schwoerbel J. (1966) *Methoden der Hydrobiologie*. Stuttgart: Kosmos.

Siebeck O. (1960) Die Bedeutung von Alter und Geschlect für die Horizontalverteilung planktischer Crustaceen im Lunzer Obersee. *Int. Rev. Gesmten Hydrobiol.*, **45**, 125–131.

Smyly W.J.P. (1968) Some observations on the effect of sampling technique under different conditions on numbers of some freshwater planktonic Entomostraca and Rotifera caught by a water bottle. *J. Nat. Hist.*, **2**, 569–575.

Tonolli V. (1949a) Struttura spaziale del poplamento mesoplanctico. Eterogeneità delle densità dei popolamenti orizzontali e sua variazione in funzione della quota. *Mem. Ist. Ital. Idrobiol.*, **5**, 189–208.

Tonolli V. (1949b) Ripartizione spaziale e migrazioni verticali dello zooplancton. Ricerche e considerazioni. *Mem. Ist. Ital. Idrobiol.*, **5**, 209–228.

Tonolli V. (1971) Methods of collection. Zooplankton. In W.T.Edmondson & G.G.Winberg (eds.), *A Manual on Methods for the Assessment of Secondary Productivity in Fresh Waters*. IBP Handbook No. 17, Oxford: Blackwell.

Tranter D.J. & Heron A.C. (1965) Filtration characteristics of Clarke Bumpus samplers. *Aust. J. Mar. Freshwat. Res.*, **16**, 281–291.

Tranter D.J. & Heron A.C. (1967) Experiments on filtration in plankton nets. *Aust. J. Mar. Freshwat. Res.*, **18**, 89–111.

Tranter D.J. & Smith P.E. (1968) Filtration performance. In *Zooplankton Sampling. Monographs on Oceanographic Methodology*. Paris: UNESCO.

Waite S.W. & O'Grady S.M. (1980) Description of a new submersible filter-pump apparatus for sampling plankton. *Hydrobiologia*, **74**, 187–191.

Wattiez C. (1978) Agrégation et migration verticale de zooplancton dans deux petits étangs peu profond. *Hydrobiologia*, **61**, 49–67.

Wiebe P.H. (1971) A computer model study of zooplankton patchiness and its effect on sampling error. *Limnol. Oceanogr.*, **16**, 29–38.

Yentsch C.S. & Duxbury A.C. (1956) Some of the factors affecting the calibration number of the Clarke–Bumpus plankton sampler. *Limnol. Oceanogr.*, **1**, 268–273.

Yentsch C.S., Grice G.D. & Hart A.D. (1962) Some opening-closing devices for plankton nets operated by pressure, electrical and mechanical action. *Int. Counc. Expl. Sea*, No. 21.

Yocum W.L., Evans M.S. & Hawkins B.E. (1978) A comparison of pump sampling systems for live zooplankton collection. *Hydrobiologia*, **60**, 199–202.

Chapter 4. Sampling the Benthos of Standing Waters

JOHN A. DOWNING

1 Introduction

Measures of population density are the raw materials from which rates of production are calculated. If population estimates are inaccurate then the resulting production estimates are inaccurate and there is no means of correction. This chapter is, therefore, concerned with the choice of sampling techniques for benthic organisms.

Although it is difficult to choose one sampling technique from the many available, this reasoning must be performed in preparation for each set of experiments, because in most cases, the sampling technique chosen will be a function of the question asked and the system investigated. The validity of the conclusions will rest on the appropriate choice of technique. In order for the hypothesis tested to be interpretable in its intended context, the samples taken must be representative of the environment, and precise enough to test the hypothesis at hand. It is the purpose of this chapter to summarize what is known about benthos sampling techniques and to recommend procedures to be applied in future studies.

As others have done (Holme 1964, 1971; Southwood 1966; Schwoerbel 1970; Kajak 1971; Brinkhurst 1974) this chapter presents and describes a variety of sampling devices. In addition, it provides a survey of frequency-of-use and success-of-operation. It is my hope that a researcher can enter this chapter with a production or population hypothesis and exit with a knowledge of techniques that will test it efficiently.

2 The Benthos of Unconsolidated Substrates

This chapter treats the sampling of the benthos of unconsolidated substrates (e.g. mud, sand, silt, clay, gravel, detritus) first because most is known about this. Fewer ecologists have sampled the hard-substrate benthos, the benthos inhabiting aquatic macrophytes, or the microbenthos; these are treated in later sections. I hope that freshwater ecologists interested in studying epilithic and phytomacrobenthos will profit from a summary of experiences in soft substrates, and that this summary will show the general pathway through which new sampling techniques must be validated. I suggest, therefore, that all benthos ecologists read at least Sections 2.4 and 2.5 before proceeding to the section of specific interest.

2.1 Data sources

When faced with similar tasks, other authors have drawn primarily upon their personal experience. Instead, I have drawn upon the published observations of many other scientists. I feel that observations and opinions committed to print are likely to be most dependable, and that corroborating observations and opinions published independently are most likely to be correct. I hope that this approach will help make useful generalizations and will not reinforce spurious opinion.

I have used two sorts of quantitative data in this analysis. Frequency-of-use data were derived from a literature survey covering as much of the published literature as I have easy access to. This included literature received from a reprint request canvass of *Biological Abstracts* between 1964 and 1979 (key words: benthic, benthos, bottom, sediment), and a full secular literature survey (1970 to 1981) on the journals listed in Section 5. The data collected in this survey included: types of samplers used, the sediment in which it was used, the size of the sampler, the number of replicates taken, the size of the sieve used to separate animals from sediment, and the preservative used. These data were collected in order to discover which specific techniques benthic ecologists feel are appropriate to various study situations. This analysis assumes that data collected using techniques tried and found unsuccessful will not often lead to publication. A high relative frequency-of-use implies, therefore, that the technique was at least mechanically successful. This argument must be applied cautiously to new sampling techniques.

The second type of data was collected to evaluate the success of various sampling programs. I collected a large amount of quantitative data on the variability seen among replicate samples taken with various sampling gear of various sizes from various sediments. These data are the same as those I used (Downing 1979a) to show that sampling variance can be predicted accurately as a function of mean density of animals and sampler size. Downing (1979a) also suggests that samplers with higher than predicted sampling variance are probably poorer samplers which will give rise to highly variable estimates, the variance of which is probably the result of sporadic sampler inaccuracy. I use these data to draw additional conclusions regarding the type of sampling gear a benthos ecologist should use.

2.2 Samplers in frequent use

Many ecologists have modified their equipment in a manner that they feel

Table 4.1 Frequency-of-use of various sampling devices in a survey of the literature published between 1970 and 1981 in the journals listed in Section 5. The table shows that the Ekman grab is the most popular device for sampling the freshwater benthos.

Sampling device	Frequency	Percent frequency
Ekman grab	163	44
Corers	81	22
Petersen grab	41	11
PONAR grab	38	10
van Veen grab	15	4
Smith–McIntyre grab	5	1
Miscellaneous samplers	25	7

might be most successful. The result is that there exist nearly as many samplers as articles on the benthos (see Elliott & Tullet 1978, for an annotated review). Certain of these samplers are now widely available, and thus, through popularity, are implicated as being useful equipment. Below, I introduce each of the most popular samplers in order of frequency-of-use (Table 4.1) and describe published evaluations of each piece of equipment.

2.2.1 Ekman grab

The Ekman grab (Ekman 1911; Fig. 4.1) is by far the most popular sampler for the bottom fauna (Table 4.1) and has been used in over 44 % of all benthos investigations since 1970. This sampler is basically a brass or stainless steel box 100–900 cm^2 open on the top and bottom. There are doors on the top that swing open on descent, and jaws on the bottom that are closed by dropping a weight or 'messenger' down the retrieving line after penetration of the sediment. The Ekman grab has been modified by the addition of lead weights (Burton & Flannagan 1973; Milbrink & Wiederholm 1973), been made taller to avoid loss of sediments on deep penetration (Flannagan 1970), has had screens added for the same purpose (Hamilton 1971), and has been used with a handle instead of a rope by divers or in shallow waters (e.g. Solem 1973) (Fig. 4.2). A very large model (2500 cm^2) has been equipped with an hydraulic closure (Murray & Charles 1975). Moore (1979) found that the Ekman grab is preceded by a shockwave that might disturb surface sediments if dropped too fast; modifications have been made so that the top doors open more fully to reduce this problem (Johnson & Brinkhurst 1971). Because the Ekman grab's closing mechanism does not operate well if the boat is moving (Powers,

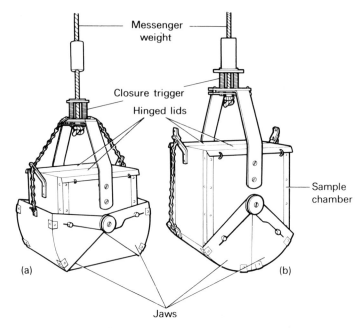

Fig. 4.1 Standard Ekman grab open (a) and closed (b). Drawings are after Welch (1948).

personal communication), Slack (1972) has modified it so that no messenger is needed for closure.

Although many modifications have been advanced for this sampling device, there is little evidence to suggest that the modifications are necessary or helpful. For example, Flannagan (1970) found that the standard Ekman grab and a tall, weighted model both yielded equally accurate population estimates. On the other hand, Hamilton (1971) found that in very soft sediments the addition of a screen over the top of the sampler allowed this modified sampler to collect significantly more organisms than the standard Ekman grab. This is because the standard sampler passed through the surface sediments where most benthic organisms live. Burton & Flannagan (1973) found that the addition of weights and locking lids allowed collection of significantly more organisms than the standard Ekman grab, while Milbrink & Wiederholm (1973) found the opposite effect. Kajak *et al.* (1978) present a comparison of the tall and standard Ekman grabs, but there is no obvious effect of the height of the sampler on sampling accuracy. It appears that the effectiveness of a sampler modification may depend upon an interaction between substrate and target population; modification of the standard Ekman grab is, therefore, not always necessary.

The Ekman grab has had limitations regarding the type of substrate it can

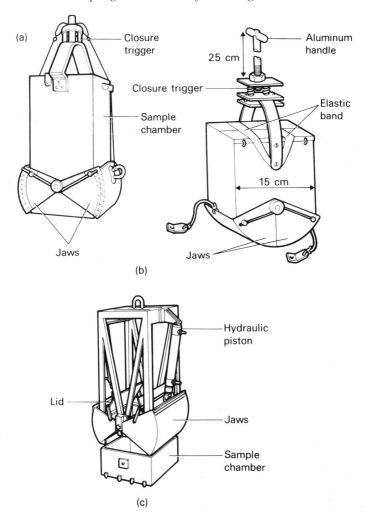

Fig. 4.2 Modified Ekman grab: (a) the tall grab for deep, soft sediments (Brinkhurst 1974); (b) a grab operated without a rope and messenger (Rowe & Clifford 1973); and (c) a very large grab with hydraulic closure (Murray & Charles 1975).

penetrate. On the basis of quantitative comparison, both Johnson & Brinkhurst (1971) and Powers & Robertson (1967) suggest that the Ekman grab does not penetrate sand well, even though Sivertson (1973) found no difference between the sampling accuracy of the Ekman and van Veen grabs in sand. Marshall (1978) found that the Ekman gave inaccurate estimates in hard sediments. Macrophytic vegetation presents another obstacle (Johnson & Brinkhurst 1971), although the Ekman has been used to sample it (Guziur *et*

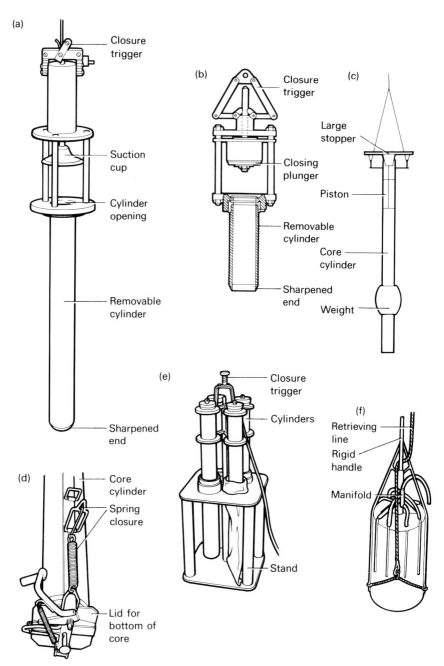

Fig. 4.3 Examples of various core samplers: (a) the single Kajak–Brinkhurst corer (Brinkhurst 1974); (b) the original Kajak corer (Kajak *et al.* (1965); (c) a similar corer that is simple to construct (Hongve 1972); (d) a special bottom closure to retain soft sediments (Giani 1974); (e) a multiple corer (Hamilton *et al.* 1970); and (f) a very large corer with hydraulic assistance for sediment penetration and sample removal (Thayer *et al.* 1975).

al. 1975), neither does the Ekman grab penetrate riverine silt well (Gale 1975). Thus, although the most popular benthos sampler, the Ekman grab has definite limitations and should be used only with caution in resistant sediments.

2.2.2 Substrate corers

Sediment corers are the second most popular type of sampling gear for the freshwater benthos (Fig. 4.3). These samplers rely on gravity to enable them to penetrate the sediments with a long, open core tube. A messenger is dropped down the line to close the top of the core tube, and the sealed top retains the sample as the core is withdrawn and hoisted to the boat.

These samplers were used in 22 % of the benthos studies surveyed (Table 4.1). The most popular of these is the Kajak–Brinkhurst corer (Kajak *et al.* 1965; Brinkhurst *et al.* 1969) which was used by 25 % of the investigators who used corers. Corers have been manufactured in a variety of sizes and sampling areas of single cores range from 3 cm² to 855 cm² (Table 4.2). Core samplers

Table 4.2 Frequency-of-use of various sized corers in a survey of the literature published between 1970 and 1981 in journals listed in Section 5. The table shows that a significant number of researchers have used corers larger than 50 cm².

Size range (cm²)	Frequency	Percent frequency
0–10	21	25
10–20	23	27
20–30	12	14
30–40	7	8
40–50	8	10
> 50	13	15

that lift more than one core at a time (multiple corers) have been designed to reduce sampling effort (Flannagan 1970; Hamilton *et al.* 1970; Hakala 1971; Milbrink & Wiederholm 1973; Carter 1978). Again, several techniques have been advanced to reduce sediment disturbance on sampler penetration. Corers can be lowered slowly to reduce bow-wave effects (Krezoski *et al.* 1978) and larger corers can be used to reduce sample compression (Kajak & Dusoge 1971; Holopainen & Sarvala 1975). Scuba divers have also been employed to ensure efficient corer penetration (Flannagan 1970). Special corers have been built for use through ice (King & Everitt 1980) and a few very simple and inexpensive closing devices have also been proposed (Milbrink 1971; Hongve

1972; Blakar 1978), but their efficiency has only been verified quantitatively in one case (Milbrink 1971).

Corers also have problems in the remote penetration of resistant sediments. Prejs (1970) states that corers are not suitable for collection of benthos from sand, gravel, or shell grit. Taylor & Erman (1980) employed a diver to force corers into hard-packed sand to assess the littoral, sand dwelling community. Similarly, corers can be pushed by hand into many shallow water substrates.

Core samplers have been used often, but only within a narrow range of substrate types. In soft substrates, corers usually provide population estimates of benthic fauna that are equal to or higher than those obtained using other sampling gear. Milbrink *et al.* (1974a) found that a corer and an Ekman grab yielded similar population estimates. Flannagan (1970) found that corers performed more accurately than the Ekman grab, PONAR grab, Benthos corer, and Shipek or Franklin–Anderson samplers, and Hakala (1971), Hamilton (1971), and Paterson & Fernando (1971) all suggest that corers yield more accurate estimates than the Ekman grab. This applies to the sampling of chironomids (Milbrink & Wiederholm 1973), *Chaoborus* (Kajak *et al.* 1978), or to samples taken in very fluid sediments (Giani 1974), or riverine silt (Gale 1975). It has also been suggested that corers are better than the Smith–McIntyre sampler for the collection of estuarine organisms in fine sand (Smith & Howard 1972). Some corers are better than others; Carter (1978) found that a multiple corer yielded higher population estimates than a Gilson corer, and Brinkhurst *et al.* (1969) found that the Kajak–Brinkhurst corer also gave higher population estimates than the FBA (Gilson) corer. Although there is some equivocation (Milbrink & Wiederholm 1973), it is clear that the popular core samplers are not only used frequently but yielded relatively accurate collections of benthic organisms.

2.2.3 The Petersen grab

The third most popular group of samplers is modeled after the Petersen grab (Petersen 1918) (Fig. 4.4). This grab consists of two large jaws that swing shut automatically when sediment penetration releases the tension on the chain or arming mechanism that holds the jaws apart. Petersen-type samplers range in size from $258\,cm^2$ to $1000\,cm^2$ and have been used in 11% of recent studies of the benthic fauna (Table 4.1). This sampler has been modified in a variety of ways to increase its accuracy and ease of operation. Because pressure waves are always a problem with free-falling sampling gear, part of the solid shell of this grab has been replaced with a screen to decrease water resistance (Koss *et al.* 1974). It has also been equipped with hydraulic closures to insure sample retention (Flury 1963).

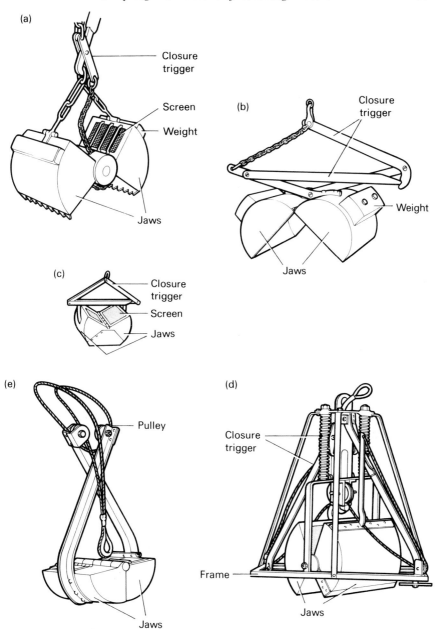

Fig. 4.4 A selection of popular grabs: (a and b) two models of the Petersen grab (Holme 1964; Welch 1948); (c) the PONAR grab (Elliott & Drake 1981); (d) the Smith–McIntyre grab (Smith & McIntyre 1954); and (e) the van Veen grab (Schwoerbel 1970).

Because the Petersen grab operates in resistant sediments that cannot be penetrated by the Ekman grab or sediment corers (Marshall 1978; Vincent 1979), it has been advanced as the best all-round piece of collection gear (Cairns & Dickson 1971). In spite of this, comparisons with other sampling equipment suggest that the Petersen grab is inferior: it yields lower population estimates than the Smith–McIntyre grab (Beeton *et al.* 1965), the van Veen grab (Kutty & Desai 1968), a short corer (Gale 1975), a Mackin corer (Baker *et al.* 1977), and an Ekman grab (Rinne 1978). Its weight and the resultant pressure wave apparently induce the loss of surface sediments (Rinne 1978). To my knowledge, the Petersen grab has never been found to yield more accurate population estimates than any sampling device.

2.2.4 *The PONAR grab*

The sampler that ranks fourth in popularity (used in 10 % of published reports) was the PONAR grab (*P*owers, *O*gle, *N*oble, *A*yers, *R*obertson; Powers & Robertson 1967; Fig. 4.4), which was developed in response to the need for a versatile piece of equipment (167–530 cm^2) able to sample the more resistant sediments, as well as mud. The two samplers of this sort previously available were the Petersen and Smith–McIntyre grabs. The Petersen is inferior in terms of sampling accuracy while the more accurate Smith–McIntyre is 'large and unwieldy, the mechanism is complicated and subject to failure, and the powerful tripping springs render it somewhat dangerous.' (Powers & Robertson 1967). The PONAR grab combines the jaw structure of the Smith–McIntyre with the safety and ease of the Petersen grab. Modification of the mesh size on the top of the PONAR affects its sampling accuracy and smaller mesh yields greater population estimates (Mozley 1974). At least one commercial version of this sampler has been modified such that it has a reduced jaw opening due to a different closure and tripping lever configuration, and the modified release is inferior to the original (C.F. Powers, personal communication).

The PONAR grab will penetrate most substrates, but its accuracy varies. For sampling the mud dwelling benthos, the PONAR yields less accurate population estimates than corers, the same accuracy as Ekman grabs, but more accurate population estimates than a Shipek grab or a modified (Franklin & Anderson 1961) Petersen grab (Flannagan 1970). Although the PONAR grab will withdraw a sample from almost any sediment, the sample will sometimes be inaccurate in soft sediments, where it often fails to close properly (P. André, personal communication). In harder substrates, the PONAR yields more accurate population estimates than either the Smith–McIntyre grab (Powers & Robertson 1967) or the van Veen grab (Ellis & Jones 1980).

2.2.5 *Smith–McIntyre and van Veen grabs*

The fifth and sixth most common sampling techniques are the van Veen (Thamdrup 1938) grabs and the Smith–McIntyre (Smith & McIntyre 1954) (Fig. 4.4). These samplers were used by 4 % and 1 % of the freshwater benthos researchers, respectively (Table 4.1). The Smith–McIntyre grab samples an area of about 500–625 cm^2 while the van Veen grab ranges in size from 200 cm^2 to 2500 cm^2. The Smith–McIntyre grab has served as the precursor to other more efficient samplers (see Section 2.2.4). Both of these samplers were designed to function in sediments ranging from mud to gravel. The Smith–McIntyre grab has been found to be more accurate than the Petersen and the orange-peel grabs in mud (Beeton *et al.* 1965), as accurate as the PONAR but more difficult to use (Powers & Robertson 1967) and less accurate than large (625 cm^2) corers in fine sand (Smith & Howard 1972). The van Veen has been found to be as accurate as the Ekman grab in sand (a difficult substrate for the Ekman to penetrate) (Sivertsen 1973), more accurate than the Petersen in some cases (Kutty & Desai 1968), and less accurate than the PONAR (Ellis & Jones 1980). A cinematographic comparison of the Smith–McIntyre and van Veen grabs suggests that the former should be preferred because it generates a smaller shockwave (Wigley 1967).

2.2.6 *Hydraulic sampling devices*

Hydraulic samplers or airlifts have been little used, since they are relatively new (Fig. 4.5) Aarefjord 1972; Mackey 1972; Pearson *et al.* 1973; Kaplan *et al.* 1974; Kritzler *et al.* 1974; also see Holme 1971). These samplers require that a corer-like device be pushed into the sediments. A stream of compressed air is fed to the bottom and the air, upon rising, entrains water, sediment, and organisms which are sieved *in situ* or else lifted and sieved in the boat. These samplers have two advantages over other sampling devices: they often yield more accurate population estimates than grabs and corers (Aarefjord 1972; Mackey 1972; Pearson *et al.* 1973), and they can be used on hard surfaces as well as mud, sand, and gravel (Aarefjord 1972; Kritzler *et al.* 1974). The main drawback is that their operation requires a diver in deep waters as well as some expensive equipment. They seem efficient and versatile and should be investigated further.

2.3 **The sampler must be suited to the substrate**

The foregoing discussion has illustrated that the accuracy of a sampling device is a function of the substrate to be sampled. Although some researchers have tried (Powers & Robertson 1967; Cairns & Dickson 1971), it is unlikely that

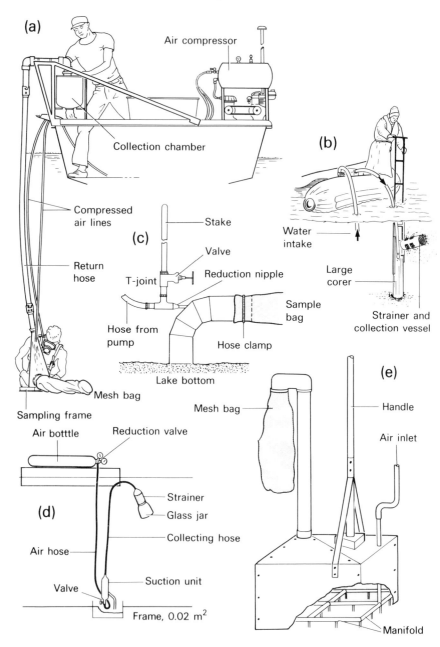

Fig. 4.5 A selection of airlift samplers. These samplers work by entraining sediment and organisms in water movement induced by the release of compressed air. Some designs are those of: (a) Kritzler *et al.* (1974); (b) van Arkel & Mulder (1975); (c) Larsen (1974); (d) Aarefjord (1972); and (e) Pearson *et al.* (1973).

anyone will be able to design or designate a single, all-purpose sampler. An accurate population survey in most lakes requires, at the very least, techniques suitable for both soft sediments like mud and silt, and techniques suitable for hard sediments like sand and gravel. This is because animals are distributed throughout the sediments and failure to penetrate the range of their distribution will yield incomplete and variable density estimations. The distribution of animals with depth in various sediments has been examined by many researchers (Prejs 1970; Bretschko 1972; Smith & Howard 1972; Giani & Lucas 1974; Goulder 1974; McGowan 1974; Meadows & Bird 1974; Kirchner 1975; Wood 1975; McLachlan & McLachlan 1976; Shiozawa & Barnes 1977; Krezoski *et al.* 1978; Marshall 1978). Most of the animals are usually aggregated in the upper 2–10 cm of sediment. This has been found for *Chaoborus* (McGowan 1974), nematodes (Bretschko 1972), chironomids (McLachlan & McLachlan 1976; Shiozawa & Barnes 1977), oligochaetes (Meadows & Bird 1974), microbenthos (Prejs 1970), and ciliates (Goulder 1974). On the other hand, significant numbers of animals often live as deep as 50 cm (Wood 1975; Ferencz 1977). Smith & Howard (1972) and Marshall (1978) have suggested that failure of a sampler to penetrate and retain sediments throughout this range of depth may cause serious underestimation of animal density. In very fluid, soft sediments, Hamilton (1971) and Giani (1974) found that samplers passing beyond the rich upper centimeters of sediment seriously underestimated populations. Due to the distribution of organisms in the sediments, a light-weight Ekman grab or corer should not be used in resistant sediments (see Gale & Thompson 1975) and a heavy grab (e.g. Smith–McIntyre, PONAR, Petersen) should not be used in softer sediments.

To see whether benthos ecologists have been sensitive to these limitations and to analyze the conventions followed regarding sampler choice for different sediments, I have analyzed frequency-of-use data extracted from the published literature. First, I ranked the sediment categories by difficulty of penetration. Sediment categories were taken from the authors' descriptions. There were eight separate categories (1 = mud, 2 = silt, 3 = detritus of vegetation, 4 = sand, 5 = clay, 6 = gravel, 7 = pebbles, 8 = stones). Mixtures of sediments were assigned ranks assuming equal contributions from each component (e.g. sand and gravel = 5; gravel, pebbles, and stones = 7; etc.). The numerical ranks were then broken into three broad categories (mud to silt = soft sediments; detritus to sand = resistant sediments; clay to stones = very resistant sediments), and frequency of sampler use was analyzed within each category.

The results of this analysis are shown in Table 4.3. This analysis shows a clear separation in use patterns of sampling gear despite some uncertainty in the ranks that I assigned and the imprecision generated by taking the average ranks of sediment mixtures. The Ekman grab and sediment corers were used

Table 4.3 Frequency-of-use table showing use patterns for the most popular sampling devices in sediments of differing resistance to sampler penetration. Data were taken from an extensive literature survey (Section 5) and sediments were ranked: 1 = mud, 2 = silt, 3 = detritus and vegetation, 4 = sand, 5 = clay, 6 = gravel, 7 = pebbles, and 8 = stones. Mixtures of sediments were assigned ranks assuming equal contributions by each component. The numerical ranks were then broken into three categories: soft = 1 to 2, resistant = 3 to 4, very resistant = 5 to 8. Frequency of sampler use was calculated within each category. The table shows that the Ekman grab and corers are used most often in soft to resistant sediments while other, heavier grabs are used in resistant to very resistant sediments.

Sampler	Sediment type		
	Soft	Resistant	Very resistant
Ekman	58 (47%)	54 (44%)	12 (9%)
Corers	24 (50%)	18 (38%)	6 (12%)
Petersen	11 (31%)	17 (47%)	8 (22%)
PONAR	8 (22%)	18 (50%)	10 (28%)
van Veen	5 (42%)	4 (33%)	3 (25%)
Smith–McIntyre	0 (0%)	3 (75%)	1 (25%)

91% and 88% of the time, respectively, in sediments less resistant to sampler penetration than clay. The Petersen, PONAR, and Smith–McIntyre grabs were used 69%, 78%, and 100% of the time, respectively, in sediments more resistant than silt. Apparently, most benthic ecologists have chosen sampling gear that is compatible with the substrates sampled. Somewhat surprising, however, was the occasional use of an Ekman grab or corer in very resistant sediments (9%–12% of the time) and the relatively frequent use of heavy Petersen, PONAR, and van Veen grabs in soft sediments (22%–42% of the time). It is clear that, although many researchers have been aware of the limitations of sampling gear, some portion of the data presented as 'quantitative' may be seriously biased.

2.4 The accuracy, precision, and efficiency of sampling gear

So far, this chapter has presented various types of sampling gear, examined the frequency-of-use of each, provided some pairwise comparisons of sampler accuracy, and has treated the question of suiting a sampling device to the substrate investigated. These constitute some of the questions involved in the planning that leads to the quantitative assessment of the benthic fauna. Wherever quantitative benthos samples are required, sampling techniques should be chosen such that the population estimates are accurate and precise (see Sutcliffe 1979) and samples are taken with the least effort for the required accuracy and precision. This section describes aspects of accuracy, precision, and efficiency as they related specifically to the freshwater macrobenthos (see also Chapter 8). First, further explanations of these concepts are presented and then protocols are devised to allow these decisions to be made.

2.4.1 Accuracy

The requirement for accurate sampling dictates that the measured density is representative of the population density within the substrate. In operational terms, this means that if there are 20 chironomids $100\,cm^{-2}$ in the substrate, then each $100\,cm^2$ sample should contain an average of 20 chironomids. If there are fewer than an average of 20 animals per sample, it is likely that the animals avoid the sampler or that the sampler fails to capture them in some other way (e.g. sediment or animal loss, insufficient penetration, too much penetration, etc.). If there are more than 20 chironomids per sampler, it is likely that the sampler attracts benthic organisms. The latter failure is probably not a problem with the sampling techniques presented here, because substrate contact time is short with respect to the speed of locomotion of the benthos. Attraction is a problem with colonization-type samplers like artificial substrates which involve long substrate contact times. Since interpretation of artificial substrate data is impossible in the context of secondary productivity (Rosenberg & Resh 1982), this method is not considered further here. In short, the accuracy of sampling technique is usually assessed indirectly through side-by-side comparisons of population density. The sampler indicating the most organisms per area is considered the most accurate technique. This is also the convention adopted here. One must be careful when using techniques that create water currents, however, because organisms could be pulled in from outside the area intended to be sampled.

Many comparisons of sampling gear have been published; thus assessment of the relative accuracy of the most common devices is possible. Some of these comparisons have been examined singly above, but Table 4.4 assembles many of these comparisons in an attempt to draw general conclusions. The conclusions are, of course, not valid for very large benthos or those that move rapidly (e.g. mysids, gammarids, crayfish, clams). Among the sampling techniques for soft sediments, sediment corers have generally been found to yield more accurate population estimates than Ekman grabs. However, the data are not unanimous and some conditions exist under which corers and Ekman grabs are equally accurate or where Ekman grabs are superior. It is also worth noting that not all corers function equally: some large area core tubes (e.g. $55\,cm^2$) have been found to be more accurate than small area core tubes (e.g. $15\,cm^2$) (Holopainen & Sarvala 1975). Multiple corers have been

Table 4.4 Comparisons of the accuracy of common sampling devices. Arrows point to the technique that collected the most organisms per unit area, open circles indicate comparisons showing no significant difference in density estimates obtained using the two techniques. Data are from citations listed in the lower left half of the table. Citation numbers refer to: (1) Flannagan (1970); (2) Paterson & Fernando (1971); (3) Giani (1974); (4) Hakala (1971); (5) Milbrink & Wiederholm (1973); (6) Milbrink _et al._ (1974a); (7) Gale (1975); (8) Kajak _et al._ (1978); (9) Marshall (1978); (10) Rinne (1978); (11) Baker _et al._ (1977); (12) Powers & Robertson (1967); (13) Sivertsen (1973); (14) Kajak (1971); (15) Thayer _et al._ (1975); (16) Kutty & Desai (1968); (17) Ellis & Jones (1980); (18) Smith & Howard (1972); (19) Beeton _et al._ (1965); (20) Wigley (1967); (21) Brinkhurst _et al._ (1969); (22) Maitland _et al._ (1972).

	Ekman	Corers	Petersen	PONAR	van Veen	Smith–McIntyre
Ekman grab		↑↑↑↑↑↑↑ 0 0 0 0 ← ←	↑ (sand) ← (mud)	↑ ↑ (sand) (mud) 0	0 ←	←
Corers	(1) (2) (3) (4) (5) (6) (7) (8) (21) (22)		← (silt) ← (mud)	←	←	←
Petersen grab	(9) (10)	(7) (11)		↑ ↑ (clay) (mud)	↑	↑
PONAR grab	(1) (12)	(1)	(12)		←	0 (sand) ←
van Veen grab	(13) (14)	(15)	(16)	(17)		↑
Smith–McIntyre grab	(1)	(18)	(19)	(1) (12)	(20)	

found to collect more organisms than Gilson corers, 'Benthos' corers, and Kajak–Brinkhurst type corers (Flannagan 1970; Milbrink & Wiederholm 1973; Carter 1978). When accuracy is important, the sampling gear of choice for soft sediment dwelling benthos should be one of the coring devices that are commonly available (e.g. Kajak–Brinkhurst; multiple corer).

Decisions regarding the accuracy of sampling gear for more resistant sediments are also quite clear, although based on fewer comparisons. Among the four most popular sampling devices of this type (Petersen, PONAR, van Veen, Smith–McIntyre) the Petersen grab is the least accurate (all others provide higher population estimates) and the PONAR is the most accurate (provides higher population estimates than all others). Although the PONAR grab out-performs the Ekman grab in both mud and sand (Powers & Robertson 1967) it should not be used in preference to a corer in mud because corers are more accurate. There are surely comparisons that I have missed in this analysis and, because fauna and sediment vary widely, all cells in Table 4.4 may not be directly comparable. Certainly, one of the studies most needed today is a simultaneous comparison of the relative accuracy of various sampling techniques for different taxa living in differing substrates.

2.4.2 Precision

The requirement of precise sampling dictates that the population estimates be repeatable. Expanding on the example in Section 2.4.1, when 10 replicate samples are taken of the chironomid population with the $100 \, cm^2$ sampler, the 95 % confidence interval (see Chapter 8) might range from 10 to 21 organisms $100 \, cm^2$. In this case, the sampling technique provides population estimates that are quite precise. If this is compared to a set of replicate population estimates made with a different sort of $100 \, cm^2$ sampler for which the 95 % confidence interval ranges from 5 to 42 organisms $100 \, cm^{-2}$, then the second device is seen to yield less precise population estimates. The latter estimates may still be accurate, however, since the known density (20 organisms $100 \, cm^{-2}$) lies within this confidence interval. It is quite possible that another, poorer sampling device would yield highly consistent underestimates of the population with a 95 % confidence interval of 16–18 organisms $100 \, cm^{-2}$. Such a device yields a precise but inaccurate estimate of population density. Generally, a sampling tool should always be accurate (unless bias can be corrected), but the precision required will depend upon the hypothesis tested. A very rough rule is that if the detection of doubling or halving of the population is desired, a standard error (SE) that is roughly 20 % of the mean density must be sought (see Chapter 8). This can be a difficult task because benthic organisms are naturally aggregated (Milbrink 1973; Calow 1974; Milbrink *et al.* 1974b; Tudorancea & Green 1975; Elliott 1977; DeSilva 1978; Juul & Shireman 1978; Ranta & Sarvala 1978; Holopainen 1979; Tudorancea *et al.* 1979), and natural population variability can yield imprecise estimates regardless of choice of sampling technique (Horká 1963; Calow 1974; Mozley 1974; Zytkowicz 1976; Ferraris & Wilhm 1977; Voshell & Simmons 1977; Carter 1978; Maesneer *et al.* 1978).

Comparisons of the sampling variability attained by various apparatus must be done with care because much of the apparent sampling variance is determined by the density of the organisms and the size of the sampler. Comparisons of sampling variability must not confuse these sources of variability with the variability induced by inadequate sampler design. Downing (1979a) presented an equation that predicts the standard deviation for a set of replicate samples from the mean density of organisms (M; numbers m^{-2}) and the size of the sampler employed (A; cm^2). A similar equation can be constructed from the same data to predict the variance of a set of samples (s^2):

$$\log_{10}(s^2) = 1 \cdot 1653 + 1 \cdot 3927 \log_{10}(M) - 5 \cdot 7 \times 10^{-4}(A) \qquad (4.1)$$

When observed sampling variances are compared with predictions from this equation, less precise samplers will yield density estimates more variable than average and will have high, positive residuals (observation − prediction). These values are shown in Table 4.5 in their logarithmic form.

There is wide variability in the degree of precision attained by different sampler types. The van Veen sampler, for example, shows the highest average residual and is thus the least precise of the popular samplers. The sample size is low (n = 3), however; thus this may not be representative of all samples taken with the van Veen grab. Only the Marukawa sampler (Rigosha & Co.) performed more poorly, with a mean residual of 0·96. This means that, on the

Table 4.5 Average residuals from equation 1 for data collected with various types of sampling gear. Data are from Downing (1979a). The residuals are reported in logarithmic (base 10) form, so that confidence intervals on mean residuals will be symmetrical and can be calculated using corresponding values of 'variance' and 'n'. A mean residual of 1·0 shows that on the average the sampler gives rise to replicate samples 10 times more variable than the mean, given its size and the density of organisms. A large mean residual suggests the sampler takes imprecise samples of the benthos, while a small mean residual suggests the sampler takes precise samples of the benthos.

Sampler	Mean residual	Variance	n
van Veen	0·887	0·210	3
'Kajak' corers	0·346	0·152	35
Smith–McIntyre Grab	0·206	0·248	20
PONAR grab	−0·007	0·390	256
Multiple corer	−0·010	0·002	4
Petersen grab	−0·014	0·222	722
Ekman grab	−0·090	0·229	301
Miscellaneous corers*	−0·161	0·575	26

* Probably commercial Kajak–Brinkhurst type corers.

average, the Marukawa sampler yielded sampling variance an order of magnitude more variable than the overall average. The most precise samplers, on the other hand, were a group of miscellaneous corers (called simply 'sediment corers' in the literature; probably Kajak–Brinkhurst corers) and the Ekman grab. These samplers yielded sampling variance 70 % and 80 % of the average, respectively. It is surprising that the corers specifically called 'Kajak-type corers' performed rather poorly, yielding variability about double the average, while multiple corers, performed much more precisely. The former could be due to the sediment compression phenomenon discussed by Kajak & Dusoge (1971) and the latter due to the close spacing of the multiple cores. The samplers used on resistant substrates performed near the average, but the Petersen grab, known to lose organisms due to bow-wave effects (Baker *et al.* 1977; Rinne 1978), had very low residuals, indicating that samples were more precise than average. It is possible that sediment losses with the Petersen grab are extremely consistent, such that population estimates are not accurate, but are precise.

2.4.3 *Efficiency*

The high cost of benthos sampling tends to limit sampling coverage. Because of this, one should choose a sampling technique that will yield accurate and precise population estimates with the least expenditure of effort. For example, an investigator might find that accurate estimates at the desired level of precision can be obtained either by taking 10 samples of $100 \, cm^2$ or by taking 8 samples of $200 \, cm^2$. The investigator must decide which of these schemes is most efficient. One plan requires the taking of 10 samples and the processing (sieving, counting, identification) of $1000 \, cm^2$ of sediment, while the other requires the taking of 8 samples, and the processing of $1600 \, cm^2$ of sediment. If it requires more effort (i.e. man-hours) to take two samples than to process an additional $600 \, cm^2$ of sediment, then the $200 \, cm^2$ sampler should be used. If sampling is not time consuming but sieving and counting is, then the $100 \, cm^2$ sampler should be used. In the benthos, most of the sampling effort is expended in sorting the sample after collection (see relative cost estimates in Wildish 1978; Cuff & Coleman 1979), and I have made this assumption below. If, under other circumstances, it is relatively time-consuming or expensive to take the samples, the appropriate adjustment can be made to these conclusions.

The size of sampling gear used is a major determinant of the efficiency with which a fauna can be sampled. Ranta & Sarvala (1978) suggest that the number of samples (n) necessary for population estimation at a required precision (P = standard error/mean density) decreases with increasing population density (M; numbers m^{-2}) and decreases with increasing sampler or quadrat size (A; cm^2). This suggestion has recently been quantified (Downing 1979a):

$$n = [(antilog(0·581 + 0·696 \log M - 2·82 \times 10^{-4}A))/PM]^2 \qquad (4.2)$$

where all logarithms are to the base 10. All taxonomic groups conform to this equation, except for the Pelecypoda for which it is significantly ($P < 0·05$) conservative (Downing 1979a). Solutions of this equation (Table 4.6) show that fewer samples are needed for a given precision if the population density is high and if samples are taken with a large sampler. The amount of sediment

Table 4.6 Number of replicate samples needed for various sampler sizes and macrobenthos densities in order that the SE of replicate samples averages 20% of the mean density. Calculations are from equation 4.2.

Density number m^{-2}	Size of sampler (cm^2)						
	20	50	100	250	500	750	1000
30	45	43	40	33	24	17	12
50	33	32	30	24	18	13	9
100	22	21	19	16	12	8	6
300	11	11	10	8	6	4	3
500	8	8	7	6	4	3	2
1000	5	5	5	4	3	2	<2
5000	<2	<2	<2	<2	<2	<2	<2
10 000	<2	<2	<2	<2	<2	<2	<2

that must be processed for each population estimate can be calculated by multiplying the necessary number of samples by the size of the sampler (Table 4.7). This relationship upholds the suggestion of Ranta & Sarvala and shows that for any population density the amount of sediment that must be processed for a given precision increases with increasing size of sampler. In short, small area samplers are most efficient (see also Kajak 1963). Table 4.5 also shows that any size of sampler can be inefficient if it induces variability in replicates. Thus, a sampler should be chosen that is not prone to sediment loss and pressure-wave effects, is large enough not to yield many zero values (Anderson 1965), but is as small as possible to decrease sediment processing time. Adherence to this scheme could result in 10- to 50-fold decreases in the sampling effort (at $P = 0·2$; Downing 1979a) and significant increases in accuracy of population estimates.

2.5 *Sieving and preservation*

After sediment samples are collected, but before animals are identified and

Table 4.7 Area of sediment (cm^2) that must be sampled, sieved and sorted in order that the SE of replicate samples averages 20% of the mean density, for various sampler sizes and macrobenthos densities. Figures are number of samples multiplied times sampler area, taken from Table 4.6.

Density number m^{-2}	Size of sampler (cm^2)						
	20	50	100	250	500	750	1000
30	900	2150	4000	8250	12000	12750	12000
50	660	1600	3000	6000	9000	9750	9000
100	440	1050	1900	4000	6000	6000	6000
300	220	550	1000	2000	3000	3000	3000
500	160	400	700	1500	2000	2250	2000
1000	100	250	500	1000	1500	1500	2000
5000	40	100	200	500	1000	1500	2000
10000	40	100	200	500	1000	1500	2000

counted, the samples are usually passed through a sieve in order to separate animals from sediment materials. The size of sieve used will greatly affect the apparent population and composition of animals in the sample. The question addressed will always dictate the sort of sieve used. Studies of life cycles and population dynamics require very fine sieves (e.g. <0.1 mm aperture) (Paterson & Walker 1974), while general surveys for questions of environmental impact or control might use meshes of greater size (e.g. $>$ 0.5 mm) (Wiederholm 1974). In all cases, apparent population levels are negatively correlated with mesh size (Särkkä 1975) and thus may give rise to wide variability (Jónasson 1958). The use of 0.3 mm sieves instead of 0.1 mm mesh causes the loss of early instars of *Chironomus* (Shiozawa & Barnes 1977). The effect of mesh size on population estimates is subject to seasonal variation (Barber & Kevern 1974) and, therefore, correction factors cannot be applied. Sieving of any kind can destroy some taxa; thus in some cases it cannot be used at all (Boddington & Mettrick 1974). The use of fine mesh greatly increases the amount of time taken to remove animals from sediment (Gale 1975). This problem hinders most benthos studies because often a trade-off is made between sampling accuracy (mediated by sieve size) and number of samples taken at different stations. As Table 4.8 shows, most benthic ecologists have 'traded' in favour of sampling coverage. The median mesh size used recently has been 0.5 mm (range: 0.02–1.3 mm) contrary to Jónasson's (1958) warning. This renders the accuracy of many population estimates suspect. Better use of sieves or the development of other techniques such as ultrasonic treatment (Maitland *et al.* 1972; Thiel *et al.* 1975), sugar flotation (Anderson 1959; Kajak *et al.* 1968), dyes and stains (Mason & Yevich 1967; Williams &

Table 4.8 Frequency-of-use of various sieve sizes used in sorting benthic organisms from sediments and detritus. The data are from a survey of the literature published between 1970 and 1981 in the journals listed in Section 5. The table shows that the most common sieve size is around 0·5 mm.

Sieve size (mm)	Frequency	Percent frequency
0·00–0·15	26	8
0·15–0·30	74	23
0·30–0·45	55	17
0·45–0·60	125	39
0·60–0·75	14	4
0·75–0·90	15	5
0·90–1·05	2	1
1·05–1·20	7	2
1·20–1·35	2	1

Williams 1974), density gradient centrifugation (see Chapter 7), or electrical sorting (Bayless 1961; Fahy 1972; Bisson 1976; Messick & Tash 1980) is needed before benthos population estimates can be interpreted with confidence.

After sieving, organisms are usually preserved prior to identification and counting. The choice of preservative is critical if ingestion rates (see Chapter 9) or biomasses (see Chapter 7) are to be estimated. Howmiller (1972) found that preservation of tubificids or chironomids in 4% formaldehyde or 70% isopropanol before weighing resulted in 10%–40% underestimation of fresh weight after 24 h, and 25%–75% underestimation after 44 days. All preservatives, and even freezing, resulted in underestimation of dry weight. Formaldehyde was judged the best preservative but its use also results in inaccurate weight estimation. Wiederholm & Eriksson (1977) have criticized Howmiller's work and have suggested that, for some benthic taxa, alcohol preservation yields accurate weight estimates. Stanford (1972) has shown that weight loss in alcohol can be as low as 5%, but is widely variable among species. Donald & Paterson (1977) performed a similar comparison and recommend the use of 4% formaldehyde for chironomids. Caution recommends that weights should be estimated immediately, at least for sample organisms (see regression technique of Smock 1980; also discussion in Chapter 7), so that biomass and production estimates can be made more accurately. It should also be remembered that variations in preservation time among samples before weighing might induce spurious variability or bias in biomass data.

As a guide to the use of preservatives where post-collection weight

Table 4.9 Frequency-of-use of preservatives in recent (1970–1981) published benthos studies. Data are from an extensive literature survey (Section 5). The 2% of studies not shown here used mixtures of alcohols and formaldehyde, other alcohols or glycerine.

Preservative	Frequency	Percent frequency
Formaldehyde	100	65
Ethanol	27	18
'Alcohol'	15	10
None	7	5

measurements are not made, Table 4.9 shows the frequency-of-use of various preservatives in the published literature. The most popular preservative is formaldehyde, followed by alcohols and no preservation. An alarming percentage of the studies surveyed (30%) failed to report the preservation technique used, even though this was often important to the interpretation of biomass figures. The concentrations of preservatives used were also quite variable (Table 4.10). There was often confusion between formalin and formaldehyde concentrations (10% formalin = 4% formaldehyde); it was not clear whether this confusion was semantic or actual. Formaldehyde should be used with extreme care because its fumes may present a significant health hazard to the researcher (Swenberg *et al.* 1980). S.C.Mozley suggests (personal communication) that no formaldehyde preserved sample should be 'picked' without first thoroughly rinsing the preserved material in water. Soft bodied forms such as ephemeropterans, amphipods, and trichopterans can disintegrate or be rendered unidentifiable if simply preserved in alcohol or formaldehyde. Edmunds *et al.* (1976) suggest that soft bodied animals should

Table 4.10 Frequency-of-use of formaldehyde preservative concentrations in a survey of the literature published between 1970 and 1981 (Section 5). The Table shows that most benthos researchers use formaldehyde concentrations of 4% or less.

Formaldehyde concentration	Frequency	Percent frequency
0–2%	47	40
2–4%	60	51
4–6%	4	3
6–8%	1	1
8–10%	5	4
>10%	0	0

be collected directly into Carnoy fluid (glacial acetic acid: 10 %/95 % ethanol:60 %/chloroform:30 %) or Kahle's fluid (formalin:11 %/95 % ethanol:28 %/glacial acetic acid:2 %/water:59 %), then after 24 hours the original fluid is replaced with 80 % alcohol. They also suggest that sample vials be filled completely and handled with extreme care. Using this technique, the animals keep their color well, are firm, and appendages do not detach as readily (also see Wiggins 1977). B.Hicks (personal communication) suggests that preservation in formaldehyde for a few days, then transfer to alcohol for long-term storage may have a similar effect on oligochaetes and softer crustaceans. Regardless of preservative, a few ml of glycerine should be added to samples stored in volatile solutions to avoid sample desiccation (Howmiller 1972).

3 Sampling Other Fauna

Because most studies of benthic organisms have examined the macrofauna of unconsolidated sediments, a full treatment of sampling gear and sampling considerations has been possible. Many of the considerations are the same for sampling other fauna, but the paucity of data does not allow an analysis of the accuracy or precision of these techniques. Below, I present a reconnaissance of techniques for sampling the benthos dwelling on hard substrates, those living on aquatic macrophytes, and those animals that are too small to be surveyed by standard techniques. It is my hope that ecologists will pay more attention to these important yet neglected animals.

3.1 *Sampling the benthos of hard substrates*

The surfaces of large rock faces and fields of boulders, stones, and cobble are probably the most difficult of all substrates to sample. Rock faces must be cleared of living material *in situ*, a feat which can rarely be accomplished using a remote sampling device. The most popular method is to enclose the surface using a core tube or similar container, and then clean the surface and remove the attached materials. In deep waters, this usually requires a diver. A hydraulic sampler or suction hose (Zimmerman & Ambühl 1970; Gulliksen & Derås 1975) is probably the best method for sampling hard substrates. A more complicated apparatus has been proposed by Gale & Thompson (1975) (Fig. 4.6). In some cases, plate-like pieces of rock can be removed from the water body. McElhone (1978) took advantage of this situation to study the epilithic benthos. He placed a core tube (5 cm diameter) over a portion of the face of the rock before gentle removal from the water. The enclosed animals and detritus were then scraped into a sample jar. Another sampler that might be modified to remove similar samples *in situ* is that proposed for periphyton

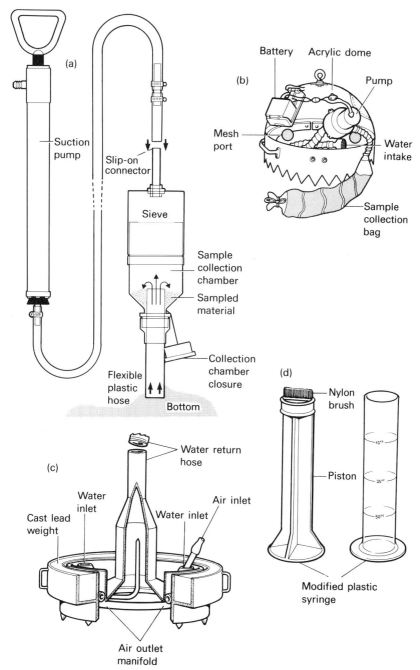

Fig. 4.6 Techniques for sampling hard substrates such as bedrock or large rocks: (a) a diver-operated suction sampler (Gulliksen & Derås 1975); (b) a dome-shaped suction sampler (Gale & Thompson 1975); (c) an air-flow operated suction sampler (Verollet & Tachet 1978). A modification of Stockner & Armstrong's (1971) periphyton sampler (d) might also work for this purpose.

by Stockner & Armstrong (1971). This field requires imagination and creativity—what is needed is a sampler that can remove samples from rock faces quickly, safely, and accurately.

Sampling boulder, stone, and cobble bottoms is also difficult (see Calow 1972 for a review) because large stones jam grab samplers of all types (Ruggio & Saraceni 1972; Elliott & Drake 1981). There are two basic methods through which population estimates are made on rocky bottoms. One technique is to encircle a portion of the bottom with a quadrat of known area, and gently remove the rocks that make up the cobble (Sapkarev 1975). In deep waters, rocks must usually be removed by diving (Lang 1974) and are placed in nets or plastic bags (Macan 1980) for transport to shore. Rocks are then held over a tray and animals are scrubbed or washed from the surface, sometimes using a spray of water (Macan & DeSilva 1979).

A modification of this technique uses an enclosed box sampler similar to the Surber sampler (see Chapter 5) to enclose the bottom (Wise & O'Sullivan 1980; Hiley *et al.* 1981). All sides of the box are made of mesh except the lower edge which is open to the substrate. Rocks are collected in a mesh bag and treated as above, while the bottom can be agitated and the loosened animals collected with a hand-net. This type of enclosure reduces loss of animals on collection of rocks. Possibly the best means of collecting the organisms enclosed in a quadrat is by scrubbing and the use of a suction hose (Zimmerman & Ambühl 1970) or the use of one of the new airlift or hydraulic samplers (Mackey 1976b; Barton & Hynes 1978; Verollet & Tachet 1978). Pearson *et al.* (1973) have found that these samplers function as accurately as Surber samplers or grabs. The device of Gale & Thompson (1975) can also be used for this type of substrate (Fig. 4.6).

The second means of quantitative sampling of the stone dwelling benthos is a regression estimation technique (Cochran 1963) which is a type of stratified sampling scheme (Elliott 1977; see also Chapter 8). Calow (1972, 1974) has suggested that the number of animals living on a stone's surface can be related empirically to the size of the stone (Fig. 4.7). If a good empirical relationship exists, then quadrat sampling for animal density is not necessary. The size distribution and density of stones can be measured instead, and the animal density can be calculated from it using the relationship between stone size and animal density. This technique may be found very useful but comparisons should be made between regression, quadrat, and air lift methods to determine which is most accurate, precise, and efficient.

3.2 *Sampling the benthos dwelling on aquatic macrophytes*

The macrobenthic organisms living on the surface of aquatic macrophytes are called 'phytomacrobenthos' and are one of the most important faunas because

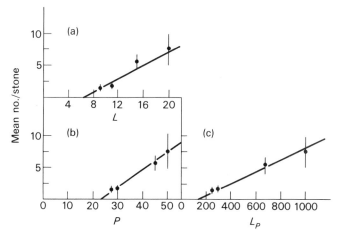

Fig. 4.7 The linear relationship between the number of *Ancylus fluviatilis* per stone and the size of the stone: L = longest length (cm); P = largest perimeter (cm), and vertical bars indicate 95 % confidence limits. This sort of determination might save much effort in the estimation of the benthos populations of boulder and cobble covered bottoms (from Calow 1974).

they are abundant, highly productive (Guziur *et al.* 1975; Howard-Williams & Lenton 1975), and constitute a major source of fish food in freshwaters (Gascon & Leggett 1977; Werner *et al.* 1978). The difficulty of estimating populations of these organisms has been reviewed by Pieczyńska (1973) who catalogued four different types of methods. These four types of techniques are differentiated on the basis of the units in which population estimates are expressed:

(1) Density per unit bottom surface
(2) Density per unit water volume
(3) Density per unit of plant surface
(4) Density per unit of plant biomass

In practice, the sampling techniques to obtain these figures fall into two categories: those in which random samples are taken of the whole environment (1 and 2), and those in which random samples are taken of the macrophytes alone (3 and 4).

Techniques that take random samples of the environment as a whole (Fig. 4.8) are the most common. The most popular of these is the least quantitative. Many researchers have simply swept a pond net randomly through weed beds for a set period of time and related the sample either to a volumetric unit or as a relative measure of macrophytobenthos density and composition (Lawton 1970; Wilson *et al.* 1975; Armitage 1977; Macan 1977). Pond net sweeps have also been used to sample the smaller phytomicrofauna

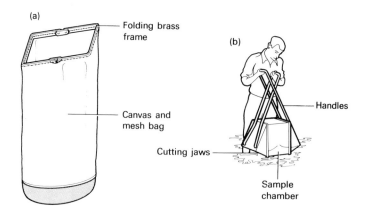

(a) Folding brass frame / Canvas and mesh bag

(b) Handles / Cutting jaws / Sample chamber

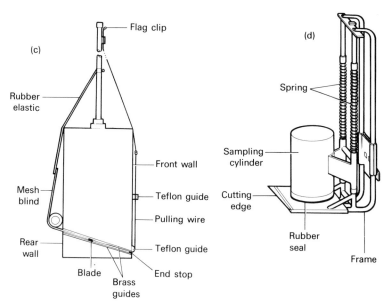

(c) Flag clip / Rubber elastic / Front wall / Mesh blind / Teflon guide / Pulling wire / Rear wall / Teflon guide / Blade / End stop / Brass guides

(d) Spring / Sampling cylinder / Cutting edge / Rubber seal / Frame

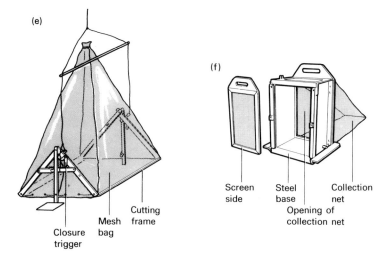

(e) Closure trigger / Mesh bag / Cutting frame

(f) Screen side / Steel base / Opening of collection net / Collection net

such as cladocerans, copepods, and rotifers (Bigelow 1928; Ward 1940; Sebestyeń 1948; Daggett & Davis 1975; Armitage 1977). Macan (1977) has suggested that sweep nets can yield quantitative estimates of population levels. However, nets can be highly selective and variable (Macan 1974) and thus can only be used when simultaneously calibrated by a quantitative technique. It is difficult to imagine how sweep net samples could ever give more information than the calibration itself, thus this technique should not be used.

Techniques which are more quantitative seek to isolate a set area of the bottom while macrophytes and attached benthos are collected. Mackey (1976a) and Soszka (1975) have simply enclosed macrophytes in a quadrat and clipped the plants at the base, collecting them in plastic bags. Mesh bags have also been used (DeCoster & Persoone 1970; Calow 1973), and are more convenient but are not more accurate (Downing, in preparation). The danger exists that phytomacrobenthos fall or swim off the plants upon collection. Other mesh collection bags have been equipped with special cutting rims on the open end (Peterka 1972). A stand of macrophytes is enclosed by lowering the bag from the surface, cutting the macrophytes at the sediment surface, and closing the bag. The bag can then be removed from the water and the sample can be agitated and sieved to separate animals from plants and detritus. This method has also been used to sample the phytomicrobenthos (Andrews & Hasler 1943).

A similar purpose has been served by rigid enclosures. Gerking (1957) proposed two different box-like samplers that are lowered over the macrophytes and pressed into the sediments. Macrophytes are clipped with grass clippers and the phytomacrobenthos sample is retained by inserting a sliding mesh baffle into the box at the sediment surface. The sampler can then be removed from the water and the sample backwashed into a container. Major problems with this sampler are that it does not always remove macrophytes at the sediment surface, it is difficult to clip macrophytes without disturbance, and it is unwieldy to drain and rinse (Downing, unpublished data). Similar but simpler samplers have been manufactured as aluminium drums (Chambers 1977), tubes (Smyly 1957), and clear, plastic boxes (Daggett & Davis 1974).

Some more complex pieces of sampling apparatus have been proposed for the phytomacrobenthos. The phytobenthic sampler of Macan (1949) is

---

Fig. 4.8 Devices for sampling the phytomacrobenthos: (a) a folding quadrat sampler with attached net bag (Welch 1948); (b) Macan's sampler (Macan 1949); (c) Minto's sampler with moving blade (Minto 1977); (d) McCauley's sampler for submerged and floating vegetation (McCauley 1975); (e) a remotely closing quadrat/net-bag that cuts macrophytes at the sediment surface (Shapovalova & Vologdin 1979); and (f) a box sampler (Hiley *et al.* 1981).

perhaps the best known, and is basically a box sampler with a bottom that can be opened and closed by means of two handles that protrude from the top (Fig. 4.8). The sampler is pushed into the vegetation, the handles are used to close the bottom, cutting the macrophyte stems. The sample is retrieved and drained, and the plants are rinsed into a receiving vessel. This technique has recently been criticized (Minto 1977) because it samples a large area (1000 cm^2) and can only be used in shallow water. Macan has also criticized this technique himself (personal communication), suggesting that it pushes some macrophytes out of the way, and is thus biased. Minto (1977) has proposed a new, smaller sampler (225 cm^2) that may be used from a boat in depths up to 2·5 m (Fig. 4.8). McCauley (1975) has also proposed a sampler which cuts plants automatically. Another very interesting grab-like closing mesh-bag sampler (Fig. 4.8) has been designed by Shapovalova & Vologdin (1979). This device is a hinged frame with a cutting edge, attached to a mesh bag. The sampler frame is dropped so that the bag encloses the macrophytes. Upon closure, the frame folds, cutting the stems above the sediment surface and the macrophytes are hauled to the surface. The authors claim that this sampler is efficient in collecting both fast- and slow-moving organisms. This device seems of useful design and deserves further investigation. There are many other types of phytomacrofauna samplers in use by Soviet ecologists (Pieczyńska 1973; Shapovalova & Vologdin 1979). An illustrated review of Soviet samplers including a quantitative analysis of sampling experiences would be welcome.

Other sampling techniques have been advanced for special situations. Junk (1979) has developed a special net for sampling floating mats of macrophytes. *Sphagnum* has been sampled with a box sampler (Minto 1977) and a strengthened Ekman grab (Beattie 1979). The organisms living on the stems of emergent macrophytes, such as *Typha* or *Scirpus*, have been sampled by scraping and washing animals off the macrophyte stems (Mason & Bryant 1975; Pieczyński 1977) and a tube-like sampler for isolating these types of plants has been proposed by McCauley (1975). Fairchild (1981) has advanced an apparatus for sampling animals inhabiting plants with floating leaves while Petr (1970) has developed techniques for sampling the benthos inhabiting the surfaces of waterlogged trees in newly-formed reservoirs. Virtually, any substrate can be sampled but the sampling of some habitats requires ingenuity and creativity.

One disturbing aspect of these samplers is their very large size (Table 4.11). As discussed in Section 2.4.3, large samplers can often lead to excess sampling effort, perhaps at the expense of precision. Table 4.11 shows that the amount of effort required to sieve and count the animals in each sample will be a function not only of the size of the sampling device, but also of the density of macrophytes. This table also illustrates that hundreds of organisms will be

Table 4.11 The hypothetical amount of macrophyte (g dry wt.) and number of animals processed for each single replicate phytomacrobenthos sample at median and high (in parentheses) macrophyte densities. Calculations are made for samplers of various sizes. The calculations assume that benthos densities are near the average figure (36 organisms per g dry wt. of macrophyte) given for one species (black fly larvae) found by Niesiolowski (1980), and the macrophyte biomasses are either at median densities (170 g dry wt. m^{-2}) or at maximum densities (7000 g dry wt. m^{-2}) (Wetzel 1975). The table shows that the use of large samplers will require the processing (weighing, sieving, counting) of large amounts of macrophyte and animal material, and that the amount of work involved in sampling the phytomacrobenthos increases rapidly with macrophyte density.

Sampler used by:	Sampler size, cm^2	g Macrophyte processed per sample	Animals counted per sample
Macan 1974	75	1·3 (53)	47 (1916)
Androkovics 1975,			
Minto 1977	225	3·8 (158)	140 (5749)
Mackey 1976a	400	6·8 (280)	248 (10 220)
Gerking 1957	756	12·9 (529)	469 (19 316)
McLachlan 1975	900	15·3 (630)	558 (22 995)
Macan 1949,			
Peterka 1972	1000	17·0 (700)	621 (25 550)
Welch 1948	1332	22·6 (932)	827 (34 033)
Gerking 1957	1980	33·7 (1386)	1229 (50 589)
Calow 1973,			
Andrikovics 1975,			
McLachlan 1975,			
Soszka 1975,			
Chambers 1977,			
Junk 1977	2500	42·5 (1750)	1551 (63 875)
McLachlan 1975,			
Soszka 1975	10 000	170·0 (7000)	6205 (225 500)

contained in each sample even for a moderately sized sampler at median macrophyte density. Many thousands of organisms must be processed using large samplers at high plant densities; this can render the random, areal sampling of the phytomacrofauna prohibitively time consuming (Minto 1977).

The effort involved in taking random samples of the environment on an areal or volumetric basis has given rise to the second set of techniques. In previous techniques, the areal variability of the organisms has been measured directly through replicate sampling of quadrats. Because phytomacrofauna live on a substrate (macrophytes) that is spatially aggregated, the areal variability of phytomacrobenthic animals is made up of two components. The average density of organisms is determined by the average number of organisms per unit macrophyte, as well as the average density of macrophytes per unit bottom area. Large area samples of macrophytes lead to macrophyte density estimates of low error (Westlake 1969), but also lead to the processing (sieving, identifying, counting, etc.) of huge amounts of animal material. Because of this, some researchers have sought to estimate the average density of animals per unit macrophyte separately from macrophyte density estimates (Pieczyńska 1973).

For example, given the same assumptions as in Table 4.11, ten, 1 g (dry weight) samples of the macrophytes at any macrophyte density could yield very precise estimates of average number of organisms per g dry wt. These estimates would require the expenditure of little effort. If animals are distributed randomly on plant material at this spatial scale, then the coefficient of variation (CV) given an estimate of 36 animals g^{-1} (Table 4.11) would be only 17 (because $s^2 = \bar{x}$, and $CV = 100s/\bar{x}$). If macrophyte biomass could be estimated with similar precision through large quadrat sampling, the CVs for animal densities on an areal basis could be less than 50. Coefficients of variation for laborious large quadrat sampling of phytomacrofauna have been found to average around 75 (Shapovalova & Vologdin 1979). This technique may yield more precise estimates of the density of phytomacro-benthos than areal or volumetric sampling and would require much less sampling effort. This technique is similar to the ratio or regression estimation techniques presented by Cochran (1963).

The use of regression or ratio techniques rests upon the estimation of the density of organisms per unit macrophyte. This has been done in two ways. One method is to pack a jar tightly with macrophytes (Hynes 1970; Niesiolowski 1980). The animals are later collected from the surface of the macrophytes by agitation or mild narcotization using CO_2, ETOH, or weak formaldehyde. The assumption is made that a jar of plant material will yield a standard sample (e.g. same ratio of stems to leaves; same ratio of deep to shallow plants; etc.) and it is also assumed that animals are not lost as plants are collected. These seem to be poor assumptions, especially because similar volumes of different plant species may possess different dry weights or may have leaves that are articulated differently. In addition, dry weight to volume relationships for macrophytes may vary seasonally.

Biochino & Biochino (1980) have collected small amounts of emergent and submergent macrophytes from a reservoir and correlated the number of invertebrates on the macrophytes with the dry weight and surface area of the macrophytes. Using this technique, the slope of the functional regression line (see Winsor 1946) of number of phytomacrobenthos as a function of the dry weight of macrophyte would yield the average number of animals per unit weight. A plot of these data would show whether sampling accuracy varies with size of sample. Ideally, the plot should be linear and pass through the origin. Biochino & Biochino (1980) have found that the number of phytophilous invertebrates correlates much better with surface area than weight of macrophytes. For this reason, slopes of functional regressions of number of organisms on the surface area of sampled macrophyte would yield good estimates of animal density. These can be converted to population estimates per unit lake bottom after measurement of plant surface area per unit lake bottom. Cattaneo (in preparation) has developed a rapid fluorescent dye technique for measuring macrophyte surface areas. The samples required to produce animal density regressions can be collected using plastic bags or nets if collection by these means can be shown to be gentle and unbiased. Alternatively, the chambers described by Downing & Peters (1980) or Cattaneo & Kalff (1979) (Fig. 9.7) yield quantitative collections of macrophyte material. I have found that the slow, careful closure of such chambers does not even disrupt the feeding of littoral cladocerans (Downing 1979b) or scare away small fishes. Therefore, they may well yield unbiased population estimates.

The relative merits of the techniques for sampling the phytomacrofauna remain unverified. Kajak (1971) suggested that comparisons of the various methods and studies of the reliability of estimates obtained using these techniques are necessary before results can be relied upon. Ten years have passed since Kajak's suggestions and comparisons of techniques are still lacking. Determination of the relative accuracy, bias, and precision of these techniques would be a real contribution to aquatic science.

3.3 Microbenthos

The previous section not only presented methods for sampling the macrofauna associated with macrophytes, but also reviewed a few techniques used to sample the phytomicrofauna. This section will examine methods used for the study of populations of small organisms in deep, unconsolidated benthic environments. The micro- or meiobenthos are usually ignored in benthos investigations but may comprise the majority of the organisms and as much biomass as the macrofauna (Stańczykowska & Przytocka-Jusiak 1968). The microbenthos consists primarily of cladocerans, harpacticoid and cyclopoid copepods, nematodes, small oligochaetes and chironomids, ostracods, protozoans, rotifers, and tardigrades.

Special problems in sampling the microbenthos are mostly associated with the tiny size of the animals. Because sieve apertures used to separate macrobenthic animals from sediments are usually very large (Table 4.8), most small organisms are either lost through the sieves (Evans & Stewart 1977) or are crushed. Although suction samplers are sometimes used (Grabacka 1971;

Bērziņš 1972), the microbenthos is usually sampled in much the same manner as the macrobenthos; either with grabs (Sebestyeń 1947; Frenzel 1979) or small diameter corers (Elmgren 1973; Evans & Stewart 1977).

Corers used to sample the microbenthos have ranged in size from $10\,cm^2$ (Stańczykowska & Pryztocka-Jusiak 1968; Prejs & Stańczykowska 1972; Stańczykowska 1973) to $40 \cdot 7\,cm^2$ (Evans & Stewart 1977), under normal circumstances. Very small glass tubes (approximately $0 \cdot 6\,cm^2$) have been used for sampling littoral sediments (Prejs & Stańczykowska 1972) and the small protozoans and metazoans of arctic ponds (Fenchel 1975). Animals are separated from the sediments using sieves which range in aperture from $45\,\mu m$ (Stańczykowska 1973) to $156\,\mu m$ (Evans & Stewart 1977) and by rinsing gently or applying pressurized streams of water (Särkkä 1975). Some very small organisms, such as ciliates, can be counted directly in small droplets without removal from the sediments (see Finlay *et al.* 1979 for a review). Fenchel (1975) has counted zooflagellates and other small protozoans using epifluoroescence microscopy (Fenchel 1970) without sieving. Sediments are removed from corers with a pipette, are placed on glass slides and stained with acridine orange. Under ultraviolet or deep blue illumination the protozoans fluoresce bright yellow-green. This may be a promising technique to use for other microbenthos as well because copepods, cladocerans (Lane *et al.* 1976; Downing 1980), chironomids, and oligochaetes (Downing, unpublished) all stain well with acridine orange. Some other fluorescent dyes or more specific stains (Fliermans & Schmidt 1975) might also prove useful. The problems involved in estimating populations of microbenthic organisms should be solved because the microbenthos may have an importance that is disproportional to our knowledge of it.

4 Conclusions

As yet, we have little information on the sampling of hard bottoms, littoral areas, and small organisms. Experience in soft sediments shows that most benthic ecologists have used too few replicates (median = 2 replicates), and samplers that are too large (Table 4.1). The large amount of sediment that must be processed (Table 4.7) demands a sieve aperture too big to retain many animals (Table 4.8), because small aperture sieves take much longer to use. The result is that benthos population estimates have not been accurate and are highly variable; hence our records of actual populations are incomplete and inadequate. The remedy that I offer is to use more replicates of smaller samplers, and to process sediments using smaller sieve apertures. For most fauna, improved population estimates can be made using available technology. These better estimates can probably be made with less effort than is currently expended on poor ones.

A final note which has been suggested by S.C.Mozley is that we might also profit from the redesign of equipment. Most of the samplers discussed in this chapter have been designed by biologists, not engineers. Technology is advancing so rapidly that it is inconceivable that new materials, components, or procedures could not give us significantly better samplers. The cost of professional design may be quite low relative to the money wasted on the analysis of unrepresentative samples. Benthos ecologists should use any technique that can be demonstrated to be effective; the results of studies could then be interpreted in the intended context.

5 Appendix

Journals reviewed to obtain data on frequency-of-use of sampling and sample treatment techniques between 1970 and 1981.

* Acta Zoologica Fennica
* The American Midland Naturalist
* Annales de Limnologie
* Archiv für Hydrobiologie
* Archiv für Hydrobiologie (suppl.)
* Australian Journal of Marine and Freshwater Research
* Canadian Journal of Fisheries and Aquatic Science (formerly Journal of the Fisheries Research Board of Canada)
* Ecological Monographs
* Ecology
* Ekologia Polska
* Freshwater Biology
* Hydrobiologia
* Internationale Revue der gesamten Hydrobiologie
* Journal of Animal Ecology
* Journal of Applied Ecology
* Limnologica
* Limnology and Oceanography
* Memorie dell'Istituto Italiano di Idrobiologia
* Mitteilungen von den Internationale Vereinigung für Theoretische und angewandte Limnologie
* Oecologia
* Polsie Archiv für Hydrobiologie
* Schweizerische Zeitschrift für Hydrobiologie
* Verhandlungen der Internationalen Vereinigung für Theoretische und angewandte Limnologie
* Water Research

6 References

Aarefjord F. (1972) The use of an air-lift in freshwater bottom sampling; comparison with the Ekman bottom sampler. *Verh. Int. Ver. Limnol.*, **18**, 701–705.

Anderson F.S. (1965) The negative binomial distribution and the sampling of insect populations *Proc. XII Int. Cong. Ent.* **395**.

Anderson R.O. (1959) A modified flotation technique for sorting bottom fauna samples. *Limnol. Oceanogr.*, **4**, 223–225.

Andrews J.D. & Hasler A.D. (1943) Fluctuations in the animal populations of the littoral zone in Lake Mendota. *Trans. Wisc. Acad. Sci.*, **35**, 175–186.

Andrikovics S. (1975) Macrofaunal biomass in the submerged vegetation stands of Lake Velence. *Symp. Biol. Hung.*, **15**, 247–254.

Armitage P.D. (1977) Development of the macroinvertebrate fauna of Cow Geen Reservoir (Upper Teesdale) in the first five years of its existence. *Freshwat. Biol.*, 7, 441–454.

Baker J.H., Kimball K.T. & Bedinger C.A., Jr. (1977) Comparison of benthic sampling procedures: Petersen grab *vs.* Mackin corer. *Water Res.*, **11**, 597–601.

Barber W.E. & Kevern N.R. (1974) Seasonal variation of sieving efficiency in a lotic habitat. *Freshwat. Biol.*, **4**, 293–300.

Barton D.R. & Hynes H.B.N. (1978) Seasonal study of the fauna of bedrock substrates in the wave zones of Lakes Huron and Erie. *Can. J. Zool.*, **56**, 48–54.

Bayless J.D. (1961) The use of electrical stimuli in live picking organisms from bottom samples. *Proc. 15th Ann. Conf. S.E. Assoc. Game Fish Comm.* Atlanta, Georgia, USA.

Beattie D.M. (1979) A modification of the Ekman-Birge bottom sampler for heavy duty. *Freshwat. Biol.*, **9**, 181–182.

Beeton A.M., Carr J.F. & Hiltunen J.K. (1965) Sampling efficiencies of three kinds of dredges in southern Lake Michigan. *Proc. 8th Conf. Grt. Lakes Res.*, *Univ. Mich.*, *Grt. Lakes Res. Div. Publ.*, **13**, 209 (Abstract).

Bērziņś B. (1972) Eine Mikrobenthostudie an Rotatorien. *Hydrobiologia*, **40**, 447–452.

Bigelow N.K. (1928) The ecological distribution of microscopic organisms in Lake Nipigon. *Toronto Univ. Dept. Biol. Publ., Ont. Fish. Res. Lab.*, **35**, 59–74.

Biochino A.A. & Biochino G.I. (1980) Quantitative estimation of phytophilous invertebrates. *Hydrobiol. J.*, **15**, 74–76.

Bisson P.A. (1976) Increased invertebrate drift in an experimental stream caused by electrofishing. *J. Fish. Res. Board Can.*, **33**, 1806–1808.

Blakar I.A. (1978) A flexible gravity corer based on a plastic funnel closing principle. *Schweiz. Z. Hydrol.*, **40**, 191–198.

Boddington M.J. & Mettrick D.F. (1974) The distribution, abundance, feeding habits, and population biology of the immigrant triclad *Dugesia polychroa* (Platyhelminthes: Turbellaria) in Toronto Harbour, Canada. *J. Anim. Ecol.*, **43**, 681–699.

Bretschko G. (1972) Benthos of a high mountain lake: Nematoda. *Verh. Int. Ver. Limnol.*, **18**, 1421–1428.

Brinkhurst R.O. (1974) *The Benthos of Lakes*. London: Macmillan.

Brinkhurst R.O., Chua, K.E. & Batvosingh E. (1969) Modifications in the sampling procedures as applied to studies on the bacteria and tubificid oligochaetes inhabiting aquatic sediments. *J. Fish. Res. Board Can.*, **26**, 2581–2593.

Burton W. & Flannagan J.F. (1973) An improved Ekman type grab. *J. Fish. Res. Board Can.*, **30**, 287–290.

Cairns J. & Dickson K.L. (1971) A simple method for the biological assessment of the effects of waste discharges on aquatic bottom dwelling organisms. *J. Water Poll. Control Fed.*, **43**, 755–772.

Calow P. (1972) A method for determining the surface areas of stones to enable quantitative density estimates of littoral stone dwelling organisms to be made. *Hydrobiologia*, **40**, 37–50.

Calow P. (1973) Gastropod associations within Malham Tarn, Yorkshire. *Freshwat. Biol.*, **3**, 521–534.

Calow P. (1974) Some observations on the dispersion patterns of two species-populations of littoral, stone-dwelling gastropods (Pulmonata). *Freshwat. Biol.*, **4**, 557–576.

Carter C.E. (1978) The fauna of the muddy sediments of Lough Neagh, with particular reference to eutrophication. *Freshwat. Biol.*, **8**, 547–559.

Cattaneo A. & Kalff J. (1979) Primary production of algae growing on natural and artificial aquatic plants: a study of interactions between epiphytes and their substrates. *Limnol Oceanogr.*, **24**, 1031–1037.

Chambers M.R. (1977) A comparison of the population ecology of *Asellus aquatica* (L.) and *Asellus meridanus* (Rac.) in the reed beds of Tjeukemeer. *Hydrobiologia*, **53**, 147–154.

Cochran W.G. (1963) *Sampling Techniques*. 2nd edition, New York: Wiley.

Cuff W. & Coleman N. (1979) Optimal survey design: lessons from a stratified random sample of macrobenthos. *J. Fish. Res. Board Can.*, **36**, 351–361.

Daggett R.F. & Davis C.C. (1974) A seasonal quantitative study of the littoral Cladocera and Copepoda in a bog pond and an acid marsh in Newfoundland. *Int. Rev. ges. Hydrobiol.*, **59**, 667–683.

Daggett R.F. & Davis C.C. (1975) Distribution and occurrence of some littoral freshwater microcrustaceans in Newfoundland. *Naturaliste Can.*, **102**, 45–55.

DeCoster W. & Persoone G. (1970) Ecological study of gastropoda in a swamp in the neighbourhood of Ghent (Belgium). *Hydrobiologia*, **36**, 65–80.

DeSilva P.K. (1978) Evidence for aggregation from a field study of a flatworm population. *Arch. Hydrobiol.*, **81**, 493–507.

Donald G.L. & Paterson C.G. (1977) Effect of preservation on wet weight biomass of chironomid larvae. *Hydrobiologia*, **53**, 75–80.

Downing J.A. (1979a) Aggregation, transformation, and the design of benthos sampling programs. *J. Fish. Res. Board Can.*, **36**, 1454–1463.

Downing J.A. (1979b) *Foraging Responses of Littoral Cladocerans*. Dissertation. McGill University, Montreal, Canada.

Downing J.A. (1980) Inhibition of cladoceran feeding by staining with acridine orange. *Trans. Am. Micros. Soc.*, **99**, 398–403.

Downing J.A. & Peters R.H. (1980) The effect of body size and food concentration on the *in situ* filtering rate of *Sida crystallina*. *Limnol. Oceanogr.*, **25**, 883–895.

Edmunds G.F. Jr., Jensen S.L. & Berner L. (1976) *The Mayflies of North and Central America*. Minneapolis: University of Minnesota Press.

Ekman S. (1911) Neue Apparate zur qualitativen und quantitativen Erforschung de Bodenfauna der Seen. *Int. Rev. ges. Hydrobiol.*, **3**, 553–561.

Elliott J.M. (1977) *Some Methods for the Statistical Analysis of Samples of Benthic*

Invertebrates. Scientific Publication Number 25, Ambleside: Freshwat. Biol. Assoc.

Elliott J.M. & Drake C.M. (1981) A comparative study of seven grabs used for sampling benthic macroinvertebrates in rivers. *Freshwat. Biol.*, **11**, 99–120.

Elliott J.M. & Tullett P.A. (1978) *A Bibliography of Samplers for Benthic Invertebrates.* Occasional Publication Number 4, Ambleside: Freshwat. Biol. Assoc.

Ellis D.V. & Jones A.A. (1980) The PONAR grab as a marine pollution monitoring sampler. *Can. Res.*, June/July, 23–25.

Elmgren R. (1973) Methods of sampling sublittoral soft bottom meiofauna. *Oikos (suppl.)*, **15**, 112–120.

Evans M.S. & Stewart J.A. (1977) Epibenthic and benthic microcrustaceans (copepods, cladocerans, ostracods) from a near-shore area in southeastern Lake Michigan. *Limnol. Oceanogr.*, **22**, 1059–1066.

Fahy E. (1972) An automatic separator for the removal of aquatic insects from detritus. *J. Appl. Ecol.*, **9**, 655–658.

Fairchild G.W. (1981) Movement and microdistribution of *Sida crystallina* and other littoral microcrustacea. Ecology, **62**, 1341–1352.

Fenchel T. (1970) Studies on the decomposition of organic detritus derived from the turtle grass *Thalassia testudinum*. *Limnol. Oceanogr.*, **15**, 14–20.

Fenchel T. (1975) The quantitative importance of the benthic microfauna of an arctic tundra pond. *Hydrobiologia*, **46**, 445–464.

Ferencz M. (1977) Data on the vertical distribution of zoobenthos in saline 'lakes' and rivers. *Acta Biol. Szegea*, **23**, 108–116.

Ferraris C. & Wilhm C. (1977) Distribution of benthic macroinvertebrates in an artificially destratified reservoir. *Hydrobiologia*, **54**, 169–176.

Finlay B.J., Laybourn J. & Strachan I. (1979) A technique for the enumeration of benthic ciliated protozoa. *Oecologia*, **39**, 375–377.

Flannagan J.F. (1970) Efficiencies of various grabs and corers in sampling freshwater benthos. *J. Fish. Res. Board Can.*, **27**, 1691–1700.

Fliermans C.B. & Schmidt E.L. (1975) Fluorescence microscopy: direct detection, enumeration, and spatial distribution of bacteria in aquatic systems. *Arch. Hydrobiol.*, **76**, 33–42.

Flury J. (1963) A modified Petersen grab. *J. Fish. Res. Board Can.*, **20**, 1549–1550.

Franklin W.R. & Anderson D.V. (1961) A bottom sediment sampler. *Limnol. Oceanogr.*, **6**, 233–234.

Frenzel P. (1979) Zonosen des litoralen Mikrozoobenthos im Bodensee. *Schweiz. Z. Hydro.*, **41**, 383–394.

Gale W.F. (1975) Bottom fauna of a segment of pool 19, Mississippi River, near Fort Madison, Iowa, 1967–1968. *Iowa State J. Res.*, **49**, 353–372.

Gale W.F. & Thompson J.D. (1975) A suction sampler for quantitatively sampling benthos on rocky substrates in rivers. *Trans. Am. Fish. Soc.*, **104**, 398–405.

Gascon D. & Leggett W.C. (1977) Distribution, abundance, and resource utilization of littoral zone fishes in response to a nutrient/production gradient in Lake Memphremagog. *J. Fish. Res. Board Can.*, **34**, 1105–1117.

Gerking S.D. (1957) A method of sampling the littoral macrofauna and its applications. *Ecology*, **38**, 219–226.

Giani N. (1974) Description d'un nouveau type de carottier pour les sédiments très fluides. *Ann. Limnol.*, **10**, 99–108.

Giani N. & Lucas C. (1974) Les sédiments d'un lac de haute Montagne; structure, nature, et peuplement. *Ann. Limnol.*, **10**, 223–244.

Goulder R. (1974) The seasonal and spatial distribution of some benthic ciliated Protozoa in Esthwaite Water. *Freshwat. Biol.*, **4**, 127–147.

Grabacka E. (1971) Ciliata in bottom sediments of fingerling ponds. *Pol. Arch. Hydrobiol.*, **18**, 225–233.

Gulliksen B. & Derås K.M. (1975) A diver-operated suction sampler for fauna on rocky bottoms. *Oikos*, **26**, 246–249.

Guziur J., Lossow K. & Widuto J. (1975) Wybrane elementy charakterystyki hydrobiologicznej jeziora Klawój, pow. Biskupiec Reszedski. *Zesz. nauk. ART Olszt.*, **4**, 3–33.

Hakala I. (1971) A new model of the Kajak bottom sampler and other improvements in the zoobenthos sampling technique. *Ann. Zool. Fenn.*, **8**, 422–426.

Hamilton A.L. (1971) Zoobenthos of fifteen lakes in the Experimental Lakes Area, Northwestern Ontario. *J. Fish. Res. Board Can.*, **28**, 257–263.

Hamilton A.L., Burton W. & Flannagan J.F. (1970) A multiple corer for sampling profundal benthos. *J. Fish. Res. Board Can.*, **27**, 1867–1869.

Hiley P.D., Wright J.F. & Berrie A.D. (1981) A new sampler for stream benthos, epiphytic macrofauna, and aquatic macrophytes. *Freshwat. Biol.*, **11**, 79–85.

Holme N.A. (1964) Methods of sampling the benthos. *Adv. Mar. Biol.*, **2**, 171–260.

Holme N.A. (1971) Macrofauna sampling. In N.A.Holme & A.D.McIntyre (eds.). *Methods for the Study of Marine Benthos.* IBP Handbook No. 16, Chapter 6. Oxford: Blackwell.

Holopainen I.J. (1979) Population dynamics and production of *Pisidium* species (Bivalva, Sphaeridae) in the oligotrophic and mesohumic lake Paajarvi, south Finland. *Arch. Hydrobiol. (Suppl.)*, **54**, 466–508.

Holopainen I.J. & Sarvala J. (1975) Efficiencies of two cores in sampling soft-bottom invertebrates. *Ann. Zool. Fenn.*, **12**, 280–284.

Hongve D. (1972) En bunnhenter som er lett å lage. *Fauna*, **25**, 281–283.

Horká J. (1963) To the statistical evaluation of the pond botton fauna sampling accuracy. *Vest. Cesk. Spol. Zool. Acta Soc. Zool. Boh.*, **27**, 280–294.

Howard-Williams C. & Lenton G.M. (1975) The role of the littoral zone in the functioning of a shallow tropical lake ecosystem. *Freshwat. Biol.*, **5**, 445–459.

Howmiller R.P. (1972) Effects of preservatives on weights of some common macrobenthic invertebrates. *Trans. Am. Fish. Soc.*, **101**, 743–746.

Hynes H.B.N. (1970) *The Ecology of Running Waters.* Toronto: Univ. Toronto Press.

Johnson M.G. & Brinkhurst R.O. (1971) Associations and species diversity in benthic macroinvertebrates of Bay of Quinte and Lake Ontario. *J. Fish. Res. Board Can.*, **28**, 1683–1697.

Jónasson P.M. (1958) The mesh factor in sieving techniques. *Verh. Int. Ver. Limnol.*, **13**, 860–866.

Junk W.J. (1977) The invertebrate fauna of the floating vegetation of Bung Borapet, a reservoir in central Thailand. *Hydrobiologia*, **53**, 229–238.

Juul R.B. & Shireman J.V. (1978) A biological assessment of fish and benthic populations inhabiting a kraft mill effluent channel. *Water Res.*, **12**, 691–701.

Kajak Z. (1963) Analysis of quantitative benthic methods. *Ekol. Pols.*, **11**, 1–56.

Kajak Z. (1971) The benthos of standing waters. In W.T. Edmondson & G.G. Winberg (eds.), *A manual for the assessment of secondary productivity in fresh waters*, IBP Handbook No. 17, p. 25–65. Oxford: Blackwell.

Kajak Z. & Dusoge K. (1971) The regularities of vertical distribution of benthos in bottom sediments of three Masurian Lakes. *Ekol. Pols.*, **19**, 485–499.

Kajak Z., Dusoge K. & Prejs A. (1968) Application of the flotation technique to assessment of absolute numbers of benthos. *Ekol. Pols.*, **16**, 607–620.

Kajak Z., Kacprzak K. & Polkowski R. (1965) Chwytacz rurowy do pobierana pròb dna, tubular bottom sampler. *Ekol. Pols. Ser. B.*, **11**, 159–165.

Kajak Z., Rybak J. & Ranke-Rybicka B. (1978) Fluctuations in numbers and changes in the distribution of *Chaoborus flavicans* (Meigen) (Diptera, Chaoboridae) in the eutrophic Mikolajskie Lake and dystrophic Lake Flosek. *Ekol. Pols.*, **26**, 259–272.

Kaplan E.H., Welker J.R. & Krause M.G. (1974) A shallow-water system for sampling macrobenthic infauna. *Limnol. Oceanogr.*, **19**, 346–350.

King E.W. & Everitt D.A. (1980) A remote sampling device for under-ice water, bottom biota, and sediments. *Limnol. Oceanogr.*, **25**, 935–938.

Kirchner W.B. (1975) The effect of oxidized material on the vertical distribution of freshwater benthic fauna. *Freshwat. Biol.*, **5**, 423–429.

Koss R.W., Jensen L.D. & Jones R.D. (1974) Benthic invertebrates. Chapter 7. In L.D.Jensen (ed.), *Environmental Response to Thermal Discharges from Marshall Steam Station, Lake Norman, North Carolina.* Report No. 11, Palo Alto: Electric Power Research Institute.

Krezoski J.R., Mozley S.C. & Robbins J.A. (1978) Influence of benthic macroinvertebrates on mixing of profundal sediments in southeastern Lake Huron. *Limnol. Oceanogr.*, **23**, 1011–1016.

Kritzler H., Hiskey R.M. & Thomas P.J. (1974) A system for quantitative sampling of shallow water benthos. *Int. Rev. ges. Hydrobiol.*, **59**, 621–627.

Kutty M.K. & Desai B.N. (1968) A comparison of the efficiency of the bottom samplers used in benthic studies off Cochin. *Mar. Biol.*, **1**, 168–171.

Lane P.A., Klug M.J. & Louden L. (1976) Measuring invertebrate predation *in situ* on zooplankton assemblages. *Trans. Am. Micros. Soc.*, **95**, 143–155.

Lang C. (1974) Macrofaune des fonds de cailloux du Léman. *Schweiz. z. Hydrol.*, **36**, 301–350.

Larsen P.F. (1974) A remotely operated shallow water benthic suction sampler. *Chesapeake Sci.*, **15**, 176–178.

Lawton J.H. (1970) A population study on larvae of the damselfly *Pyrrhosoma nymphula* (Sulzer) (Odonata: Zygoptera). *Hydrobiologia*, **36**, 33–52.

Macan T.T. (1949) A survey of a moorland fishpond. *J. Anim. Ecol.*, **18**, 160–187.

Macan T.T. (1974) *Freshwater Ecology.* London: Longman Group Ltd.

Macan T.T. (1977) The fauna in the vegetation of a moorland fishpond as revealed by different methods of collecting. *Hydrobiologia*, **55**, 3–15.

Macan T.T. (1980) Changes in the fauna of the stony substratum of lakes in the English Lake District. *Hydrobiologia*, **72**, 159–167.

Macan T.T. & DeSilva P.K. (1979) On the occurrence of *Dendocoelum lacteum* (Muller) and *Asellus aquaticus* (L.) as predator and prey in the stony substratum of Windermere. *Arch. Hydrobiol.*, **86**, 95–111.

Mackey A.P. (1972) An air-lift for sampling freshwater benthos. *Oikos*, **23**, 413–415.

Mackey A.P. (1976a) Quantitative studies on the Chironomidae (Diptera) of the Rivers Thames and Kennet. *Arch. Hydrobiol.*, **78**, 240–267.

Mackey A.P. (1976b) Quantitative studies on the Chironomidae (Diptera) of the Rivers Thames and Kennet. II. The Thames flint zone. *Arch. Hydrobiol.*, **78**, 310–318.

Maeseneer J., de Pauw M. & Waegeman D. (1978) Influence of the mud layer of the

'Wetersportbann' at Ghent on some aquatic life forms, especially Chironomid larvae and *Filenia* spp., *Hydrobiologia*, **60**, 151–158.

Maitland P.S., Charles N.W., Morgan N.C., East K. & Gray M.C. (1972) Preliminary research on Production of Chironomidae in Loch Levan, Scotland. In Z.Kajak & A.Hillbricht-Ilkowska (eds.) *Productivity Problems in Freshwaters.* Proc. IBP–UNESCO Symposium on Productivity Problems of Freshwaters, pp. 795–812.

Marshall B.E. (1978) Aspects of the ecology of benthos fauna in Lake McIlwaine, Rhodesia. *Freshwat. Biol.*, **8**, 241–249.

Mason C.F. & Bryant R.J. (1975) Periphyton production and grazing by chironomids in Alderfen Broad, Norfolk. *Freshwat. Biol.*, **5**, 271–277.

Mason W.T., Jr. & Yevich P.P. (1967) The use of Phloxine B and Rose Bengal stains to facilitate sorting benthic samples. *Trans. Am. Micros. Soc.*, **86**, 221–223.

McCauley V.J.E. (1975) Two new quantitative samplers for aquatic phytomacrofauna. *Hydrobiologia*, **47**, 81–89.

McElhone M.J. (1978) A population study of littoral dwelling Naididae (Oligochaeta) in a shallow mesotrophic lake in north Wales. *J. Anim. Ecol.*, **47**, 615–626.

McGowan L.M. (1974) Ecological studies on *Chaoborus* (Diptera, Chaoboridae) in Lake George, Uganda. *Freshwat. Biol.*, **4**, 483–505.

McLachlan A.J. (1975) Factors restricting the range of *Glyptotendipes paripes* Edwards (Diptera: Chironomidae) in a bog lake. *J. Anim. Ecol.*, **45**, 105–113.

McLachlan A.J. & McLachlan S.M. (1976) Development of the mud habitat during filling of two new lakes. *Freshwat. Biol.*, **6**, 59–67.

Meadows P.S. & Bird A.H. (1974) Behavior and local distribution of the freshwater oligochaete *Nais Pardalis* (Piguet) (Fam. Naididae). *Hydrobiologia*, **44**, 265–275.

Messick C.F. & Tash J.C. (1980) Effects of electricity on some benthic stream insects. *Trans. Am. Fish. Soc.*, **109**, 417–422.

Milbrink G. (1971) A simplified tube bottom sampler. *Oikos*, **22**, 260–263.

Milbrink G. (1973) Communities of Oligochaeta as indicators of the water quality in Lake Hjalmaren. *Zoon*, **1**, 77–88.

Milbrink G. & Wiederholm T. (1973) Sampling efficiency of four types of mud bottom samplers. *Oikos*, **24**, 479–482.

Milbrink G., Lundquist S. & Pramsten H. (1974a) On the horizontal distribution of the profundal bottom fauna in a limited area of central Lake Malaren, Sweden, I. Studies on the distribution of the bottom fauna. *Hydrobiologia*, **45**, 509–526.

Milbrink G., Lundquist S. & Pramsten H. (1974b) On the horizontal distribution of the profundal bottom fauna in a limited area of central Lake Malaren, Sweden, II. Statistical treatment of the data. *Hydrobiologia*, **45**, 527–542.

Minto M.L. (1977) A sampling device for invertebrate fauna of aquatic vegetation. *Freshwat. Biol.*, **7**, 425–430.

Moore J.W. (1979) Some factors influencing the distribution, seasonal abundance, and feeding of subarctic Chironomidae (Diptera). *Arch. Hydrobiol.*, **85**, 302–325.

Mozley S.C. (1974) Preoperational distribution of benthic macroinvertebrates in Lake Michigan near Cook Nuclear Power Plant. In E.Seible & J.C.Ayers (eds.) *The Biological, Chemical, and Physical Character of Lake Michigan in the Vicinity of the Donald C. Cook Plant.* Univ. Mich. Grt. Lakes Res. Div. Spec. Rep. **51**, p. 5–138.

Murray T.D. & Charles W.N. (1975) A pneumatic grab for obtaining large, undisturbed mud samples: its construction and some applications for measuring growth of larval and emergence of adult Chironomidae. *Freshwat. Biol.*, **5**, 205–210.

Niesiolowski S. (1980) Studies on the abundance, biomass, and vertical distribution of larvae and pupae of black flies (Simuliidae, Diptera) on plants of the Grabia River, Poland. *Hydrobiologia*, **75**, 149–156.

Paterson C.G. & Fernando C.H. (1971) A comparison of a simple corer and an Ekman grab for sampling shallow water benthos. *J. Fish. Res. Board Can.*, **28**, 365–368.

Paterson C.G. & Walker K.F. (1974) Seasonal dynamics and productivity of *Tanytarsus barbitarsus* Freeman (Diptera: Chironomidae) in the benthos of a shallow, saline lake. *Austr. J. Mar. Freshwat. Res.*, **25**, 151–165.

Pearson R.G., Litterick M.R. & Jones N.V. (1973) An air-lift for quantitative sampling of the benthos. *Freshwat. Biol.*, **3**, 309–315.

Peterka J.J. (1972) Benthic invertebrates in Lake Ashtabula Reservoir, North Dakota. *Am. Midl. Nat.*, **88**, 408–418.

Petersen C.G.J. (1918) The sea bottom and its production of fish food. *Rep. Dan. Biol. Stn.*, **25**, 62 pp.

Petr T. (1970) Macroinvertebrates of flooded trees in the man-made Volta Lake (Ghana) with special reference to the burrowing Mayfly *Povella adusta* (Navas). *Hydrobiologia*, **36**, 373–398.

Pieczyńska E. (1973) Experimentally increased fish stock in the pond type Lake Warniak. XIII. Numbers and biomass of the fauna associated with macrophytes. *Ekol. Pols.*, **21**, 595–610.

Pieczyński E. (1977) Numbers and biomass of the littoral fauna in Mikolajski Lake and in other Masurian lakes. *Ekol. Pols.*, **25**, 45–57.

Powers C.F. & Robertson A. (1967) Design and evaluation of an all-purpose benthos sampler. *Grt. Lakes Res. Div. Univ. Mich. Spec. Rep.*, **30**, 126–131.

Prejs K. (1970) Some problems of the ecology of benthic nematodes (Nematoda) of Mikolajskie Lake. *Ekol. Pols.*, **18**, 225–242.

Prejs K. & Stańczykowska A. (1972) Spatial differentiation and changes in time of zoomicrobenthos in three Masurian lakes. *Ekol. Pols.*, **20**, 733–745.

Ranta E. & Sarvala J. (1978) Spatial patterns of littoral meiofauna in an oligotrophic lake. *Verh. Int. Ver. Limnol.*, **20**, 886–890.

Rinne J.N. (1978) Standing crops of Chironomidae and Tubificidae in two desert reservoirs, central Arizona. *Hydrobiologia*, **57**, 217–224.

Rosenberg D.M. & Resh V.H. (1982) The use of artificial substrates in the study of freshwater macroinvertebrates. In J.Cairns, Jr. (ed.), *Artificial Substrates*. Ann Arbor: Ann Arbor Science Publishers.

Rowe G.T. & Clifford C.H. (1973) Modifications of the Birge-Ekman box corer for use with scuba or deep submergence research vessels. *Limnol. Oceanogr.*, **18**, 172–175.

Ruggio D. & Saraceni C. (1972) A statistical study of the distribution of the bottom fauna of a lake undergoing accelerated eutrophication. *Mem. Ist. Ital. Idrobiol.*, **29**, 169–187.

Sapkarev J.A. (1975) Composition and dynamics of the bottom animals in the littoral zone of Dojran Lake, Macedonia. *Verh. Int. Ver. Limnol.*, **19**, 1339–1350.

Särkkä J. (1975) The numbers of *Tubifex tubifex* and its cocoons in relation to mesh size. *Biol. Res. Rep. Univ. Jyväskylä*, **1**, 9–13.

Schwoerbel J. (1970) *Methods of Hydrobiology*. Oxford: Pergamon.

Sebestyeń O. (1947) Cladocera studies in Lake Balaton. *Arch. Biol. Hungarica*, **17**, 1–17.

Sebestyeń O. (1948) Cladocera studies in Lake Balaton. II. Littoral Cladocera from the northwestern shores of Tihany Peninsula. *Arch. Biol. Hungarica*, **18**, 101–116.

Shapovalova I.M. & Vologdin M.P. (1979) Procedure for quantitative estimation of submerged vegetation and the phytophilous fauna. *Hydrobiol. J.*, **15**, 89–91.

Shiozawa D.K. & Barnes J.R. (1977) The microdistribution and population trends of larval *Tanypus stellatus* (Coquellet) and *Chironomus frommeri* (Atchley & Martin) (Diptera: Chironomidae) in Utah Lake, Utah. *Ecology*, **58**, 610–618.

Sivertsen B. (1973) The bottom fauna of Lake Huddingsvatn, based on quantitative sampling. *Norw. J. Zool.*, **21**, 305–321.

Slack H.D. (1972) A lever operated Ekman grab. *Freshwat. Biol.*, **2**, 401–405.

Smith K.L., Jr. & Howard J.D. (1972) Comparison of a grab sampler and large volume corer. *Limnol. Oceanogr.*, **17**, 142–145.

Smith W. & McIntyre A.D. (1954) A spring loaded bottom sampler. *J. Mar. Biol. Assoc. U.K.*, **33**, 257–264.

Smock L.A. (1980) Relationship between body size and biomass of aquatic insects. *Freshwat. Biol.*, **10**, 375–383.

Smyly W.J.P. (1957) Distribution and seasonal abundance of Entomostraca in moorland ponds near Windermere. *Hydrobiologia*, **11**, 59–72.

Solem J.O. (1973) The bottom fauna of Lake Lille-Jonsvann, Trondelag, Norway. *Norw. J. Zool.*, **21**, 227–261.

Soszka G.J. (1975) The invertebrates on submerged macrophytes in three Masurian Lakes. *Ekol. Pols.*, **23**, 371–391.

Southwood T.R.E. (1966) *Ecological Methods with Special Reference to the Study of Insect Populations*. London: Methuen.

Stańczykowska A. (1973) Experimentally increased fish stock in the pond type Lake Warniak. X. Numbers and distribution of zoomicrobenthos. *Ekol. Pols.*, **2**, 575–581.

Stańczykowska A. & Przytocka-Jusiak M. (1968) Variations in abundance and biomass of microbenthos in three Masurian Lakes. *Ekol. Pols.*, **16**, 539–559.

Stanford J.A. (1972) A centrifuge method for determining live weights of aquatic insect larvae with a note on weight loss in preservative. *Ecology*, **54**, 449–451.

Stockner J.G. & Armstrong F.A.J. (1971) Periphyton of the Experimental Lakes Area, Northwestern Ontario. *J. Fish. Res. Board Can.*, **28**, 215–229.

Sutcliffe D.W. (1979) Some notes to authors on the presentation of accurate and precise measurements in quantitative studies. *Freshwat. Biol.*, **9**, 397–402.

Swenberg J.A., Kerns W.D., Mitchell R.I., Gralla E.J. & Pavkov K.L. (1980) Induction of squamous cell carcinomas of the rat nasal cavity by inhalation exposure to formaldehyde vapor. *Cancer Res.*, **40**, 3398–3402.

Taylor T.P. & Erman D.C. (1980) The littoral bottom fauna of high elevation lakes in Kings Canyon National Park. *Calif. Fish Game*, **66**, 112–119.

Thamdrup H.M. (1938) Der van Veen Bodengreifer. Vergleichsversuche über die Leistungsfähigkeit des van Veen und des Petersen Bodengreifers. *J. Cons. perm. Int. Explor. Mer.*, **13**, 206–212.

Thayer G.W., Williams R.B., Price T.J. & Colby D.R. (1975) A large corer for quantitatively sampling benthos in shallow water. Limnol. Oceanogr., **20**, 474–481.

Thiel H., Thistle D. & Wilson G.D. (1975) Ultrasonic treatment of sediment samples for more efficient sorting of meiofauna. *Limnol. Oceanogr.*, **20**, 472–473.

Tudorancea C. & Green R.H. (1975) Distribution and seasonal variation of benthic fauna in Lake Manitoba. *Verh. Int. Ver. Limnol.*, **19**, 616–623.

Tudorancea C., Green R.H. & Huebner J. (1979) Structure, dynamics and production of the benthic fauna in Lake Manitoba. *Hydrobiologia*, **64**, 59–95.

Van Arkel M.A. & Mulder M. (1975) A device for quantitative sampling of benthic organisms in shallow water by means of a flushing technique. *Neth. J. Sea Res.*, **9**, 365–370.

Verollet G. & Tachet H. (1978) Un échantillonneur à succion pour le prélèvement du zoobenthos fluvial. *Arch. Hydrobiol.*, **84**, 55–64.

Vincent B. (1979) Étude du benthos d'eau douce dans le haut estuaire du Saint-Laurent (Québec). *Can. J. Zool.*, **57**, 2171–2182.

Voshell J. R., Jr. & Simmons G.M. (1977) An evaluation of artificial substrates for sampling macrobenthos in reservoirs. *Hydrobiologia*, **53**, 257–269.

Ward E. B. (1940) A seasonal population study of pond Entomostraca in the Cincinnati region. *Am. Midl. Nat.*, **23**, 635–691.

Welch P.S. (1948) *Limnological Methods.* New York: McGraw-Hill.

Werner E.E., Hall D.J. & Werner M.D. (1978) Littoral zone fish communities of two Florida lakes and a comparison with Michigan lakes. *Env. Biol. Fish.*, **3**, 163–172.

Westlake D.F. (1969) Sampling macrophytes. In R.A. Vollenweider (ed.) *A Manual on Methods for Measuring Primary Production in Aquatic Environments.* IBP Handbook No. 12, Oxford: Blackwell.

Wetzel R.G. (1975) *Limnology.* Philadelphia: Saunders.

Wiederholm T. (1974) Bottom fauna and eutrophication in the large lakes of Sweden. *Acta Univ. Upsal.*, **270**, 12 pp.

Wiederholm T. & Eriksson L. (1977) Benthos of an acid lake. *Oikos*, **29**, 261–267.

Wiggins G.B. (1977) *Larvae of the North American Caddisfly Genera (Trichoptera).* Toronto: University of Toronto Press.

Wigley R.L. (1967) Comparative efficiencies of van Veen and Smith-McIntyre grab samplers as revealed by motion pictures. *Ecology*, **48**, 168–169.

Wildish D.J. (1978) Sublittoral macro infaunal grab sampling reproducibility and cost. *Fish. Mar. Ser. Tech. Rep.*, No. 770, Ottawa: Minister of Supply and Services Canada.

Williams D.D. & Williams N.E. (1974) A counter staining technique for use in sorting benthic samples. *Limnol. Oceanogr.*, **19**, 152–154.

Wilson R.S., Maxwell T.R.A., Mance G., Sleigh M.A. & Milne R.A. (1975) Biological aspects of Chew Valley and Blagdon Lakes, England. *Freshwat. Biol.*, **5**. 379–393.

Winsor C.P. (1946) Which regression? *Biometrics*, **2**, 101–109.

Wise E.J. & O'Sullivan A. (1980) Preliminary observations on the benthic macroinvertebrate community of Rose Bay, a polluted area of Lough Leane, South West Ireland. *Water Res.*, **14**, 1–13.

Wood L.W. (1975) Role of oligochaetes in the circulation of water and solutes across the mud water interface. *Verh. Int. Ver. Limnol.*, **19**, 1530–1533.

Zimmerman U. & Ambühl H. (1970) Zur methodik der quantitativen biologische Probenahmen in stark strömenden Flüssen. *Schweiz. Z. Hydrol.*, **32**, 340–344.

Zytkowicz R. (1976) Production of macrobenthos in Lake Tynwald. *Acta Univ. Nicolai Cpernici Nauk. Matem.*, **38**, 75–97.

Chapter 5. Sampling the Stream Benthos

BARBARA L. PECKARSKY

1 Introduction

Numerous original papers and reviews have been published on sampling of stream or river benthos before and since Hynes' (1971) review of this topic in the first edition of this manual. The most inclusive have been those of Macan (1958), Cummins (1962), Mason (1976), Mundie (1971), Resh (1979), Waters & Resh (1979), and Merritt *et al.* (1978). These studies discuss available samplers, problems unique to sampling the stream benthos, and recommendations for choosing the appropriate methodology. I do not intend to reiterate ideas reviewed in the above papers in great detail, but refer you to these reviews, and to other papers cited in this chapter, for more information. My objective is to comment on the available technology for sampling benthos in running waters, and to introduce another approach to choosing appropriate methodology.

Although 10 years have passed since Hynes' (1971) chapter, no revolutionary break-throughs have occurred to rectify the largely unresolved problems of estimating secondary productivity in running waters. I hope to encourage those attempting to study this problem to avoid the existing, error-ridden techniques, and to apply creativity to the task of quantifying productivity of stream benthos.

This chapter is organized as follows: First, I review some traditional qualitative and quantitative methods for sampling stream benthos, contrast available techniques, and point out existing problems and needs. Next, I discuss experimental design for special problems requiring quantitative measurement of stream benthos. Finally, I conclude with a section on choosing the appropriate sampling methodology.

2 Review of traditional sampling techniques

The design of any sampling scheme and the choice of apparatus should depend largely upon the questions being asked. The procedure for measuring the density of invertebrates in a riffle will differ from that for estimating diversity. Estimating the production of each species requires a unique approach, specific to the distribution, life history, and habits of that species. For example, measuring the production of surface-dwelling water striders (Gerridae) presents different problems to estimating production of interstitial stoneflies, or of net-spinning caddisflies. One must implement a sampling program that incorporates the special conditions that apply to each species and to the parameter being estimated.

In the past, this procedure has not generally been followed. Most measures of standing crop biomass or numbers, densities, diversity, and production of stream invertebrates have used a similar methodology: random samples with a standard stream sampler (Surber sampler or box sampler), or modifications of these (Merritt *et al.* 1978) (Fig. 5.1), and the number of samples taken has been

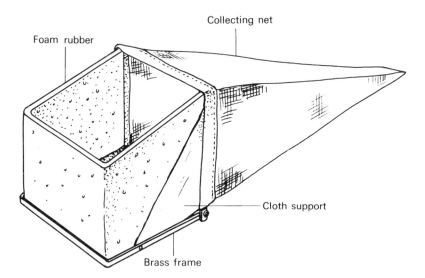

Fig. 5.1 Modified Surber sampler.

based on practicality or avoidance of destruction of a small habitat (see reviews cited above). Although these samplers may be unreliable or inappropriate to the organisms or streams being studied, and unreasonable and destructive numbers of samples may be required to estimate benthic density, biomass, diversity or production, the same methods continue to appear in the literature (Resh 1979).

Several examples illustrate the potential imprecision of standard stream sampling techniques. These studies were designed to test the effectiveness of certain methods of estimating the standing crop of invertebrates in stream riffles. Needham & Usinger (1956) systematically took 100 samples in a 10 × 10 latin square design in a 'uniform' riffle in Prosser Creek, California. Five people took 10 Surber samples each over a two-day period. (Ideally, replicate samples should be taken instantaneously.) These data allowed the authors to determine the variability among samples, and to calculate the number of samples necessary to estimate the benthic standing crop with 95 % confidence intervals within 40 % of the mean. Their estimates of 73 (numbers) and 194 samples (biomass) were later shown by Chutter (1972), to be too high. Chutter also showed that a sample size of 448 was necessary to estimate numbers of invertebrates within 5 % of the mean.

This impractical and destructive number of samples is required to make reasonable population estimates due to the patchy distribution of benthic invertebrates in this seemingly 'uniform' riffle. The number of animals collected per sample ranged from two to 198. Radford & Hartland-Rowe (1971) and Frost *et al.* (1971) calculated that similarly impractical numbers of Surber samples would be necessary to obtain a reasonable estimate of standing crop in seemingly uniform riffles. Resh (1979) took 26 pairs of Surber samples side by side in an Indiana stream to estimate the patchiness of the net-spinning Trichopteran larvae, *Cheumatopsyche pettiti* (Hydropsychidae). If the distribution of these larvae was uniform, one would expect a positive correlation between the numbers of *C. pettiti* collected by the two investigators in adjacent samples. The result, however, showed that the distribution of these insects was contagious, requiring 24 samples to obtain estimates of standing crop within 40 % of the mean.[1]

Some of the variation in numbers of invertebrates per sample could be due to differences in sampling technique or efficiency of different people. Needham & Usinger (1956) showed that only four or five people were consistent in the range of numbers of animals obtained. Pollard (1981) implemented a standard traveling kick method (STKM) using a simple dip net to estimate standing crop of benthos in a Colorado stream. A net was held in place on the substrate, and the investigators moved downstream, vigorously kicking the substrate for a prescribed distance and time interval. Pollard compared the results of samples taken by different investigators, and between samples taken for 30 sec over a 3 m^2 of substrate to those for 15 sec over 1·5 m^2 of substrate. He found significant differences between samples taken by different investigators in depauperate reaches, and showed that samples taken for twice the time over twice the substrate area did not yield twice the standing crop, although fewer discrepancies occurred in faunal-rich reaches. Pollard concluded that there is an unknown relationship between length of kick, substrate area sampled, and faunal richness.

Another popular methodology has been the use of artificial substrate samplers, such as basket samplers and multiplate samplers (Fig. 5.2). These may be useful for collecting selected taxa that prefer such introduced habitats;

1. *Editor's Note:* see Section 5.2 for a treatment of sample size and precision.

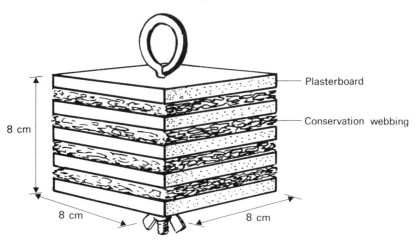

Plasterboard

Conservation webbing

8 cm

8 cm   8 cm

Fig. 5.2 Dendy multiplate artificial substrate sampler.

however, caution must be exercised when using artificial substrates to avoid obtaining biased samples. For example, I attempted to estimate the composition of the benthic invertebrate community in Otter Creek, Wisconsin, during the summer of 1975 using various different sampling techniques, including Surber samplers, Dendy samplers, drift net samples, and mesh cages filled with natural stream substrates (Fig. 5.3). I compared estimates of percent composition of the four major orders between the different methods (Fig. 5.4). Surbers and drift nets obtained similar numbers of Ephemeroptera, but drift nets captured more Plecoptera and Trichoptera, and fewer Diptera than Surber samplers. Cage samples contained a slightly higher percentage of Ephemeroptera, more Plecoptera, fewer Diptera, and the same proportion of Trichoptera as Surbers. Dendy samplers gave the most divergent picture of percent composition at the ordinal level, with much higher estimates of Plecoptera, and smaller proportions of Trichoptera and Diptera (Peckarsky 1979b). Had I used Dendy samples to estimate the standing crop or production of benthos in Otter Creek, I could have made a serious error.

Many authors (e.g. Hilsenhoff 1969; Brooks 1972; Rosenberg & Resh 1982) have summarized the potential disadvantages of the use of artificial substrate samplers to characterize stream benthos:

(1) They differentially attract some taxa, as illustrated above.
(2) The time required for colonization to reach equilibrium may be impractically long.
(3) Organisms may be lost upon retrieval unless precautions are taken.
(4) Passers-by may tamper with these devices.

Given knowledge of these possible problems, artificial substrate samplers can

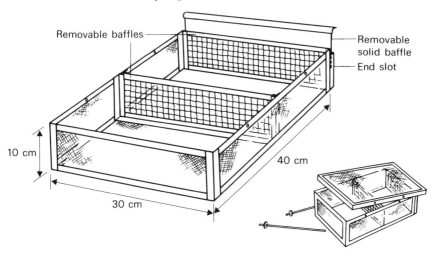

Fig. 5.3 Colonization cage, first generation designed by S.I.Dodson (from Peckarsky 1979a).

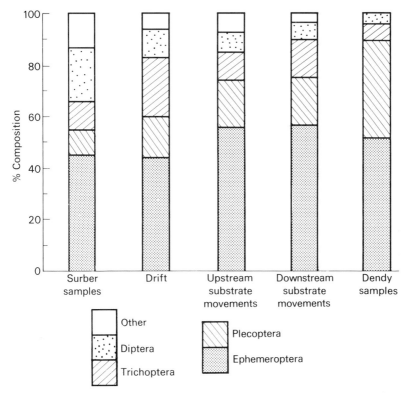

Fig. 5.4 Percent composition (by order) of samples taken with Surber samplers, drift nets, cages, and Dendy samplers in Otter Creek, Wisconsin.

be implemented if they are an efficient means of collecting certain taxa. Extrapolation of results to estimates of absolute benthic density or production may be erroneous. However, they can be effective in comparison of the production of a taxon from site to site.

Core samples have been used to measure the vertical distribution of hyporheic benthos by several investigators (Bishop 1973; Coleman & Hynes 1970; Hynes 1974; O'Conner 1974; Williams & Hynes 1974; Godbout & Hynes 1983). Historically, these studies identified a habitat that had been overlooked by surface sampling techniques, and suggested that estimates of standing crops based on surface samples might be serious underestimates. These techniques may be appropriate in certain substrates (loose gravel or sand), but impractical in cobble, rubble, and substrates where hardpan exists a few centimeters below the surface. Furthermore, criticisms of surface samples as underestimates may only apply to penetrable substrates. Caution must be exercised in retrieval of core samples, as in other artificial substrate samplers, so that animals are not lost.

Resh (1979) presents a tabular summary (see Appendix, Section 5.1) of factors that affect various benthic sampling devices and may result in sampling bias. Even more useful, he includes possible remedies to the problems of each sampler. This table is extremely important to all investigators who must choose between the available devices within the limitations of each particular study. Use of the information given in Resh (1979) will ensure more responsible implementation of traditional benthic sampling techniques.

A different number of samples and type of sampling program may be appropriate to estimates of standing crop, production, and species composition. Needham & Usinger (1956) showed that fewer samples were required to estimate diversity than standing crop, but that samples needed to be taken over a wider range of substrate types. Two to three samples were enough to collect the most common Ephemeroptera, Plecoptera, Trichoptera, and Diptera. Nelson & Scott (1962) found that 96 % of the taxa recovered in 12 Surber samples were included in the first four samples. Random samples are most likely to give unbiased estimates of standing crop or production of the entire benthic community. However, stratified random sampling, concentrating more effort in habitats rich in fauna (riffles *versus* pools), or systematic sampling, such as transects, may be more efficient at gathering information about specific taxa given information about their life histories and distribution (Resh 1979; Tanner 1978; see also Chapter 8).

I am not aware of any simple solutions to the impracticality associated with obtaining good estimates of benthic standing crop or production in streams. At the very least, we should be aware of the potential error in our calculations of production or standing crop, given the limitations of sampling patchily distributed organisms. Merritt *et al.* (1978) describe methods for analyzing stream bottom samples to arrive at estimates of standing crop biomass and numbers (cf. their Fig. 3.1, p. 14). Gillespie & Benke (1979), Benke (1979), Krueger & Martin (1980), and Menzie (1980) have contributed to techniques for calculating production of stream insects. Krueger & Martin (1980) emphasize the importance of carrying out separate calculations on species with different voltinisms, maximum sizes, growth rates, and trophic levels. Cushman *et al.* (1978) present a comparison of the removal-summation, instantaneous growth, and size-frequency methods of calculating production, based on a computer simulation considering such variables as sampling interval and growth rate. In addition, Whittaker (1972) and Peet (1974) have defined the problems and appropriateness of various diversity indexes for use in ecological studies. Kaesler & Herricks (1979) apply the concept of diversity indexes to problems of environmental impact assessment.

These studies provide sound advice based on the mathematical constraints of various available measures of production and diversity. For example, Cushman *et al.* (1978) showed that the removal-summation technique for calculating production was the most robust over different simulated growth curves and mortality, as well as over different sampling intervals. Peet (1974) showed that indexes of species richness (S = number of species) are affected by arbitrary choice of sample size (N). One can actually predict the rate of increase of S with increasing N. Peet also notes that different types of heterogeneity indexes that take both richness and the distribution of individuals within each species (evenness or equitability) into account are sensitive to different changes. The commonly used Shannon type index is more responsive to changes in rare species, whereas the Simpson type index is more sensitive to changes in common species. All heterogeneity indexes give ranges which are comparable qualitatively but not statistically, due to peculiarities in the underlying distribution of the index values. They also assume an infinite community of known proportions. Peet suggests that one who uses any heterogeneity index should develop a 'response curve', that is, graph the components of the index summed over all species. This will show how the changes in the sample composition affect the index.

Other types of heterogeneity indexes have been adapted from information theory (Brillouin type) (see Kaesler & Herricks 1979). These indexes are not dependent upon sample size, but are very cumbersome to calculate. Cuba (1981) developed an index that separates the influences of S and evenness, and gives values that indicate how close the observed sample is to a theoretical sample of equivalent S and N where numbers of individuals are evenly distributed among species. This index always gives higher values with larger S, which is not always true of other heterogeneity indexes. Equitability indexes are also reviewed by Peet (1974). Most require a knowledge of the number of species in the sampling universe, and increase with species richness. Alatalo

(1981) suggests that Hill's ratio is the least ambiguous, is not dependent on sample size, and does not require a knowledge of S. It is, however, quite new and has not been fully explored.

No matter how sophisticated the manipulation of data, however, standing crop biomass, production, or diversity estimates are unreliable unless they have been calculated from appropriately gathered data. The precision of each of these measures is dependent upon adequate sample sizes, generally in excess of the actual number of samples taken (see Appendix, Section 5.2). The most elegant calculations cannot overcome the shortcomings of a poor sampling program.

In summary, stream biologists are faced with the frustrating problem of lacking adequate methods to determine accurately how many organisms inhabit lotic ecosystems. What can we do to resolve this dilemma? Rather than abandoning the challenge altogether, or lowering our standards of desired levels of precision, I suggest that a problem-oriented approach may improve the precision with which data are gathered, and allow us to answer some of these difficult questions.

3 Experimental design for special problems

Below are case histories as examples of studies in which creativity has been applied to quantitative problem solving in investigations of stream benthos. The studies discussed cover a broad range of questions that may be of interest to stream ecologists, such as density or production estimates, life histories, benthic distributions, dispersal, stream invertebrate behavior, and biological interactions among benthic invertebrates.

3.1 *Benthic density: production studies*

In a study of the leech fauna of Lake Esrom, Denmark, Dall (1979) introduced a technique that can be applied to measuring the density of stream-dwelling species on relatively homogeneous mineral substrates. Using a circular iron ring with a diameter of 15·3 cm (185 cm^2 area), Dall estimated the surface area of the stones in randomly selected samples taken at two-week intervals. Unembedded stones ($> 2·5 \times 2·5 \times 1·0$ cm) were collected and measured. Buried stones, gravel, and sand were considered as a separate fraction. Sampling was terminated when 100 stones, an average of 13·8 sample units, had been collected. Leeches and stones were also collected from a 1 m^2 horizontal surface of the substrate.

Dall calculated the surface area of the unembedded stones by the formula

$$S = \pi/3(LW + LH + WH) \tag{5.1}$$

measuring length (L), width (W), and height (H) of each stone to the nearest 0·5 cm. He discussed the biological importance of this parameter as a measure of available habitat for negatively phototactic animals such as leeches (and most stream invertebrates). In addition, he was able to deduce the mean stone surface area per m² of bottom (2·77) from the 1 m² samples. This factor is a more accurate representation of actual habitable space for stone-dwelling organisms than is horizontal surface area of the substrate, and should be considered when estimating the density of these organisms.

This study exemplifies a carefully conceived scheme by which the author obtained valuable information regarding the growth and production of leeches. Not only did he recheck his primary sampling technique with the square meter sampling, but he incorporated additional systematic sampling designed to collect rarer leech species. Dall thereby accounted for the biology and distribution of the taxa being studied, and double-checked the adequacy of his primary sampling technique to provide improved estimates of growth and production of leeches. This study can be used as a model, and modified to obtain similar information on lotic inhabitants with known biological characteristics on similar substrates.

3.2 Life history studies

Resh (1979) pointed out the need for consideration of life history information in the design of studies of benthic production. Conversely, if one wishes to determine life history information such as growth rates, mortality, ontogenetic movement patterns or dispersal, and timing of hatching, diapause, pupation or emergence, specific techniques must be employed to ensure proper interpretation of data. Resh (1979) described the distribution of *Cheumatopsyche pettiti* (Trichoptera; Hydropsychidae) in Rock Creek, Carroll Co., Indiana. All five instars of *C. pettiti* coexist in single riffles, but different instars construct filtering nets with different mesh sizes, requiring different optimal current regimens.

Resh emphasized that sampling design must include the entire range of habitats for all five instars to accurately assess population parameters such as growth and migration. Resh (1975) suggested systematic transect sampling as a technique that maximizes information per unit sampling effort in single-species studies, and enhances the collection of early instars. The procedure is deliberately biased to increase the range of habitat types sampled. Mesh size of sampling nets must also be carefully chosen to avoid overlooking the smallest instars.

The number of samples necessary to estimate population sizes may vary throughout the life cycle of a species. Sampling at regular intervals may not be appropriate for obtaining adequate information; it may be necessary to sample more frequently during periods when the population is changing more rapidly. Unfortunately, *a priori* information from which a sampling program can be designed is not always available. Ideally, an investigator should obtain as much relevant information on the biology of a species as possible, either from preliminary samples or from the literature, before designing the sampling program. If this is not possible, Resh (1979) suggested short-interval sampling when populations are in early age classes, and a gradual increase in the length of sampling intervals as the growth rate declines. Another practical solution is to begin a sampling program with short intervals, and then to lengthen intervals if changes in the populations are slow enough to sample less frequently without losing a great deal of information.

3.3 Distributional studies

As we have already seen, complications necessarily arise when populations that are not dispersed evenly in space are to be sampled. Greater numbers of samples are required to accurately estimate population densities as distributions diverge from random, and as sample means become smaller (Elliott 1977; Resh 1979). Since aggregated spatial patterns are so common for stream benthos (see studies summarized in Section 2), techniques must be designed to meet the challenge of measuring these distributions. For example, Downing (1979) described an index of aggregation based on the exponent of the power relationship between density and variance as a means by which to predict the degree of patchiness. He then showed how to plan a sampling program based on this index, and how to transform data for analysis.

Peckarsky (1979a, b) developed a technique by which the factors mediating distributions of stream benthos could be determined as an alternative to multiple regressions of concurrent samples of biotic and abiotic variables. Cages constructed of stainless steel screen and filled with natural substrate were buried in the substrate to allow colonization by invertebrates (Fig. 5.3). These cages were placed along transects to determine the spatial patterns of stream benthos relative to distance from the stream bank, and were stacked vertically to measure the vertical distribution of invertebrates (Fig. 5.5). Substrate type was also manipulated to test the effect of substrate size and heterogeneity on the distribution of benthos.

This technique is very useful since the screen cages contain 'natural' substrate, do not present the obstruction problems of some artificial substrate samplers, mentioned by Hynes (1971) and discussed in Section 2, are relatively light-weight and easily manageable, and allow manipulation of a number of different habitat variables. The experimental technique is more incisive than a correlative sample survey approach for determining factors mediating distributions, since differences between experimental and control treatments

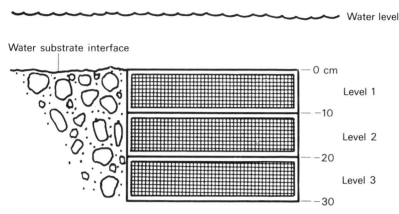

Fig. 5.5 Cross-section of stream showing vertical arrangement of cages. This technique is useful in measuring vertical stratification of benthic distribution in the substrate.

can be interpreted with less ambiguity. However, the cages are themselves an artefact, and may be partially responsible for the observed results (Hulberg & Oliver 1980).

Recently, stream ecologists have introduced association techniques, such as ordination (Culp & Davies 1980), that can handle large sets of data, but, if poorly designed, these can produce ambiguous data subject to a variety of interpretations. Individuals implementing ordination techniques should realize that they reduce information in order to extract it, and thus simplify complex situations. They are also an *a posteriori* analytical tool, and are less adapted to show causal relationships, but they can be a powerful method for identifying associations among variables under natural conditions. Again, caution should be used in interpreting data based on methods with the limitations discussed in Section 2.

3.4 Dispersal, colonization studies

A modification of the cages described above can be used to determine the direction and distance of dispersal of stream invertebrates within the substrate (Fig. 5.6). Mesh baffles on two sides of the cage allow colonization of benthos from a maximum of two directions. Cages can be attached end-to-end and arranged in a longitudinal pattern with respect to the current velocity (Fig. 5.7). Direction of migration can be controlled by the use of restrictive mesh size baffles on the upstream or downstream end of the colonization cage. Other types of apparatus applied to this question are described by Bishop & Hynes (1969b), Elliott (1971a), Hughes (1970), Hultin *et al.* (1969), and Keller (1975). They include boxes, tapered mesh bags, and artificial troughs.

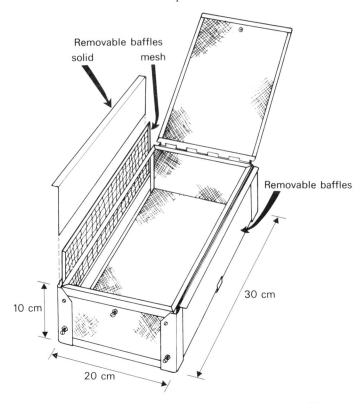

Fig. 5.6 Second generation colonization cage; lids held in place with neoprene fasteners.

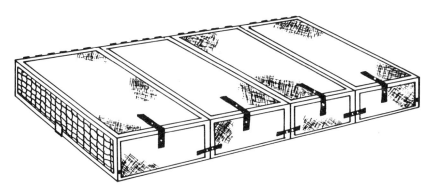

Fig. 5.7 Schematic representation of an experiment to measure the directional migration of stream benthos in the substrate; cages held together with neoprene fasteners.

Effective colonization devices allow analysis of the colonization pattern of individual species and factors affecting the rate of colonization. Devices can be removed after different periods of time to test the effect of duration of availability of 'new habitat' on the migration of invertebrates. Cages buried with different initial benthic densities allow patterns of density-dependent and density-independent colonization to be measured and equilibrium densities to be predicted (Peckarsky 1979a, 1981). The effect of experimentally introduced detritus on habitat choice can also be measured using colonization cages (Peckarsky 1980a). This technique has also been shown to be an effective indicator of environmental disturbance (Peckarsky & Cook 1981). Baffles of intermediate mesh sizes can be constructed such that large predators, such as Perlidae (Plecoptera), may be confined within the cages, while small prey species (Ephemeroptera, other Plecoptera, some Trichoptera and Diptera) are given access to the cage habitat. In this way, theories concerning the avoidance of predators and effects of predators on prey colonization can be tested (Peckarsky & Dodson 1980a).

An area of considerable interest to stream ecologists has been the study of invertebrate drift. Drift is usually sampled by placing nets in the stream to 'trap' organisms as they travel downstream in the current (Fig. 5.8) (Extensive reviews by Waters 1972; Müller 1974; Wiley & Kohler, in press). This drift net technique can suffer from potential backwash, clogging, inappropriate mesh size, and other logistical problems (see Resh 1979; Section 5.1). A drift net essentially reveals the number of animals that drifted past a certain point in the stream over a specified time period. It does not, however, tell you where the individuals came from, how far they would have drifted had they not been trapped in the net, why they released hold of the substrate, or why they would have settled. Elliott (1971b), Keller (1975), and Müller (1974) review methods for determining drift distances. Hypotheses on causal factors of drift behavior from studies of a correlative nature are reviewed extensively by Waters (1972) and Müller (1974). Here, I describe a few controlled experiments designed to determine some of the causal variables of invertebrate drift.

Ciborowski, Corkum, and associates have conducted refined experiments within a laboratory system to generate data on settling distances, and on the effects of certain variables, such as food, current, photoperiod, substrate, and predators, on drift behavior of some species of stream insects (Ciborowski 1979; Ciborowski & Corkum 1980; Ciborowski *et al.* 1977; Corkum 1978a, b; Corkum & Clifford 1980; Corkum & Pointing 1979; Corkum *et al.* 1977). They manipulated these variables and tested the drift responses of certain animals in the laboratory in a plexiglass elliptical channel powered by an Archimedes screw (Ciborowski *et al.* 1977). Studies of this type and similar work in laboratory streams of other designs by Wiley & Kohler (1980), Walton (1980a, b; Walton *et al.* 1977), and Hildebrand (1974) have provided

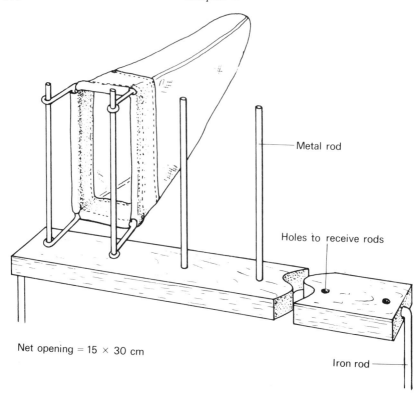

Metal rod

Holes to receive rods

Net opening = 15 × 30 cm

Iron rod

Fig. 5.8 A drift net design.

more easily interpretable information than field drift net studies on the factors mediating drift behavior. However, the artificiality of laboratory conditions must be taken into account when extrapolating the results to explain field phenomena.

Another technique for measuring effects of exogenous variables on drift is that employed by Peckarsky (1980b). Mayflies were observed in the field within streams in plexiglass observation boxes with screen ends (Fig. 5.9). Drifting behavior was quantified as a response to encounters with large stonefly predators. *Baetis* (Ephemeroptera, Baetidae) species, commonly trapped in drift nets, were found to enter the water column primarily to avoid the large predators. Wiley and Kohler (1981) also filmed drift events as a response to foraging invertebrate predators in the field. This direct observational approach provided definitive support for the importance of predator avoidance as a causal factor of invertebrate drift in some species.

Finally, a question of considerable importance to those interested in stream production is whether the numbers drifting from substrates cause significant reduction in benthic standing crop. Estimates of the proportion of

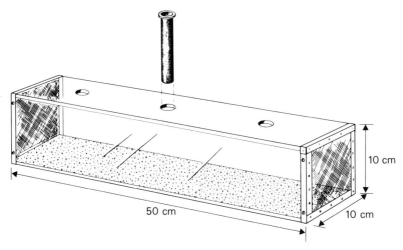

Fig. 5.9 Observation box—first generation; plexiglass sides and top, screen ends, sand substrate spray-painted in place.

the benthos in the drift are quite variable across species, in different streams, and depending upon the procedure used in calculation. Some examples are 0·0002–0·004 % of the benthos in the drift at any given time (Bishop & Hynes 1969a), 0·00059 %m^{-2} sec^{-1} (Elliott 1971a), and a mean drift (100 m^{-3} discharge): benthos ratio (0·1 m^{-2}) of 0·24–5.31 (Lehmkuhl & Anderson 1972). Waters (1966) showed that drift has no denuding effect on upstream reaches and suggested that drift removes animals in excess of the carrying capacity of the stream, a hypothesis that has received little empirical support (Dimond 1967; Pearson & Kramer 1971). Hildebrand (1974), Kroger (1972), Reisen & Prins (1972), and others present data that do not support this hypothesis. Recently, Waters (1981) demonstrated that production of *Gammarus pseudolimneaus* is sufficient to compensate for the observed drift.

3.5 Behavioral studies

Stream ecologists may be interested in quantifying behavior of benthic invertebrates to obtain information related to their distribution and abundance. This information can be used to help plan sampling programs or interpret distributional data. Predator avoidance responses such as crawling and posturing were measured for mayflies that did not drift or swim from encounters with stonefly predators in plexiglass observation boxes (Peckarsky 1980b). The mechanisms by which prey detect predators were also determined using this technique. Predators were presented visually (within test tubes), chemically (within screen tubes), and free (tactilely), and prey responses were recorded. The effect of predator presence on prey activity was also quantified. Pilot experiments have been conducted with a slightly modified observation box (Fig. 5.10) that improves the versatility and convenience of this observation technique. Questions concerning predator search behavior, feeding rates, effects of competitors on activity and distribution, effects of alarm substances on prey behavior, and many others can be answered using this approach.

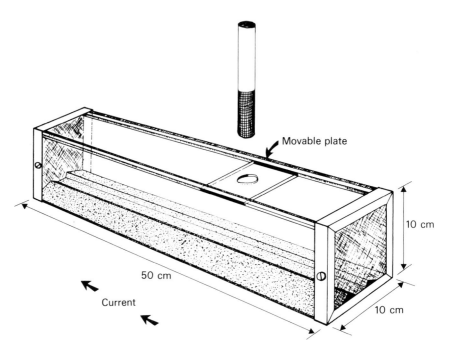

Fig. 5.10 Observation box—second generation; substrate with longidutinal depressions, sliding plexiglass plate on top.

Others have implemented direct observational techniques to monitor stream insect behavior. Hart & Resh (1980) quantified the foraging patterns of a diurnal, pool-dwelling caddisfly, *Dicosmoecus gilvipes* in a California stream by SCUBA. Mackay (1977) and Gallepp (1974) observed the behavior of caddisfly larvae in laboratory stream systems. Wiley & Kohler (1980) designed a simple laboratory technique by which to measure positioning changes of mayfly nymphs in relation to oxygen and current regimens. In addition, they implemented an elegant system whereby behavior of stream benthos was filmed *in situ* using a super-8 movie camera taking individual frames on an automatic timer (Wiley & Kohler 1981). The use of this type of film technology has much potential in the study of the behavior of stream benthos.

In summary, knowledge of the behavior of stream invertebrates can be incorporated into the design of effective programs to investigate secondary production.

3.6 Studies on biological interactions

A few investigators have begun to examine biological interactions such as predation and competition, which may be influential in determining production as well as the community structure of stream benthos. Hildrew and Townsend (1976, 1977) and Townsend and Hildrew (1978, 1979a, b) used primarily the traditional sample-survey approach, which, again, limits our interpretative ability to associations among predator-prey and competitor distributions. The experimental design employed by Peckarsky & Dodson (1980a, b) allows controlled manipulations of predator, prey, or competitor densities within cages (Figs. 5.3, 5.6); experiments were conducted to measure the causal role of such biological factors in determining distributions or colonization of stream benthos.

4 Choosing the appropriate methodology: summary and conclusions

Reviews by Hynes (1971), Resh (1979), and others discuss general rules for the choice of an appropriate sampling scheme. I have mentioned many of these in Section 2. Here I present a list of guidelines that can be useful to a stream ecologist in designing an effective sampling program.

First, identify the objectives of your research. What are the questions? Are you measuring diversity, production, standing crop numbers or biomass, dispersal? Each of these requires unique treatment. Second, decide upon a desired level of precision. Do you wish to estimate density within 5% of the mean or 40% of the mean? This decision will affect the choice of number of samples. Third, and very critical, gather as much information as possible on the biology of the taxa in question. The size of the animals will dictate proper mesh sizes; the life history, behavior, and distribution of different instars will be important in determining the scheduling of sampling intervals and the choice of sampling design (random, stratified, etc.). The habits and preferred habitat of the group will also be important in choice of sampling design. The dispersion pattern (even *versus* clumped) will be important in choosing sample sizes and design. Finally, the density of animals should be taken into account when choosing the size of a sample unit and the number of replicate samples. Preliminary samples should be taken to obtain as much of this information as possible.

Whatever methodology is chosen, a responsible investigator should understand the strengths and weaknesses of each technique so that data can be interpreted appropriately. For example, sample-survey designs can be subject to large error due to variability among samples if one attempts to use these data to extrapolate to absolute numbers, biomass, or production. Use of Surber samplers to compare estimates of benthic invertebrates in different riffles or in the same riffle over time, or above and below a disturbance, can be quite informative if the procedure for obtaining samples is standardized (same investigator, same volume of substrate sampled for the same time period, using the same sorting technique). Association techniques may generate testable hypotheses from large data sets, but causal relationships are least ambiguously elucidated through controlled experimentation.

In conclusion, I strongly encourage stream ecologists to design new and original apparatus, and to implement unique sampling schemes with considerable forethought so that hypotheses concerning productivity of stream benthos can be rigorously tested. It is hoped that the case studies presented in Section 3 can serve as examples that can be modified into individualized experimental designs appropriate to questions involving particular species. We must remember that the most sophisticated data analyses cannot override weaknesses in experimental design.

5.1 *Appendix 1*

The following table lists selected examples of factors that affect benthic sampling devices and may result in sampling bias (Table 1 from Resh 1979).

5.1 Appendix 1, (contd)

Factor	Samplers affected	Problems created	Remedy
	A. Factors related to characteristics of the samplers		
Backwash created in sampler by water not being able to pass through net	Netted and kick samplers	4–30% loss of benthos around sides of sampler (Badcock 1949; Macan 1958; Mundie 1971; Frost et al. 1971)	Increase the net's surface area and/or decrease size of net opening (Macan 1958); use enclosed double netted sampler (Mundie 1971); alternatively use a hand-operated Ekman grab or cylinder box sampler (Hynes 1971)
Washout of surface organisms upon placement of sampler	Hess sampler	Turbulence scours substrate surface (Macan 1958)	Use permeable sides (Waters & Knapp 1961)
Disruption of substrate surface by shockwave when sampler strikes bottom	Corer and Grab samplers	Loss of small organisms and surface dwellers (Flannagan 1970; Howmiller 1971; Milbrink & Wiederholm 1973)	Modify Ekman grab by removing screens and incorporating heavier materials in design (Burton & Flannagan 1973); alternatively use a pneumatic grab (Murray & Charles 1975), a box sampler (Jónasson & Olausson 1966; Farris & Crezee 1976), or a modified corer (Brinkhurst et al. 1969; Kajak 1963, 1971)
Disturbance of biota	Surber sampler and Allan grab	Underestimation of biota due to disruption when sampler is set in place (Surber: Kroger 1972; Allan grab: Kajak 1971)	Modify Allan grab by adding screened openings on top
	Shovel sampler	Loss of motile organisms (Macan 1958; Hynes 1970)	

(continued)

5.1 Appendix 1, (contd)

Factor	Samplers affected	Problems created	Remedy
Variable depth of penetration into substrate by sampler	Grabs	Inconsistent volume of sediment sampled; loss due to overfilling (Flannagan 1970) or incomplete closure (Kajak 1963; Gale 1971)	Leave 5-cm space above substrate (Flannagan 1970); alternatively use a corer whenever possible (Kajak 1963; Gale 1971)
	Surber	Failure to consider stream hyporheic zone	Two stage sampling, surface and hyporheic
Variable area sampled	Shovel sampler	Area sampled laterally is variable (Macan 1958)	
Sampler mesh size too coarse	Netted samplers	Early instars, small and slender organisms missed (Zelt & Clifford 1972; Frost et al. 1971; Mundie 1971; DeBovee et al. 1974)	Finer mesh, or preferably a double bag sampler (Macan 1958; Frost et al. 1971; Mundie 1971; Zelt & Clifford 1972; Barber & Kevern 1974)
Sampler mesh too fine	Netted samplers	May cause backwash (see above)	Coarser mesh as in double bag samplers
Sampler dimension too large	All samplers	Increase sorting time; may not detect population aggregations (Elliott 1977)	Smaller samples (Elliott 1977; Voshell & Simmons 1977)
	Grab samplers and corers	Inefficient cost/sample ratio (Karlsson et al. 1976)	When density > several hundred/m^2 use corer, when < use Ekman grab (Kajak 1963); alternatively use multiple corer (Brinkhurst et al. 1969; Flannagan 1970; Hakala 1971)
Sampler dimension too small	All samplers	May not detect aggregations; variability increased due to edge effect (Elliott 1977)	Use nested sampler to determine optimal sampler dimension

Operator inconsistency	All samplers	Systematic error in population estimates (Needham & Usinger 1956)	Single operator; or correction factor for each operator (Chutter 1972)

B. Factors related to characteristics of the environment

Water depth limitations in lotic environments	Surber and Hess samplers	Surber sampler limited to <30 cm depth (Macan 1958; Albrecht 1959; Chutter 1972)	From 0·5 to 4 m use an airlift sampler (Mackey 1972; Pearson *et al.* 1973); 0·4 to 10 m deep, SCUBA and dome suction sampler (Gale & Thompson 1975) or modified Hess sampler (Rabeni & Gibbs 1978); or use a modified Allan hand operated grab (Allan 1952; Kajak 1971) or bottombasket samplers (e.g. Crossman & Cairns 1974; Rabeni & Gibbs 1978)
Substrate—stony	Grab samplers, corers	Grabs may not close (Kajak 1971); cylinder sampler cannot penetrate (Ulfstrand 1968)	Substitute airlift or dome suction sampler and artificial substrate as above
Substrate—mixed	Grab samplers, corers	Differential penetration	Flannagan (1970) recommends specific samplers for different substrate types; stratified sampling (Scherba & Gallucci 1976)
Current too slow	Surber and kick samplers	Organisms do not drift into net	Enclosed sampler such as modified Surber or Hess sampler (Leonard 1939; Waters & Knapp 1961)
Current too fast	Netted samplers	Backwash, resulting in a loss of organisms	Substitute a modified sampler with controlled flow (Mundie 1971)
Current fluctuations	All samplers	Rapid change in flow may scour study area	

(*continued*)

5.1 Appendix 1, (contd)

Factor	Samplers affected	Problems created	Remedy
Low air temperatures	Netted samplers	Samples freeze in net before organisms are removed	Catch bottle or a zippered net (Waters & Knapp 1961; Lane 1974)
Sampling in vegetation	All samplers	Loss of organisms during removal; inability to close sampler	Use samplers described by Welch (1948), Macan (1949), Gerking (1957), Gillespie and Brown (1966), Mackie & Qadri (1971), Minto (1977), or artificial vegetation (Glime & Clemons 1972; Higler 1977; Macan 1977a)
Sampling in open water	Lotic: drift samplers; lentic: all samplers	Lotic: net clogging and changes in current and flow pattern affect estimation of water volume sampled (Pearson & Kramer 1969); lentic: sampling a consistent volume of water; scattering of organisms (Legner et al. 1975)	Lotic: use Parshall flume drift net (Hales & Gaufin 1969) or waterwheel drift sampler (Pearson & Kramer 1969); lentic: use column samplers (e.g. Legner et al. 1975; Enfield & Pritchard 1977; Henrickson & Oscarson 1978) or pull-up trap (Higer & Kolipinski 1967)
Habitat small	All samplers	Sampling destroys habitat (Chutter 1972; Mason 1976)	Smaller sampler dimension; artificial substrates (Glime & Clemons 1972; Macan 1976, 1977a, b)
Water chemistry	All samplers	Presence of springs, man-made outfalls, and other conditions may influence microhabitat distribution of biota	Reconnaissance

5.2 *Appendix 2*

Figure reproduced from Resh (1979, Fig. 7) showing the required number of samples for estimating the mean density (number m^{-2}) of stream benthos samples with 95 % confidence limits ± 20 % and ± 40 % of the mean, based on the general formula of Elliott (1977; see also Chapter 8, Section 2.1.3). Data were collected using a Surber sampler and are from Needham & Usinger (1956, Table 3) and Chutter & Noble (1966, Table 1). Each point represents a taxon. These figures can be used by reading values from the relationship: one must take 'Y' samples if the density is 'X'. See similar treatment for lake benthos in Chapter 4.

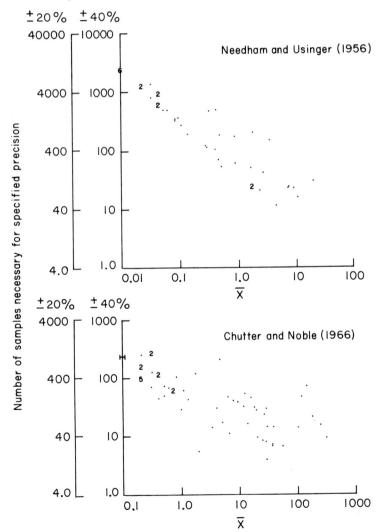

6 References

Alatalo R.V. (1981) Problems in the measurement of evenness in ecology. *Oikos*, **37**, 199–204.

Albrecht M.L. (1959) Die quantitative Untersuchung der Bodenfauna fliessender Gewässer (Untersuchungsmethoden und arbeitsergebnisse). *Z. Fisch.*, **8**, 481–550.

Allan I.R.H. (1952) A hand operated quantitative grab for sampling river beds. *J. Anim. Ecol.*, **21**, 159–160.

Badcock R.M. (1949) Studies in stream life in tributaries of the Welsh Dee. *J. Anim. Ecol.*, **18**, 193–208.

Barber W.E. & Kevern N.R. (1974) Seasonal variation of sieving efficiency in a lotic habitat. *Freshw. Biol.*, **4**, 293–300.

Benke A.C. (1979) A modification of the Hynes method for estimating secondary production with particular significance for multivoltine populations. *Limnol. Oceanogr.*, **24**, 168–170.

Bishop J.E. (1973) Observations on the vertical distribution of the benthos in a Malaysian stream. *Freshw. Biol.*, **3**, 147–156.

Bishop J.E. & Hynes H.B.N. (1969a) Downstream drift of invertebrate fauna in a stream ecosystem. *Arch. Hydrobiol.*, **66**, 56–90.

Bishop J.E. & Hynes, H.B.N. (1969b) Upstream movements of benthic invertebrates in Speed River, Ontario. *J. Fish. Res. Board Can.*, **26**, 279–298.

Brinkhurst R.O., Chua K.E. & Batoosingh E. (1969) Modifications in sampling procedures as applied to studies on the bacteria and tubificid oligochaetes inhabiting aquatic sediments. *J. Fish. Res. Board Can.*, **26**, 2581–2593.

Brooks J.G. (1972) *Artificial substrate samplers as indicators of water quality.* Dissertation. University of Wisconsin, Madison, USA.

Burton W. & Flannagan J.F. (1973) An improved Ekman-type grab. *J. Fish. Res. Board Can.*, **30**, 287–290.

Chutter F.M. (1972) Reappraisal of Needham and Usinger's data on the variability of a stream fauna when sampled with a Surber sampler. *Limnol. Oceanogr.*, **17**, 139–141.

Chutter F.M. & Noble R.G. (1966) The reliability of a method of sampling stream invertebrates. *Arch. Hydrobiol.*, **62**, 95–103.

Ciborowski J.J.H. (1979) The effects of extended photoperiods on the drift of the mayfly *Ephemerella subvaria* McDunnough (Ephemeroptera: Ephemerellidae). *Hydrobiologia*, **62**, 209–214.

Ciborowski J.J.H. & Corkum L.D. (1980) Importance of behavior to the re-establishment of drifting Ephemeroptera. In J.F.Flannagan & K.E.Marshall (eds.), *Advances in Ephemeroptera Biology*. New York: Plenum Press.

Ciborowski J.J.H., Pointing P.J. & Corkum L.D. (1977) The effect of current velocity and sediment on the drift of the mayfly, *Ephemerella subvaria* McDunnough. *Freshw. Biol.*, **7**, 567–572.

Coleman M.J. & Hynes H.B.N. (1970) The vertical distribution of the invertebrate fauna in the bed of a stream. *Limnol. Oceanogr.*, **15**, 31–40.

Corkum L.D. (1978a) The influence of density and behavioural type on the active entry of two mayfly species (Ephemeroptera) into the water column. *Can. J. Zool.*, **56**, 1201–1206.

Corkum L.D. (1978b) Is benthic activity of stream invertebrates related to behavioral drift? *Can. J. Zool.*, **56**, 2457–2459.

Corkum L.D. & Clifford H.F. (1980) The importance of species associations and substrate types to behavioural drift. In J.F.Flannagan & K.E.Marshall (eds.), *Advances in Ephemeroptera Biology*. New York: Plenum Press.

Corkum L.D. & Pointing P.J. (1979) Nymphal development of *Baetis vagans* McDonnough (Ephemeroptera: Baetidae) and drift habits of large nymphs. *Can. J. Zool.*, **57**, 2347–2354.

Corkum L.D., Pointing P.J. & Ciborowski J.J.H. (1977) The influence of current velocity and substrate on the distribution and drift of two species of mayflies (Ephemeroptera). *Can. J. Zool.*, **55**, 1970–1977.

Crossman J.S. & Cairns J., Jr. (1974) A comparative study between two different and artificial substrate samplers and regular sampling techniques. *Hydrobiologia*, **44**, 517–522.

Cuba T.R. (1981) Diversity: a two level approach. *Ecology*, **62**, 278–279.

Culp J.M. & Davies R.W. (1980) Reciprocal averaging and polar ordination as techniques for analyzing lotic macroinvertebrate communities. *Can. J. Fish. Aquat. Sci.*, **37**, 1358–1364.

Cummins K.W. (1962) An evaluation of some techniques for the collection and analysis of benthic samples with special emphasis on lotic waters. *Am. Midl. Nat.*, **67**, 477–504.

Cushman R.M., Shugart H.H., Jr., Hildebrand S.G. & Elwood J.W. (1978) The effect of growth curve and sampling regime on instantaneous growth, removal-summation, and Hynes/Hamilton estimates of aquatic insect production: A computer simulation. *Limnol. Oceanogr.*, **23**, 184–189.

Dall P.C. (1979) A sampling technique for littoral stone dwelling organisms. *Oikos*, **33**, 106–112.

DeBovee F., Soyer J. & Albert P.H. (1974) The importance of mesh size for the extraction of the muddy bottom meiofauna. *Limnol. Oceanogr.*, **19**, 350–354.

Dimond J.B. (1967) Evidence that drift of stream benthos is density related. *Ecology*, **48**, 855–857.

Downing J.A. (1979) Aggregation, transformation, and the design of benthos sampling programs. *J. Fish. Res. Board Can.*, **36**, 1454–1463.

Elliott J.M. (1971a) Upstream movements of benthic invertebrates in a Lake District stream. *J. Anim. Ecol.*, **40**, 235–252.

Elliott J.M. (1971b) The distances travelled by drifting invertebrates in a Lake District stream. *Oecologia*, **6**, 350–359.

Elliott J.M. (1977) *Some Methods for the Statistical Analysis of Samples of Benthic Invertebrates*. 2nd ed. Ambleside: Freshwater Biol. Assoc. Sci. Publ. 25.

Enfield M.A. & Pritchard G. (1977) Methods for sampling immature stages of *Aedes* spp. (Diptera: Culicidae) in temporary ponds. *Can. Ent.*, **109**, 1435–1444.

Farris R.A. & Creeze M. (1976) An improved Reineck box for sampling coarse sand. *Int. Rev. Gesamten Hydrobiol.*, **61**, 703–705.

Flannagan J.F. (1970) Efficiencies of various grabs and corers in sampling freshwater benthos. *J. Fish. Res. Board Can.*, **27**, 1691–1700.

Frost S., Huni A. & Kershaw W.E. (1971) Evaluation of a kicking technique for sampling stream bottom fauna. *Can J. Zool.*, **49**, 167–173.

Gale W.F. (1971) A shallow water core sampler. *Prog. Fish Cult.*, **33**, 238–239.

Gale W.F. & Thompson J.D. (1975) A suction sampler for quantitative sampling on rocky substrates in rivers. *Trans. Am. Fish. Soc.*, **104**, 398–405.

Gallepp G.W. (1974) Behavioral ecology of *Brachycentrus occidentalis* Banks during the pupation period. *Ecology*, **55**, 1238–1294.

Gerking S.D. (1957) A method of sampling the littoral macrofauna and its application. *Ecology*, **38**, 219–226.

Gillespie D.M. & Benke A.C. (1979) Methods for calculating cohort production from field data—some relationships. *Limnol. Oceanogr.*, **24**, 171–176.

Gillespie D.M. & Brown C.J.D. (1966) A quantitative sampler for macroinvertebrates associated with aquatic macrophytes. *Limnol. Oceanogr.*, **11**, 404–406.

Glime J.M. & Clemons R.M. (1972) Species diversity of stream insects on *Fontinalis spp.* compared to diversity on artificial substrates. *Ecology*, **53**, 458–464.

Godbout L. & Hynes H.B.N. (1983) The three dimensional distribution of the fauna in a single riffle in a stream in Ontario. *Hydrobiologia*, **97**, 87–96.

Hakala I. (1971) A new model of the Kajak bottom sampler and other improvements in the zoobenthos sampling technique. *Ann. Zool. Fenn.*, **8**, 422–426.

Hales D.C. & Gaufin A.R. (1969) Comparison of two types of stream insect drift nets. *Limnol. Oceanogr.*, **14**, 459–461.

Hart D.D. & Resh V.H. (1980) Movement patterns and foraging ecology of a stream caddisfly larva. *Can. J. Zool.*, **38**, 1174–1185.

Henrickson L. & Oscarson H. (1978) A quantitative sampler for air-breathing aquatic insects. *Freshw. Biol.*, **8**, 73–77.

Higer A.L. & Kolipinski M.C. (1967) Pull-up trap: a quantitative device for sampling shallow-water animals. *Ecology*, **48**, 1008–1009.

Higler L.W.G. (1977) Macrofauna-cenoses on *Stratiotes* plants in Dutch broads. *Rijksinstituut voor Natuurbeheer Verh.*, **11**, 86 pp.

Hildebrand S.G. (1974) The relation of drift to benthos density and food in an artificial stream. *Limnol. Oceanogr.*, **19**, 951–957.

Hildrew A.G. & Townsend C.R. (1976) The distribution of two predators and their prey in an iron rich stream. *J. Anim. Ecol.*, **45**, 41–57.

Hildrew A.G. & Townsend C.R. (1977) The influence of substrate on the functional response of *Plectrocnemia conspera* (Curtis) larvae (Trichoptera: Polycentropodidae). *Oecologia*, **31**, 21–26.

Hilsenhoff W.L. (1969) An artificial substrate device for sampling benthis stream invertebrates. *Limnol. Oceanogr.*, **14**, 465–471.

Howmiller R.P. (1971) A comparison of the effectiveness of Ekman and Ponar grabs. *Trans. Am. Fish. Soc.*, **100**, 560–564.

Hughes D.A. (1970) Some factors affecting drift and upstream movements of *Gammarus pulex. Ecology*, **51**, 301–305.

Hulberg L.W. & Oliver J.S. (1980) Caging manipulations in marine soft-bottom communities: importance of animal interactions or sedimentary habitat modification. *Can. J. Fish. Aquat. Sci.*, **37**, 1130–1139.

Hultin L., Svensson B. & Ulfstrand S. (1969) Upstream movements of insects in a south Swedish small stream. *Oikos*, **20**, 553–557.

Hynes H.B.N. (1970) *The Ecology of Running Waters*. Toronto: Univ. of Toronto Press.

Hynes H.B.N. (1971) Benthos of flowing water. In W.T.Edmondson & G.C.Winberg (eds.), *A Manual on Methods for the Assessment of Secondary Productivity in Fresh Waters*. IBP Handbook No. 17. Oxford: Blackwell.

Hynes H.B.N. (1974) Further studies on the distribution of stream animals within the substratum. *Limnol. Oceanogr.*, **19**, 92–99.

Jónasson A. & Olausson E. (1966) New devices for sediment sampling. *Mar. Geol.*, **4**, 365–372.

Kaesler R.L. & Herricks E.E. (1979) Hierarchical diversity of communities of aquatic insects and fish. *Wat. Res. Bull.*, **15**, 1117–1125.

Kajak Z. (1963) Analysis of quantitative benthic methods. *Ekol. Pol.*, **11**, 1–56.

Kajak Z. (1971) Benthos of standing water. In W.T.Edmondson & G.G.Winberg (eds), *A Manual on Methods for the Assessment of Secondary Productivity in Fresh Waters*. IBP Handbook No. 17. Oxford: Blackwell.

Karlsson M., Bohlin T. & Stenson J. (1976) Core sampling and flotation: Two methods to reduce costs of chironomid population study. *Oikos*, **27**, 336–338.

Keller V.A. (1975) [The drift and its ecological significance. Experimental investigation on *Ecdyonurus venosus* (Fabr.) in a stream model.] *Swiss J. Hydrobiol.*, **37**, 294–331. (German, English summary).

Kroger R.L. (1972) Underestimation of the standing crop by Surber sampler. *Limnol. Oceanogr.*, **17**, 475–478.

Krueger, C.C. & Martin F.B. (1980) Computation of confidence intervals for the size-frequency (Hynes) method of estimating secondary production. *Limnol. Oceanogr.*, **25**, 774–777.

Lane E.D. (1974) An improved method of Surber sampling for bottom and drift fauna in a small stream. *Prog. Fish. Cult.*, **36**, 20–22.

Legner E.F., Medved R.A. & Sjogren R.D. (1975) Quantitative water column samples for insects in shallow aquatic habitats. *Proc. Calif. Mosq. Control Assoc.*, **43**, 110–115.

Lehmkuhl D.M. & Anderson N.H. (1972) Microdistribution and density as factors affecting the downstream drift of mayflies. *Ecology*, **53**, 661–667.

Leonard J.W. (1939) Comments on the adequacy of accepted stream bottom sampling technique. *Trans. N. Am. Wildl. Conf.*, **4**, 288–295.

Macan, T.T. (1949) Survey of a moorland fishpond. *J. Anim. Ecol.*, **18**, 160–186.

Macan T.T. (1958) Methods of sampling the bottom fauna in stony streams. *Mitt. Int. Ver. Limnol.*, **8**, 1–21.

Macan T.T. (1976) A twenty-one year study of the water-bugs in a moorland fishpond. *J. Anim. Ecol.*, **45**, 913–922.

Macan T.T. (1977a) The fauna in the vegetation of a moorland fishpond as revealed by different methods of collecting. *Hydrobiologia*, **55**, 3–15.

Macan T.T. (1977b) A twenty-one year study of the fauna in the vegetation of a moorland fishpond. *Arch. Hydrobiol.*, **81**, 1–24.

Mackay R.J. (1977) Behavior of *Pyncnopsyche* (Trichoptera: Limnephilidae) on mineral substrates in lab streams. *Ecology*, **58**, 191–195.

Mackey A.P. (1972) An air-lift for sampling freshwater benthos. *Oikos*, **23**, 413–415.

Mackie G.L. & Qadri S.V. (1971) A quantitative sampler for aquatic phytomacro-fauna. *J. Fish. Res. Board Can.*, **28**, 1322–1324.

Mason J.C. (1976) Evaluating a substrate tray for sampling the invertebrate fauna of small streams, with comment on general sampling problems. *Arch. Hydrobiol.*, **78**, 51–70.

Menzie C.A. (1980) A note on the Hynes method of estimating secondary production. *Limnol. Oceanogr.*, **25**, 770–773.

Merritt R.W., Cummins K.W. & Resh V.H. (1978) Collecting, sampling, and rearing methods for aquatic insects. In R.W.Merritt & K.W.Cummins (eds.), *An Introduction to the Aquatic Insects of North America*, Dubuque, Iowa, USA: Kendall–Hunt Publ. Co.

Milbrink G. & Wiederholm T. (1973) Sampling efficiency of four types of mud bottom samplers. *Oikos*, **24**, 479–482.

Minto M.L. (1977) A sampling device for the invertebrate fauna of aquatic vegetation. *Freshw. Biol.*, **7**, 425–430.

Müller K. (1974) Stream drift as a chronobiological phenomenon in running water ecosystems. *Ann. Rev. Ecol. Syst.*, **5**, 309–323.

Mundie J.H. (1971) Sampling benthos and substrate materials down to 50 microns in size in shallow streams. *J. Fish. Res. Board Can.*, **28**, 849–860.

Murray T. D. & Charles W.N. (1975) A pneumatic grab for obtaining large, undisturbed mud samples: its construction and some applications for measuring the growth of larvae and emergence of adult Chironomidae. *Freshw. Biol.*, **5**, 205–210.

Needham P.R. & Usinger R.L. (1956) Variability in the macrofauna of a single riffle in Prosser Creek, California, as indicated by the Surber sampler. *Hilgardia*, **14**, 383–409.

Nelson D.J. & Scott D.C. (1962) Role of detritus in the productivity of a rock outcrop community in a piedmont stream. *Limnol. Oceanogr.*, **7**, 396–413.

O'Conner J.F. (1974) An apparatus for sampling gravel substrates in streams. *Limnol. Oceanogr.*, **19**, 1007–1011.

Pearson R.G., Litterick M.R. & Jones N.V. (1973) An air-lift for quantitative sampling of the benthos. *Freshw. Biol.*, **3**, 309–315.

Pearson W.D. & Kramer R.H. (1969) A drift sampler driven by a waterwheel. *Limnol. Oceanogr.*, **14**, 462–465.

Pearson W.D. & Kramer R.H. (1971) Drift and production of two aquatic insects in a mountain stream. *Ecol. Monogr.*, **42**, 365–386.

Peckarsky B.L. (1979a) Biological interactions as determinants of the distributions of benthic invertebrates in the substrate of stony streams. *Limnol. Oceanogr.*, **24**, 59–68.

Peckarsky B.L. (1979b) *Experimental manipulations involving the determinants of the spatial distribution of benthic invertebrates within the substrate of stony streams.* Dissertation. University of Wisconsin, Madison.

Peckarsky B.L. (1980a) The influence of detritus on colonization of stream insects. *Can J. Fish. Aquat. Sci.*, **37**, 957–963.

Peckarsky B.L. (1980b) Predator-prey interactions between stoneflies and mayflies: behavioral observations. *Ecology*, **61**, 932–943.

Peckarsky B.L. (1981) Reply to comment by Sell. *Limnol. Oceanogr.*, **26**, 982–987.

Peckarsky B.L. & Cook K.Z. (1981) Effects of Keystone Mine effluent on colonization of stream benthos. *Environ. Entom.*, **10**, 864–871.

Peckarsky B.L. & Dodson S.I. (1980a) Do stonefly predators influence benthic distributions in streams? *Ecology*, **61**, 1275–1282.

Peckarsky B.L. & Dodson S.I. (1980b) An experimental analysis of biological factors contributing to stream community structure. *Ecology*, **61**, 1283–1290.

Peet R.K. (1974) The measurement of species diversity. *Ann. Rev. Ecol. Syst.*, **5**, 258–307.

Pollard J.E. (1981) Investigator differences associated with a kicking method for sampling macroinvertebrates. *J. Freshw. Ecol.*, **1**, 215–224.

Rabeni C.F. & Gibbs K.E. (1978) Comparison of two methods used by divers for sampling benthic invertebrates in deep rivers. *J. Fish. Res. Board Can.*, **35**, 332–336.

Radford D.S. & Hartland-Rowe R. (1971) Subsurface and surface sampling of benthic invertebrates in two streams. *Limnol. Oceanogr.*, **16**, 114–120.

Reisen W.K. & Prins R. (1972) Some ecological relationships of the invertebrate drift in Praters Creek, Pickens County, S. Carolina. *Ecology*, **53**, 876–884.

Resh V.H. (1975) The use of transect sampling in estimating single species production of aquatic insects. *Verh. Int. Ver. Limnol.*, **19**, 3089–3094.

Resh V.H. (1979) Sampling variability and life history features: basic considerations in the design of aquatic insect studies. *J. Fish. Res. Board Can.*, **36**, 290–311.

Rosenberg D.M. & Resh V.H. (1982) The use of artificial substrates in the study of freshwater macroinvertebrates. In J.Cairns, Jr. (ed.), *Artificial Substrates*. Ann Arbor: Ann Arbor Science Publishers.

Scherba S. Jr. & Gallucci V.F. (1976) The application of systematic sampling to a study of infauna variations in a soft substrate environment. *Fish. Bull.*, **74**, 937–948.

Tanner J.T. (1978) *Guide to the Study of Animal Populations*, Knoxville, Tenn.: University of Tennessee Press.

Townsend C.R. & Hildrew A.G. (1978) Predation and resource utilization by *Plectrocnemia conspersa* (Curtis) (Trichoptera: Polycentropodidae). In M.I.Crichton (ed.), *Proceedings of the Second International Symposium on Trichoptera*. The Hague: D.W.Junk.

Townsend C.R. & Hildrew A.G. (1979a) Foraging strategy and co-existence in a seasonal environment. *Oecologia*, **38**, 321–234.

Townsend C.R. & Hildrew A.G. (1979b) Resource partitioning by two freshwater invertebrate predators with contrasting foraging strategies. *J. Anim. Ecol.*, **48**, 909–920.

Ulfstrand S. (1968) Benthic animal communities in Lapland streams. *Oikos (Suppl.)*, **10**, 1–120.

Voshell J.R. & Simmons G.M. (1977) An evaluation of artificial substrates for sampling macrobenthos in reservoirs. *Hydrobiologia*, **53**, 257–269.

Walton E.O. Jr. (1980a) Active entry of stream benthic macroinvertebrates into the water column. *Hydrobiologia*, **74**, 129–139.

Walton E.O. Jr. (1980b) Invertebrate drift from predator-prey associations. *Ecology*, **61**, 1486–1497.

Walton E.O. Jr., Reice S.R. & Andrews R.W. (1977) The effects of density, sediment particle size, and velocity on drift of *Acroneuria abnormis* (Plecoptera). *Oikos*, **28**, 291–298.

Waters T.F. (1966) Production rate, population density and drift of stream invertebrates. *Ecology*, **47**, 595–604.

Waters T.F. (1972) The drift of stream insects. *Ann. Rev. Entom.*, **17**, 253–272.

Waters T.F. (1981) Seasonal patterns in production and drift of *Gammarus pseudolimneaus* in Valley Creek, Minnesota. *Ecology*, **62**, 1458–1466.

Waters T.F. & Knapp R.J. (1961) An improved stream bottom fauna sampler. *Trans. Am. Fish. Soc.*, **90**, 225–226.

Waters T.F. & Resh V.H. (1979) Ecological and statistical features of sampling insect populations in forest and aquatic environments. In G.P.Patil & M.Rosenzweig (eds.), *Contemporary Quantitative Ecology and Related Econometrics*, Fairland, Maryland: Int. Co-op. Publ. House.

Welch P.S. (1948) *Limnological Methods.* New York: McGraw-Hill.

Whittaker R.H. (1972) Evolution and measurements of species diversity. *Taxon*, **21**, 213–251.

Wiley M.J. & Kohler S.L. (1980) Positioning changes of mayfly nymphs due to behavioral regulation of oxygen consumption. *Can. J. Zool.*, **58**, 618–622.

Wiley M.J. & Kohler S.L. (1981) An assessment of biological interactions in an epilithic stream community using time-lapse cinematography. *Hydrobiologica*, **78**, 183–188.

Wiley M.J. & Kohler S.L. (in press) Behavioral adaptations of aquatic insects. In V.H.Resh & D.M.Rosenberg (eds.), *The Ecology of Aquatic Insects.* New York: Praeger Press.

Williams D.D. & Hynes H.B.N. (1974) The occurrence of benthos deep in the substratum of a stream. *Freshw. Biol.*, **4**, 233–256.

Zelt K.A. & Clifford H.F. (1972) Assessment of two mesh sizes for interpreting life cycles, standing crop and percentage composition of stream insects. *Freshw. Biol.*, **2**, 259–269.

Chapter 6. Sampling Aquatic Insect Emergence

I.J. DAVIES

1 Why Sample Insect Emergence?

In the last stage of their life cycle, aquatic insects undergo both a metamorphosis to the adult form and a transition from the aquatic to the terrestrial environment. This transition, or emergence, of adults is a prerequisite for reproduction and dispersal of each species. As a quantity, emergence represents the final component of insect production, a measure of the cumulative effects of growth, natural mortality and predation throughout the life cycle, and a potential net export of insect material from an aquatic system. Because the taxonomy of larval forms is so often poorly developed, the adults also provide the only means of identifying some insects.

After they have emerged, insects may be sampled by hand collecting, pitfall traps, sticky traps, sweep nets or light traps. Although each of these methods can yield a large number of specimens, catches often contain a high proportion of terrestrial species and give little information about the point of origin or absolute numbers of emerging insects.

Alternatively, aquatic insects can be intercepted on their way to the water surface or contained, once there, by a wide variety of funnel, tent, or box shaped devices known as emergence traps. These traps are passive samplers used to provide continuous or periodic records of emergence from fixed locations. Because traps are generally inexpensive to construct, easy to use, and yield specimens that do not have to be sorted from the sediment, many stations can be monitored with the minimum of effort. Emergence traps are often the only practical way of sampling habitats where boulders, gravel, bedrock or dense vegetation preclude the use of corers and grabs for sampling larval insects. In addition, the temporal sequence of emergence provides important information on insect life history and may be used in monitoring programs to document the effects of sudden environmental change.

The first published account on the use of emergence traps was given by Needham (1908): 'Quite as an experiment, and without expecting any large results, we made a tent of cheese cloth . . . and set it directly in the bed of Beaver Meadowbrook, just above the fish ponds, to capture and retain such winged insects as might upon transformation arise from the surface of the water beneath it. . . . Our first peep into it on the morning of the 16th was revelation. Insects of five orders in astonishing numbers had transformed beneath it, and were assembled under the ridge cord, waiting to be picked off. There were several square feet of Chironomidae in the top, and stone flies and crane flies and caddis flies and May flies were scattered all over the sides.'

Following this initial application, emergence traps have become widely used in the study of aquatic insect communities. Many of the common designs and trapping techniques have been previously summarized by Kajak (1957), Morgan (1971), and Mundie (1956, 1971a). The goals of this chapter are to update this information, review what is known about trap performance and the factors that affect it, discuss patterns of insect emergence, and examine some of the practical aspects of using emergence traps as sampling devices.

2 Some General Comments on Emergence Traps

Ideally, emergence traps should sample without bias, capture and retain both adults and exuviae, and allow subimagoes to continue their transformation into the full adult stage. Traps should protect individual specimens from damage by wind, waves, extremes of temperature and deterioration after death. Specimens inside a trap should be safe from predation by fish, invertebrates, and birds. Traps should also be easy to construct, install, and operate; they must be rugged, portable, relatively free of maintenance problems such as algal build-up and deterioration due to sunlight or rust; and, finally, they should be inexpensive. In practice, few traps approach this ideal standard. Problems arise because the spectrum of insect habitat is so diverse that no single trap design is adequate for all applications. To cope with local conditions of wind, waves, water depth, or emergent vegetation, design compromises must be made, with the result that a large number of specialized trap designs have evolved.

The process of choosing or designing a trap involves four distinct phases. First, the sampling requirements of an experiment or monitoring program must be defined. Considerations of sample size, adequate coverage of all habitats and ease of trap use may be of primary importance when emergence sampling is used to establish a species list, but is of little concern in an experimental program where traps of high sampling efficiency are needed to provide an accurate estimate of emergence. Second, trap choice is further restricted by the emergence habits of the taxa under study. For instance, many hemimetabolous species leave the water before eclosion—nymphs climb emergent vegetation and stones, or crawl shoreward onto the bank. Included in this group are the Odonata, most species of Plecoptera, and some Ephemeroptera. Among holometabolous insects, the Megaloptera and some species of Diptera and Trichoptera, also emerge from shore. Traps designed to monitor shore-emerging taxa must span the region between terrestrial and aquatic habitats without acting as a bridge or impeding the migrations of larvae or nymphs. Third, physical constraints of the habitat, such as water depth, current speed, wave action, and the occasional presence of large amounts of vegetation, play a role in the choice of a trap. As a general rule, traps should alter the sampling environment as little as possible. Final considerations include cost, portability, ease of trap use, and the required frequency of servicing. A number of published trap designs are outlined below. Details of their construction and operation are given in the Appendices, Sections 9.1, 9.2 and 9.3.

3 Trap Designs

3.1 Open water traps

Floating traps, illustrated in Fig. 6.1, enclose an area of lake surface (usually 0·25–0·5 m²) inside a tent or cage supported by a framework of wood or metal. Designs are kept light-weight and transparent by employing as much clear plastic or mesh in their construction as possible. Except for two models that operate in the semi-submerged mode (Fig. 6.1c, d), surface traps float with their open bases just below the water surface. Plastic coverings such as celluloid, acrylic sheet or polyethylene film (see Table 6.1) protect the catch from damage by wind or rain, but some screen covering is always necessary to reduce condensation build-up. Mesh with a 250 μm opening will retain even the smallest insects. To remove the catch, traps are generally lifted out of the water with their bases covered and insects are collected by hand or with the aid of an entomological aspirator. Although some models lessen this work by including a removable sample bottle (Fig. 6.1c, d, e), insects often remain in the body of the trap and must still be recovered by lifting the trap. Floating traps offer the advantage of being able to collect large numbers of insects because they can be built to almost any dimension. Disadvantages are that surface traps are somewhat cumbersome to use, are susceptible to damage by wind, waves and vandals, and, except for Mundie's pyramidal design (Fig. 6.1c), do not retain pupae or floating insect exuviae. Details on the design and use of floating traps are given in Appendix 9.1.

Traps suspended in the water column are free of the influences of wind, rain, and the condensation problems associated with surface models. Submerged traps can also be made relatively immune to damage by wave action, depending on how they are suspended. Because the emergence of pupae or nymphs is restricted to an air space inside a removable bottle, collections of insects and exuvia can be made by simply removing and capping the sample bottle while holding it inverted under the water surface.

Chapter 6

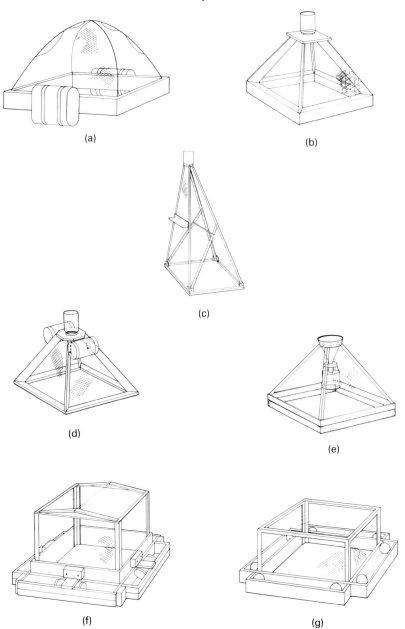

Fig. 6.1 Floating traps for open water. Designs originally described by: (a) Miller (1941), (b) Scott & Opdyke (1941), (c) Mundie (1971a), (d) Wohlschlag (1950), (e) Boyle (1979), (f) Macan (1949), (g) Morgan (1958).

Table 6.1 Properties of common plastics used to make emergence traps.

Type	Relative cost	Properties	Solvent or bonding technique
Acrylic (sheet)	High	Colourless, transparent, strong, degrades very slowly in sunlight, brittle, good resistance to oil and gasoline, S.G.[1] = 1·2, R.I.[2] = 1·5.	Methylene chloride*, Methyl-ethyl-ketone.
Cellulose acetate (sheet)	Medium	Colourless, good transparency, flexible, quickly discolours and becomes brittle in sunlight, good resistance to oil and gasoline, thermoforming[3], S.G. = 1·3, R.I. = 1·5.	Acetone*, Chloroform, Ethyl acetate, Methyl-ethyl-ketone.
Cellulose acetate butyrate (sheet)	Medium	Colourless, good transparency, flexible, degrades slowly in sunlight (embrittles, discolours), good resistance to oil and gasoline, thermoforming, S.G. = 1·2, R.I. = 1·5.	Acetone*, Ethyl acetate, Methyl-ethyl-ketone, Methyl cellosolve.
Cellulose acetate propionate (sheet)	Medium	Colourless, good transparency, flexible, degrades at a moderate rate in sunlight (embrittles, discolours), thermoforming, S.G. = >1.	Ethyl acetate, Methyl-ethyl-ketone, Methyl cellosolve.
Polycarbonate (sheet)	High	Colourless, good transparency, flexible, high impact strength, high temperature resistance, degrades slowly in sunlight, S.G. = 1·2, R.I. = 1·6.	Methylene chloride*.
Polyethylene (film)	Low	Colourless, slight opacity, flexible, chemically inert degrades at a moderate rate in sunlight, S.G. = 0·91–0·94, R.I. = 1·5.	Not soluble, Glues ineffective, Heat sealing*.
Polystyrene	Medium	Colourless, good transparency, light-weight, brittle, degrades quickly in sunlight, poor resistance to oil and gasoline, S.G. = 1·1, R.I. = 1·6.	Toluol, Xylol, 'Model Cement'.
Vinyl (sheet)	Medium	Colourless, good transparency, flexible, thermoforming, S.G. = 1·2 (see Flannagan & Lawler (1972) for light transmission characteristics).	Tetrahydrofuran, Methylene chloride, Cyclohexanone, Ethyl acetate, Heat sealing.

[1] S.G. = Specific gravity
[2] R.I. = Refractive index
[3] will soften and can be easily worked at temperatures <100 °C
* indicates best solvent or method of bonding

Disadvantages of the submerged design include the rapid build-up of algae and detritus on the trap, which reduces its transparency, the tendency of the sample bottle to become clogged with blue-green algae or tree pollen, the limited volume of air inside to house insects and keep them alive once they have emerged, and the fact that Ephemeroptera or other hemimetabolous insects seldom complete the transition from subimagoe to adult inside the trap. Further, restrictions on the size of the trap, imposed by the capacity of the sample bottle, structural strength of materials and manageability, usually limit sampling area to between 0·10 and 0·25 m².

Early versions of the submerged funnel (Fig. 6.2 and Fig. 6.3a) were constructed from metal mesh supported and strengthened by a stiff wire frame. These traps were heavy, expensive, time consuming to build, and rather opaque. Plastics dominate the list of construction materials in more recent

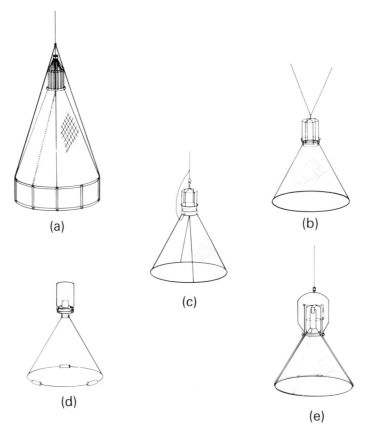

Fig. 6.2 Submerged traps for open water. (I) Designs originally described by: (a) Grandilewskaja-Decksbach (1935), (b) Brundin (1949), (c) Mundie (1955), (d) Palmén (1955), (e) Jónasson (1954).

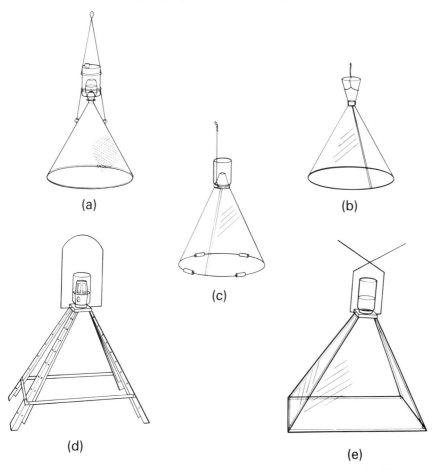

Fig. 6.3 Submerged traps for open water. (II) Designs originally described by: (a) Borutsky (1955), (b) Sublette & Dendy (1959), (c) Hamilton (1965), (d) Fast (1972), (e) Welch (1973).

models (Fig. 6.3b, c, d, e); the properties of common plastics are given in Table 6.1, as an aid to designers. Details of several models of submerged funnel traps are summarized in Appendix 9.1.

To illustrate some practical aspects of trap construction, installation and use, I have chosen as an example an inexpensive and versatile version of Hamilton's (1965) design for further description.

3.1.1 Construction of a submerged funnel trap

Referring to Fig. 6.4a, the two parameters which define sampling area (A) and shape of a submerged funnel trap are: its basal diameter (2R′); and height (h)

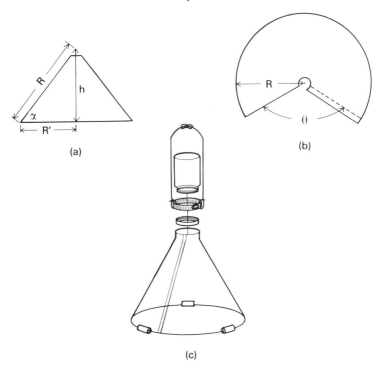

(a)

(b)

(c)

Fig. 6.4 Construction details of a submerged funnel trap. (a) Basic specifications, (b) pattern design, (c) exploded view of the final trap.

or pitch angle (α) of the cone [where $R' = +\sqrt{A/\pi}$ and $\alpha = \tan^{-1}(h/R')$]. Once these specifications have been finalized, a pattern for forming the cone from sheet plastic (Fig. 6.4b) can be drawn. The radius (R) of the circular pattern equals $R'/\cos\alpha$ and the angle of the pie shaped cut-out (θ) is 360 − (360 × cos α) degrees. Note than an extra 1 cm of material is left to allow for seam overlap.

Although a variety of clear plastics may be used to form the cone, cellulose acetate butyrate (0·75–1·00 mm thickness) offers some advantages over other materials listed in Table 6.1. It has good mechanical, chemical and optical properties, can be easily shaped when heated (i.e. is a thermoforming plastic), is quite resistant to degradation by sunlight, and is widely available at moderate cost.

Trap blanks cut according to the pattern (Fig. 6.4b) are made into cones by bringing the two straight sides together and clamping them between wood strips to form an overlapping seam. A small amount of acetone dispensed from a hypodermic syringe along the edge of the overlap will be drawn in between the two layers of plastic by capillary action to create a solvent weld.

Clamps may be removed after five minutes, but the seam should be left to harden overnight before proceeding.

Once the seam has set, the apex of the cone is softened, either in boiling water or with a 'heat gun', and formed into a cylindrical collar by pushing a glass jar or other object of the correct diameter through the hole in the top of the cone from the inside. A Bakelite jar lid, with its center portion removed to within 6 mm of the rim, is fitted into the collar (Fig. 6.4c) and held in place by a gear-type stainless hose clamp, set over the outside of the collar and tightened. The lid reinforces the cone and serves as a threaded attachment point for a glass sample bottle. Reheating the neck of the trap shrinks the acetate plastic tightly around the lid. Excess material can now be cut away. Split lead weights (gill net leads) in 2–3 cm lengths are crimped over the basal edge of the cone to provide trap stability. These weights grip well if the surface of the plastic has been roughened at the attachment points by burning in shallow grooves or holes with a soldering iron.

A loop of 45 kg breaking strength, nylon monofilament (marine fishing line) tied around the hose clamp forms a suspension bridle. Wear on the bridle can be reduced by wrapping the clamp with vinyl tape and by stringing a short length of stiff vinyl or rubber tube onto the monofilament to prevent the bridle from kinking when the trap is hung from a surface float by a piece of strong fishing line. An alternate suspension scheme, employed for its shock absorbing characteristics, uses a bridle made of surgical rubber tubing attached either to the neck of the trap (Dr. H.E. Welch, Freshwater Institute, personal communication), or directly to the cone (Rosenberg *et al.* 1980).

3.1.2 Anchoring techniques

The choice of an anchoring system can greatly influence trap performance. While a trap that sits directly on the bottom requires only a single line to raise and lower it or attach it to a marker float, suspended traps require a more complex mooring.

The simplest technique uses a single rock anchor attached to a float (Fig. 6.5a) to hold the trap in position. Unfortunately, this method does not stabilize traps against wind and wave action. Float movements may tangle the trap in the anchor line or confound the interpretation of spatial patterns of emergence in areas where the substrate is not uniform. During periods of calm, the trap may hang directly over the portion of the bottom disturbed by the anchor, or the mooring line may interfere by tilting the trap.

The advantage gained by adding a second anchor (Fig. 6.5d) usually outweighs the additional cost and effort involved. Anchors should be placed parallel to the prevailing wind and far enough apart so the ropes rise to the surface at an angle of 50–60 degrees. By keeping the lines tight, a trap can be

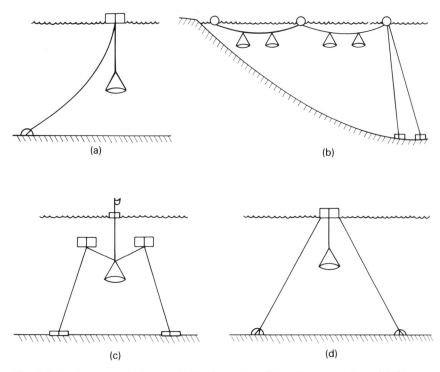

Fig. 6.5 Anchoring techniques. (a) Single anchor, (b) cable suspension with floats, (c) a submerged suspension scheme (d) double anchored surface float.

held on station, free of interference from anchors or mooring ropes. The effect of wave action is also reduced as waves tend to break over the float rather than lift it. To lessen strain on the mooring ropes, small floats should be used at the most exposed stations.

Submerged buoys (Fig. 6.5c), described by Welch (1973), are a practical alternative to surface floats. Although somewhat more costly and time consuming to install they allow traps to be hung beneath ice. Submerged floats can also be used to keep traps secure from wave action or to make stations less conspicuous and therefore less susceptible to unwanted inspections or vandalism.

Mundie (1971a) described a method for suspending traps from a taut cable (Fig. 6.5b) held at one end by a large anchor in deep water, supported by floats along its length, and fastened to shore. Although the method allows an investigator access to traps simply by pulling a small boat along the cable from station to station, it is cumbersome to install, may present a hazard to navigation, and does not protect traps from damage by wave action that causes vertical oscillations in the cable.

3.1.3 Floats

Foam plastics dominate the list of flotation materials because they are convenient to use and widely available. Polyethylene and polypropylene foams are extremely durable but most expensive; closed cell urethane foam is less costly but has poor abrasion resistance. Expanded polystyrene, sold either in closed cell form (Styrofoam®) or as beads bonded into sheets or blocks, is the most commonly used material even though it has low resistance to abrasion and may become rapidly colonized by burrowing insect larvae (see Section 4.4). These disadvantages may be partially overcome by sealing floats in polyethylene bags (Fig. 6.6a). Plastic strapping (industrial banding) clamped around the float makes a convenient attachment point for ropes. Flotation materials can also be sandwiched between two pieces of plywood which are then bolted together (Fig. 6.6b). Foams can easily be cut with a knife, saw, or hot wire, although some plastics give off toxic gases when heated. Air-filled floats made from sealed plastic pipe or empty containers provide useful alternatives to foam in many situations.

Ice cover in northern latitudes poses a special problem where emergence must be monitored at the same location over several years. Ropes and floats left to freeze in place will be dragged off station during spring break-up. If floats are removed and lines sunk below the maximum depth of ice cover it is often impossible to find them again.

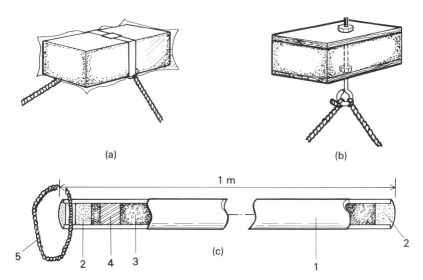

(a) (b) (c)

Fig. 6.6 Float designs. (a) Expanded polystyrene sealed in polyethylene film, (b) expanded polystyrene/plywood construction, (c) 'winter' marker float (shown in partial section view with components as follows; (1) aluminum tube, (2) silicone sealant, (3) foam polyethylene, (4) lead weight, (5) attachment rope).

To solve this problem I have developed an inexpensive 'winter float' (Fig. 6.6c) which marks stations in the autumn and allows anchor lines to be retrieved without damage the following spring. The float is a one meter length of seamless aluminium tube (22 mm o.d. × 1 mm wall), sealed at either end with a plug of silicone adhesive to make it air tight. Closed cell polyethylene foam rod (used in the concrete construction industry) provides back-up flotation, should any air leaks occur, and holds a lead weight (85–90 g) firmly against one end of the tube. The weight keeps the tube floating upright in the water with 80 % of its length submerged. Lines attached to the float are held beneath the ice when the top part freezes in place. In the spring, heat from sunlight, warm air or meltwater is rapidly distributed to all parts of the ice in contact with the aluminium, and the tube melts free along its entire length. As ice breaks away from shore and begins to move, tension on the anchor ropes pulls the tube through the hole melted around it, allowing it to float safely under the ice.

3.2 Traps for shallow standing water

Many of the previously mentioned open water traps can be used or adapted to sample shallow ponds or inshore areas; however, a number of traps have been made specifically for this purpose. Unlike their open water counterparts, built to withstand wind and waves, these shallow water traps have been designed to accommodate emergent vegetation, prevent condensation or anaerobic conditions from developing inside the trap, and allow insects to move freely into the shallows prior to emergence.

Staked or floating traps for heavily vegetated areas, illustrated in Fig. 6.7 and described in detail in Appendix 9.2, are tall form structures with basal areas between 0·1 to 0·7 m², built to stand over emergent plants. These traps are either installed with their bases above the substrate or moved frequently to accommodate the migrations of larvae or nymphs in this habitat. Some designs are equipped with removable sample bottles, but, because the efficiency of these collecting devices is variable, the entire trap should be emptied at frequent intervals to prevent catch loss.

Traps shown in Fig. 6.8 and described in Appendix 9.2 are intended for surface or semi-submerged use in shallow areas without emergent vegetation. With the exception of a floating silk cone (Frank 1965; Fig. 6.8d), none of these traps was designed to collect insect exuviae.

Figures 6.9 and 6.10 illustrate traps which are set directly on the substrate in the shallows. Details of their construction and operation are given in Appendix 9.2. Fully submerged models in this category retain both insects and exuviae in an apical sample bottle and are set or emptied in the same manner as open water funnel traps. One notable exception is the design of

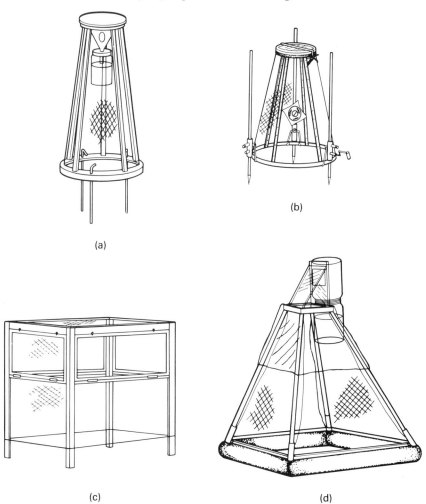

Fig. 6.7 Traps for shallow vegetated habitats. Traps originally described by: (a) Lammers (1977), (b) Corbet (1965), (c) Judd (1949), (d) LeSage & Harrison (1979).

Lindeberg (1958; Fig. 6.9c) which functions as a fully submerged funnel in shallow rockpools containing only a few centimetres of water. Exuviae may be collected from semi-submerged traps if the bottom of the trap is closed off with a screen prior to lifting it from the water (Butler 1980; Fig. 6.10c). Alternatively, exuviae can be contained within a cylinder at the surface (Kajak 1957; Fig. 6.9a) and collected after the upper trap portion has been removed. Traps set directly on the bottom should be well vented to prevent anaerobic conditions from developing inside. Sampling locations should also be changed periodically to avoid containment effects.

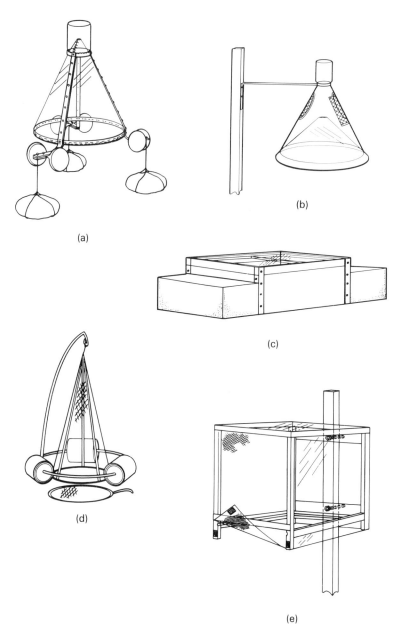

(a)

(b)

(c)

(d)

(e)

Fig. 6.8 Traps for shallow protected areas with little or no emergent vegetation. Designs originally described by: (a) Mundie (1956), (b) McCauley (1976), (c) Street & Titmus (1979), (d) Frank (1965), (e) Kimerle & Anderson (1967).

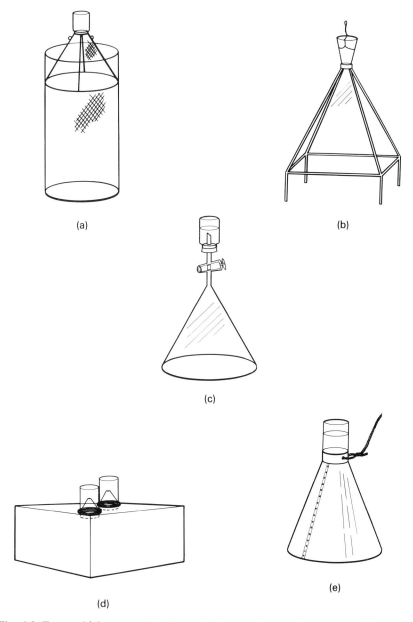

(a)

(b)

(c)

(d)

(e)

Fig. 6.9 Traps which are set directly on the bottom in standing water. (I) Designs originally described by: (a) Kajak (1957), (b) Sublette & Dendy (1959), (c) Lindeberg (1958), (d) Cheng (1974), (e) Mulla *et al*. (1974).

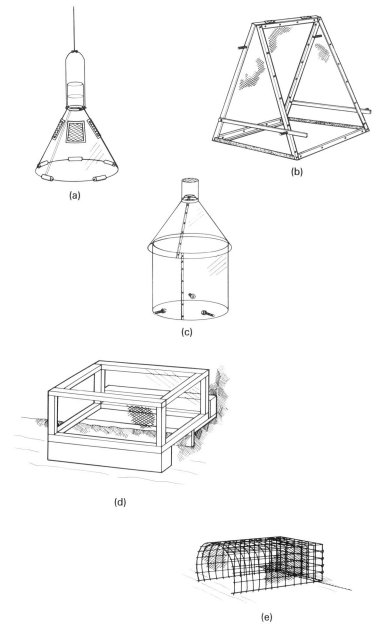

Fig. 6.10 Traps which are set directly on the bottom in standing water. (II) Designs originally described by: (a) Davies (1980), (b) Ettinger (1979), (c) Butler (1980), (d) Morgan (1971), (e) Cook & Horn (1968).

The water's edge is, perhaps, the most difficult of all shallow habitats to sample. Traps must not obstruct the movement of larvae or nymphs as they crawl shoreward to emerge, yet they must capture and retain adults. Two models illustrated here are a modified box (Morgan 1971; Fig. 6.10d) set with half its open base on land and the other half floating on the water, and a wire cage, lined with screen, built by Cook & Horn (1968) to monitor damselfly emergence from a pond (Fig. 6.10e). On rock shorelines with irregular shapes, a tent rather than a cage may make a more useful type of trap.

3.3 Traps for running water

Techniques for sampling insect emergence from flowing water differ somewhat from those employed in standing or open water habitats. Trap construction must be sufficiently robust to withstand 'worst-case' conditions, even though these may occur infrequently. Without some mechanism to compensate for fluctuating water levels, traps can become stranded during periods of low flow or inundated by a spate. In addition, a number of different trap designs may be needed to adequately sample the bank, pool, and riffle habitats present in a small section of stream.

A popular technique for monitoring emergence from small streams uses a tent or screen covered cage (0.5–1.0 m^2 basal area) set directly on the stream bottom with the edge of its open base below the water surface (Fig. 6.11a, b; Appendix 9.3). Drifting insects are exluded from these samplers, but, because the base is not sealed against the substrate, crawling larvae and nymphs are free to enter or leave. Debris accumulations on the upstream side of the cage can be minimized if the stream is allowed to flow through the trap under flaps along its base (Fig. 6.11c). With this technique, however, surface drift is also included in the estimate of emergence. As with floating traps used in open or standing water, the maximum mesh opening of the tent or cage covering should be 250 μm to retain the smallest insects. Except for the pyramid design shown in Fig. 6.11b, which is emptied from the outside via a sleeve in the wall, investigators must enter tents or cages to make collections. Care must be taken during this operation to avoid disturbing the substrate inside the trap.

A greenhouse (Fig. 6.11d), built to completely enclose an 11.1 m^2 area of a small brook and its banks, is an expanded version of the cage concept. While several workers have successfully used the design (Appendix 9.3), it is an expensive and relatively permanent structure that is poorly suited to most applications.

Whenever stream depth exceeds more than a few centimeters, floating or suspended traps become a practical alternative to stationary cages. Under conditions of low to moderate flow, many of the floating traps used to sample standing water can be adapted for this purpose. Surface drift can be excluded

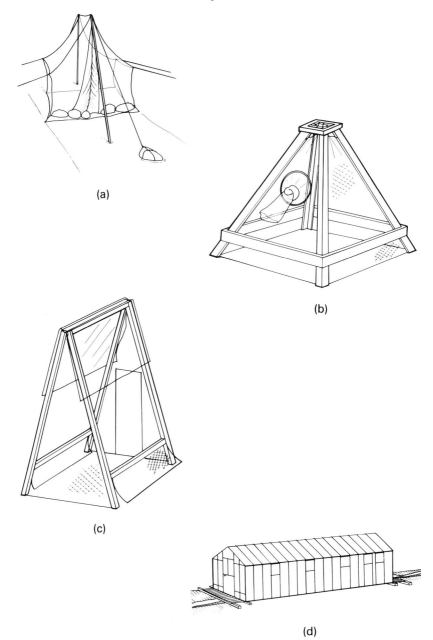

(a)

(b)

(c)

(d)

Fig. 6.11 Traps for shallow running water. Designs originally described by: (a) Needham (1908), (b) Harper & Magnin (1971), (c) Anderson & Wold (1972), (d) Illies (1971).

if the trap sides extend several centimetres into the water around the entrance. This modification also helps create a still pool inside, which reduces the number of insects that are washed away by current. Adding an entrance baffle similar to those illustrated in Fig. 6.12c and d further protects against catch loss. Where flows are more extreme, traps may be protected from upset by currents or floating debris by trailing them in the lee of a floating boom (Fig. 6.12b) or by enclosing the sampler in a rugged, boat-like float (Fig. 6.12a, but see also Section 4.4 on float colonization). Further details on the construction and use of floating traps are given in Appendix 9.3.

The problem with using surface traps to estimate emergence from running water is that effective sampling area and origin of the specimens cannot be easily discerned. Samples are a composite made up of insects from the substrate beneath the trap, those from the subsurface drift, and, in the case of some large species of Ephemeroptera and Trichoptera, those that arrive with the surface drift and simply crawl into the trap to use it for refuge or as a convenient place to oviposit.

Several traps have been built to selectively sample each of these catch components. A triangular pyramid (Fig. 6.13a), set with its base just above the substrate, and an open-bottom box with screened ends (Fig. 6.13b) placed directly on the stream bed, each sample insects from an area directly beneath and exclude drifting insects. The trap shown in Fig. 6.13c samples only the drift component. Surface or subsurface flow enters the trap through a narrow slit and exits from a large, partially screened opening at the rear and insects emerge into a pyramid-shaped air chamber located over the exit screen. Similarly, a plankton net attached to a wedge-shaped headpiece with a slit entrance (Mundie 1971b) can be used to collect drifting insects and exuviae from streams. A composite sample of drifting and emerging insects originating from a known area of stream bed can be obtained by constructing an experimental channel (Fig. 6.13d) which has a collecting net over its outlet and a fine mesh ($200\,\mu$m) screen attached to the upstream end to exclude stream drift from the outside. Finally, tent or cage traps similar to those previously mentioned for use in standing water can be set along the edge of the stream to monitor bank-emerging species, although, as Williams (1982) estimated, this component of emergence may represent less than 10 % of the total for a small, north-temperate stream.

As an alternative to sampling insects directly, Thienemann (1910) suggested that pupal exuviae, which are distinctive for most species, could be collected and used to monitor emergence. This method has been used by Humphries (1938) and Carrillo (1974) for lakes and by Coffman (1973) to study emergence phenology in a stream. While the sampler shown in Fig. 6.13c or the modified drift net of Mundie (1971b) (Appendix 9.3) can be used to collect exuviae from the surface drift, experiments by Wilson & Bright (1973) suggest

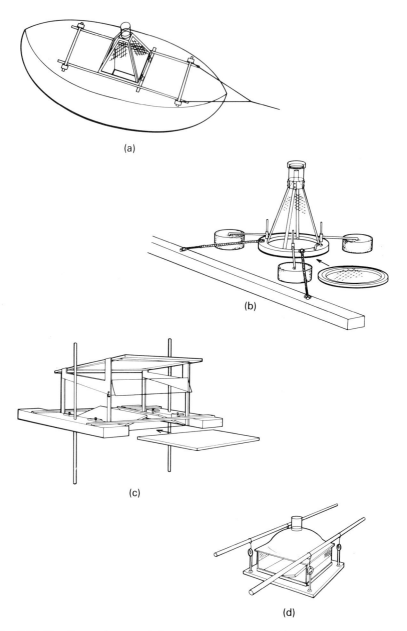

(a)

(b)

(c)

(d)

Fig. 6.12 Floating and suspended traps for streams and rivers. Designs originally described by: (a) Langford & Daffern (1975), (b) Corbet (1966), (c) Boerger (1981), (d) Nordlie & Arthur (1981).

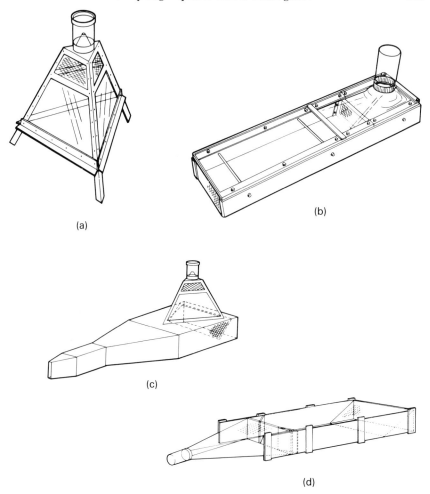

Fig. 6.13 River and stream traps designed for use directly on the substrate by: (a) Mundie (1956), (b) Hamilton (1969), (c) an enclosed bottom, drift sampler (Mundie 1964), (d) an experimental channel (Wartinbee & Coffman 1976).

that, at best, this method yields a qualitative sample of local populations. They concluded that exuviae only remain afloat in a stream for about 2 h and that many of these were washed up onto the bank or became entangled in weeds.

4 Factors Which Influence the Performance of Emergence Traps

Although much effort has been devoted to the design of emergence traps, few attempts have been made to understand the basic principles that govern their performance. Evidence to support claims that a particular design attribute improves trap performance or that one design is superior to another is often anecdotal, qualitative, or based on single experimental trials with little or no replication. It should not be assumed that these data are misleading or suspect, but rather that testing has been inadequate and that the list of variables which control trap sampling efficiency is incomplete.

4.1 Transparency

Light plays an important modifying role in insect emergence. For most species, patterns of emergence show a diel periodicity that is closely correlated with ambient light levels. Many species exhibit strong positive phototaxis, a behavior which Scott & Opdyke (1941) tried unsuccessfully to use to attract insects toward a clear glass sample bottle at the top of a darkened cage trap. Over a seven day test period the total number of insects accumulated in daily collections from a darkened trap was only 12 % of the emergence measured by an adjacent unshaded trap (Fig. 6.14), suggesting that pupae and nymphs actively avoided the darker one. This avoidance reaction was particularly noteworthy because most emergence occurred during low light conditions at dusk, with a second minor peak at dawn. Mundie (1957), Sublette & Dendy (1959) and Morgan *et al.* (1963) also mentioned that insects tended to avoid opaque traps.

A field experiment by Kimerle & Anderson (1967) compared the catch performance of clear and opaque versions of three trap types: a submerged pyramid, a floating pyramid and their staked box design, and showed consistent catch reductions of 80 % for opaque traps of each model (Fig. 6.14). Similar results were obtained when they used clear and blackened funnel traps to monitor emergence from a tank in two sets of well replicated laboratory experiments. Fast (1972) also noted catch reductions when he covered his traps with black plastic instead of the usual clear polyethylene.

Boerger (1981) used floating box traps to empirically define the relationship between trap opacity and relative sampling efficiency over a range of transparencies from 0 % to 80 %, in increments of 20 %. Within the limits of experimental error, results (Fig. 6.14) showed a threshold effect for chironomid emergence. No significant differences in efficiency were noted among traps that transmitted more than 60 % of ambient light, but below this level, catches were abruptly halved.

In the first of a set of three experiments in which I examined the effect of trap transparency on the catch performance of submerged funnels, a straight line relationship existed (Fig. 6.14, 1978 data) between these two variables when traps set 0·5–1·0 m above the bottom were used to sample chironomid emergence from a shallow (2 m) bay. Below 50 % transparency, submerged

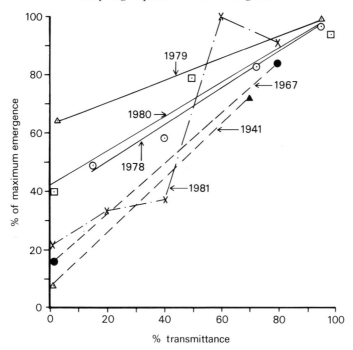

Fig. 6.14 Emergence trap transparency as a percent of surface light and its effect on trap capture efficiency. A linear decrease was assumed for all data except that of Boerger (1981) who proposed a threshold effect. Scott & Opdyke (1941), ▲, floating pyramid; Kimerle & Anderson (1967), ●, staked box; I.J.Davies (1978 ⊙, 1979 △, 1980 ⊡ unpublished data), submerged funnel; Boerger (1981), ×, floating box.

traps always sampled with a higher relative efficiency than the surface designs tested by Scott & Opdyke (1941), Kimerle & Anderson (1967) and Boerger (1981). In this and subsequent experiments a minimum of three traps of the Hamilton (1965) type, modified as shown in Fig. 6.4c, were used for each transparency. Funnels were sprayed on the outside surface with grey paint to achieve the required opacity and transparency was measured *in situ* with an underwater light meter. Sample bottles were not painted. Traps were sampled for one 24 h period each week throughout the ice free season and emergence rates for the periods between samplings were estimated by linear extrapolation in order to calculate season totals, which formed the basis of comparison among traps (see Section 8 for calculation details).

In order to determine whether the reduction measured in the first experiment applied when the distance between trap and substrate was increased, I hung clear and opaque traps 1 m below the lake surface over a deeper (5 m) location. Although individual estimates of emergence (Fig. 6.14,

1979 data) were quite variable, the mean value for opaque traps was 60 % of that for clear traps, suggesting that part of the observed reduction at shallow stations could be attributed to a bottom shading effect.

In a third experiment, traps set within 1 m of the bottom at a 2 m deep location, were removed between sampling periods to minimize their influence on periphyton growth or larval activity prior to emergence. Results (Fig. 6.14, 1980 data) were identical to those of the first experiment; thus either shading effects were established very rapidly or they did not cause pupae to migrate away from the area prior to emergence.

Regardless of whether the relationship is a linear or a threshold phenomenon, traps made from opaque materials catch fewer insects than clear traps of the same type. In practice, most standard traps transmit between 70 % and 95 % of ambient light. Unless design changes produce a major increase in transparency, improvements in catch performance will probably be obscured by normal sampling variance. However, algae and detritus build-ups, which prevent the traps from operating at maximum efficiency, and larval insects that colonize the trap surface and may eventually contaminate the catch should be periodically removed by brushing.

4.2 *Effect of trap size on catch*

The catch performance of an emergence trap can be influenced by size in two ways. First, effectiveness and reproducibility of a trap are related to the area which it samples. Large traps are best suited to collecting a few rare species along with numerous common insects, while small traps catch fewer specimens but generally show less sampling variability. Second, the efficiency of a trap may change with size; if the entire trap is enlarged or reduced characteristics such as internal temperature, shading, pupal avoidance or catch retention may change disproportionately. For example, in the arctic, where insect flight is often impaired by low temperatures, the percentage of the total catch entering the apical sample bottle of a floating pyramid trap will diminish as the trap is enlarged if height changes in proportion to basal area. Problems can also arise when some trap dimensions are scaled disproportionately. If the basal area of a submerged funnel trap is enlarged without increasing the size of the sample bottle, the air space inside may be too small to accommodate all of the specimens during periods of peak emergence. Many insects may then die due to overcrowding and fall back onto the water surface where they, along with the exuviae that remain, decay and sink or block the entrance of pupae into the sample bottle. I shall refer to this temporary decrease of capture efficiency as 'trap saturation'.

Although size and area are important variables in trap design, little has been done to quantify their relationship to catch performance. Scott &

Opdyke (1941) suggested that, on the basis of catch per unit area, floating pyramid traps with a basal opening of $0.25\,m^2$ were more efficient than $1.0\,m^2$ versions of the same design, used the previous year. Morgan *et al.* (1963) compared the catches of three adjacent box traps of basal areas 0.37, 0.46 and $0.70\,m^2$ and concluded that the mid-size trap was the most efficient. No optimum size should have been assigned in either case. Experimental designs were incomplete, unreplicated and ignored either spatial or temporal variations in emergence patterns.

Mundie (1956) suggested that ascending pupae might find it difficult to avoid large traps; capture efficiency should, therefore, be directly related to trap area. Palmén (1962), however, reported that submerged funnel traps with basal areas of 0.25, 0.50 and $1.0\,m^2$ sampled with equal efficiency, but no data were presented. In a well replicated experiment, Rosenberg & Wiens (1983) showed that submerged funnel traps with basal areas of 0.10 and $0.28\,m^2$ gave equal mean estimates of chironomid emergence from a reservoir over a 93 day experimental period. Although the means were equal, samples with the highest variability were consistently obtained from large traps.

The results of a short experiment which I conducted to determine relative capture efficiency of submerged funnel traps, each with the same size sample bottle but different basal areas, are shown in Table 6.2. All traps caught chironomids with equal efficiency and showed no evidence of saturation at an average emergence rate of 49 individuals $m^{-2}\,d^{-1}$. Coefficients of variation indicate the relative uniformity of emergence throughout the test location.

Table 6.2 Chironomid emergence measured at a $2\,m$ deep location in Lake 226 NE, Experimental Lakes Area (ELA), with submerged funnel traps of four different basal areas. All types were equipped with 375 ml (58 mm cap diameter) glass sample bottles. Tabulated values are estimates of total emergence (number m^{-2}) for each trap over a 37 day experimental period, calculated as the integral of 8 separate 24 h collections (see Section 8). Mean and coefficient of variation (C.V. = standard deviation as a percentage of the mean) are also listed for traps of each size.

Replicate No.	Trap area (m^2)			
	0.05	0.10	0.15	0.25
1.	1631	700	2641	1995
2.	2161	1707	2164	1330
3.	2874	1597	1021	—
Mean =	2222	1335	1942	1663
C.V.	28.1%	41.3%	42.9%	28.3%

4.3 Tilting of the trap

Jónasson (1954) and Morgan *et al.* (1963) speculated that submerged funnels may have underestimated emergence because the effective sampling area decreased each time the traps were tilted by wave action. The size of this reduction can be calculated by simplifying trap movements and expressing them as simple harmonic motion.

Consider a funnel with a cone pitch of 50°, driven by wave action so that it swings like a bell through an angle of 45° in each direction. Further angular displacement would cause air loss from the bottle and identify samples as invalid. At the maximum height of each swing, a projected view of the trap base becomes an elipse covering 71% of the maximum sampling area. An analytical solution to the equation of extreme trap motion shows that a time-averaged reduction of basal area is only 13% (F.A.J.Armstrong personal communication). In a real system, where such motion is rare, differences should routinely be less than 5%; an insignificant level of error.

4.4 Float colonization

A serious source of sample bias comes from the use of foam plastic floats around the basal entrance of surface traps. These plastics are rapidly colonized by insect larvae or nymphs that eventually mature and emerge into the trap. Langford & Daffern (1975) showed that, over the course of one season, foam polystyrene which surrounded the underwater entrance to their trap became heavily colonized by Ephemeroptera nymphs. Wrubleski & Rosenberg (in press) noted abnormally high catches of two species of *Glyptotendipes* (Chironomidae) in a version of the LeSage & Harrison (1979) trap. The source of these adults was a large colony of *Glyptotendipes* larvae that had established itself in the foam polystyrene floats around the base of the trap.

Minor modifications to trap design can usually eliminate or reduce sample bias caused by float colonization. Hollow plastic floats, available from commercial fishing supply outlets, empty plastic containers, or lengths of plastic pipe and standard plumbing fittings (of PVC or ABS plastic) can be used to construct air-filled floats in a variety of shapes and sizes. These floats can easily be kept free of larvae by periodically cleaning them, but because they can develop leaks, they lack the inherent reliability of foam materials. Alternatively, foam floats can be sealed in polyethylene bags or simply placed away from the trap entrance. Where water depth and current permit, the latter solution can be achieved by using submerged traps or by extending the entrance of a surface model considerably below the floats, a modification which also prevents catch loss when wave action breaks float contact with the water surface.

4.5 Trap depth

The interpretation of catch data from emergence traps used to sample standing or open water habitats depends on the premise that trap catch accurately reflects the distribution and abundance of larvae or nymphs in the substrate beneath. Implicit in this assumption is the understanding that insects rise vertically through the water column without being displaced horizontally and that fish predation is minimal as larvae or nymphs swim to the surface.

At shallow stations there is reasonable evidence to support this view. Borutsky (1939a) observed only a 4 % difference in the catches from traps set near the bottom and those hung just below the water surface. Palmén (1955) reported that a pair of funnel traps placed directly on the substrate and two traps suspended 0·5 m above the bottom at a 1·5 m deep station caught similar numbers of chironomids. In a separate study, Palmén (1962) found that pairs of traps set on the bottom, and at 1 m and 2 m above the bottom all gave the same estimate of emergence.

The extent to which fish prey on insects emerging from the profundal is also unknown. Predation can be eliminated by placing traps directly on the bottom, but, apart from the inconvenience of raising and lowering submerged traps over any distance, the method suffers from a technical problem related to the effect of pressure on gas volume and solubility. For each 10 m increment of depth, pressure increases by one atmosphere. Gas solubility is directly proportional to pressure, while gas volume varies as the reciprocal of pressure. Consequently, the air space inside a submerged trap is first compressed to some fraction of its original volume as the sampler is lowered into position, and continues to shrink as the air dissolves in the surrounding water; thus placing a practical lower limit of about 6–10 m depth on this technique. Jónasson (1954) noted an additional problem: traps set near the bottom at deeper stations caught chironomid pupae, most of which died or failed to emerge. An air bubble, which forms in the thoracic region under the pupal skin just prior to emergence, expands as pupae rise through the water column. It is possible that expansion of this gas bubble aids in the eclosion process. Pressure change may, therefore, be a necessary prerequisite for successful emergence.

Bretschko (1974) designed a funnel trap which sampled directly from the bottom, but, unlike previous designs, did not have to be lifted to be emptied. A long hose (25 mm diameter) connected the trap apex to a detachable sample bottle at the water surface. Preliminary results indicated that the hose did not inhibit emergence, as the number of adults in the trap corresponded roughly to the decrease in developing larval populations beneath.

4.6 Design of the sample chamber

Once insects are inside, the utility of an emergence trap is largely determined by the design of the sample chamber. In its simplest form, the chamber is an open-bottomed, air-filled cavity into which insects emerge. Commonly, no provisions are made to retain dead insects, keep specimens in good condition, or to prevent fish from feeding on the catch. Specimen removal is also difficult if the chamber is large. Several modifications have been introduced to improve on this basic design.

To facilitate sample removal, the entire catch of a submerged trap is contained within an emergence chamber formed by an air space inside a sample bottle. If a funnel (Fig. 6.3c) or 'stand pipe' (Fig. 6.2d, e) entrance is added at the mouth of the bottle, catch retention is improved, but the condition of the specimens remains a function of the number of insects in the chamber and the length of time which they are left there. Although sample retention is improved by this technique, overall sampling efficiency may be decreased if the modification blocks or discourages insects from entering the sample bottle, or if the presence of additional specimens damages other insects in the catch (Rosenberg & Wiens 1983).

A sloping baffle, added to some designs of surface trap (Figs. 6.1c, 6.8b, 6.12c, d), forms a one-way entrance that prevents catch loss. Baffles placed below the water surface inside a trap retain imagoes, pupae and exuviae but may do little to prevent fish predation; when placed above the water line (e.g. Fig. 6.12c, d) they keep adults dry in the upper portion of the trap and away from fish. Disadvantages of the latter arrangement are that pupae, exuviae and adults that fail to fly past the baffle are not included in the sample.

To simplify the job of removing insects from tent or cage traps, several models have been fitted with a removable sample bottle, usually located at the highest point of the funnel or pyramid-shaped emergence chamber, where flying insects tend to congregate. A funnel-shaped entrance (Fig. 6.7a) or an auxillary cone in the sample bottle (Fig. 6.8a) ensures that specimens which enter are retained. The efficiency of this sample collector will depend on the amount of light at the top of trap, the strength of the phototactic response and flight activity of the specimens. Each of these variables is related to time of day and air temperature, so the effectiveness of the collector will vary accordingly.

The use of preservatives (usually alcohol or formalin based) in the sample bottle of submerged (Fig. 6.3a) or surface traps (Figs. 6.1e, 6.7a, d, 6.12b) is not recommended. Although such preservatives may keep the catch from deteriorating, insects may not be saved in optimum condition. For example,

Mundie (1964) stated that chironimid wings do not inflate properly if the adults die immediately after emerging. Long periods of record may also be lost if preserving traps are left to sample for an extended time and become damaged or upset. Furthermore, Potter & Learner (1974) showed that some preservatives can adversely affect catch performance. Traps with 70 % alcohol or 4 % formalin (1·5 % aqueous formaldehyde) caught fewer insects than those containing a saline-detergent-copper sulfate solution.

4.7 *Temperature and frequency of emptying*

While the thermal tolerance limits of many insect species differ, their lifespans and decomposition rates after death are temperature dependent processes. High temperature inside a trap can cause significant mortality, such as that reported by Sandrock (1978) for the greenhouse design of Illies (1971). Although traps set over water tend to moderate daily extremes, mean temperature plays an important role in determining how frequently traps should be emptied.

For lake temperatures below 5 °C, Welch (1973) found no evidence of chironomid mortality when submerged traps were emptied at three day intervals. Laville (1971a) concluded that weekly collections were sufficient for traps at a cold alpine study site, whereas Mundie (1956) recommended that submerged traps with funnel entrances be emptied at least twice a week in temperate summer climates, and Palmén (1962) advised daily servicing.

Trap design also plays an important role in determining the frequency of sample collections. Experiments by Morgan & Waddell (1961) and Morgan *et al.* (1963) showed that open-bottom box traps emptied several times a day gave the same total estimate of emergence as those emptied once daily. No mortality occurred in the box traps, but several dead insects were found in a submerged funnel after only one day. Boerger (1981) found that over a four day sampling period, floating box traps with entrance baffles (Fig. 6.12c) retained specimens in good condition. Traps without baffles yielded the same total number of insects if sampled daily, but considerably fewer if left for the full four days. Tests by McCauley (1976) showed that catch loss from surface funnel traps (Fig. 6.8b), which were stocked with known numbers of one-day-old chironomid adults, remained fairly constant at 5 % of the catch per day over a 10 day experiment. In addition, loss rate was independent of stocking density up to a simulated emergence rate of 100 individuals $m^{-2} d^{-1}$.

4.8 *Predation*

Several studies have shown that predation is a problem in emergence traps. Reported instances of insect predators include: Empididae (Sprules 1947:

Morgan *et al.* 1963); Trichoptera larvae (Jónasson 1954); halipid and gyrinid beetles (Morgan *et al.* 1963); spiders (Morgan *et al.* 1963); mites (Mundie 1956); dragonflies and damselflies (LeSage & Harrison 1979). In addition, Palmén (1962) reported losses of pupal exuvia to amphipods.

The narrow, upper portions of surface traps, where insects tend to congregate, is a favourite hunting place for the spiders and dragonflies which are frequently caught when traps are set over vegetation. Even if traps are equipped with a sample bottle containing preservative, predators will usually avoid it and continue to capture insects as they emerge into the trap. The only practical solution is to inspect traps frequently and remove predators at least once a day.

Fish are rarely mentioned as predators in emergence traps, even though insects are one of their major dietary items. Mundie (1956) found larval minnows < 8 mm long in submerged traps, but concluded that they were probably too small to eat insects. An examination of the adult:exuviae ratio in the catch of submerged funnel traps, used at the Experimental Lakes Area (ELA) suggested that fish predation was a problem at some stations (Davies, unpublished data). Dipteran adults and exuviae generally occurred in equal numbers in the catch, except when water temperatures exceeded 22 °C and exuviae deteriorated rapidly (i.e. $A:E > 1$). Occasionally ratios $\ll 1$ were recorded for some stations. A small cone placed in the sample bottle of traps at these locations retained cyprinids and larval fish that entered the trap, thus confirming the predation problem. Attempts to exclude these fish by redesigning the entrance to the sample bottle have failed; the only sure solution has been to set traps directly on the bottom, a method that sometimes creates more problems than it solves.

5 Tests of Sampling Efficiency

Emergence traps have been in use for more than 75 years, yet there is surprisingly little data to indicate whether the samples that they provide are accurate or simply qualitative. Initially, traps were used as qualitative samplers to make taxonomic collections, study emergence phenology (temporal sequence) as an aid to understanding life histories, and to investigate phenomena such as the diel periodicity of emergence. More recently, traps have been used to make quantitative collections for estimating total emergence, but evidence to support their use in this role is far from conclusive.

5.1 *Absolute accuracy*

Three lines of investigation have been used to determine the accuracy of emergence traps:

(1) Field observations.
(2) Analysis of catch data.
(3) Comparison of total measured emergence with an expected value, calculated either as the difference in larval abundance before and after the emergence period, or as the number of mature larvae in the sediment just prior to emergence.

Using the first two methods, several authors have shown that traps were inappropriate samplers or gave biased estimates of emergence for some species. Wohlschlag (1950) noted that large species of caddisflies, mayflies and dragonflies were able to crawl out of his partially submerged pyramid trap. Corbet (1964) suggested that during periods of windy weather dragonflies may preferentially seek out surface traps for shelter. A sex ratio that differed greatly from the expected value of one, led Illies (1971) to conclude that female Simuliidae (*Odagmia ormata*) used his greenhouse trap as a refuge. The data of Flannagan & Lawler (1972) show that, for several species of Trichoptera, submerged funnel traps caught large numbers of females but few males, indicating a possible trap bias.

Table 6.3 summarizes the results of several attempts to measure trap sampling efficiency by the third, or experimental, approach. In each case, submerged funnels were used to sample chironomid emergence. Overall, the results are inconclusive and highly variable, but it may be unreasonable to expect otherwise, given the number of species and methods involved in these tests. It is instructive, however, to consider the errors associated with such experimental estimates. First, the technique ignores mortality and predation losses that occur between the time that the larvae are sampled and the onset of emergence. Welch (1976) showed that these losses could amount to more than half of the standing crop of fourth instar larvae present just prior to emergence, and corrected his estimates accordingly. Real sampling efficiency of traps may, therefore, be considerably higher than values reported in Table 6.3. A second source of error which causes an underestimate of trap efficiency was reported by Potter & Learner (1974) who found that blue-green algae accumulated in the top of their traps and blocked pupal access to the sample bottle. Under the same conditions, floating box traps were 2–3 times more efficient, presumably because they did not concentrate the algae and allowed more surface area for emergence. A third source of error, an underestimate of larval abundance, may give rise to an inflated value of trap efficiency. Except where calculated efficiencies exceed 100 %, this type of error can easily go undetected. If larvae are sampled after the onset of emergence or if they continually migrate into a habitat, an underestimate of their abundance will result. While the latter hypothesis is convenient, there is little published evidence to support the claim that chironomid larvae in lakes undergo purposeful migrations just prior to emerging (see Section 6.1).

Table 6.3 Sampling efficiency of submerged funnel traps, calculated by expressing numbers of captured Chironomidae as a percentage of the decrease in larval standing stock. Larval abundances were not corrected for mortality or predation losses except by Welch (1976). Potter & Learner's (1974) results are given only for species $\geq 5\%$ of the total trap catch.

Study	Chironomid	Trap efficiency
Borutsky (1939a)	*Chironomus plumosus*	13%–17%
Borutsky (1939b)	Tanypodinae	55%–76%
Jónasson (1954)	*Chironomus anthracinus*	54%
Mundie (1956)	Tanypodinae	79%
	Chironomus plumosus	15%
	Tanytarus sp.	2%–6%
Hamilton (1965)	Overall	~36%
Sandberg (1969)	Overall (mud bottom)	12%–16%
	Overall (*Cladophora*)	74%
Laville (1971a)	Overall (deep stations)	30%–63%
	Overall (shallow stations)	24%–83%
Bretschko (1974)	*Lauterbornia coracina*	93%
	Micropsectra contracta	>43%
	Heterotrissocladius marcidus	220%
	Heterotrissocladius grimshawi	97%
	Paratanytarsus austriacus	190%
	Protanypus forcipatus	>31%
	Estimated overall	~50%
Potter & Learner	*Procladius choreus*	15% and 7%
(1974)	*Psilotanypus rufovittatus*	18%
	Glyptotendipes paripes	3% and 2%
	Microtendipes sp.	12% and 16%
	Tanytarsus inopertus	8% and 3%
	Tanytarsus lugens	10% and 6%
Welch (1976)	*Pseudodiamesa arctica*	343%
	Lauterbornia sp. nov.	26%
	Trissocladius sp. nov.	31%
	Orthocladius spp.	125%
	Overall	46%

The results of two experiments suggest that some traps provide accurate estimates of emergence under laboratory conditions. Kimerle & Anderson (1967) and McCauley (1976) measured total emergence from a screen-covered tank or pool stocked with sediment and chironomid larvae. In each case, these totals were compared on an areal basis to simultaneous estimates of emergence from traps set inside the experimental enclosure. Kimerle &

Anderson found that surface traps made from plastic funnels gave a 10 % overestimate of total emergence, while McCauley, using clear vinyl funnels set as surface traps, found that actual and estimated totals of emergence were not significantly different.

5.2 *Comparative efficiency*

5.2.1 *Submerged versus surface traps*

Most tests of trap efficiency compare the relative catch performance of two different designs and comparisons are usually undertaken to select traps that give the highest catch per unit effort, to calibrate a new model against some standard trap, or to demonstrate that two designs sample with the same efficiency. Tests therefore reflect the relative merit of each trap as a sampler in a particular application; under other circumstances, the sampling efficiency of each design can be considerably different.

To illustrate this variability, consider a popular test in which the catch performance of submerged funnels is compared with that of floating or staked box traps. Guyer & Hutson (1955) claimed that funnel traps made of sheet metal and floating box design of Macan (1949) sampled with equal efficiency. Morgan *et al.* (1963) showed that a pair of floating box traps (Morgan & Waddell 1961) each caught three times the number of insects and 60 % more species than a single submerged funnel (Jónasson 1954) of the same basal area. Kimerle & Anderson (1967) compared their staked box design with a submerged pyramid of equal sampling area. Over a 33 day experiment, the sum of daily collections from the box totalled 20 times the number of insects sampled by the submerged trap. A repeat of the Kimerle & Anderson experiment (Davies, unpublished data) based on a full season comparison between three staked box traps and three submerged funnels (Fig. 6.4c), basal area of all traps = $0.2 \, \text{m}^2$) in a shallow, well-sheltered bay of Lake 239 (ELA), showed that annual estimates of chironomid emergence from box traps were twice that of the funnels.

These differences are difficult to interpret because critical pieces of evidence are missing. Laboratory studies (Kimerle & Anderson 1967, McCauley 1976) have shown that, under controlled conditions, surface traps sample with 100 % efficiency; however, no comparable experiments have been performed with submerged traps. Absolute sampling efficiency of submerged funnel traps has been measured in several field experiments, but the results are quite variable and inconclusive (Table 6.3). Similarly, an attempt by Potter & Learner (1974) to estimate the accuracy of floating box traps showed that for species making up more than 5 % of the total catch, trap efficiency varied between 14 % and 65 % of the potential emergence yield.

Kajak (1958) proposed a mechanism to explain why surface traps catch more than submerged models. He noted in an experiment that funnel traps caught the same number of insects when placed directly on the bottom as they did at the surface when they were mounted inside a close fitting mesh cylinder that extended down to the sediment. Traps floated on the surface without cylinders caught between three and six times more than those with cylinders, implying that the floating traps caught more because they attracted pupae or adults. Kajak speculated that insects with nocturnal or crepuscular habits were attracted by the reduced light regimen inside the muslin covered traps, but this mechanism contradicts the usual inverse relationship between transparency and catch performance and fails to explain the results of Morgan *et al.* (1963) and Kimerle & Anderson (1967), who each used highly transparent traps. It is possible, however, that pupae were attracted to the calm water inside the floating traps. Although it is not clear whether pupae can distinguish sheltered areas, it would be a selective advantage for the eclosion process if they could. This attraction hypothesis is consistent with the observation that catches are always highest in surface traps. It also explains why in the Lake 239 experiment, where the water was usually calm and there was little to distinguish between the inside and outside of a surface trap, the differences in catch between surface and submerged traps were smaller than those observed in the open water comparisons done by others.

Regardless of whether insects are attracted to surface traps or avoid submerged ones, the source of the consistent catch difference observed between the two types must be resolved by further testing before emergence traps can be used with confidence to obtain accurate estimates of insect emergence for standing water habitats.

5.2.2 Stream traps

Floating box traps with open bottoms perform poorly in streams. A test by Gledhill (1960) showed that a benthic pyramid trap (Mundie 1956) retained its catch, while a floating box (Macan 1949) did not. Macan (1964) repeated the experiment and included an additional comparison between his box trap and a floating cone (Mundie 1956). Boxes trapped more Ephemeroptera, but fewer Trichoptera per unit area than the cones, and only 64% of the trichopteran species found in the cones. The pyramid trap consistently gave the highest estimate of total emergence and caught more species of Ephemeroptera, Plecoptera and Trichoptera than the other traps. Macan suggested that catch loss, particularly from the box trap, was the major reason for the observed differences. Boerger (1981) showed that chironomid losses from floating box traps could be drastically reduced or eliminated if traps were equipped with entrance baffles.

Catch loss can also be reduced by placing traps on the stream bottom. To test whether the sampling efficiency of these 'containment' traps was a function of size or design type, Flannagan (1978) used large cage traps (1·0 m² base) and small (0·1 m² base) low-profile samplers (Hamilton 1969) to sample a stream. Both models were set directly on the bottom and each gave similar estimates of trichopteran emergence on an areal basis. The data of Sandrock (1978) suggested that greenhouse traps collected fewer insects per unit area than smaller tent traps; insect mortality due to high temperature inside the greenhouse seemed to be the principle reason for this difference. Apart from these few studies, there is little other evidence to evaluate the efficiency of stream traps.

6 Patterns of Emergence

During their brief period of sexual maturity, adult insects must survive predation and the rigors of the terrestrial environment until they can reproduce successfully. Many aquatic insect species accomplish this by emerging in a highly synchronized fashion at a distinct time each season. This mass emergence of a few species at a time maximizes the chances of mating success, prevents interference from other insects and helps to keep losses to a minimum by briefly 'saturating' the predation mechanisms. Other aquatic insects choose asynchronous emergence as a reproductive strategy. The net result is a temporal series of species emerging in pulses throughout the season, superimposed on a lower, more continuous background rate of emergence.

In addition to separations in time, the emergence of some species is further localized by habitat. These spatial patterns, such as the general decline of total emergence with depth in a lake, or the close association between leaf-mining Chironomidae and specific types of vegetation, may reflect the food habits of the larvae. A second type of habitat association comes from specific emergence requirements, such as the need for Odonata nymphs to crawl to shore, or climb onto rocks or vegetation before eclosion can take place.

Corbet (1964) identified four basic temporal patterns: continuous, sporadic, seasonal, and rhythmic. Continuous emergence shows no seasonal trends and occurs mainly in the tropics. Elsewhere, a few species of stream insects and some members of the genus *Cricotopus* exhibit this behaviour in temperate systems that do not freeze. Sporadic emergence is exemplified by *Hexagenia* sp., which emerges along a 960 km reach of the Mississippi River at intervals of 6–11 days (Fremling 1960). Progressions of peak emergence along the river give the illusion of adult migrations. Seasonal emergence is common at temperate and polar latitudes. The length of the season, which shortens as one moves northward, is defined by the period of open water, except in arctic lakes, where ice cover occasionally remains all year round, forcing insects to emerge through cracks in the ice and from open areas around the shore (Welch 1973, 1976). The timing of emergence within each of the previous categories may be strongly rhythmic. In rare cases, as with the marine chironomid *Clunio marinus*, timing is derived from lunar cycles (Caspers 1951); however, emergence in most species shows a distinct diel periodicity.

Temperature and photoperiod are the variables most likely to control and synchronize emergence, but the relationships are complex and poorly understood. Weather also exerts a modifying influence; insect emergence measured in floating or submerged traps is lowest on stormy or windy days and reaches its highest value during clear, calm periods (Vallentyne 1952; Davies unpublished data).

The onset of chironomid emergence in the spring appears to require a minimum threshold temperature, which ranges from 6·5 °C (Carrillo 1974) to 8 °C (Morgan 1958) for temperate latitudes, 7 °C in alpine climates (Laville 1971a), between 4 °C and 5 °C for high-arctic tundra ponds (Danks & Oliver 1972), and as low as 2 °C for high-arctic lakes (Welch 1973). As water temperature rises, overall emergence increases to a peak value in the first half of the season, then tapers off, sometimes with a minor pulse in the latter half of the season, and ceases before freezeup. Among individual species, though, the timing of emergence and the length of the emergence period is quite variable.

For species that exhibit synchronous habits, the emergence period may extend from a few days to a month or more, but lasts on average about two weeks (Palmén 1955; Flannagan & Lawler 1972). Within a population, protandry (the tendency for the onset of male emergence to precede that of the females) is frequently observed (Palmén 1962; Sandberg 1969; Harper & Magnin 1971; Danks & Oliver 1972; Flannagan & Lawler 1972; Welch 1973; Sandrock 1978).

Distribution of emergence throughout the day is also characteristic for each species. Trichoptera and Chironomidae (particularly the Chironomini and Tanypodinae) emerge primarily around dusk or shortly thereafter, with a second minor peak at dawn (Scott & Opdyke 1941; Sprules 1947; Potter & Learner 1974; Friesen *et al.* 1980; Ali 1980), although Miller (1941) found that maximum chironomid emergence occurred between 04:00 h and 07:00 h daily. The diel pattern may be somewhat more variable for members of other chironomid subfamilies. For example, Potter & Learner (1974) reported that peak emergence of Orthocladiinae occurred at dawn, followed by a lower continuous rate throughout the day with a mid-afternoon minimum, but LeSage & Harrison (1980) found that *Cricotopus* spp. adhered to the common dusk-dawn pattern described above. Simuliidae emerge during daylight hours (Sprules 1947), or from noon until dusk, but seldom after dark (Davies 1950). Ephemeroptera are primarily evening emergers (Sprules 1947; Friesen *et al.*

1980), although seasonal differences may occur (Friesen *et al.* 1980). Flannagan (1978) noted a strong seasonal modification of diel periodicity in trichopteran emergence: in the spring, Trichoptera emerged during the day; by mid-summer, full darkness was preferred; in the fall, peak emergence had reverted to the early evening. Flannagan hypothesized that caddisflies were able to optimize conditions for flight and minimize the risk of desiccation by shifting the timing of emergence according to seasonal conditions. Overall, the emergence of most species is minimum between 09:00 h and 11:00 h (solar time) daily, making this an ideal time to clear or set emergence traps.

6.1 *Larval migrations prior to emergence*

Spatial and temporal patterns of emergence can sometimes be interpreted in more than one way, giving radically different explanations for a set of observations. For example, it has been noted in several studies that standing crops of larvae in the littoral areas of lakes, measured prior to emergence, seemed insufficient to account for the total number of insects trapped from that area (Borutsky 1939b; Wohlschlag 1950; Bretschko 1974; Bagge *et al.* 1980). The reverse seemed true for the profundal. For each study it was proposed that larvae migrated shoreward just prior to emergence. While such a redistribution may be possible with the highly mobile larvae of *Chaoborus*, and has been shown to occur for one species of chironomid colonizing a newly flooded reservoir (Cantrell & McLachlan 1977), data presented by Borutsky and the others could not rule out the possibility that the apparent migrations may have been an artefact caused by underestimates of larval standing crop (Scott & Opdyke 1941). Alternatively, emergence may be an estimate of production, not standing crop (Illies 1971; Speir & Anderson 1974; Davies 1980), and the apparent disparity between larval abundance and number of adults may simply reflect differences in generation times between warm littoral and cold profundal regions. The issue of larval migrations raised here deserves close attention in future studies because it is fundamental to our understanding of emergence mechanisms.

7 Sampling Strategies and Analytical Techniques

The design of an emergence study follows a simple hierarchical structure. First, a clear definition of a central study purpose is required. Spatial and temporal patterns of emergence, physical restrictions on sampling, habitat diversity and an estimate of the precision needed to answer the question are examined, in turn, to determine where, when and how to sample. Considerations of cost, time and available manpower will further modify the strategy and determine trap type, number of traps and a sampling schedule.

Qualitative studies, aimed at characterizing the insect fauna of a habitat or documenting changes in species composition that result from environmental disruptions, require extensive collections from all parts of the habitat. Except where a single species or group is being monitored, characterization studies usually require a minimum of one full season's data. Where long-term changes are being measured, annual variation in species composition must also be considered. Emergence collections are often made in conjunction with larval sampling programs. Larval material can be used to derive life history information, while examination of emergent adults is often the only way of establishing the taxonomic identity of larvae. To obtain adequate samples from all habitats, a variety of trap designs may be needed. Although it is important that these traps collect all species of interest, estimates of abundance may not be required, so accuracy can sometimes be sacrificed in favour of other criteria. As a result, large, inexpensive traps that are simple to construct and easy to use are often chosen to give the maximum number of specimens for the least cost and sampling effort.

By comparison, quantitative studies are primarily concerned with accuracy and minimizing sample variance. To achieve these goals, the scope of investigations is often narrowed to include only single groups of insects or habitats. Traps are chosen for their ability to sample accurately or with the same relative efficiency at all locations. Trap design should be standardized, whenever possible, to permit comparisons within and between studies. Finally, the emphasis in sampling must be shifted towards replication to allow statistical analysis of the data.

For control versus treatment comparisons involving one variable, such as a test of the relative catch efficiency of two trap designs, simple random sampling with replication is adequate. Where possible, a uniform location should be selected for the tests to minimize random errors. If the abundance of an insect group is measured in several different habitats, estimates of overall variance calculated from a simple random sample will usually be too high. Stratified random sampling (Elliott 1971) can often reduce overall variance, but choice of the stratification criteria is critical (see Chapter 8). In cases where a variable that controls the abundance of insects, such as vegetation density or bottom type, varies along a well defined gradient (e.g. depth), transect sampling approximates the stratified random approach, particularly if the position of the transect is randomized in a direction perpendicular to the gradient. In addition, transect sampling offers two practical advantages over other techniques. First, positional effects, such as orientation to the sun or prevailing wind direction, are held constant along the transect. Second, the orderly arrangement of stations makes them easy to find and minimizes travel time between traps.

To illustrate some of the practical aspects of a quantitative study, consider the problem of designing a sampling program to give an estimate of total chironomid emergence from a lake. Chironomid abundance is usually a function of habitat type and lake depth at a given location. Because the distribution of emergence is not uniform, a simple random sampling scheme is inappropriate. For shallow lakes with several distinct habitats, stratified random sampling is recommended, with sampling effort distributed among habitats in proportion to their size. Where habitat seems relatively uniform around the lake, a depth-stratified sampling scheme is more appropriate. Trap placement at equal intervals of depth, however, tends to overemphasize the importance of deep stations.

Sampling effort can be equalized by dividing the lake into several intervals of depth and distributing a number of traps among the intervals in proportion to the area that each occupies. If a fixed number of stations is required, however, the lake can be divided into equal intervals of area on a hypsographic plot (area *versus* depth) and the corresponding depth intervals read from the curve.

The choice of a trap will be largely determined by its sampling efficiency, ease of use, cost, and the wind and wave conditions of the lake. Traps should be large enough to ensure that zero counts are rare during periods of emergence. Beyond this minimum, size has no apparent effect (Table 6.2) or a detrimental effect (Rosenberg & Wiens 1983) on sample variance. The number of traps required at each sample location will depend on the aims of the study. While there is some evidence to suggest that a single trap may catch between 80 % and 90 % of the maximum numbers of insects at any location (Laville 1971a) and approximately 60 % of the species (Sandberg 1969; Rosenberg *et al.* 1980), the practice is not recommended. For some specified level of error, it is possible to calculate the number of traps that are required from a preliminary estimate of mean and variance (see Chapter 8). However, an understanding of how the variance of emergence estimates is distributed in lakes may help to assign a reasonable level of expectation of accuracy.

Estimates of the spatial variability of chironomid emergence at a shallow location are given in Table 6.2. Coefficients of variation (C.V.) ranged between 28·1 % and 42·9 %, and appeared to be independent of trap size. Similarly, five submerged funnels (0·1 m^2), suspended 1 m above the bottom at a 2 m depth location in Lake 239 (ELA), gave estimates of 11 496, 12 324, 8401, 10 997 and 9228 chironomids m^{-2} yr^{-1}, a mean of 10 501, and a C.V. of 15·4 % (Davies, unpublished data). Considering that trap locations in each experiment were chosen for apparent uniformity of the substrate, these estimates probably represent minimum expected variability among 2 m deep stations in each lake.

Rosenberg *et al.* (1980) measured spatial variability of chironomid emergence in a newly flooded northern reservoir. Clay shorelines were particularly unstable and drowned forest and sunken debris were common in most areas. Table 6.4 summarizes their results. Variability was highest in the shallows and declined sharply with depth. Although species composition differed at each location, mean emergence at a given depth was similar among shoreline types.

These examples suggest that, beyond a 2 m depth, estimates of emergence can be obtained with a $\pm 30\%$ level of precision from a minimum of two or three replicates at each location. Many more replicates are needed at shallow

Table 6.4 Spatial variability of chironomid emergence and its dependence on depth (from Rosenberg *et al.* 1980, Table 1). Reported values are mean emergence, X (number $m^{-2} yr^{-1}$), and coefficient of variation, C.V. ($\%$), for 4 submerged funnel traps ($0.1 m^2$), monitored continuously at each of 4 depths and 3 shoreline types.

Depth (m)	Clay		Bedrock		Marsh	
	X	C.V.	X	C.V.	X	C.V.
1·0	1867	128·9	1765	61·1	769	107·8
2·0	2985	44·9	2509	45·3	2161	20·1
3·5	1356	22·8	1561	15·8	1818	38·9
4·5	764	27·0	1012	19·7	1081	16·7

stations to give the same estimate of precision. Because most areas of the lake do not require extra traps, a decision must be made to either abandon the concept of equal sampling effort, or to accept higher levels of variability in the shallows and minimize the contribution that these stations make to an overall estimate of emergence by increasing the number of sampling strata, thus isolating areas of high variability. The latter solution is usually preferred because it uses fewer traps.

An estimate of long-term fluctuations in insect abundance must be considered whenever systems are compared over several years or when current conditions are referred to previous baseline data, to test for differences. The results of a long-term study to determine temporal variation of emergence at a fixed location are shown in Table 6.5. Single traps, at each of four depths, were used to measure annual emergence of Diptera ($>90\%$ Chronomidae) over 9 consecutive years (Davies, unpublished data). Annual catch differences were highest in the shallows, but variability, expressed as a percentage of the long-term mean for each location, was lowest at the 1 m station and increased with depth. Lake averages were less variable than the results for any individual station. While additional stations were used in the calculation of lake averages, the major reason for the discrepancy is that stations did not respond proportionately to, or even in the same direction, as the overall trend for a

Table 6.5 Long-term variability of dipteran emergence in Lake 226 SW (Experimental Lakes Area). Entries are estimates of emergence (number m^{-2} yr^{-1}) from a single location at each of 4 depths over 9 years, with means ($\bar{X}$) and coefficients of variation (C.V.). Lake-average emergence is corrected for lake morphometry (number m^{-2} yr^{-1}). Bold type indicates years in which emergence increased.

Depth (m)	Year									$\bar{X}$	C.V.
	1973	1974	1975	1976	1977	1978	1979	1980	1981		
1	4403	**11 134**	8138	**11 901**	**14 112**	11 332	6227	**10 228**	10 186	9740	30·8
3	4711	**9 616**	4151	**4 322**	3477	1399	**3054**	2 212	**6 259**	4356	55·8
5	2486	2 473	280	**1 591**	1111	679	**982**	769	**3 969**	1593	73·8
7	19	**697**	70	**140**	**406**	65	**224**	**435**	237	248	92·0
Lake-average	1855	**2 984**	1825	**2 709**	**3 024**	1921	1675	1 563	**2 992**	2283	27·4

given year, so that individual deviations tended to cancel each other out. Lake-average (or total) emergence appears, therefore, to be the most useful indicator of long-term change. In the absence of whole-lake data, littoral collections made from the same locations each year (a technique used to reduce the spatial component of variability), provide a potentially stable alternative, while the small size and relatively high variability of profundal estimates make them unsuitable as indicators of long-term change.

Emergence trapping programs may be operated on a continuous or periodic basis. Continuous trapping yields more rare species than periodic sampling, but is a time-consuming, labour-intensive practice, so fewer stations, in total, can be monitored. For studies concerned with estimating overall emergence and examining major species, returns can be maximized for a given amount of work by using a large number of traps and operating them discontinuously. Rosenberg *et al.* (1980) showed that, compared to continuous records, information loss was minimal when traps were operated for one 48 h period each week.

A seasonal record of emergence for stations which have been sampled discontinuously may be constructed by plotting daily rates of emergence and extrapolating between the points with straight lines. Total emergence is then equal to the area under the curve between the first and last sampling days (i.e. the integral of daily emergence m^{-2} over the season) and may be calculated as:

$$\text{Integral Emergence} = \sum_{i=1}^{d-1} \frac{X_i + X_{i+1}}{2} \cdot (T_{i+1} - T_i) \qquad (6.1)$$

where: d is the total number of sampling periods in a season. X_i is emergence unit-area^{-1} day^{-1} in the ith sampling period, T_i is the mid-point time of the ith sampling period [i.e. (the day that traps were set – the day they were cleared)/2], and $(T_{i+1} - T_i)$ is the number of days between sampling periods.

Lake total emergence for the season is therefore:

$$\text{Lake total emergence} = \sum_{j=1}^{n} E_j \cdot A_j \qquad (6.2)$$

where: n is the number of sample strata, E_j is the mean seasonal emergence unit area^{-1} (average of sample replicates) in the jth sample stratum, A_j is the area of the jth sample stratum.

Short term comparisons between trap replicates, habitats, or whole systems may yield spurious differences, caused solely by variations in the timing of emergence. Without data for a full season, even species differences should be interpreted with caution. Seasonal data provide the only logical basis for comparing systems, particularly if the total periods of emergence are dissimilar due to latitude or climatic effects. Except where differences in emergence distribution are considered, comparisons between lakes should be made with annual, lake-average data (seasonal total emergence/lake surface area), a figure which reflects the relative productivity of each system, independent of its size or morphometry.

8 Predicting Insect Emergence

A generalized relationship between the standing crop of benthic organisms and lake trophic status has been recognized for some time (Johnson 1974), but is poorly understood. Vallentyne (1952) showed that the concept could be extended to insect emergence by calculating that total chironomid emergence equalled 0·3 % of annual sedimentation in a lake, a process that was presumed to be a covariate of productivity. Similarly, the relationship between chironomid emergence and the C:N ratio of sediments (Laville 1971b) suggested a link between primary production and emergence, because the C:N ratio of sediments increases as lakes become more eutrophic (Welch 1973). More direct connections with productivity were established by Teal (1957), who estimated that total insect emergence was equal to 4·6 % of gross photosynthesis in a cold, temperate spring, and by Welch (1967), who found that total dipteran emergence amounted to approximately 1 % of gross primary production in a small eutrophic pond. Other studies (summarized in Davies 1980, Table 2) have shown that dipteran emergence accounts for 0·1 %–2·2 % of gross phytoplankton production in a wide variety of lakes.

A number of empirical relationships between dipteran emergence and phytoplankton production (Davies 1980) are summarized in Table 6.6. These relationships were derived from long-term data sets on a number of small shield lakes in the Experimental Lakes Area, ranging in terms of phytoplankton production from oligotrophic ($21 \cdot 0 \, gC \, m^{-2} \, yr^{-1}$) to eutrophic ($116 \cdot 7 \, gC \, m^{-2} \, yr^{-1}$) (Fee 1980).

Lake-average emergence, as biomass or numbers of Diptera, was strongly correlated with phytoplankton production (equations 1 and 2 of Table 6.6) when data averaged over several years were compared. The depth distribution of emergence was also a function of lake trophic status. Emergence tended to be concentrated in the shallow littoral areas of eutrophic lakes, but spread over a much wider range of depth in oligotrophic systems according to a pattern which paralleled the depth distribution of phytoplankton production in the water column. Thus, equation 3 of Table 6.6 could be used to predict the biomass of emergence at each depth from an estimate of phytoplankton production at that depth, for all lakes, regardless of their overall trophic state. Insect size, however, was related to lake productivity. The average size of an individual adult was largest in eutrophic systems (equation 4, Table 6.6), but within each lake, size was also a function of depth. The number of insects emerging from a given depth, therefore, could not be calculated by dividing

Table 6.6 Empirical relationships between dipteran emergence in lakes and phytoplankton production.

Equation No.	Relationship[1]		Definition of symbols and units
1	$\bar{B} = -0.0111 + 0.00867\overline{PP}$	$\bar{B}$	Lake-average dry biomass of emergent Diptera, corrected for morphometry ($g\,m^{-2}\,yr^{-1}$).
2	$\bar{E} = 1147.5 + 40.815\overline{PP}$	B_{zi}	Average integral dry biomass of Diptera emerging per unit area from the ith depth interval ($g\,m^{-2}\,yr^{-1}$).
3	$B_{zi} = 0.160 + 0.050 PP_{zi}$	B_{95}	The depth above which 95 % of the lake-total biomass of Diptera emerges (m).
4	$\bar{W} = -0.138 + 0.069\ln\overline{PP}$	$\bar{E}$	Lake-average number of emergent Diptera, corrected for morphometry (Number $m^{-2}\,yr^{-1}$).
5	$\bar{N} = 72432(\overline{PP})^{-1.202}$	E_{zi}	Average integral number of Diptera emerging per unit area from the ith depth interval (Number $m^{-2}\,yr^{-1}$).
6	$E_{zi} = \bar{N} \times PP_{zi}$	E_{95}	The depth above which 95 % of the lake-total number of Diptera emerge (m).
7	$B_{95} = -1.154 + 0.972\bar{Z}_c$	$\bar{N}$	Average number of Diptera emerging per gC of PP_{zi}. Units of number $m\,gC^{-1}$ results when estimates of E_{zi} are divided by B_{zi} for each interval of depth.
8	$E_{95} = -0.106 + 0.819\bar{Z}_c$	$\overline{PP}$	Lake-average phytoplankton production corrected for morphometry ($gC\,m^{-2}\,yr^{-1}$).
		PP_{zi}	Average integral phytoplankton production per unit volume in ith depth interval ($gC\,m^{-3}\,yr^{-1}$).
		$\bar{W}$	Mean dry weight of an individual dipteran adult (mg).
		$\bar{Z}_c$	Mean depth of 1 % of surface irradiance during the ice free season (m).

[1] from Davies (1980).

biomass (B_{zi}, equation 3) by the average weight of an adult ($\overline{W}$, equation 4). Instead, an empirical factor $\overline{N}$ was derived (equation 5) which could be used in equation 6 to calculate numbers of Diptera emerging at each depth from a water column distribution of annual phytoplankton production. Because emergence and phytoplankton production were so closely related, and primary production, in turn, was light-dependent, the mean depth of the euphotic zone was closely correlated with the lower depth limit of emergence (equations 7 and 8).

Although these relationships seem to be powerful tools, they have important limitations. They were derived for lakes in a single geographic and climatic region, from long-term data in systems where phytoplankton were the major primary producers. The relationships might be obscured in individual years by annual variability, or may break down in systems where macrophytes or allochthonous carbon inputs dominate the energy supply. While initial tests suggest that these equations do work in a much broader context, their real value is a conceptual one. They demonstrate a new potential use of emergence studies and emphasize the need for more quantitative work in the field.

9 Appendices

9.1 Emergence traps for open water habitats

Reference and illustration	Description	Comments
Floating traps		
Adamstone & Harkness (1923)	Wood frame base supporting wire hoops covered with a muslin tent.	Trap must be lifted to permit catch removal. Exuviae are not retained.
Miller (1941) Fig. 6.1a	Wood frame base supporting wire hoops covered with a muslin tent. Hollow metal floats are attached to the outside of the frame. Sampling area: $0.37\,\mathrm{m}^2$.	Trap must be lifted to permit catch removal. Exuviae are not retained.
Scott & Opdyke (1941) Fig. 6.1b	A wood frame pyramid covered with coarse mesh over a muslin tent. Sampling area: $0.25\,\mathrm{m}^2$.	Use of an apical sample bottle abandoned in favour of emptying as above. Wire mesh covering protects the trap from animals. Exuviae are not retained.

(continued)

Section 9.1 (contd)

Reference and illustration	Description	Comments
Macan (1949) Fig. 6.1f	A wood frame box, covered on the top and three sides with cellulose acetate sheet and on fourth side with fine nylon mesh. A wooden raft with hollow metal floats fits around the trap such that the open base of the box is held just below the water surface. Sampling area: $0·3\,m^2$.	To retrieve the catch, the box is lifted free of the raft and closed off at its base. Insects are then collected by hand or with the aid of an entomological aspirator. Exuviae are not retained.
Wohlschlag (1950) Fig. 6.1d	A wood frame pyramid covered inside with plastic screen and equipped with a removable glass sample bottle at its apex. Hollow metal floats are attached near the top of the frame. Sampling area: $0·25\,m^2$.	In use, only the sample bottle floats above the water surface. Exuviae not easily sampled.
Morgan & Waddell (1961) Fig. 6.1g	Similar to Macan's (1949) floating box trap except that the top is a flat piece of acrylic sheet and all four sides are mesh-covered. Sampling area: $0·46\,m^2$.	Exuviae are not retained. See also: Morgan (1958), Morgan *et al.* (1963), Edwards *et al.* (1964) and Morgan (1971).
Mundie (1971a) Fig. 6.1c	An aluminum (duralumin) frame pyramid with one vertical, mesh-covered side ($250\,\mu m$ opening), three sides and an internal baffle covered with polyethylene film, and a removable glass sample bottle at the apex. All coverings are held in place by aluminum strips bolted to the frame. Sampling area: $0·25\,m^2$.	The trap can be operated as a surface, semi-submerged or fully submerged unit. The angled internal baffle prevents catch loss.
Boyle (1979) Fig. 6.1e	A wood frame pyramid covered with nylon mesh and supported by foam plastic floatation at its base. A funnel, with holes around the top and the lid of the sample bottle glued to its stem, is set in the apex of the	Although the reported efficiency of the sample collector is high, some insects may remain in the body of the trap. Exuviae are not retained.

Section 9.1 (contd)

Reference and illustration	Description	Comments
	trap and covered with a glass plate. Insects entering the funnel fall into the sample bottle where they are retained. Sampling area: $0.5\,m^2$.	
Submerged traps Grandilewskaja-Decksbach (1935) Fig. 6.2a	A metal frame funnel covered with screen or mesh.	Further details not available.
Borutsky (1939a)	A metal frame covered with screen or mesh.	Further details not available.
Brundin (1949) Fig. 6.2b	A cone of brass screen with its base reinforced with copper wire and a sample bottle bound to the apex with twine. All metal seams are welded. Sampling area: $0.25\,m^2$.	The trap is suspended by a cord from a surface float attached to a wire yoke, wrapped around a glass sample bottle. Exuviae float on the water surface inside the sample bottle.
Jónasson (1954) Fig. 6.2e	A conical frame of galvanized wire, covered with galvanized mesh and attached to an apical tube. Wire and sheet metal form a hinged bracket to hold a glass sample bottle over the tube with its rim sealed against the outside of the mesh cone. Sampling area: $0.25\,m^2$.	Apical tube prevents insects from escaping from the sample bottle.
Borutsky (1955) Fig. 6.3a	A conical metal frame covered with metal mesh, and equipped with a dual chambered collecting vessel.	Emergence occurs in the inner chamber of the sample collector. Insects fly vertically into the surrounding outer chamber which contains preservative.
Guyer & Hutson (1955)	A sheet metal cone with a removable glass sample bottle. Sampling area: $0.42-0.84\,m^2$.	Exuviae float on the water surface inside the sample bottle.

(continued)

Section 9.1 (contd)

Reference and illustration	Description	Comments
Mundie (1955) Fig. 6.2c	A conical brass-wire frame, covered with copper gauze, and equipped with a threaded copper collar at its apex which holds a removable glass sample bottle. Sampling area: $0.25 \, m^2$.	A wire yoke around the sample bottle serves to attach the trap to a cable support from the surface. A safety chain prevents trap loss when the bottle is changed. Both adults and exuviae are retained.
Palmén (1955) Fig. 6.2d	A cone of stainless steel gauze with a tube welded to its apex. A weighted wire circle is attached to the base for strength and ballast. Sampling area: $1.0 \, m^2$.	The sample bottle is friction-fitted onto a rubber stopper which encircles the tube at the top of the trap. Both adults and exuviae are retained.
Kajak (1957)	A conical wire frame covered with cotton ('Miller gauze'). Sampling area: $0.2 \, m^2$.	Various configurations and sample containers were tested.
Sublette & Dendy (1959) Fig. 6.3b	A galvanized wire frame covered with polyethylene film that is heat bonded to form a cone. An inverted Erlenmeyer flask, attached to the top of the cone by elastic bands, acts as a sample collector. Sampling area: $0.09 \, m^2$.	Wire tied around the flask serves to attach the trap to a surface float. Both insects and exuviae are collected.
Hamilton (1965) Fig. 6.3c	A removable glass sample bottle, containing an auxiliary plastic cone to prevent catch loss, is attached to the top of a cellulose-acetate-butyrate funnel by a plastic jar lid with its center portion removed, A stiff wire, fixed to a hose clamp at the apex, forms an attachment point for suspending the trap. Split lead weights are clamped to the basal rim of the funnel. Sampling area: $0.1 \, m^2$.	The trap, which was primarily intended for sampling chironomids, has also been used to capture Trichoptera and Ephemeroptera by Flannagan & Lawler (1972). Also see Davies (1980) and Fig. 6.4 for modifications and construction details. Adults and exuviae are retained within the sample bottle.

Section 9.1 (*contd*)

Reference and illustration	Description	Comments
Fast (1972) Fig. 6.3d	A pyramidal frame of welded angle iron with sides covered by polyethylene film, held in place by redwood lath strips. A removable glass sample bottle is attached to the top of the frame by the rim of a metal jar lid. Extensions of the frame hold the trap base above the substrate. Sampling area: $0·5\,m^2$.	A perforated styrofoam cup inside the sample jar prevents catch loss.
Welch (1973) Fig. 6.3e	A square pyramid of clear acrylic with a removable glass sample bottle at its apex. The trap is suspended from a submerged float via a wire bridle (see Fig. 6.5c). Sampling area: $0·25\,m^2$.	Divers can be used to tend the traps during periods of ice cover. Exuviae float on the water surface inside the sample bottle.
Bretschko (1974)	Large funnels ($1\,m^2$) set directly on the lake bottom have a $2·5\,cm$ diameter hose leading from the top of the trap to a sample bottle floating on the lake surface.	Maximum hose length $10\,m$. Deeper stations must be tended by divers. Both adults and exuviae retained in the sample bottle.
Davies (1980) Fig. 6.4	A slightly modified version of Hamilton's (1965) trap. Sampling area: $0·1\,m^2$.	See Section 3.1.1 for construction details.

9.2 Emergence traps for shallow water habitats

Reference and illustration	Description	Comments
Traps for Areas with Emergent Vegetation		
Judd (1949) Fig. 6.7c	An open-bottomed, wood frame cage covered on the top and sides with copper screen. The upper portion of each side is a hinged door to allow access to the trap interior for specimen	Exuviae are not retained.

(continued)

Section 9.2 (contd)

Reference and illustration	Description	Comments
	removal. A cage is set over vegetation and supported, with its base below the water surface, on four stakes driven into the sediment. Sampling area: $0.7\,m^2$.	
Edwards *et al.* (1964)	The floating box trap of Morgan & Waddell (1961), Fig. 6.1g, modified slightly by adding stoppered holes to the roof. Sampling area: $0.18\,m^2$.	Catch removed by inserting an insect aspirator through the holes in the trap roof. Exuviae are not retained.
Corbet (1965) Fig. 6.7b	A truncated cone frame made of aluminum with a glass plate top, covered on the sides by fine plastic screen, held in place by aluminum strips bolted to the frame. Metal rod legs slip through sleeves on the frame and are secured in place by set screws. A rubber sampling port is fixed to one side. Sampling area: $0.1\,m^2$.	This lightweight, stackable design can be set over vegetation and emptied with the aid of an aspirator while viewing through the glass plate. Exuviae are not easily collected.
Lammers (1977) Fig. 6.7a	A tall form trap made from pine struts on a plywood ring base and covered on the inside with nylon mesh. A funnel-and-sample-bottle collector hangs from a plastic cover plate at the top of the trap. Steel rods through the base of the trap can be driven into the substrate to provide stability. Sampling area: $0.5\,m^2$.	Insects enter the sample bottle, which contains preservative, through holes in the side of the funnel. Exuviae are not retained.
LeSage & Harrison (1979) Fig. 6.7d	As one of several versions described, this trap consists of a nylon mesh tent supported externally by a wooden pyramidal frame attached at its base to a sealed, plastic pipe float. An acrylic headpiece with an opening near the top funnels	Suggested preservative: 70% ethanol mixed with glycerine or ethylene glycol. Exuviae are not retained.

Section 9.2 *(contd)*

Reference and illustration	Description	Comments
	insects toward a removable sample bottle, partially filled with preservative. A poly-ethylene skirt around the top of the trap protects the catch from rain. Sampling area: 0·37 m².	

Floating and staked designs[1]

Reference and illustration	Description	Comments
Mundie (1956) Fig. 6.8a	An internal aluminum frame supporting a nylon mesh or cellulose acetate cone. The mesh or plastic is held by aluminum strips bolted to the frame and by copper staples around the base. A removable glass sample bottle containing an auxiliary acetate cone threads into a collar at the trap apex. Hollow metal floats are fixed to extensions of the trap frame at its base. Sampling area: 0·25 m².	The trap is intended for partially submerged operation, but can be set as a surface sampler. The cone in the sample bottle prevents catch loss. Exuviae are not retained.
Frank (1965) Fig. 6.8d	A cone of silk or fine nylon is suspended upside down from an arm attached to a ring float made of wire and empty tin cans. Fabric tape and stiff wire strengthen the cone and hold its base open. Sampling area: 0·06 m².	A cloth disc stretched over a wire frame attached to a long wood handle is used to seal the base and lift the trap out of the water without loss of exuviae or adults.
Kimerle & Anderson (1967) Fig. 6.8e	A wood frame cube, covered on the top and 3 sides with polyethylene film and on the front with nylon mesh. Coverings are held on with wooden lath strips, stapled or nailed to the frame. The trap bottom can be closed off by raising a flap of the mesh front and sliding a square of plastic	The trap, with its base extending a few cm below the water surface, is held in position by bolting it to a stake that has been driven into the sediment. The bottom of the trap is open during sampling, but closed off prior to removal to prevent loss of

1. Also see Appendix 9.1, Floating Traps.

(continued)

Section 9.2 (contd)

Reference and illustration	Description	Comments
	or masonite hardboard along a groove cut in the inside edge of the bottom portion of the frame. Velcro® strips can be used to secure the lower edges of the mesh to the frame. Sampling area: $0.23\,m^2$.	specimens. Exuviae are not retained.
McCauley (1976) Fig. 6.8b	Two clear vinyl cones pitched at different angles are stacked and glued together at their bases to form a chambered trap. A screw cap with a hole in it is clamped to the apex of the outer cone to serve as an attachment for a removable sample vial. Nylon mesh vents cover holes in the outer cone. Sampling area: $0.1\,m^2$.	The trap is attached to a stake via a bracket so that its base rests just below the water surface. The catch is removed by inverting the trap and washing insects into the vial with preservative, sprayed through the vent windows. Exuviae are not easily sampled.
Street & Titmus (1979) Fig. 6.8c	A metal frame box with plastic or metal sides and a removable glass plate top, painted on its underside with a film of fruit tree grease-band (Boltac® or Tanglefoot®). Foam poly-styrene blocks on two sides provide floatation. Trap adapted from Green (1970). Sampling area: $0.1\,m^2$.	Emerging insects rise to the top of the trap and become stuck to the glass plate. The grease can be dissolved with acetone to remove insects. Exposed plates should be kept in sealed containers to avoid catching other insects. Exuviae are not retained.

Traps Set Directly on the Bottom

Kajak (1957) Fig. 6.9a	A conical surface trap (see Appendix 9.1: Kajak), adapted as a free-standing model by attaching it to the inside of a close-fitting cylinder made of wire and covered with 'Miller gauze'. The bottom of the cylinder is pressed into the sediment. Sampling area: $0.20\,m^2$.	The whole assembly should periodically be cleaned and moved to a different location to overcome colonization or containment effects. Exuviae remain on the water surface inside the cylinder.

Section 9.2 (contd)

Reference and illustration	Description	Comments
Lindeberg (1958) Fig. 6.9c	An inverted glass funnel with a stopcock in the stem, topped with a removable sample bottle, press-fitted onto a rubber stopper surrounding the stem. Use: (1) invert funnel over a shallow pool, (2) open stopcock and fill the funnel with water by suction, (3) close the stopcock, (4) quickly invert a sample bottle $\frac{2}{3}$ full of water over the stopper and seal in position, (5) open the stopcock. Sampling area: $0.07\,m^2$.	External air pressure keeps the trap full of water, thus giving the sampling convenience of a submerged trap in extremely shallow habitats. Emergence of large insects may be inhibited by the small diameter of the funnel stem.
Sublette & Dendy (1959) Fig. 6.9b	A polyethylene covered wire-frame pyramid which stands above the substrate on leg-like extensions of the frame to allow water circulation within the trap. Wire tied around the detachable sample flask at the apex of the pyramid provides an attachment point for a rope to raise or lower the trap from the surface. Sampling area: $0.09\,m^2$.	The trap may be operated either partially or fully submerged, although in the latter mode, it is easier to empty. Adults and exuviae are contained within the sample flask.
Paasivirta (1972)	Stainless mesh cone (see Appendix 9.1: Palmén), set directly on the bottom at shallow stations. Sampling area: $0.5\,m^2$.	Also see Paasivirta (1975).
Cheng (1974) Fig. 6.9d	An open-sided metal box with vials fitted into holes in the top. Sample vials contain auxiliary cones to prevent catch loss. Sampling area: $0.25\,m^2$.	In the fully submerged mode both adults and exuviae are retained.
Ali & Mulla (1979) Fig. 6.9e	A submerged funnel trap made of galvanized sheet metal with a removable glass sample bottle. Sampling area: $0.3\,m^2$.	Trap does not permit water circulation. Consequently, anoxia may develop inside.

(continued)

Section 9.2 (contd)

Reference and illustration	Description	Comments
Ettinger (1979) Fig. 6.10b	A folding tent of nylon mesh with two sides stretched over rectangular aluminum frames, hinged together at the top. Triangular mesh sides supported by rubber bands at the base are held taut during sampling by hinged metal stays which slip over pins in the frame to keep the trap open. Side panels are tucked inwards when the trap is folded flat for removal. Sampling area: $0.1\,m^2$.	By closing the trap with its base held under the water surface, both adults and exuviae are retained. Because traps are lightweight and fold flat, they are extremely portable.
Butler (1980) Fig. 6.10c	A free-standing semi-submerged trap made from polycarbonate sheet. Side seams are held together with bolts. The cone and cylinder are joined and sealed with silicone adhesive. The rim of a jar lid, glued to the outside of the cone at its apex, serves to attach a sample bottle with a screen-covered end. Brass bolts extending outward from the base of the cylinder support weights and help to stabilize the trap in soft sediment. Sampling area: $0.05\,m^2$.	Insects and exuviae are removed by lifting the trap out of the water with its base covered, inverting the unit, and washing specimens into the sample bottle with a spray of preservative.
Davies (1980) Fig. 6.10a	A modification of the trap illustrated in Fig. 6.4. Vents, cut in the body of the trap, to allow water circulation are covered with nylon mesh ($250\,\mu m$) which is held in place by acetate plastic strips, glued around the perimeter of each vent. Extra weights around the base assure trap stability under mild wave action. Sampling area: $0.1\,m^2$.	Traps operate in the fully submerged mode. Adults and exuviae are contained within the sample bottle.

Section 9.2 *(contd)*

Reference and illustration	Description	Comments
Traps for Shore		
Cook & Horn (1968) Fig. 6.10e	A sturdy box, open along the bottom and at one end, made from heavy fence wire, and lined inside with fibreglass screen. Sampling area: $0.28\,m^2$.	A qualitative trap for sampling Odonata that is set with its open end sloping downward toward the water.
Morgan (1971) Fig. 6.10d	A wood frame box with an open bottom, nylon mesh front, and acrylic sheet covering the top, back and sides. Bank material is cut away and replaced by a wooden board with a vertical front lip that is sunk into the bank at the water's edge to stop burrowing insects from crawling underneath the board. The trap front is supported just beneath the water surface by a float. Sampling area: unspecified.	This trap requires calm waters and sand or soil-covered banks. On rocky shorelines a tent may make a more useful trap.

9.3 *Emergence traps for running water*

Reference and illustration	Description	Comments
Cages and Tents		
Needham (1908) Fig. 6.11a	A muslin tent with a flap entrance. The trap base is sealed against the stream bed with stones. Sampling area: $0.56\,m^2$.	First recorded use of an emergence trap. Investigator must enter the trap to make collections.
Ide (1940)	A wood frame cube covered on the top and four sides with copper screen ($\sim 1000\,\mu m$ mesh). Base extends below the water surface, but does not seal against the substrate. Access to the trap interior is through a door in one side. Sampling area: $0.83\,m^2$.	Investigator must enter the trap to make collections.

(continued)

Section 9.3 *(contd)*

Reference and illustration	Description	Comments
Sprules (1947)	Trap style: see Ide (1940). A corner seat minimizes the time the investigator spends standing on the substrate inside the trap. Sampling area: $0.83\,m^2$.	Investigator must enter the trap to make collections.
Davies (1950)	Trap style: see Ide (1940). A finer mesh covering is used to retain Simuliidae. Sampling area: $0.83\,m^2$.	Investigator must enter the trap to make collections.
Harper & Magnin (1971) Fig. 6.11b	A pyramid shaped tent of nylon mesh supported by an external wood frame. A mesh sleeve, sewn to a hole in the tent wall, is tied off close to the tent to prevent insects from becoming caught in the folds of material. Sampling area: $0.5\,m^2$.	Specimens can be collected without lifting the trap, by reaching inside through the sleeve. Also see Harper & Cloutier (1979).
Illies (1971) Fig. 6.11d	A commercial greenhouse built to cover the complete cross section of a stream and its banks. Dimensions (L, W, H): $12.2 \times 2.8 \times 2.3\,m$, coverage: $11.1\,m^2$ of stream. See Böttger (1975) and Lehman (1979) for less expensive polyethylene-film-on-wooden-frame versions. Also see Malicky (1976), Zwick (1977), Sandrock (1978), Malicky (1980).	Investigators must enter the greenhouse to make collections. Advantages: (1) stream flow not restricted, (2) no substrate disruption during sampling, (3) large sample area, all habitats sampled. Disadvantages: (1) relatively permanent, (2) expensive to construct, (3) time consuming to sample, (4) thermal effects and intensive sampling may alter the habitat.
Anderson & Wold (1972) Fig. 6.11c	An 'A' frame of wood covered with fiberglass screen. Polyethylene film, secured to the upper third of the sloped sides, protects the catch from rain. A door in one end provides access to the trap. Screen flaps along the base of each angled side allow peak flows and debris to pass	Investigator must enter the trap to make collections.

Section 9.3 *(contd)*

Reference and illustration	Description	Comments
	through the trap. Dimensions: base = 1 m², height = 2 m.	
Masteller (1977)	A plastic mesh (500 μm) tent which covers the entire width of a stream and its banks. Dimensions: base = 15·8 m², L = 5·2 m, W = 3·1 m. The trap is similar in concept to the greenhouse of Illies (1971), but inexpensive by comparison.	Investigator must enter the trap to make collections. Apart from permanence and cost, the advantages and disadvantages listed for Illies' (1971) greenhouse apply.
Flannagan (1978)	A wood frame cube similar to that of Ide (1940) with 400 μm Nitex® cloth covering 3 sides, a Nitex covered door on the fourth side, a vinyl sheet roof, and a metal cross-bar to stand on while inside. Sampling area: 1·0 m².	Investigator must enter the trap to make collections. Vinyl roof protects specimens from rain.

Floating and Suspended Traps

Reference and illustration	Description	Comments
Judd (1957)	A slightly modified version of Miller's (1941) floating tent trap. Sampling area: 0·37 m².	Useful only during conditions of low flow.
Macan (1964) Fig. 6.1f and Fig. 6.8a	The box trap of Macan (1949) and Mundie's (1956) cone trap. Traps float on the water surface, held in place by a rope bridle attached to opposite banks of a small stream. Sampling area: Box = 0·33 m², cone = 0·25 m².	Useful only during conditions of low flow.
Corbet (1966) Fig. 6.12b	A partially submerged trap for use in rivers. A saran mesh cone, supported by a plywood ring base and aluminum struts, is attached to an apical aluminum collar. A machined sample container with a removable top and inverted funnel entrance fits into the collar. The position of foam floats attached to the trap base	Stability of the trap in strong currents or waves is improved by tethering it to the lee side of a wood boom. Prior to lifting the trap for sample removal, the base is sealed with a mesh-covered ring to retain both insects and exuviae.

(continued)

Section 9.3 *(contd)*

Reference and illustration	Description	Comments
	via metal rods and adjustable sleeves sets the height of the trap in the water. Sampling area: not reported, but $\sim 0.5\,m^2$.	
Langford & Daffern (1975) Fig. 6.12a	An aluminum frame pyramid, covered with nylon mesh and hinged at its base over a rectangular hole in a boat-shaped foam polystyrene float. Intended for use in rivers that are subject to wide fluctuations in level and may carry heavy loads of debris, the trap is trailed by a rope bridle from anchor points on opposite shores. Sampling area: $0.25\,m^2$.	The apical sample bottle used in initial experimental trails was omitted in subsequent models. Float material was colonized by Ephemeroptera nymphs.
LeSage & Harrison (1979) Fig. 6.7d	The previously discussed floating tent design or a truncated version, for improved stability at windy locations, can be used to sample streams. Further modifications include a sleeve on the side of the tent [see Appendix 9.3, Cages and Tents, Harper & Magnin (1971)], to allow easy access to the trap interior. Sampling area: $0.37\,m^2$.	Not suited to conditions of high flow.
Boerger (1981) Fig. 6.12c	A wood frame box trap with a hinged lid, mesh-covered sides and a sloping polyethylene covered roof. Two acrylic baffles in the base angle inward to prevent catch loss. A sliding panel, which fits into grooves cut in the frame, is used to close off the trap. The box rests on a float made of foam polystyrene blocks. Aluminum rods placed through holes in	Trap can move vertically as water levels change in the stream. A flexible, polyethylene skirt at the front of the hinged top permits access to the trap interior without risking catch loss. Exuviae are not retained.

***Section 9.3** (contd)*

Reference and illustration	Description	Comments
	each float are driven into the stream bed to hold the trap in place. Sampling area: 0·1 m².	
Nordlie & Arthur (1981) Fig. 6.12d	An acrylic plastic box with an open bottom, an angled baffle inside to prevent loss of insects, screen-covered windows for ventilation, and a commercially available domed acrylic skylight top. A removable sample bottle with a mesh bottom is attached to a hole in the centre of the dome by the rim of a jar lid. Plastic strips, glued to the outside of the box, support it on a square acrylic collar, which is suspended above the water surface from pipes laid across an experimental stream channel. Sampling area: 0·18 m².	Trap height must be adjusted frequently to cope with fluctuating water levels. The base of the box can be closed off with a sliding panel prior to lifting the trap free of the collar for emptying.

Traps Set Directly on the Bottom

Mundie (1956) Fig. 6.13a	A triangular pyramid frame made of heavy metal, covered on two sides with acrylic sheet and on the third side and around the top by copper mesh (250 μm opening). A removable sample jar containing a small cone to prevent insects from returning to the body of the trap is threaded into a collar at the top of the pyramid. Ropes or wires anchor the trap to the streambed or shore. Sampling area: 0·16 m².	Trap can be operated either partially or fully submerged and is designed to allow water to flow over the substrate. See also: Gledhill (1960), Macan (1964), and Mundie (1971a).
Hamilton (1969) Fig. 6.13b	An open-bottomed low profile box with stainless steel sides, a clear plastic top, and removable entrance and exit screens which allow water to flow through the	The trap functions in the fully submerged mode in streams as little as 12 cm deep. Also see a modified design by Williams (1982).

(*continued*)

Section 9.3 (contd)

Reference and illustration	Description	Comments
	trap but prevent drifting organisms from entering. Above the rear screen, which is angled upward, a shallow vinyl pyramid supports a removable glass sample bottle attached to a threaded collar. Sampling area: $0 \cdot 1 \, m^2$.	Exuviae float on the water surface inside the sample bottle.

Drift Samplers and Miscellaneous Designs

Mundie (1964) Fig. 6.13c	A long sheet metal box, tapering in two stages from a narrow vertical slit, which is the trap's only entrance, to a large exit at the rear. An oblique exit screen slopes upward from a narrow gap at its base, directing drift organisms towards an air-filled chamber where insects emerge and become trapped. The upper third of this triangular pyramid chamber is screened to prevent condensation build-up inside and is topped with a removable sample bottle containing a small cone to prevent insects from falling back into the water. Entrance slit $= 2 \cdot 5 \, cm \times 20 \, cm$.	This trap can be set directly on the bottom in shallow streams or supported by lateral floats where water depth exceeds the height of the entrance. In place of the vertical slit entrance, a short length of pipe can be used as a subsurface intake to exclude surface drift. Sample volume is a function of intake size, stream depth and water velocity. Also see Mundie (1966) and Williams (1982).
Mundie (1971b)	A wedge-shaped metal box, with a slit entrance, used as a headpiece for a plankton net. The sampler collects insect drift from a stream.	The wedge-shaped design protects the net from debris and eliminates any bow wave (back-pressure) at the front of the sampler by allowing through only a small fraction of the net's straining capacity.
Carrillo (1974)	Plywood box trap, used on lakes to collect only the floating exuviae of emerging insects. These boxes are open on the top and bottom and covered on	Collections of exuviae are made by periodically skimming the water surface inside the box with a fine mesh dip net.

Section 9.3 *(contd)*

Reference and illustration	Description	Comments
	the outside with foam polystyrene floatation. Sampling area: $1–2\,m^2$ depending on box dimensions.	
Wartinbee & Coffman (1976) Fig. 6.13d	Experimental channels with wooden sides, set several cm into the stream bed, and high enough to contain the entire depth of flow. Fine mesh nets (200 μm opening), attached to the upstream and downstream ends of the channel, stop drift from entering the channel and collect both drift and emerging insects originating from within the channel. Sampling area: $0\cdot6–3\cdot5\,m^2$ depending on dimensions.	Advantages: (1) A large but closely defined sampling area. Disadvantages: (1) large sample size, (2) labour intensive sampling, (3) installation and servicing disrupt the surrounding stream bed. Also see Wartinbee (1979).

10 References

Adamstone F.B. & Harkness W.J.K. (1923) The bottom organisms of Lake Nipigon. *Univ. Toronto Stud., Biol.*, **22**, 121–170.

Ali A. (1980) Diel adult eclosion periodicity of nuisance chironomid midges of central Florida U.S.A. *Environ. Ent.*, **9**, 365–370.

Ali A. & Mulla M.S. (1979) Diel periodicity of eclosion of adult chironomid midges in a residental recreational lake. *Mosq. News*, **39**, 360–364.

Anderson N.H. & Wold J.L. (1972) Emergence trap collections of Trichoptera from an Oregon stream. *Can. Ent.*, **104**, 189–201.

Bagge P., Ilus E. & Paasivirta L. (1980) Emergence of insects (esp. Diptera, Chironomidae) at different depths in the archipelago of Lovisa (Gulf of Finland) in 1971. *Ann. Ent. Fenn.*, **46**, 89–100.

Boerger H. (1981) Species composition, abundance and emergence phenology of midges (Deiptera:[SIC] Chironomidae) in a brown-water stream of west-central Alberta, Canada. *Hydrobiologia*, **80**, 7–30.

Borutsky E.V. (1939a) Dynamics of the biomass of *Chironomus plumosus* in the profundal of Lake Beloie. *Arb. Limnol. Sta. Kossino*, **22**, 156–195.

Borutsky E.V. (1939b) Dynamics of the total benthic biomass in the profundal of Lake Beloie. *Proc. Kossino Limnol. Stn.*, **22**, 196–218. (English translation by M. Ovchynnyk, Mich. State Univ., Mich. Dep. Conserv. 26 pp. + 9 Figs.).

Borutsky E.V. (1955) A new trap for the quantitative estimation of emerging chironomids. (In Russian). *Trud. Vsesoyuz. Gidrobiol. Obschch*, **6**, 223–226.

Böttger K. (1975) Produktionsbiologische studien an dem zentralafrikanischen. Bergbach Kalengo. (Studies on the productivity of the Kalengo-stream in Central Africa). *Arch. Hydrobiol.*, **75**, 1–31. (German with English abstract and summary).

Boyle T.P. (1979) New floating trap for capturing and preserving emerging aquatic insects. *Prog. Fish-Cult.*, **41**, 108–109.

Bretschko G. (1974) The chironomid fauna of a high-mountain lake (Vorderer Finstertaler See, Tyrol, Austria 2237m asl). *Ent. Tidskr.*, **95**, *Suppl.*, 22–33.

Brundin L. (1949) Chironomiden und andere Bodentiere der Südschwedischen Urgebirgsseen. *Rep. Inst. Freshw. Res. Drottning.*, **30**, 1–914.

Butler M.G. (1980) *The Population Ecology Of Some Arctic Alaskan Chironomidae (Diptera)*. Dissertation. Univ. of Michigan, Ann Arbor, 170 pp.

Cantrell M.A. & McLachlan A.J. (1977) Competition and chironomid distribution patterns in a newly flooded lake. *Oikos*, **29**, 429–433.

Carrillo R.J. (1974) *Emergence Dynamics Of A Lentic Chironomidae (Diptera) Community In Northwestern Pennsylvania*. Dissertation. Univ. of Pittsburgh, 316 pp.

Caspers H. (1951) Rhythmische Erscheinungen in der Fortpflanzung von *Clunio marinus* (Dipt. Chiron.) und das Problem der lunaren Periodizität bei Organismen. *Arch. Hydrobiol. Suppl.*, **18**, 415–594.

Cheng L. (1974) A simple emergence trap for small insects. *Pan-Pacific Ent.*, **50**, 305–307.

Coffman W.P. (1973) Energy flow in woodland stream ecosystem: II The taxonomic composition and phenology of the Chironomidae as determined by the collection of pupal exuviae. *Arch. Hydrobiol.*, **71**, 281–322.

Cook P.P. Jr. & Horn H.S. (1968) A sturdy trap for sampling emergent Odonata. *Ann. Ent. Soc. Am.*, **61**, 1506–1507.

Corbet P.S. (1964) Temporal patterns of emergence in aquatic insects. *Can. Ent.*, **96**, 264–279.

Corbet P.S. (1965) An insect emergence trap for quantitative studies in shallow ponds. *Can. Ent.*, **97**, 845–848.

Corbet P.S. (1966) Diel periodicities of emergence and oviposition in riverine Trichoptera. *Can. Ent.*, **98**, 1025–1034.

Danks H.V. & Oliver D.R. (1972) Seasonal emergence of some high arctic Chironomidae (Diptera). *Can. Ent.*, **104**, 661–686.

Davies D.M. (1950) A study of the blackfly populations of a stream in Algonquin Park, Ontario. *Trans. R. Can. Inst.*, **59**, 121–160.

Davies I.J. (1980) Relationships between dipteran emergence and phytoplankton production in the Experimental Lakes Area, northwestern Ontario. *Can. J. Fish. Aquat. Sci.*, **37**, 523–533.

Edwards R.W., Egan H., Learner M.A. & Maris P.J. (1964) The control of chironomid larvae in ponds using TDE (DDD). *J. Appl. Ecol.*, **1**, 97–117.

Elliott J.M. (1971 reprinted 1973) *Some Methods for the Statistical Analysis of samples of Benthic Invertebrates. Freshw. Biol. Assoc. Sci. Publ.*, **25**, 148 pp.

Ettinger W.S. (1979) A collapsible insect emergence trap for use in shallow standing water. *Entomol. News*, **90**, 114–117.

Fast A.W. (1972) A new aquatic insect trap. *Mich. Acad.*, **5**, 115–124.

Fee E.J. (1980) Important factors for estimating annual phytoplankton production in the Experimental Lakes Area. *Can. J. Fish. Aquat. Sci.*, **37**, 513–522.

Flannagan J.F. (1978) Emergence of caddisflies from the Roseau River, Manitoba. In: *Proc. of the 2nd. Int. Symp. on Trichoptera.* M.I.Crichton (ed.), The Hague: W.Junk, p. 183–197.

Flannagan J.F. & Lawler G.H. (1972) Emergence of caddisflies (Trichoptera) and mayflies (Ephemeroptera) from Heming Lake, Manitoba. *Can. Ent.*, **104**, 173–183.

Frank G.H. (1965) The hatching pattern of five species of chironomid from a small reservoir in the eastern Transvaal Lowveld as revealed by a new type of trap. *Hydrobiologia*, **25**, 52–68.

Fremling C.R. (1960) Biology of a large mayfly, *Hexagenia bilineata* (Say), of the Upper Mississippi River. *Iowa Agric. Home Econ. Exp. Stn. Res. Bull.*, **482**, 842–852.

Friesen M.K., Flannagan J.F. & Laufersweiler P.M. (1980) Diel emergence patterns of some mayflies (Ephemeroptera) of the Rouseau River (Manitoba, Canada). In: *Advances in Ephemeroptera Biology.* J.F.Flannagan & K.E.Marshall (eds.), New York: Plenum, p. 287–296.

Gledhill T. (1960) The Ephemeroptera, Plecoptera and Trichoptera caught by emergence traps in two streams during 1959. *Hydrobiol.*, **15**, 179–188.

Grandilewskaja-Decksbach M.L. (1935) Materialien zur Chironomidenbiologie verschiedener Becken. Zur Frage über die Schwankungen der Anzahl und der Biomasse der Chironomidenlarven. *Proc. Kossino Limnol. Sta.*, **19**, 145–182.

Green M.B. (1970) Insect populations of sludge drying beds. *Wat. Pollut. Contr.*, **69**, 399–408.

Guyer G. & Hutson R. (1955) A comparison of sampling techniques utilized in an ecological study of aquatic insects. *J. Econ. Ent.*, **48**, 662–665.

Hamilton A.L. (1965) *An Analysis Of A Freshwater Benthic Community With Special Reference To The Chironomidae.* Dissertation. Univ. British Columbia, Vancouver, B.C. 92 + 216 pp.

Hamilton A.L. (1969) A new type of emergence trap for collecting stream insects. *J. Fish. Res. Board Can.*, **26**, 1685–1689.

Harper F. & Magnin E. (1971) Émergence saisonière de quelques éphémeroptères d'un ruisseau des Laurentides. *Can. J. Zool.*, **49**, 1209–1221.

Harper P.P. & Cloutier L. (1979) Chironomini and Pseudochironomini of a Quebec highland stream (Diptera: Chironomidae). *Ent. Scand. Suppl.*, **10**, 81–94.

Humphries C.F. (1938) The chironomid fauna of the Grossen Plöner See, the relative density of its members and their emergence period. *Arch. Hydrobiol.*, **33**, 535–584.

Ide F.P. (1940) Quantitative determination of the insect fauna of rapid water. *Univ. Toronto Stud., Biol. Ser.*, **47**, 1–13.

Illies J. (1971) Emergenz 1969 in Breitenbach, Schlitzer produktionsbiologische Studien (1). (Emergence 1969 on Breitenbach (Schlitz studies on productivity, No.1). *Arch. Hydrobiol.*, **69**, 14–59. (German with English Abstract and Summary.)

Johnson M.G. (1974) Production and productivity. In: *The Benthos of Lakes.* R.O. Brinkhurst (ed.), London: Macmillan, p. 46–64.

Jónasson P.M. (1954) An improved funnel trap for capturing emerging aquatic insects, with some preliminary results. *Oikos*, **5**, 179–188.

Judd W.W. (1949) Insects collected in the Dundas Marsh, with observations on their period of emergence. *Can. Ent.*, **81**, 1–10.

Judd W.W. (1957) A study of the population of emerging and littoral insects trapped as adults from tributary waters of the Thames River at London, Ontario. *Amer. Midl. Nat.*, **58**, 394–412.

Kajak Z. (1957) Metody ilościowego połowa imagines Tendipedidae. (Methods of the Quantitative capture of emerging imagines and pupae of the Tendipedidae). *Ekol. Pol.* (*B*), **3**, 49–61. (Polish with English Summary).

Kajak Z. (1958) Próba interpretacji dynamiki liczebności fauny bentonicznej w wybranym środowisku lachy wiślanej 'Konfederatka'. *Ekol. Pol*, **6**, 205–291. (Preliminary interpretation of the dynamics of benthic fauna abundance in a chosen environment of the Konfederatka Pool (Old River Bed) adjoining the Vistula River) English Trans., 1965, from Office of Technical Services, U.S. Dept. of Commerce, Washington, D.C., No. OTS 63-11396. 77 pp.

Kimerle R.A. & Anderson N.H. (1967) Evaluation of aquatic insect emergence traps. *J. Econ. Ent.*, **60**, 1255–1259.

Lammers R. (1977) Sampling insects with a wetland emergence trap: design and evaluation of the trap with preliminary results. *Amer. Midl. Nat.*, **97**, 381–389.

Langford, T.E. & Daffern J.R. (1975) The emergence of insects from a British river warmed by power station cooling-water. Part I—The use and performance of insect emergence traps in a large, spate-river and the effects of various factors on total catches, upstream and downstream of the cooling-water outfalls. *Hydrobiologia*, **46**, 71–114.

Laville H. (1971a) Recherches sur les chironomides (Diptera) lacustres du Massif de Néouvielle (Hautes-Pyrénées). Première partie: systématique, écologie, phénologie. *Ann. Limnol.*, **7**, 173–332. (In French).

Laville H. (1971b) Recherches sur les chironomides (Diptera) lacustres du Massif de Néouvielle (Hautes-Pyrénées). Deuxieme partie: communautés et production. *Ann. Limnol.*, **7**, 335–414. (In French).

Lehman J. (1979) Chironomidae (Diptera) aus Fliessgewässen Zentralafrikas (Systematik, Ökologie, Verbreitung und Produktionsbiologie. Teil I: Kivu-Gebiet, Ostzaire. (Chironomids from running waters of Central Africa (Diptera) (Systematic, Ecology, distribution and production biology). Part I: Region of Kivu, east-Zaire). *Spixiana Suppl.*, **3**, 1–144. (In German).

LeSage L. & Harrison A.D. (1979) Improved traps and techniques for the study of emerging aquatic insects. *Ent. News*, **90**, 65–78.

LeSage L. & Harrison A.D. (1980) The biology of *Cricotopus* (Chironomidae: Orthocladinae) in an algal-enriched stream. Part I: Normal biology. *Arch. Hydrobiol. Suppl.*, **57**, 375–418.

Lindeberg B. (1958) A new trap for collecting emerging insects from small rockpools with some examples of the results obtained. *Ann. Ent. Fenn.*, **24**, 186–191.

Macan T.T. (1949) Survey of a moorland fishpond. *J. Anim. Ecol.*, **18**, 160–186.

Macan T.T. (1964) Emergence traps and the investigation of stream faunas. *Rivista di Idrobiologia*, **3**, 75–92.

Malicky H. (1976) Trichoptera—Emergezn in zwei Lunzer Bächen, 1972–74. (Emergence of Trichoptera in 1972–74 from two streams near Lunz (Austria)). Schlitzer Produktionsbiologische Studien Nr. 14. *Arch. Hydrobiol.*, **77**, 51–65. (German with English abstract and summary).

Malicky H. (1980) Evidence for seasonal migrations of larvae of two species of philopotomid caddisflies (Trichoptera) in a mountain stream in lower Austria. *Aquat. Insects.*, **2**, 153–160.

Masteller E.C. (1977) An aquatic emergence trap on a shale stream in western Pennsylvania, U.S.A. *Melsheimer Ent. Ser.*, **23**, 10–15.

McCauley V.J.E. (1976) Efficiency of a trap for catching and retaining insects emerging from standing water. *Oikos*, **27**, 339–345.

Miller R.B. (1941) A contribution to the biology of the Chironomidae of Costello Lake, Algonquin Park, Ontario. *Univ. Toronto. Stud. Biol.*, **49**, 1–63.

Morgan N.C. (1958) Insect emergence from a small Scottish loch. *Int. Ver. Theor. Angew. Limnol. Verh.*, **13**, 823–825.

Morgan N.C. (1971) Factors in the design and selection of insect emergence traps. In: IBP Handbook No. 17, *A Manual on Methods for the Assessment of Secondary Productivity in Fresh Waters*. W.T.Edmondson and G.G.Winberg (eds.). Oxford: Blackwell, p. 93–108.

Morgan N.C. & Waddell A.B. (1961) Insect emergence from a small trout loch, and its bearing on the food supply of fish. *Sci. Invest. Freshwat. Fish. Scot.*, **25**, 1–39.

Morgan N.C., Waddell A.B. & Hall W.B. (1963) A comparison of the catches of emerging aquatic insects in floating box and submerged funnel traps. *J. Anim. Ecol.*, **32**, 203–219.

Mulla M.S., Norland R.L., Ikershoji T. & Kramer W.L. (1974) Insect growth factors for the control of aquatic midges. *J. Econ. Ent.*, **67**, 165–170.

Mundie J.H. (1955) On the distribution of Chironomidae in a storage reservoir. *Int. Ver. Theor. Angew. Limnol. Verh.*, **12**, 577–581.

Mundie J.H. (1956) Emergence traps for aquatic insects. *Int. Ver. Theor. Angew. Limnol. Mitt.*, **7**, 1–13.

Mundie J.H. (1957) The ecology of Chironomidae in storage reservoirs. *Trans. R. Ent. Soc. Lond.*, **109**, 149–232.

Mundie J.H. (1964) A sampler for catching emerging insects and drifting materials in streams. *Limnol. Oceanogr.*, **9**, 456–459.

Mundie J.H. (1966) Sampling emerging insects and drifting materials in deep flowing water. *Gewässer*, **41/42**, 159–162.

Mundie J.H. (1971a) Techniques for sampling emerging aquatic insects. In: *IBP Handbook No. 17, A Manual for Methods for the Assessment of Secondary Productivity in Fresh Waters*. W.T.Edmondson & G.G.Winberg (eds.), Oxford: Blackwell, p. 80–93.

Mundie J.H. (1971b) The diel drift of Chironomidae in an artificial stream and its relation to the diet of Coho Salmon Fry, *Oncorhynchus kisutch* (Waulbaum [SIC]). *Can. Ent.*, **103**, 289–297.

Needham J.G. (1908) Report of the entomological field station conducted at Old Forge, N.Y. in the summer of 1905. *Bull. N.Y. St. Mus.*, **124**, 167–172.

Nordlie K.J. & Arthur J.W. (1981) Effects of elevated water temperature on insect emergence in outdoor experimental channels. *Environ. Pollut. Ser. A.*, **25**, 53–65.

Paasivirta L. (1972) Taxonomy, ecology and swarming behaviour of *Tanytarsus gracilentus* Holmgr. (Diptera, Chironomidae) in Valassaaret, Gulf of Bothnia, Finland. *Ann. Zool. Fenn.*, **9**, 255–264.

Paasivirta L. (1975) Insect emergence and output of incorporated energy and nutrients from the oligotrophic lake Pääjärvi, southern Finland. *Ann. Zool. Fenn.*, **12**, 126–140.

Palmén E. (1955) Diel periodicity of pupal emergence in natural populations of some chironomids (Diptera). *Ann. Zool. Soc. Vanamo.*, **17**, 1–30.

Palmén E. (1962) Studies on the ecology and phenology of the Chironomids (Dipt.) of the Northern Baltic. 1. *Allochironomus crassiforceps* K. *Ann. Ent. Fenn.*, **28**, 137–168.

Potter D.W.B. & Learner M.A. (1974) A study of the benthic macro-invertebrates of a shallow eutrophic reservoir in South Wales with emphasis on the Chironomidae (Diptera); their life histories and production. *Arch. Hydrobiol.*, **74**, 186–226.

Rosenberg D.M. & Wiens A.P. (1983) Efficiency of modifications in the design and use of submerged funnel traps for sampling Chironomidae (Diptera). *Hydrobiologia*, **98**, 113–118.

Rosenberg D.M., Wiens A.P. & Bilyj B. (1980) Sampling emerging Chironomidae (Diptera) with submerged funnel traps in a new northern Canadian reservoir, Southern Indian Lake, Manitoba. *Can. J. Fish. Aquat. Sci.*, **37**, 927–936.

Sandberg G. (1969) A quantitative study of Chironomid distribution and emergence in Lake Erken. *Arch. Hydrobiol. Suppl.*, **35**, 119–201.

Sandrock F. (1978) Vergleichende Emergenzmessung an zwei Bächen des Schliterzerlandes (Breitenbach und Rohrwiesenbach 1970–1971). Schlitzer Produktionsbiologische Studien (24). (A comparison of the insects emerging from two brooks in the region of Schlitz (Breitenbach and Rohrwiesenbach 1970–1971)). (Schlitz studies on productivity, no. 24). *Arch. Hydrobiol. Suppl.*, **54**, 328–408.

Scott W. & Opdyke D.F. (1941) The emergence of insects from Winona Lake. *Invest. Ind. Lakes*, **2**, 3–14.

Speir J.A. & Anderson N.H. (1974) Use of emergence data for estimating annual production of aquatic insects. *Limnol. Oceanogr.*, **19**, 154–156.

Sprules W.M. (1947) An ecological investigation of stream insects in Algonquin Park, Ontario. *Univ. Toronto. Stud., Biol. Ser.*, **56**, 1–81.

Street M. and Titmus G. (1979) The colonisation of experimental ponds by Chironomidae (Diptera). *Aquat. Insects*, **1**, 233–244.

Sublette J.E. & Dendy J.S. (1959) Plastic material for simplified tent and funnel traps. *Southwestern Nat.*, **3**, 220–223.

Teal J.M. (1957) Community metabolism in a temperate cold spring. *Ecol. Monogr.*, **27**, 283–302.

Thienemann A. (1910) Das Sammeln von Puppenhäuten de Chironomiden. Eine Bitte um Mitarbeit. *Arch. Hydrobiol.*, **6**, 213–214.

Vallentyne J.R. (1952) Insect removal of nitrogen and phosphorus compounds from lakes. *Ecol.*, **33**, 573–577.

Wartinbee D.C. (1979) Diel emergence patterns of lotic Chironomidae. *Freshwat. Biol.*, **9**, 147–156.

Wartinbee D.C. & Coffman W.P. (1976) Quantitative determination of Chironomid emergence from enclosed channels in a small lotic ecosystem. *Am. Midl. Nat.*, **95**, 479–485.

Welch H.E. (1967) *Energy Flow Through The Major Macroscopic Components Of An Aquatic Ecosystem*. Dissertation. Univ. Georgia, Athens, Ga. 97 pp.

Welch H.E. (1973) Emergence of Chironomidae (Diptera) from Char Lake, Resolute, Northwest Territories. *Can. J. Zool.*, **51**, 1113–1123.

Welch H.E. (1976) Ecology of Chironomidae (Diptera) in a polar lake. *J. Fish. Res. Board Can.*, **33**, 227–247.

Williams D.D. (1982) Emergence pathways of adult insects in the upper reaches of a stream. *Int. Revue ges. Hydrobiol.*, **67**, 223–234.

Wilson R.S. & Bright P.L. (1973) The use of chironomid pupal exuviae for characterizing streams. *Freshwat. Biol.*, **3**, 283–302.

Wohlschlag D. (1950) Vegetation and invertebrate life in a marl lake. *Invest. Ind. Lakes*, **3**, 321–372.

Wrubleski D.W. & Rosenberg D.M. (in press) Overestimates of Chironomidae (Diptera) abundance from emergence traps with polystyrene floats. *Am. Midl. Nat.*

Zwick P. (1977) Plecopteren-Emergenzweier Lunzer Bäche, 1972–1974, Schlitzer Produktionsbiologische studien Nr. 30. (Plecoptera emerging from two streams at Lunz, 1972–1974). *Arch. Hydrobiol.*, **80**, 458–505 (German with English abstract and summary).

Chapter 7. The Estimation of the Abundance and Biomass of Zooplankton in Samples

EDWARD MCCAULEY

1 Introduction

Techniques of enumeration are essential for generating observations that can be used to test predictions derived from theories or to provoke questions leading to new areas of investigation. The ability to distinguish between estimates of important ecological variables, such as the abundance and biomass of species, directly influences our ability to test predictions and, therefore, to conduct our science. These estimates also form the basis of empirical theories or relationships that can make quantitative predictions about the distribution and abundance of organisms in nature. It is important, therefore, for ecologists to assess their techniques for producing estimates of these basic ecological variables routinely and critically.

The scope of this review is restricted to discussing techniques for determining the number of individuals of a particular size class or cohort present in a sample of zooplankton and the average mass of these individuals. These are the two essential quantities required to calculate the production of a population since multiplying the number of individuals by their average mass yields an estimate of the biomass of the size class or set of individuals in the population being considered and the rate of production is defined as the biomass accumulated by a population per unit time (Chapter 2).

My goals are simple:

(1) To describe techniques, including their assumptions, commonly used to estimate the biomass of individuals and populations in samples.
(2) To evaluate the accuracy and precision of these techniques by presenting estimates of these quantities gathered from actual studies.
(3) To illustrate how the information concerning assumptions, accuracy and precision can be used to make decisions about the utility of the various techniques.

The limitations, in achieving these goals, are not in the descriptive aspects, but in the availability of data to evaluate both the accuracy and the precision of estimates from the various techniques. When empirical estimates are not available, I attempt to discuss the differences in assumptions between alternative techniques and suggest ways in which these can be tested.

Biomass describes the mass of material concentrated in a group of organisms. It is estimated by combining the number of individuals (N) in a size class, cohort, or species and their average mass ($\bar{M}$) to yield an estimate of the biomass (B) of a population:

$$B = N \cdot \bar{M}. \tag{7.1}$$

Throughout this chapter, the terms mass and weight are used interchangeably; although mass is the correct term most ecologists refer to the average weight of individuals. To test several quantitative theories in ecology, a scientist requires an accurate estimate of population biomass with a certain level of precision. Because B is estimated as the product of two variables its precision, as estimated by the fractional coefficient of variation ($CV_B = S/\bar{B}$), is given by:

$$CV_B \simeq ((CV_N)^2 + (CV_M)^2)^{0.5} \tag{7.2}$$

where CV_N and CV_M are the respective coefficients (Chapter 8; Colquhoun 1971) for estimates of N and $\bar{M}$. Once a level of precision for the estimate of B is decided upon, then this places constraints on the precision of the individual estimates required to calculate B. I will use equation 7.2 to discuss the relative merits of alternative techniques for weighing and counting organisms.

I begin with the premise that the approximate level of precision for B which is required to test a particular hypothesis (Chapter 8) can be determined prior to processing the sample. The magnitude of this level will vary, depending upon the ability of different theories to make quantitative predictions. If we know or determine the CVs for alternative procedures of weighing and for alternative techniques of counting a sample, then we can decide on a particular combination of techniques which yields an estimate of B with the desired level of precision. Since human energy is considered a premium, then the choice of technique will be tempered to minimize energy input while still achieving the goal.

Consider the following examples in which we wish to estimate the biomass of a population in a sample with $CV_B = 0.20$. Suppose that only one technique was available to estimate the mean weight of the individuals and its CV_M was determined to be 0.15. From equation 7.2, given $CV_B = 0.20$, we would require a maximum CV_N of 0.13. We would then have to adopt procedures for counting the sample which yielded a CV_N of 0.13. This places limitations on the technique and may help to make a decision. Now suppose that the CV_N of a counting technique was fixed for some reason, perhaps by human energy input, at 0.10 and that two alternative techniques were available for determining the average weight of individuals, which possessed CV_Ms of 0·10 and 0·25, respectively. By solving equation 7.2 for each of the values, it can be seen that the second technique is not appropriate for our stated purpose since it produces estimates of CV_B which are larger than the required level.

The following sections present descriptions of various techniques used to estimate $\bar{M}$ and N for zooplankton and observations collected from the literature on the coefficients of variation for these techniques. I begin with techniques for weighing individuals and then discuss enumeration techniques. The material is presented in this order since one of the most important decisions in estimating biomass is to determine the counting effort. This decision requires prior knowledge from the analyses of weighing techniques. Within each section, I have chosen to discuss techniques for crustacean zooplankton first and then consider comparable problems for rotifers and protozoans. This order will illustrate serious discrepancies in our ability to enumerate different taxa and I hope that, in proceeding from the taxa which have been most studied to those studied least, suggestions as to how these discrepancies could be eliminated will present themselves.

2 Estimating the Mass of Crustacean Zooplankton

To determine what scientists consider to be an estimate of biomass of an individual, I blatantly pirated the approach used by J. Downing (Chapter 4) and conducted a survey of published biomass values for the last decade (Table 7.1). Of the 42 studies cited, 9·5 % equated biomass with fresh weight or wet weight and 83 % reported dry weights of individuals. Of the studies which determine wet weight, 50 % converted these estimates to dry weight by multiplication with some constant. Only 16 % of the studies determined the carbon content of individuals. I therefore concentrated my efforts on describing and comparing alternative techniques used to determine the dry weight of individuals. Recent advances in analyzing the carbon content of individuals are presented in a later section.

The most frequently used technique (Table 7.1) calculates the average dry weight of the population from an estimate of average length. This approach has become popular since Dumont *et al.* (1975) published length-dry weight regression equations for a large variety of species. Subsequently, Bottrell *et al.* (1976) summarized the equations derived from the IBP studies which expanded the potential for this technique considerably. This technique is also used to estimate the dry weight of benthic organisms (Smock 1980). In the following section, I will describe how to make a prediction using an estimate of length, discuss the assumptions involved and perform an analysis to determine expected levels of precision. I will then describe how to measure the length of organisms and to obtain estimates of their dry weights.

Table 7.1 A survey of studies reporting values of biomass for crustacean zooplankton between 1972 and 1982. Biomass is reported as fresh weight (FW), dry weight (DW) and carbon content (C). Among the reports of dry weight, direct weight measurements (DM) versus weight determined from length–weight regressions (LW) are distinguished. Finally, the origin of the regression used in the study is presented as being derived from the original study (LW_O) as opposed to those from the literature (LW_L).

Study	FW	DW DM	DW LW	DW LW_O	DW LW_L	C
Adalsteinsson (1979)	×					
Baudouin & Ravera (1972)						×
Burgis (1974)			×	×		
Coveney et al. (1977)	×					
de Bernardi & di Cola (1976)			×		×	
DeMott (1982)			×		×	
Doohan (1973)		×				
Duncan (1975)		×				
George & Edwards (1974)	×					
Gophen (1978)		×				
Hawkins & Evans (1979)		×				
Herzig (1974)			×	×		
Herzig (1979)			×		×	
Jacobsen & Comita (1976)			×	×		
Lair (1977)			×		×	
Lair (1978)			×		×	
Lampert (1977)						×
Lampert & Krause (1976)						×
Latja & Salonen (1978)			×		×	×
Lehman (1976)			×		×	
Lehman (1980)			×		×	
Lemcke & Lampert (1975)						×
Makarewicz & Likens (1979)			×	×		×
McCauley & Kalff (1981)			×		×	
Mires & Soltero (1981)			×		×	
O'Brien & de Noyelles (1974)			×	×		
Pace & Orcutt (1981)			×	×		
Pedersson et al. (1976)			×		×	
Persson & Ekbohm (1980)			×	×		
Porter et al. (1982)			×	×		
Redfield & Goldman (1981)			×		×	
Redfield & Goldman (1978)		×				
Rosen (1981)			×	×		
Roth & Horne (1980)			×		×	
Schindler & Noven (1971)		×	×	×		
Skogheim & Rognerud (1978)		×				
Smyly (1973)	×					
Snow (1972)			×	×		×
Swift & Hammer (1979)		×				
Threlkeld (1976)			×		×	
Watson & Carpenter (1974)			×	×		
Wattiez (1981)			×		×	

2.1 *Predicting dry weight from estimates of length*

To make a prediction of the mean dry weight of a population using length–weight regressions, the investigator requires an estimate of the representative length of individuals in the population, the appropriate length–weight regression equation, and some simple statistics from both the regression analysis and the length measurements. While it is common to use the first two elements in the above list, the importance of the third is not recognized (Persson & Ekbohm 1980). In addition, although this technique is the most frequently used to estimate the weight of a population (Table 7.1), the accuracy and precision of estimates are rarely considered.

Using regression equations to predict estimates is a simple matter. All of the length–weight regressions which have been collected from the literature and collated in Table 7.2 have been converted to the general form:

$$\ln w = \ln a + b\,\overline{\ln L} \qquad (7.3)$$

where lnw is the natural logarithm of the dry weight (μg), lna the estimate of the intercept, b the estimate of the slope, and $\overline{\ln L}$ the geometric mean length of individuals in the sample population. $\overline{\ln L}$ is calculated as the mean of the transformed length measurements (L in mm). Let s_L^2 represent the estimated variance of $\overline{\ln L}$. I will use the subscripts yx and L to denote contributions from the regression analysis and length measurements, respectively. To predict lnw, the estimate of $\overline{\ln L}$ should be entered into equation 3 and lnw calculated. The variance of lnw ($s_{\ln w}^2$) has been given by Persson & Ekbohm (1980) as:

$$s_{\ln w}^2 = s_{yx}^2\left(n^{-1} + \frac{(\overline{\ln L} - \bar{X})^2 - s_L^2}{\Sigma x^2}\right) + b^2 \cdot s_L^2 \qquad (7.4)$$

where s_{yx}^2 is an estimate of the residual mean square of the regression, n the number of paired observations used to derive the regression, $\bar{X}$ is the mean of the $\overline{\ln L}$ measurements from the regression and Σx^2 is equal to $\Sigma(X - \bar{X})^2$ from the regression (Steel & Torrie 1960).

To arrive at an unbiased estimate of w(μg), the following equation (Brownlee 1967; Baskerville 1972; Persson & Ekbohm 1980) should be used:

$$w = e^{(\ln w + s_{\ln w}^2/2)} \qquad (7.5)$$

where e is the base of the natural logarithm and $s_{\ln w}^2$ is as equation 7.4. The use of equation 7.5 is necessary to correct for the skew which arises in converting logarithmic values back to arithmetic units (Baskerville 1972). Only one of the regression equations presented in Table 7.2 provides the information required to calculate $s_{\ln w}^2$. Differences in the estimates between using equation 7.5 and simply untransforming values are not trivial. For example, the estimate of the dry weight for a population of *Daphnia longispina* having a $\overline{\ln L}$ of 0·5 is more than 8 % higher using equation 7.5 as compared to simply untransforming the value of lnw. A brief inspection of several equations in Table 7.2, suggests that the expected bias in not using equation 7.5 varies between 2 and 11 %. This bias may vary differentially among species, depending on the relative magnitudes of $s_{\ln w}^2$ and lnw.

An estimate of precision (Persson & Ekbohm 1980) is provided by the confidence interval calculated as:

$$CL(w) = \ln w \pm t_{(1-\alpha)} \left\{ s_{yx}^2 \left(n^{-1} + \frac{(\overline{\ln L} - \bar{X})^2 - s_L^2}{\Sigma x^2} \right) + b^2 \cdot s_L^2 \right\}^{0·5} \quad (7.6)$$

where t is from the Students' t-distribution evaluated at α and $n-2$; n is the number of paired observations used to derive the regression, $\bar{X}$ the mean of $\overline{\ln L}$ from the regression, Σx^2 is the $\Sigma (X - \bar{X})^2$ (Steel & Torrie 1960), b and s_L^2 as above. This formula is different from equation 8.50 since it has two variance components, one from the regression analysis and one from estimating the mean length of $\overline{\ln L}$ (Persson & Ekbohm 1980). If the variance in $\overline{\ln L}(s_L^2)$ is assumed to be zero, then equation 7.6 reduces to equation 8.50. The explicit nature of equation 7.6 is important, since it allows the examination of how the variance from the original regression analysis and the variance from the length measurements interact to influence the precision of estimated weight values. An estimate of the variance of the estimated mean weight in arithmetic units (Baskerville 1972), is given by:

$$s_w^2 = e^{(2s_{\ln w}^2 + 2\ln w)} - e^{(s_{\ln w}^2 + 2\ln w)}. \quad (7.7)$$

The terms of this equation are defined above. Values from this equation can be used to calculate the coefficient of variation when accompanied by arithmetic estimates from equation 7.5.

2.1.1 An analysis of the precision of estimates

In using length–weight relationships the general assumption has been made that the error contributed by their use is small relative to other factors, such as sampling variability (Chapter 3) and counting error (Chapter 8). The acceptance of this assumption, along with their general convenience, may account for their prevalence over alternative techniques. This assumption has not been adequately examined, with the notable exception of work by Persson & Ekbohm (1980). To estimate precision levels one simply needs to calculate them using equation 7.6. Few authors, however, report the information required to make a prediction and calculate the level of precision; only one of the 88 equations presented in Table 7.2, has the necessary information.

Table 7.2 Length–weight relationships for crustacean zooplankton collected from the literature. The slope (b), intercept (ln a), pertinent statistics (F/R; F value or correlation coefficient), number of observations (N), residual mean square (RMS) and range of length measurements (mm) are presented for the general relationship:

$$\ln w = a + b \overline{\ln L}$$

where lnw is the logarithm of the dry weight estimate (µg). Preserved samples are indicated with a plus sign.

References (R) for these equations are: (1) Dumont *et al.* (1975), (2) Bottrell *et al.* (1976), (3) Pace & Orcutt (1981), (4) Rosen (1981), (5) Persson & Ekbohm (1980), (6) Burns (1969), (7) O'Brien & deNoyelles (1974), (8) Burgis (1974), (9) Jacobsen & Comita (1976).

The lengths measured (L) refer to: (1) total length not including caudal setae, (2) from the eye to the point of insertion of the caudal spine, (3) only thoracal segments measured, (4) do not include furcal rami, (5) distance between the *setae natores* and the terminal claw of the post-abdomen. Instars refer to nauplii (N), copepodites (C), and adults (ad).

Species	ln a	b	F/R	N	RMS	Range	P	L	Instar	R
(A) CLADOCERA										
(1) *Daphnia*										
D. parvula	1·44	1·80	0·80	44		0·44–1·22	–	1		3
D. parvula	1·08	2·16	0·86	52		0·44–1·22	+	1		3
D. parvula	1·6026	3·632	0·98	25–50		0·40–1·50	+	1		4
D. retrocurva	1·4322	3·129	0·95	25–50		0·50–2·00	+	1		4
D. longispina	1·0727	2·8915	1590	402		0·60–2·35	+	1		2
D. longispina	1·34	2·57			0·155		+	1		2
D. longispina	1·37	2·5567	423	73			+	1		2
D. galeata	1·51	2·56					+	1		1
D. galeata	2·64	2·54				0·60–2·20	+	1		2
D. hyalina	2·46	2·52	191	372		0·60–2·20	+	1		2
D. hyalina	1·4369	2·7680		22	0·0809	0·78–2·21	+	1		2
D. ambigua	1·54	2·29					+	1		1
D. pulex	1·9445	2·72	0·98				+	1		7
D. pulex	1·4663	3·1932	1212	245	0·1629	0·95–3·40	+	1		2
D. pulex	1·59	2·77					+	1		1

Species										
D. pulex	2·48	2·63					0·55–1·60	+	1		6
D. pulex	-0·71	3·13					0·30–0·40	+	1	Ephippial	1
D. pulex	3·1246	0·526	90–240	1581			1·00–2·50	−	2		9
D. schodleri	2·30	3·10					0·82–4·00	+	1		6
D. magna	1·6729	2·6880	1359	245	0·1860		0·84–4·83	+	1		2
D. magna	1·8268	2·7854	6902	516	0·0627			+	1		2
D. magna	2·20	2·63						+	1		6
D. magna	2·51	1·80					1·40–3·60	+	1		1
D. magna	2·36	2·25						+	1		1
D. magna	2·12	2·61						+	1	Ephippial	1
(2) *Ceriodaphnia*										
C. quadrangula	2·5623	3·3380	107		0·1463		0·30–0·71	+	1		2
C. quadrangula	2·3266	2·26		19			0·28–0·60	+	1		1
C. quadrangula	7·1610	7·722	0·99	23				+	1		4
C. reticulata	2·83	3·15	0·90					−	1		3
C. reticulata	3·0727	3·29	0·96					+	1		7
C. reticulata	1·9148	2·02						+	1		1
(3) *Holopedium*										
H. gibberum	5·3976	2·0555	179	8	0·0577		0·08–0·43	+	5		2
H. gibberum	6·4957	3·190	0·87	142	0·201		3·01–3·37	−	5		5
H. gibberum	6·2625	3·052	0·94	107				−	5		5
(4) *Diaphanosoma*										
D. brachyrum	1·2894	3·039	0·91				0·40–1·20	+	1		4
D. brachyrum	1·3252	2·11						+	1		1
D. brachyrum	1·6242	3·0468	1488	106	0·1370		0·44–1·44	+	1		2
(5) *Bosmina*										
B. longirostris	2·7116	2·5294	88	17	0·051		0·28–0·54	+	1		2
B. longirostris	3·28	3·13						+	1		2
B. longirostris	4·68	4·27						+	1	+ eggs	2
B. longirostris	4·9344	4·849	0·99				0·20–0·50	+	1		4
B. longispina	2·7312	2·0665	322	26	0·0172		0·44–0·95	+	1		2
B. longispina	3·5274	3·5859	70	34	0·0936		0·38–0·50	+	1		2

(continued)

Table 7.2—(contd)

	Species	ln a	b	F/R	N	RMS	Range	P	L	Instar	R
	B. obtusirostris	3·2359	2·928	0·90	108	0·077	2·64–3·22	–	1		5
	B. coregoni	2·7839	2·505	0·90	84			–	1		5
(6)	*Chydorus*										
	C. sphaericus	4·5430	3·636	0·97			0·20–0·40	+	1		4
	C. sphaericus	4·4935	3·93					+	1		1
	C. sphaericus	4·8211	4·08					+	1		1
(7)	*Leptodora*										
	L. kindtii	−0·8220	2·670	0·97	10–25		1·00–5·00	+	1		4
(8)	*Polyphemus*										
	P. pediculus	2·7792	2·152	0·98	25–50		0·30–1·10	+	1		4
(9)	*Sida*										
	S. crystallina	2·0539	2·189	0·90	25–50		0·80–2·30	+	1		4
(10)	*Scapholeberis*										
	S. kingi	2·8713	3·079	0·99	25–50		0·30–0·80	+	1		4
(11)	*Ilyocriptus*										
	I. sordidus	5·9913	7·942	0·98	25–100		0·30–0·60	+	1		4
(12)	*Disparalona*										
	D. rostrata	3·5276	3·264	0·99	25–100		0·30–0·50	+	1		4
(B)	**COPEPODA**										
(1)	*Copepod nauplii*	0·6977	0·469	0·98	50–100		0·16–0·30	+	1		4
(2)	*Diaptomus*										
	D. pallidus	1·5013	1·730	0·85	25–50		0·30–1·40	+	4		4
	D. siciloides	1·05	2·46	0·59	26			–	1		3
	D. gracilis	1·2431	2·2634	213	23	0·1422	0·30–1·85	+	1	N-ad	2
(3)	*Cyclops*										
	C. vernalis	2·2266	3·230	0·99	25–50		0·40–1·20	+	4		4
	C. vernalis	2·4511	0·7825	0·66	21	0·2123	1·22–1·73	+	4	CV-ad	2
	C. scutifer	1·4919	1·985	0·81		0·138	0·14–0·73	–	1		5

	Taxon										Stage	
	C. scutifer	1·3048	2·500	0·89					−	1	N1–N6	5
	C. scutifer	2·5442	2·3696		76	6	0·0257	0·14–0·29	+	1	CI-ad	2
	C. scutifer	1·2286	2·6398		67	7	0·0782	0·45–1·20	+	1	N1-ad	2
	C. scutifer	1·0866	1·5493		105	13	0·1652	0·14–1·20	+	1	ad	2
	C. viridis	2·7412	1·6785		11	29	0·0837	1·60–2·45	+	4	N-CV	2
	C. vicinus	1·4497	2·1160		1336	27	0·0578	0·17–1·60	+	4	N-ad♀	2
	C. vicinus	2·0577	2·5530		2938	111	0·0471	0·17–2·18	+	4		2
	C. vicinus	2·4342	1·9694		67	84	0·2400	1·25–2·18	+	4	ad♀	2
	C. vicinus	2·0186	1·9948		64	120	0·2471	1·12–2·18	+	4		2
	C. strenuus	1·5386	2·3418		362	20	0·0757	0·24–1·72	+	1	N-ad	2
	C. abyssorum	2·2128	2·2947		305	52	0·0806	0·66–1·70	+	1	CII-ad	2
(4)	*Mesocyclops*											
	M. edax	1·6602	3·968	0·97		25–50		0·30–1·50	+	1		4
	M. leuckarti	1·3035	2·49					0·30–1·10	+	1		8
	M. leuckarti	1·2700	2·2570		134	23	0·1031	0·33–1·14	+	4	C-ad	2
(5)	*Heterocope*											
	H. appendiculata	1·1356	2·996	0·88			0·150	0·36–0·99	−	1		5
	H. appendiculata	1·4678	2·908	0·98					−	1		5
	H. saliens	2·0365	1·8911		132	9	0·0238	0·18–0·79	+	1	N1–N6	2
	H. saliens	1·8977	2·0374		460	8	0·0112	0·66–2·08	+	1	CI-ad	2
	H. saliens	1·8551	1·9756		1972	17	0·0190	0·18–2·08	+	1	N1-ad	2
(6)	*Eudiaptomus*											
	E. graciloides	1·6296	3·192	0·88			0·139	0·36–0·81	−	1		5
	E. gracilis	1·6097	2·529	0·94					−	1		5
(7)	*Thermocyclops*											
	T. hyalinus	1·3035	2·49					0·30–1·10	+	1		8
	T. hyalinus	0·6772	0·8928		44	25	0·1131	0·31–0·68	+	4	C-ad	2
(8)	*Arctodiaptomus*											
	A. spinosus	2·8519	3·6520		57	48	0·1699	0·32–0·60	+	3	C	2
	A. spinosus	2·3409	2·4409		135	86	0·0284	0·65–1·02	+	3	ad♂	2
	A. spinosus	2·2614	3·5724		278	107	0·0497	0·76–1·16	+	3	ad♀	2
	A. spinosus	2·3392	2·9835		2778	241	0·0797	0·32–1·16	+	3	C-ad	2

Table 7.3 This table shows how the error in estimating the length of an organism will influence the error of the dry weight estimate. Estimates of precision (95% confidence limits—C.L.) expressed as a percentage (%) of the estimated dry weight (ln w) are presented for different levels of assumed variation in length measurements (s_L^2). 's.d.' is the square root of s_{lnw}^2 as calculated in equation 7.4. These levels of variance are expressed as a percentage of the mean length (lnL). Part A presents these estimates evaluated at the mean of the length–weight regression for four different species of crustaceans. Part B evaluates the estimates at the upper limit of the regression.

Species	s_L^2	s.d.	lnw	C.L.	%
(A) Evaluated at the mean of the regression:					
(1) *Daphnia longispina*	20	0·6323	1·7637	1·7392	245
	10	0·4473	1·7637	0·8767	140
(lnL = 0·239)	5	0·3166	1·7637	0·6205	85
	1	0·1427	1·7637	0·2796	32
	0	0·0197	1·7637	0·0386	3
(2) *Daphnia parvula*	20	0·3410	1·1138	0·6820	98
	10	0·2421	1·1138	0·4842	68
(lnL = −0·1812)	5	0·1725	1·1138	0·3450	42
	1	0·0816	1·1138	0·1632	18
	0	0·0299	1·1138	0·0598	6
(3) *Ceriodaphnia reticulata*	20	1·1195	0·8301	2·3106	908
	10	0·7926	0·8301	1·6359	413
(lnL = −0·63488)	5	0·5619	0·8301	1·1597	218
	1	0·2566	0·8301	0·5296	70
	0	0·0577	0·8301	0·1192	13
(4) *Diaptomus siciloides*	20	0·2628	1·1877	0·5403	72
	10	0·1885	1·1877	0·3876	48
(lnL = 0·05597)	5	0·1368	1·1877	0·2813	32
	1	0·0727	1·1877	0·1495	16
	0	0·0438	1·1877	0·0901	9
(B) Evaluated at the upper limit of the regression:					
(1) *Daphnia longispina*	20	1·0769	3·077	2·1107	725
	10	0·7620	3·077	1·4935	345
(lnL = 0·6932)	5	0·5390	3·077	1·0574	187
	1	0·2436	3·077	0·4775	62
	0	0·0384	3·077	0·0752	8
(2) *Daphnia parvula*	20	0·3692	1·800	0·7384	109
	10	0·2695	1·800	0·5390	72
(lnL = 0·200)	5	0·2019	1·800	0·4038	50
	1	0·1237	1·800	0·2474	28
	0	0·0946	1·800	0·1893	22

Table 7.3—*contd.*

Species	s_L^2	s.d.	lnw	C.L.	%
(3) *Ceriodaphnia reticulata*	20	0·7514	1·948	1·5508	372
	10	0·5376	1·948	1·1096	203
$(\overline{\ln L} = -0·280)$	5	0·3888	1·948	0·8025	123
	1	0·2023	1·948	0·4175	52
	0	0·1155	1·948	0·2384	27
(4) *Diaptomus siciloides*	20	0·4805	1·517	0·9879	168
	10	0·3418	1·517	0·7027	101
$(\overline{\ln L} = 0·1900)$	5	0·2446	1·517	0·5029	65
	1	0·1193	1·517	0·2453	28
	0	0·0531	1·517	0·1092	12

Fortunately, M. Pace provided me with the statistics for the equations presented in Pace & Orcutt (1981), which allowed me to examine this assumption on three more species of crustaceans.

I evaluated the expected levels of precision (Table 7.3) by assuming certain levels of variation in $\overline{\ln L}$, the independent variable, which are not uncommonly found when estimating $\overline{\ln L}$ for natural populations. The results are presented as approximate 95 % confidence limits expressed as a percentage of the predicted weight. These limits are calculated for two values of $\overline{\ln L}$; one at the mean of L used in the original regression analysis, and the second value near the upper limit of L. In addition, the limits were calculated assuming zero variance in length measurements (this is the most conservative estimate possible since variation is derived only from the regression analysis).

The results are striking (Table 7.3). Small variation in $\overline{\ln L}$ causes the 95 % confidence limits to increase dramatically. Assuming zero variance in $\overline{\ln L}$, the 95 % confidence limits were of the order of 3–12 % at the mean of $\overline{\ln L}$ and 8–27 % at the upper limit of $\overline{\ln L}$. If one percent variance is assumed these limits change to 17–32 % and 28–61 % at the mean and upper limits, respectively. This decrease in precision is considerable given the low level of variance assumed for length measurements, and the analysis suggests that estimates of length for a population should be as precise as possible. The reasons for this are evident upon inspection of equation 7.6. The variance contributed by measurement of L is multiplied by the square of the slope from the log length–log weight regression. In addition, these regressions describe power relationships whereby small deviations in L produce considerable increases in the weight estimate because of the magnitude of the slope. Model 1 regression analysis assumes that there is no error associated with the independent variable, and, although this is rarely true when real data are used, it is assumed that the effect of this small variation is insignificant. Perhaps this assumption is not true for relationships described by power functions.

The 95 % confidence limits are conservative estimates of precision. They are somewhat greater than the Least Significant Difference (LSD) used in analyses of variance procedures (Steel & Torrie 1960). I also calculated the coefficients of variation for the technique given different levels of variation in estimating $\overline{\ln L}$ (Table 7.4). The trend is similar to that described for the 95 % confidence limits. These values can be used to compare the relative abilities of alternative techniques to produce estimates of biomass.

Investigators wanting to use the equations (Table 7.2) to predict dry weight from an estimate of $\overline{\ln L}$ should be sure that $\overline{\ln L}$ is within the range of the original regression analysis. When there is more than one equation for a species, it is impossible at present to make recommendations on which one to use. There have been few systematic studies to test which factors influence the parameters of the equations (Lemcke & Lampert 1975), and many attempts to explain intraspecific variation in the parameters on the basis of habitat differences are anecdotal (Dumont *et al.* 1975). As more regressions are collected, this variation may be found to be related to simple variables such as the altitude, latitude, temperature or phytoplankton biomass of the study site. These relationships could then be used by the investigator to decide between alternative equations. Until more empirical evidence is available, I would recommend using the equation which has a mean $\overline{\ln L}$ closest to the measured $\overline{\ln L}$ (Tables 7.3 and 7.4).

2.2 *Measuring the length or dimensions of an organism*

The previous section showed that the lengths of individuals must be measured with the highest possible accuracy and precision if they are to be used to predict weight estimates, since even small deviations in length can produce large deviations in weight estimates due to the nature of the regression equations. In addition, accurate measures of the linear dimensions of individuals are necessary for the calculation of volume as an estimate of biomass for rotifers and protozoans (see Sections 7.3 and 7.4). The length of an individual crustacean can be measured using a dissecting microscope equipped with an ocular micrometer or, in the case of rotifers and protozoans, using an inverted compound microscope (Edmondson & Winberg 1971). An ocular micrometer is an optical instrument which focuses a scaled line or grid onto the plane of the specimen being examined and is not simply a scale or Whipple disc placed in the eyepiece and calibrated with a stage micrometer. The use of an ocular micrometer reduces, but does not remove, the possibility of error in measurements due to variation in the angle and distance between the eye of the observer and the eyepiece of the microscope. Variation in the

Table 7.4 The coefficient of variation (CV = S/W) for arithmetic estimates of dry weight (W) and its variance (s_W), assuming different levels of variance in measuring lnL (s_L^2; expressed as a percentage of lnL). See Table 7.3 for results of the analysis in logarithmic values.

Species	s_L^2	s_W	$W\,(\mu g)$	CV
(A) Evaluated at the mean of the regression:				
(1) *Daphnia longispina*	20	4·9952	7·1249	0·7011
	10	3·0346	6·4478	0·4706
$\overline{(\ln L} = 0·239)$	5	1·9917	6·1338	0·3247
	1	0·8453	5·8937	0·1434
	0	0·1150	5·8351	0·0197
(2) *Daphnia parvula*	20	1·1336	3·2283	0·3511
	10	0·7706	3·1365	0·2457
$\overline{(\ln L} = -0·1812)$	5	0·5373	3·0916	0·1738
	1	0·2498	3·0561	0·0817
	0	0·0911	3·0473	0·0299
(3) *Ceriodaphnia reticulata*	20	6·7886	4·2919	1·5820
	10	2·9359	3·1400	0·9350
$\overline{(\ln L} = -0·63488)$	5	1·6365	2·6858	0·6093
	1	0·6184	2·3703	0·2609
	0	0·1327	2·2074	0·0578
(4) *Diaptomus siciloides*	20	0·9078	3·3948	0·2674
	10	0·6349	3·3383	0·1902
$\overline{(\ln L} = 0·05597)$	5	0·4550	3·3104	0·1374
	1	0·2394	3·2827	0·0728
	0	0·1439	3·2827	0·0438
(B) Evaluated at the upper limit of the regression:				
(1) *Daphnia longispina*	20	57·3162	38·7394	1·4795
	10	25·7305	29·0008	0·8872
$\overline{(\ln L} = 0·6932)$	5	14·5648	25·0848	0·5806
	1	5·5254	22·0848	0·2473
	0	0·8339	21·7092	0·0384
(2) *Daphnia parvula*	20	2·4749	6·4763	0·3822
	10	1·7218	6·2734	0·2745
$\overline{(\ln L} = 0·200)$	5	1·2594	6·1742	0·2040
	1	0·7570	6·0961	0·1242
	0	0·5762	6·0768	0·0948
(3) *Ceriodaphnia reticulata*	20	8·1032	9·3027	0·8711
	10	4·6920	8·1052	0·5789
$\overline{(\ln L} = -0·280)$	5	3·0562	7·5654	0·4040
	1	1·4633	7·1592	0·2044
	0	0·8183	7·0616	0·1159
(4) *Diaptomus siciloides*	20	2·6074	5·1163	0·5096
	10	1·7013	4·8327	0·3520
$\overline{(\ln L} = 0·1900)$	5	1·1663	4·6970	0·2483
	1	0·5497	4·5911	0·1197
	0	0·2426	4·5650	0·0531

accuracy of measurements can derive from fatigue of the observer (this alters the position of the head relative to the eyepiece) and also from differences among observers (R. Lamarche personal communication).

Recently, Sprules *et al.* (1981) presented a microcomputer-based technique which uses a caliper system linked to a microcomputer through an analog-digital converter (Fig. 7.1). The image of the individual organism or characteristic to be measured is projected onto the viewing screen of a microscope. The caliper is then spread and positioned to make the measurement. The spreading of the caliper varies the voltage across its potentiometer; this is then relayed to the computer through the analog-digital converter. A complete description of the caliper plus construction details are provided by Sprules *et al.* (1981). They report that using this technique 400–700 organisms can be measured in 15–20 minutes. The estimated cost of assembling the system is approximately $US2800–3500 (1981), excluding the microscope and assuming shop facilities for constructing the caliper. Their

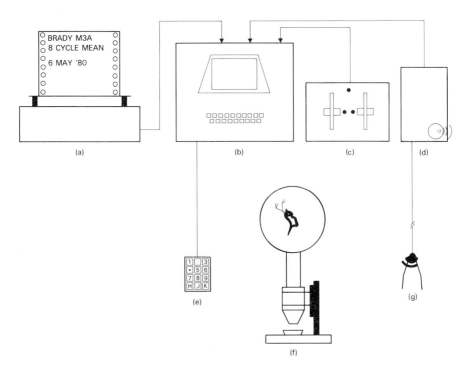

Fig. 7.1 The design for a computer assisted technique to measure the length or dimensions of microscopic organisms. It consists of a caliper system (g) linked to a computer (b) through an analog-digital converter (d). Data entry is controlled using a key pad (e) (From Sprules *et al.* 1981).

system also has the advantage of data processing, storage, and retrieval using the associated microcomputer. A similar system is presented by McAlister & Planck (1981) for measuring larger organisms such as fish which do not require optical magnification.

Different anatomical characteristics have been used for length measurement in various zooplankton species. It is important to check exactly what length measurements are required to derive an estimate of weight when using either length–weight regression (Table 7.2) or volume calculations (Table 7.5). In the Cladocera, the most commonly measured characteristic is total length of the individual, as measured from the top of the head to the point of insertion of the tail spine. The length from a point in the eye region, either in the centre of the eyespot or its exterior aspect, to the point of insertion of the tail spine is also frequently used in some species of *Daphnia* that possess helmets. For *Holopedium gibberum* which is a particularly flexible species, the distance between the *setae natores* and the terminal claw of the post-abdomen has been used since this structure is more rigid (Persson & Ekbohm 1980). Similar variation in the characteristics measured can be found in the equations describing length–weight relationships for the Copepoda (Bottrell *et al.* 1976). Measurements are made from the tip of the cephalothorax to various points on the urosome, usually excluding the furcal rami (Table 7.2). An interesting suggestion for a means of avoiding ambiguity in measuring lengths of marine copepods was that maximum width of the body be used rather than length (Pearre 1980). He found that regression equations of width–wet weight relationships made more precise estimates than length–wet weight relationships. Perhaps this modification would yield similar improvements if applied to freshwater copepods. In all cases, care should be taken that the specimen being measured is lying flat so that the measurement is in one plane.

2.3 *Measuring the dry weight of individuals*

The techniques described in this section are applicable for determining the dry weight of individuals or the average dry weight of populations. These weights may then be used to calculate the biomass of a population or to construct length–weight regressions. Although preservation techniques are described in Chapter 3, I will briefly discuss their effects as they relate to determining the accuracy of the dry weight estimate. I will then present the techniques for weighing and discuss their precision.

2.3.1 *Preservation effects*

There is some question as to the importance of dry weight loss upon preservation of samples with formalin. Dumont *et al.* (1975) compared dry weights of preserved and freshly frozen individuals of the rotifer *Asplanchna brightwelli* and the cladoceran *Daphnia pulex* and concluded that weight loss is insignificant after formalin preservation. Recently, Pace & Orcutt (1981) found a significant difference between length–weight regressions of fresh and formalin preserved individuals of *Daphnia parvula*, the dry weight of *D. parvula* was significantly underestimated using formalin preserved individuals. This result is consistent with observations on dry weight loss of marine zooplankton (Omori 1978). Schram *et al.* (1981) found a dry weight loss in *Ceriodaphnia lacustris* of up to 47 % after preservation in 3 % formalin, and they also demonstrated a temporal component to this loss process. Individuals of *C. lacustris* lost 25 % and 47 % of their dry weight after 15 and 45 days of preservation, respectively. This time element could account for the discrepancy among observations on dry weight loss from the different studies. Dry weights of *Daphnia pulex* were compared only after a period of 24 h in the study by Dumont *et al.* (1975) and although they report no difference in the weight of *Asplanchna brightwelli* after 9 years of preservation, it is not clear how this test was performed. The evidence suggests that dry weight loss upon preservation in formalin is significant and it should not be ignored as was previously suggested by Bottrell *et al.* (1976).

Based on their findings, Pace & Orcutt (1981) elected to construct length–weight relationships using fresh specimens. On the other hand, Schram *et al.* (1981) recommended that samples be preserved and then measured only after a certain period of time (the time required being that needed to produce stable results). This time period would have to be determined for each species of interest. In addition, they recommend that a standard concentration of formalin be used; the use of different concentrations might result in variable weight loss ratios after stabilization. Obviously, the use of fresh specimens has disadvantages in the necessity of making measurements on freshly collected samples; however, this inconvenience may be minor relative to the energy required to implement the recommendations of Schram *et al.* (1981).

2.3.2 *Estimating dry weight*

To determine the dry weight of crustaceans, individuals are isolated from the sample using a pipette or a fine dissecting needle (this can be hooked under the antennae of several of the larger species to enable the individual to be lifted out of the tray without damage). Furnass & Findley (1975) present an apparatus which can be attached to the stage of the dissecting microscope and used to sort individuals without picking them up manually. Individuals can be delivered into the field of view of the microscope with a stream of water, and then redirected to another sample jar by using a valve to change the direction of the flow. If the weights are for length–weight relationships, then eggs embryos, and gelatinous sheaths should be removed prior to weighing (Dumont *et al.* 1975; Persson & Ekbohm 1980). The decision on whether to weigh individuals or groups of animals can be made on the basis of the expected weight of an individual. Dumont *et al.* (1975) suggested that the minimum amount of weighed material should exceed $5.0 \mu g$, given that the sensitivity of the most commonly used balances—the Cahn Electrobalance® and the Mettler Microbalance®—is reported as $0.1 \mu g$. The animals should be rinsed with distilled water if they are from preserved samples. The animals are then placed on tared aluminium foil pans or boats (Dumont *et al.* 1975; Makarewicz & Likens 1979). The material used as a weighing pan varies among studies; for example, Rosen (1981) used small pieces of prewashed fiberglass filter paper which had been oven dried to constant weight. Whatever the material used, the weight of the pan should be kept to a minimum (Edmondson & Winberg 1971). The animals, on their trays, are then placed in an oven and dried for 24–48 h at 60 °C. The temperature and duration of drying also varied considerably among studies. The highest temperature recorded was 110 °C (Snow 1972; Baudouin & Ravera 1972; Dumont *et al.* 1975), the lowest was 55 °C (Jacobsen & Comita 1976) and the most commonly used was 60 °C (Burns 1969; Makarewicz & Likens 1979; Pace & Orcutt 1981; Persson & Ekbohm 1980; Rosen 1981; Schram *et al.* 1981). Drying time varied between 2 and 48 h with 24 h being the most frequently used. After drying, the samples are allowed to cool in a desiccator for 1–2 h and are then transferred to the balance and weighed using counterbalance techniques to maximize the accuracy of the reading. A small container of desiccant should be placed in the chamber of the balance to absorb moisture picked up while transferring the sample. Placing a container of desiccant inside the housing of the balance and sealing this space also improves the stability of the reading (J. Downing, personal communication). Weighings should be delayed for a short period of time, to allow for stabilization.

To obtain an estimate of precision, replicates of individuals or groups can be weighed. The number of replicates can then be varied to give a desired level of precision. Gophen (1978) reported weights and 95 % confidence limits for different developmental stages of *Mesocyclops leuckarti*. He found that these limits varied between 4 and 6 % of the average dry weights, weighing 100 animals. Swift & Hammer (1979) present mean weights and 95 % confidence limits for four different developmental stages of *Diaptomus* at several times during the growing season. The limits vary in magnitude among stages; however, on average they appear to be less than 10 % of the mean dry weight. Five samples of 10–150 individuals of each stage were weighed for each sampling date. Individual weights were calculated from the sample dry weights and the number of individuals per sample. Hawkins & Evans (1979) report seasonal variations in weights and precision for 5 different species of crustaceans from Lake Michigan. Although the results appear in graphical form, the 95 % confidence limits are approximately $\leq 10\%$ for most species and sampling dates. I determined the coefficients of variation for these estimates by back calculation using equations presented in Chapter 8 and found that these varied between 0·01 and 0·08. There was no consistent pattern with the different sizes of individuals being measured. Unfortunately, none of the studies which provide estimates of precision give any indication of the time required to obtain the desired level of precision. This time period would vary with the number of species involved, their size, and the number of samples to be processed.

The discussion of whether to use length–weight techniques or direct weighing will be reserved until the last section of this chapter, once analyses for enumeration techniques are described.

3 Estimating the Mass of Rotifers

There are two different techniques employed to measure the dry weight of rotifers. One technique estimates dry weight through the use of geometrical formulae which approximate the volume of an individual. The second technique estimates dry weight directly by weighing individuals of a species using a microbalance. Ruttner-Kolisko (1977) suggests that volume determination is currently more efficient because of the considerable time required to weigh individuals and the large error associated with the measured weights. Some workers may feel that directly weighing individuals, which provides an error estimate, is more appropriate in testing their hypothesis than determining weights from volume estimates which possess a number of assumptions, outlined below.

To estimate dry weight using geometrical approximations, several different dimensions are measured and then used to calculate a volume estimate from simple formulae which depend upon the shape of the species. Ruttner-Kolisko (1977; Appendix 1 Bottrell *et al.* 1976) presents a complete description of the technique, including a list of formulae and the appropriate dimensions required to calculate the volumes of over 20 genera (Table 7.5). The dimensions should be estimated on slightly narcotized, living adult specimens, that have not been flattened by a coverslip (Ruttner-Kolisko 1977). Once the volume has been calculated, it is converted to fresh weight assuming a specific gravity of 1. Bottrell *et al.* (1976) present a range of fresh weights for various rotifers determined from volume calculations. Fresh weight is then converted to dry weight assuming some constant value. Schindler & Noven (1971) assumed a ratio of 0·05 (dry:wet); while, Pace and Orcutt (1981) used a value of 0·1, as was determined by Doohan (1973) for *Brachionus plicatus*.

Table 7.5 Formulae for calculating the volume of rotifers (from Ruttner-Kolisko 1977).

Genus	(1) Geometric formula used	(2) Calculation formula	(3) Simplified formula when:	then:	(4) Appendices in % of body volume (b.v.)	measurement used for formula	(5) a = length, b = width, c = height of body
Anuraeopsis	trilateral truncated pyramid: $\dfrac{2G \cdot h}{2}$	$v = 0.33 \times abc$	$b = 0.5a$; $c = 0.2a$;	$v = 0.03a^3$	-.-.-.-.-	$a = h$; $\dfrac{bc}{2} = G$	
Ascomorpha	general ellipsoid: $\dfrac{4\pi \cdot r_1 r_2 r_3}{3}$	$v = 0.52 \times abc$	$b = 0.6a$; $c = 0.4a$;	$v = 0.12a^3$	-.-.-.-.-	$a = 2r_1$; $b = 2r_2$; $c = 2r_3$	
Asplanchna	ellipsoid of revolution: $\dfrac{4\pi \cdot r^2 r_3}{3}$	$v = 0.52 \times ab^2$	$b = c = 0.7a$;	$v = 0.23a^3$	-.-.-.-.-.-	$a = 2r_3$; $b = c = 2r$	
Brachionus	general ellipsoid: $\dfrac{4\pi \cdot r_1 r_2 r_3}{3}$	$v = 0.52 \times abc$	$b = 0.6a$; $c = 0.4a$;	$v = 0.12a^3$	foot: 10% of b.v.	$a = 2r_1$; $b = 2r_2$; $c = 2r_3$	
Conochilus colony	sphere: $\dfrac{4r^3\pi}{3}$	$v(col.) = 4.2a^3$	a:b has to be measured	$v(col.) = 4.2a^3$		$b = c = 2r$	
individual	cone: $\dfrac{r^2\pi h}{3}$	$v(ind.) = 0.26 \times ab^2$		$v(ind.) = 0.26ab^2$	-.-.-.-.-	$a = h$	

(continued)

Table 7.5—(contd).

Genus	(1)	(2)	(3)	(4)	(5)
Collotheca	cone: $\dfrac{r^2\pi h}{3}$	$v = 0.26 \times ab^2$	$a = 7b$; $v = 1.8\,b^3$	gelatinous hull: 150–200% of b.v.	$b = 2r$ $a = h$
Euchlanis	1/2 general ellipsoid: $\dfrac{2\pi \cdot r_1 r_2 r_3}{3}$	$v = 0.52 \times abc$	$b = 0.6\,a$ $c = 0.3\,a$; $v = 0.1\,a^3$	foot: 5% of b.v.	$a = 2r_1$ $b = 2r_2$ $c = r_3$
Filinia	ellipsoid of revolution: $\dfrac{4\pi \cdot r_1 r_1 r_3}{3}$	$v = 0.52 \times ab^2$	$b = 0.5\,a$; $v = 0.13\,a^3$	1% of b.v. $\times \dfrac{\text{length of setae}}{\text{length of body (a)}}$	$a = 2r_3$ $b = c = 2r_1 = 2r_2$
Gastropus	elliptic cylinder: $r_1 r_2 \pi \cdot h$	$v = 0.8 \times abc$	$b = 0.7\,a$ $c = 0.4\,a$; $v = 0.20\,a^3$	—·—·—·—·—	$b = 2r_1$ $c = h$ $a = 2r_2$
Hexarthra	cone: $\dfrac{r^2\pi h}{3}$	$v = 0.26 \times ab^2$	$b = 0.75\,a$; $v = 0.13\,a^3$	33% of bv.	$a = h$ $b = c = 2r$
Kellikottia	cone: $\dfrac{r^2\pi h}{3}$	$v = 0.26 \times ab^2$	$b = 0.33\,a$; $v = 0.03\,a^3$	1.5% of b.v. $\times \dfrac{\text{caudal + frontal setae}}{\text{body length}}$	$a = h$ $b = 2r$
Keratella quadrata group	Parallelepiped: abc	$v = abc$	$b = 0.7\,a$ $c = 0.33\,a$; $v = 0.22\,a^3$	5% of b.v. $\times \dfrac{\text{caudal spines}}{\text{body length}}$	a, b, c

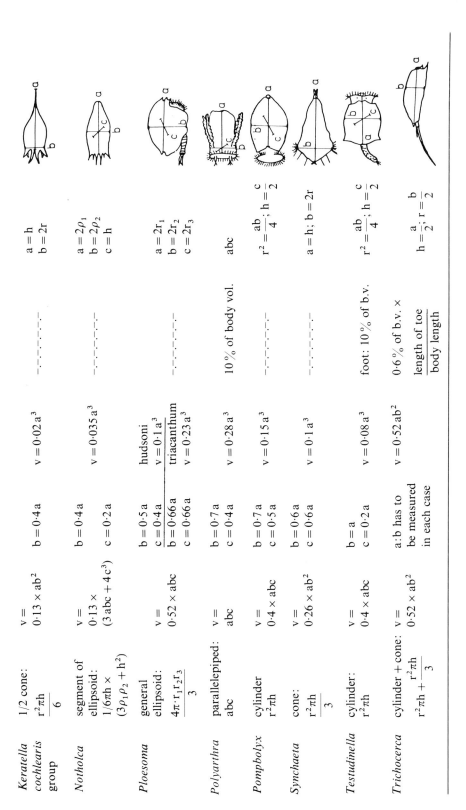

Keratella cochlearis group	1/2 cone: $\dfrac{r^2\pi h}{6}$	$v = 0.13 \times ab^2$	$b = 0.4a$	$v = 0.02a^3$	—·—·—·—·—·—	$a = h$ $b = 2r$
Notholca	segment of ellipsoid: $1/6\pi h \times (3\rho_1\rho_2 + h^2)$	$v = 0.13 \times (3abc + 4c^3)$	$b = 0.4a$ $c = 0.2a$	$v = 0.035a^3$	—·—·—·—·—	$a = 2\rho_1$ $b = 2\rho_2$ $c = h$
Ploesoma	general ellipsoid: $\dfrac{4\pi \cdot r_1 r_2 r_3}{3}$	$v = 0.52 \times abc$	$b = 0.5a$ $c = 0.4a$ $b = 0.66a$ $c = 0.66a$	hudsoni $v = 0.1a^3$ triacanthum $v = 0.23a^3$	—·—·—·—·—	$a = 2r_1$ $b = 2r_2$ $c = 2r_3$
Polyarthra	parallelepiped: abc	$v = abc$	$b = 0.7a$ $c = 0.4a$	$v = 0.28a^3$	10% of body vol.	abc
Pompholyx	cylinder $r^2\pi h$	$v = 0.4 \times abc$	$b = 0.7a$ $c = 0.5a$	$v = 0.15a^3$	—·—·—·—·—	$r^2 = \dfrac{ab}{4}; h = \dfrac{c}{2}$
Synchaeta	cone: $\dfrac{r^2\pi h}{3}$	$v = 0.26 \times ab^2$	$b = 0.6a$ $c = 0.6a$	$v = 0.1a^3$	—·—·—·—·—	$a = h; b = 2r$
Testudinella	cylinder: $r^2\pi h$	$v = 0.4 \times abc$	$b = a$ $c = 0.2a$	$v = 0.08a^3$	foot: 10% of b.v.	$r^2 = \dfrac{ab}{4}; h = \dfrac{c}{2}$
Trichocerca	cylinder + cone: $r^2\pi h + \dfrac{r^2\pi h}{3}$	$v = 0.52 \times ab^2$	a:b has to be measured in each case	$v = 0.52ab^2$	0.6% of b.v. × $\dfrac{\text{length of toe}}{\text{body length}}$	$h = \dfrac{a}{2}; r = \dfrac{b}{2}$

The major assumptions using this technique to estimate dry weight are that:

(1) The geometric formulae provide accurate descriptions of the volume of individuals.
(2) The specific gravity of all species in all habitats equals one.
(3) Dry weight is a constant fraction of fresh weight irrespective of the species being considered.

It is difficult to examine the validity of these assumptions since there is very little published evidence to either support or reject them. There have been no systematic studies of how individual variation in the dimensions needed to calculate volume influences the precision of these estimates; therefore the determination of the number of individuals that should be measured to arrive at a volume estimate with a desired level of precision remains difficult. The assumption concerning specific gravity has not been examined, even though Bottrell *et al.* (1976) recommended that it be determined through density gradient analysis using a non-osmotic solution. This test has recently been carried out on several species of phytoplankton using isopycnic gradient centrifugation (Oliver *et al.* 1981). It seems reasonable to expect that the specific gravity of individual rotifer species could be determined using these techniques with minor modification. The conversion factor from fresh to dry weight should also be determined for a larger number of species to assess its variability.

The second technique used to estimate dry weight involves making direct weight measurements, although the small size of rotifers makes it impossible to weigh individual animals of most species. The sensitivity of the two commonly used balances (the Cahn Electrobalance® and the Mettler Microbalance®) is reported to be $0.10\,\mu g$, but most individual weights (Dumont *et al.* 1975; Bottrell *et al.* 1976) are an order of magnitude below this. Owing to their small size, individuals of a species have to be weighed as a group and the mean weight determined by accounting for the number of individuals used. Makarewicz & Likens (1979) described this procedure clearly. Preserved animals are first rinsed for a brief period in distilled water. They are then placed on tared aluminum foil pans and dried for 24–48 h at 60 °C. The samples are cooled for 1 h in a desiccator before being weighed. Using this technique, Makarewicz & Likens (1979) report mean weights for nine different species and obtain confidence limits on these estimates which vary between 2 and 35 % of the mean. Dumont *et al.* (1975) dried specimens at 110 °C for 2 h, followed by a cooling period of 30 min in a desiccator. Numbers of animals were chosen which would produce a minimum of 5 μg dry weight— for rotifers this is 50–2000, depending on their size. Dumont *et al.* (1975) do not provide error values for the reported weights. Doohan & Rainbow (1971) present a cumulative weighing technique to measure mean weights. Sets of approximately 50 rotifers were counted accurately, washed briefly in distilled water and dried on cavity slides placed in a $CaCl_2$ desiccator at room temperature for 48 h. A sample was then transferred to the scale pan of a Cahn Electrobalance® using tungsten needles or fine hairs and weighed. Additional samples were then added and the weights recorded upon each addition. Each weighing was delayed for a short period to allow moisture absorbed during transfer to be removed by the desiccant in the balance chamber. If the cumulative weights are plotted as a function of the cumulative number of individuals weighed, the slope of this relationship is an estimate of the weight of an individual and an estimate of its precision is provided by the confidence limits of the slope (Chapter 8). Doohan & Rainbow (1971) report 95% confidence limits of approximately 2% of the mean weight for one species, *Keratella quadrata*. More data are required on the relative merits of these techniques before any recommendations can be made concerning their respective efficiency. Although the precision of the estimate using the cumulative technique is on the lower limit of the range found by measuring a group, Makarewicz & Likens (1979) estimated the weights of nine species as opposed to the one measured by Doohan & Rainbow (1971).

The large variability in weights of individuals of the same species from different habitats (Dumont *et al.* 1975; Bottrell *et al.* 1976) suggests that mean weights drawn from the literature should not be used except where they have been determined by the investigator on samples relevant to those that are being processed. Dry weight determinations from direct weighing have the advantage of yielding data that are comparable to information gathered for crustacean zooplankton, without assuming any conversion factor from fresh to dry weight, as with the volumetric technique. Until more information is presented on the accuracy and precision of the volumetric technique and also on the relative efficiency of direct weighing, it is not possible to make recommendations on which technique should be employed. Hopefully, the descriptions of the techniques and their assumptions presented in this section will assist individual investigators in making the appropriate choice.

4 Determining the Mass of Protozoans

4.1 Estimating the mass from volume measurements

The small size of protozoans precludes measuring their weight directly using current technology. The measurement of biomass is derived from calculation of the volume of individuals, assuming that their specific gravity is unity. Volume is determined by first approximating the complex shape of individuals with simple geometric formulae, such as spheres, ellipses, prolate spheroids, and cones (Laybourn & Finlay 1976). The measurements required to calculate an estimate of volume using these formulae are them made. There has been no systematic study on the effect of preservation on the shape of individuals, but Pace (1982) observed that the natural shape of some species appeared to be altered on contact with preservative. The addition of a narcotizing agent prior to preservation may avoid this problem (c.f. Gannon & Gannon 1975; Chapter 3). The dimensions of 10–20 individuals of each species are usually measured either directly with a microscope (Bownik-Dylinska 1975; Hecky & Kling 1981; Laybourn & Finlay 1976; Pace 1982) or by taking measurements from a photomicrograph of the individual (Laybourn & Finlay 1976). It seems logical to avoid compressing the individual and thus distorting its shape during measurement, but Fenchel (1980) compressed cells with the coverslip 'until they had plane parallel sides, drawing the outline of the squeezed cell with a camera lucida and measuring the thickness of the preparation with the micrometer screw'. The advantages of this technique over making measurements of individuals settled in plankton chambers are not explained by Fenchel (1980) nor is there any discussion as to how this treatment might affect cell shape and thereby alter the volume estimate.

The calculated volumes of many species of protozoans are presented for comparison in Bownik-Dylinska (1975), Pace (1982), Fenchel (1980), Beaver & Crisman (1982), Finlay & Uhlig (1981), and Schonborn (1977). In addition, Laybourn & Finlay (1976) calculate the dry weights for 5 ciliate species assuming a conversion factor of $0.17\,pg\,\mu m^{-3}$, as determined from a laboratory culture. Bottrell *et al.* (1976) present the mean dry weights for 6 representatives of the Protozoa from the Japanese IBP/PF; however, no description of how these dry weights were determined was provided and they appear to be much higher than other estimates.

It is difficult to assess the accuracy and the precision of the techniques currently used to estimate protozoan biomass. Unfortunately, intraspecific variation in measurements of volume are not reported and it is, therefore, impossible to make recommendations concerning how many individuals of a population should be measured in order to obtain a predetermined level of precision. Perhaps the guidelines presented in the section on crustaceans could be used by the authors listed above to answer this important question. Accuracy might be improved by adopting more complex formulae (Kovala & Larrance 1966) which provide better approximations.

4.2 *Preservation of protozoans*

Three different solutions have been used to preserve planktonic protozoans: formalin (2%), Lugol's iodine, and a saturated solution of mercuric chloride. Hecky & Kling (1981) compared samples preserved in formalin (2%) with live material and concluded that formalin was a satisfactory preservative; however, they provide neither the data nor statistical analyses to support this conclusion. Pace & Orcutt (1981) compared all three preservatives and found that both mercuric chloride (10 ml of a saturated solution of mercuric chloride in a sample volume of 230 ml) and Lugol's iodine solution provided significantly higher counts of protozoans than those performed on formalin (2%) preserved samples. They also suggest that the addition of a drop of bromophenol blue (0·04%) stain to a sample aids in recognizing individuals and provides an advantage over Lugol's solution since the latter stains individuals the same colour as other particulate matter.

5 Estimating Mass as Carbon Content

Although carbon content is an ideal measure of biomass, since it relates weight to the energetic content of the organism, few authors routinely use it (Table 7.1). Perhaps this is because the equipment required to estimate the carbon content of individuals is quite sophisticated and expensive, relative to other techniques used to estimate biomass. Most of the techniques rely on wet oxidation or high temperature combustion of the material and measurement of either changes in temperature, as with calorimetry, or of the evolution of carbon dioxide. Wet oxidation techniques are not popular because of the problems in assuring complete digestion of the material. Complete descriptions of calorimetry procedures and a critical analysis of alternative techniques can be found in Cummins & Wuycheck (1971).

Recently, Latja & Salonen (1978) proposed a new technique for determining the carbon content of individuals which requires high temperature combustion of the sample and measurement of the carbon dioxide evolved using an infra-red gas analyzer. It requires 10 000 times less material and processes samples 20 times faster than current methods of calorimetry (Salonen 1979).

Using this technique, submicrogram quantities of carbon (sensitivity 0·01 μg) can be measured; this sensitivity is considerably better than the best microbalance, and the carbon content of an individual animal as small as a rotifer can be determined in <1 min (Latja & Salonen 1978). An individual is transferred to the combustion tube using forceps, and then combusted at 950 °C. If the animal is transferred with a pipette, then the carbon content of the volume of water used must be determined and subtracted from the weight of the animal. The carbon dioxide produced is measured using an infra-red gas analyzer. A complete description of the apparatus, its calibration, recovery statistics, and design for constructing the quartz combustion tube can be found in Salonen (1979).

Latja & Salonen (1978) present a comprehensive analysis of the accuracy and precision of the technique by comparing measured values for rotifers and copepods with those presented in the literature. They also report the 95 % confidence limits and coefficients of variation found for measuring individuals of 8 rotifer and 2 copepod species. The average carbon weight of an individual rotifer ranged from 0·008 to 0·500 μg C and the 95 % confidence limits were 10–20 % of the mean (CV = 0·05–0·50). The 95 % confidence limits for individual copepods was < 10 % of the mean (CV = 0·15–0·30). The sensitivity of this technique and its short processing time may increase the popularity of measuring carbon content in organisms. Unfortunately estimated costs are not provided and Salonen (1979) considers the technique 'moderately expensive'.

6 Estimating the Abundance of Zooplankton in a Sample

The sample usually consists of a volume of water in a jar containing an assemblage of species. Because of the large number of organisms present, it is generally unpractical to count every individual in the sample. This necessitates that the sample be 'sampled' using subsampling procedures. The best way to treat these procedures is to imagine that you are sampling organisms in the environment. The requirements for subsampling are the same as those for sampling the benthos (Chapter 4) or any other taxonomic group: the subsample should be representative and precise. Because the task is directly analagous to field sampling, it would be expedient for the investigator to read Chapters 4 and 8 prior to processing the samples.

Techniques for subsampling are described by Schwoerbel (1970), Edmondson & Winberg (1971) and Bottrell *et al.* (1976). The minimum requirements of this procedure is the production of a random distribution of organisms in the sample through mixing and the taking of a representative subsample. The recommended technique (c.f. Edmondson & Winberg 1971) is to use a swirling flask and Stempel pipette. This pipette is a wide bore piston apparatus which can capture a large (2·5–5·0 ml) volume of liquid. The sample is accurately brought to the desired volume and then poured into the flask. It is then swirled in a figure eight pattern until mixed. While in motion, the Stempel pipette is inserted into the flask and the subsample taken. The wide bore of the pipette ensures that organisms will not be selected against on the basis of size. Edmondson & Winberg (1971) suggest that the opening of any pipette used to take subsamples, whether automatic or manual, should exceed 4 mm. Bottrell *et al.* (1976) found that the coefficient of variation for subsampling in this way stabilized at 0·08 when the density of organisms in the subsample exceeded 60 individuals. Since the volume of the pipette is fixed, the volume of the sample should be altered to give subsampling densities > 60 individuals per subsample.

McCallum (1979) compared these techniques with a simpler and less expensive technique; he found that bubbling a sample by blowing into it through a graduated pipette and then sucking up a subsample, gave comparable results. This was tested for both rotifers and crustacean zooplankton. Although this technique should not be used for samples preserved with harmful chemicals (e.g. $HgCl_2$) bubbling could be carried out in these cases using an alternative air supply, and subsampling with an automatic pipette.

The chamber for counting the sample will vary with the optical equipment used. A dissecting microscope has sufficient magnification for counting most crustaceans; however, higher magnifications are often needed for taxonomic identification. Rotifers, protozoans, and nauplii are counted with a compound or inverted microscope using either a Sedgewick–Rafter cell or a sedimentation chamber (Edmondson & Winberg 1971). Makarewicz & Likens (1979) found no difference between counts obtained using these two chambers.

The chamber used to count crustaceans is usually a tray with partitions or grooves which confine the subsample to tracks of a constant width. Gannon (1971) presents photographs of two alternate designs. The tray is constructed to hold 5–10 ml of sample, and the width of the grooves in the tray is less than the width of the field at the counting magnification. Once the subsample is placed in the chamber, the individuals are counted by moving the tray and tallying the individuals encountered in the field of the microscope. Since all of the organisms in the subsample are usually counted, a homogeneous distribution in the tray is not needed, although the volume of the sample should be adjusted so that organisms do not pile up on one another. Repeated subsamples are then taken until the desired number of individuals have been counted (see Section 7.7).

For rotifers and protozoans, samples are placed in sedimentation chambers (1–25 ml) and allowed to settle (approximately 2 h per cm height). Sedimentation chambers are preferred since these allow more flexible volume changes than Sedgewick–Rafter cells. After settling, the chamber is placed on the stage of the inverted microscope and individuals counted. As described below, it is best that the contents of the whole chamber be enumerated to simplify statistical considerations. This can be achieved by altering the volume of liquid in the sample and the subsample to bring the number of organisms in the chamber to the desired level. It is important that all manipulations of sample volume are recorded and are as accurate as possible so that the original concentration of organisms in the sample may be calculated.

It is essential to determine statistically whether subsampling conforms to a random distribution, since this information is required in determining estimates of counting precision. The statistical techniques required to perform this test are presented in Chapter 8. The procedure involves counting replicate subsamples (without replacement) and testing the observed distribution of counts using a Chi-square analysis. Lund *et al.* (1958) recommend that at least 10 sets, each containing ≥ 5 replicate counts, should be tested for randomness. It is important to test subsampling procedures on a variety of samples if the density of individual organisms varies considerably among the samples to be enumerated (Rassoulzadegan & Gostan 1976). If the counts of discrete plankton organisms from a sample are random and the number of individuals counted is small relative to the total population (this is generally the case with enumerating plankton; Lund *et al.* 1958; Cassie 1971), then the counts can be assumed to be distributed according to a Poisson series. If the counts are not random, then there is no recourse but to count the entire sample.

The conformity of counts to a Poisson distribution enables calculation of expected precision levels as a simple function of the number of individuals counted. This distribution has the property that the variance is equal to the mean number of organisms counted. Thus, in counting randomly distributed organisms from a large population the precision depends only upon the number of individuals counted (Cassie 1971), and the coefficient of variation is equal to the inverse of the square root of the number of individuals counted.

In counting protozoans, some investigators do not count the entire subsample, but select randomly distributed fields or strips and count only a portion of the chamber area. Essentially, this procedure is subsampling a subsample, and all of the above tests for determining the accuracy of subsamples have to be repeated for the new procedure. Rassoulzadegan & Gostan (1976) tested these assumptions using samples of marine ciliates. They found that subsampling from jars followed a Poisson series (Chi-square analysis), with the exception of subsamples taken from the most concentrated samples. They also tested counts from randomly selected fields and found that the null hypothesis from the Chi-square analysis could be rejected; at high cell densities, there was a significant deviation in the expected relationship between the mean and the variance; at these densities, therefore, the counts were not random. In these cases, transformation procedures can be applied to the counts prior to calculating the precision of the estimate (Cassie 1971; Rassoulzadegan & Gostan 1976). Non-randomness may result from the way the subsample is deposited in the chamber or from the inclination of the surface on which the chamber is placed while settling occurs. Both of these procedures can be altered to try to achieve a random distribution of individuals within the chamber. In most cases, however, counting the entire subsample of protozoans is feasible and recommended, given the densities of protozoans found in the samples (Pace 1982).

Knowledge that the subsampling regime is random simplifies the calculation of the precision of a count. As mentioned above, the coefficient of variation is equal to the inverse of the square root of the number of individuals counted ($CV = 1/\sqrt{N}$). For example, if 50 individuals were counted then the coefficient of variation would be approximately 0·14. An investigator can use this relationship to determine how many individuals should be counted to obtain a desired level of precision for the estimate of the density of organisms in a sample. In the next section, I will examine how this coefficient and the coefficient for the weight estimate interact to determine the final coefficient for a biomass estimate of a population in a sample.

7 Estimating the Biomass of a Population: Decisions, Decisions, Decisions

Deciding among alternative techniques and procedures is one of the most difficult tasks which an investigator faces. There are many variables which have to be considered: time elements, number of samples to process, availability of equipment, cost, and the statistical requirements for the estimate. The importance of each one of these variables will vary among investigators and with the theory being tested. In the analyses from the previous sections I have attempted to present observations on each of these variables. Unfortunately, most of the observations are qualitative; for example, one technique is more time consuming or expensive compared to another. However, I have presented quantitative values for the precision of several techniques and I will now show how this information could be used in making decisions about estimating the biomass of a population.

The precision of a biomass estimate for a population, in a single sample, is a function of the precision of estimates of the average weight and number of individuals present in the sample (Section 1, equation 7.2). It is important to minimize precision levels of single sample estimates for two reasons:

(1) These levels are often used to test for differences among samples in the case of rotifers and protozoans.
(2) These levels will influence the precision of the average biomass derived from replicate samples.

The precision of a biomass estimate from replicate samples will be a function of the error contributed by sampling variability (Chapter 3) and the variability of measurements from single samples. To minimize the contribution from single samples, the coefficient of variation for these measurements must be less than the coefficient of variation expected among samples. In Chapter 3, the fractional coefficient of variation for various sampling devices on different species of zooplankton ranged from approximately 0·15 to 1·50. Therefore, the coefficient of variation for biomass estimates from single samples should be less than approximately 0·15. How much less should be determined from quantitative relationships between variation in the coefficient of variation for single samples and the precision of the final estimate derived from replicate samples. Unfortunately, these important relationships have not been developed. For illustrative purposes, I have adopted a maximum allowable coefficient of variation of 0·15 for estimates from single samples.

Suppose we wish to determine the biomass of a population of crustacean zooplankton in a sample with a coefficient of variation ($CV_B = S/\bar{X}$) of 0·15. To achieve this goal, we must know how many individuals in the sample should be counted in order to estimate the density, and which weighing technique should be used to estimate the mean weight of individuals in the population. From equation 7.2, we can determine the combination of values which can produce an estimate of biomass with $CV_B = 0·15$. In Table 7.6 I have presented values

Table 7.6 Calculated values (equation 7.2) of the coefficient of variation (expressed in fractional form) of biomass estimates. These estimates are presented for different combinations of the coefficient of variation in dry weight estimates (W) and the number of individuals counted in a sample. The calculation assumes that subsampling is random and counts follow a Poisson distribution.

| No. counted | Coefficient of variation in W | | | | | | |
	0·01	0·05	0·10	0·15	0·20	0·25	0·30
50	0·142	0·150	0·173	0·206	0·245	0·287	0·332
100	0·100	0·112	0·141	0·180	0·224	0·269	0·316
150	0·082	0·096	0·129	0·171	0·216	0·263	0·311
200	0·071	0·087	0·122	0·166	0·212	0·260	0·308
250	0·064	0·081	0·118	0·163	0·210	0·258	0·307
300	0·059	0·076	0·115	0·161	0·208	0·257	0·306
600	0·042	0·065	0·108	0·155	0·204	0·253	0·303

for the coefficient of variation for a biomass estimate as a function of the coefficient of variation in weight estimates (CV_M) and the number of individuals counted in a sample. These calculations assume that counting follows a Poisson distribution, which enables the coefficient of variation for density estimates to be calculated as a simple function of the number of individuals counted. I have arranged the successive rows in Table 7.6 to show how increasing the number counted (the counting effort) affects the precision of the biomass estimate. The range of values for the columns encompass the range of CV_M's found for the different weighing techniques.

There are only a few combinations of coefficients for counting and weighing which produce the value of 0·15 for the above example (Table 7.6); this puts constraints on the technique for weighing since any technique producing estimates with a CV_M above 0·10 is not satisfactory. Suppose that CV_M is equal to 0·10, then >50 individuals would have to be counted to produce estimates of biomass with the desired level of precision. Thus, Table 7.6 can be used to estimate the number of individuals which should be counted and to indicate when increases in counting effort are advantageous. For example, moving down a column at a fixed CV_M indicates the gain in precision with successive increases of counting effort.

The relationships presented in Table 7.6 can also help in choosing between techniques. In the above example, a CV_M of $\leq 0\cdot10$ was required. There are two techniques to determine dry weight: direct weighing or length–weight relationships. The CV_M for direct weighing is within the required range. Recall that CV_M for length–weight relationships varied as a function of the variance in $\overline{\ln L}$ measurements (Tables 7.3 and 7.4). To obtain a CV_M of $0\cdot10$, the variance of $\overline{\ln L}$ would have to be less than 1% for most species examined (Table 7.4), a level which may be difficult to attain for most natural populations. These observations would suggest that direct weighing would be more profitable than predicting weights from length measurements. There are many theories for which length–weight relationships would be an entirely adequate technique to use for estimating dry weights. In these cases, direct weights should not be used since measurements are more time-consuming than length–weight relationships.

The calculated values of precision presented in Table 7.6 are based on a number of assumptions and should not be used without determining whether or not these assumptions are true for processing a particular sample. I hope that this analysis has indicated ways in which quantitative observations on the properties of techniques might be used to decide upon their efficiency and applicability for a stated purpose.

8 Estimating the Biomass of Groups of Species

In testing certain ecological theories, estimates of biomass are often required which concern groups of species or size classes rather than single populations of a species. There are a number of ways to arrive at these estimates. The most conventional way is simply to follow the techniques for single species, described in the previous sections, and to sum these values to arrive at an estimate for the entire assemblage. Alternative techniques have been presented which, in most cases, require that the assemblage under consideration be separated from the rest of the sample by some treatment, such as filtration through different sized screens or nets.

Carpenter (1974) proposed a method for determining zooplankton biomass by separating phytoplankton from zooplankton through *in situ* sampling procedures, followed by selective filtration and weight determinations. Zooplankton are sampled by vertical net haul (64 µm mesh size) and this sample is filtered onto a glass fiber filter. Upon weighing, this yields an estimate of net zooplankton plus net phytoplankton and the weight of any other particulate matter retained by the net. An integrated tube sample is taken to the same depth as the net haul, and this sample is passed through mesh of the same size as the net haul. The material retained is filtered onto a glass fiber filter and weighed. This provides an estimate of net phytoplankton biomass and particulate matter retained by the net; the assumption is made that zooplankton completely avoid the integrated tube sampler. After correcting for the volume of water sampled, an estimate of net zooplankton biomass can be obtained by subtracting the weights of the two samples.

Duncan (1975) estimated the biomass of zooplankton in two reservoirs by simply taking vertical net hauls (240 μm mesh size) and filtering the samples onto glass fiber filters which were then dried and weighed. The weights of 10 replicates from one station yielded 95 % confidence limits of < 10 % of the mean dry weight.

The advantages of these techniques are that tedious counting procedures are avoided and that a large number of samples can be processed relative to other techniques. The short processing time may facilitate taking more samples from the environment or experimental situation. Unfortunately, few studies have examined the accuracy of these techniques. Watson & Carpenter (1974) estimated the biomass of crustacean zooplankton using conventional techniques (C) of counting and weighing, and by a slightly modified filter technique (F) similar to that proposed by Carpenter (1974). They visually compared the seasonal variation of these two estimates (C and F) and concluded that F provided a good approximation of C and that when it did not the variation was due to contributions from phytoplankton biomass (P). I examined their data using statistical analyses and found that C and F were significantly related (p < 0·001); variation in F accounted for 60 % of the variation in C. The percent variation was determined from a log-log regression of the two variables. I also tested their assumption that variation in P accounted for differences between C and F using multiple regression analysis, and found that P did not explain a significant amount of residual variation. These results are promising, but more data are required to compare filtration techniques for estimating zooplankton biomass with more time consuming enumeration techniques. The methods also fail to account for microzooplankton biomass, which may be a large portion of the total biomass.

There are other methods, besides selective filtration, which are currently being investigated as means of separating zooplankton from the rest of the sample. Schmitz & McGraw (1981) applied density–gradient centrifugation techniques to separate zooplankton from net seston in preserved lake samples. After centrifugation, the fraction representing the zooplankton was filtered onto a glass fiber filter, dried and weighed. Schmitz & McGraw (1981) compared these weights with total zooplankton biomass determined by hand sorting and weighing subsamples of equal volume. They found that dry weight estimates derived from the centrifugation technique was, on average, 80·5 % of total zooplankton dry weight; there was, however, considerable variation associated with this result, and this they attributed to the presence of filamentous algae. Their technique for processing samples is simpler and requires much smaller sample volumes than similar systems for isolating marine zooplankton (Price *et al.* 1977), but has the disadvantage that rotifers and protozoans are not separated from the sample. Borkott (1975) describes a method to quantitatively separate ciliated protozoans from samples, based on their swimming properties in an electrical current, but no data are provided.

Processing samples to determine total zooplankton biomass is a difficult task, requiring considerable energy and taxonomic expertise, and it is extremely difficult to assess the error propagation involved in the procedures. Estimates are often arrived at by enumerating individual species and summing these values. It is recommended that considerable effort be directed at ensuring the accuracy and precision of the species or taxonomic group which contributes most of the biomass estimate, since the errors among estimates should be additive. More fundamental problems remain. The biomass estimates of smaller individuals rest on assumptions, many of which are testable using today's technology. The validity of these assumptions influence the confidence we have in these estimates and our ability to test predictions.

9 Conclusion

I have attempted to provide accurate descriptions of the current techniques used by scientists to estimate basic ecological variables. These techniques will undoubtedly change within the next few years as theories dictate that new variables should be measured and as new technology becomes more accessible to ecologists. Perhaps the approach I have presented to assess existing techniques will be useful in evaluating future innovations.

10 References

Adalsteinsson H. (1979) Zooplankton and its relation to available food in Lake Mývatn. *Oikos*, **32**, 162–194.

Baskerville G.L. (1972) Use of logarithmic regression in the estimation of plant biomass. *Can. J. Forest. Research*, **2**, 49–53.

Baudouin M.F. & Ravera O. (1972) Weight, size, and chemical composition of some freshwater zooplankters: *Daphnia hyalina* (Leydig). *Limnol. Oceanogr.*, **17**, 645–649.

Beaver J.R. & Crisman T.L. (1982) The trophic response of ciliated protozoans in freshwater lakes. *Limnol. Oceanogr.*, **27**, 246–253.

Borkott H. (1975) A method for quantitative isolation and preparation for particle-free suspensions of bacteriophagous ciliates from different substrates for electronic counting. *Arch. Protistenkd.*, **117**, 261–268.

Bottrell H.H., Duncan A., Gliwicz Z.M., Grygierek E., Herzig A., Hillbricht-Ilkowska A., Kurasawa H., Larsson P. & Weglenska T. (1976) A review of some problems in zooplankton production studies. *Norw. J. Zool.*, **24**, 419–456.

Bownik-Dylinska L. (1975) Ecosystem of the Mikolajskie Lake. Dynamics and biomass of free living planktonic protozoans. *Pol. Arch. Hydrobiol.*, **22**, 65–72.

Brownlee K.A. (1967) *Statistical Theory and Methodology in Science and Engineering.* New York: Wiley and Sons.

Burgis M.J. (1974) Revised estimates for the biomass and production of zooplankton in Lake George, Uganda. *Freshwat. Biol.*, **4**, 535–541.

Burns C.W. (1969) Relation between filtering rate, temperature, and body size in four species of *Daphnia. Limnol. Oceanogr.*, **14**, 693–700.

Carpenter G.F. (1974) A proposed method suitable for large-scale surveys of biomass in lakes. *J. Fish. Res. Board Can.*, **31**, 327–328.

Cassie R. (1971) Sampling and statistics. In W.T.Edmondson & G.G.Winberg (eds.), *A Manual on Methods for the Assessment of Secondary Productivity in Fresh Waters.* IBP Handbook no. 17. Oxford: Blackwell.

Colquhoun D. (1971) *Lectures on Biostatistics.* Oxford: Clarendon Press.

Coveney M.F., Cronberg G., Enell M., Larsson K. & Olofsson L. (1977) Phytoplankton, zooplankton and bacteria-standing crop and production relationships in a eutrophic lake. *Oikos*, **29**, 5–21.

Cummins K.W. & Wuycheck J.C. (1971) Caloric equivalents for investigations in ecological energetics. *Mitt. Int. Ver. Limnol.*, **18**, 1–158.

de Bernardi R. & Di Cola G. (1976) Instantaneous growth rates and production estimation in natural zooplankton populations. *Mem. Ist. Ital. Idrobiol.*, **33**, 105–123.

DeMott W.R. (1982) Feeding selectivities and relative ingestion rates of *Daphnia* and *Bosmina. Limnol. Oceanogr.*, **27**, 518–527.

Doohan M. (1973) An energy budget for adult *Brachionus plicatilis* Muller (Rotatoria). *Oecologia*, **13**, 351–362.

Doohan M. & Rainbow V. (1971) Determination of dry weights of small Aschelminthes. *Oecologia*, **6**, 380–383.

Dumont H.J., van de Velde I. & Dumont S. (1975) The dry weight estimate of biomass in a selection of Cladocera, Copepoda and Rotifera from the plankton, periphyton and benthos of continental waters. *Oecologia*, **19**, 75–97.

Duncan A. (1975) Production and biomass of three species of *Daphnia* coexisting in London reservoirs. *Verh. Internat. Verein. Limnol.*, **19**, 2858–2867.

Edmondson W.T. & Winberg G.G. (eds.) (1971) *A Manual on Methods for the Assessment of Secondary Productivity in Fresh Waters.* IBP Handbook no. 17. Oxford: Blackwell.

Fenchel T. (1980) Suspension feeding in ciliated Protozoa: Functional response and particle size selection. *Microb. Ecol.*, **6**, 1–11.

Finlay B.J. & Uhlig G. (1981) Calorific and carbon values of marine and freshwater Protozoa. *Helgolander Meeresunters.*, **34**, 401–412.

Furnass T.I. & Findley W.C. (1975) An improved sorting device for zooplankton. *Limnol. Oceanogr.*, **20**, 295–297.

Gannon J.E. (1971) Two counting cells for the enumeration of zooplankton microcrustacea. *Trans. Am. Microsc. Soc.*, **90**, 486–490.

Gannon, J.E. & Gannon F.A. (1975) Observations on the narcotization of crustacean zoolankton. *Crustaceana*, **28**, 220–224.

George D.G. & Edwards R.W. (1974) Population dynamics and production of *Daphnia hyalina* in a eutrophic reservoir. *Freshwat. Biol.*, **4**, 445–465.

Gophen M. (1978) The productivity of *Mesocyclops leuckarti* in Lake Kinneret. *Hydrobiologia.*, **60**, 17–22.

Hawkins B.E. & Evans M.S. (1979) Seasonal cycles of zooplankton biomass in southeastern Lake Michigan. *J. Great Lakes Res.*, **5**, 256–263.

Hecky R.E. & Kling H.J. (1981) The phyto- & protozooplankton of the euphotic zone of L. Tanganyika: species composition, biomass, chlorophyll content and spatio-temporal distribution. *Limnol. Oceanogr.*, **26**, 548–564.

Herzig A. (1974) Some population characteristics of planktonic crustaceans in Neusiedlersee. *Oecologia*, **15**, 127–141.

Herzig A. (1979) The zooplankton of the open lake. In H. Loffler (ed.) *Neusiedlersee: The Limnology of a Shallow Lake in Central Europe. Monographiae Biologicae*, **37**.

Jacobsen T.R. & Comita G.W. (1976) Ammonia-nitrogen excretion in *Daphnia pulex*. *Hydrobiologia.*, **51**, 195–200.

Kovala P.E. & Larrance J.D. (1966) Computation of phytoplankton cell numbers, cell volume, cell surface, plasma volume per liter from microscopical counts. *Univ. Wash. Dept. Oceanogr. Spec. Rep.*, **38**.

Lair N. (1977) Biomasse et production dans deux lacs du Massif Central français. *Arch. Hydrobiol.*, **79**, 247–273.

Lair N. (1978) Repartition spatio-temporelle biomasse et production des populations zooplanktonique du Lac d'Aydat en periode estivale. *Hydrobiologia.*, **61**, 237–256.

Lampert W. (1977) Studies on the carbon balance of *Daphnia pulex* as related to environmental conditions. 3. Production and production efficiency. *Arch. Hydrobiol. (Suppl.)*, **48**, 336–360.

Lampert W. & Krause I. (1976) Zur Biologie der Cladocere *Holopedium gibberum* Zaddach in Windgfällweiher (Schwarzwald). *Arch. Hydrobiol. (Suppl.)*, **48**, 262–286.

Latja R. & Salonen K. (1978) Carbon analysis for the determination of individual biomass of planktonic animals. *Verh. Internat. Verein. Limnol.*, **20**, 2556–2560.

Laybourn J. & Finlay B.J. (1976) Respiratory energy losses related to cell weight and temperature in ciliated Protozoa. *Oecologia*, **24**, 349–355.

Lehman J.T. (1976) Aspects of nutrient dynamics in freshwater communities. Dissertation. University of Washington, Seattle, USA.

Lehman J.T. (1980) Nutrient recycling as an interface between algae and grazers in freshwater communities. In C.W.Kerfoot (ed.). *Evolution and Ecology of Zooplankton Communities*. Spec. Symp., 3. Seattle: Am. Soc. Limnol. Oceanogr.

Lemcke H.W. & Lampert W. (1975) Veränderungen in Gewicht und der chemischen Zusammensetzung von *Daphnia pulex* im Hunger. *Arch. Hydrobiol. (Suppl.)*, **48**, 102–137.

Lund J.W., Kipling C. & LeCren E.D. (1958) The inverted microscope method of estimating algal numbers and the statistical basis of estimation by counting. *Hydrobiologia*, **11**, 143–170.

Makarewicz J.C. & Likens G.E. (1979) Structure and function of the zooplankton community of Mirror Lake New Hampshire. *Ecol. Monogr.*, **49**, 109–127.

McAllister D.E. & Planck R.J. (1981) Capturing fish measurements and counts with calipers and probe interfaced with a computer or pocket calculator. *Can. J. Fish. Aquat. Sci.*, **38**, 466–470.

McCallum I.D. (1979) A simple method of taking a subsample of zooplankton. *N. Z. J. Mar. Freshwat. Res.*, **13**, 559–560.

McCauley E. & Kalff J. (1981) Empirical relationships between phytoplankton and zooplankton biomass in lakes. *Can. J. Fish. Aquat. Sci.*, **38**, 458–463.

Mires J.M. & Soltero R.A. (1981) Changes in the zooplankton community of Medical Lake, WA, subsequent to its restoration by a whole lake alum treatment and the establishment of a trout fishery. *J. Freshwat. Ecol.*, **1**, 167–178.

O'Brien W.J. & deNoyelles F. Jr. (1974) Relationship between nutrient concentration, phytoplankton density and zooplankton density in nutrient enriched experimental ponds. *Hydrobiologia*, **44**, 105–125.

Oliver R.L., Kinnear A.J. & Ganf G.G. (1981) Measurements of cell density of three freshwater phytoplankters by density centrifugation. *Limnol. Oceanogr.*, **26**, 285–294.

Omori M. (1978) Some factors affecting on dry weight, organic weight and concentration of carbon and nitrogen in freshly prepared and in preserved zooplankton. *Int. Rev. Gesamt. Hydrobiol.*, **63**, 261–269.

Pace M.L. (1982) Planktonic ciliates: Their distribution, abundance and relationship to microbial resources in a monomictic lake. *Can. J. Fish. Aquat. Sci.*, **39**, 1106–1116.

Pace, M.L. & Orcutt J.D., Jr. (1981) The relative importance of protozoans, rotifers and crustaceans in a freshwater zooplankton community. *Limnol. Oceanogr.*, **26**, 822–830.

Pearre S. Jr. (1980) The copepod width-weight relation and its utility in food chain research. *Can J. Zool.*, **58**, 1884–1891.

Pederson G.L., Welch E.B. & Litt A.H. (1976) Plankton secondary productivity and biomass: Their relation to lake trophic state. *Hydrobiologia*, **50**, 129–144.

Persson G. & Ekbohm G. (1980) Estimation of dry weight in zooplankton populations: Methods applied to crustacean populations from lakes in the Kuokkel Area, Northern Sweden. *Arch. Hydrobiol.*, **89**, 225–246.

Porter K.G., Gerritsen J. & Orcutt J.D. Jr. (1982) The effect of food concentration on swimming patterns, feeding behavior, ingestion, assimilation, and respiration by *Daphnia*. *Limnol. Oceanogr.*, **27**, 935–949.

Price C.A., St. Onge-Burns J.M., Colton J.B. & Joyce J.E. (1977) Automatic sorting of zooplankton by isopycnic sedimentation in gradients of silica: performance of a Rho spectrometer. *Mar. Biol.*, **42**, 225–231.

Rassoulzadegan F. & Gostan J. (1976) Répartition des ciliés pélagiques dans les eaux de Ville franche-sur-Mer. *Ann. Inst. Océanogr.*, **52**, 175–188.

Redfield G.W. & Goldman C.R. (1981) Diel vertical migration by males, females copepodids and nauplii in a limnetic population of *Diaptomus* (Copepoda). *Hydrobiologia*, **74**, 241–248.

Redfield G.W. & Goldman C.R. (1978) Diel vertical migration and dynamics of zooplankton biomass in the epilimnion of Castle Lake, California. *Verh. Internat. Verein. Limnol.*, **20**, 381–387.

Rosen R.A. (1981) Length-dry weight relationships of some freshwater zooplankton. *J. Freshwat. Ecol.*, **1**, 225–229.

Roth J.C. & Horne A.J. (1980) Algal nitrogen fixation and microcrustacean abundance: An unregarded interrelationship between zoo- and phytoplankton. *Verh. Internat. Verein. Limnol.*, **21**, 333–338.

Ruttner-Kolisko A. (1977) Suggestions for biomass calculations of plankton rotifers. *Arch. Hydrobiol. Beih. Ergebn. Limnol.*, **8**, 71–76.

Salonen K. (1979) A versatile method for the rapid and accurate determination of carbon by high temperature combustion. *Limnol. Oceanogr.*, **24**, 177–182.

Schindler D.W. & Noven B. (1971) Vertical distribution and seasonal abundance of zooplankton in two shallow lakes of the Experimental Lakes Area, Northwestern Ontario. *J. Fish. Res. Board Can.*, **28**, 245–256.

Schmitz E.A. & McCraw J.T., Jr. (1981) Density-gradient separation of zooplankton from total net seston for dry weight estimates. *Trans. Am. Micros. Soc.*, **100**, 94–98.

Schonborn W. (1977) Production studies on Protozoa. *Oecologia*, **27**, 171–184.

Schram M.D., Ploskey G.R. & Schmitz E.H. (1981) Dry weight loss in *Ceriodaphnia lacustris* following formalin preservation. *Trans. Am. Micros. Soc.*, **100**, 326–329.

Schwoerbel J. 1970. *Methods of Hydrobiology*. Oxford: Pergamon Press.

Skogheim O.K. & Rognerud S. (1978) Recent changes in plankton communities and present trophic state of Lake Steinsfjord. *Arch. Hydrobiol.*, **83**, 179–199.

Smock L.A. (1980) Relationships between body size and biomass of aquatic insects. *Freshwat. Biol.*, **10**, 375–383.

Smyly W.J.P. (1973) Bionomics of *Cyclops strenuus abysorum* Sars (Copepoda: Cyclopoida). *Oecologia*, **11**, 163–186.

Snow N.B. (1972) The effect of season and animal size on the caloric content of *Daphnia pulicaria*. *Limnol. Oceanogr.*, **17**, 909–912.

Sprules W.G., Holtby L.B. & Griggs G. (1981) A microcomputer-based measuring device for biological research. *Can. J. Zool.*, **59**, 1611–1614.

Steel R.G.D. & Torrie J.H. (1960). *Principles and Procedures in Statistics*. New York: McGraw-Hill.

Swift M.C. & Hammer V.T. (1979) Zooplankton population dynamics and *Diaptomus* production in Waldsea Lake, a meromictic lake in Saskatchewan. *J. Fish. Res. Board Can.*, **36**, 1430–1438.

Threlkeld S.T. (1976) Starvation and the size structure of zooplankton communities. *Freshwat. Biol.*, **6**, 489–496.

Watson N.H.F. & Carpenter G.F. (1974) Seasonal abundance of crustacean zooplankton and net plankton biomass in lakes Huron, Erie and Ontario. *J. Fish. Res. Board Can.*, **31**, 309–317.

Wattiez C. (1981) Biomasse du zooplancton et productivité des cladocères d'eaux de degré trophique différent. *Annls. Limnol.*, **17**, 219–236.

Chapter 8. Some Statistical Methods for the Design of Experiments and Analysis of Samples

ELLIE E. PREPAS

1 Introduction

Statistical analysis can be a very powerful tool for the researcher, but its power comes mainly from interpreting data which were collected for a specific analysis. This chapter introduces the reader to some of the analyses used routinely by researchers and to aspects of sampling design which should be considered prior to the collection of field or laboratory data. It is not intended as a substitute for a text in applied statistics (e.g., Zar 1974, Snedecor & Cochran 1980, and Sokal & Rohlf 1981); rather it directs the reader to specific tests and problems which are common in aquatic invertebrate research.

This chapter is divided into five parts. The introduction deals with commonly used sample statistics and distributions. The second section focuses on design of the experiment and the sampling program. Preparation of data for analysis, including enumeration, volume weighting, smoothing, determining the distribution, and transformation are introduced in the third part. Section four deals mainly with the comparison of means, such as the t-test, nonparametric alternatives, multiple comparisons between means, and problems to be aware of when doing an analysis of variance. This section also looks at tests for homogeneity of sample variances and combining probabilities from independent tests of significance. Finally, standard regression and correlation, and alternative methods are discussed in terms of searching for patterns, estimating parameters and making predictions.

Many of the statistical models discussed will be illustrated with examples from the literature, although the analyses may differ from those undertaken by the original authors.

1.1 Descriptive statistics

There are two basic kinds of sample statistics: indices of central tendency and dispersion.

1.1.1 Indices of central tendency

The most frequently used measure of central tendency is the *arithmetic mean*.

266

The arithmetic mean $\bar{X}$ is the average of a set of n observations X_i:

$$\bar{X} = \frac{\sum\limits_{i=1}^{n} X_i}{n} \tag{8.1}$$

The statistic $\bar{X}$ is an estimate of the parameter μ, the true population mean. (Greek letters such as μ are used in statistics to describe actual as opposed to estimates of population parameters.) The mean is the measure of central tendency used in most statistical analyses. It is thus the most powerful index of central tendency.

The median, the value with an equal number of observations on either side of it, is another measure of central tendency used in biological studies. It is a useful statistic for describing a population with a skewed distribution because, unlike the mean, it is not unduly influenced by outliers. Other indices such as the geometric mean, harmonic mean, and mode, are rarely used in analyses of biological data.

1.1.2 Indices of dispersion

The most commonly used indices of dispersion are the variance (s^2) and the standard deviation (s). The variance is calculated from the sum of the squared deviations of each observation from the mean (i.e., sum of squares), corrected for sample size. The mean sum of squares tends to underestimate the true population variance σ^2 and thus it is divided by $n-1$ rather than n:

$$s^2 = \frac{\sum\limits_{i=1}^{n} (X_i - \bar{X})^2}{n-1} \tag{8.2}$$

In practice the formula used to calculate the variance is:

$$s^2 = \frac{\sum\limits_{i=1}^{n} X_i^2 - \dfrac{\left(\sum\limits_{i=1}^{n} X_i\right)^2}{n}}{n-1} \tag{8.2i}$$

The standard deviation is the square root of the variance. Variance and standard deviation are the most powerful measures of dispersion because they, like the mean, are used for statistical analyses.

The range (i.e., the distance between the maximum and minimum values) is also used to describe sample variation. The range is affected by outlying values and sample size and thus is only a rough estimate of dispersion.

1.1.3 The coefficient of variation

The coefficient of variation, CV, is a relative measure of dispersion in a sample. It is the ratio of the standard deviation, s, to the mean:

$$CV = \frac{s}{\bar{X}} \tag{8.3}$$

A large CV indicates substantial variation in the samples, whereas, a small CV (i.e., 0·20 or less) indicates that the $\bar{X}$ is representative of the true population mean μ and, in samples where the s^2 is not dependent on the $\bar{X}$, that the s^2 is representative of the true population variance σ^2. The CV is often used to compare the variability of data sets measured in different units (e.g., feet as opposed to centimeters).

The calculation of descriptive statistics is illustrated in Table 8.1 using data from Ricker (1938) on the number of *Daphnia* in replicate samples collected at one location and at random locations in Cultus Lake.

1.2 Distribution of the data

Most statistical analyses assume that random processes are responsible for the variation observed in a population. This variation may be described by different models depending on whether the variable is discontinuous or continuous. The binomial and related distributions are used to describe certain discontinuous or discrete data, such as number of organisms per sample with a particular attribute, whereas the normal distribution is used for continuous variables, such as weight, and can also be used for most discrete variables.

The binomial distribution is based on the parameters p, the proportion of the population containing a particular attribute, and q, which is defined as $1 = p$. The events acting on the population are assumed to be independently distributed and p is assumed to be constant. For a sample of size n, $\mu = np$ and $\sigma^2 = npq$. Suppose 100 copepods are taken from each of several random samples collected from a lake. Suppose also that there is an equal sex ratio in the population and that male copepods are randomly distributed. Then the number of male copepods per sample should follow the binomial distribution, with $p = 0·5$ and $n = 100$.

As the sample size increases, the binomial distribution tends quickly to the normal distribution, particularly when p is close to 0·5. The normal approximation is usually considered adequate if the mean of the population ($\mu = np$) is greater than 15. Where p is small and $\mu = np < 15$ the Poisson distribution, which has the useful property $\mu = \sigma^2$, is used. If the individuals in a rare population are randomly distributed in a lake then the number of

Table 8.1 Calculation of sample statistics for the number of *Daphnia* collected in Cultus Lake, British Columbia, from one central location and at several randomly selected open water locations (data are from Ricker 1938).

Haul number	Location	
	Centre	Random
1	37	63
2	48	54
3	37	91
4	46	83
5	38	104
6	38	79
7	50	71
8	33	—
9	35	—
10	50	—
total $\left(\sum\limits_{i=1}^{n} X_i \right)$	412	545
sample size, n	10	7
mean $\bar{X}\left(\dfrac{\sum\limits_{i=1}^{n} X_i}{n} \right)$	$\dfrac{412}{10} = 41\cdot2$	$\dfrac{545}{7} = 77\cdot9$
median	$\rightarrow$ $\begin{array}{c} 33,\ 35,\ 37,\ 37 \\ 38,\ 38 \\ 46,\ 48,\ 50,\ 50 \end{array} = 38$	$\rightarrow$ $\begin{array}{c} 54,\ 63,\ 71, \\ 79 \\ 83,\ 91,\ 104 \end{array} = 79$
variance, s^2 $\left(\dfrac{\sum\limits_{i=1}^{n} X_i^2 - \dfrac{\left(\sum\limits_{i=1}^{n} X_i \right)^2}{n}}{n-1} \right)$	$\dfrac{17\,360 - \dfrac{(412)^2}{10}}{9}$ $= 42\cdot8$	$\dfrac{44\,153 - \dfrac{(545)^2}{7}}{6}$ $= 286\cdot8$
range	33–50	54–104
standard deviation, s $(\sqrt{s^2})$	6·54	16·9
CV $\left(\dfrac{s}{\bar{X}} \right)$	$\dfrac{6\cdot54}{41\cdot2} = 0\cdot16$	$\dfrac{16\cdot9}{77\cdot9} = 0\cdot22$
$s^2/\bar{X}$	1·04	3·68
$s_{\bar{X}} \left(\dfrac{s}{\sqrt{n}} \right)$	2·07	6·40

these individuals collected in random samples should follow the Poisson distribution. The Poisson distribution is also used to describe counts of organisms from replicate samples.

A simple way to determine whether counts are randomly distributed is to examine the s^2 to $\bar{X}$ ratio. This ratio is close to 1 if the distribution is random and > 1 if it is clumped or contagious. The data on *Daphnia* collected at one station (Table 8.1) appear to follow the Poisson distribution because the s^2 to $\bar{X}$ ratio is very close to unity. On the other hand, samples collected at randomly selected stations have a s^2 to $\bar{X}$ ratio which is substantially > 1, suggesting a contagious distribution. A χ^2-test can be used to determine whether the s^2 to $\bar{X}$ ratio is significantly different from unity (see Section 3.5).

The normal distribution has a symmetrical bell-shaped curve about the population mean μ. The breadth of the curve is determined by the variance (σ^2). The normal distribution works well for measurements such as length or weight when the population is not skewed towards large or small individuals, although many measurements made in biology do not conform to the normal distribution. However, as the sample size increases, the sample means approach normality even when the raw data are not normally distributed. In addition, it may be possible to transform the data to a normal distribution (see Sections 3.4–3.6). Methods of calculating the binomial, Poisson, and normal distributions are covered in most statistical texts. Other methods for analyzing patterns of discrete variables are discussed in detail in the ecological literature (e.g., Lloyd 1967; Pielou 1977; Elliott 1977; Iwao 1977; Green 1979).

2 Sampling Design

Preliminary data on the distribution or the characteristics of the organisms under study can be used to estimate the number of samples required for a given level of accuracy, to determine the best method of sampling, e.g., random, systematic, or stratified, and where appropriate, the time interval between samples.

2.1 Random sampling

To locate random stations for sampling, a random number table is usually employed. For example, the stations marked on Baptiste Lake in Fig. 1 were chosen randomly. A grid with 99 units was marked on both the north and east sides of the lake. To arbitrarily choose a starting location, a coin was thrown on a random number table. The first two numbers to the right of this location were used for the east-west coordinates and the next two as the north-south coordinates for the first point and so on for the 10 locations (Fig. 8.1). Only those points located on the lake were used.

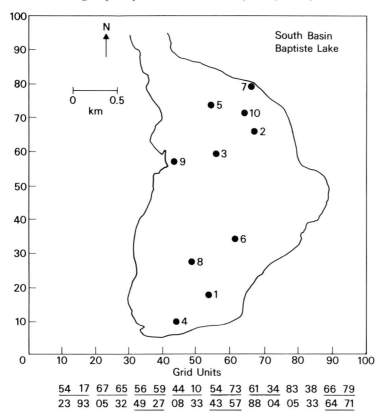

54 17 67 65 56 59 44 10 54 73 61 34 83 38 66 79
23 93 05 32 49 27 08 33 43 57 88 04 05 33 64 71

Fig. 8.1 Randomly chosen sampling locations marked on an outline of the southern basin of Baptiste Lake, Alberta. Numbers below are from a random number table; the numbers underlined were used to select the locations. The grid used to locate the stations is indicated to the top and side of the lake.

Once a set of random samples has been collected and analyzed, a mean ($\bar{X}$) can be calculated for the samples. The precision of the mean or confidence interval can be estimated for samples which are approximately normally distributed.

2.1.1 Confidence intervals

A confidence interval is based on the standard deviation of the mean, usually referred to as the standard error of the mean. The formula for calculating the standard error of the mean ($s_{\bar{X}}$) is:

$$s_{\bar{X}} = \frac{s}{\sqrt{n}} \tag{8.4}$$

where s is the sample standard deviation and n is the sample size. The standard error of the mean is also sometimes abbreviated SE. When the sample mean is calculated from a large number of observations, statistical theory states that it is approximately normally distributed even when the original population is not normal. Confidence limits are usually set at the 95% level. When the sample mean is approximately normally distributed the 95% confidence limits are calculated from the expression:

$$\bar{X} \pm s_{\bar{X}} t \tag{8.5}$$

where t is the Student's t value for $P = 0.05$ and $(n - 1)$ degrees of freedom (df). For example, 30 plankton samples were collected from randomly located stations in a lake to estimate the average number of *Daphnia* per sample. The mean and standard deviation for these samples were $\bar{X} = 10.0$ and $s = 3.20$ (*Daphnia* per sample), therefore:

$$s_{\bar{X}} = \frac{3.20}{\sqrt{30}} = 0.584$$

The value in Student's t-table (found in most statistics texts) for $P = 0.05$, df $= 29$ is 2.045. Thirty observations is usually a sufficient number to ensure that the mean will approach a normal distribution. Thus the 95% confidence limits for the mean number of *Daphnia* (per sample) can be calculated from equation 8.5:

$$10.0 \pm (2.045)(0.584) = 10.0 \pm 1.2$$

Ninety-five percent of all confidence levels calculated will include the population mean μ.

This method of calculating the standard error of the mean is for infinite populations, i.e. the number of individuals sampled is extremely small relative to the size of the population. This is true for virtually all samples collected in the field. In laboratory work it is possible to sample a significant number n of a total population of size N. In this case, a finite population correction is applied to the standard error of the mean:

$$s_{\bar{X}} = -\frac{s}{\sqrt{n}} \sqrt{1 - \frac{n}{N}} \tag{8.6}$$

The ratio n/N determines the size of the correction. For example, if 20% of a population is randomly sampled with mean $\bar{X} = 55.0$, the unadjusted standard error of the mean $s_{\bar{X}} = 3.67$ is 12% higher than the adjusted standard error of the mean:

$$s_{\bar{X}} = 3.67 \sqrt{1 - \frac{20}{100}} = 3.28$$

When the entire population is sampled, then the standard error is zero (as $n/N \to 1$, $s_{\bar{x}} \to 0$).

2.1.2 The pilot survey

Often, an investigator would like to collect enough samples to ensure that the confidence intervals will be no larger than a set percentage of the mean. This requires an estimate of the mean (μ) and variance (σ^2) of the population under study. These statistics can be estimated from a previous study of similar fauna (e.g., for benthic invertebrates see Downing 1979) or by carrying out a pilot survey. For the latter, several random samples which can be used to estimate the population μ and σ^2 are collected at the start of the study. A large number of small samples gives a better estimate of the population mean and variance than a few large ones.

2.1.3 The number of samples

At an early stage in the design of an experiment, the question 'How many samples should I collect?' must be considered. Although a precise answer may not be easy to find, the problem can be attacked in a rational way. Clearly the investigator wants to avoid two extremes: collecting too few samples to make the estimate useful or collecting so many samples that the estimate exceeds the precision desired. The method of calculating the appropriate number of samples depends on the distribution of the population.

If it is reasonable to assume a normal distribution for the population then first decide upon the allowable error of the population estimate and the desired confidence level associated with this error. This information along with an estimate of the variance (s^2) from the pilot study is used to calculate the required number of samples (n). The formula for n is:

$$n = \frac{t^2 s^2}{L^2} \qquad (8.7)$$

where t is the value of the Students' t-distribution for the df associated with the estimate of variance and the desired confidence level and L is the allowable error in the sample mean. For example, suppose that 30 samples were collected, the mean number of animals $\bar{X} = 25$ and the variance $s^2 = 20$. If the 95% confidence level is chosen, $t = 2 \cdot 045$ ($P = 0 \cdot 05$, df $= 29$), and if 20% of the mean or five animals is the allowable error, then the number of samples which would suffice is:

$$n = \frac{(2 \cdot 045)^2 (20)}{(5)^2} \simeq 3$$

Often, the distribution of aquatic invertebrates does not approximate the normal distribution. In cases where the data approximate either a Poisson or a contagious distribution then the variance will be either equal to or greater than the mean, respectively. In these cases the sampling intensity should increase as the density increases. Alternatively, Elliott (1977) has proposed a method for estimating the number of samples required when the distribution is unknown. First, decide the allowable size of the ratio of the standard error to the mean, D. This information, along with an estimate of the population mean $\bar{X}$ and variance s^2, is then used to calculate the required number of samples n. The formula for n is:

$$n = \frac{s^2}{D^2 \bar{X}^2} \qquad (8.8)$$

For example, the mean number of *Daphnia* per sample at the central station in Table 8.1 was 41·2, the variance was 42·8, and the standard error of the mean was 2·07. If the desired ratio of the standard error to the mean is 0·1 (10%), then the required number of samples is

$$n = \frac{42 \cdot 8}{(0 \cdot 10)^2 41 \cdot 2^2} \simeq 3$$

which is less than the 10 originally collected. As the estimated ratio of the variance to mean increases, so does the number of samples required to keep the same ratio of standard error to mean. For example, if the mean number of *Daphnia* per sample remained at 41·2 but the variance was 128·4 rather than 42·8, then the standard error of the mean would be 3·58 and the number of samples needed to keep the ratio of the standard error to the mean at 10% would be:

$$n = \frac{128 \cdot 4}{(0 \cdot 10)^2 41 \cdot 2^2} \simeq 8$$

Elliott (1977) also provides separate formulae for samples with known distributions.

If samples are being collected with the goal of comparing means then there are two important points to remember. Replicates are required to estimate a standard error of the mean. The smaller this error and the larger the number of replicates the easier it will be to find real differences. In addition, statistical tests which assume a normal distribution are less sensitive to violations of this assumption with increased replication.

The sampling methodology discussed so far assumes that the sampling routine is random. The stratified, systematic and ratio sampling methods are also used in studies of aquatic invertebrates.

2.2 *Stratified random sampling*

Often, the environment sampled has a number of fairly homogeneous patches, but there may be large differences among individual patches. In these circumstances a stratified random sampling regimen can add considerable precision to the population estimate with a minimum of additional effort. First, the study area is divided into a number of strata. Next, samples are collected individually in each stratum. The mean for the population, $\bar{X}_W$, is a weighted mean:

$$\bar{X}_W = \frac{\sum\limits_{i=1}^{k} W_i \bar{X}_i}{W} \tag{8.9}$$

where k is the number of strata, W_i and $\bar{X}_i$ are the size and mean for the *i*th stratum respectively, and W is the sum of the weights,

$$W = \sum\limits_{i=1}^{k} W_i \tag{8.9i}$$

The standard error for the weighted mean, $s(\bar{X}_W)$, is also weighted,

$$s(\bar{X}_W) = \sqrt{\sum\limits_{i=1}^{k} \left(\frac{W_i}{W}\right)^2 \frac{s_i^2}{n_i}} \tag{8.10}$$

where s_i^2 and n_i are the variance and number of samples in the *i*th stratum, respectively. There is a gain in precision when using a stratified sampling routing because only the variation within strata, and not that among strata, contributes to the sampling error.

The formulae for a weighted mean and variance can be simplified if the ratio of W_i to W is the same for all strata, or if the variances are equal for all strata (Snedecor & Cochran 1980). In addition a finite population correction should be applied to the standard error of the mean if more than 10% of the population is sampled in any stratum, such that:

$$s(\bar{X}_W) = \sqrt{\sum\limits_{i=1}^{k} \left(\frac{W_i}{W}\right)^2 \frac{s_i^2}{n_i}\left(1 - \frac{n_i}{N_i}\right)} \tag{8.11}$$

where n_i/N_i is the fraction of the total population sampled in stratum i.

An optimal sampling regimen for estimation of the population mean can be designed when preliminary data are available for the mean $\bar{X}$ and variance s^2 in individual strata. The number of units sampled in each stratum is determined by the relative weight of the stratum and its standard deviation. The process is illustrated with the artificial example in Table 8.2, where the sediment area of a lake was divided into three strata according to percent vegetative cover to estimate chironomid density. In a pilot survey, four

8.2 Example to illustrate the technique of stratified random sampling.
Number of chironomids (cm^{-2}) in four random samples collected in each of three
strata, A, B, and C with vegetative cover over $>75\%$, $<75\%$ & $>50\%$, and
$<50\%$ of the area, respectively. The zones represent 20, 30, and $50 \times 10^2 \, m^2$,
respectively.

	Stratum		
	A	B	C
	50	20	5
	40	15	6
	60	25	9
	30	20	2
$\bar{X}_i$	45	20	5·5
$\sum\limits_{i=1}^{4} X_i$	180	80	22
$\sum\limits_{i=1}^{4} X_i^2$	8600	1650	146
s_i^2	166·67	16·667	8·333
W_i	20	30	50
$\dfrac{W_i}{W}$	0·2	0·3	0·5

samples were collected in each stratum. A quick inspection of the data shows
that the density estimates in section A are much more variable than in either
sections B or C. A weighted mean $(\bar{X}_W)$ and standard deviation of the weighted
mean $(s(\bar{X}_W))$ are calculated following equations 8.9 and 8.10:

$$\bar{X}_W = \frac{20(45) + 30(20) + 50(5·5)}{100}$$

$$= 17·75$$

and

$$s(\bar{X}_W) = \left(0·2^2 \left(\frac{166·67}{4} \right) + 0·3^2 \left(\frac{16·667}{4} \right) + 0·5^2 \left(\frac{8·333}{4} \right) \right)$$

$$= 1·6 \text{ chironomids cm}^{-2}$$

A decision can then be made about the total number of samples to be
collected. The sampling fraction in each stratum should be proportional to the
weight W_i and standard deviation s_i in each stratum. As illustrated in Table
8.3, a weighted standard deviation $W_i s_i$ is calculated for each stratum. These

Table 8.3. Calculations for obtaining the optimum sample size of individual strata. The calculations are based on data from Table 8.2.

Stratum	Surface area represented ($\times 10^2$ m^2) W_i	Mean number chironomids (cm^{-2}) $\bar{X}_i$	Standard deviation s_i	$W_i s_i$	Relative sample size	Actual sample size
A	20	45	12·91	258·2	0·4917	59
B	30	20	4·082	122·5	0·2333	28
C	50	5·5	2·887	144·4	0·2750	33
Total	100			525·1	1·0000	120

values are then summed over all strata. The relative sample size for each stratum is the ratio of $W_i s_i$ to $\sum_{i=1}^{k} W_i s_i$. As a consequence of the high standard deviation(s) in stratum A, the relative size of this sample is 49 %, or more than twice its relative weight W_i/W. If, for example, the total sample size was 120 samples then the optimum sampling programme would be to collect 59 samples in stratum A, as opposed to 24 samples based on proportional representation alone. The sampling strategy which collects a number of samples in each stratum proportional to the product of the weight and the standard deviation of the stratum reduces the standard error. Thus, if it is assumed that the sample variance (s^2) is a good estimate of the population variance (σ^2) in the example in Table 8.3, then the weighted standard error of the mean is 25 % lower with the optimal as opposed to a proportional sampling regimen (i.e., $s(\bar{X}_W) = 0·48$ as compared to 0·60). Various modifications of the randomized stratified sampling method are described by Stuart (1962) and Cochran (1977).

2.3 Systematic sampling

Systematic samples are evenly spaced throughout a designated area with the initial sampling point chosen randomly. For example, a random point was chosen on a small lake and samples were collected at that point and at five points 0·2 km apart in a westerly direction. Systematic sampling is more even than random sampling and easier to set up. It is often used for plankton samples when individual samples are pooled. It does, however, have two disadvantages over the random sample: it is not accurate if there is a periodicity over the same distance as the interval between samples. In addition, there is no general formula to estimate standard error, although there are formulae for some situations (e.g., Cochran 1977).

2.4 Ratio and regression estimates

The ratio estimate is another way of estimating population size. It is used when the size X of one population is known, the size Y of a second population is unknown, and the ratio of Y to X, R, is known. The information sought is the size of Y. The parameters X and Y could be the same population in two different years. If the mean rather than total numbers are of interest, then X and Y are replaced by $\bar{X}$ and $\bar{Y}$, respectively. The value of Y is estimated from:

$$Y = RX \qquad (8.12)$$

The ratio estimate is designed for situations where R, the ratio of Y to X, is relatively constant over the study population. For example, suppose there was a constant ratio of mean zooplankton ($\bar{Y}$) to mean phytoplankton ($\bar{X}$) biomass in a group of lakes. If, in one of these lakes, the phytoplankton but not the zooplankton biomass has been measured the ratio estimate could be used to predict the standing crop of zooplankton. The method of calculating a standard error for Y is described in Snedecor & Cochran (1980).

Sometimes the ratio of Y to X is not constant, but a straight line relationship appears to exist between them, i.e., there is a linear relationship with a non-zero intercept. In this case a regression estimate is appropriate (see Section 5.1). This technique is described in Cochran (1977). Both the ratio and regression estimations are useful for survey information, although information on distribution is lost.

2.5 Gradients in space

Vertical and horizontal gradients in planktonic and benthic organisms must be considered when designing a sampling routine. Since there are so few studies in the literature, pilot surveys (see Section 2.1.2) on the extent of spatial gradients in the population become an invaluable tool. From papers which have published data on spatial variation in plankton it is clear that the variation over a whole lake is greater than at a single location, as illustrated in Table 8.1.

2.6 Composite samples

Aquatic biologists often collect several samples to estimate one parameter, these samples being pooled to create a composite sample. Although information on spatial variation is lost in composite samples, this process is often necessary when it is not feasible to analyze all of the individual samples. The sampling programme for composite samples should take into account the natural variation in the community. Samples may be pooled along the main axis of the variation; for example, plankton samples have been taken at evenly spaced stations on the axis running from the leeward to the windward end of the lake. The composite sample should also be created with consideration for the volume of water or sediment area represented by the individual samples. For example, if individual samples are taken from a shallow and a deep station, representing 80 % and 20 % of the lake, respectively, then 80 % of the composite sample should be from the shallow station and 20 % from the deep station (see Sections 2.2 and 3.2). Wherever possible, replicate composite samples should be taken so that the population variance can be estimated.

3 Preparation of Samples for Statistical Analysis

This section covers the estimation of population numbers, determining the distribution of the data set, and an introduction to transformation of variables.

3.1 Enumeration of samples

There are two ways to estimate the number of organisms in a sample—either the entire sample is counted or subsamples are counted. Subsamples are used when random subsamples which contain sufficient numbers of each organism to give repeatable results can be obtained. The number of many of the larger aquatic invertebrates (e.g., *Chaoborus* larvae) cannot be accurately estimated from subsamples because these animals are not randomly distributed in the sample. In these cases there is little alternative to counting the entire sample. On the other hand, the distribution of small organisms is often random (e.g., Ricker 1938). Counts of several subsamples should be performed to check whether the variance to mean ratio conforms with a random distribution for each kind of organism.

The estimate of the mean is usually accurate when each subsample contains 50–150 individuals. Replicate subsamples with numbers in this range should have relatively low coefficients of variation (CV). On the other hand, small counts give very inaccurate results. For example, Ricker (1937) counted six groups of zooplankton in 20 subsamples taken from a single sample. In three groups, the mean number of organisms per subsample ranged from 58 to 122 and the CVs were low, ranging from 0·06 to 0·17. The three other groups of zooplankton had mean densities per subsample ranging from 1 to 14 and high CVs ranging from 0·31 to 1·06. Since the CVs in the first three groups were low, the subsample mean is a good estimate of the sample mean; in the second three groups the subsample mean is not accurate. If there are too many animals in the counting chamber, they tend to clump (e.g., Kott 1953) and the counts may also be inaccurate. See Chapter 7 for a fuller treatment of sample enumeration and its implications.

3.2 Estimation of population numbers

The process of converting subsample numbers to population estimates is illustrated in Table 8.4 with numbers of *Daphnia* collected from five separate strata. In this example, a smaller fraction is subsampled from the deeper strata rather than the upper strata since the animals are more dense in the deeper strata. As a result, the total number of *Daphnia* counted per subsample is within the limits of 50–150 animals (as suggested in Section 3.1). The sample

Table 8.4 The conversion of the numbers of *Daphnia* in subsamples to the number in the lake. The subsamples were from samples collected at five depths and each sample represents 1 m³ of water.

Stratum (m)	Fraction of the sample counted	*Daphnia* in subsample	*Daphnia* in sample	Volume of water per stratum ($\times 10^6$ m³)	*Daphnia* per stratum ($\times 10^6$)
0–1	0·10	52	520	32	16 640
1–2	0·10	73	730	20	14 600
2–3	0·10	95	950	11	10 450
3–4	0·02	102	5 100	5	25 500
4–5	0·02	87	4 350	2	8 700
Total			11 650	70	75 890

numbers are obtained by dividing the number of *Daphnia* counted by the fraction of the sample counted. Since each sample represents 1 m³ of water, the sample numbers are per m³. In this example the samples represent strata of unequal size. The sample estimates (X_i) are multiplied by the volume of water they represent to get a total population estimate X:

$$X = \sum_{i=1}^{k} X_i V_i \tag{8.13}$$

where k is the number of strata and V_i is the volume of water in stratum i. In this example the population estimate based on strata of different volumes is lower than an estimate based on strata of equal volumes (i.e., $75\,890 \times 10^6$ as compared to $163\,100 \times 10^6$). This difference occurs because the larger animal densities were found in samples which represent smaller volumes of water.

3.3 Smoothing data

Estimates of changes in the number of aquatic organisms over time are often relatively imprecise because of inadequate sampling. When looking for trends with time, smoothing of population numbers is recommended (e.g., Edmondson 1960; covered in detail in Tukey 1977). Smoothing involves replacing population estimates on individual dates by moving averages, usually from three or five consecutive dates. If population estimates for three consecutive dates are X_{i-1}, X_i and X_{i+1}, then the three-date moving average $\bar{X}_i$ is:

$$\bar{X}_i = \frac{X_{i-1} + X_i + X_{i+1}}{3} \tag{8.14}$$

The number of dates included in moving averages should be inversely related to the confidence which is placed in individual population estimates. In Table 8.5, population estimates prior to smoothing and three- and five-week running averages are presented. In this example, smoothing eliminates the small fluctuation in population numbers between the third and seventh weeks and reduces the peak value recorded for the ninth week. Smoothing reduces the possibility of attributing causes to short-term population fluctuations which are the result of sampling inadequacies. On the other hand, some information on short- term change is lost, and erroneous conclusions can be drawn from moving averages (e.g. Cole 1954, 1957).

Table 8.5 An example to illustrate smoothing of data.

Week i	Observed population numbers X_i	Running average $\bar{X}_i$	
		3 week	5 week
1	76		
2	90	84	
3	86	94	95
4	105	103	101
5	117	109	109
6	106	118	122
7	130	129	201
8	150	260	205
9	500	263	208
10	140	253	202
11	120	119	
12	98		

Table 8.6 Array of total shell length (cm) of 122 snails, *Thais lamellosa.* Data were collected at Bamfield Marine Station by R.Palmer.

Snail number	Length (cm)	Snail number	Length (cm)	Snail number	Length (cm)
001	3·8	043	2·3	085	2·7
002	3·3	044	2·3	086	2·2
003	3·4	045	2·2	087	2·5
004	3·1	046	2·0	088	2·6
005	3·6	047	2·0	089	3·6
006	3·2	048	2·2	090	2·6
007	3·0	049	2·0	091	2·5
008	2·7	050	2·3	092	2·4
009	3·0	051	2·4	093	2·2
010	3·0	052	2·0	094	2·2
011	3·0	053	2·0	095	2·2
012	2·5	054	1·8	096	2·3
013	2·8	055	1·8	097	2·5
014	2·6	056	2·0	098	2·7
015	2·2	057	1·7	099	2·5
016	2·7	058	1·7	100	2·4
017	2·5	059	1·6	101	2·3
018	3·2	060	1·6	102	2·4
019	3·3	061	1·5	103	2·3
020	2·7	062	1·5	104	2·3
021	4·2	063	1·5	105	2·4
022	3·3	064	1·5	106	2·4
023	3·3	065	1·6	107	2·4
024	3·1	066	1·4	108	2·1
025	2·8	067	1·2	109	1·8
026	3·0	068	3·4	110	2·0
027	2·6	069	3·0	111	2·1
028	3·3	070	3·0	112	1·8
029	3·4	071	3·0	113	1·8
030	2·8	072	2·8	114	1·9
031	2·9	073	2·8	115	1·9
032	2·8	074	2·8	116	1·7
033	3·0	075	2·9	117	1·8
034	2·7	076	2·8	118	1·8
035	2·9	077	2·7	119	1·5
036	2·3	078	3·0	120	1·8
037	2·9	079	2·9	121	1·6
038	2·8	080	2·0	122	2·4
039	2·6	081	2·7		
040	2·3	082	2·5		
041	2·5	083	2·3		
042	2·6	084	2·5		

3.4 Determining the distribution of the data

The approximate distribution of a data set can be determined simply with a frequency histogram, although reasonable sample size is required to make this a useful exercise. To illustrate this process the shell lengths of 122 adult snails (*Thais lamellosa*) collected at the Bamfield Marine Station by R. Palmer will be used (Table 8.6). The snails range in length from 1·2 to 4·2 cm, with mean $\bar{X} = 2·47$ cm and variance $s^2 = 0·329$ cm. The range was divided into 11 equal categories extending from 1·1 to 4·3 cm. The observed frequency for each category was recorded (Table 8.7) and this information used to draw the frequency histogram in Fig. 8.2. The graphical presentation suggests that the snail lengths approximate the normal distribution.

There are a number of methods used to test whether data are normally distributed. A graphical method based on a cumulative frequency distribution uses arithmetic probability paper (see Fig. 8.3). On this graph paper the abscissa scale is linear and the ordinate is the cumulative percentage rising from 0·01 to 99·99. The ordinates are stretched at both ends such that when the percentages of the observations which are less than or equal to each of the upper class limits are plotted, the points will be on a straight line if the distribution is normal. To plot points on probability paper the data are

Table 8.7 Calculation of expected normal frequency distribution. The data are shell length of snails in cm from Table 8.6; $n = 122$; $\bar{X} = 2·47$; $s = 0·574$. Data were collected at Bamfield Marine Station by R.Palmer.

Class limits		Observed frequency	Expected frequency	Z value	Area under the normal curve (A)	Cumulative area under the normal curve	Expected class probability
Practical	Implied						
1·1–1·3	$-\infty$–1·35	1	3·1	−1·95	0·4744	0·0256	0·0256
1·4–1·6	1·35–1·65	10	6·2	−1·43	0·4236	0·0764	0·0508
1·7–1·9	1·65–1·95	13	12·8	−0·91	0·3186	0·1814	0·1050
2·0–2·2	1·95–2·25	17	20·8	−0·38	0·1480	0·3520	0·1706
2·3–2·5	2·25–2·55	27	24·9	0·14	0·0557	0·5557	0·2037
2·6–2·8	2·55–2·85	23	23·1	0·66	0·2454	0·7454	0·1897
2·9–3·1	2·85–3·15	17	16·5	1·18	0·3810	0·8810	0·1356
3·2–3·4	3·15–3·45	10	9·2	1·71	0·4564	0·9564	0·0754
3·5–3·7	3·45–3·75	2	3·7	2·23	0·4871	0·9871	0·0307
3·8–4·0	3·75–4·05	1	1·2	2·75	0·4970	0·9970	0·0099
4·1–4·3	4·05–∞	1	0·4	∞	0·500	1·000	0·0030
Total		122	121·9				1·00

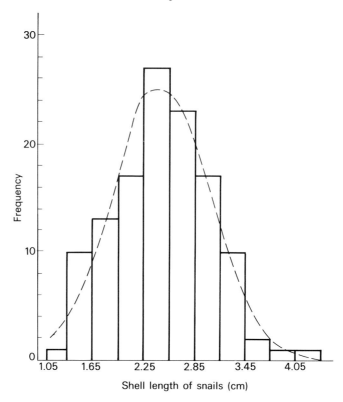

Fig. 8.2 Histogram of total shell length of 122 snails, *Thais lamellosa*. The dashed curve is the normal distribution with mean $\mu = 2\cdot47$ and variance $\sigma^2 = 0\cdot329$. Data were collected at Bamfield Marine Station by R.Palmer.

divided into equal size classes, the frequency is calculated for each class, and the cumulative frequency is plotted against the upper class limit. A straight line is drawn by hand through the points, giving most weight to the points between the cumulative frequencies of 25 % to 75 %. This method is illustrated in Fig. 8.3 using the snail data from Table 8.8. The points in Fig. 8.3 fall close to a straight line and thus appear to be normally distributed, as they were in Fig. 8.2. This method works well for large samples ($n > 60$); however, for small samples, a more suitable graphical test for normality of a frequency distribution is the Rankit method. Both of these graphical methods are for continuous data and are described in Cassie (1963) and Sokal & Rohlf (1981).

Another approach to determine whether data follow a normal distribution is to calculate the theoretical or expected distribution and compare this with the observed distribution—this is suitable for large samples sizes. It will be illustrated with the calculation of an expected normal frequency distribution

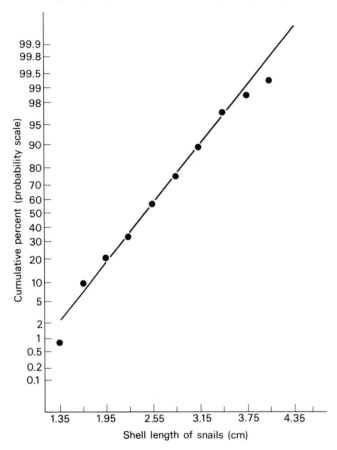

Fig. 8.3 Shell length of snails, *Thais lamellosa*, plotted on probability paper. Data were collected at Bamfield Marine Station by R. Palmer.

for the snail data (Table 8.7). There are five steps in calculating an expected normal frequency distribution.

(1) A standard deviation unit or Z value is calculated for each upper class limit X_u:

$$Z = \frac{X_u - \bar{X}}{s} \tag{8.15}$$

In the example, the first upper class limit is $1 \cdot 35$ cm, the mean ($\bar{X}$) and standard deviation (s) are $2 \cdot 47$ and $0 \cdot 574$ cm, respectively, and the Z value is:

$$Z = \frac{1 \cdot 35 - 2 \cdot 47}{0 \cdot 574} = -1 \cdot 95$$

Table 8.8 The calculations required to use arithmetic probability paper to test for normality of a frequency distribution. The data are shell length of snails in cm from Table 8.7. Data were collected at Banfield Marine Station by R.Palmer.

Class mean	Upper class limit	Observed frequency	Cumulative frequency	Percent cumulative frequency
1·2	1·35	1	1	0·82
1·5	1·65	10	11	9·1
1·8	1·95	13	24	19·7
2·1	2·25	17	41	33·6
2·4	2·55	27	68	55·7
2·7	2·85	23	91	74·6
3·0	3·15	17	108	88·5
3·3	3·45	10	118	96·7
3·6	3·75	2	120	98·4
3·9	4·05	1	121	99·18
4·2	4·35	1	122	100·0
Total		122		

(2)   The area under the normal curve (A) is then read from a table of the cumulative normal frequency distributions (available in most statistical texts).

  For example, when $Z = 1·95$ (which is the case for the first category in the snail data) $A = 0·4744$.

(3)   The cumulative area under the curve is calculated for each class as follows: for negative Z, use $(0·5 - A)$; for positive Z, use $(0·5 + A)$. The cumulative area under the portion of the curve extending from $-\infty$ to $1·35$ cm is thus $(0·5 - 0·4744) = 0·0256$.

(4)   The expected class probabilities are calculated by subtracting successive cumulative probabilities. For the first category in the snail data ($-\infty$ to $1·35$ cm) the expected class probability is $(0·0256 - 0) = 0·0256$.

(5)   To obtain the expected frequencies, the class probabilities are multiplied by the sample size, which is 122 in the example used here.

For the snail data the expected frequencies appear similar to the observed frequencies (Table 8.7). To test whether the observed distribution fits the expected distribution, the χ^2-test is normally applied (see Section 3.5.1). Alternatively, when the sample size is small the Kolmogorov–Smirnov test for goodness-of-fit should be applied because it is more powerful (see Sokal & Rohlf 1981).

3.5 The χ^2-test

The χ^2-test is used to determine whether an observed distribution conforms with a theoretical or expected distribution for both discrete and continuous variables. It is also used to test whether two or more sets of discrete data have similar distributions. The general formula for the χ^2 is:

$$\chi^2 = \sum_{i=1}^{k} \frac{(f_i - F_i)^2}{F_i} \tag{8.16}$$

where k is the total number of classes and f_i and F_i are the observed and expected frequencies of the ith class, respectively. The calculated χ^2 value is compared to a χ^2-distribution with $(k-1)$ degrees of freedom less 1 degree of freedom for every parameter of the expected distribution estimated from the data. When a χ^2-test is performed with 1 degree of freedom, a continuity correction is applied:

$$\chi^2 = \sum_{i=1}^{k} \frac{(|f_i - F_i| - 0 \cdot 5)^2}{F_i} \tag{8.17}$$

where $|f_i - F_i|$ is the absolute value of the difference $(f_i - F_i)$. Four examples are presented to illustrate some uses of χ^2.

3.5.1 χ^2-Test of goodness-of-fit

An expected normal frequency distribution for the snail data was calculated in the previous section. The calculations necessary to compare this expected frequency distribution with the observed distribution are shown in Table 8.9. The expected probabilities (F_i) used in a χ^2 should be >1 (Cochran 1954). To comply with this rule, classes with expectations <1 are merged: in Table 8.9 the last two classes were combined to comply with this rule. For each class the contribution to the χ^2 is the squared difference between the observed and expected values, divided by the appropriate expected value. These individual contributions to the χ^2 are summed and the total, 5·60, is compared to a χ^2 table with $(k-3)$ degrees of freedom. There are $(10-3) = 7$ degrees of freedom in this example because there are 10 classes after the merging of the last two classes, one degree of freedom is lost automatically, and two more are lost because the sample mean ($\bar{X}$) and variance (s^2) were used to calculate the expected values. The probability (P) associated with a χ^2 value of 5·60 with 7 degrees of freedom is $>0·5$. Thus the null hypothesis that the observed frequency distribution is similar to the normal distribution is not rejected.

In a second example, which is hypothetical, the problem is to determine whether there are differences in the number of eggs carried by 50 adult *Daphnia pulex* collected in each of four strata in a small lake. The expected

Table 8.9 The χ^2 goodness-of-fit test. The observed frequencies of snail shell lengths are from Table 8.7 and the expected frequencies are calculated assuming a normal frequency distribution.

Class mean	Observed frequency (f)	Expected frequency (F)	$f - F$	Contribution to χ^2
1·2	1	3·1	−2·1	1·42
1·5	10	6·2	3·8	2·34
1·8	13	12·8	0·2	0·00
2.1	17	20·8	−3·8	0·69
2·4	27	24·9	2·1	0·18
2·7	23	23·1	−0·1	0·00
3·0	17	16·5	0·5	0·02
3·3	10	9·2	0·8	0·07
3·6	2	3·7	−1·7	0·78
3·9	1 ⎫ 2	1·2 ⎫ 1·6	0·4	0·10
4·2	1 ⎭	0·4 ⎭		
Total	122	121·9		5·60

frequency for each stratum is the total number of observations divided by the number of strata, as illustrated in Table 8.10. The expected frequency was computed on the basis of the expected ratio of 1:1:1:1. This expected ratio is extrinsic to the sampled data and thus no additional degrees of freedom are lost. The χ^2 value of 11·58 is compared to a χ^2-distribution with 3 degrees of freedom. Since the calculated χ^2 value has a $P < 0.01$, the data are not consistent with the null hypothesis that the distribution of *Daphnia* eggs in the four strata is homogeneous.

Table 8.10 The χ^2 goodness-of-fit test where the hypothesis is extrinsic to the sampled data. The data are number of eggs carried by 50 adult *Daphnia pulex* selected randomly from samples collected in each of four strata in a lake.

Stratum	Observed frequency (f)	Expected frequency (F)	$f - F$	Contribution to χ^2
1	106	82	24	7·02
2	83	82	1	0·01
3	75	82	−7	0·60
4	64	82	−18	3·95
Total	328	328		11·58

3.5.2 χ^2-Test for the variance to mean ratio

A χ^2-test is also used to compare the sample variance to mean ratio with that expected from a Poisson distribution. For a Poisson distribution, the variance to mean ratio multiplied by the degrees of freedom:

$$\frac{s^2}{\bar{X}}(n-1) \qquad (8.18)$$

has approximately a χ^2-distribution with $(n-1)$ degrees of freedom, where n is the sample size. In Table 8.1, statistics were presented for *Daphnia* collected in replicate samples at one station and at random stations. The variance to mean ratio was 1·04 with 9 degrees of freedom for the samples collected at one station and 3·68 with 6 degrees of freedom for the samples collected at random stations. The ratio for the fixed station ($\chi^2 = 9\cdot35$ with 9 degrees of freedom) is not significant ($P > 0\cdot25$) whereas for the random stations ($\chi^2 = 22\cdot1$ with 6 degrees of freedom) the ratio is significant ($P < 0\cdot005$). Thus the null hypothesis that *Daphnia* are randomly distributed is not rejected for the samples collected at a single station, but is rejected for the samples collected at random locations.

3.5.3 χ^2-Test for homogeneity

The χ^2-test for homogeneity of samples is used to test whether two or more observed distributions are drawn from the same population. This test is illustrated with data on the proportion of five prey types found in the stomach and intestine of 56 mysids (from Murtaugh 1981, unpublished). The data were arranged in cells: each cell contains a unique combination of a prey type and a location (Table 8.11). The expected values for each cell are the product of the corresponding row R and column C totals divided by the overall number of observations. The calculations for the χ^2-test are illustrated in Table 8.11. The number of degrees of freedom for this test is $(R-1)(C-1)$: in this example there are five rows and two columns of cells and thus 4 degrees of freedom. The χ^2 value for the mysid data (1·89) is very low ($P > 0\cdot75$). Thus, there is no reason to reject the null hypothesis that prey type and location in the digestive tract are independent.

3.6 Transformations

When data do not conform to the basic assumptions for a parametric statistical test, a transformation of these observations into another scale often makes them suitable for the test. Transformations are used to reduce data non-normality, the heterogeneity in the variances, and the non-additivity of

Table 8.11 The χ^2 test for homogeneity of samples. The observed and expected frequencies are for the numbers of various groups of planktonic organisms in the digestive tract of the predator *Neomysis mercedis*. Data are from P.A.Murtaugh (1981, unpublished).

Prey type	Location		Row total
	Stomach	Intestine	
	Observed numbers f		
Daphnia	452	102	554
Calanoid copepods	41	9	50
Cylopoid copepods	28	3	31
Rotifers	51	9	60
Other (e.g. *Bosmina*)	5	1	6
Column total	577	124	701

	expected numbers F	
Daphnia	$\dfrac{(577)\,(554)}{701} = 456$	$\dfrac{(124)\,(554)}{701} = 98\cdot0$
Calanoid copepods	41·2	8·84
Cylopoid copepods	25·5	5·48
Rotifers	49·4	10·6
Others (e.g. *Bosmina*)	4·94	1·06

$$\chi^2 = \sum_{i=1}^{n} \frac{(f_i - F_i)^2}{F_i} = \frac{(452 - 456)^2}{456} + \frac{(41 - 41\cdot2)^2}{41\cdot2} + \cdots + \frac{(1 - 1\cdot06)^2}{1\cdot06} = 1\cdot89$$

the treatment effects. A transformation involves taking each observation X_i and converting it to a new number, X_i', which is then used in subsequent calculations. Three commonly used transformations, the logarithmic, the square root, and the arcsine, will be discussed in this section.

Once a transformation has been applied, the data should be rechecked to determine whether the transformation has corrected the problem. Several methods have been developed to determine the best transformation, such as the Box and Cox (1964) method for non-normal data (described briefly in Sokal & Rohlf 1981), Taylor's (1961) method for variance stabilization and Tukey's (1949) method for non-additivity (described in Snedecor & Cochran 1980). One of these, Taylor's method for variance stabilization, will also be discussed below.

3.6.1 Logarithmic transformation

This is the most commonly used transformation for biological data, and there are two forms: logs to the base 10 and natural logarithms, i.e.

$$X'_i = \log_{10}(X_i) \tag{8.19}$$

and

$$X'_i = \log_e(X_i), \tag{8.19i}$$

respectively. If there are very small numbers or zeros then the transformation is applied to $(X_i + 1)$ instead of X_i. The logarithmic transformation is illustrated in Section 5.1.1.

3.6.2 Square root transformation

The square root transformation:

$$X'_i = \sqrt{X_i} \tag{8.20}$$

is normally applied to data that follow the Poisson distribution. If there are zero values, then the transformation:

$$X'_i = \sqrt{X_i + 0.5} \tag{8.20i}$$

is applied (e.g., Kutkuhn 1958).

3.6.3 Arcsine transformation

Data which are expressed as percentages or proportions and lie between 0–30 % and 70–100 % are usually non-normal, i.e., there are too many values at the tails of the distribution relative to the centre. The arcsine or angular transformation:

$$X'_i = \arcsin \sqrt{X_i} \tag{8.21}$$

reduces the scale in the middle of a distribution and extends the tails.

3.6.4 Taylor's method for variance stabilization

Taylor (1961) showed that, for data on the abundance of organisms, there is a simple power law relationship between the variance (s^2) and the mean ($\bar{X}$):

$$s^2 = a\bar{X}^b \tag{8.22}$$

Where a and b are parameters describing the study population, and that the appropriate transformation is:

$$X'_i = X_i^{1-0.5b} \tag{8.23}$$

or

$$X'_i = (X_i + c)^{1-0.5b} \tag{8.23i}$$

where c is a constant such as 0·5 or 1 and b is the coefficient from equation 8.22. When $b = 0$, the distribution is regular and no transformation is necessary. The distribution is Poisson and a square root transformation ($\sqrt{X} \equiv X^{0.5}$) is suggested when $b = 1$. A logarithmic transformation is recommended when $b = 2$, and when $b > 2$ a negative power function is the appropriate transformation.

Taylor's method is useful only for cases where numerous estimates of the μ and σ^2 can be collected. Downing (1979) gathered enough data to examine the relationship between the mean and variance for benthic invertebrates that were collected with several types of samplers and from various substrates. He found that a fourth root transformation was the most appropriate for the samples examined. Further investigations are required to determine the general applicability of Downing's fourth root transformation to data on the abundance of aquatic invertebrates (Taylor 1980).

4 Comparison of Means and Related Topics

This section focuses on the t-test as a method for comparing two or more means. Alternatives to the standard t-tests are also introduced, although the most important alternative, the analysis of variance (ANOVA), is discussed only briefly. A test for combining probabilities from independent tests of significance is considered in this section. Since most statistical tests for the comparison of means assume that the sample variances are homogeneous, three tests for homogeneity of sample variances are also reviewed.

4.1 Calculation of an average variance and tests for homogeneity of sample variance

An estimate of average variance is required for most t-tests. If there are k independent estimates ($s_1^2, s_2^2, \ldots, s_k^2$) of the same population variance σ^2, with $(n_1 - 1)$, $(n_2 - 1)$, ..., $(n_k - 1)$ degrees of freedom, respectively, a single estimate of σ^2 is given by the weighted average of sample variances:

$$\bar{s}^2 = \frac{\sum\limits_{i=1}^{k} (n_i - 1)s_i^2}{\sum\limits_{i=1}^{k} (n_i - 1)} \tag{8.24}$$

The calculation of an average variance is illustrated in Table 8.12 with data from Peters & Rigler (1973) on the reproductive rate of adult *Daphnia* fed three different concentrations of yeast.

This calculation of an average variance (equation 8.24) assumes that the estimated variances are consistent with one another. Three ways to test whether the variances are homogeneous will be outlined.

Table 8.12 Reproductive rate of adult *Daphnia rosea* fed on three different concentrations of *Rhodotorula*. Data are from Peters & Rigler (1973).

	Food concentration (cells ml^{-1})		
	0.125×10^5	0.5×10^5	1×10^5
Mean, reproductive rate $\bar{X}_i$ (ng P animal^{-1} hr^{-1})	0.64	1.74	1.89
Variance s_i^2	0.0256	0.3136	0.2209
Sample size n_i	5	6	10

$$\bar{s}^2 = \frac{4(0.0256) + 5(0.3136) + 9(0.2209)}{4 + 5 + 9} = 0.203\,25 \text{ ng P animal}^{-1} \text{ hr}^{-1}$$

4.1.1 Standard F-test

When there are only two sample variances, s_1^2 and s_2^2, the *F*-test

$$F = \frac{s_1^2}{s_2^2} \tag{8.25}$$

with $(n_1 - 1)$, $(n_2 - 1)$ degrees of freedom is used to compare sample variances. This is a two-tailed test of significance, although the *F*-table is usually set up for one-tailed tests. Therefore, the ratio is formed with $s_1^2 > s_2^2$ and the tabular probability is doubled.

For example, the length of *Diaptomus minutus* was examined by Rigler & Langford (1967) for lakes in which the congenitor *D. oregonensis* was absent and present. As illustrated in Table 8.13, the variance in length of males, but not females, appears to be much greater in lakes when it occurs together with *D. oregonensis* than when it occurs alone. A ratio of the larger variance to the smaller variance is computed for both sexes. The *F*-ratio of 4·5 for the lengths of male *D. minutus* has 38 and 12 degrees of freedom associated with it. For a one-tailed test the tabular probability for this ratio is <0.005 and for a two-tailed test it is doubled, i.e., $P < 0.01$. The hypothesis that the variances are homogeneous is, therefore, rejected for the male *D. minutus* ($F = 4.5$; df = 38, 12; $P < 0.01$), whereas it cannot be rejected for female *D. minutus* ($F = 1.97$; df = 35, 13; $P > 0.10$). Similar patterns are seen in the variances of male and female *D. oregonensis* in the same article. These differences suggest that the presence of congenitors may effect male growth rates more than female growth rates in *Diaptomus*.

4.1.2 Maximum F-ratio Test

The F_{max}-test is a simple test for comparing more than two variances. It can be

Table 8.13 Total length (mm) of *Diaptomus minutus* in lakes in which the congenitor *D. oregonensis* was absent and present. Data are from Rigler & Langford 1967).

	Males		Females	
	Alone	Together	Alone	Together
Mean $\bar{X}_i$	0·92	1·01	1·00	1·08
Variance s_i^2	0·001 05	0·004 72	0·003 58	0·007 06
Sample size n_i	13	39	14	36
s_i^2/n_i	0·000 08	0·000 12		

	F-test for homogeneity of variances	
F-ratio	$\dfrac{0·004\,72}{0·001\,05} = 4·5**$	$\dfrac{0·007\,06}{0·003\,58} = 1·97$
Degrees of freedom df	38, 12	35, 13
Probability *P*	$(<0·005 \times 2) = \,<0·01$	$(>0·05 \times 2) = \,>0·10$

used when there are up to six variances, all based on the same number of degrees of freedom. For this test the ratio:

$$F_{max} = \frac{\max(s^2)}{\min(s^{2)}} \tag{8.26}$$

is formed. This value cannot be compared to the standard *F*-table which can be used to compare only two variances at a time; there are tables available, however, which make proper allowance for the selection of extremes (David 1952; reproduced as Table 17 from Rohlf & Sokal 1981).

The data in Table 8.14 (from Kott 1953) are used to illustrate this test. In an investigation of an apparatus for subsampling a cladoceran species based on three separate plankton hauls, the maximum variance was 400·3 animals

Table 8.14 Variances in number of the cladoceran *Penilia smaekeri* in subsamples collected with a modified whirling apparatus from three separate plankton hauls. Data are from Kott (1953).

Haul	Number of subsamples collected	Sample variance
1	10	92·2
2	10	400·3
3	10	290·0

per compartment and the minimum variance was 92·2 animals per compartment. The F_{max} value,

$$F_{max} = \frac{400\cdot3}{92\cdot2} = 4\cdot34$$

for the three variances all with 9 degrees of freedom, is less than the critical value ($P = 0\cdot05$) of 5·34. Thus, heterogeneity of the three sample variances is not clearly indicated.

4.1.3 Bartlett's test of homogeneity of variances

When there are more than two estimates of variance s_i^2, i.e., $k > 2$, Bartlett's test of homogeneity can be applied. This is an approximate χ^2-test, which, in most cases, is more efficient than the F_{max}-test. However, the calculations for Bartlett's test are more extensive and it has been criticized as being too sensitive to departures from normality in the data. This test requires:

$$l_i = \log_e s_i^2 \tag{8.27}$$

for each sample variance s_i^2, and:

$$L = \log_e \bar{s}^2 \tag{8.27i}$$

from the weighted average variance $\bar{s}^2$.

The quantity:

$$M = \left[\left(\sum_{i=1}^{k} n_i - 1 \right) L - \sum_{i=1}^{k} (n_i - 1) l_i \right] \tag{8.27ii}$$

can then be compared after correction to the χ^2-distribution for $(k - 1)$ degrees of freedom. A correction factor:

$$C = 1 + \frac{1}{3(k - 1)} \left[\sum_{i=1}^{k} \frac{1}{(n_i - 1)} - \frac{1}{\sum_{i=1}^{k} (n_i - 1)} \right] \tag{8.27iii}$$

is applied to equation 8.27ii because the χ^2 value tends to be too large. When the correction is required, M/C is compared with the χ^2-distribution. C is always slightly greater than 1 and therefore only needs to be calculated if M is slightly larger than the critical χ^2 value.

The data in Table 8.12 on reproductive rates of *Daphnia* grown in three different food concentrations are used to illustrate this test. The calculations are shown in Table 8.15. The M value 5·37 is compared to a χ^2-distribution with 2 degrees of freedom. This is a small χ^2 value for 2 degrees of freedom ($P > 0\cdot05$) and there is, therefore, no reason to assume that the variances are not homogeneous.

Table 8.15 Bartlett's test for homogeneity of variances. The data are mean reproductive rate of *Daphnia* grown in three separate food concentrations (from Table 8.12). Data are from Peters & Rigler (1973).

Step 1	Calculate l_i for each food concentration			
	Food concentration (cells ml^{-1})	$n_i - 1$	s_i^2	$l_i = \ln s_i^2$
	$0 \cdot 125 \times 10^5$	4	0·0256	−3·665 16
	$0 \cdot 5 \ \ \times 10^5$	5	0·3136	−1·159 64
	$1 \cdot 0 \ \ \times 10^5$	9	0·2209	−1·510 05

Step 2   Calculate L
Since $\bar{s}^2 = 0 \cdot 203\,25$, $L = \ln\,(0 \cdot 203\,25) = -1 \cdot 593\,32$

Step 3   Calculate M

(i) $\sum_{i=1}^{k} (n_i - 1)l_i = 4(-3 \cdot 665\,16) + 5(-1 \cdot 159\,64) + 9(-1 \cdot 510\,05)$

$$= -34 \cdot 049\,29$$

Since the average variance $\bar{s}^2$ is based on 18 df

(ii) $M = 18(-1 \cdot 593\,32) - (-34 \cdot 049\,29) = 5.37$
with $k - 1$ or $3 - 1 = 2$df

4.2 *t-Test for comparison of a sample mean with the population mean*

To determine if a sample mean is significantly different from an assumed population mean, a *t*-test is used. The *t* value is the ratio of the deviation of a sample mean ($\bar{X}$) from the population mean (μ) to the standard error of the mean ($s_{\bar{x}}$).

$$t = \frac{\bar{X} - \mu}{s_{\bar{x}}} \tag{8.28}$$

This *t* value is compared with the Student's *t*-distribution with ($n - 1$) degrees of freedom. It is assumed that the sample mean ($\bar{X}$) is normally distributed.

This test is illustrated with data from Lampert (1974) in which he investigated whether filter feeders showed preferences for certain food items. *Daphnia pulex* were fed a mixture of labelled bacteria and algae. A coefficient of selection, *S*, was calculated to determine to what extent bacteria were preferred to algae. If there was no food preference the coefficient of selection would be $S = 1$. In one experiment with four observations the average coefficient of selection $\bar{S}$ was 1·65 and the sample variance s^2 was 0·0784. In order to test whether this value of 1·65 ($\bar{X}$) is different from 1 (μ), a standard error of the mean $s_{\bar{x}}$ is first calculated:

$$s_{\bar{x}} = \sqrt{\frac{0 \cdot 0784}{4}} = 0 \cdot 14$$

The t value,

$$t = \frac{1 \cdot 65 - 1}{0 \cdot 14} = 11 \cdot 8$$

is compared with the Student's t-distribution with 3 degrees of freedom. Since the Student's t value for $P = 0 \cdot 005$ and 3 degrees of freedom is $7 \cdot 45$, the null hypothesis that *Daphnia* show no preference for food organisms is rejected.

4.3 Comparison of two independent means

4.3.1 Standard t-test

The standard method for comparison of two independent means, $\bar{X}_1$ and $\bar{X}_2$, is the t-test. This test assumes that:

(1) The observations which are used to calculate $\bar{X}_1$ and $\bar{X}_2$ are independent.
(2) The means $\bar{X}_1$ and $\bar{X}_2$ are normally distributed.
(3) The variances in the two populations are homogeneous.

This comparison requires the standard error of the difference between two means:

$$s_{\bar{X}_1 - \bar{X}_2} = \sqrt{\bar{s}^2 \left(\frac{1}{n_1} + \frac{1}{n_2} \right)} \qquad (8.29)$$

where $\bar{s}^2$ is the average variance (see Section 4.1) and n_1 and n_2 are the number of observations used to compute $\bar{X}_1$ and $\bar{X}_2$, respectively. To test whether the difference between the means is different from zero, the value:

$$t = \frac{\bar{X}_1 - \bar{X}_2}{s_{\bar{X}_1 - \bar{X}_2}} \qquad (8.29\mathrm{i})$$

is calculated and compared to a Student's t-table with $(n_1 + n_2 - 2)$ degrees of freedom.

The standard t-test is illustrated with mean length data for female *D. minutus* when they occur alone and with a congenitor (Table 8.13). There are three calculations required: from equation 8.24, an average variance:

$$\bar{s}^2 = \frac{13(0 \cdot 00358) + 35(0 \cdot 00706)}{48} = 0 \cdot 00612 \, \mathrm{mm}$$

from equation 8.29, a standard error of the difference between the means:

$$s_{\bar{X}_1 - \bar{X}_2} = \sqrt{0 \cdot 006 \, 12 \left(\frac{1}{14} + \frac{1}{36} \right)} = 0 \cdot 024 \, 64 \, \mathrm{mm}$$

and finally the value:

$$t = \frac{1\cdot00 - 1\cdot08}{0\cdot024\,64} = 3\cdot25$$

This t value is compared with a two-tailed t-distribution with 48 degrees of freedom. Since the probability is $<0\cdot005$, the hypothesis that the mean length of female *D. minutus* is unaffected by the presence of the congenitor is rejected.

4.3.2 t-Test for samples with heterogeneous variances

The standard t-test makes the assumption that the sample variances are homogeneous. When this assumption does not hold the investigator has two choices—either transform the variables to reduce the heterogeneity or use a modified t-test to compare the means. If the variances are heterogeneous, a standard t-test is not accurate: the null hypothesis will be rejected too few times if the larger sample has the larger variance and too many times if the larger sample has the smaller variance. If heterogeneity of variances is suspected and is not corrected by a transformation of the data, the standard t-test must be modified so that the t value will approximate a t-distribution (Snedecor & Cochran 1980). A weighted variance is not used to calculate the standard error of the mean $s'_{\bar{X}_1 - \bar{X}_2}$, rather:

$$s'_{\bar{X}_1 - \bar{X}_2} = \sqrt{\frac{s_1^2}{n_1} + \frac{s_2^2}{n_2}} \qquad (8.30)$$

and:

$$t' = \frac{\bar{X}_1 - \bar{X}_2}{s'_{\bar{X}_1 - \bar{X}_2}} \qquad (8.30i)$$

where $\bar{X}_1$ and $\bar{X}_2$, s_1^2 and s_2^2, and n_1 and n_2 are the means, variances and sample size for the first and second samples, respectively. The degrees of freedom are also modified:

$$df' = \frac{(s_{\bar{X}_1}^2 + s_{\bar{X}_2}^2)^2}{\left(\dfrac{s_{\bar{X}_1}^4}{n_1 - 1} + \dfrac{s_{\bar{X}_2}^4}{n_2 - 1}\right)} \qquad (8.31)$$

The t' value is then compared with the Student's t-distribution with df' degrees of freedom.

This test is illustrated with a comparison of the mean lengths of male *D. minutus* in the presence and absence of a congenitor. The variances for this example are heterogeneous (Table 8.13). This t-test requires a standard error of the differences between two means:

$$s'_{\bar{X}_1 - \bar{X}_2} = \sqrt{0 \cdot 000\ 08 + 0 \cdot 000\ 12} = 0 \cdot 014\ 14 \text{ mm}$$

a t' value:

$$t' = \frac{0 \cdot 92 - 1 \cdot 01}{0 \cdot 014\ 14} = -6 \cdot 37$$

and degrees of freedom:

$$df' = \frac{(0 \cdot 000\ 08 + 0 \cdot 000\ 12)^2}{\left(\dfrac{(0 \cdot 000\ 08)^2}{12} + \dfrac{(0 \cdot 000\ 12)^2}{38}\right)} = 44$$

The sign of the t' value is ignored and it is compared with a Student's t-distribution with 44 degrees of freedom. This t' value is highly significant ($P < 0 \cdot 001$) and thus the hypothesis that the mean length of male *D. minutus* is unaffected by the presence of the congenitor is rejected. Calculations for the standard t-test would result in a t value of $4 \cdot 53$ with 50 degrees of freedom. Both of these values would be incorrect, although, for this example, the same conclusions would be drawn.

4.3.3 Nonparametric alternative to the t-test

In cases where the distribution of the samples is unknown or the data cannot be transformed to approximate the normal distribution, a nonparametric alternative is recommended. Nonparametric tests make fewer assumptions than standard tests; for example, there are no assumptions about the distribution of the data nor of variance homogeneity. However, these tests tend to be less powerful than their parametric alternatives, especially when the sample size is small.

The Mann–Whitney or Wilcoxon rank sum test is a nonparametric alternative to the standard t-test. As in many nonparametric tests, the first step is to rank the data. The ranks are then summed for each sample and the results compared with specially prepared tables. Additional calculations are required when the sample sizes are not equal and when the sample size is outside the limits of the table (e.g., Conover 1980; Snedecor & Cochran 1980; Sokal & Rohlf 1981). This test is illustrated with data from Grant & Bayly (1981) which are reproduced in Table 8.16. They investigated the effect of crest development in cladocerans on their vulnerability to predation. These data are expressed as percentages and, as a result, may not be normally distributed. Thus, it is appropriate to use a nonparametric test to determine whether there are differences between the vulnerability of the two prey types. The first step is to

Table 8.16 Vulnerability of crested and uncrested *Daphnia cephalata* to predation by *Anisops*. The values in brackets are ranks. Data are from Grant & Bayly (1981).

Trial number	% *Daphnia* killed Crested	% *Daphnia* killed Uncrested
1	28 (3)	50 (6)
2	25 (1)	64 (8)
3	31 (4·5)	75 (10)
4	26 (2)	66 (9)
5	31 (4·5)	59 (7)
Total	(15·0)	(40·0)

rank the data from smallest to largest, with the smallest value being given a rank of 1, as illustrated in Table 8.16. Average values are used when ties occur. The ranks are totalled for each sample and the smaller of the two totals, $T = 15$, is compared to a table for the Wilcoxon two-sample rank test (e.g., Table A10 Snedecor & Cochran (1980); Table 29 Rohlf & Sokal (1981)). The critical values for two samples with five observations each are 17 and 15 for $P = 0.05$ and $P = 0.01$, respectively. Thus the differences are highly significant ($P = 0.01$) and the hypothesis that crest development does not influence prey vulnerability is rejected.

4.3.4 One-way analysis of variance

When there are more than two means, an analysis of variance (ANOVA) is used to compare the means. In this analysis an *F*-test is used to determine whether there are significant differences among treatments. The steps involved in the analysis of variance are too extensive to be detailed here; they are, however, given in most standard statistical textbooks and are covered in detail in books such as Scheffé (1959). Nonparametric alternatives to the analysis of variance are outlined in texts such as Siegel (1956) and Conover (1980).

The model comparable to the standard *t*-test is a one-way analysis of variance. The assumptions of this test are similar to those for a standard *t*-test:

(1) The observations should be independent.
(2) The errors should be normally distributed.
(3) The error variances should be constant among groups.

When planning an experiment to be analyzed by analysis of variance, remember that the test is more robust when treatments are based on equal sample sizes.

When only two treatments are compared, the standard t-test (Section 4.3.1) and the one-way analysis of variance give identical statistical results. However, the t-test requires the calculation of a sample variance for each treatment, thus facilitating comparison of variances and making it the preferred method when comparing only two treatment means.

4.4 Paired comparisons

When there is a deliberate or natural pairing of subjects for treatments then a paired t-test is the appropriate test for the comparison of two means. In this test the differences between pairs D_i are analyzed rather than individual observations X_i. These differences are assumed to be normally and independently distributed. The paired design makes the comparison of paired samples more accurate since all differences between samples except for the treatment differences are removed.

The first step in this test is to calculate a standard deviation of the differences:

$$s_D = \sqrt{\frac{\sum\limits_{i=1}^{n} D_i^2 - \dfrac{\left(\sum\limits_{i=1}^{n} D_i\right)^2}{n}}{n-1}} \tag{8.32}$$

where D_i is the difference between the ith pair and n is the number of pairs. A standard error of the differences $s_{\bar{D}}$ is then calculated:

$$s_{\bar{D}} = \frac{s_D}{\sqrt{n}} \tag{8.33}$$

This statistic, along with the mean difference $\bar{D}$, is used to calculate the t value:

$$t = \frac{\bar{D}}{s_{\bar{D}}} \tag{8.34}$$

The result is compared with the Student's t-table with $(n-1)$ degrees of freedom.

A paired t-test was used to determine whether two solvents extracted similar amounts of chlorophyll a from phytoplankton. Twenty-nine duplicate sets of lake water samples were analyzed by both methods. The data are presented in Table 8.17, along with the differences between each pair (Prepas & Trew 1983, unpublished). To test the null hypothesis that there is no difference between the efficiencies of the two methods, a t value is computed:

$$t = \frac{0 \cdot 25}{0 \cdot 37} = 0 \cdot 68$$

Table 8.17 Concentration of chlorophyll a ($mg\,m^{-3}$) in replicate samples of lakewater analyzed by two separate methods. Data are from Prepas & Trew (1983, unpublished).

Sample number	Solvent		$D = X_1 - X_2$
	acetone X_1	ethanol X_2	
1	66·2	68·4	−2·2
2	60·2	67·0	−6·8
3	20·5	21·1	−0·6
4	3·3	4·9	−1·6
5	4·9	6·6	−1·7
6	7·6	5·8	1·8
7	5·2	4·5	0·7
8	4·8	3·5	1·3
9	13·4	10·2	3·2
10	4·3	4·0	0·3
11	6·3	6·4	−0·1
12	63·2	61·8	1·4
13	5·5	4·5	1·0
14	8·4	9·1	−0·7
15	4·2	3·3	0·9
16	5·1	4·7	0·4
17	7·4	8·8	−1·4
18	27·2	29·4	−2·2
19	6·4	4·5	1·9
20	13·6	14·4	−0·8
21	3·7	2·9	0·8
22	6·2	6·5	−0·3
23	12·0	11·9	0·1
24	14·7	13·2	1·5
25	12·8	9·9	2·9
26	20·6	19·6	1·0
27	9·0	7·6	1·4
28	19·0	16·2	2·8
29	17·3	15·0	2·3
Total	453·0	445·7	7·3
mean	15·62	15·36	0·25
variance	308·28	342·00	4·06

$$\sum_{i=1}^{n} D_i^2 = 115·61$$

$$s_D^2 = \frac{115·61 - \dfrac{(7·3)^2}{29}}{28} = 4·06$$

$$s_{\bar{D}} = \sqrt{\frac{4·06}{29}} = 0·37 \, mg\,m^{-3} \text{ chlorophyll } a$$

When this value is compared with a Student's t-table, the probability is >0.5. Thus the null hypothesis that the two solvents extract similar amounts of chlorophyll is not rejected.

The advantage of the paired t-test, as opposed to an unpaired or standard t-test, is that the standard error reflects only the differences within pairs and not between pairs. This usually results in a smaller standard error, as illustrated with the chlorophyll example where the differences between pairs are far greater than within pairs. In this example, the standard error of the difference between the means $s_{\bar{X}_1 - \bar{X}_2}$ is $4.74 \, \text{mg m}^{-3}$ chlorophyll a, which is much higher than the standard error of the differences $s_{\bar{D}} = 0.37 \, \text{mg m}^{-3}$ chlorophyll a. The smaller error term in the paired design provides a better opportunity to detect real differences.

If there is doubt over whether the distribution of the differences is normal then the data can be transformed prior to the application of the paired t-test. Alternatively, a nonparametric test such as the Wilcoxon signed-rank test can be performed. When there are more than two treatments, the randomized block analysis of variance is the appropriate statistical design.

4.5 Multiple comparisons among a set of means

When there are more than two means involved in an experiment the investigator may wish to make specific comparisons. A standard t-test is used to make these comparisons when they are planned or *a priori*. However more conservative tests are required when unplanned or *a posteriori* comparisons are made, since if standard tests are used in these circumstances, i.e., on hypotheses generated after viewing the data, the probability of erroneously rejecting the null hypothesis at a significance level of 0.05 is greater than 5%. Three tests have been developed for unplanned comparisons.

(1) Dunnett's which is used for comparisons of a control with all treatment means.
(2) Newman–Keul's for the comparison of all treatment means.
(3) Scheffé's for specific comparisons decided on after the data are collected.

Dunnett's is the least conservative of these tests and Scheffé's is the most conservative. These three tests along with the standard t-test will be considered in this section.

4.5.1 Standard t-test

This is an appropriate test for planned comparisons. In this case the numerator L is some linear combination of the k means $\bar{X}_k$:

$$L = \lambda_1 \bar{X}_1 + \lambda_2 \bar{X}_2 + \cdots + \lambda_k \bar{X}_k \qquad (8.35)$$

where the λ_i's are fixed numbers and :

$$\sum_{i=1}^{k} \lambda_i = 0$$

The denominator is the standard error of L:

$$s_L = \sqrt{\bar{s}^2 \sum_{i=1}^{k} \frac{\lambda_i^2}{n_i}} \tag{8.35i}$$

where $\bar{s}^2$ is the average variance (or MS(error) in analysis of variance) of all k treatments and n_i is the number of observations in the ith treatment. The test is then:

$$t = \frac{L}{s_L} \tag{8.35ii}$$

with the same degrees of freedom as for the average variance with $\bar{s}^2$. The same comparison can be done in an analysis of variance, with the aid of orthogonal coefficients [explained on p. 226 in Snedecor & Cochran (1980), and p. 232 in Sokal & Rohlf (1981)].

Table 8.18 Mean density (per litre) of the copepod *Epischura nevadensis* collected in replicate samples from an offshore station and two inshore stations in a large lake.

	Area		
	Offshore	Inshore 1	2
Mean $\bar{X}_i$	0·25	0·68	0·83
Sample size n_i	20	15	18
Mean variance $\bar{s}^2 = 0·72$			

This method will be illustrated with the artificial example given in Table 8.18 where the mean density of a copepod species collected at an offshore station $\bar{X}_1$ is compared with the mean densities collected at two inshore stations, $\bar{X}_2$ and $\bar{X}_3$. Since we are comparing $\bar{X}_1$ with the average of $\bar{X}_2$ and $\bar{X}_3$, $\lambda_1 = 1$, $\lambda_2 = -\frac{1}{2}$ and $\lambda_3 = -\frac{1}{2}$. The numerator L is then:

$$L = 1(0·25) - \tfrac{1}{2}(0·68 + 0·83) = 0·505$$

the denominator s_L is:

$$s_L = \sqrt{0·72\left(\frac{1}{20} + \frac{0·25}{15} + \frac{0·25}{18}\right)} = 0·240\,84$$

and the resulting t value is:

$$t = \frac{0.505}{0.240\,84} = 2.10$$

When this t value with 50 degrees of freedom is compared with the Student's t-table the significance probability is <0.05, and the null hypothesis is rejected. We conclude that there is a lower density of the copepod species offshore than onshore.

4.5.2 Dunnett's test

Where one of the means is a control and the others are treatment means, Dunnett's test (Dunnett 1955) is used to compare each treatment mean $\bar{X}_i$ (where i goes from 2 to k and k is the total number of treatments) with the control mean $\bar{X}_c$. In this test, the t-ratios are:

$$t = \frac{\bar{X}_c - \bar{X}_i}{\sqrt{\bar{s}^2 \left(\dfrac{1}{n_c} + \dfrac{1}{n_i}\right)}} \qquad (i = 2, k) \qquad (8.36)$$

where $\bar{s}^2$ is the overall average variance [or MS(error)] and n_c and n_i are the number of observations in the control and treatment groups, respectively. These t values are compared to a suitably modified t-table (Table A9 Steel & Torrie 1960; Dunnett 1964) with two values; the degrees of freedom for the average variance:

$$\sum_{i=1}^{k} n_i - k$$

(where n_i is the number of observations in the ith treatment) and the total number of treatments including the control, k.

4.5.3 Newman–Keuls method

Where it seems reasonable to compare all pairs of means, the Newman–Keuls (or Studentized Newman–Keuls) method (Newman 1939; Keuls 1952) is the appropriate test. The calculations for this test will be illustrated in five steps with the data from Table 8.12. The question is whether there is a statistical difference in adult *Daphnia* reproductive rates among any of the three food concentrations.

(1) The means are arranged from smallest to largest, as in Table 8.12.
(2) A error term $s_{\bar{X}}$ is calculated:

$$s_{\bar{X}} = \sqrt{\frac{\bar{s}^2}{2}\left(\frac{1}{n_a} + \frac{1}{n_b}\right)} \qquad (8.37)$$

where $\bar{s}^2$ [or MS(error)] is the overall average variance and n_a and n_b are the number of observations used to compute the two means being compared. In our example, the first comparison is between the smallest mean, $\bar{X}_1 = 0.64$, and the largest mean, $\bar{X}_3 = 1.89$. In this case:

$$s_{\bar{x}} = \sqrt{\frac{0.203\,25}{2}\left(\frac{1}{5} + \frac{1}{10}\right)} = 0.174\,61$$

(3)   A Q value ($P = 0.05$) for the total number of treatments and degrees of freedom associated with the overall average variance $\bar{s}^2$ is taken from a table of the studentized range (e.g., May 1952; Table A15 in Snedecor & Cochran 1980; and Table 18 in Rohlf & Sokal 1981). The Q value for $P = 0.05$, 3 treatments, and 18 degrees of freedom is 3.61.

(4)   The product of $s_{\bar{x}}$ (equation 8.37) and the Q value

$$D = (s_{\bar{x}})\,(Q\text{ value}) \tag{8.38}$$

is calculated. In the example:

$$D = 0.174\,61(3.61) = 0.630\,33$$

If the difference between the smallest and largest mean is greater than D, then this difference is significant, and the other differences can then be tested. If not, there are no significant differences at the 5% level. In our example:

$$\bar{X}_3 - \bar{X}_1 = (1.89 - 0.64) = 1.25$$

there is, therefore, a significant difference between the largest and smallest reproductive rates.

(5)   Values for $s_{\bar{x}}$, Q, and D are calculated for the second largest difference. A new Q and $s_{\bar{x}}$ value may be required for each comparison. The Q value is looked up with the same degrees of freedom as for the first comparison but with one less treatment, since the means being compared are the smallest and largest from a group with one less treatment than in the first case. The value $s_{\bar{x}}$ must be recalculated for each comparison if the means are not based on equal sample sizes. The second largest difference:

$$\bar{X}_2 - \bar{X}_1 = 1.10$$

is compared to D where the Q value ($P = 0.05$) with two treatments and 18 degrees of freedom is 2.97 and $s_{\bar{x}}$ is 0.193 03. In this second comparison:

$$D = 0.193\,03(2.97) = 0.573\,30$$

is smaller than the observed difference and thus significant at the 95% confidence level.

This process is continued until D is greater than the largest difference remaining in the set of means. In this example, one difference remains:

$$\bar{X}_3 - \bar{X}_2 = 0.015$$

For this third comparison the Q value remains the same as in the previous comparison, 2·97, $s_{\bar{X}}$ is 0·164 62, and the minimum difference:

$$D = 0.164\,62(2.97) = 0.488\,92$$

In this last case the difference between the means is not significant.

The results of this test can be presented neatly in a $k \times k$ table, where k is the number of treatments, as illustrated in Table 8.19. In the example taken

Table 8.19 Newman–Keuls Method for comparisons among all means for the data on *Daphnia* reproductive rates at three food levels (from Table 8.12). The calculation of D is explained in the text. Differences between means are indicated as either significant (*) or not significant (ns). Data are from Peters & Rigler (1973).

	Food concentration		
	0.125×10^5	0.5×10^5	1×10^5
0.125×10^5		$D = 0.57$ $\bar{X}_2 - \bar{X}_1 = 1.10*$	$D = 0.63$ $\bar{X}_3 - \bar{X}_1 = 1.25*$
0.5×10^5			$D = 0.49$ $\bar{X}_3 - \bar{X}_2 = 1.15^{ns}$
1×10^5			

from Table 8.12, the hypothesis that there is no difference between reproductive rate and food level is rejected for comparisons between the lowest food concentration and the two higher levels and is not rejected for comparisons at the two highest concentrations.

4.5.4 Scheffé's test

Scheffé's test (Scheffé 1959) is used for specific comparisons which are suggested by the data. This test is suitable wherever L (equation 8.35) and s_L (equation 8.35) can be formed. The resulting t-value:

$$t = \frac{L}{s_L}$$

is significant only if it exceeds $\sqrt{(k-1)F_{0.05}}$ where k is the total number of treatments and $F_{0.05}$ is the 95% confidence level for the F value from a standard table with degrees of freedom $(k-1)$ and degrees of freedom of the average variance $\bar{s}^2$ [or MS(error)].

By looking at the data in Table 8.12 it might be suspected that the mean reproductive rate for *Daphnia* at the two higher food levels is different from the reproductive rate at the lower food concentration. In this case, $\lambda_1 = 1$ and $\lambda_2 = \lambda_3 = -0.5$.

$$L = 0.64 - 0.5(1.74 + 1.89) = 1.175$$

$$s_L = \sqrt{0.203\,25\left(\frac{1}{5} + \frac{0.25}{6} + \frac{0.25}{10}\right)} = 0.232\,81$$

and:

$$t = \frac{1.175}{0.232\,81} = 5.05$$

The corresponding F value ($P = 0.05$) with 2 and 18 degrees of freedom is 3.55, and:

$$\sqrt{(k-1)F_{0.05}} = \sqrt{2(3.55)} = 2.66$$

which is smaller than the calculated t value. Thus, the null hypothesis that there is no difference in *Daphnia* reproductive rates at the lowest food level as compared with the two higher concentrations is rejected.

4.6 Notes of analysis of variance

Analysis of variance is used to determine the significance of the differences between means. An F-test is used to compare a treatment variance with an error term. The analysis of variance is a very powerful technique for statistical analysis; like all techniques, however, it can give misleading results when incorrectly applied. In the more complex designs such as two-way (two factor), factorial (three or more factor), and nested, the choice of the correct model for the analysis is crucial. The appropriate model is determined by the experimental design and the type of variables used. Choice of appropriate design is a topic too extensive to be discussed here (see Scheffé 1959; Sokal & Rohlf 1981); however, the designation of variable or treatment type is generally overlooked in the aquatic literature and will be discussed.

4.6.1 Choice of variable type: Illustrated with a factorial experiment

Variables are classified into two categories for analysis of variance, fixed and random. In a fixed treatment, the different levels of specific interest are under the control of the investigator, e.g., variations of food concentrations in the laboratory to determine how these specific levels effect growth rates; or two locations on a stream, one near an industrial effluent and the other away from the effluent, used to test whether the effluent effects benthic biomass at these specific locations. In a random treatment the different levels are not completely under the control of the experimenter and are considered to be representative of other possible levels, e.g., the food concentration found in lakes used to determine if food concentration effects growth rate, or locations on a lake chosen to see if there is spatial heterogeneity in biomass. In most analyses of variance, the variable type is important in determining the appropriate error term used to test each component. In this section an experiment (Fleminger & Clutter 1965) analyzed with a factorial design will be used to illustrate how inappropriate conclusions can be drawn from incorrectly applying statistical tests.

The study was of the effect of three factors, light intensity, net size, and zooplankton population density, on the number of mysids collected by plankton nets and it involved towing nets over a fixed distance in an enclosed sea water pond. The experiment was repeated a total of 108 times under three light levels, full, reduced, and dark (550, 22, and 0 lux at the water surface, respectively), with three sizes of plankton net, large, medium, and small (1600, 800, and 400 cm² openings, respectively) and with two zooplankton densities, low and high. There were thus $(3 \times 3 \times 2) = 18$ treatments each replicated six times. The mean numbers of mysids collected under this experimental design are shown in Table 8.20.

The investigators performed a three-way analysis of variance on the mysid data to determine whether there was a significant difference between the various treatments as illustrated in Table 8.21. A three-factor experiment has three main effects (i.e., population size, net size, and light level), three first order interactions (population size × net size, net size × light level, and

Table 8.20 Mean number of mysids collected for three light conditions, three net sizes and two population densities. Each mean is based on six replicates. Data are from Fleminger & Clutter (1965).

Light condition	Zooplankton population density					
	Small			Large		
	Net size			Net size		
	Large	Medium	Small	Large	Medium	Small
Full	12·8	6·3	2·0	17·5	15·7	16·0
Reduced	7·8	6·7	2·0	30·3	19·3	28·0
Dark	13·3	10·0	4·7	154·8	123·7	71·3

Table 8.21 Three-way factorial analysis of variance for mysid data based on a fixed-effects model (Column 5) and a mixed-model (columns 6 and 7). F values are indicated as nonsignificant (ns) or significant $P < 0.01$ (**), $P < 0.001$ (***). Data are from Fleminger & Clutter (1965).

Source of variation		Degrees of freedom	Sum of squares	Mean squares	F value assuming fixed effects	Ratio for a mixed-model	F value for a mixed-model
Population size (P)		1	76·03	76·03	148 ***	P/Error	as before
Net size (N)		2	12·11	6·05	11·8***	$N/(P \times N)$	1·76^{ns}
Light level (L)		2	31·60	15·80	30·8***	$L/(P \times L)$	2·86^{ns}
Replicates		5	3·334	0·669	1·3^{ns}		
Population × net ($P \times N$)		2	6·874	3·437	6·7**	$(P \times N)/\text{Error}$	
Population × light ($P \times L$)		2	11·80	5·900	11·5***	$(P \times L)/\text{Error}$	
Net × light ($N \times L$)		4	0·821	0·2052	0·4^{ns}	$(N \times L)/(P \times N \times L)$	
Population × net × light ($P \times N \times L$)	Residual						
Error		89	45·66	0·513			

population size × light level), a second order interaction (population size × net size × light level), an error term, and, in this case, a replicate term. In their analysis the error and second order interaction terms were combined and used to test all the main effects and first order interactions (see Table 8.21). The authors gave the following summary of their study:

> 'statistical treatment of the results showed that smaller nets were more efficiently avoided [than larger nets and] more mysids . . . were caught in the darkness than in light.'

However, a re-analysis of their data suggests that these conclusions were not justified.

They treated their data as being suitable for a fixed-effects model, since the residual was used to test all of the interactions and main effects. If this was a fixed-effects model, then the statistical results were not interpreted correctly since two of the three first order interaction terms were significant (Table 8.21). For a fixed-effects model, the presence of significant interaction terms implies that there is no consistent pattern in the corresponding main effects. As a result, statistical tests of the corresponding main effects are not meaningful. In this example, the number of mysids caught decreases seven-fold as light levels increase at the higher zooplankton density, whereas at the lower density there is essentially no change in numbers caught with changing light levels (Fig. 8.4). The correct inference, therefore, is that light intensity affects numbers of mysids collected at the higher but not the lower density.

However, these data are not suitable for a fixed-effects model. Light level and net size are fixed treatments since the investigators were interested in the specific light levels and net sizes used. However, population size is a random effect, since the investigators wished to know the effect of density but the specific densities were not of interest. A mixed-model design is suitable for these data, as illustrated in Sokal & Rohlf (1981, Box 12.1). In mixed models, some of the main effects and first order effects contain additional error components and thus the appropriate choice of the error terms is crucial for a meaningful analysis. The appropriate error terms needed to calculate the F values in the mysid example are illustrated in column 6, Table 8.21. The error terms for two of the main effects, net size and light level have changed. When the new F values are calculated, net size and light level change from being highly significant to nonsignificant treatments ($P > 0.25$ for both cases). Thus, the null hypothesis that there is no effect of light level or net size on number of mysids collected cannot be rejected and the major conclusions of the original authors are not supported.

4.6.2 *Nested analysis of variance*

This design, where the main treatments are subdivided into randomly chosen

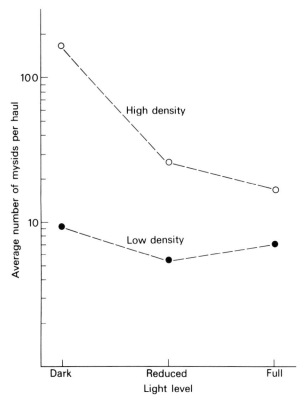

Fig. 8.4 An illustration of an interaction effect with the mysid data. The change in mysid numbers collected under three light levels at two zooplankton densities. Data are from Fleminger & Clutter (1965).

subgroups, can be very useful for sampling aquatic invertebrates, although it is seldom used. If, for example, duplicate zooplankton samples are collected at each of two separate stations and duplicate subsamples are taken from each sample for zooplankton enumeration, the design is nested. An example of the nested design applied to the collection and enumeration of aquatic invertebrates is given in Kutkuhn (1958).

4.7 *Combining probabilities from independent tests of significance*

When there are a number of experiments testing the same scientific hypothesis and these experiments are based on small sample sizes, the results are often suggestive but not conclusive. Fisher (1954) (also in Sokal & Rohlf (1981) Box 18.1) developed a test which allows the combination of probabilities P_i from independent tests to determine whether a statistically significant trend exists.

The natural logarithm ($\log_e = \ln$) is determined for each probability value P_i and the statistic:

$$-2 \sum_{i=1}^{k} \ln P_i \tag{8.39}$$

is calculated where k is the number of independent tests and is distributed as a χ^2 with $2k$ degrees of freedom.

This test is illustrated with results from four independent feeding trials where the predator *Neomysis* was offered a choice between two groups of prey, *Daphnia* sp. and *Diaptomus ashlandi* (from Murtaugh 1981). For each experiment the clearance rates (liters per predator per day) were compared with a nonparametric equivalent to the *t*-test, the Wilcoxon rank sum test. The

Table 8.22 Results of feeding experiments where *Neomysis* were offered a choice between *Daphnia* and *Diaptomus*. Probability values, P_i, are from a one-tailed Wilcoxon rank sum test. Data are from Murtaugh (1981).

Experiment (no. mysids)	Prey	Median clearance rate (L mysid^{-1} day^{-1})	P_i	$\ln P_i$
1 ($n_1 = 6$)	*Daphnia*	2·31	0·021	−3·863 23
	Diaptomus	0·62		
2 ($n_2 = 4$)	*Daphnia*	1·22	0·243	−1·414 69
	Diaptomus	0·64		
3 ($n_3 = 7$)	*Daphnia*	0·93	0·180	−1·714 80
	Diaptomus	0·53		
4 ($n_4 = 9$)	*Daphnia*	0·87	0·081	−2·513 31
	Diaptomus	0·35		
Total				−9·506 03

$$-2 \sum_{i=1}^{4} \ln P_i = -2(-9 \cdot 506\,03) = 19 \cdot 01$$

significance probability levels for each experiment are given in Table 8.22. Only one of the four tests was significant at the 95 % confidence level. However, when the probabilities are combined as illustrated in Table 8.22, the resulting value is 19·01 and is compared with a χ^2-distribution with 8 degrees of freedom. This result has a significance probability level between 0·025 and 0·01. Therefore, the null hypothesis that *Neomysis* has no food preference when offered a choice of *Daphnia* and *Diaptomus ashlandi* is rejected.

5 Regression and Correlation

The analyses that have been considered so far involve single measurements on each subject. However, the investigator is often interested in the dependence of one variable on a second variable. This functional relationship is called regression. Regression has many uses in biology, e.g., to describe the relationship between water temperature and growth rate of an invertebrate. The constants estimated in linear regression can be tested to determine whether they are statistically different from zero or from any other number chosen *a priori*. These constants can also be compared with those derived from other populations. Finally, the linear regression model can be used for prediction of one variable from another variable. If there is more than one independent factor acting on the independent variable, a multiple regression may be suitable.

The correlation coefficient is another measure of the relationship between two variables. In correlation analysis there is no implied causal relationship of one variable on the other, rather the interest is in the closeness of the relationship. The correlation coefficient can be tested for significance, and, if the sample size is sufficiently large, it can be used to describe the fraction of the variability which can be explained by regression. However, correlation is more limited than regression analysis because it cannot be used for making predictions.

In this section the standard linear regression model is introduced and compared with alternative models, the correlation coefficient is illustrated, and more complex regression techniques are dealt with very briefly. The reader is encouraged to consult textbooks which specialize in regression analysis (e.g., Snedecor & Cochran 1980; Draper & Smith 1966) for a more extensive account of these techniques.

5.1 Standard linear regression

This is a parametric technique often referred to as Model I regression (Sokal & Rohlf 1981). The estimation procedure used in standard linear regression is that of least squares, and minimizes the squared deviations between each pair of observed and predicted points. The linear model for a sample is:

$$Y = a + bX \qquad (8.40)$$

where X and Y are the independent and dependent variables, respectively, and a and b are the regression coefficients.

To develop a regression model, the independent and dependent variables are defined. The independent variables should be under the control of the investigator and be measured with relatively little error, whereas the dependent variable varies freely. The independent variable should, ideally, be evenly spaced throughout its range. Notions of cause and effect are implicit in the choice of the variables.

In laboratory situations, the independent variable can be controlled but this is often difficult or impossible in field situations. There are alternative regression models which do not make assumptions about investigator control of the independent variable. These approaches, referred to as Model II regressions, are however, generally less powerful and the mathematics on which they are based are poorly understood relative to the standard model. Two of these alternative regression methods are discussed in a subsequent section.

In standard linear regression, three assumptions are made about the relationship between Y and X.

(1) If several Ys are chosen randomly for each X, these Ys are normally distributed.
(2) The population of Ys chosen for each X has a mean (μ_Y):

$$\mu_Y = \alpha + \beta X \qquad (8.40i)$$

where α and β are constants, i.e., μ_Y for different values of X lie on a straight line.
(3) The variances about the mean μ_Y are assumed to be homogeneous, i.e., the scatter around a mean regression line is similar over the entire range of X.

In many cases, these assumptions cannot be tested and are assumed. However, abnormal heterogeneity in the variances can be detected by graphical means. This technique will be illustrated in the next section.

5.1.1 Preparation of data for analysis

Graphical techniques are useful for determining whether data are suitable for linear regression. The independent variable is always placed on the horizontal axis of a two-dimensional graph and the dependent variable on the vertical axis. This technique is illustrated in Figs. 8.5 and 8.6 with data from McCauley & Kalff (1981) (raw data supplied by E. McCauley) on the phytoplankton-zooplankton relationship measured on individual dates in 13 lakes (Fig. 8.5a) and the average values for 17 lakes (Fig. 8.6a). The phytoplankton-zooplankton relationship appears to be linear in both cases; however, neither set of raw data is suitable for standard linear regression analysis. In Fig. 8.5a the variance increases as the phytoplankton biomass increases, and in both Figs. 8.5a & 8.6a the independent variables are not evenly spaced; in Fig. 8.6a there is one extreme outlier and in Fig. 8.5a the data become progressively thinner as the phytoplankton biomass increases.

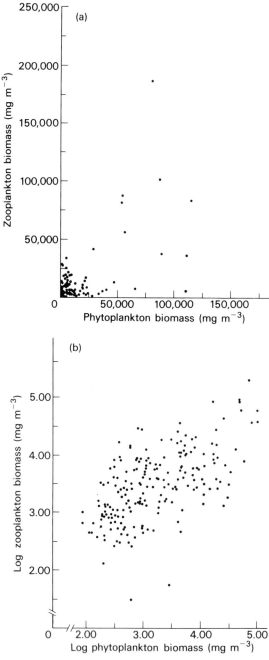

Fig. 8.5 Plots of zooplankton biomass against phytoplankton biomass based on (a) indvidual observations from 13 lakes and (b) $\log_{10}$ individual observations from 13 lakes. Data are from McCauley & Kalff (1981; E.McCauley, personal communication).

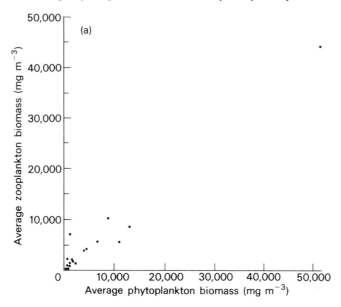

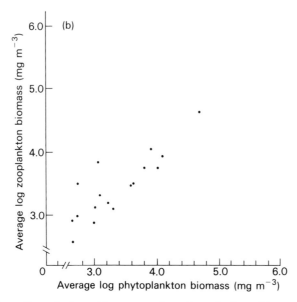

Fig. 8.6 Plots of zooplankton biomass against phytoplankton biomass based on (a) average observations from 17 lakes and (b) $\log_{10}$ average observations from 17 lakes. Data are from McCauley & Kalff (1981; E.McCauley, personal communication).

Both sets of data are, however, suitable for linear regression after a logarithmic transformation has been applied (Figs. 8.5b and 8.6b). This transformation reduces the variation around the relationship in Fig. 8.5a and decreases the spread between the higher values in both Figs. 8.5a and 8.6a.

5.1.2 The calculations

The calculations for regression are tedious and, except for the simplest cases, are better done by a programmable calculator, a computer program or computer packages such as BMDP, SAS, or SPSS (e.g. Dixon 1975; Helwig & Council 1979). Prior to using a package program to analyze new data the package should be tested with a data set where the answers are known. The results of this test run are used to interpret the program output and its precision. Regression statistics are imprecise when the calculations are done with a small number of decimal places—this is often a problem with small, poorly documented packages. It is recommended that package programs that are well maintained and documented, such as those listed above, be used whenever possible.

The calculation for standard linear regression are illustrated with the average phytoplankton-zooplankton data reproduced in Table 8.23. To construct a least squares linear regression line, six parameters are required, mean $X(\bar{X})$, mean $Y(\bar{Y})$, the number of pairs of points n, the sum of squares of X and Y. and the cross products of X and Y, where X and Y are the independent and dependent variables, respectively. The last three parameters will be labelled $[x^2]$, $[y^2]$, and $[xy]$, respectively, and they are calculated as follows:

$$[x^2] = \sum_{i=1}^{n} X_i^2 - \frac{\left(\sum_{i=1}^{n} X_i\right)^2}{n} \tag{8.41}$$

$$[y^2] = \sum_{i=1}^{n} Y_i^2 - \frac{\left(\sum_{i=1}^{n} Y_i\right)^2}{n} \tag{8.42}$$

and

$$[xy] = \sum_{i=1}^{n} X_i Y_i - \frac{\sum_{i=1}^{n} X_i \sum_{i=1}^{n} Y_i}{n} \tag{8.43}$$

The equation used to calculate the slope of the regression is:

$$b = \frac{[xy]}{[x^2]} \tag{8.44}$$

By definition, the regression line always goes through the point $(\bar{X}, \bar{Y})$. These

Table 8.23 Average phytoplankton and zooplankton biomass $(mg\,m^{-3})$ expressed as $\log_{10}$ for 17 lakes. Data are from McCauley & Kalff (1981; E.McCauley, pers. comm.).

| | Measured | | Predicted | | |
	phytoplankton biomass X_i	zooplankton biomass Y_i	zooplankton biomass $\hat{Y}_i$	residual $(\hat{Y}_i - \hat{Y}_i)$	residual^2 $(Y_i - \hat{Y}_i)^2$
	2·631	2·912	2·893	0·018 63	0·000 35
	2·651	2·575	2·907	−0·332 5	0·110 56
	2·708	2·997	2·949	0·047 84	0·002 29
	2·756	3·489	2·984	0·504 7	0·254 72
	3·000	2·871	3·161	−0·290 4	0·084 33
	3·017	3·131	3·174	−0·043 04	0·001 85
	3.086	3·833	3·224	0·609 3	0·371 25
	3·125	3·310	3·252	0·058 31	0·003 40
	3·234	3·187	3·331	−0·144 6	0·020 91
	3·322	3·103	3·395	−0·292 7	0·085 67
	3·612	3·469	3·606	−0·137 6	0·018 93
	3·643	3·504	3·629	−0·124 6	0·015 53
	3·825	3·745	3·761	−0·016 43	0·000 27
	3·950	4·004	3·852	0·151 6	0·022 98
	·4·037	3·743	3·915	−0·172 2	0·029 65
	4·122	3·929	3·977	−0·048 56	0·002 36
	4·715	4·620	4·408	0·212 2	0·045 03
Total	57·436	58·421		0	1·070 08
mean	3·378 56	3·436 55			
standard deviation					
s	0·601 94	0·508 25			

values are substituted into the regression equation (equation 8.40) along with the value calculated for b to obtain the intercept:

$$a = \bar{Y} - b\bar{X} \qquad (8.45)$$

The variance about a regression line, called the residual variation, σ_{yx}^2, is estimated from the sum of squared deviations of each observed value Y_i from the corresponding predicted value $\hat{Y}_i = a + bX_i$, divided by the degrees of freedom for the regression line:

$$s_{y\cdot x}^2 = \frac{\left(\sum_{i=1}^{n} Y_i - \hat{Y}_i\right)^2}{n-2} \qquad (8.46)$$

The degrees of freedom associated with a regression line is equal to the number of pairs of points n, minus one degree of freedom for each coefficient which is estimated. In the linear regression equation (equation 8.40), a and b are required and there are, therefore, $(n-2)$ degrees of freedom. To calculate the deviation between observed and predicted values is tedious and hence the equation:

$$s_{y \cdot x}^2 = \frac{[y^2] - b[xy]}{n-2}$$ (8.46i)

is used to calculate the residual variance.

In the biomass example (Table 8.23), $\bar{X} = 3 \cdot 378\,56$, $\bar{Y} = 3 \cdot 436\,55$, $n = 17$, $[x^2] = 5 \cdot 797\,31$, $[y^2] = 4 \cdot 133\,09$ and $[xy] = 4 \cdot 213\,89$ so that:

$$b = \frac{4 \cdot 213\,89}{5 \cdot 797\,31} = 0 \cdot 726\,87$$

and:

$$a = 3 \cdot 436\,55 - 0 \cdot 726\,87(3 \cdot 378\,56) - 0 \cdot 980\,76$$

The linear relationship between average phytoplankton and zooplankton biomass is thus:

$\log_{10}$ zooplankton biomass =
$0 \cdot 980\,76 + 0 \cdot 726\,87 \log_{10}$ phytoplankton biomass   (8.47)

and this is illustrated in Fig. 8.7. The estimated residual variation $s_{y \cdot x}^2$ for this regression line is calculated from equation 8.46 and the data in Table 8.23:

$$s_{y \cdot x}^2 = \frac{1 \cdot 070\,08}{15} = 0 \cdot 071\,34$$

Remember that regression is only valid if: (1) the independent variables X_i are independent of one another, (2) there are no outliers in the data set used, and (3) the variance about the regression line is relatively constant throughout the range of X.

5.1.3 Testing the significance of regression coefficients

A t-test is used to determine if a linear relationship is significant, i.e., to test whether the slope b is different from zero. A standard error of the slope s_b is calculated from the equation:

$$s_b = \sqrt{\frac{s_{y \cdot x}^2}{[x^2]}}$$ (8.48)

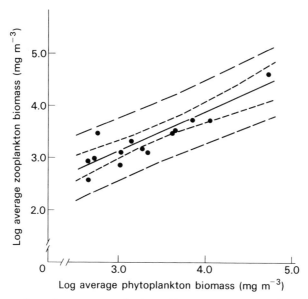

Fig. 8.7 Regression of average zooplankton biomass on average phytoplankton biomass. The narrower set of confidence bands is for the predicted value of the mean μ_Y at point X and the wider set is for the predicted value of Y for a new member of the population. Data are from McCauley & Kalff (1981; E.McCauley, personal communication).

where $s^2_{y \cdot x}$ is the residual variation and $[x^2]$ the sum of squares of X. The ratio:

$$t = \frac{b - 0}{s_b} \qquad (8.48\mathrm{i})$$

is compared with a Student's t-distribution with $(n - 2)$ degrees of freedom. In the biomass example:

$$s_b = \sqrt{\frac{0 \cdot 071\,34}{5 \cdot 797\,31}} = 0 \cdot 110\,93$$

and:

$$t = \frac{0 \cdot 726\,87}{0 \cdot 110\,93} = 6 \cdot 55$$

This t value is compared with a Student's t-distribution with 15 degrees of freedom. Since the significance probability is $< 0 \cdot 0001$, the null hypothesis that the slope of the regression line is not different from zero is rejected.

Confidence intervals for the slope are calculated from the relationship:

$$b \pm s_b t \qquad (8.48\mathrm{ii})$$

where s_b is the standard error of the slope, and t is the value in the Student's t table for the desired significance level, with $(n - 2)$ degrees of freedom. The value in the Student's t table for $P = 0.05$ and 15 degress of freedom is 2.131. The 95% confidence interval for the slope $b = 0.727$ is:

$$0.727 \pm (0.1109)(2.131) = 0.963 \text{ to } 0.491$$

This confidence interval is relatively large, plus or minus almost a third of the slope.

The investigators (McCauley & Kalff 1981) were interested in whether the zooplankton biomass increases more slowly than the phytoplankton biomass as overall lake productivity increases. This can be tested with a t-test similar to equation 8.48i, where the slope of the regression line is compared with 1. The ratio:

$$t = \frac{b - 1}{s_b} \tag{8.48iii}$$

is formed and compared with a Student's t-distribution with $(n - 2)$ degrees of freedom.

In this example:

$$t = \frac{0.726\,87 - 1}{0.110\,93} = -2.46$$

The sign is ignored and this value is compared to a Student's t-distribution with 15 degrees of freedom. Since the significance probability is <0.05 the null hypothesis that the slope is not different from one is rejected. This result supports the hypothesis that the zooplankton biomass increases more slowly than the phytoplankton biomass as overall lake productivity increases.

The intercept can also be compared with various other values, although zero is the most usual value. The standard error of the intercept s_a is given by:

$$s_a = s_{y \cdot x} \sqrt{\frac{1}{n} + \frac{(0 - \bar{X})^2}{[x^2]}} \tag{8.49}$$

and the t-ratio is formed,

$$t = \frac{a - 0}{s_a} \tag{8.49i}$$

This t value is compared to a Student's t-distribution with $(n - 2)$ degrees of freedom. This test is only meaningful when $X = 0$ is near the range of the independent variable. In the biomass example (Table 8.23), zero is outside the range of the independent variable, thus there is no sense in testing the significance of this intercept.

5.1.4 Confidence intervals about predicted values

There are different confidence intervals for two types of predicted values. To calculate the confidence interval for the mean $\mu_{\hat{y}} = \alpha + \beta X$ at point X_i, a standard error of the predicted value $s(\mu_{\hat{y}})$ is required:

$$s(\mu_{\hat{y}}) = s_{y \cdot x} \sqrt{\frac{1}{n} + \frac{(X_i - \bar{X})^2}{[x^2]}} \qquad (8.50)$$

where $s_{y \cdot x}$ is the square root of the residual variation, n is the number of pairs of points, $[x^2]$ is the sum of squares of X, and $\bar{X}$ is the mean of the independent values. The 95% confidence interval is calculated from the formula:

$$\mu_{\hat{y}} \pm s(\mu_{\hat{y}})t \qquad (8.50i)$$

where t is the value in the Student's t table with $(n - 2)$ degrees of freedom and probability level 0·05.

For example, for a phytoplankton biomass ($\log_{10}$) of 3·950 mg m^{-3} the predicted mean zooplankton biomass ($\log_{10}$) is 3·852 mg m^{-3} (Table 8.23). The standard error of this predicted value $\mu_{\hat{y}} = 3·852$ mg m^{-3} is:

$$s(\mu_{\hat{y}}) = 0·2671 \sqrt{\frac{1}{17} + \frac{(3·950 - 3·3786)^2}{5·797\,31}} = 0·0906$$

and the 95% confidence interval is:

$$3·852 \pm 0·0906(2·131) = 4·045 \text{ to } 2·040 \text{ mg m}^{-3}$$

as illustrated in Fig. 8.7. The size of the confidence interval increases with the distance between X_i and $\bar{X}$: when the measured phytoplankton biomass is 4·715 mg m^{-3}, the predicted mean zooplankton biomass is 4.408 mg m^{-3}. The standard error of $\mu_{\hat{y}} = 4·408$ is:

$$s(\mu_{\hat{y}}) = 0·2671 \sqrt{\frac{1}{17} + \frac{(4·715 - 3·3786)^2}{5·797\,31}} = 0·1618$$

and the confidence interval is $\pm 0·3448$ as compared to $\pm 0·1931$ mg m^{-3} in the previous example.

A regression equation can also be used to predict the value of Y for an individual that was not used to construct the regression line. The predicted value $\hat{Y}$ is calculated from the standard equation $\hat{Y} = a + bX$; there is, however, greater uncertainty associated with the prediction of $\hat{Y}$ than the mean $\mu_{\hat{y}}$, which is reflected in a larger error term. The equation used to calculate this standard error $s_{\hat{Y}}$ is:

$$s_{\hat{Y}} = s_{y \cdot x} \sqrt{1 + \frac{1}{n} + \frac{(X_i - \bar{X})^2}{[x^2]}} \qquad (8.51)$$

The value of $s_{\hat{Y}}$ also increases as the distance between the measured value X_i and the mean $\bar{X}$ increases. The formula for the 95% confidence interval is

$$\hat{Y} \pm S_{\hat{Y}}t \qquad (8.51\text{i})$$

where t is the value in the Student's t table with $(n-2)$ degrees of freedom and probability level 0·05.

For example, the standard errors of the predicted ($\log_{10}$) zooplankton biomass of 3·852 and 4·408 mg m^{-3} for new individual lakes with measured ($\log_{10}$) phytoplankton biomass of 3·950 and 4·715 mg m^{-3} are

$$s_{\hat{Y}} = 0\cdot2671\sqrt{1 + \frac{1}{17} + \frac{(3\cdot950 - 3\cdot3786)^2}{5\cdot79731}} = 0\cdot2820$$

and

$$s_{\hat{Y}} = 0\cdot2671\sqrt{1 + \frac{1}{17} + \frac{(4\cdot715 - 3\cdot3786)^2}{5\cdot79731}} = 0\cdot3123$$

respectively. The 95% confidence limits for $\hat{Y} = 3\cdot852$ are $\pm0\cdot6009$ mg m^{-3} and for $\hat{Y} = 4\cdot408$ they are $\pm0\cdot6655$ mg m^{-3}. These are much larger than the confidence intervals for the mean zooplankton biomass at the same X_is, as illustrated in Fig. 8.7.

If predictions are made for several new members of the population, the confidence interval for each of the new members is larger than the confidence interval obtained if there was only one new member. For example, if confidence intervals are constructed from equation 8.51i for each of 12 new lakes, the probability that all 12 confidence intervals include the correct values of the new Ys is substantially less than 0·95. The method for calculating confidence intervals for several values of $\hat{Y}$ is detailed in Snedecor and Cochran (1980, p. 166).

Since the relationship for individuals outside the range of the values in the original data set is unknown, predictions should not be attempted for such individuals. Thus, equation 8.47 should not be used to make predictions when the average phytoplankton biomass is $<2\cdot631$ or $>4\cdot715$ ($\log_{10}$) mg m^{-3}.

5.2 *Alternatives to standard linear regression*

Standard linear regression makes certain assumptions which are often not satisfied by biological data, particularly those which are collected in the field. For example, the independent variable should either be measured without error or be under investigator control. However, the phytoplankton data (Table 8.23) do not satisfy this assumption. In such circumstances the investigator may turn to alternative models which make fewer assumptions.

In this section two alternative methods, the geometric mean regression and Bartlett's three-group method will be illustrated using biomass data, and the uses and limitations of these nonstandard or functional models will be discussed.

Geometric mean regression was introduced to aquatic biology by Ricker (1973). It makes no assumption about investigator control of error for the independent variable. The geometric mean model:

$$Y = c + dX \qquad (8.52)$$

is similar to a standard regression line. However, the slope, d, is simply the ratio of the standard deviations of the dependent to independent variables:

$$d = \sqrt{\frac{[y^2]}{[x^2]}} \qquad (8.53)$$

where $[x^2]$ and $[y^2]$ are the sum of squares for X and Y, respectively. The sign for d ($+$ or $-$) must be added by the investigator. The intercept c is calculated in the standard way:

$$c = \bar{Y} - d\bar{X} \qquad (8.54)$$

In the biomass example,

$$d = \sqrt{\frac{4 \cdot 133\,09}{5 \cdot 797\,31}} = 0 \cdot 844$$

and

$$c = 3 \cdot 437 - 0 \cdot 844(3 \cdot 379) = 0 \cdot 585$$

The resulting regression line is given in Table 8.24. An alternative method to calculate d is:

$$d = \frac{b}{r} \qquad (8.53i)$$

where b is the slope from a least squares regression line (equation 8.44) and r is the correlation coefficient (see Section 5.3). Since the correlation coefficient has a maximum value of 1, the slope for the geometric mean regression is larger than for the standard method, as illustrated in Table 8.24 with the biomass data. There is no independent estimate of error for the geometric mean regression; this method is thus severely limited when it comes to testing the significance of the coefficients. In addition, the slope, d, will equal zero only when the sum of squares of Y equals zero (see equation 8.53), and thus it makes little sense to test whether the slope equals zero (Sokal & Rohlf 1981).

Bartlett's three-group method also makes no assumption of investigator

Table 8.24 Regression lines fit to the phytoplankton (X), zooplankton (Y) biomass data (mg m^{-3}) in Table 8.23. Data are from McCauley & Kalff (1981; E. McCauley, pres. comm.).

Standard linear regression

$$\log_{10} Y = 0{\cdot}981 + 0{\cdot}727 \log_{10} X$$

Geometric mean regression

$$\log_{10} Y = 0{\cdot}585 + 0{\cdot}844 \log_{10} X$$

Bartlett's three-group method

$$\log_{10} Y = 0{\cdot}938 + 0{\cdot}739 \log_{10} X$$

---

control of error in the independent variable. The regression has the same form as the previous models:

$$Y = e + fX \tag{8.55}$$

To estimate the regression coefficient f, the data are arranged in ascending order with respect to X, as in Table 8.23. Then they are divided into three groups of approximately equal size. The first and last group must be of equal size, as illustrated in Table 8.25. Mean X and Y values are calculated for groups one ($\bar{X}_1$, $\bar{Y}_1$) and three ($\bar{X}_3$, $\bar{Y}_3$), in order to calculate the regression coefficients:

$$f = \frac{\bar{Y}_3 - \bar{Y}_1}{\bar{X}_3 - \bar{X}_1} \tag{8.56}$$

and:

$$e = \bar{Y} - f\bar{X} \tag{8.57}$$

In the biomass example:

$$f = \frac{3{\cdot}924 - 2{\cdot}996}{4{\cdot}049 - 2{\cdot}794} = 0{\cdot}739$$

$$e = 3{\cdot}437 - 0{\cdot}739\,44(3{\cdot}379) = 0{\cdot}938$$

and the regression line is given in Table 8.24. Confidence intervals for this method involve several additional calculations, as illustrated in Sokal & Rohlf (1981, Box 14.12).

The two functional regression lines for the biomass data are different from each other and from the least squares equation (see Table 8.24), and, therefore, the question of which regression line should be used arises. Unfortunately, the mathematical basis of functional regression is not sufficiently well worked out to answer this question. There are other weaknesses with both functional regression methods outlined here (e.g., Ricker 1973; Kuhry & Marcus 1977). For example, it is still uncertain what

Table 8.25 First third and last third of ($\log_{10}$) phytoplankton biomass (mg m^{-3}) and ($\log_{10}$) zooplankton biomass (mg m^{-3}) from Table 8.23. Data are from McCauley & Kalff (1981; E.McCauley, pers. comm.).

	First third		Last third	
	X_1	Y_2	X_3	Y_3
	2·631	2·912	3·643	3·504
	2·651	2·575	3·825	3·745
	2·708	2·997	3·950	4·004
	2·756	3·489	4·037	3·743
	3·000	2·871	4·122	3·929
	3·017	3·131	4·715	4·620
Mean	2·794	2·996	4·049	3·924

the coefficients actually represent; as a result the standard method is still the best approach for predictive models. On the other hand, strong evidence (e.g., Ricker 1973) has been put forward for using a functional regression model to describe the relationship between two variables when both have large errors associated with them.

Particular care should be taken when reporting results from functional regression analyses because there is no standard approach. The method used should be clearly spelled out, and only one method should be used for a particular analysis. Also, to facilitate the comparison of data sets, the values needed to calculate the least squares coefficients, n, $\bar{X}$, $\bar{Y}$, $[x^2]$, $[y^2]$, $[xy]$ should be listed.

5.3 Correlation

Correlation is a measure of the closeness of the linear relationship between two variables. Both variables are treated in the same way in correlation since there is no reason to label one the independent and the other the dependent variable. The variables are labeled X_1 and X_2.

The correlation coefficient or product moment correlation coefficient r is calculated from three parameters:

$$r = \frac{[x_1 x_2]}{\sqrt{[x_1^2][x_2^2]}} \tag{8.58}$$

where $[x_1 x_2]$ is the cross product of X_1 and X_2 and $[x_1^2]$ and $[x_2^2]$ are the sum of squares of X_1 and X_2, respectively. The calculations for $[x_1^2]$, $[x_2^2]$, and $[x_1 x_2]$ are as in equations 8.41–8.43, with $X_1 = X$ and $X_2 = Y$. The correlation coefficient is a dimensionless number which can range from -1 to $+1$. A correlation coefficient of zero indicates no correlation whereas a coefficient of

Table 8.26 Total phosphorus loading (Lp, $g m^{-2} yr^{-1}$) and number of crustaceans (cm^{-2}) in four Great Lakes. Data are from Patalas (1972).

Lake	$\begin{array}{c}L_p\\X_1\end{array}$	$\begin{array}{c}\text{Crustaceans}\\X_2\end{array}$	$X_1 X_2$	X_1^2	X_2^2	Rank	
						Lp	Crustaceans
Superior	0·03	43	1·29	0·0009	1 849	1	1
Huron	0·15	167	25·05	0·0225	27 889	2	2
Ontario	0·86	306	263·16	0·7396	93 636	3	3
Erie	0·98	400	392·00	0·9604	160 000	4	4
Total	2·02	916	681·50	1·7234	283 374		

$$[x_1 x_2] = 681 \cdot 5 - \frac{(2 \cdot 02)(916)}{4} = 218 \cdot 92$$

$$[x_1^2] = 1 \cdot 7234 - \frac{(2 \cdot 02)^2}{4} = 0 \cdot 7033$$

$$[x_2^2] = 283\,374 - \frac{(916)^2}{4} = 73\,610$$

$$r = \frac{218 \cdot 92}{\sqrt{(0 \cdot 7033)(73\,610)}} = 0 \cdot 96$$

1 indicates that the correlation is perfect. The calculations for a correlation coefficient are illustrated in Table 8.26 with data from Patalas (1972) on the levels of phosphorus loading and crustacean numbers in four Great Lakes.

Correlation has two frequent uses. In regression it describes the proportion of the variation in Y that can be attributed to its linear regression on X. It is also used to determine whether the correlation between two variables is significantly different from zero. This latter requires that the points are independent and follow a bivariate normal distribution. A bivariate normal distribution is a cloud of points in an elliptical band, similar to those in Fig. 8.5b.

The square of the correlation coefficient, r^2, is the fraction of the variance of X_2 that can be attributed to its linear regression on X_1 when the sample size is large. Although an r^2 value could be calculated for the crustacean biomass example, a sample size of four is too small for the results to be meaningful. On the other hand, an r^2 value can be interpreted for the logged individual phytoplankton-zooplankton biomass data, illustrated in Fig. 8.5b. Since $[x_1^2] = 106 \cdot 32$, $[x_2^2] = 72 \cdot 66$, and $[x_1 x_2] = 53 \cdot 48$ for this example, the correlation coefficient is:

$$r = 0 \cdot 61$$

and

$$r^2 = 0.37$$

Thus, 37% of the variance of the zooplankton data in Fig. 8.5b can be attributed to its linear regression on phytoplankton biomass.

To test if the correlation coefficient is significantly different from zero, it is compared to the critical values for correlation coefficients with $(n - 2)$ degrees of freedom. The crustacean biomass data in Table 8.26, with $r = 0.96$ and a sample size $n = 4$ will be used as an illustration. For 2 degrees of freedom, the 5% value of r in a table of critical values is 0.95. The observed r is statistically significant and the null hypothesis that there is no correlation between phosphorus loading and crustacean biomass in the Great Lakes is rejected.

The crustacean biomass example is not entirely suitable for testing the significance of the product moment correlation coefficient because a sample size of four is too small to know whether either of the variables was from a normally distributed population. Some tables for the critical values do not even cover 2 degrees of freedom (e.g., Snedecor & Cochran 1980). The nonparametric alternative to the product moment correlation coefficient is the Spearman rank correlation coefficient. This is used when neither variable follows the normal distribution; it is less powerful than the parametric equivalent for small samples and quite tedious to perform for large samples. In this procedure, X_1 and X_2 are both converted to rankings as illustrated with the crustacean biomass data in Table 8.27. The difference between the ranks for each pair of points, d_i, is used to calculate the rank correlation coefficient:

$$r_s = 1 - \frac{6 \sum\limits_{i=1}^{n} d_i^2}{n(n^2 - 1)} \tag{8.59}$$

where there are n pairs of points. In the crustacean biomass example, $r_s = 1$, suggesting a strong correlation. However, there is no critical value at the 95% confidence level for a Spearman rank correlation coefficient when the sample

Table 8.27 The ranks of the paired variables; total phosphorus loading (Lp) and number of crustaceans in four Great Lakes from Table 8.26. Data are from Patalas (1972).

Lake	Rank Lp	Rank Crustaceans	Difference d_i
Superior	1	1	0
Huron	2	2	0
Ontario	3	3	0
Erie	4	4	0

size is 4. Thus, the null hypothesis that phosphorus loading and crustacean biomass are not correlated in the Great Lakes cannot be rejected with this test.

In order to illustrate the limitations of nonstandard correlation and regression tests, the same examples were used for more than one test. In practice, data should be analyzed by only one method, chosen prior to the analysis. This is because a variety of analyses may give more than one result and the decision of the investigator to choose one method over the others may be based on the results. As illustrated, crustacean numbers and phosphorus loading in the Great Lakes are significantly correlated at the 95% confidence level with a standard correlation but not with a rank correlation. The choice of method will obviously influence the result in this case.

Correlation is most meaningful when it is carried out on data selected to test a specific hypothesis. When data are available on several parameters it is often tempting to run correlations on all possible sets of parameters. However, when a shotgun approach is used, the probability of erroneously reporting significant results increases, i.e., if you look at data in enough ways, patterns will be found even if the data are generated randomly (e.g., Cole 1954, 1957).

5.4 Some other regression models

In this section other models in regression—multiple linear, polynomial, and nonlinear—and the comparison of regression lines or analysis of covariance are mentioned. These are complex subjects and users are encouraged to consult texts such as Draper & Smith (1966) and Snedecor & Cochran (1980) for an introduction to them.

5.4.1 Multiple linear regression

Multiple linear regression is the linking of two or more independent variables to a single dependent variable. When there are two independent variables X_1 and X_2 the multiple linear regression equation for a sample is:

$$Y = a + b_1 X_1 + b_2 X_2 \tag{8.60}$$

where a, b_1, and b_2 are sample coefficients, and Y is the predicted value. The coefficients b_1 and b_2 can be tested for significance to determine if a multiple regression is more suitable than a linear regression.

For example, Grant & Bayly (1981) used both a measure of turbulence and the density of an invertebrate predator *Anisops* to predict variation in crest size in *Daphnia cephalata*. The measure of turbulence accounted for 78% of the variation in crest size in a linear regression, whereas when the measure of turbulence was combined with density of predators in a multiple regression, they accounted for 88% of the variation in crest size. In this case, a multiple regression explained significantly more of the variation than the simple regression.

Multiple linear regression, like many other complex models in regression, requires a much larger sample size than simple regression. The variables X_1 and X_2 should be independent of each other, so that appropriate values can be assigned to the coefficients b_1 and b_2.

5.4.2 Nonlinear regression

The relationship between two variables is often not a straight line. If the population size is sufficiently large a polynomial regression of the form:

$$Y = a + b_1 X + b_2 X^2 + \cdots + b_n X^n \tag{8.61}$$

can describe the relationship between two variables X and Y, where a, b_1, b_2,...., b_n are coefficients, and n is the order of the polynomial.

For example, based on laboratory results, Frank *et al.* (1957) described the relationship between age and volume of *Daphnia pulex* with the polynomial equation:

$$Y = 0.1928 + 0.327X - 6.514 \cdot 10^{-3} X^2 + 51\,569 \cdot 10^{-5} X^3$$

where X is age in days and Y is number cm^{-3}. For these data a third degree polynomial described 99% of the variance.

Many other nonlinear regression models are available, e.g., the exponential growth model:

$$Y = (a)(b^X) \tag{8.62}$$

and the exponential decay model:

$$Y = (a)(b^{-X}) \tag{8.63}$$

where X and Y are the independent and dependent variables, respectively, and a and b are the coefficients. The exponential growth model is commonly used to describe the change in weight of young organisms (Y) over time (X). The exponential decay model can be used to describe development time (Y) of immature stages of aquatic organisms at various temperatures.

The coefficients in regression models should always be tested for significance. If several parametric models seem appropriate, the one which has significant coefficients and accounts for the highest fraction of the variation should be used.

5.4.3 Analysis of covariance

The relationship between two or more variables can be compared for various treatments with an analysis of covariance. For example, Cooley (1977) used an analysis of covariance to examine the effect of pulp mill effluent on filtering rates of *Daphnia retrocurva*. He measured the filtering rates (ml per animal per day) and carapace lengths (mm) of *Daphnia* in lake water (with labeled algae added) with and without pulp mill effluent. Filtering rate was regressed on body size for each treatment and the regression lines were compared. These results could have been analyzed by an analysis of variance if animals of identical size were used in both treatments. However, as this is virtually impossible with *Daphnia*, and since body size has an important influence on filtering rate, an analysis of covariance is the appropriate analytical method. Analysis of covariance should only be used when the covariates (such as body size) are drawn from the same population.

Comparison of regression lines in analysis of covariance is done in three parts. First, the residual variances of the individual regression lines are compared. If these variances are homogeneous, a common residual variance is calculated and the individual slopes are compared. If these slopes are not significantly different, a common slope is calculated along with an adjusted common residual variance and the individual adjusted intercepts are compared. When more than two regression lines are compared, the methods outlined for multiple comparisons of means (Section 4.5) are applied.

6 Summary

The trend in data analysis is towards more sophisticated techniques. However, as the complexity of the analysis grows, there is a tendency to lose sight of the original biological questions and the analysis tends to take on a meaning independent of the original intention of the investigation. I am reminded at this point of a paper which appeared recently in a major journal. Multivariate analyses were applied to a large data set and the results were spelled out in great detail, yet there was no mention of the variables used in the analysis, let alone how they were determined.

The contribution of any analysis is dependent upon three factors; the experimental design, the quality of the data, and the suitability of the method of analysis for the data. Weakness in any one of these areas can override any significant results. When writing up an experiment, one should present sufficient information so that the results are clearly understood and demonstrated by the data. In summary:

(1) The data should be collected with specific analysis in mind.
(2) The samples should be of sufficient size for the analyses.
(3) The data should be examined carefully for suitability for the selected analyses.

(4) The raw data should be presented or at least a summary should be given (e.g., mean, standard deviation, and sample size).

(5) The results of the analyses should be clearly spelled out and related to the scientific questions asked.

7 References

Box G.E.P. & Cox D.R. (1964) An analysis of transformation. *J. Roy. Stat. Soc., Ser. B*, **26**, 211–243.

Cassie R.M. (1963) Tests of significance for probability paper analysis. *N.Z. J. Sci.*, **6**, 474–482.

Cochran W.G. (1954) Some methods for strengthening the common χ^2 tests. *Biometrics*, **10**, 417–451.

Cochran W.G. (1977) *Sampling Techniques*. New York: Wiley.

Cole L.C. (1954) Some features of random population cycles. *J. Wildlife Management*, **18**, 2–24.

Cole L.C. (1957) Biological clock in the unicorn. *Science*, **125**, 874–876.

Conover W.J. (1980) *Practical Nonparametric Statistics*. (2nd ed.) New York: Wiley.

Cooley J.M. (1977) Filtering rate performance of *Daphnia retrocurva* in pulp mill effluent. *J. Fish. Res. Board Can.*, **34**, 863–868.

David H.A. (1952) Upper 5 and 1 % points of the maximum F-ratio. *Biometrika*, **39**, 422–424.

Dixon W.J. (1975) BMDP. Biomedical computer programs. Berkeley: University of California Press.

Downing J.A. (1979) Aggregation, transformation, and the design of benthos sampling programs. *J. Fish. Res. Board Can.*, **36**, 1454–1463.

Draper N. & Smith H. (1966) *Applied Regression Analysis*. New York: Wiley.

Dunnett C.W. (1955) A multiple comparison procedure for comparing several treatments with a control. *J. Amer. Statistical Assoc.*, **50**, 1096–1121.

Dunnett C.W. (1964) New tables for multiple comparisons with a control. *Biometrics*, **20**, 482–491.

Edmondson W.T. (1960) Reproductive rates of rotifers in natural populations. *Mem. Ist. Ital. Idrobiol.*, **12**, 21–77.

Elliott J.M. (1977) *Some Methods for the Statistical Analysis of Samples of Benthic Invertebrates*. Scientific publ. No. 25 (2nd ed.) Freshwater Biol. Assoc.

Fisher R.A. (1954) *Statistical Methods for Research Workers*. (12th ed.) Edinburgh: Oliver & Boyd.

Fleminger A. & Clutter R.I. (1965) Avoidance of towed nets by zooplankton. *Limnol. Oceanogr.*, **10**, 96–104.

Frank P.W., Boll C.D. & Kelly R.W. (1957) Vital statistics of laboratory cultures of *Daphnia pulex* De Geer as related to density. *Physiol. Zool.*, **4**, 288–305.

Grant J.W.G. & Bayly I.A.E. (1981) Predator induction of crests in morphs of the *Daphnia carinata* King complex. *Limnol. Oceanogr.*, **26**, 201–218.

Green R.H. (1979) *Sampling design and statistical methods for environmental biologists*. New York: Wiley.

Helwig J.T. & Council K.A. (1979) The SAS user's guide. Raleigh, North Carolina, USA: SAS Institute, Inc.

Iwao S. (1977) The m*-m statistic as a comprehensive method for analyzing spatial patterns of biological populations and its application to sampling problems *Jpn. Int. Biol. Prog. Syn.*, **17**, 21–46.

Keuls M. (1952) The use of 'studentized range' in connection with an analysis of variance. *Euphytica*, **1**, 112–122.

Kott P. (1953) Modified whirling apparatus for the subsampling of plankton. *Aust. J. Mar. Freshw. Res.*, **4**, 387–393.

Kuhry B. & Marcus L.F. (1977) Bivariate linear models in biometry. *Syst. Zool.*, **26**, 201–209.

Kutkuhn J.H. (1958) Notes on the precision of numerical and volumetric plankton estimates from small-sample concentrates. *Limnol. Oceanogr.*, **3**, 69–83.

Lampert W. (1974) A method for determining food selection by zooplankton. *Limnol. Oceanogr.*, **19**, 995–998.

Lloyd M. (1967) Mean crowding. *J. Anim. Ecol.*, **36**, 1–30.

May J.M. (1952) Extended and corrected tables of the upper percentage points of the 'studentized' range. *Biometrika*, **39**, 192–193.

McCauley E. & Kalff J. (1981) Empirical relationships between phytoplankton and zooplankton biomass in lakes. *Can. J. Fish. Aquat. Sci.*, **38**, 458–463.

Murtaugh P.A. (1981) Selective predation by *Neomysis mercedis* in Lake Washington. *Limnol. Oceanogr.*, **26**, 445–453.

Newman D. (1939) The distribution of range in samples from a normal population expressed in terms of an independent estimate of standard deviation. *Biometrika*, **31**, 20.

Patalas K. (1972) Crustacean plankton and the eutrophication of St. Lawrence Great Lakes. *J. Fish. Res. Board Can.*, **29**, 1451–1462.

Peters R.H. & Rigler F.H. (1973) Phosphorus release by *Daphnia. Limnol. Oceanogr.*, **18**, 821–839.

Pielou C.E. (1977) *Mathematical Ecology*. New York: Wiley.

Prepas E.E. & Trew D.O. (1983) Evaluation of the phosphorus-chlorophyll relationship for lakes off the Precambrian Shield in western Canada. *Can. J. Fish. Aquat. Sci.*, **40**, 27–35.

Ricker W.E. (1937) Statistical treatment of sampling processes useful in the enumeration of plankton organisms. *Arch. Hydrobiol.*, **31**, 68–84.

Ricker W.E. (1938) On adequate quantitative sampling of pelagic net plankton of a lake. *J. Fish. Res. Board Can.*, **4**, 19–32.

Ricker W.E. (1973) Linear regressions in fishery research. *J. Fish. Res. Board Can.*, **30**, 409–434.

Rigler F.H. & Langford R.R. (1967) Congeneric occurrences of species of *Diaptomus* in southern Ontario lakes. *Can. J. Zool.*, **45**, 81–90.

Rohlf F.J. & Sokal R.R. (1981) *Statistical Tables*. San Francisco: Freeman.

Scheffé H. (1959) *The Analysis of Variance*. New York: Wiley.

Siegel S. (1956) *Nonparametric Statistics for the Behavioural Sciences*. New York: McGraw-Hill.

Snedecor G.W. & Cochran W.G. (1980) *Statistical Methods*. (7th ed.) Ames, Iowa: State Univ. Press.

Sokal R.R. & Rohlf F.J. (1981) *Biometry*. San Francisco: Freeman.

Steel R.G.D. & Torrie J.H. (1960) *Principles and Procedures of Statistics*. New York: McGraw-Hill.

Stuart A. (1962) *Basic Ideas of Scientific Sampling.* London: Latimer, Trend & Co.

Taylor L.R. (1961) Aggregation, variance, and the mean. *Nature*, **189**, 732–735.

Taylor L.R. (1980) Comment on 'Aggregation, transformation, and the design of benthos sampling programs.' *Can. J. Fish. Aquat. Sci.*, 215–219.

Tukey J.W. (1949) One degree of freedom for non-additivity. *Biometrics*, **5**, 232–242.

Tukey J.W. (1977) *Exploratory Data Analysis.* Reading, Massachusetts: Addison-Wesley.

Zar J.H. (1974) *Biostatistical Analysis.* Englewood Cliffs, N.J.: Prentice-Hall.

Chapter 9. Methods for the Study of Feeding, Grazing and Assimilation by Zooplankton

ROBERT HENRY PETERS

1 Introduction

In terms of energy or mass flow, ingestion represents the greatest of all interactions between an animal and its environment (Spomer 1973). Consequently, many aquatic ecologists have attempted to describe and measure the feeding process of zooplankton. They have evolved a formidable number of methods.

Any investigation must be tailored to the hypotheses to be tested; it is, therefore, important to consider briefly the major questions to which zooplankton ingestion and assimilation are relevant. At a practical level, there are two: we wish to know the future amount and composition of the algal community and we wish to predict fish stocks. The former is determined, in part, by the pressure of zooplanktonic grazing on the algae and the latter, in part, by the amount of zooplankton production available to the fish. Of course, accurate descriptions of the feeding process of zooplankton alone will not permit predictions about fish stocks or algal composition: such descriptions can only be used as components in larger models of the aquatic ecosystem which will yield such predictions. At a more academic level, zooplankton lend themselves to the testing of ecological theory because of the animals' small size, ease of culture, aquatic habitat and the seemingly reduced heterogeneity of their environment. Determinations of ingestion and grazing rates have been used in studies dealing with energy flow (Slobodkin and Richman 1956; Richman 1958), mineral cycling (Johannes 1968; Peters & Rigler 1973), competition (Dodson 1970; Hall *et al.* 1976; Lynch 1977), optimal foraging (Lam & Frost 1976; Lehman 1976), and predator-prey interactions (Holling 1959; Wilson 1973) among others. Beyond these general theories lie an unlimited number of specific hypotheses regarding the fine structure of aquatic communities and the behavior of their components. This review primarily presents the basic methods which have been used to measure feeding, grazing and assimilation rates. I hope these methods will not be adopted uncritically by other workers but will be adapted to suit their own needs and their questions.

2 Basic Concepts

2.1 Definition of terms

The same term or concept may apply to values which necessarily differ because they were determined in different ways and under different assumptions. For example, the term 'grazing rate' is applied both to values determined using Gauld's (1951) formula (which implies an exponential decline in food concentration) and to values from short-term radiotracer experiments (which assume a linear reduction in food concentration). These two estimates can differ considerably (Rigler 1971a) despite their conceptual identity. Because the three terms in the title (feeding, grazing, and assimilation) are used widely and variously in the literature, one must clarify their usage each time they are presented by giving their method of calculation. Consequently, only idealized definitions are given in this section. The appropriate method of calculation for each technique will be provided later.

2.2 Feeding and grazing

Feeding rate (f), or ingestion rate, is a measure of mass or energy flow into the animal. It is usually expressed in cells ingested individual^{-1} time^{-1}. However, differences in cell size and animal weight render such a formulation difficult to interpret for most quantitative purposes. A preferable, though far less common formulation, would express ingestion rate in terms of ingested biomass, which can be presented as cell volume, dry weight, elemental composition, energy content, etc. No standard expression has been accepted in the literature, but perhaps dry weight or volume might be suggested as a compromise, for these are easily determined and can approximate other units through relatively simple conversions.

Grazing rate (G) is the volume of food suspension from which a zooplankter would have to remove all cells in a unit of time to provide its measured ingestion. Synonyms in the literature include searching rate, filtering rate, filtration rate, clearance rate, and volume of water cleared per unit time. Each of these terms involves a mechanistic image of the food collection process which may be false. Suspension-feeding organisms may not actively search and zooplankton do not always (and may never) force the suspension through a sieve-like device and so may never actually filter-feed. Similarly animals do not remove cells from suspension with an efficiency of 100 % and so it is misleading to speak of clearance. For these reasons the more neutral term, grazing rate, has been preferred in this account; however, even this may imply a false homology with terrestrial grass-eaters. It is unlikely that such a suggestion for terminological change will find widespread acceptance because all terms are entrenched in the literature. Consequently, we should be careful not to over interpret the intentions behind such synonyms when they are encountered. Perhaps it is easier to change our interpretations of these phrases than to change the phrases themselves.

Feeding rate, which is equal to the product of grazing rate and food concentration, is an approximation of the sustenance which an animal draws from its environment. It is most appropriate in considering problems of zooplankton production for fish stocks, while grazing rate is more appropriate in considering the effect of zooplankton on algae, for it is equivalent to the mortality rate of algae per zooplankter. Both feeding and grazing rates vary with the environmental conditions of the animals.

2.3 *The feeding process*

Before discussing assimilation or techniques for the measurement of feeding and grazing, I will review the current descriptions of feeding and grazing by zooplankton, in part to review terms and in part to outline our current conception of the process. It is this imagery which often determines our approach to the subject. For example, it was once thought that grazing was an automatic behavior and that each species had a typical clearance rate independent of external conditions. If this were true, grazing rate could be determined in very artificial laboratory conditions and the results could then be applied readily to nature. We now know the process to be far more sensitive and our prerequisites for laboratory measurement and field application of grazing rates are far more demanding.

Our conception of the mechanism of suspension feeding is currently undergoing a revolution. 'Pre-revolutionary' conceptions are still widely held and continue to influence experimental design. Consequently this account begins with a traditional picture of filter-feeding and then provides a brief sketch of a contemporary alternative.

The processes involved in food collection by zooplankton were studied in detail by many authors (Naumann 1921; Cannon 1928, 1933; Storch 1928; Eriksson 1934; Lowndes 1935; Fryer 1957a; Gauld 1959, 1966). Their accounts sometimes differ in detail, but a traditional picture of feeding by the major groups of zooplankton may be had without doing great violence to any particular researcher.

The most studied suspension-feeding zooplankton are calanoid copepods and cladocerans. Traditionally, both animals were said to force a current of water through a fine mesh of setae and setules which sieve food particles from the water. These particles should then pass to the mouth where they are swallowed, with or without mastication. The other major group of freshwater, planktonic crustaceans, the cyclopoid copepods were thought not to depend on filtering currents but were considered raptorial feeders. Protozoans and rotifers were similarly not thought to filter-feed because neither group is obviously equipped with sieve-like appendages, although rotifers certainly create feeding currents and Fenchel (1980a) believes that ciliates use their cilia as screens. Most research effort has concentrated on cladocerans and calanoids which will be given disproportionate coverage here. This account ignores suspension feeding by the zoobenthos, which has been less studied. Cummins & Klug (1979) and Wallace & Merritt (1980) provide points of entry to this literature.

Among calanoids, the feeding current is traditionally thought to consist of secondary eddies created by the locomotory activity of the second antennae and by movement of the mouth parts. This current would draw water and suspended food forward into a filtering chamber bounded dorsally by the body, laterally by the filtering setae of the maxillae and ventrally by the forward-directed abdominal appendages. Water flows through the setae of the maxillae which strain out suspended matter; this then collects between the appendages (Fig. 9.1). Actions of the mouth parts then propel the food forward to the mandibles which push the food between the labrum and the body to the mouth (Lowndes 1935; Gauld 1966). Conover (1966a) found that marine calanoids, and presumably their freshwater relatives, are capable of two other modes of food collection when confronted by larger particles. The maxillipeds may be extended below the filter basket to seine for food or they may be extended, praying mantis-like, to grasp larger prey. The mandibles serve to masticate large prey before swallowing. Rosenberg (1980) found that the marine calanoid, *Acartia*, will use its thoracic legs to supplement the seining action of the mouth parts.

Cladocerans are classically thought to create a filtering current by the active, rhythmic pumping of their thoracic legs. This action would draw water and suspended food into the anterior part of the filter chamber formed dorsally by the ventral body wall, posteriorly by the post-abdomen, and laterally and ventrally by the moving filtering appendages. Water in the filtering chamber would then pass through the setae of these appendages, towards the valves of the carapace and then away from the animal, leaving the food to collect in the food groove between the filtering appendages along the ventral body wall whence it passes, propelled by water currents, to the mandibles and the mouth (Naumann 1921; Cannon 1933). The post-abdomen is used to clean the food groove and the filtering appendages of excess or undesirable material (Cannon 1933; McMahon & Rigler 1963; Burns 1968a).

For both groups, the significant aspects of the process are the rate of movement of the appendages creating the current, the volume of flow, the efficiency of retention of the filtering setae, the efficiency of transfer of the collected food to the mouth, and the amount of nutrient extracted in the gut.

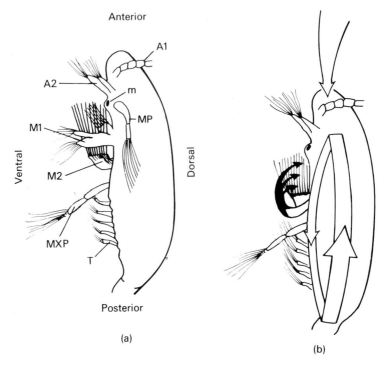

Fig. 9.1 The feeding appendages (a) and the traditional conception of filter-feeding (b). Only the left appendage of each pair is shown in schematic form. Movement of the appendages draws water from in front of the animal into a large posterio-lateral whorl. A portion of this swirling water is sucked anterio-medially by the outward swing of the maxillipeds. The inward swing then forces water through the fine meshes of the maxillipeds' setae which strains food from the water. Arrows with a large head and narrow shaft indicate movement out of the plane of the page and towards the reader. A thick shaft and narrow head indicate medial movement away from the reader. A1: first antenna; A2: second antenna; m: mouth; MP: mandibular palp; M1: first maxilla; M2: second maxilla; MXP: maxilliped; T: Thoracic or swimming legs (modified from Koehl & Strickler 1981).

The image of suspension feeding as a seiving of particles larger than the filter's mesh from a stream of flowing water may not be accurate. Rubenstein and Koehl (1977) point out that such filters may collect particles by direct interception, inertial impaction, gravitational deposition, motile particle deposition, or by electrostatic impaction. Gerritsen and Porter (1982) found that charge associated with the food particle may affect filtering rate.

Recently, Strickler has suggested that the conception of zooplankton as sieves or filters is grounded in misconception. He believes that, given the viscosity of water and the rapid rates of movement of the appendages, it is impossible that water should flow through the tiny apertures between the setae. Instead the appendages must act like paddles pushing food particles out of the feeding current to the mouth (Fig. 9.2) and the concept of filtration by suspension-feeders must be abandoned. Instead, all food collection is essentially a raptorial selection of individual particles. An increasing amount of information appears to support this interpretation of 'filter'-feeding (Alcaraz *et al.* 1980; Friedman 1980; Zaret 1980; Koehl & Strickler 1981; Gerritsen & Porter 1982; Paffenhöfer *et al.* 1982). These arguments may eventually have far reaching effects on experimental studies of suspension-feeders: for example, studies of the intersetule distance (i.e. filter mesh size) are rendered largely irrelevant under this conception of suspension feeding (Porter *et al.* in press).

It is less easy for this writer to imagine how experimental determinations of feeding or grazing rates themselves would distinguish between these hypotheses. The value of any alternative scientific hypothesis rests in the critical experiments they suggest to distinguish between competing theories. For example, B.Marcotte (personal communication) pointed out that Strickler's conception allows a greater role for prey selection by grazers. This

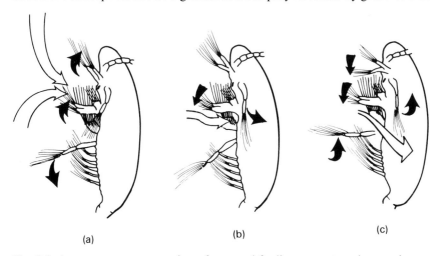

(a)   (b)   (c)

Fig. 9.2 A more contemporary view of copepod feeding currents and appendage movements showing how outward movement of the second antennae and maxillipeds sucks water towards the maxillae (a), postero-medial movement of the first maxillae and dorso-lateral movement of mandibular palps sucks water laterally (b), inward movements of second antennae and maxillipods coupled with dorso-lateral movement of mandibular palps shoves water postero-laterally. The second maxillae collect (and reject) food particles carried in the feeding current (c). Appendage movements are indicated by closed arrows and water currents as open arrows. Movement out of the plane of the page is indicated by varying widths of the arrows as noted in Fig. 9.1 (modified from Koehl & Strickler 1981).

may provide a basis for critical tests. In any case, our earlier conceptions and misconceptions about suspension feeding have been extremely fruitful. Their simplicity has allowed development of theories and methods for feeding behavior which are second to none.

2.4 *Assimilation*

Assimilation rate is usually defined as the amount of material or energy which passes from the lumen of the gut into the body of the animal, per unit time. It must be expressed in terms of a particular element (P, C, N, etc.) or compound (glucose, vitamin B_{12}, etc.) or energy (Joules), for different materials are assimilated to different degrees. Assimilation (A) is often expressed as assimilation efficiency (A.E.), the percentage of the ingested food (I) which is assimilated.

$$A.E. = (A/I) \times 100 \qquad (9.1)$$

where A and I are in the same units. In the physiological literature, assimilation often implies the difference between ingestion and the sum of excretion and defecation. Johannes & Satomi (1967) suggest that 'retention' be used for this concept.

This section has described current, widely held conceptions of food collection by zooplankton. Ideally, the quantities measured by our methods would correspond closely to these concepts. However, since alternative techniques with the same conceptual goal yield different values, it seems that this ideal is not always achieved. This lack of correspondence between measured value and concept argues that the researcher take as many approaches as possible. Although this is a truism for good research, it provides a strong rationale for a short examination of the advantages and disadvantages of at least the most popular methods used to measure the feeding behavior of zooplankton.

3 Techniques for Measurement of Feeding and Grazing Rates

3.1 *Morphology and microscopy*

Although careful examination of the feeding appendages has yielded a great deal of information, this approach has been less extensively employed in recent years. Most basic descriptions were completed in the nineteenth century by Daday, Leydig, Sars and others, even if questions of detail remain. These early authors did not usually deal with function; this was investigated most intensively in the early part of this century (e.g. Naumann 1921; Cannon 1928; Lowndes 1935). The ecological significance of the morphology of the feeding apparatus is still an open question.

In general, plumose setation and flat, grinding mandibles are associated with herbivorous species whereas carnivores are armed with spiny, widely spaced setae and carinate mandibles (Naumann 1921; Anraku & Omori 1963). The mandibles of herbivorous copepods also carry long sharp projections which may imply a cracking rather than grinding function. (Sullivan *et al.* 1975). There is, however, no sharp division in diet between these types and opportunistic feeding is to be expected (Marshall 1924, 1973; Fryer 1975b). The inter-setular distance has been measured (Marshall 1973; Nival & Nival 1976; Geller & Müller 1981) as an indicator of minimum food size, for the filtering apparatus may function as a 'leaky sieve' (Boyd 1976) allowing small particles to pass (Peterson *et al.* 1978). Gliwicz (1977, 1980; Gliwicz & Siedlar 1980) has analyzed the width of the opening between the valves of cladocerans since this could set a maximum size to the edible particle, as could the so-called guard setae which protect the entry to the filter basket of calanoid copepods (Gauld 1966). Egloff & Palmer (1971) measured the filtering area of the thoracic appendages of two *Daphnia* species in an attempt to test apparently conflicting hypotheses (McMahon & Rigler 1963; Burns & Rigler 1967; Burns 1969a) regarding the relationship of grazing rate (and, by their reasoning, filter area) and animal size. Strickler and his coworkers (Strickler & Bal 1973; Friedman & Strickler 1975; Strickler 1975; Friedman 1980) have used electron microscopy to identify putative chemoreceptors and thigmoreceptors on the appendages of copepods. Such receptors would be required if these animals are capable of selective feeding on the basis of taste or of response to moving prey at some distance, respectively. Gut and fecal analyses have been used more widely (Fryer 1957b; Porter 1973, 1975; Infante 1973, 1981; Pourriot 1977; among others). Despite these initiatives, microscopic examinations are used too rarely in the modern testing of ideas and the following comments are written in the hope that future workers will employ them more frequently.

Animals may be studied from whole mounts or sections of animals and exuvia (Frey 1973; Fryer 1968) or from dissections of the limbs. Since isolated parts may misrepresent the function of the whole, it is good practice to compare dissections with whole mounts and living animals. Care should be taken in preserving material since killing agents, such as formalin, may distort the animals. Haney and Hall (1973) recommend that animals be anaesthetized with carbonated water before killing with a solution of 4 % formalin and sucrose. Prepas (1978) reported that chilling the formalin and sugar solution reduces distortion still more. Manipulations of the limbs or animals is simplified if performed in a viscous medium like glycerol or polyvinyl lactophenol (Frey 1973; Fryer 1968).

It is often not necessary to stain the animals. However, Egloff and Palmer (1971) used a chitin stain, crystal violet, to examine the setae of *Daphnia* and Eriksson (1934) found that methyl violet B was useful in observing hairs and bristles'. Fryer (1968) recommends Mallory's triple stain for most uses. Polarized light and a camera lucida or other drawing system (Frey 1973) have also been employed. Researchers hoping to use such techniques can refer to Pantin (1964), a microscopical handbook or, in the case of drawing aids, to the manufacturer's directions. Electron microscopy is finding increasing application in the analysis of the fine structures associated with feeding (Sullivan *et al.* 1975; Geller & Müller 1981; Gerritsen & Porter 1982).

Gut contents of zooplankton have long been a focus of study: the presence or absence of food in the gut may identify diel rhythms of feeding behaviour (Fuller 1937; Gauld 1953; Kajak & Ranke-Rybickova 1970; Singh 1972) and the identification of food types in the gut may reflect selective feeding and food preferences (Lebour 1922; Lowndes 1935; Fryer 1957b; Gliwicz 1969; Rapport *et al.* 1972; Infante 1973; Porter 1973, 1975, and others). However, such analyses should be treated critically. Handling and fixing of the animals may cause regurgitation or defecation of the gut contents (Gauld 1953; Swift & Fedorenko 1973; Hayward & Gallup 1976). This should be avoided by narcotizing the animals: Gannon & Gannon (1975) compared 20 different narcotizing and killing agents and finally recommended that the animals be anaesthetized by adding carbonated water to their container (1:20 by volume). Many animals will not completely empty their gut even after prolonged starvation (Cannon 1928; Lowndes 1935; Lemcke & Lampert 1975), thus empty guts may not indicate fasting and food in the gut may not indicate recent feeding.

The interpretation of analyses of gut contents also requires considerable caution. A number of food organisms, especially naked flagellates, disintegrate in the gut and analysis may show only a green mush. Gliwicz (1969) found identifiable remains in less than 10% of the 150 animals he examined and Infante (1973) obtained results from only one third of the animals she dissected. Marshall (1924) found that only 52% of the *Calanus* she studied contained recognizable remains. Moreover, a long series of observations have shown that some cells, although ingested by zooplankton, may pass through the gut apparently unharmed (Lefèvre 1942; Fryer 1957b; Grygierek 1971; Porter 1973, 1975, 1976; Pourriot 1977). Identification of prey in the gut of predators is made difficult because the animals frequently ingest only a part of their prey (Confer 1971; Ambler & Frost 1974; Dagg 1974; Brandl & Fernando 1975); in addition, the food of the prey may appear in the predator's gut (Fryer 1957b). Murtaugh (1981) found no evidence for differential digestion of animal prey in the guts of *Neomysis*. The implications of these problems are very serious. Because only a small, highly resistant portion of the gut contents is identifiable, analyses invariably deal with an unrepresentative sample. Because food must be destroyed in the gut, whereas indigestible items are unaffected, the presence of a particular item in the gut does not indicate that it is food and its absence is no proof that the animal does not eat that item. Nevertheless, the presence of a particle in the gut proves ingestion, while the presence of cell fragments or empty tests shows mortality of the cell and probably indicates utilization of the cells by the zooplankton.

The examination of the gut contents is usually performed by gently crushing the dissected gut (Marshall 1924; Fryer 1957b) or the entire animal (Porter 1973; Pourriot 1977) between slide and coverslip. This extrudes the gut contents. Fryer (1957b) suggests that the extruded material be further macerated and claims that many difficulties in identification of the gut contents could be reduced by this step. It may be advantageous to examine the gut contents in living animals, for the gut peristalsis allows the researcher to see the food from different angles (Gliwicz 1969). The discrete fecal pellet produced by copepods allows their gut contents to be identified by examining the pellets rather than the gut (Marshall & Orr 1955).

Chemical analyses can offer a less time-consuming alternative to microscopic examination of the gut. Gut enzymes may provide important clues to food type and digestibility (Hasler 1937; Mayzaud 1980; Mayzaud & Mayzaud 1981). Fluorescence analysis for chlorophyll derivatives in extracts from whole zooplankton (Mackas & Bohrer 1976; Dagg & Grill 1980) has been used to study diel variation in feeding activity (Boyd *et al.* 1980).

In summary, gut analyses and morphological studies can yield useful and rare information. However, the techniques are time-consuming and require great patience; they are open to misinterpretation and the results should be compared to the behavior of living animals.

3.2 Behavioral studies

Close examination of the actions of individual, living animals complements both static, morphological observations and feeding or grazing rate determinations, which tend to be 'black-box' experiments. Behavioral studies have provided the descriptions of the feeding process outlined above and have given strong evidence that zooplankton are not automatic filtering machines, but are capable of a considerable range of feeding behaviors (Porter *et al.* 1982). McMahon (1968; McMahon & Rigler 1963) discovered that the reduced grazing rate of *Daphnia magna* in high concentrations of food is achieved by a reduction in the rate of movement of the thoracic appendages and by rejection of excess food in the food groove by the post-abdomen. Burns (1968a) showed that this same movement can be used to discard undesirable foods, such as blue-green algae. This behavior is widespread in cladocerans (Hayward & Gallup 1976; Webster & Peters 1978; Porter & Orcutt 1980), although gut analyses of both laboratory and field specimens have shown that not all blue-green algae are rejected (Bogatova 1965; Arnold 1971; Infante

1973, 1981; Geller 1975; Nadin-Hurley & Duncan 1976; and others) and some rotifers (Starkweather 1981) and cladocerans are capable of assimilation (Lampert 1977a), growth and reproduction on a diet containing blue-green algae (Hrbáčkova-Esslova 1963; de Bernardi *et al.* 1981). Studies of the behavior of calanoids have added greatly to our picture of their feeding process. *Calanus* may feed discontinuously (Conover 1966a; Paffenhöfer 1971; Rosenberg 1980), a habit which could cause considerable variation in short-term measurements of feeding rate. Conover (1966a) also noted that these animals may shred larger food particles and lose some fragments. This observation involves modification of the cell size spectrum, which has implications for the interpretation of feeding or grazing rates determined from the size spectra produced by electronic size analyzers like the Coulter counter and may result in overestimation of ingestion rates based on microscopic determinations of the food cell mortality through cell counts. Cells which are collected in the filter basket are not always successfully ingested (Conover 1966a; Alcaraz *et al.* 1980); moreover *Calanus* uses different behaviors to deal with foods of different size (Conover 1966a; Gauld 1966) and may persist in one mode despite changes in food type. Others (Poulet & Marsot 1980) argue for more opportunistic switching among foods. These observations suggest that the animals feed less effectively on certain foods at particular times. Active selection of foods has also been observed in cyclopoids (Williamson 1980), rotifers (Gilbert & Starkweather 1977; Gilbert & Bogdan 1981), and ciliates (Rapport *et al.* 1972). Obviously, most of these studies require observation through a microscope, but useful information can be gained by simply watching zooplankton in an aquarium. For example, both *Diaptomus* (Lowndes 1935) and *Daphnia* (McMahon & Rigler 1963; Burns 1969b; Horton *et al.* 1979) were observed to scavenge or browse on container surfaces when the suspended food concentration is low. This implies that suspended food concentration may not reflect available food for zooplankton in shallow lakes or in the littoral zone.

Microscopic examination of the feeding process requires that the animal be enclosed in a small volume of water, and this frequently means that it is fixed in position. Observation chambers may be as large as a watch glass or syracuse dish (Gauld 1966; Conover 1966a; Williamson 1980) but small animals may be observed in a depression slide (Fryer 1968, 1974) or in a drop of water suspended from a coverslip (Edmondson 1965; Brandl and Fernando 1975). Closer observation requires that the animals be held in position. Cladocerans may be constrained by enclosing the animal in a very small drop of water and then pressing the dorsal surface of the carapace into a small dab of petroleum jelly or stopcock grease, care should be taken to allow the swimming antennae and thoracic appendages free movement. The animal is then given more water and mounted under a microscope with the ventral surface towards the microscope's objective lens (McMahon & Rigler 1963; Webster & Peters 1978). This gives the animal an abnormal position with respect to gravity, although a side mounted microscope partially circumvents this problem (Burns 1968a). Ringelberg (1969) has positioned *Daphnia magna* by driving a fine pin through the brood pouch and using a side mounted microscope with dorsally directed illumination. This should permit the animal free rotation to assume a more natural position. The same effect may be had with less damage to the animals if they are fixed to the end of a fine wire (Fox *et al.* 1951) or a glass rod (Porter *et al.* 1979) with petroleum jelly or glued onto a hair (Alcaraz *et al.* 1980). These are probably the only measures suitable for copepods (Alcaraz *et al.* 1980). All manipulations are greatly facilitated by the use of fine Erwin loops (Sargent-Welch Co.) which minimize damage to the animals. Webster & Peters (1978) felt that restrained small cladocerans may reject food more frequently than free-swimming animals, but McMahon & Rigler (1963) found no such effect with *Daphnia magna*. The effect of such restraints must be investigated further.

It is difficult to believe that the behavior of planktonic animals is unaffected by these conditions of observation. Paffenhöfer *et al.* (1982) feel that tethering copepods may reduce the range of behaviors of free-living animals. Fryer (1968) argues that no benthic cladoceran behaves normally on a clean, brightly lighted, slide. Certainly, light should be as dim as possible. The spectral composition of light may influence animal behavior (Baylor & Smith 1954; Hairston 1976): red illumination is sometimes used to reduce any light effect but the insensitivity of zooplanktonic crustaceans to red light is by no means a certainty (Lumer 1932; Viaud 1951; Smith & Baylor 1953; Stearns 1975). *Daphnia* do not respond to infra-red light (Baylor 1959; Young 1974) and Strickler (1970, 1977) used infra-red light with the appropriate film to follow the behavior of cyclopoid copepods. Since microscope lights may inadvertently heat the animal's water, one should take care to control the water temperature by the use of water jackets, flow-through chambers or simply by using a relatively large volume of water and a short observation period. Small chambers may also distort laminar flows generated by calanoid copepods when feeding, thus inhibiting food particle perception and capture (B. Marcotte, personal communication).

Observation chambers have been used to describe the feeding currents produced by the animals. Food cells, inorganic particles, or dye are introduced to such systems and the patterns of flow observed. Among the substances used have been methylene blue, coloured starch particles (Cannon 1928), charcoal, carmine red (Naumann 1921) and India ink (Eriksson 1934; Koehl & Strickler 1981).

More quantitative studies have determined the rate of movement of the feeding apparatus. The appendages move at a greater speed than one can normally count by eye, although larger cladocerans may move slowly enough for manual methods (McMahon & Rigler 1963, McMahon 1968) and for some purposes zooplankton may be slowed down by the use of an anaesthetic like MS222 (Conover 1966a) or chloral hydrate (Eriksson 1934), by starvation (Rigler 1961) or by thickening the water with methyl cellulose (Fryer 1968). However, such techniques are intentionally unnatural and should be compared with normal behavior whenever possible. A number of mechanical aids have been used to resolve the problem of rapid movement. For example, if the movement is continuous and rhythmic, one can 'freeze' the actions of the appendages stroboscopically. An animal is fixed under a microscope and the light directed to the eye is pulsed. When the rate of pulsing is equivalent to the rate of movement of the appendages (or to any integral multiple of that rate) the appendages appear to stand still; slightly higher or slower pulse rates slow the motion of the appendages. This 'freezing' can be achieved by pulsing the light source but rapidly fluctuating light may upset the animals unnecessarily. A more effective device is the stroboscope (Cannon 1928; Gray 1930; Tonolli 1947; Schröder 1961): a dark dish, slit at regular intervals around its perimeter, is rotated between the objective and the animal, so that the animal is only visible through the slits. The speed of rotation is increased until appendage motion appears to cease. At that point, the speed of the appendages (in cycles per unit time) equals the product of the number of slits and the rate of revolution of the disk. For effective stroboscopic measurements, the animal must move its legs at a fixed speed for some time. Lowndes (1935) concluded that the stroboscope was ineffective for the study of calonoid copepods but Schröder (1961) obtained stroboscopic estimates which were comparable to those obtained cinemagraphically by Lowndes (1800–3600 versus 600–2400 beats per minute, respectively). In any case, the stroboscope cannot reveal inter-flash or irregular behaviors, which may also play a significant role in food collection (B.Marcotte, personal communication), McMahon (1968) and Burns (1968a) have circumvented the problem of discontinuous and arrhythmic movement by continuous and automatic recording. A photocell replaced one of the oculars of a stereoscopic microscope which was focused on the moving appendages. These movements produced changes in light intensity, and, therefore, in the current through the photocell, which were automatically recorded on a strip chart recorder. Porter et al. (1982) have used a similar device. High speed cinematography has provided an alternative means of observation for many years (Erikkson 1934; Lowndes 1935). Strickler (1975) filmed zooplankton at 250 frames/sec and subsequently (Alcaraz et al. 1980; Koehl & Strickler 1981; Paffenhöfer et al. 1982) at 500 frames/sec; such films can then be viewed in slow motion and a wealth of information extracted. Videotape can provide a useful alternative to film and is preferable in that the tape can be viewed immediately. However, the resolution provided by the television screen is less than that of film and the range of filming speeds is reduced. Technological advance may soon permit the application of equipment with much higher time resolution which is now prohibitively expensive. (J.A.Downing, personal communication).

To date, much of the literature has been confined to verbal descriptions of processes without attempts to quantify or score such behavior. Altmann (1974) suggests that such studies are best seen as initial reconnaissance preparatory to further quantitative investigation. She maintains that the danger of biased description based on selective observations is too great to be ignored; such studies must be followed with careful testing of selected hypotheses based on objective systems of scoring behavior. One danger of quantification by the development of unambiguous criteria for scoring is that one may study events which are easily scored but of little or no ecological relevance. Marler & Hamilton (1967, Chapter 20) point out that compromise may be necessary between the significance of the behavior to the researcher's ultimate objectives and the ease with which it may be measured. Such trade-offs are commonplace in ecological research.

Behavioral studies can provide independent tests of mechanistic models of zooplankton feeding and are a rich source of ideas and inspiration for hypotheses to be tested with other techniques. They also permit the biologist to treat zooplankton as complex and interesting organisms rather than simple pump-and-filter automata. However, many ethological studies of zooplankton feeding have limited themselves to qualitative descriptions and often do not provide objective tests of hypotheses.

3.3 Laboratory determinations of feeding and grazing rate

Most studies of zooplankton feeding have concentrated on the estimation of G and f in laboratory vessels. The animals are introduced to a suspension of food and the rate of accumulation of food by the animals or its rate of loss from suspension is measured. The former method usually involves labeling the food with a radioactive tracer and the latter involves sequential estimates of food biomass (cell number, cell volume, chlorophyll, carbon, etc.). Both approaches are quantitative, relatively rapid and conceptually simple, but uncritical use can confuse the interpretation of results.

3.3.1 Cell counts

The oldest technique for estimating grazing and ingestion rates is based on the observed change in the number of suspended cells counted before and after a suitable period of exposure to feeding animals. The change in food concentration is then considered a measure of the amount of food eaten. The grazing rate (G, in ml animal^{-1} unit time^{-1}) is calculated as:

$$G = V(\ln C_0 - \ln C_t)/(tN) \qquad (9.2)$$

where V is the volume of the container in ml, t is the length of time the animals were allowed to feed, N is the number of animals in the container, C_0 is the initial cell concentration and C_t is the final cell concentration. This, of course, simply assumes that cell number is reduced by a constant fraction per unit time (i.e. that grazing rate is unaffected by changes in cell concentration) and is thus a simple negative exponential relationship. This formula is popularly referred to as Gauld's (1951) equation. Since subsequent studies (Rigler 1961; Mullin 1963; Richman 1966; Burns & Rigler 1967; Frost 1972; Corner *et al.* 1976; and many others) have shown that above some critical concentration (Fig. 9.3), termed the 'incipient limiting level' (Rigler 1961), grazing rate is a negative function of food concentration, the assumptions of Gauld's equation do not apply universally. In his seminal paper, Gauld (1951) was careful to ensure that the cell concentration did indeed decline exponentially, but this precaution has often been ignored by other workers. Rigler (1971a) has calculated that this oversight may result in as much as a 100% overestimate of feeding rate. Above the incipient limiting level, feeding rate (f) is constant (Burns & Rigler 1967; Frost 1972; Mullin *et al.* 1975; Corner *et al.* 1976; Harris & Paffenhöfer 1976a) or nearly so (McMahon 1965; Mullin 1963; Parsons and LeBrasseur 1970; Geller 1975; Horton *et al.* 1979) and f (in cells animal^{-1} unit time^{-1}) can be calculated as:

$$f = V(C_0 - C_t)/(Nt) \qquad (9.3)$$

(The reader should be aware that precise identification of the incipient limiting level may not be possible and that it depends on the model used to describe the effect of food concentration on feeding behavior—see Section 3.6). Although grazing rate is not constant above the incipient limiting level and feeding rate is not constant below, it may sometimes be necessary to calculate these values, regardless. At low concentrations of food, an average value for the food concentration (C) can be estimated as:

$$C = VC_0 \exp(-GNt/V) - 1/tGN \qquad (9.4)$$

(modified from Frost 1972) and an average feeding rate (f) as:

$$f = CG \qquad (9.5)$$

Above the incipient limiting level, an average G can be calculated as:

$$G = (C_0 - C_t)2/t(C_0 + C_t) \qquad (9.6)$$

and C can be taken as the arithmetic mean of the initial and final cell concentrations ($[C_0 + C_t]/2$). Both calculations are only approximations of

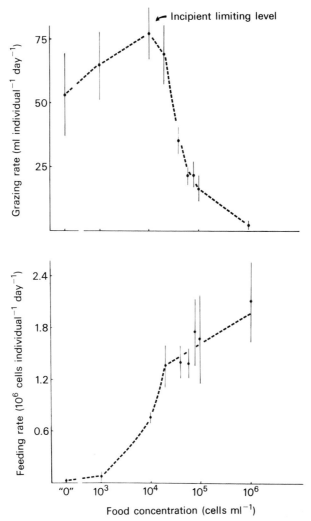

Fig. 9.3 The effect of food concentration on filtering and feeding rates of *Daphnia pulex* (Horton *et al.* 1979) showing the decline in filtering rate and near plateau of feeding rate above the 'incipient limit concentration'.

the animals' changing behavior over the period of the experiment. The errors involved are increased as the reduction in food concentration during the experiment (Rigler 1971a) becomes greater.

At the incipient limiting food concentration, animals pass from a concentration at which feeding rate is constant to one in which grazing rate is constant. A survey of the literature (Fig. 9.4) suggests that this change occurs between 1 and 10 p.p.m. (vol./vol.) of food, and experiments conducted in this

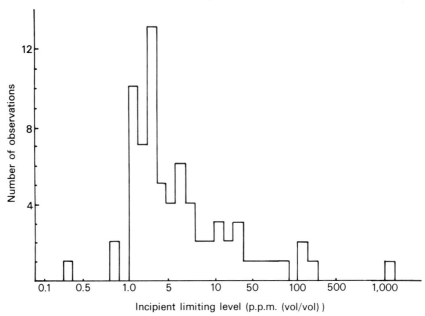

Fig. 9.4 Frequency distribution of reported incipient limiting food concentrations
(p.p.m., wet weight/volume) for calanoid copepods (Richman 1966, Kibby 1969,
McAllister 1970, Corner *et al.* 1972, Esaias & Curl 1972, Frost 1972, Gaudy 1974,
Poulet 1977) Cladocera (Ryther 1954, Rigler 1961, McMahon 1965, McMahon &
Rigler 1965, Burns & Rigler 1967, Crowley 1973, Infante 1973, Geller 1975,
Hayward & Gallup 1976, Kersting and van der Leeuw 1976, Kring & O'Brien
1976) and rotifers (Gilbert & Starkweather 1977a). When necessary, wet weight of
cells was calculated from volumes published elsewhere for the same species or by
conversion from other indices of biomass such as carbon content or dry weight. In
general, the incipient limiting level lies between 1 and 10 p.p.m.

range should include assurance that change in cell concentration is
approximated either by a linear (i.e. f constant) or by a negative exponential
(i.e. G constant) function of time. Otherwise, the researcher should use
radiotracer or electronic cell counting techniques, which minimize the change
in cell concentration, or simply avoid working over this range of
concentrations.

A number of problems have arisen in using cell counts. Because relatively
long exposures (2–24 h) are required, algal sedimentation may produce
variations in cell concentration. This problem may be alleviated by using
motile algae like *Chlamydomonas* (Marshall & Orr 1955), but most
researchers now routinely stir or rotate the experimental vessels. Anraku
(1964) and Nauwerck (1959) both report an increase in observed feeding rates
during stirring but neither Mullin (1963) nor Schindler (1968) found a

significant effect. Ryther (1954) found that agitation of the experimental container stopped feeding. Long exposures also raise the possibility that algal growth may seriously influence the change in cell numbers (Nauwerck 1963; Sheldon *et al.* 1973; Nival & Nival 1976) even with little or no light (Anraku 1964; Roman & Rublee 1980). Most workers try to reduce algal growth by keeping their experimental flasks in dim light and a number have corrected their estimates of grazing rate by following the increase in cell numbers in control flasks without zooplankton. Coughlan (1969) reviews the equations for such a correction which reduce to the consideration of the food growth rate in the control flask assuming an exponential increase. The initial (CC_0) and final (CC_t) concentrations in the control are determined and a growth rate constant (b) is calculated as:

$$b = [\ln(CC_t) - \ln(CC_0)]/t \qquad (9.7)$$

A similar calculation for changes (C_t and C_0) in the experimental chamber yields 'a' (a negative value which is equal to Gauld's G [equation 9.2] times N/V):

$$a = (\ln C_t - \ln C_0)/t \qquad (9.8)$$

The grazing rate can then be calculated as:

$$G = V(b - a)/N \qquad (9.9)$$

Since a is usually negative this estimate of G is larger than that estimated by equation 9.2. The average cell concentration is calculated by substituting $(b - a)$ for GNt/V in equation 9.4 (Frost 1972).

Strictly interpreted, these corrections can only be applied when both the algal growth rate in the controls and its rate of decline in the experimental vessels are shown to be exponential. Such determinations are rarely made because the number of cell counts required is considered prohibitive unless electronic counting systems are used (Sheldon 1979). The possibility exists that any external control is inappropriate because the growth rate of algae in the experimental flask may be enhanced by the excretions of zooplankton (Gliwicz 1975; Porter 1976; Roman & Rublee 1980). If this is so, feeding and grazing rates will be underestimated, but strong evidence for zooplanktonic enhancement of algal growth is scarce (Frost 1972). The conditions for algal growth must vary greatly with experimental conditions and no set rule about the magnitude of error introduced can be established. A maximum value of b ($= r_{max}$: day^{-1}) for algal growth can be established on the basis of the allometric equation of Blueweiss *et al.* (1978):

$$r_{max} = 33M^{-0.26} \qquad (9.10)$$

where M is the wet weight of the food cell in pg. This would usually overestimate algal growth under the conditions provided by grazing rate experiments, since such conditions are rarely ideal for algal growth.

When microscope counts are used to determine cell concentrations, care should be taken to obtain representative counts. This is rarely a problem with pure cultures, but in mixed cultures of food cells or natural waters, one may be tempted to push the method beyond its limits and to count cells for which statistically meaningful counts are unobtainable. Hobero & Willén (1977) recommend:

(1) The use of KI_2 as a preservative.
(2) The use of an Utermöhl inverted microscope as a counting system.
(3) The counting of at least 100 cells per species.
(4) The counting of only the most abundant species.

Theoretically, cells should settle randomly in an Utermöhl chamber and the variance around each count should be equal to the mean; hence the standard deviation for a count of 100 cells is 10 (see Chapter 7). However, since the cells frequently settle unevenly, a Poisson distribution cannot be assumed and the variance in counts should be determined directly (Nauwerck 1963). Because grazing rate is calculated as the ratio of the means of C_0 and C_t (i.e. $\ln C_t - \ln C_0 = \ln C_t/C_0$) the standard deviation of the filtering rate is increased over that of the estimates of C_0 and C_t:

standard deviation of C_t/C_0

$$= (\text{variance of } C_t)/C_0^2 + (\text{variance of } C_t)/C_t^2 \qquad (9.11)$$

(Mood *et al.* 1974). Because G is calculated from the logarithm of this ratio, the probability distribution of G is negatively skewed and extremely low values of G will be more frequent than extremely high values. Most publications of grazing rates have ignored statistical treatments of the individual estimates, apparently more by tradition than by design. An exception to this rule is the work of Downing (1979, 1981; Downing & Peters 1980).

A frequent ploy in cell count experiments is to confine a large number of animals in a small volume of water so that large changes in cell concentration will be achieved in a relatively short time. This sould be avoided since crowding has been shown to influence metabolic rates (Zeiss 1963; Hargrave & Geen 1968; Santomi & Pomeroy 1968) and to depress feeding rates of zooplankton (Anraku 1964; Hargrave & Geen 1970). Marine calanoids appear to increase their grazing rates with increases in volume up to at least 7 liters (Paffenhöfer 1971, 1976; Harris & Paffenhöfer 1976b; Paffenhöfer & Harris 1976; Paffenhöfer & Knowles 1978). However, these workers consistently use equation 9.9, which gives higher values of G than the calculations used by others. Hayward & Gallup (1976) have found that the grazing rate of

Daphnia pulex is inhibited when the animals are held at concentrations of > 1 animal per 20 ml. Apparently, this is the only investigation of the effects of crowding on feeding by freshwater animals.

A number of authors have suggested that zooplankton feed on detritus (Nauwerck 1962; Tappa 1965; Paffenhöfer & Strickland 1970; Saunders 1972; Corner *et al.* 1974; Buscemi & Puffer 1975; Nadin-Hurley & Duncan 1976; Lenz 1977). Detrital feeding cannot be effectively measured with visual counts; detrital particles are practically impossible to count with a microscope and because the particles vary so greatly in size and shape that the size of each must be measured individually. This is best left to automatic particle counters.

Despite their disadvantages, direct counts can provide more information than any other estimate of feeding rate, and they are particularly useful in determining differential rates of algal mortality in suspensions of mixed species and in natural waters (Gliwicz 1969; McQueen 1970; Gaudy 1974). Because the method necessarily deals with large numbers of animals and longer periods of exposure, it circumvents the variations introduced by diel patterns in feeding activity (Nauwerck 1963; Duval & Geen 1975; Haney & Hall 1975; Starkweather 1978), discontinuous activity, and individual variations (Conover 1966a; Paffenhöfer 1971). Cell count techniques avoid the dangers of radiotracers (Section 3.3.5) and the ambiguities of electronic particle counters (Section 3.3.2). They also require equipment which is less expensive and widely available. It is unfortunate, if understandable, that this time-consuming approach has not been used more often.

3.3.2 Electronic particle analysis

Coulter counters®, and their analogues (e.g. Coulter's 'Cell Sorter'® system, or image analyzers like Bausch and Lomb's Omnicon® and Quantimet's 720®) represent a significant advance in the techniques of cell counting. These systems alleviate many of the problems and most of the tedium involved in microscopical cell counts and are rapidly finding acceptance among marine workers. Only the Coulter counter has been widely used and this discussion is limited to that machine. Again, while the device is extremely powerful, uncritical use can be misleading (Sheidon & Parsons 1967a, b: Allen 1975; Deason 1980a; Harbison & McAlister 1980).

The basis of the Coulter counter is very simple (Sheldon & Parsons 1967a). The particles to be counted are suspended in an electrolyte and passed through a small aperture containing an electric field. As they pass through this field, the cells change the suspension's resistance (R) and, because the change in resistance is very nearly proportional to the cell volume, both the volume (V_i) of cells and their number can be determined from the relationship:

$$R = q \cdot V_i(r_p - r_e)/r_p \qquad (9.12)$$

where q is a constant of proportionality, V_i is the cell volume, r_p is the resistivity of the particle and r_e is the resistivity of the electrolyte. Usually, r_p is assumed to be so large that the term $(r_p - r_e)/r_p$ is practically unity. The value of q is determined by calibration of the instrument with different particles of known size, usually pollen grains (Sheldon & Parsons 1967a; Allen 1975). For smaller particles, the electric current must be increased, but since very high currents cause the electrolyte to boil there is a minimum particle size of about 0·8 μm (Allen 1975). This excludes the use of the machine for very small cells such as populations of natural bacteria (Peterson *et al.* 1978). The size of the aperture sets a maximum limit to diameter ($= 0·4 \times$ aperture diameter), but utilization of a series of three apertures permits the sizing of phytoplankton up to 800 μm in diameter (Sheldon & Parsons 1967a) which is sufficient for most uses. Analysis of the output from the counter is greatly facilitated by the use of a Coulter Channelyzer which determines and prints a copy of the particle distribution in the suspension.

Coulter counters determine the total cell volume in each of a series of up to 100 channels of size classes for each aperture used. Each class corresponds to a range of cell volumes (say V_1 to V_2) and results are expressed as total volume or number of cells each of which cause a change in resistance equivalent to that produced by a cell with a volume between V_1 and V_2. The scales are frequently converted to 'equivalent spherical diameters' calculated as $(6 . V_1/\pi)^{0·333}$ to $(6 . V_2/\pi)^{0·333}$.

The Coulter counter readily analyzes the size spectrum of particles in natural waters. The range is usually so great that the size classes are plotted on a logarithmic scale, usually to the base 2 (Sheldon & Parsons 1967b) so that the size range doubles over each class. This requires some mental flexibility in interpretation, since a doubling of diameter implies an 8-fold increase in volume whereas a doubling in volume only entails a 26 % increase in diameter. The range of diameters or volumes in each class, expressed in μm or μm^3, increases exponentially with increasing logarithmic size class (i.e. 1–2, 2–4, 4–8, . . . , 1024–2048, etc.). The counter measures the size of all particles and so the recent trend to refer to measured volumes as 'biovolumes' appears to introduce a misnomer; the volumes need not be biotic at all. The approach is sometimes frustrating to the biologist in that our traditional taxonomic categories and distinctions between living and non-living particles are necessarily ignored. However, these difficulties are perhaps more apparent than real and diminish with familiarity.

The great advantage of these systems is that they can count and measure thousands of particles in a matter of seconds. Researchers can, therefore, determine statistically significant effects of feeding from small changes in cell concentration and without crowding their animals or using long exposure times. In practice, however, both animal concentration and exposure times have often been similar to those employed for the cell count methods.

The Coulter counter has a number of sources of error. The number of small cells may be underestimated and dense cultures can cause an underestimate of cell number if two or more cells pass the aperture together (Allen 1975). The volume of large particles may be underestimated (Paffenhöfer & Knowles 1978; Vanderploeg 1981) and large particles may block the aperture (Sheldon & Parsons 1967a). The equality of cell volumes determined microscopically and electronically has rarely (Harbison & McAlister 1980) been investigated over a range of cell sizes and types. Harbison & McAlister (1980) list 6 sources of variation in Coulter counts:

(1) Variations in particle shape.
(2) Changes in the geometry of the orifice.
(3) Differences in particle path.
(4) Variations in applied current.
(6) Variations in the conductivities of the medium.
(6) Variations in the conductivities of the particles.

They cite C.Boyd as holding that the first three items can produce an error of 20%. Allen (1975) warns that electronic failure may go undetected and result in erroneous counts. He suggests that, notwithstanding the simplicity of operation, users should be 'experienced'. Presumably, frequent controls and calibrations would eliminate the dangers of equipment failure. It is possible that osmotic stress created by the electrolyte may distort or destroy small freshwater cells, such as naked flagellates. Perhaps the greatest problem with Coulter counters is the cost: in 1980, the price of a Coulter TA-2 counting system in Canada was $32 000·00.

Once the counts in each channel are obtained in both control and experimental vessels (or before and after feeding), grazing rates and feeding rates are calculated from the same formulae used in the cell count method. The ease and rapidity of the method allows the experimenter to work with very small changes in cell concentration and one can easily determine the relationships of cell growth and mortality over time required for accurate assessment of feeding and grazing rate. Occasionally, grazing rates, calculated from Coulter counts, are presented as ml individual^{-1} litre^{-1} unit time^{-1} (Berman & Richman 1974; Duval & Geen 1975). These units are converted to the more usual ml individual^{-1} unit time^{-1} on multiplication by the volume of water in the experimental vessel.

The Coulter counter has been used extensively to investigate the selection of foods of different size by zooplankton (Richman & Rogers 1969; Poulet 1973, 1974; Berman & Richman 1974; Allan *et al.* 1977; Richman *et al.* 1977). These studies purport to show that marine calanoids, and perhaps even freshwater cladocerans, demonstrate a remarkable capacity to 'track' or feed selectively upon the most abundant size class of food particles, to the exclusion of less abundant particles from the diet. When the food size spectrum is more evenly distributed, the animals feed non-selectively. This would be an extremely exciting discovery, for it would imply that zooplankton impose a density dependent control on their food and greatly influence the course of algal succession. Unfortunately, two sources of error could, under certain assumptions, produce the same results even though the animals feed non-selectively at all times (Poulet & Chanut 1975; Poulet 1976; Vanderploeg 1981).

Peter Starkweather (personal communication) points out that the variance associated with grazing rate estimates decreases as the number of particles counted increases (equation 9.11). Thus, if the animals removed a constant proportion of all size classes, statistically significant estimates of G would first be obtained in the most abundant class; with time, and hence with further reduction in the number of particles in this most abundant class, significant reductions in cell numbers would be observed in other classes. A naive interpreter might think that the animals fed selectively when once class was very abundant but increased the range of particle size ingested as the number of cells in the most abundant class fell. The solution is obviously to give the confidence limits for grazing rate in each channel; these should be determined by repetitive counts rather than by assuming a Poisson distribution.

A second source of error arises because the animals may modify the size spectrum of suspended particles in ways other than by simply consuming cells. For example, defecated or masticated cell fragments may be released into the medium and be counted as food particles. Since most food particles are likely to be derived from the most abundant size class, a disproportionate number of defecated aggregations or cell fragments would appear in other channels, reducing the observed changes in these channels. The results could then be falsely interpreted to indicate selective feeding on the most abundant size classes (Nival & Nival 1976; Poulet 1974; Frost 1977).

Many observations suggest that particle modification could occur. Both calanoids and cladocerans lose masticated fragments of larger cells (Conover 1966a; Lampert 1978) and the animals break apart chains of algal cells (Martin 1970; O'Connors *et al.* 1976; Alcaraz *et al.* 1980; Deason 1980b); both processes result in the production of smaller particles. Even gentle agitation may disrupt some cells (Harbison & McAlister 1980) and the feces of cladocerans quickly disintegrate once released into the water (Rigler 1971b). The feces of copepods are frequently contained by the peritrophic membrane of the fecal pellet and may be less likely to influence the counts generated by electronic analysis. Although some fecal pellets are very resistant (Ferrante & Parker 1977), Marshall & Orr (1955) observed that others disintegrate immediately after defecation. Lautenschlager *et al.* (1978) observed that the peritrophic membrane of *Gammarus* disappears in 7–24 h at 10 °C and Turner (1977) believes that the fecal pellets of some marine calanoids lack peritrophic membranes altogether. Conover (1966a) has observed that calanoids may tear open and then discard fecal pellets. Kersting & Holterman (1973) suggest that the Coulter counter may record electrolyte-filled tests from the feces as cell fragments because of their changed resistance. All of these effects must increase cell counts in at least some channels and so reduce grazing rates for those size classes.

Kersting & Holterman (1973) showed that defecation gives the impression of selective feeding although none occurs. They used a Coulter counter to follow the decline in cell concentration induced by previously starved *Daphnia magna*. The animals appeared to feed selectively only after the onset of defecation, when released cell fragments appeared in some channels. Harbison & McAlister (1980) warn that sieves sense particle size by largest linear dimension while sensing zone counters sort by volume: this difference in sorting may give the appearance of selectivity where none exists. They show that a metal screen can select cells of intermediate volume (but greater length) over volumetrically larger but shorter cells. Runge & Oman (1982) showed that cells do not necessarily orient along one axis when passing through a sieve.

Although it has long been recognized that Coulter counters cannot distinguish between particle modification and selective feeding (Sheldon & Parsons 1967a), many workers continue to interpret all net reductions in cell number as the result of selective feeding alone. Typically, only channels which show a net gain in cells (and therefore negative feeding and grazing rates) are thought to show particle modification; the grazing and feeding rates in these channels are arbitrarily set to zero. Channels in which the net change is reduced (but not reversed) are treated quite differently, for in them the role of particle modification is ignored. Current models of cladoceran feeding do not permit much selection; because Coulter counters seem to show remarkable powers of selection in *Daphnia* (Berman & Richman 1974), one is lead to doubt the evidence for selection in copepods, although their richer behavioral repertoire should permit more selective feeding. Deason (1980a) used a computer simulation to show that Coulter counters are effective only in estimation of total ingestion rate, not of ingestion rate on any one size class.

Recently, the phrase 'particle modification' has become increasingly applied to the results of electronic particle counters. Unfortunately, the change seems cosmetic not conceptual: the phrase 'particle modification' is becoming a synonym for 'feeding'. In summary, alternative approaches and methodologies are required to test the models based on particle counter techniques and to resolve the doubts they have engendered. Nevertheless the discriminatory power and ease of operation of particle counters hold great promise for increasing our knowledge of suspension feeding.

3.3.3 *Other estimates of biomass*

Although cell numbers are the most frequently used representation of biomass in expression of feeding rate, a number of other estimators have been used which are probably preferable for comparisons among studies. The Coulter counter provides one appropriate alternative, cell volume, which has found wide acceptance. Energy or carbon content are also suitable, but dry weight seems the most easily obtained of the various measures. Chlorophyll concentration has been used to estimate algal biomass but the ratio of chlorophyll to cell volume is quite variable (Krey 1958; Nicholls & Dillon 1978). In each case, the initial and final concentrations of biomass replace C_0 and C_t in equations 9.2 through 9.9. Again, defecation and cell growth can lead to underestimates of ingestion and grazing rates.

It will frequently be necessary to convert among the different indices. Cell volume is approximately three times cell dry weight (Parsons *et al.* 1961; Nalewajko 1966). Cell carbon (C_0 in pg) is 40–50 % of dry weight or may be estimated from cell volume (V_i in μm^3) as:

$$C_c = 0.40 V_i^{0.712} \qquad (9.13)$$

(Strathmann 1967). The ratio of chlorophyll to cell volume varies from 0.001 to 0.097 pg/μm^3 (Nicholls & Dillon 1978) with a median of about 0.008.

3.3.4 *Beads and inorganic particles*

Many characteristics of the food cells influence grazing and ingestion rates, thus comparisons among experiments with different foods often entail simultaneous changes in more than one variable. Since strong conclusions are difficult to draw from such multivariate experiments, several attempts have been made to standardize the particles. For example, Frost (1972) investigated the effect of cell size on the feeding rate of *Calanus* by using different sized clones of the same alga. Other workers have used various non-food particles to achieve the same standardization: Burns (1968b) and Gliwicz (1977) used plastic spheres, Wilson (1973) used glass beads, and Gliwicz (1969) used sand and natural diatomite. Poulet and Marsot (1978, 1980) have manufactured membrane bound particles which permitted the flavouring of these artificial cells with different materials. Burky & Benjamin (1979) describe a rapid spectrophotometric analysis for filtering rate of latex beads. All such beads provide the animals with a standard 'food' which is not destroyed by digestion.

These experiments are much the same as those which use natural cells. Animals are allowed to feed in a bead suspension. After a short time, they are killed and rates of feeding and grazing are estimated from the number of particles removed from the water or present in the gut (Gliwicz 1969a, 1977).

The calculations required are analogous to those used in the cell count method, and the problems encountered are identical. Since these particles may be resuspended after gut passage, experimental exposures should be less than the gut passage time. An alternative to shortened feeding times is to determine gut passage time (G_p) then to expose the animals for a longer period of time, count the number of beads (B) in the gut and calculate feeding rate (f) in beads per unit time per individual as:

$$f = B/G_p \qquad (9.14)$$

Grazing rate could be calculated from the concentration of beads in suspension (S):

$$G = B/(SG_p) \qquad (9.15)$$

For such use, gut passage time should be determined for the experimental conditions. This is probably an inappropriate measure for ingestion by some zooplankton, since *Bosmina* and *Daphnia longiremis* apparently select against all beads (Burns 1968b) as do *Acartia clausi* (Donaghay & Small 1979; Donaghay 1980). In practice, beads are not normally used to provide absolute estimates of feeding rates. Instead, they provide an index of selective feeding among particles which are similar in all respects but size (Burns 1968b, 1969b, Gliwicz 1969) or taste (Poulet & Marsot 1978). Grazing rates obtained from beads in the guts are frequently (Wilson 1973; Frost 1977; Gliwicz 1977), but not always (Gliwicz 1969), lower than those determined with other techniques. Rigler (unpublished data) compared the number and size distribution of both natural and artificial particles in the guts and the environment of *Limnocalanus macrurus*. He found that, although these copepods grazed beads at a lower rate than natural foods, the size distribution of both particles was similar. This suggests that beads are best used to determine feeding selectivity, not feeding rate. Gerritsen & Porter (1982) found that the surface charge of the beads influences grazing rate determinations. This may be a widespread phenomenon and may indicate the inadequacy of size alone in determining selection behavior.

Because the volume of a zooplankton gut is small and analyses are tedious, the number of beads counted is frequently low. Moreover, the most interesting regions in the size frequency distributions (usually the larger size categories) are usually represented by the smallest number of particles because size distributions of offered particles are skewed. Small sample size imposes wider statistical limits on any counts of these beads and may lead to misinterpretations. Such estimates must include a statement of properly calculated statistical variation (equation 9.11) and researchers should ignore size classes in which only a few beads are counted.

One should also recognize that hard, spherical beads are only imperfect models of natural foods. Since natural particles may be more easily ingested (Nadin-Hurley & Duncan 1976) or may be broken in ingestion (Infante 1973), natural particles eaten by cladocerans may be larger than the maximum sizes suggested by experiments with glass beads (Burns 1968b).

3.3.5 Radiotracer techniques

The prime alternatives to cell counts for the determination of feeding and grazing rates are obtained through estimates of the amount of radioactivity that animals accumulate from a suspension of radioactively labeled cells. If the activity of N animals is A_a after t minutes of exposure in a suspension of particles with a radioactivity as A_s (ml^{-1}), then grazing rate on the tracer particles (G, in ml individual^{-1} h^{-1}) is:

$$G = A_a 60/A_s Nt \qquad (9.16)$$

Feeding rate (f) in units of biomass per individual per unit time can be calculated as:

$$f = GS \qquad (9.17)$$

where S is the food concentration ml^{-1} expressed in the appropriate units (cell number, volume, dry weight, carbon, etc.). Equation 9.17 is simply a more general statement of equation 9.5. In most modern studies, t is less than the time required for food to pass through the gut. The great precision of this technique makes it extremely useful in dealing with short exposure times, single animals and dilute food concentrations. Since exposure times are short there is no need to correct for changes in cell concentration as in cell count methods. However, determination of selection among a variety of foods or of feeding and grazing over extended periods requires considerably more effort than would estimates from Coulter counting.

The older literature contains several variations on this basic experiment. Marshall & Orr (1955) measured the loss of tracer from suspension and Sorokin (1966) advocated monitoring the gain in incorporated tracer plus fecal radioactivity over periods of up to several hours. Both approaches require the quantitative recovery of all tracer in the body, eggs and feces and both assume that no radioactive material will be respired or excreted during the experiment. Early work suggested that these assumptions may hold (Marshall & Orr 1955; Sorokin 1966; Schindler 1968), but more recent studies (Sorokin 1968; Conover & Francis 1973; Brandl & Fernando 1975; Peters 1975a; Lampert 1977a) suggest that a considerable proportion of assimilated tracer is excreted in only an hour. Lampert (1977a) suggests that previous checks for respiration losses of ^{14}C-CO_2 were insufficiently sensitive to detect rapid dilution of a small labile pool of ^{14}C which mediates all tracer exchange: as the animals feed upon labeled food this labile compartment excretes significant amounts of ingested tracer but such excretion ceases soon after the labeled food is removed. The similarity of various models for carbon (Brandl & Fernando 1975; Lampert 1975) and phosphorus (Conover 1961; Peters & Rigler 1973) metabolism for both copepods (Conover 1961; Brandl & Fernando 1975) and cladocerans (Peters & Rigler 1973; Lambert 1975) suggests that tracer excretion is probably a general phenomenon. Since it is improbable that defecated or excreted tracer can be completely recovered, it is unlikely that long-term tracer experiments will yield accurate data. In consequence, only short-term radiotracer experiments will be considered here. Those interested in longer term experiments may refer to Sorokin (1966).

Selection of an appropriate radioisotope is obviously a first step. A number of radionuclides have been used in feeding experiments: ^{14}C (Nauwerck 1959; Geller 1975; Lampert 1981), ^{59}Fe (McMahon 1970), ^{3}H (Gophen *et al.* 1974; Lampert 1974; Hollibaugh *et al.* 1980; DeMott 1982), ^{32}P (Rigler 1961; Webster & Peters 1978) and many others are possibilities. Primarily, one seeks a label which is easily incorporated by the food cell (usually algae, bacteria or yeast), inexpensive, and which emits low energy particles for safety's sake. For Geiger–Müller counting, the most practical isotope is ^{32}P. Although this is a hard beta emitter and is potentially more dangerous than ^{14}C or ^{3}H, a higher energy particle is necessary to avoid self-absorption, i.e. the absorption of the emitted particle by the body of the animal. Less penetrating isotopes can be used with these counting systems if self-absorption corrections are applied (Sorokin 1966, 1968; Rigler 1971a). Correction is necessary because the calculation of grazing rate (equation 9.16) compares the number of disintegrations per minute in the animals' bodies to that in a sample of dried food suspension which has low self-absorption. Generally, zooplankton absorb 15–40% of the low energy beta particles emitted by ^{14}C in their guts (Richman 1966; Bell & Ward 1968; Kibby 1969) although the exact amount depends greatly on animal size (Sorokin 1966, 1968). Even using ^{32}P, the counting efficiency of the Geiger–Müller system (i.e. the number of counts per 100 disintegrations) is less than that of liquid scintillation counters. Despite these disadvantages, Geiger–Müller counting is simpler and cheaper than liquid scintillation and does not involve the use of dangerous fluors and organic solvents. Moreover, liquid scintillation systems are in continuous use in many institutes where Geiger–Müller systems are left unused. Nevertheless, liquid scintillation counting is preferred for most work because of the greater range of possible isotopes, higher counting efficiencies, the capacity to count two or more isotopes simultaneously and because these systems can be serviced more readily. In either case, the isotope should be chosen in relation to available counting systems. The most economical isotopically-labeled compounds are ^{14}C-bicarbonate and ^{32}P-phosphoric acid.

Labeling of an appropriate food is quite simple. If ^{32}P is used, the cells may simply be grown in or exposed to a medium containing ^{32}P-PO$_4$ and low levels of ^{31}P-PO$_4$. Such a system will label both heterotrophic and autotrophic cells (Rigler 1961; Burns & Rigler 1967; Haney 1973; Gilbert & Starkweather 1977; Downing & Peters 1980). Primary producers are easily labeled with ^{14}C-bicarbonate, but labeled organic materials are required to label heterotrophes with ^{14}C or ^{3}H (Sorokin 1966, 1968; Gophen *et al.* 1974; Lampert 1974; Hollibaugh *et al.* 1980; De Mott 1982). Since both C and H will be lost from the culture as gases, special precautions should be taken to render the vessel air-tight if long experiments are anticipated (Sorokin 1966; Conover & Francis 1973; Copping & Lorenzen 1980). Many workers have chosen to label cultures for short periods of 6–24 h. This treatment may result in incomplete labeling of the cells—a point of minor interest in feeding rate estimates if pure cell cultures are used but a crucial problem in measurements of feeding rates in multispecific cultures or assimilation (Conover & Francis 1973). Radiotracer estimates of assimilation must derive from cells which were grown in an environment of constant specific activity.

In some cases, ^{14}C (Nauwerck 1959, 1963; Bogdan & McNaught 1975; Griffiths & Caperon 1979), ^{3}H (Hollibaugh *et al.* 1980) and ^{32}P (Webster & Peters 1978) have been used to label natural sestonic assemblages which were subsequently used to estimate grazing rates. It is improbable that the label is spread evenly or consistently among all potential food particles (Knoechel & Kalff 1978); hence the nature of the labeled food must change from day to day and lake to lake. This method is appropriate only for simultaneous comparisons within a single study, and not for quantitative comparisons among different studies or dates, unless uniform labeling can be shown.

Radiotracer techniques usually involve pure cultures. The amount of radioactivity introduced to the culture cannot be specified because variations in counting efficiency, exposure time, and growth conditions will strongly affect the amount of tracer collected by each cell. Ideally, each estimate of A_a in equation 9.16 should be based on a total of 10 000 counts. If small numbers or small animals are to be used, this level may be difficult, though not impossible, to attain. To increase the counts in the animals, workers try to keep the specific activity of the food cell medium as high as possible, usually by reducing the amount of 'carrier' (non-radioactive isotope) to a minimum. Downing & Peters (1980) obtained very radioactive food particles by first introducing a small inoculum of log phase yeast cells to a ^{32}P-labeled carrier-free medium for 1 day and then promoting cell growth by the addition of small amounts of P-rich yeast extract. Smith & Wiebe (1977) found that algae could be made highly radioactive with ^{14}C by incubating the cultures in water which had been purged of dissolved inorganic carbon. The concentration of food cells achieved in a nutrient medium is frequently much greater than that in nature and also, therefore, greater than that which should be used in feeding experiments. This means that levels of radioactivity in the cell cultures must be elevated in order to allow for subsequent dilution of the cell suspension.

After exposure of the food to the tracer for a period ranging from several hours to several days, the cells are usually centrifuged, the supernatant drained off, and the cells resuspended in unlabeled medium. A second or third rinse is a wise precaution. However, excretion by cells may be so rapid (Johannes 1964; Brock & Brock 1969; Hollibaugh *et al.* 1980) that such washes are effective only immediately before the experiment. The actual level of particulate activity should be determined during the experiment by filtering at least 5 ml of feeding solution through a 25 mm, $\leq 0.45\,\mu m$ porosity membrane filter. Absorption of dissolved tracer by the filters produces significant overestimates of particulate tracer if larger filters or smaller volumes are used (Arthur & Rigler 1967). The radioactivity of the material retained on the filter can then be used to determine A_s in equation 9.16.

Unless the researcher wishes to investigate the effects of sudden change on rates of food collection (Runge 1980), the animals should be acclimatized to the experimental concentration of food. The length of this 'pre-feeding' period is normally determined as the time the animals require to feed on unlabeled cells in order to yield consistent feeding rates. Typically, animals are allowed to feed on unlabeled cells for a short time and then grazing and feeding rates are determined. These decline to a more or less constant value after a finite period of feeding, which then determines the minimum pre-feeding time (McMahon and Rigler 1963, 1965; Geller 1975). The appropriate length of the pre-feeding period appears to be 30–60 min for cladocerans (McMahon & Rigler 1963, 1965; Geller 1975) but may last several days in the case of marine calanoids (Mullin 1963; Rigler 1971a; Frost 1972). For those animals, one can only wonder if rates measured early or late in acclimatization approximate normal values.

Soon after the tracer cells are added, the animals must be removed from the suspension, using filtration (Burns & Rigler 1967) before (Haney 1971; Geller 1975) or after (Hayward & Gallup 1976; Horton *et al.* 1979) narcotization with carbonated water or after gentle heating (Saunders, in Rigler 1971a). A number of methods have been proposed to stop feeding. Burns and Rigler (1967) allowed their animals a 2 min 'post-feeding' period in unlabeled cells to allow ingestion or rejection of any radioactive cells in the food groove, while Rigler (1971a) recommends that animals be rinsed to remove any adhering particles. However, any manipulation may cause the animals to lose tracer (Peters & Lean 1973) and it is not possible to recommend any one method. Until careful comparative studies are performed, one can only caution that the method of removal from the feeding suspension should be as gentle as possible.

    Exposure time must be less than gut passage time; this should be
determined in separate experiments, and two methods are commonly used.
The microscopic method involves feeding the animals in a suspension of one
colour and then transferring the animals to a suspension of contrasting
colour. Suspensions of chalk dust, India ink, green algae and yeast have all
been used (Naumann 1921; Bond 1933; Pacaud 1939; Burns & Rigler 1967;
Peters 1972). This produces a sharp transition which moves down the gut with
time. By sampling a number of such animals over time (or following the
movement of the edge in one animal) one can determine the time required for
food to pass through the gut. The same parameter may be estimated
isotopically (Nauwerck 1959; Rigler 1961; Burns & Rigler 1967; Haney 1971),
with the amount of tracer accumulated by different animals feeding on
identical radioactive food for various lengths of time being measured. As
Fig. 9.5 shows, tracer is accumulated at a constant rate, presumably as the gut
fills, until a break in the uptake curve appears. This is presumed to be the point
at which defecation begins. Isotopic and microscopic estimates of gut passage
time concur (Peters 1972; Starkweather & Gilbert 1977b). Gut passage time
increases with body size (Geller 1975), with decreasing temperatures, and
with decreasing food concentrations (Peters 1972). Copepods may have longer
gut passage times than cladocerans (Table 9.1).

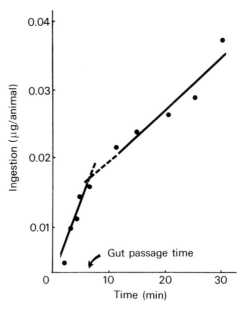

Fig. 9.5 The accumulation of radioactive phosphorus by *Daphnia rosea* feeding on
radioactively labeled yeast showing the decline of tracer uptake rate when
defecation begins (Peters 1972).

Table 9.1 The gut passage time (*GPT*, in min) for zooplankton of different types and weights (W, in µg dry weight) feeding upon different foods. The food concentrations (C, in mg dry weight per litre) are also listed.

Animal	W	Food	C	GPT	Ref.
Calliopus laeviusculus	6000	*Calanus*	—	210	1
Calanus hyperboreus	3100	Large Cells		40	2
		Small Zooplankton			
Rhincalanus nasutus	475	*Prorocentrum*	2	37	3
Pleuromamma xiphias	450	*Streptotheca*	3	28	3
Daphnia pulex	410	Phytoplankton	—	60	4
D. magna	290	*Chlorella*	5	50	5
D. magna	250	*Saccaromyces*	5	45	6
D. magna	140	—	—	55	7
D. magna	140	*Chlorella*	—	25	8
D. pulex	50	—	—	25	7
D. pulex	50	*Scenedesmus*	0·4	59	9
D. pulex		*Asterionella*	1·1	28	9
D. pulex		*Nitzschia*	1·7	48	9
Sida crystallina	30	—	—	60	10
S. crystallina	30	Phytoplankton	—	60	11
Centropages	25	*Gymnodinium*	2	125	3
D. schodleri	20	*Ankistrodesmus*	0·4	135	12
Diaptomus sicilis	11	Phytoplankton		200	13
Daphnia rosea	10	Phytoplankton	—	6	14
D. rosea	10	*Rhodotorula*	5	5	15
D. longispina	10	—	—	25	10
D. longispina	10	—	—	15	7
Diaptomus	8	—	—	30	7
Eudiaptomus gracilis	8	Phytoplankton	—	60	16
Holopedium	7	—	—	15	10
Acartia tonsa	7	*Prorocentrum*	1	55	3
		Prorocentrum	2	60	3
		Prorocentrum	10	37	3
A. tonsa	7	Neutral red	—	25	17
Ceriodaphnia	6	—	—	15	10
Ceriodaphnia	6	Phytoplankton	—	4	14
Daphnia galeata	5	Phytoplankton	—	5	14
D. galeata	5		—	4	7
Bosmina	5	Nannoplankton	—	15	10
Scapholeberis	4	—	—	15	10
Chydorus sphaericus	1	*Rhodotorula*	—	40	11
Brachionus calyciflorus	0·2	*Euglena*	70	20	18
Tintinnid	0·0001	Starch grains		20	19

References: (1) Dagg 1974; (2) Conover 1966a; (3) Arashkevich 1975; (4) Bell & Ward 1970; (5) McMahon 1970; (6) Rigler 1961; (7) Bond 1933; (8) Schindler 1968; (9) Geller 1975; (10) Naumann 1921; (11) Downing 1979; (12) Hayward & Gallup 1976; (13) Kibby 1969; (14) Haney 1971; (15) Burns & Rigler 1967; (16) Nauwerck 1963; (17) Hargis 1977; (18) Starkweather & Gilbert 1977b; (19) Heinbokel 1978b.

Since animals are exposed to labeled cells for a short time, the disturbance involved in adding labeled cells or removing animals may result in anomalous feeding rates. Experiments such as that in Fig. 9.5, should reveal such effects as a discontinuity in tracer uptake after very short (< 5 min) exposures. If such a plot extrapolates through zero one may assume that ingestion rates were constant over the course of the experiment.

The animals should be removed quickly from the sieve or rinse water and placed on planchets or in liquid scintillation vials (Downing & Peters 1980). Delays at this point may result in leaching of tracer to the rinse water by autolysis (Golterman 1964; Krause 1964), by loss of the haemolymph (Rigler 1971a; Ikeda *et al.* 1982) or by defecation of the gut contents. Such losses may reduce grazing rate estimates by up to 70 % (Downing & Peters 1980; Holtby & Knoechel 1981) depending on post-experimental treatment of the animals. Holtby & Knoechel (1981) suggest that losses from ^{32}P-labeled yeast and ^{14}C-labeled algae are minimized if ethanol or Lugol's solution, respectively, serve as killing agents or if chemical preservatives are avoided entirely. They recommend killing in near boiling water and then drying. Downing & Peters (1980) chose only to minimize the lag between collection and plating of the animals.

If Geiger–Müller counting systems are used, the animals should be placed in a single stratum close to the centre of the planchet to increase counting efficiency. If a weakly penetrating isotope is used, they should be dismembered. The animals may be covered with Parafilm® discs to prevent loss of material and to ease subsequent handling (Rigler 1971a).

If liquid scintillation is anticipated, two methods of counting may be employed, depending on the isotope. Hard beta emitters, like ^{32}P, produce a light called Cerenkov radiation, which may be effectively counted by a liquid scintillation system though the glass liquid scintillation vial contains only water (Haberer 1966; Fox 1976; J.Haney, personal communication). Weaker emitters are normally digested overnight in tissue solubilizer, an organic base like NCS®, Protosol®, or Soluene® (Ward *et al.* 1970; Lampert 1977a) before adding the scintillation 'cocktail'. Addition of tissue solubilizers to scintillation cocktails can alter their pH, causing high background counts due to chemoluminescence and unpredictable shifts in apparent energy spectra. It is a wise precaution to acidify the sample with a small amount of glacial acetic acid—Hall (1978) added 0·3 ml of acid per litre of scintillation fluid, Downing (1979) suggests 30 μl or 'two tiny drops' and DeMott (1982) 50 μl of glacial acetic acid per 10 ml of cocktail. Combustion of animals and food in an oxygen atmosphere either manually (Bell & Ward 1968) or automatically (using a system like Intertechnique's Oximat®) for ^{14}C and ^{3}H provide alternatives to digestion in an organic base. In any liquid scintillation system, there is a possibility that emissions will be 'quenched' to different degrees, because contaminants in the sample absorb some of the scintillations. Quench corrections must be routinely applied to all work. Researchers who intend to use any radioisotopic technique should acquaint themselves with the basic of these methods by reference to standard works (e.g. Wang & Willis 1965; Fox 1976).

Liquid scintillation can distinguish between isotopes which emit particles of different energy (e.g. ^3H and ^{14}C; ^{14}C and ^{32}P; ^{32}P and ^{33}P). This allows simultaneous estimation of grazing on two different particles (Lampert 1974; Starkweather & Gilbert 1978; Downing 1981a). In such experiments, the activity of the low energy emitter is counted over one, low, range or 'window' of emitted energies and the activity of the high energy emitter in three. Standard curves permit an estimation of 'crosstalk', the proportion of all counts in the lowest window which are derived from the high energy particle, from the ratio of counts in the two upper windows. Although this method is much more limited than Coulter counters, it can be used to compare grazing rates on similar sized particles and could be used to check Coulter counter estimates. Dual isotope experiments are also possible with Geiger–Müller counters. If one selects two isotopes with different decay characteristics, levels of activity of each isotope may be determined.

(1)   By curve splitting (Riggs 1970) using plots of total activity against time.
(2)   By waiting until one isotope disappears and then determining initial levels of the decayed isotope by difference.
(3)   By using isotopes that penetrate different materials to different degrees.

In the latter case, the counts are determined before and after the weak emitter is blocked by some material such as aluminum foil, and the counts of each isotope are determined by difference; self-absorption corrections will be necessary. Although these possibilities have existed for some time they have rarely been exploited.

There are several limitations to radioactive estimates of feeding rate. Because the experiments must be short, discontinuous feeding (Conover 1966a; Rosenberg 1980) or diel patterns in feeding behavior (Haney & Hall 1975; Starkweather 1975) can result in considerable variations. The necessary disturbance of the animals caused by adding the labeled cells and removing the zooplankton may create unnatural rates. If natural foods or mixtures of species are used, it is impractical to have identical labeled and unlabeled cell suspensions for pre-feeding and experimental food. Instead, highly radio-active cells of one species, usually yeast (Burns & Rigler 1967), small algae (Chisholm *et al.* 1975), or bacteria (Haney 1973) are introduced into the food suspension at a very low concentration (<1000 cells ml^{-1}). Such experiments yield grazing rates on this radioactive particle, but rates on the unlabeled cells are often assumed to be the same. The validity of this assumption has not been rigorously tested (Haney 1973). Loss of tracer by excretion or mastication usually results in underestimates of only a few percent (Rigler 1971a; Peters 1975a) but mastication loss may rise to 10–15 % if large cells are used, at least for *Daphnia* (Lampert 1978).

3.4 *Field estimates of feeding and grazing*

If our laboratory experiments are to be of ecological significance they must be relevant to the field. A number of workers have tried to extend laboratory estimates of ingestion to lakes by multiplication of laboratory feeding or grazing rates and population densities (Heinle 1974; Nauwerck 1963). The usual goal of such calculations is to show whether zooplankton ingestion can significantly affect phytoplankton populations. Thus Jassby & Goldman (1974) were able to show that, in Castle Lake, zooplankton populations were far too low (apparently $< 11^{-1}$) to explain algal population dynamics. Coveney *et al.* (1977) reached the same conclusions for a small eutrophic lake with much higher zooplankton densities. Lampert & Schober (1978) applied laboratory feeding rates to field population densities and showed that zooplankton may control summer phytoplankton density in Lake Constance. Gliwicz & Hilbricht-Ilkowska (1975; Gliwicz 1970) considered both grazing rate and food selection by zooplankton and found that, in eutrophic lakes, phytoplankton are less affected by zooplankton grazing than are bacteria. Nauwerck (1963) and Gulati (1975) calculated that observed primary production was insufficient to meet the demands of zooplankton; they suggested that bacteria and detritus must be utilized by the animals.

These calculations are extremely interesting, but unless field rates can be shown to correspond to laboratory values, one should treat such extrapolations with suspicion. Unfortunately, few field measurements have been made and still fewer have been made in a manner which would allow comparisons with laboratory data.

The simplest approximation to field measurements is achieved by placing animals in a beaker of natural lake water. Grazing rate can then be estimated by either microscopic (McQueen 1970) or electronic (Allan *et al.* 1977; Poulet 1977; Richman *et al.* 1977) cell counts or by changes in suspended carbon or chlorophyll (Hargis 1977; Taguchi & Ishi 1972). Radiotracer estimates are possible, using either radioactively labeled phytoplankton (Nauwerck 1959, 1963; Zankai & Ponyi 1974a, 1974b, 1976; Bogdan & McNaught 1975; Gulati 1975) or by introducing a low concentration of radioactively labeled cells of one species (Burns & Rigler 1967) into the lake water. Such experiments require handling, enclosure, and changes in a number of other factors; it is, therefore, questionable how accurately these measurements reflect field rates.

The measurement of grazing rates on natural bacteria presents a special problem. Such cells are so small (Peterson *et al.* 1978), that they lie below the lower limit of the Coulter counter, and they are not obvious under normal microscopy: These can be isotopically labeled but there is a risk of uneven labeling of freshly collected natural populations, and cultured bacteria cannot be used because they are much larger in size. The only practicable alternative appears to be cell counts after staining the bacteria with a fluorescing stain such as 4'6-diamidino-2-phenyl indole (DAPI; Coleman 1980; Porter & Feig 1980) or fluorescein isothiocyanate (FITC: Fliermans & Schmidt 1976).

Very few workers have attempted to measure feeding rates *in situ*, and most of the experiments have been performed using some modification of Gliwicz's (1968) experimental chamber (Fig. 9.6). This is a clear plastic

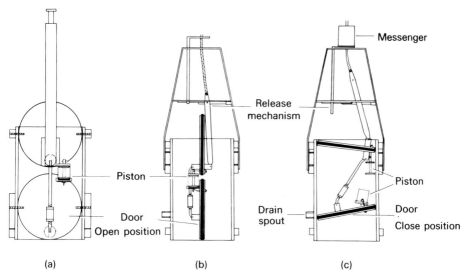

Fig. 9.6 Haney's (1971) modification of Gliwicz' (1968) *in situ* grazing chamber for the measurement of filtering rate by planktonic filter feeders (modified from Haney 1971).

plankton trap or water sampler which, when lowered into a lake and closed, encloses a volume of water and simultaneously opens a small piston inside the chamber. Gliwicz (1968) used two such samplers—one simply trapped and held zooplankton in lake water at a particular depth; the other released a narcotic (physostigmium salicyclum) from the piston into the water. This substance stopped zooplankton feeding in 5–30 min. Both chambers were then held at the collection depth and inverted every 20 min to prevent settling of the seston. After 4 h, subsamples from each chamber were preserved for later microscopic determination of the number of particles in each chamber, from which the feeding rates of the zooplankton community were calculated.

The obvious advantage of this system is the reduction of any change in the physical, chemical, or biological environment of the animals.

Haney (1971) used a similar device for *in situ* radiotracer experiments: the piston was filled with ^{32}P-labeled cells (yeast, bacteria or algae) and the closure of the chamber released and mixed these particles into the water. After 5 min, the trap was withdrawn from the lake and drained through a sieve. The animals were then anaesthetized with carbonated water and killed with formalin. Haney (1971, 1973; Haney & Hall 1975) then either measured the radioactivity in the entire sample for total grazing rates of the zooplankton community or picked animals from the sieve for individual grazing rates. This technique has most of the advantages of Gliwicz's approach but is much more rapid and permits estimates of both spatial and temporal variation in grazing rates. Using this approach, Haney (1973) identified a new parameter for lake ecosystems, community grazing rate. (G_c, day^{-1}) which is calculated as:

$$G_c = A_a 60 \times 24/VA_s t \qquad (9.18)$$

where A_a is the radioactivity of all animals in the feeding chamber (c.p.m.) at the end of the experiment, A_s is the radioactivity of the suspended food (c.p.m./ml), V is the volume of the chamber (ml) and t is time the animals were allowed to feed (min). Community grazing rate represents the mortality that the entire animal plankton imposed on all algae which are as suitable as the tracer particle as food. Haney found that the predation pressure on the nannoplankton was far more intense in eutrophic than in oligotrophic or dystrophic lakes. This might lead to increased sedimentation in the latter systems, affecting both patterns of nutrient flow and the balance between benthic and planktonic secondary production in lakes (Rigler, personal communication). Regrettably, few researchers have adopted Haney's technique and those who have used it (Kibby & Rigler 1973; Peters 1975b; Waite 1976) have usually measured individual rather than community rates.

These *in situ* techniques are not without problems. Only one type of radioactive particle is used at a time, so that measured grazing rates refer only to this particle type. Sieving of the animals at the end of the feeding period may be a harsh treatment which results in loss of radioactivity. The method measures the animal's behavior only over a small segment of time, and repetitive sampling is necessary to determine daily rates (Haney & Hall 1975). However, the method requires less effort than laboratory radiotracer measurements and certainly yields data which are closer to nature.

Haney's method has been modified to measure the feeding rate of littoral animals associated with macrophytes (Downing & Peters 1980). A 6-litre plexiglass box was placed around a macrophyte (Fig. 9.7), trapping animals associated with the plant. A suspension of radioactively labeled yeast cells was injected from a syringe into the chamber. After 10 min, the chamber was

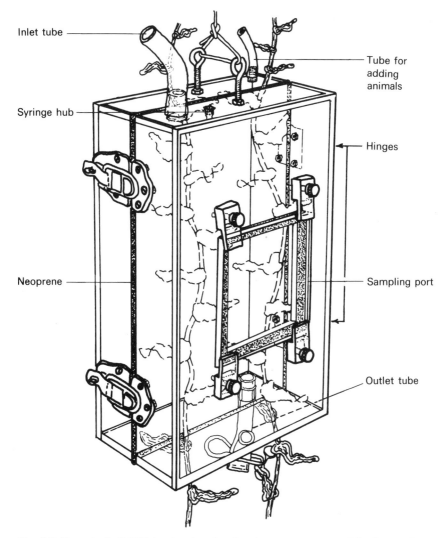

Fig. 9.7 Downing's (1981) *in situ* chamber for the measurement of feeding and filtering by littoral microcrustaceans.

drained through a Nitex® screen. Animals so collected were anaesthetized with carbonated water and then preserved in sucrose-formalin solution (Haney & Hall 1973) until they could be separated into individual liquid scintillation vials. Grazing rates were calculated from equation 9.16 and feeding rates were approximated as the product of grazing rate and the concentration of seston which passed a 35 μm mesh screen.

Downing (1981) further modified this technique to estimate the rates of ingestion of both suspended and periphytic foods. After the plant was enclosed, he injected $0.1-0.5$ mCi of $^{32}PO_4$ solution into the chamber. After 1–3 days, the tracer was distributed proportionately among different size fractions. Suspended ^{32}P was then reduced to a minimum by pumping unlabeled lake water through the chamber. Animals already in the chamber were unsuitable for feeding experiments because they were, of course, labeled with ^{32}P. Instead, animals were collected from nearby plants and introduced into the chamber with a wide bore syringe. Immediately afterwards, a suspension of tritium-labeled yeast cells was also injected into the chamber. Samples of macrophyte were then withdrawn to determine the amount of $^{32}P(A_p)$ in 'loose' periphytic material (Cattaneo & Kalff 1978) per unit weight of macrophyte. Samples of suspension were taken for later estimates of the amounts of tritium (A_{st}) and $^{32}P(A_{sp})$ in suspension. After 10 min the animals were collected as above and the amounts of tritium (A_{at}) and $^{32}P(A_{ap})$ in each animal was measured. Grazing rates $(G, ml\ day^{-1})$ were determined from the tritium counts using equation 9.16. Rates of ingestion of periphytic material $(I_p,\ in\ \mu g\ animal^{-1}\ day^{-1})$ were calculated as:

$$I_p = 24(A_{ap} - G.A._{sp}.t/24)/A_p t \qquad (9.19)$$

where t is the length of the experiment in hours.

An approximation of *in situ* feeding rates may be made from the contents of animals' guts and the turnover time of these contents or gut passage time (Mackas & Bohrer 1976; Boyd *et al.* 1980; Dagg & Grill 1980). First, one estimates fullness of the gut at a series of sample times. Gut passage time is then estimated in separate experiments. The sampling interval divided by the gut passage time yields an estimate of the number of times that the gut has filled over the interval. Multiplication by gut contents gives ingestion over the interval and division by interval yields the feeding rate. Grazing rate is calculated by division by food concentration in the medium. This is a very rough estimate because gut passage time is variable (Table 9.1) and 'food concentration' of natural waters is difficult to assess.

3.5 *Feeding rates of other organisms*

Estimates of predation rate (number of prey killed individual^{-1} unit time^{-1}) and ingestion rate of predaceous zooplankton such as cyclopoids (Anderson 1970; Smyly 1970; Confer 1971; Brandl & Fernando 1975), calanoids (Anraku & Omori 1963; Ambler & Frost 1974; Dodson 1974) raptorial cladocerans like *Leptodora* (Hillbricht-Ilkowska & Karabin 1970) and dipterous larvae like *Chaoborus* (Kajak & Ranke-Rybickova 1970; Swift & Fedorenko 1973; Lewis 1977) are becoming more frequent in the literature. The basic techniques and problems are identical to those used in the cell count method except that small animals, nauplii, copepodites, rotifers, or cladocerans, replace algal or bacterial cells. The prey are counted at intervals and their mortality rate is calculated, generally by assuming an exponential decline in prey numbers (equation 9·2). Since many predators only partly ingest their prey (Ambler & Frost 1974; Dagg 1974; Brandl & Fernando 1975), measurement of mortality rate of the prey will give an overestimate of the amount of food ingested and researchers should, therefore, be careful to collect discarded animal parts if ingestion rates are important to their study. Lawton (1970) points out that prey animals may lose a considerable proportion of their weight if not fed during experiments (Lemcke & Lampert 1975; Threlkeld 1976), thus ingestion rate would be over-estimated if initial prey weights were used in calculation. Since animal prey are more motile than algae they can aggregate in parts of the experimental vessel, producing heterogeneous prey distribution. This might result in apparent food selectivity due to differential availability of prey and will certainly affect estimates of prey density. Finally, some prey can escape from certain predators more easily than others (Confer 1971; Dodson 1974; Fedorenko 1975; Kerfoot 1977; Lewis 1977), so that the type of prey offered may influence the results of experiments. Ambler & Frost (1974) say that the widely used *Artemia* nauplius is slow compared to other tiny zooplankton and estimates based on these prey items may overestimate both predation and ingestion rates.

Less effort has been placed on the measurement of feeding and grazing rates by rotifers or ciliates than on crustaceans. Studies of rotifers (Hirayama & Ogawa 1972; Doohan 1973; Gilbert & Starkweather 1977; Pilarska 1977; Pourriot 1977; Starkweather & Gilbert 1977a; Gilbert & Bogdan 1981; Starkweather 1981) have usually employed variations of the cell count or radioisotopic methods. These can also be applied to ciliates (Laybourne 1975; Laybourn & Stewart 1975). Fenchel (1975) has employed an interesting technique, similar to that of Mackas & Bohrer (1976), to measure the ingestion rate of protozoans. After a feeding period on algae or bacteria, he stained the animals with acridine orange and determined the rate constant of decline in the number of food cells in vacuoles. He then assumed that the number of vacuolar food items was maintained in the field by an ingestion rate which balanced these laboratory loss rates and calculated ingestion rate as the product of the number of food particles in field specimens and the rate constant of loss. Subsequently, Fenchel (1980b) has determined the grazing rate of ciliates in a suspension of latex beads by counting the number of beads in the food vacuoles. Rassoulzadegan & Etienne (1981) have successfully used a Coulter counter technique to estimate feeding rates of a tintinnid ciliate. Heinbokel (1978a, 1978b) has also estimated the feeding rates of tintinnids using cell counts in laboratory cultures and by counting starch grains ingested by natural protozoan populations.

Gliwicz's chamber has also been used to measure rates of predation. Hillbricht-Ilkowska & Karabin (1970) placed several *Leptodora kindtii* in the piston and measured the reduction in zooplankton populations after closure of the chamber relative to the lake. Kajak & Ranke-Rybickova (1970) used a similar technique with *Chaoborus*, but used a second sampler without *Chaoborus* as a control. Lane *et al.* (1975) put prey organisms, marked with acridine orange, in the piston and counted the decline of these organisms. Both approaches require handling of either prey or predators but again seem preferable to experiments performed completely in the laboratory. It should be noted that some brands of acridine orange are toxic to cladocerans (Downing 1980); this could have contributed to the very high rates of zooplankton mortality reported by Lane *et al.* (1975). In addition, stain may be lost from potential prey in the course of longer experiments. Lasenby (1979) believes that realistic predation rates may be estimated using this basic technique even if a Haney trap is unavailable. He marked *Limnocalanus* with Rhodamine b and added a known number to carboys containing *Mysis* and uncounted, unmarked copepods. He then estimated mortality rate from the loss of marked animals and the final concentration of unmarked copepods. Lasenby (1979) warns that prolonged staining (> 3 min) increased mortality and that neither cyclopoids nor cladocerans stain well. Other stains might circumvent some of these problems.

3.6 *Factors influencing grazing and feeding rates*

It is not my purpose to review the published literature exhaustively (see Jørgensen 1966; Marshall 1973; Porter 1977; Pourriot 1977; Conover 1978). However, the researcher who intends to work with suspension feeding should be aware of the range of factors which have been shown to be important, if only so that more effective controls may be devised.

Although there may be disagreement as to the magnitude of effect, physical and chemical factors which influence metabolic rates of any animal may be assumed to influence grazing and feeding by zooplankton. There is typically a thermal optimum (Anraku 1964; Zankai & Ponyi 1974; Geller 1975; Kersting & van der Leeuw 1976), which is influenced by acclimatization (Kibby 1971). Low oxygen levels (20–40 % saturation) reduce grazing rates of *Daphnia* (Fox *et al.* 1951; Heisey & Porter 1977; Hoshi & Kobayashi 1971; Kring & O'Brien 1976a). The intensity and quality of light have not been shown, unequivocally, to influence feeding rate (McMahon 1965; Buikema 1973, 1975), although they obviously influence behavior (e.g. Smith & Baylor 1953; Hairston 1976; Horton *et al.* 1979). Haney & Hall (1975) argue that diel changes in light intensity at dawn and dusk induce a strong increase in the grazing rate of cladocerans, but not of copepods. Similar observations have subsequently been made in the laboratory (Starkweather 1975, 1978). The effect of pH also seems highly variable (Ivanova 1969; Ivanova & Klebowski 1972) perhaps reflecting, in part, physiological plasticity (Kring & O'Brien 1976b).

The physiological status of the zooplankter may influence rates of food collection: male calanoids graze more slowly than females (Conover 1956; Nauwerck 1959; Harris & Paffenhöfer 1976b) but the reverse may be true for cladocerans (Hayward & Gallup 1976). Egg-bearing *Diaptomus*, which are presumably healthy animals, graze faster than non-ovigerous females (Nauwerck 1959; Zankai and Ponyi 1976) and ephippiate *Daphnia* graze at slower rates than parthenogenetic females (Haney & Hall 1975). There is some evidence that the grazing rate of juvenile animals may be less affected by experimental conditions than that of adults. Haney & Hall (1975) report that diel variations are more pronounced among larger daphnids. Chisholm *et al.* (1975) found that large *Daphnia* are more sensitive to temperature than small animals. Both feeding and grazing rates increase with animal body size (McMahon & Rigler 1963; Suschenya 1967, 1970; Burns 1969a; Kibby & Rigler 1973; Allan *et al.* 1977; Paffenhöfer & Knowles 1978; and many others).

As one would expect, zooplankton have some maximum and minimum sizes for foods which they consume and, within this range, some food sizes are more effectively handled than others. While Gliwicz (1977) offers some evidence for this, most studies on the effect of food size depend upon gut analyses without effective statistical treatment (Burns 1968b; Wilson 1973; Nadin-Hurley & Duncan 1976), or on Coulter counter experiments which confuse ingestion and particle modification. As a result, there is little good evidence for size selection. Figure 9.8 shows that experimenters believe that cladocerans prefer smaller cells than copepods, and these frequency distributions may summarize our intuitions regarding food sizes eaten by members of the two groups. Feeding experiments suggest that calanoids may feed less effectively upon small particles (McQueen 1970; Kibby & Rigler 1973; Paffenhöfer & Knowles 1978) but their behavior is quite variable (Bogdan & McNaught 1975; Gliwicz 1977). It is also possible that freshwater copepods prefer smaller particles than their marine relatives. Cladocerans, and especially small cladocerans, may prefer smaller particles (Nadin-Hurley & Duncan 1976; Gliwicz 1977) but the size range over which effective collection is possible ranges from $0.1 \ \mu m^3$ to $10^6 \ \mu m^3$ (McMahon & Rigler 1963; Peterson *et al.* 1978; Porter *et al.* 1979).

A number of authors have found that the quality of the food organism influences feeding rates. In particular, blue-green algae are frequently rejected as food (Burns 1968a; Webster & Peters 1978; Porter & Orcutt 1980) or are grazed at a lower rate (Tezuka 1971; Crowley 1973; Infante 1973; Geller 1975; Lampert 1981). Some interactions probably occur among food types. For

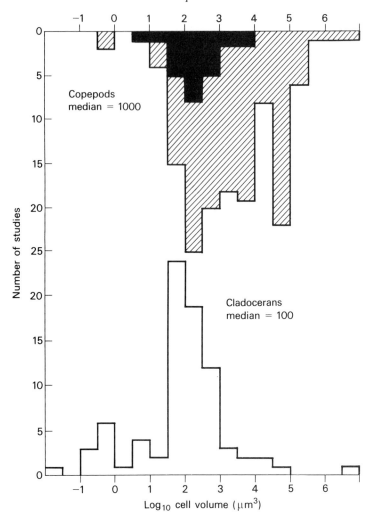

Fig. 9.8 Frequency distribution of food sizes used in the measurement of feeding as filtering rates for calanoids and cladocerans. The contribution of freshwater copepods is indicated by the solid histogram. This figure suggests that most researchers believe that cladocerans prefer smaller particles than do calanoid copepods.

example, rejection of a food bolus containing blue-green algae must reduce feeding rates on all cells. The presence of larger algal cells appears to increase feeding rates on smaller bacterial foods (DeMott 1982). Not all strains of blue-green algae have this effect (O'Brien & DeNoyelles 1974; Porter & Orcutt 1980) and some animals ingest and grow on a diet of blue-greens (Arnold 1972; De Bernardi *et al.* 1981). Esaias & Curl (1972) found that bioluminescent dinoflagellates were eaten less readily than non-luminescent cultures.

Finally, food concentration has a marked influence on both feeding and grazing rates. A number of mathematical formulae have been applied to curves such as those in Fig. 9.3 (Rigler 1971a) which relate feeding rate (f) to food concentration (S). These are usually called:

(1) The rectilinear model, which implies a constant grazing rate below the incipient limiting food concentration.
(2) The curvilinear model, which implies a decelerating grazing rate as food concentration increases.
(3) The Ivlev model, which permits a reduction in grazing rate at very low food concentrations (Fig. 9.9).

Porter *et al.* (1982) found that a power curve ($f = aS^b$), a logarithmic curve ($f = a + b \ln S$), and a hyperbolic curve ($f = a + b/S$) also fit such data. However, attempts to distinguish which of these various models is best (Frost 1972; Mullin *et al.* 1975; Corner *et al.* 1976; Harris & Paffenhöfer 1976a; Heinbokel 1978a) have not been able to identify any one as better than the others. The rectilinear model typically has higher correlation coefficients. However, since the same data (i.e. food concentrations) are frequently incorporated in both axes, these plots involve a degree of autocorrelation and least squares regression may be biased and inappropriate. If low enough food levels are used, plots of grazing rate against food concentration can distinguish the rectilinear model from others (Fig. 9.9). By plotting grazing, rather than feeding, rate against food concentration, Frost (1975) has clearly shown that *Calanus* will reduce its grazing rate at very low concentrations.

The foregoing factors may be expected to have an influence in nature and we should obviously control for their effects in laboratory experiments.

Factors which are clearly artefacts of our experimental techniques also influence our determinations of feeding and grazing rates. Crowding reduces the grazing rate of both copepods (Lucas 1936; Hargrave & Geen 1970) and cladocerans (Hayward & Gallup 1976). Starvation may lead to rapid initial rate of grazing and feeding (Lucas 1936; McMahon & Rigler 1963; McAllister 1970; Frost 1972; Hirayama & Ogawa 1972; Geller 1975). A number of workers have found that the grazing rate of copepods is reduced in very small vessels (Marshall & Orr 1955; Cushing 1958; Anraku 1964; Corner *et al.* 1972), but most of this earlier work assumed that maximum and natural rates were achieved in the largest container used (about 500 ml). Paffenhöfer (1971, 1976; Harris & Paffenhöfer 1976a, 1976b; Paffenhöfer & Harris 1976; Paffenhöfer & Knowles 1978) have since shown that the rates can increase another order of magnitude if vessels of several litres are used. This raises the possibility that most published values for calanoids are underestimates.

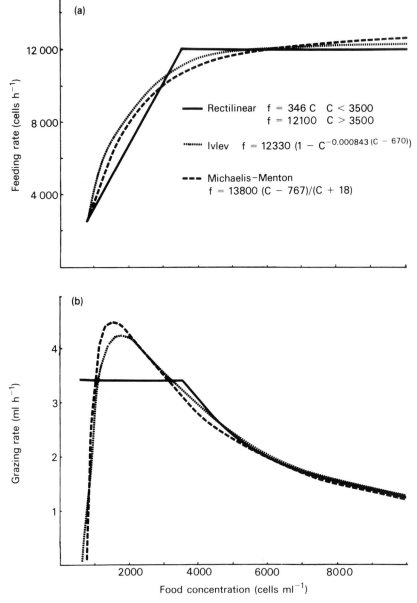

Fig. 9.9 Three models which describe feeding rate as a function of food concentrations (a) and their solution to provide grazing rates (b). Each model is an equally good description of the data (Frost 1972) on which the models are based. Panel (a) is modified from Mullin *et al.* (1975). The rectilinear model provides quite different descriptions of filtering rate at low food concentrations and this may permit one to distinguish the appropriate model (Frost 1975).

Finally, the age of the cell culture used in feeding experiments has been shown to influence feeding; senescent cultures are eaten less readily than those in exponential growth (Ryther 1954; McMahon & Rigler 1963; Mullin 1963; Marshall & Orr 1966).

The effects of these sources of variation on estimates of feeding or grazing rates are difficult to judge. Certainly, they reduce the absolute value; however, it is also possible any qualitative trends observed in such experiments—such as the effects of food size or animal body weight—are also unnatural. Rigler (1971a) pleaded for greater care in experimentation and further study of these artefacts. Although most of us are not interested in the behavior of starving animals feeding on unpalatable and monotonous foods, crowded into small beakers etc., these effects can bias our results. We should put more effort into the evaluation of such effects.

3.7 *Average experimental conditions*

The number of factors which can influence determinations of grazing and feeding rates may daunt a researcher seeking to enter this field. Ideally, one would examine the effect of all aspects of the experimental treatment on the animals and the results. However, few of us have the time to study all potential sources of error, and we must turn instead to the literature for some direction in planning our experiments.

Such searches are often haphazard. To provide a more quantitative summary of some aspects of experimental design, the literature surveyed in preparing this review is summarized in Table 9.2. This shows the mean, median, mode and range of values reported for seven variables which are likely to affect grazing rate estimation. One cannot assume that any of these values are good, in the sense that observations made under these conditions are unbiased. At best, one can only hope that such values are no worse than others in the literature.

For comparison, it may be instructive to consider the range which such variables may take in nature. Straškraba (1980) compiled the average annual surface temperature of moderate-sized lakes. He found a range between 1 and 20°C and a range of 0–30°C is probably sufficient to represent the range in lakes. Ponds and puddles may be somewhat warmer. The concentration of naturally occurring phytoplankton varies between 0·3 and 100 p.p.m. by volume (McCauley & Kalff 1981). Nannoplankton concentrations, which may better reflect available food, range from 0·1 to 10 p.p.m. (Watson & Kalff 1981). Planktonic crustacean concentrations range from 0·06 to 70 p.p.m. (by volume). This corresponds to about 1–700 animals, each weighing 10 μg dry weight, per litre. The volume of water per animal is therefore between 1·4 and 1000 ml.

Table 9.2 Summary of typical conditions and independent variables used in the estimation of filtering and feeding rates of cladocerans and calanoid copepods. The values listed in this table summarize those used in the literature and do not represent recommended values. W = animal dry weight, μg; S = food concentration, p.p.m. by volume; V_i = cell volume, μm^3; T = temperature, °C; H = volume per animal, ml; M = experimental duration, min; L = total volume of experimental vessel, litres.

	Median	Mode	Mean	Range	n
Cladocerans					
W	20	10	26	0·5–300	191
S	4·5	0·8	4·5	0·38–180	160
V_i	50	50	68	0·1–6 150 000	190
T	20	20	18·6	5–35	179
H	6	8	15·8	1–80	86
M	30	30	198	2–1440	158
L	0·125	0·125	0·441	0·004–10	190
Calanoids					
W	11	195	35	0·4–74 000	429
S	2·8	0·5	2·9	0·02–510	411
V_i	2500	2500	5370	0·5–6 900 000	303
T	15	15	12·4	2–35	340
H	20	3	88·7	1–400	245
M	1440	1440	1219	5–13 300	364
L	0·500	0·700	0·187	0·010–10	352

3.8 Comparison of methods

Surprisingly, few scientists have made direct comparisons of available methods for the estimation of feeding by zooplankton. To augment these comparisons, I have plotted weight specific rates of grazing for calanoid copepods and cladocerans measured with four basic techniques. Figure 9.10 shows first that workers with cladocerans have favoured short-term tracer experiments while workers studying calanoids prefer to use Coulter counters.

Grazing rates generated by the various techniques are quite variable and hence there is considerable overlap among methods. Long-term tracer experiments may yield values slightly lower than other techniques. Those grazing rates obtained using Coulter counters or cell counts are the most variable. However, the variability of grazing rates (5 orders of magnitude) makes it difficult to separate the distributions for different techniques.

When frequency diagrams of the weight specific grazing rates of the two groups are prepared, ignoring the methods used, the histograms in Fig. 9.11

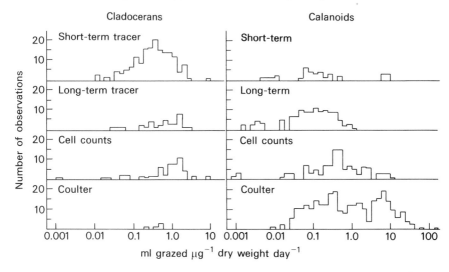

Fig. 9.10 Frequency distribution of weight specific grazing rates for cladocerans and calanoid copepods measured with four different techniques. Data were collected from an intensive literature survey, but only one point for each combination of food type and zooplankton species was taken from each publication. The variance in the literature does not seem to result from methodological differences.

are obtained. These show that, although calanoid copepods may filter at higher rates than cladocerans and show more variation, the median values for the two groups are identical. The higher variation in copepods probably represents their greater range of feeding behavior and their greater sensitivity to experimental conditions. The high values almost always reflect the use of large (i.e. $\geq 2 \cdot 5$ l) experimental vessels. Figures 9.12 and 9.13 are similar plots for feeding rate.

The similarity of the median values is in contrast to the results of several experiments which compared cladoceran and calanoid grazing rates (Nauwerck 1963; Haney 1973; Bogdan & McNaught 1975). These suggest that copepods graze at lower rates than cladocerans. However, most of these experiments used methods (small volumes, small cells) which are more appropriate for cladocerans and may underestimate the potential of copepods.

The comparisons in Figs 9.10 and 9.12 are necessarily coarse and they must be interpreted in the light of direct experimental confrontation obtained by various methods. Conover & Francis (1973) measured grazing rate with cell

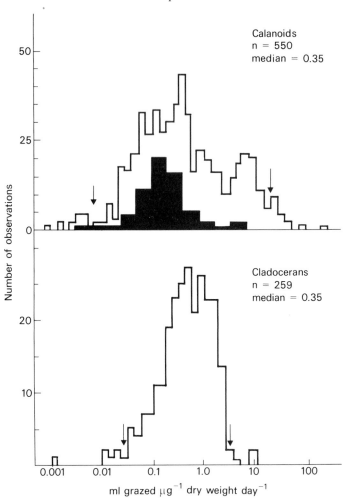

Fig. 9.11 Frequency distribution of weight specific grazing rates for cladocerans and calanoid copepods, regardless of method used. 95% of all points lie between the arrows. Although calanoids have shown a greater range in measured rates the median values are similar. Freshwater calanoids are represented by the solid histogram, which uses a larger interval.

counts and long-term tracer experiments. They concluded that the latter underestimate G and so confirmed the reservations of Sorokin (1968). Nauwerck (1959, 1963) employed both cell counts and short-term tracer experiments and found that the cell count method gave somewhat higher values (5 versus 3 ml individual^{-1} day^{-1}). However, his experiments were not paired and he preferred the tracer method because of its greater rapidity and

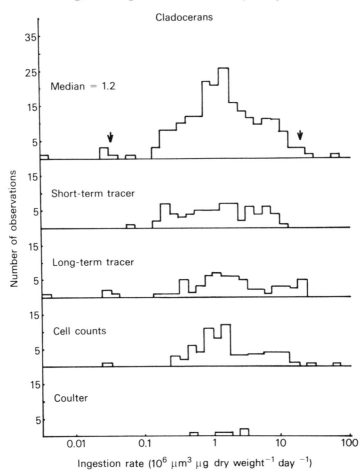

Fig. 9.12 Frequency distributions of weight specific ingestion rates for cladocerans measured with four different techniques. The upper panel shows a cumulative distribution ignoring methodology.

precision. Richman & Rogers (1969) measured the feeding rate of *Calanus* on single and paired cells using a Coulter counter and a radiotracer technique. They reported that Coulter counts showed higher grazing rates on double than on single cells, but the short-term radiotracer estimate for animals feeding on a labeled mixture of both types was as high as that measured for paired cells using a Coulter counter. This suggests that breakage of the paired cells resulted in underestimates of the grazing rates on single cells as measured by the Coulter counter. If both methods were equally effective the tracer estimate would have been lower than observed. Taguchi & Fukuchi (1975) and Taguchi & Ishi (1972) compared the grazing rate of *Calanus* measured from changes in

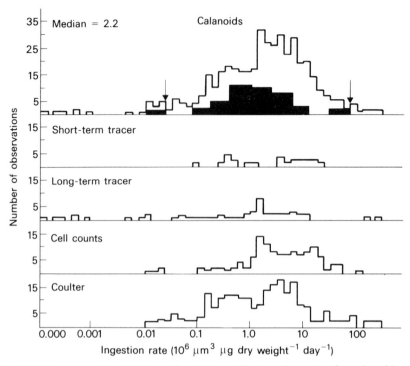

Fig. 9.13 Frequency distributions of weight specific ingestion rates for calanoids measured with four different techniques. The upper panel shows a cumulative distribution ignoring methodology. Freshwater calanoids are represented by the solid histogram which uses a larger interval.

cell number, chlorophyll concentration, sestonic carbon concentration, and (in smaller vessels) long-term incorporation of ^{14}C from labeled cells. They found that chlorophyll and ^{14}C gave similar estimates but were lower than grazing rates estimated from changes in carbon concentration or cell counts. Hargis (1977) compared the grazing rates of *Acartia* on small natural phytoplankton using Coulter counts, change in chlorophyll and short term uptake of ^{14}C from labeled cells. His results were quite variable and no statistical difference existed among the methods. Haney's (1973) *in situ* estimates of the grazing rate of *Daphnia* can be compared to those obtained by adding radioactive cells to a sample of lake water in a beaker (Burns & Rigler 1967). Although these experiments were conducted in different years, both studies used the same species of zooplankton from the same lake, and measured grazing rate using short-term tracer experiments in which ^{32}P-labeled *Rhodotorula* was the tracer particle. Both experiments gave grazing rates which were $\frac{1}{2}$ to $\frac{1}{6}$ of those predicted on the basis of measured grazing rates in single species suspensions of food.

These comparisons suggest that long-term tracer experiments may underestimate grazing rates and that the other techniques are roughly comparable. However, no set of comparisons has been conducted under a range of conditions and available comparisons often differ in more than the method of evaluating changes in cell concentration. More intensive study is required before any one method can be unhesitatingly recommended.

3.9 Calculated grazing and feeding rates

One often wishes to estimate the feeding or grazing rates of zooplankton but is unable to invest the time and effort required to make adequate measurements. To meet this need, Peters & Downing (in preparation) performed multiple regression analyses of the data used to construct Figs. 9.10–9.13. These analyses predict grazing rate (in ml animal^{-1} day^{-1}) or feeding rate (in μg wet weight of food animal^{-1} day^{-1}) from animal dry weight (W, in μg), food concentration (S, in p.p.m. volume/volume), individual food cell size (V_i, in μm^3), temperature (T, in degrees centigrade), volume of water per animal (H, in ml), experiment duration (M, in minutes), and container volume (L, in liters). Of these factors only those which had a significant ($p < 5\%$) effect were retained in their regression equations. For cladocerans, the equations are:

$$\log_{10} G = 0.173 + 0.75 \log_{10} W - 0.43 \log_{10} S - 0.33L + 0.014H$$
$$(n = 70;\ R^2 = 0.68) \qquad (9.20)$$

$$\log_{10} f = -1.34 + 0.49 \log_{10} S + 0.59 \log_{10} W + 0.014H$$
$$- 0.16(\log_{10} V_i)^2 + 0.89 \log_{10} V_i + 0.027T$$
$$(n = 81;\ R^2 = 0.66) \qquad (9.21)$$

For marine calanoids, they found:

$$\log_{10} G = -1.25 + 0.53 \log_{10} W + 0.13L + 0.68 \log_{10} V_i$$
$$- 0.000\,18M - 0.067(\log_{10} V_i)^2$$
$$(n = 272;\ R^2 = 0.69) \qquad (9.22)$$

$$\log_{10} f = -0.039 + 0.37 \log_{10} W - 0.000\,30M + 0.48 \log_{10} S$$
$$+ 0.59 \log_{10} V_i - 0.060(\log_{10} V_i)^2$$
$$(n = 246;\ R^2 = 0.52) \qquad (9.23)$$

For all data including cladocerans, calanoids plus rotifers, euphausiids etc.:

$$\log_{10} G = 0.11 + 0.55 \log_{10} W - 0.26 \log_{10} S + 0.099L$$
$$+ 0.12 \log_{10} V_i - 0.000\,20M$$
$$(n = 350;\ R^2 = 0.66) \qquad (9.24)$$

$$\log_{10} f = -0.353 + 0.54 \log_{10} W + 0.58 \log_{10} S - 0.000\,22M$$
$$+ 0.47 \log_{10} V_i + 0.060L - 0.045(\log_{10} V_i)^2$$
$$(n = 355;\ R^2 = 0.63) \qquad (9.25)$$

The order of entry of the independent variables in the above equations reflects their partial significance in the multiple regression analysis. The most significant factor is listed first. The equations use all data available to the authors and so must include erroneously high and erroneously low values. Residual analysis of these regressions suggests that rotifers and fresh water calanoids feed and graze more slowly than other animals. Radioisotopic techniques give lower values than average, while cell and Coulter counts give higher values. The average equations represent the most complete composite value which can be derived from the literature and this cannot be assumed to be more correct than carefully measured rates. However, these equations are more representative than a casual selection of values from the literature.

3.10 *The expression of selectivity*

The past decade has seen increased interest in the food preferences of zooplankton and other animals. Increased grazing mortality on any one food class and the possibility that animals may switch their preferences with food availability have powerful implications for patterns of phytoplankton succession and competition. Since zooplankton are no longer thought to have a similar effect on all potential food items, grazing rates must be adjusted to account for differences in catchability (Gliwicz 1970) if they are applied to real systems. Measurement of these capacities requires a quantitative index of food preference.

Many indices of selectivity or electivity have been suggested and several reviews of these proposals have recently been published (Jacobs 1974; Chesson 1978; Cock 1978; Paloheimo 1979; Vanderploeg & Scavia 1979). All indices seek to compare the proportion of each food type in the environment with the proportion in the diet—high values of whatever index is used should indicate preference and low values should indicate avoidance. Lechowicz (1982) reviews the desirable characteristics of electivity indices and compares the adequacy of the existing alternatives.

For zooplankton, the amount of available food of each type in the environment is determined from plankton samples; the amount of each food type in the diet is determined from feeding experiments or by gut analyses. Both estimates are only operational approximations. Zooplankton can, and do, browse on surfaces and in sediments (Lowndes 1935; Nadin-Hurley & Duncan 1976; Horton *et al.* 1979) so plankton samples may not reflect available food resources, at least in shallow waters. Since particle modification may affect estimates of feeding rate, and differential digestion obviously affects gut analyses, the actual diets may be quite different from those determined. These pitfalls in the experimental methods cannot be circumvented by the choice of index.

The most common indices used are the forage ratio (F.R.) and Ivlev's index (I) (Cock 1978). For both, the experimenter must determine the proportion of food type i which is eaten (r_i), from the number of this type in the ration or gut (N_{r_i}):

$$r_i = N_{r_i}/\Sigma N_{r_i} \qquad (9.26)$$

and p_i, the proportion of food type i in the environment is determined from counts (N_{p_i}) of each type in the environment:

$$p_i = N_{p_i}/\Sigma N_{p_i} \qquad (9.27)$$

The forage ratio is then calculated as:

$$FR = r_i/p_i \qquad (9.28)$$

and Ivlev's index as:

$$I = (p_i - r_i)/(r_i + p_i) \qquad (9.29)$$

Both indices have serious disadvantages.

(1) Both change as the ambient proportion of various foods change through grazing (Jacobs 1974), even though the animals maintain the same behavior.

(2) The value of the index for any one food type is not independent of the other values; thus, positive selection on one class imposes negative selection on the others (Boyd 1976) and an error in counts in one class imposes an error on all other classes.

(3) Because both indices are ratios of ratios, the values obtained will have very broad statistical limits (equation 9.11) and are subject to bias (Chapter 8).

Several alternatives to these indices have been presented (Jacobs 1974; Chesson 1978; Cock 1978; Vanderploeg & Scavia 1979), however those of us who work with suspension-feeders need not consider these alternatives in detail since they amount to comparisons of mortality rate in each class which, of course, is the same as a comparison of grazing rates on each class. Grazing rate is a simple, effective and practical index of selectivity among a series of food classes: the class on which grazing rate is highest is that most selected. In theory, the grazing rate on each class is independent of the other classes and this value is calculated as a simple ratio rather than as a ratio of ratios. More complex or obscure formulations give no more information.

Larger animals will have higher grazing rates than smaller ones, although they may be no more selective in the sense that their predation draws a greater proportion from some food class. In comparison of the impact of animals of different size of algal succession, this is quite appropriate because larger animals will have more effect. However, if one desires to compare the selective behavior of two such animals, the data may be standardized by plotting the results on graphs of identical size (i.e. in cm) (Richman *et al.* 1977; Allan *et al.* 1977). The same effect is achieved by dividing the measured grazing rate on each class by the sum of all grazing rates (Vanderploeg & Scavia 1979). Because food selection is a complex behavior which depends at least upon the relative and total densities of predator and prey, it should not be compressed into a single, one-dimensional measure or index. The only exception to this is the case in which only two foods are available or in which pair-wise comparisons are made. In this case, the ratio of the grazing rates on the two foods would suffice.

Theoretically, grazing rate in ml cleared individual^{-1} day^{-1} is equal to the mortality rate imposed on algae in 1 ml of water by a single zooplankter. Multiplication of G by the concentration of animals per ml yields a value which is the mortality rate of the algae or food particles, the dimensions of which are day^{-1}. This should be a useful index of electivity in other systems as well.

4 Assimilation

Viable gut passage (Porter 1973, 1975) and differential digestability (Lefèvre 1942; Arnold 1971; Lampert 1977a) of food cells underline the difference between the ingestion of food by zooplankton and its use in secondary production or respiration. The absorption of material from the gut, or its ecological assimilation, is in part measured in an attempt to differentiate between these processes. Although assimilation rate is not measured as frequently as grazing and feeding rates, a number of methods have been developed.

4.1 Estimates based on defecation rates

The simplest approach, conceptually, to the determination of assimilation rate is based on the measurements of rates of ingestion and defecation:

$$\text{Assimilation rate} = \text{Ingestion rate} - \text{defecation rate} \qquad (9.30)$$

in which all rates are expressed in the same units. Because techniques for the estimation of ingestion rates have been reviewed above only the measurement of defecation need be considered in this section.

Defecation rates are measured from quantitative collection of feces produced over a known time interval. These feces are then weighed (if gravimetric analyses are intended), burned (if calorimetric estimates of assimilation are necessary), or analyzed chemically (if the assimilation rates of some element or compound are sought). The amount of material defecated is then divided by the length of the collection period to yield a defecation rate.

The conceptual simplicity of this method should not obscure its practical complexity. Since the estimate will be subtracted from the ingestion rate it is essential that the conditions of the experiment should be identical to those used in the accompanying ingestion experiments. The animals should be kept in a steady state (i.e. defecation rate should be constant over the experiment).

The method is restricted to species which always produce discrete and coherent fecal pellets—this certainly excludes cladocerans and may not include all copepods or any copepod at certain times (see Section 3.3.2). Moreover, once released from the body, fecal pellets may undergo rapid changes in composition both through bacterial colonization and loss of soluble fecal material (Johannes and Satomi 1966, 1967). Some elements, like phosphorus, quickly leach from dead plankton (Golterman 1964; Krause 1964). Coprophagy must be avoided (Frankenberg *et al.* 1967). In the absence of information to the contrary, it is prudent to assume that any fecal material will alter rapidly and so must be removed as soon as possible after release from the animal. This may prove difficult to do without disturbing the animal and thereby altering the rate of ingestion or defecation.

Fecal pellets contain not only unabsorbed food but also products of the animals themselves: the chitinous peritrophic membrane, cells sloughed from the gut, mucus, intestinal bacteria and so forth. The amount of material in the feces can, therefore, only approximate the unutilized and unabsorbed portion of the food. However, such an approximation is probably sufficient for most ecological applications.

4.2 Estimates based on fecal analysis

For some experiments, it may be inconvenient to measure the rate of feces production but quite feasible to analyze a non-quantitative sample of the feces. Conover (1966b, 1966c) has found that assimilation rate may be estimated from ingestion rate if some component of the food is completely unassimilated. If an animal has an ingestion rate (I), and the food contains an unassimilable fraction (U), such that:

$$U = \text{mass of unassimilable material/food mass} \qquad (9.31)$$

The feces will contain a higher proportion of the unassimilable fraction (U′), since a unit of this material is unaffected by gut passage but the total amount of food will have been reduced by the amount of the food which was assimilated. The assimilation rate (A) can then be calculated as:

$$A = I \times U/U' \qquad (9.32)$$

The numerator and denominator used in the calculation of U′ (equation 9.31) and U must be expressed in appropriate terms (grams, Joules, μg N, etc.).

The advantage of this technique is that it eliminates the need for quantitative collection of the defecated material. The method assumes:

(1)   That the unassimilable material is indeed unassimilated.
(2)   That the animal does not select against this indigestible substance.
(3)   That this material moves through the gut at the same rate as the digestible fraction.
(4)   That this substance is not lost from the feces once defecated (Wightman 1975).

Conover (1966b) suggested that the ratio of ash-free dry weight to ash in the food and feces be used to provide U and U'. He showed that these ratios can give estimates of assimilation which are comparable to those measured gravimetrically (Conover 1966c). However, assimilation rates of some components of the ash, such as phosphorus, have repeatedly been shown to be significant (Peters & Rigler 1973). Lasenby & Langford (1973) estimate that 70 % of the ash in the food of *Mysis relicta* is assimilated. This would lead to overestimates of assimilation rate, since U' would be decreased. Conover (1966b) supposed that U could be measured fron the ratio of ash-free dry weight to ash in plankton samples, but growing evidence for selective feeding suggests that total plankton may not represent zooplankton food.

Even if the original formulation of the method is not correct in detail, a number of modifications are possible. Calow & Fletcher (1972) proposed that an unassimilated radioactive tracer (e.g. ^{51}Cr) could be used in place of ash. Unfortunately, it is difficult to label a food cell with a material which cannot be assimilated by the cell's predator. In practice, a compromise is reached and corrections for the assimilation of this material are applied (Wightman 1975). In principle, other materials could substitute—for example, one could use the number of chitinous remains of prey animals or the tests of food cells in the feces (Rigler 1971b) as the numerator in equation 9.31. These methods would require extensive examination before use. For example, B.Marcotte (personal communication) suggests that some copepods may ingest only the contents of diatom cells, not their tests. It might be possible to label cells which are ingested but not assimilated with one isotope and other cells with a second. In any case, the tracer material must not be selected for or against, it must pass through the gut with the food but must not be assimilated, and it must not leach from the feces before collection.

4.3 *Direct measurement of assimilation*

Isotopic estimates of assimilation are possible only for elements or non-degradable compounds. Extrapolations to assimilation in terms of total mass, energy or other materials are only possible through conversion factors and should not be considered more than rough approximations.

The methods are essentially the same as those used for isotopic measurement of ingestion rate. Basically, the uptake of tracer by the animals is measured over a time series, such as that shown in Fig. 9.5. Assimilation rate is approximately proportional to the slope of the uptake curve after the inflection point which indicates the initiation of egestion of radioactive feces. If the radioactivity per animal at t_2 minutes, and later at t_3 minutes is A_2 and A_3 respectively, then assimilation rate (A) can be calculated as:

$$A = (A_3 - A_2)/(t_3 - t_2)s \qquad (9.33)$$

where s is the specific activity (radioactivity/unit mass) of the substance for which assimilation is to be determined. Lampert (1977a) has reviewed the methodological difficulties with this approach.

One of the major problems results from the excretion of assimilated tracer. This reduces the uptake rate calculated in equation 9.33. The error becomes more severe as the experiment becomes longer. Lampert (1977a) points out that the amount of excreted tracer declines rapidly after removal of the animal from its labeled food. Thus, the size of the underestimate due to tracer excretion can only be estimated by determining the reduction in tracer excretion with time after removal from the radioactive food and extrapolation to zero time (Peters & Rigler 1973; Peters 1975b) or by measuring the rate of appearance of soluble tracer simultaneous with measurement of the rate of assimilation (Lampert 1977a). The former is the only method advisable if rates of re-uptake of excreted tracer by the animals or by the remaining food cells are significant (Peters & Lean 1973; Ganf & Blazka 1974). This is certainly the case with phosphorus, but probably not so with carbon. Tracer excretion can result in underestimates of assimilation of 10 % in experiments which last only 30 minutes (Peters 1975a).

The measurement of assimilation by isotopic accumulation requires that any tracer uptake between t_2 and t_3 represents only uptake by the body of the animal. The radioactivity of the gut remains unchanged because all non-radioactive food in the gut was, in principle, flushed out before t_2. This may not be so. Smirnov (1974), Schultz & Kennedy (1976) and Marcotte (1977) report that antiperistaltic movement may lead to refluxing of the gut contents. This would lead to overestimates of assimilation rate in short-term experiments as some of the tracer accumulated after defecation begins would represent further filling of the gut. However, microscopic estimates of time to defecation suggest that the amount of mixing of the gut contents is rather small.

A more serious problem in the measurement of tracer assimilation is incomplete labeling of the food cells. This leads to low values of s in equation 9.33 and so causes overestimation of assimilation rate. Since most work has used algal cultures which were labeled for only a day (Bell & Ward 1970; Arnold 1971; Lampert 1977a) it is unlikely that all compartments within the food are fully labeled. For example, it is probable that structural components, such as cell walls, become labeled with ^{14}C-bicarbonate more slowly than metabolically active sugars. This problem may be avoided if the cell cultures are grown in a medium of constant specific activity (Conover & Francis 1973; Peters & Rigler 1973).

Lampert (1977a) checked for the influence of incomplete labeling by comparing assimilation with the sum of growth and respiration. The close correspondence probably indicates that most of the carbon in his cells was labeled. Since it is improbable that the cell walls were labeled (Lampert reported little growth in population during labeling), one must speculate that, under the culture conditions used, the cells fixed and stored a large quantity of uniformly labeled carbohydrate (Morgan 1976). A more effective check for complete labeling of the food cells may be made by dividing the cells into two or more arbitrary fractions. Cells may be sonified and filtered and the specific activity of material in the filtrate and particulate fractions determined or one may measure the specific activity of acid extractable and residual components (Lampert 1977a). In fully labeled cultures, all fractions should have identical specific activities. Since the fractions are arbitrary, it is conceivable that two such different fractions could have similar specific activities before complete labeling was achieved. If possible, two or more distinctive fractionations should be used.

In any measurement of assimilation, the researcher should be aware that absorption of the material does not indicate that the assimilated substance is used in production by the zooplankton. High assimilation rates do not necessarily correlate with high growth rates for animals feeding on that food (Arnold 1971; Lampert 1977b). This may reflect antibiotic effects of the food, some nutrient deficiency in the algae (Taub & Dollar 1968) or an error due to incomplete labeling of the cells. Researchers should test for the effect of easily assimilated foods in zooplankton growth experiments.

Finally, a comment on the presentation of assimilation rates is in order. Most estimates are presented as assimilation efficiencies (equation 9.1). In the case of the ash-free dry weight method and its analogues, assimilation efficiency must be calculated to determine assimilation rate from ingestion rate. Because assimilation efficiency is a ratio of two experimental values, the variance around the mean is magnified. Partly as a result of this, published values for assimilation are notoriously variable (i.e. 8–100%—Conover 1964; Peters 1972). Assimilation should be presented as a rate, not a ratio, whenever possible.

5 Conclusions

Every experimental technique is open to abuse and the data obtained from any method must be interpreted in light of the capabilities of the techniques employed. Careful researchers should approach their hypotheses from as many experimental directions as possible and hypotheses resting solely on one technique should be treated with a healthy scientific skepticism until tested with alternative techniques. It is not enough to state the assumptions of the method chosen; the validity of these assumptions should be tested explicitly. Techniques for the measurement of feeding and grazing by zooplankton are among the most developed, and, when used properly, give us some of the best estimates available for feeding of any group. I hope this review will increase our already high level of achievement.

The research community involved in measurements of feeding and grazing is now so large that it risks defining a 'normal science' of Zooplanktophagology, one which creates and tests theories which are interesting only to members of that community. We must continually examine and re-affirm the ecological relevance of our studies. While the minute aspects of zooplankton feeding may be of interest to us, we must also consider their utility and relevance. The techniques for the measurement of feeding, grazing, and assimilation rates are powerful; it is for us to find a place for these measurements in the broad scheme of material and energy flow both in lakes and ecosystems in general.

6 References

Alcaraz M., Paffenhöfer G.A. & Strickler J.R. (1980) Catching the algae: a first account of visual observations on filter-feeding calanoids. In W.C.Kerfoot (ed.), *The Evolution and Ecology of Zooplankton Communities.* Hanover, N.H.: University Press of New England.

Allan J.D., Richman S., Heinle D.A. & Huff R. (1977). Grazing in juvenile stages of some estuarine calanoid copepods. *Mar. Biol.*, **43**, 317–332.

Allen T. (1975) *Particle Size Measurement.* 2nd ed. London: Chapman and Hall Ltd.

Altmann J. (1974) Observational study of behavior sampling methods. *Behavior*, **44**, 227–267.

Ambler J.W. & Frost B.W. (1974) The feeding behavior of a predatory planktonic copepod, *Tortanus discaudatus. Limnol. Oceanogr.*, **19**, 446–451.

Anderson R.S. (1970) Predator prey relations and predation rates for crustacean zooplankters from some lakes in Western Canada. *Can. J. Zool.*, **48**, 1229–1240.

Anraku M. (1964) Some technical problems encountered in quantitative studies of grazing and predation by marine planktonic copepods. *J. Oceanogr. Soc. Japan*, **20**, 19–29.

Anraku M. & Omori M.O. (1963) Preliminary survey of the relationship between the feeding habit and the structure of the mouthparts of marine copepods. *Limnol. Oceanogr.*, **8**, 116–126.

Arashkevich Y.G. (1975) Duration of food digestion in marine copepods. *Trudy. Inst. Okean. P.P. Shirshova*, **102**, 351–357.

Arnold D.E. (1971) Ingestion, assimilation, survival and reproduction by *Daphnia pulex* fed seven species of bluegreen algae. *Limnol. Oceanogr.*, **16**, 906–920.

Arthur C.R. & Rigler F.H. (1967) A possible source of error in the ^{14}C method of measuring primary productivity. *Limnol. Oceanogr.*, **12**, 121–124.

Baylor E.R. (1959) Infrared observation and cinematography of microcrustacea. *Limnol. Oceanogr.*, **4**, 498–499.

Baylor E.R. & Smith F.E. (1953) The orientation of cladocera to polarized light. *Amer. Nat.*, **87**, 97–101.

Bell R.K. & Ward F.J. (1968) Use of liquid scintillation counting for measuring self absorption of ^{14}C in *Daphnia pulex*. *J. Fish Res. Board Can.*, **25**, 2505–2508.

Bell R.K. & Ward F.J. (1970) Incorporation of organic carbon by *Daphnia pulex*. *Limnol. Oceanogr.*, **15**, 713–725.

Berman M.S. & Richman S. (1974). The feeding behavior of *Daphnia pulex* from Lake Winnebago, Wisconsin. *Limnol. Oceanogr.*, **19**, 105–109.

Blueweiss L., Fox H., Kudzma V., Nakashima B., Peters R. & Sams (1978). Relationships between body size and some life history parameters. *Oecologia* (Berl.), **37**, 257–272.

Bogatova I.B. (1965). The food of daphnids and diaptomids in ponds. *Trudy Ugerossiskovo naucho issled ovatelskova instituta prudovo rybnovo khozyaistva, voprosy prodova rybovodstva*, **13**, 165–178 (transl. by J.F.Haney).

Bogdan K.G. & McNaught D.C. (1975) Selective feeding by *Diaptomus* and by *Daphnia*. *Verh. Internat. Verein. Limnol.*, **19**, 2935–2942.

Bond R.M. (1933) A contribution to the study of the natural food cycle in aquatic environments. *Bull. Bingham. Oceanogr. Collect*, **4**, 89 pp.

Boyd C.M. (1976) Selection of particle size by filter-feeding copepods: a plea for reason. *Limnol. Oceanogr.*, **21**, 175–180.

Boyd C.M., Smith S.L. & Cowles T.J. (1980) Grazing patterns of copepods in an updwelling system off Peru. *Limnol. Oceanogr.*, **25**, 583–597.

Brandl Z. & Fernando C.H. (1975) Food consumption and utilization in two freshwater cyclopoid copepods (*Mesocyclops edax* and *Cyclops vicinus*). *Int. Revue ges. Hydrobiol.*, **60**, 471–494.

Brock T.D. & Brock M.L. (1969). The fate in nature of photosynthetically assimilated ^{14}C in a bluegreen alga. *Limnol. Oceanogr.*, **14**, 604–607.

Buikema A.L. Jr. (1973) Filtering rate of the cladoceran *Daphnia pulex* as a function of body size, light and acclimation. *Hydrobiologia*, **41**, 515–527.

Buikema A.L. Jr (1975) Some effects of light on the energetics of *Daphnia pulex* and implications for the significance of vertical migration. *Hydrobiologia*, **47**, 43–58.

Burky A.J. & Benjamin R.B. (1979). An accurate microassay for measuring filtration rates of small invertebrates using latex beads. *Comp. Biochem. Physiol.*, **63A**, 483–484.

Burns C.W. (1968a) Direct observations of mechanisms regulating feeding behavior of *Daphnia* in lakewater. *Int. Revue ges. Hydrobiol.*, **53**, 83–100.

Burns C.W. (1968b) The relationship between body size of filter-feeding Cladocera and the maximum size of the particle ingested. *Limnol. Oceanogr.*, **13**, 675–678.

Burns C.W. (1969a). Relation between filtering rate, temperature and body size in four species of *Daphnia*. *Limnol. Oceanogr.*, **14**, 693–700.

Burns C.W. (1969b). Particle size and sedimentation in the feeding behavior of two species of *Daphnia*. *Limnol. Oceanogr.*, **14**, 392–403.

Burns C.W. & Rigler F.H. (1967) Comparison of filtering rates of *Daphnia rosea* in lake water and in suspensions of yeast. *Limnol. Oceanogr.*, **12**, 492–502.

Buscemi P.A. & Puffer J.H. (1975) Chemico-trophic attributes of detrital aggregates in a New Mexico alkaline reservoir. *Verh. Internat. Verein. Limnol.*, **19**, 358–366.

Calow P. & Fletcher C.R. (1972) A new radiotracer technique involving ^{14}C and ^{51}Cr for estimating the assimilation efficiencies of aquatic primary consumers. *Oecologia (Berl.)*, **9**, 155–170.

Cannon H.G. (1928) On the feeding mechanism of the copepods *Calanus finmarchicus* and *Diaptomus gracilis*. *J. Exp. Biol.*, **6**, 131–144.

Cannon H.G. (1933) On the feeding of the Brachiopoda. *Phil. Trans. Roy. Soc. Lond. B.*, **13**, 222–267.

Cattaneo A. & Kalff J. (1978) Seasonal changes in the epiphyte community of natural and artificial macrophytes in Lake Memphremagog (Qué.-Vt.). *Hydrobiologia*, **60**, 135–144.

Chesson J. (1978) Measuring preference in selective predation. *Ecology*, **59**, 211–215.

Chisholm S.W., Stross R.G. & Nobbs P.A. (1975) Environmental and intrinsic control of filtering and feeding rates in arctic *Daphnia*. *J. Fish. Res. Board Can.*, **32**, 219–226.

Cock M.J.W. (1978) The assessment of preference. *J. Anim. Ecol.*, **47**, 805–816.

Coleman A. (1980) Enhanced detection of bacteria in natural environments by fluorochrome staining of DNA. *Limnol. Oceanogr.*, **25**, 948–951.

Confer J.L. (1971) Intrazooplankton predation by *Mesocyclops edax* at natural prey densities. *Limnol. Oceanogr.*, **16**, 663–667.

Conover R.J. (1956) Biology of *Acartia clausi* and *A. tonsa*. *Bull. Bingham. Oceanogr. Collect.*, **15**, 156–223.

Conover R.J. (1961) The turnover of phosphorus by *Calanus finmarchicus*. *J. Mar. Biol. Ass. U.K.*, **41**, 484–488.

Conover R.J. (1964) Food relations and nutrition of zooplankton. *Proc. Symp. Expt. Mar. Ecol.*, Occ. Pub. no. 2. Kingston: Graduate School of Oceanography, Univ. of Rhode Island.

Conover R.J. (1966a) Feeding on large particles by *Calanus hyperboreus* (Kröyer). In H.Barnes (ed.). *Some Contemporary Studies in Marine Science*. London: George Allen and Unwin, Ltd.

Conover R.J. (1966b) Assimilation of organic matter by zooplankton. *Limnol. Oceanogr.*, **11**, 338–345.

Conover R.J. (1966c) Factors affecting the assimilation of organic matter by zooplankton and the question of superfluous feeding. *Limnol. Oceanogr.*, **11**, 346–354.

Conover R.J. (1978) Transformation of organic matter. *Mar. Ecol.*, **4**, 221–499. Wiley and Sons, London.

Conover R.J. & Francis V. (1973) The use of radioactive isotopes to measure the transfer of materials in aquatic food chains. *Mar. Biol.*, **18**, 272–283.

Copping A.E. & Lorenzen C.J. (1980) Carbon budget of a marine phytoplankton herbivore system with carbon-14 as tracer. *Limnol. Oceanogr.*, **25**, 873–882.

Corner E.D.S., Head R.N. & Kilvington C.C. (1972) On the nutrition and metabolism of zooplankton. VIII. The grazing of *Biddulphia* cells by *Calanus helgolandicus*. *J. Mar. Biol. Assoc. U.K.*, **52**, 847–861.

Corner E.D.S., Head R.N., Kilvington C.C. & Marshall S.M. (1974) On the nutrition and metabolism of zooplankton. IX. Studies relating to the nutrition of over-wintering *Calanus. J. Mar. Biol. Assoc. U.K.*, **54**, 319–331.

Corner E.D.S., Head R.N., Kilvington C.C. & Pennycuick L. (1976) On the nutrition and metabolism of zooplankton. X. Quantitative aspects of *Calanus helgolandicus* feeding as a carnivore. *J. Mar. Biol. Assoc. U.K.*, **56**, 345–358.

Coughlan V. (1969) The estimation of filtering rate from the clearance of suspensions. *Mar. Biol.*, **2**, 356–358.

Coveney M.F., Cronberg G., Enell M., Larsson K. & Olofsson L. (1977) Phytoplankton, zooplankton and bacteria-standing crop and production relationships in a eutrophic lake. *Oikos*, **29**, 5–21.

Crowley P.H. (1973) Filtering rate inhibition of *Daphnia pulex* in Wintergreen lake. *Limnol. Oceanogr.*, **18**, 394–402.

Cummins K.W. & Klug M.J. (1979) Feeding ecology of stream invertebrates. *Ann Rev. Ecol. Syst.*, **10**, 147–172.

Cushing D.H. (1958) The effect of grazing in reducing the primary production: a review. *Rapp. P.V. Réun. Cons. Perm. int. Explor. Mer*, **144**, 149–154.

Dagg M.J. (1974) Loss of prey body contents during feeding by an aquatic predator. *Ecology*, **55**, 903–906.

Dagg M.J. & Grill D.W. (1980) Natural feeding rates of *Centropages typicus* females in the New York Bight. *Limnol. Oceanogr.*, **25**, 597–609.

Deason E.E. (1980a) Potential effect of phytoplankton colony breakage on the calculation of zooplankton filtering rates. *Mar. Biol.*, **57**, 279–286.

Deason E.E. (1980b) Grazing of *Acartia hudsonica* (*A. clausi*) on *Skeletonema costatum* in Narragansett Bay (U.S.A.): influence of food concentration and temperature. *Mar. Biol.*, **60**, 101–114.

de Bernardi R., Giussani G. & Pedretti E.L. (1981) The significance of blue-green algae as food for filter feeding zooplankton: experimental studies on *Daphnia* spp. fed by *Microcystis aeruginosa. Verh. Internat. Verein. Limnol.*, **21**, 477–483.

DeMott W.R. (1982) Feeding selectivities and relative ingestion rates of *Daphnia* and *Bosmina. Limnol. Oceanogr.*, **27**, 518–527.

Dodson S.I. (1970) Complementary feeding niches sustained by size selective predation. *Limnol. Oceanogr.*, **15**, 131–137.

Dodson S.I. (1974) Adaptive change in plankton morphology in response to size selective predation: a new hypothesis of cyclomorphosis. *Limnol. Oceanogr.*, **19**, 721–729.

Donaghay P.L. (1980) Grazing interactions in the marine environment in W.C.Kerfoot (ed.) *Evolution and Ecology of Zooplankton Communities.* Hanover N.H.: New England University Press.

Donaghay P.L. & Small L.F. (1979) Food selection capabilities of the estuarine copepod *Acartia clausi. Mar. Biol.*, **52**, 137–146.

Doohan M. (1973) An energy budget for adult *Brachionus plicatilis* Müller: Rotatoria. *Oecologia (Berl.)*, **13**, 351–382.

Downing J.A. (1979) *Foraging Responses of Littoral Cladocerans.* Dissertation. McGill University, Montréal, Canada.

Downing J.A. (1980) Inhibition of cladoceran feeding by staining with acridine orange. *Trans. Am. Micros. Soc.*, **99**, 398–403.

Downing J.A. (1981) *In situ* foraging responses of three species of littoral Cladocera. *Ecol. Monogr.*, **51**, 85–103.

Downing J.A. & Peters R.H. (1980) The effect of body size and food concentration on the filtering rate of *Sida crystallina, in situ. Limnol. Oceanogr.*, **25**, 883–895.

Duval W.S. & Geen G.H. (1975) Diel rhythms in the feeding and respiration of zooplankton. *Verh. Internat. Verein. Limnol.*, **19**, 518–523.

Edmondson W.T. (1965) Reproductive rate of planktonic rotifers as related to food and temperature in nature. *Ecol. Monogr.*, **35**, 61–111.

Egloff D.A. & Palmer D.S. (1971) Size relations of the filtering area of two *Daphnia* species. *Limnol. Oceanogr.*, **16**, 900–905.

Eriksson S. (1934) Studien über die Fangapparate der Branchiopoden. Websteinigen Phylogenetischen Bermerkungen. *Zool. Bidr. Fr. Uppsala*, **15**, 23–287.

Esaias W.E. & Curl H.C. (1972) Effect of dinoflagellate bioluminescence on copepod ingestion rate. *Limnol. Oceanogr.*, **17**, 901–906.

Fedorenko A.Y. (1975) Feeding characteristics and predation impact of *Chaoborus* (Diptera, Chaoboridae) larvae in a small lake. *Limnol. Oceanogr.*, **20**, 250–258.

Fenchel T. (1975) The quantitative importance of the benthic microfauna of an arctic tundra pond. *Hydrobiologia*, **46**, 445–464.

Fenchel T. (1980a) Relation between particle size selection and clearance in suspension-feeding ciliates. *Limnol. Oceanogr.*, **25**, 733–738.

Fenchel T. (1980b) Suspension feeding in ciliated Protozoa: Functional response and particle size selection. *Microb. Ecol.*, **6**, 1–12.

Ferrante J.G. & Parker J.I. (1977) Transport of diatom frustules by copoepod fecal pellets to the sediments of Lake Michigan. *Limnol. Oceanogr.*, **22**, 92–98.

Fliermans C.B. & Schmidt E.L. (1976) Fluorescein microscopy: direct determination, enumeration, and spatial distribution of bacteria in aquatic systems. *Archiv. Hydrobiol.*, **76**, 33–42.

Fox B.W. (1976) *Techniques of Sample Preparation for Liquid Scintillation Counting.* Amsterdam: North-Holland Publishing Co.

Fox H.M., Gilchrist B.M. & Phear E.A. (1951) Function of haemoglobin in *Daphnia. Proc. R. Soc. Lond. B. Biol. Sci.*, **138**, 514–528.

Frankenberg D., Coles S.L. & Johannes R.E. (1967) The potential trophic significance of *Callianessa major* fecal pellets. *Limnol. Oceanogr.*, **12**, 113–120.

Frey D.G. (1973) Comparative morphology and biology of three species of *Eurycercus* (Chydoridae, Cladocera) with a description of *Eurycercus macrocanthus* Nov., *Int. Revue ges. Hydrobiol.*, **58**, 221–277.

Friedman M.M. (1980) Comparative morphology and functional significance of copepod receptors and oral structures. In W.C.Kerfoot (ed.) *Evolution and Ecology of Zooplankton Communities.* Hanover, N.H.: University Press of New England.

Friedman M.M. & Strickler J.R. (1975) Chemoreceptors and feeding in calanoid copepods (Arthropoda: Crustacea). *Proc. Nat. Acad. Sci. U.S.A.*, **72**, 4185–4188.

Frost B.W. (1972) Effects of size and concentration of food particles on the feeding behavior of the marine planktonic copepod, *Calanus pacificus. Limnol. Oceanogr.*, **17**, 805–815.

Frost B.W. (1975) A threshold feeding behavior in *Calanus pacificus. Limnol. Oceanogr.*, **20**, 263–267.

Frost B.W. (1977) Feeding behavior of *Calanus finmarchius* in mixtures of food particles. *Limnol. Oceanogr.*, **22**, 472–491.

Fryer G. (1957a) The feeding mechanism of some freshwater cyclopoid copepods. *Proc. Zool. Soc. Lond.*, **129**, 1–25.

Fryer G. (1957b) The food of some freshwater cyclopoid copepods and its ecological significance. *J. Animal. Ecol.*, **26**, 263–286.

Fryer, G. (1968) Evolution and adaptive radiation in the Chydoridae (Crustacea: Cladocera): a study in comparative functional morphology and ecology. *Phil. Trans. Roy. Soc. London*, **254**, 221–385.

Fryer G. (1974) Evolution and adaptive radiation in the Macrothricidae (Crustacea: Cladocera): a study in comparative and functional morphology and ecology. *Phil. Trans. Roy. Soc. London B.*, **269**, 217–274.

Fuller J.L. (1937) Feeding rate of *Calanus finmarchicus* in relation to environmental conditions. *Biol. Bull.*, **72**, 233–246.

Ganf G.C. & Blazka P. (1974) Oxygen uptake, ammonia, and phosphate excretion by zooplankton in a shallow equatorial lake (Lake George, Uganda). *Limnol. Oceanogr.*, **19**, 313–315.

Gannon J. & Gannon S. (1975) Observations on the narcotization of crustacean zooplankton. *Crustaceana*, **28**, 220–224.

Gaudy, R. (1974) Feeding of four species of pelagic copepods under experimental conditions. *Mar. Biol.*, **25**, 125–141.

Gauld D.T. (1951) The grazing rate of planktonic copepods. *J. Mar. Biol. Assoc. U.K.*, **29**, 695–706.

Gauld D.T. (1953) Diurnal variation in the grazing of planktonic copepods. *J. Mar. Biol. Assoc. U.K.*, **31**, 461–474.

Gauld D.T. (1959) Swimming and feeding in crustacean larvae: the nauplius larva *Proc. Zool. Soc. London*, **132**, 31–50.

Gauld D.T. (1966) The swimming and feeding of planktonic copepods. In H.Barnes (ed.) *Marine Science*. London: George Allen and Unwin, Ltd.

Geller W. (1975) Die Nahrungsaufnahme von *Daphnia pulex* in Abhangigkeit von der Futterkonzentration, der Temperature, der Korpergrösse und dem Hungerzustand der Tiere. *Arch. Hydrobiol. (Suppl.)*, **48**, 47–107.

Geller W. & Müller H. (1981) The filtration apparatus of Cladocera: filter mesh sizes and their implications on food selectivity. *Oceologia*, **49**, 316–321.

Gerritson J. & Porter K.G. (1982) Fluid mechanics, surface chemistry, and filter-feeding by *Daphnia. Science*, **216**, 1225–1227.

Gilbert J.J. & Bogdan K.G. (1981) Selectivity of *Polyarthra* and *Keratella* for flagellate and aflagellate cells. *Verh. Internat. Verein. Limnol.*, **21**, 1515–1521.

Gilbert J.J. & Starkweather P.L. (1977) Feeding in the rotifer *Brachionus calyciflorus*. I. Regulatory mechanisms. *Oecologia (Berl.)*, **28**, 125–131.

Gliwicz Z.M. (1968) The use of anaesthetizing substance in studies on the food habits of zooplankton. *Ecol. Pol.*, **16**, 279–295.

Gliwicz Z.M. (1969) Studies on the feeding of pelagic zooplankton in lakes with varying trophy. *Ecol. Pol.*, **17**, 663–708.

Gliwicz Z.M. (1970) Calculation of food ration of zooplankton community as an example of using laboratory data for field conditions. *Pol. Arch. Hydrobiol.*, **17**, 169–175.

Gliwicz Z.M. (1975) Effect of zooplankton grazing on photosynthetic activity and composition of zooplankton. *Verh. Internat. Verein. Limnol.*, **19**, 1490–1497.

Gliwicz Z.M. (1977) Food size selection and seasonal succession of filter feeding zooplankton in a eutrophic lake. *Ekol. Pol.*, **25**, 179–225.

Gliwicz Z.M. (1980) Filtering rates, food size selection and feeding rates in cladocerans—another aspect of interspecific competition in filter-feeding zooplankton. In W.C.Kerfoot (ed.) *Evolution and Ecology of Zooplankton Communities*. Hanover: University Press.

Gliwicz Z.M. & Hillbricht-Ilkowska A. (1975) Efficiencies of the utilization of nannoplankton primary production by communities of filter feeding animals measured *in situ*. *Verh. Internat. Verein. Limnol.*, **18**, 197–203.

Gliwicz Z.M. & Siedlar E. (1980) Food size limitation and algae interfering with food collection in *Daphnia*. *Arch. Hydrobiol.*, **88**, 155–177.

Golterman H.L. (1964) Mineralization of algae under sterile conditions or by bacterial breakdown. *Verh. Internat. Verein. Limnol.*, **15**, 544–548.

Gophen M., Cavari B.Z. & Berman T. (1974) Zooplankton feeding on differentially labelled algae and bacteria. *Nature*, **247**, 393–394.

Gray F.R.S. (1930) The mechanism of ciliary movement. VI. Photographic and stroboscopic analysis of ciliary movement. *Proc. Roy. Soc. B.*, **107**, 313–332.

Griffiths F.B. & Caperon J. (1979) Description and use of an improved method for determining estuarine zooplankton grazing rates on phytoplankton. *Mar. Biol.*, **54**, 301–309.

Grygierek E. (1971) Some data on the role of food in the biology of *Eudiaptomis zachariassi* Poppe. *Ekol. Pol.*, **19**, 277–292.

Gulati R.D. (1975) A study of the role of a herbivorous zooplankton community as primary consumers of phytoplankton in Dutch lakes. *Verh. Internat. Verein Limnol.*, **19**, 1202–1210.

Haberer K. (1966) *Measurement of Beta Activities in Aqueous Samples Utilizing Cerenkov Radiation*. Packard Technical Bulletin No. 16. Downers Grove, Illinois: Packard Instrument Co.

Hairston N.G. (1976) Photoprotection by carotenoid pigments in the copepod *Diaptomus nevadensis*. *Proc. Nat. Acad. Sci. U.S.A.*, **73**, 971–974.

Hall D.J., Threlkeld S.T., Burns C.W. & Crowley P.H. (1976). Zooplankton community structure and the size efficiency hypothesis. *Ann. Rev. Syst. Ecol.*, **7**, 177–200.

Hall T. (1978) *Nickel Uptake Retention and Loss in Daphnia magna*. Thesis. Univ. of Toronto, Toronto, Canada.

Haney J.F. (1971) An *in situ* method for the measurement of zooplankton grazing rates. *Limnol. Oceanogr.*, **16**, 970–977.

Haney J.F. (1973) An *in situ* examination of the grazing activities of natural zooplankton communities. *Arch. Hydrobiol.*, **72**, 87–132.

Haney J.F. & Hall D.J. (1973) Sugar-coated *Daphnia:* a preservation technique for Cladocera. *Limnol. Oceanogr.*, **18**, 331–333.

Haney J.F. & Hall D.J. (1975) Diel vertical migration and filter feeding activities of *Daphnia*. *Arch. Hydrobiol.*, **75**, 413–441.

Harbison G.B. & McAlister V.L. (1980) Fact and artifact in copepod feeding experiments. *Limnol. Oceanogr.*, **25**, 971–981.

Hargis J.R. (1977) Comparison of techniques for the measurement of zooplankton filtration rates. *Limnol. Oceanogr.*, **22**, 942–945.

Hargrave B.T. & Geen G.H. (1968) Phosphorus excretion by zooplankton. *Limnol. Oceanogr.*, **13**, 332–343.

Hargrave B.T. & Geen G.H. (1970) Effects of copepod grazing on two natural phytoplankton populations. *J. Fish. Res. Board Can.*, **27**, 1395–1403.

Harris R.P. & Paffenhöfer G.A. (1976a) The effect of food concentration on cumulative ingestion and growth efficiency of two small marine planktonic copepods. *J. Mar. Biol. Assoc. U.K.*, **56**, 875–888.

Harris R.P. & Paffenhöfer G.A. (1976b) Feeding, growth and reproduction of the marine planktonic copepod *Temora longcornis* (Müller). *J. Mar. Biol. Assoc. U.K.*, **56**, 675–690.

Hasler A.D. (1937) The physiology of digestion in plankton Crustacea II. Further studies on the digestive enzymes of (A) *Daphnia* and *Polyphemus*, (B) *Diaptomus* and *Calanus*. *Biol. Bull.*, **72**, 290–298.

Hayward R.S. & Gallup D.N. (1976) Feeding, filtering and assimilation in *Daphnia schoedleri* as affected by environmental conditions. *Arch. Hydrobiol.*, **77**, 139–163.

Heinbokel J.F. (1978a) Studies on the functional role of tintinnids in the southern California Bight. I. Grazing and growth rates in laboratory cultures. *Mar. Biol.*, **47**, 177–189.

Heinbokel J.F. (1978b) Studies on the functional role of tintinnids in the southern California Bight II. Grazing rates of field populations. *Mar. Biol.*, **47**, 191–197.

Heinle D.R. (1974) An alternative grazing hypothesis for the Patuxent Estuary. *Chesapeake Sci.*, **15**, 146–150.

Heisey D. & Porter K.G. (1977) The effect of ambient oxygen concentration on filtering and respiration rates of *Daphnia galeata mendotae* and *Daphnia magna*. *Limnol. Oceanogr.*, **22**, 839–845.

Hillbricht-Ilkowska A. & Karabin A. (1970) An attempt to estimate consumption, respiration and production of *Leptodora kindtii* (Focke) in field and laboratory experiments. *Pol. Arch. Hydrobiol.*, **17**, 81–86.

Hirayama K. & Ogawa S. (1972) Fundamental studies on physiology of rotifer for its mass culture. I. Filter feeding of rotifer. *Bull. Jap. Soc. Sci. Fish*, **38**, 1207–1214.

Hobero R. & Willén E. (1977) Phytoplankton counting. Intercalibration, results and recommendations for routine work. *Int. Revue. ges. Hydrobiol.*, **62**, 805–812.

Hollibaugh J.T., Furman J.A. & Azam F. (1980) Radioactivity labeling natural assemblages for use in trophic studies. *Limnol. Oceanogr.*, **25**, 172–181.

Holling C.S. (1959) Some characteristics of simple types of predation and parasitism. *Can. Ent.*, **16**, 385–398.

Holtby L.B. & Knoechel R. (1981) Zooplankton filtering rates: error due to loss of radioisotopic label in chemically preserved samples. *Limnol. Oceanogr.*, **26**, 774–780.

Horton P.A., Rowan M., Webster K.E. & Peters R.H. (1979) Browsing and grazing by cladoceran filter feeders. *Can. J. Zool.*, **57**, 206–212.

Hoshi T. & Kobayashi K. (1971) Studies on physiology and ecology of plankton. XXV. Ion-content and millimolar extinction coefficient of the *Daphnia* haemoglobin. *Sci. Rep. Niigala Univ. ser. D. (Biology)*, **8**, 65–68.

Hrbáčkova-Esslova M. (1963) The development of 3 species of *Daphnia* in the Slapy Reservoir. *Int. Revue. ges. Hydrobiol.*, **48**, 325–333.

Ikeda T., Hing Fay E., Hutchinson S.A. & Boto G.M. (1982) Ammonia and inorganic phosphate excretion by zooplankton from inshore waters of the Great Barrier Reef, Queensland. I. Relationships between excretion rate and body size. *Aust. J. Mar. Freshwat. Res.*, **33**, 55–70.

Infante A.G. (1973) Untersuchungen über die Ausnutzbarkeit verschiedener Algen durch das Zooplankton. *Arch. Hydrobiol. (Suppl.)*, **42**, 340–405.

Infante A.G. (1981) Natural food of copepod larvae from Lake Valencia, Venezuela. *Verh. Internat. Verein. Limnol.*, **21**, 709–714.

Ivanova M.B. (1969) The influence of active water reaction on the filtration rate of Cladocera. *Pol. Arch. Hydrobiol.*, **16**, 115–124.

Ivanova M.B. & Klekowski R.Z. (1972) Respiration and filtration rates in *Simocephalus vetulus* (O.F.Müller) (Cladocera) at different pH. *Pol. Arch. Hydrobiol.*, **19**, 303–318.

Jacobs J. (1974) Quantitative measurement of food selection: a modification of the forage ratio and Ivlev's electivity index. *Oecologia (Berl.)*, **14**, 413–417.

Jassby A.D. & Goldman C.R. (1974) Loss rates from a lake phytoplankton community. *Limnol. Oceanogr.*, **19**, 618–627.

Johannes R.E. (1964) Phosphorus excretion and body size in Marine Animals. Microzooplankton and nutrient regeneration. *Science*, **146**, 923–924.

Johannes R.E. (1968) Nutrient regeneration in lakes and oceans. *Adv. Microbiol. Sea.*, **1**, 203–213.

Johannes R.E. & Satomi M. (1966) Composition and nutritive value of fecal pellets of a marine crustacean. *Limnol. Oceanogr.*, **11**, 191–197.

Johannes R.E. & Satomi M. (1967) Measuring organic matter retained by aquatic invertebrates. *J. Fish. Res. Board Can.*, **24**, 2467–2471.

Jørgensen C.B. (1966) *Biology of Suspension Feeding*. London: Pergamon Press.

Kajak Z. & Ranke-Rybickova B. (1970) Feeding and production efficiency of *Chaoborus flavicans* (Meigen) (Diptera, Culicidae) larvae in eutrophic and dystrophic lake. *Pol. Arch. Hydrobiol.*, **17**, 225–232.

Kerfoot W.C. (1977) Implications of copepod predation. *Limnol. Oceanogr.*, **22**, 316–325.

Kersting K. & Holterman W. (1973) The feeding behaviour of *Daphnia magna* studied with the Coulter counter. *Verh. Internat. Verein. Limnol.*, **18**, 1435–1440.

Kersting K. & van der Leeuw W. (1976) The use of the Coulter counter for measuring the feeding rates of *Daphnia magna*. *Hydrobiologia*, **49**, 233–237.

Kibby H.V. (1969) *Energy Transformation by a Population of Diatomus gracilis*. Dissertation. Westfield College, University of London, London, England.

Kibby H.V. (1971) Effect of temperature on the feeding behaviour of *Daphnia rosea*. *Limnol. Oceanogr.*, **16**, 580–581.

Kibby H.V. & Rigler F.H. (1973) Filtering rates of *Limnocalanus*. *Verh. Internat. Verein Limnol.*, **18**, 1457–1461.

Knoechel R. & Kalff J. (1978) An *in situ* study of the productivity and population dynamics of five freshwater planktonic diatom species. *Limnol. Oceanogr.*, **23**, 195–218.

Koehl M.A.R. & Strickler J.R. (1981) Copepod feeding currents: food capture at low Reynolds number. *Limnol. Oceanogr.*, **26**, 1062–1073.

Krause H.R. (1964) Zur Chemie und Biochemie der Zersetzung von Süsswasserorganismen, unter besonder Berücksichtigung des Abbaues der organischen Phosphorkomponenten. *Verh. Internat. Verein. Limnol.*, **15**, 549–561.

Krey J. (1958) Chemical methods of estimates of standing crop of phytoplankton. *Rapp. P.V. Reun. Cons. Intern. Explor. Mer.*, **144**, 20–27.

Kring R.L. & O'Brien W.J. (1976a) Effect of varying oxygen concentration and the filtering rate of *Daphnia pulex*. *Ecology*, **57**, 808–814.

Kring R.L. & O'Brien W.J. (1976b) Accommodation of *Daphnia pulex* to altered pH conditions as measured by feeding rate. *Limnol. Oceanogr.*, **21**, 313–315.

Lam R.K. & Frost B.W. (1976) Model of copepod filtering responses to changes in size and concentration of food. *Limnol. Oceanogr.*, **21**, 490–500.

Lampert W. (1974) A method for determining food selection by zooplankton. *Limnol. Oceanogr.*, **19**, 995–998.

Lampert W. (1975) A tracer study of the carbon turnover of *Daphnia pulex*. *Verh. Internat. Verein. Limnol.*, **19**, 2913–2921.

Lampert W. (1977a) Studies on the carbon balance of *Daphnia pulex* as related to environmental conditions. I. Methodological problems of the use of ^{14}C for the measurement of carbon assimilation. *Arch. Hydrobiol. (Suppl.)*, **48**, 287–309.

Lampert W. (1977b) Studies on the carbon balance of *Daphnia pulex* de Geer as related to environmental conditions. II. The dependence of carbon assimilation on animal size, temperature, food concentration and diet species. *Arch. Hydrobiol. (Suppl.)*, **48**, 310–335.

Lampert W. (1978) Release of dissolved organic carbon by grazing zooplankton. *Limnol. Oceanogr.*, **23**, 831–834.

Lampert W. (1981) Toxicity of the bluegreen *Microcystis aeruginosa:* effective defence mechanism against *Daphnia*. *Verh. Internat. Verein. Limnol.*, **21**, 1436–1440.

Lampert W. & Schober U. (1978) Das regelmassige Auftreten von frujahres Algenmaximum und 'Klarwasserstadium' in Bodensee als Folge von Klimatischen Bedingungen und Wechselwerkungen zwischen Phyto-und Zooplankton. *Arch. Hydrobiol.*, **62**, 364–386.

Lane P., Klug M.J. & Louden L. (1975) Measuring invertebrate predation *in situ* on zooplankton assemblages. *Trans. Amer. Micros. Soc.*, **95**, 143–155.

Lasenby D.C. (1979) A method for determining predation rates of macrozooplankton. *Can. J. Zool.*, **57**, 1504–1508.

Lasenby D.C. & Langford R.R. (1973) Feeding and assimilation of *Mysis relicta*. *Limnol. Oceanogr.*, **18**, 280–285.

Lautenschlager K.P., Kaushik N.K. & Robinson J.B. (1978) The peritrophic membrane and fecal pellets of *Gammarus lacustris limnaeus* (Smith). *Freshwat. Biol.*, **8**, 207–211.

Lawton J.H. (1970) Feeding and food energy assimilation in larvae of the damselfly *Pyrrhosoma nymphula* Sulz Odonata: Zygoptera. *J. Anim. Ecol.*, **39**, 669–689.

Laybourn J.E.M. (1975) An investigation of the factors influencing mean cell volume in populations of the ciliate *Colpidium campylum*. *J. Zool. (Lond.)*, **177**, 171–177.

Laybourn J.E.M. & Stewart J.M. (1975) Studies on consumption and growth in the ciliate *Colpidium campylum* Stokes. *J. Anim. Ecol.*, **44**, 165–174.

Lebour M.V. (1922) The food of planktonic organisms. *J. Mar. Biol. Assoc. U.K.*, **12**, 644–677.

Lechowicz M.J. (1982) The sampling characteristics of electivity indices. *Oecologia (Berl.)*, **52**, 22–30.

Lefèvre M. (1942) L'utilization des algues de l'eau douce par les Cladocères. *Bull. Biol. de la France et Belgique.*, **76**, 250–276.

Lehman J.T. (1976) The filter feeder as an optimal forager and the predicted slopes of feeding curves. *Limnol. Oceanogr.*, **21**, 501–516.

Lemcke H.W. & Lampert W. (1975) Veränderungen in Gewicht und der chemischen

Zusammensetzung von *Daphnia pulex* beim Hunger. *Arch. Hydrobiol. (Suppl.)*, **48**, 108–137.

Lenz J. (1977) On detritus as a food source for pelagic filter feeders. *Mar. Biol.*, **41**, 39–48.

Lewis W.M. (1977) Feeding selectivity of a tropical *Chaoborus* population. *Freshwater. Biol.*, **7**, 311–325.

Lowndes A.J. (1935) The swimming and feeding of certain calanoid copepods. *Proc. Zool. Soc. Lond.*, **107**, 687–715.

Lucas C.E. (1936) On certain interrelations between phytoplankton and zooplankton under experimental conditions. *J. Cons. Perm. Explor. Mer.*, **11**, 343–362.

Lumer H. (1932) The reaction of certain Cladocera to colored lights of equal intensity. *Ohio J. Sci.*, **32**, 218–231.

Lynch M. (1977) Fitness and optimal body size in zooplankton populations. *Ecology*, **58**, 763–774.

Mackas D. & Bohrer R. (1976) Fluorescence analysis of zooplankton gut contents and an investigation of diel feeding patterns. *J. Exp. Mar. Biol. Ecol.*, **25**, 77–85.

Marcotte B.M. (1977) An introduction to the architecture and kinematics of harpactacoid (Copepoda) feeding: *Tisbe furcata* (Baird, 1837). *Mikrofauna Meeresboden*, **61**, 183–197.

Marler P.R. & Hamilton W.J. (1967) *Mechanisms of Animal Behaviour*. New York: Wiley & Sons.

Marshall S.M. (1924) The food of *Calanus finmarchicus* during 1923. *J. Mar. Biol. Assoc. U.K.*, **13**, 473–479.

Marshall S.M. (1973) Respiration and feeding in copepods. *Adv. Mar. Biol.*, **11**, 57–120.

Marshall S.M. & Orr A.P. (1955) On the biology of *Calanus finmarchicus*. VIII. In adult and stage V *Calanus*. *J. Mar. Biol. Assoc. U.K.*, **34**, 495–529.

Marshall S.M. & Orr A.P. (1966) Respiration and feeding in some small copepods. *J. Mar. Biol. Assoc. U.K.*, **46**, 531–535.

Martin J.H. (1970) Phytoplankton—zooplankton relationships in Narraganset Bay. IV. The seasonal importance of grazing. *Limnol. Oceanogr.*, **15**, 413–418.

Mayzaud P. (1980) Some sources of variability in the determination of digestive enzyme activity in zooplankton. *Can. J. Fish. Aquat. Sci.*, **37**, 1426–1432.

Mayzaud P. & Mayzaud O. (1981) Kinetic properties of digestive carbohydrases and proteases of zooplankton. *Can. J. Fish. Aquat. Sci.*, **38**, 535–543.

McAllister C.D. (1970) Zooplankton rations, phytoplankton mortality, and the estimation of marine phytoplankton. In J.H.Steele (ed.), *Marine Food Chains*. Berkeley: University of Calif. Press.

McCauley E. & Kalff J. (1981) Empirical relationships between phytoplankton and zooplankton biomass in lakes. *Can. J. Fish. Aquat. Sci.*, **38**, 458–463.

McMahon J.W. (1965) Some physical factors influencing the feeding behavior of *Daphnia magna* Straus. *Can. J. Zool.*, **43**, 603–611.

McMahon J.W. (1968) Environmental factors influencing the feeding behaviour of *Daphnia magna* Straus. *Can. J. Zool.*, **46**, 759–762.

McMahon J.W. (1970) A tracer study of ingestion and metabolic cycling of iron in *Daphnia magna*. *Can. J. Zool.*, **48**, 873–878.

McMahon J.W. & Rigler F.H. (1963) Mechanisms regulating the feeding rate of *Daphnia magna* Straus. *Can. J. Zool.*, **41**, 321–332.

McMahon J.W. & Rigler F.H. (1965) Feeding rates of *Daphnia magna* Straus in different foods with radioactive phosphorus. *Limnol. Oceanogr.*, **10**, 105–113.

McQueen D.J. (1970) Grazing rates and food selection in *Diaptomus oregonensis* (Copepoda) from British Columbia. *J. Fish. Res. Board Can.*, **27**, 13–20.

Mood A.M., Graybill E.A. & Boes D.C. (1974) *Introduction to the Theory of Statistics*. 3rd ed. New York: McGraw-Hill.

Morgan K. (1976) *Studies on the autecology of the freshwater algal flagellate Cryptomonas erosa* Skuja. Dissertation. McGill University, Montreal, Canada.

Mullin M.M. (1963) Some factors influencing the feeding of marine copepods of the genus *Calanus*. *Limnol. Oceanogr.*, **9**, 239–250.

Mullin M.M., Stewart E.F. & Fuglister F.V. (1975) Ingestion by planktonic grazers as a function of concentration of food. *Limnol. Oceanogr.*, **20**, 259–262.

Murtaugh P. (1981) Selective predation by *Neomysis mercedis* in Lake Washington. *Limnol. Oceanogr.*, **26**, 445–453.

Nadin-Hurley C.M. & Duncan A. (1976) A comparison of daphnid gut particles with the seston present in two Thames Valley reservoirs throughout the season. *Freshwat. Biol.*, **6**, 109–123.

Nalewajko C. (1966) Dry weight, ash and volume data for some freshwater planktonic algae. *J. Fish. Res. Board Can.*, **23**, 1285–1288.

Naumann E. (1921) Spezielle Untersuchungen über die Ernährungsbiologie des tierischen Limnoplanktons. I. Über die Technik des Nahrungserwerbs bei den Cladoceren und ihre Bedeutung für die Biologie der Gewässertypen. *Lunds Universtets Arsskrift*, **17**, 3–27.

Nauwerck A. (1959) Zur Bestimmung der Filtrierate limnischer Planktontieres. *Arch. Hydrobiol. (Suppl.)*, **25**, 83–101.

Nauwerck A. (1962) Nicht-algische Ernährung bei *Eudiaptomus gracilis* (Sars) *Arch. Hydrobiol. (Suppl.)*, **25**, 393–400.

Nauwerck A. (1963) Die Beziehungen Zwischen Zooplankton und Phytoplankton im See Erken. *Symbolae Botanicae Upsalensis*, **17**, 1–163.

Nicholls K.H. & Dillon P.J. (1978) An evaluation of phosphorus-chlorophyll-phytoplankton relationships for lakes. *Internat. Revue. ges. Hydrobiol.*, **63**, 141–154.

Nival P. & Nival S. (1976) Particle retention efficiencies of a herbivorous copepod *Arcatia clausi* (adult and copepodite stages): effects on grazing. *Limnol. Oceanogr.*, **21**, 24–28.

O'Brien W.J. & DeNoyelles F. (1974) Filtering rate of *Ceriodaphnia reticulata* in pond waters of varying phytoplankton concentrations. *Am. Midl. Nat.*, **91**, 509–512.

O'Connors H.B., Small L.F. & Donaghay P.L. (1976) Particle-size modification by two size classes of the estuarine copepod. *Acartia clausi. Limnol. Oceanogr.*, **21**, 300–308.

Pacaud A. (1939) Contribution a l'écologie des Cladocères. *Bull. Biol. France Belgique (Suppl.)*, **25**, 1–260.

Paffenhöfer G.A. (1971) Grazing and ingestion rates of nauplii, copepodids, and adults of the marine planktonic copepod, *Calanus helgolandicus*. *Mar. Biol.*, **11**, 286–298.

Paffenhöfer G.A. (1976) Feeding, growth and food conversion of the marine planktonic copepod *Calanus helgolandicus*, *Limnol. Oceanogr.*, **21**, 39–50.

Paffenhöfer G.A. & Harris R.P. (1976) Feeding growth and reproduction of the marine planktonic *Pseudocalanus elongatus* Bock. *J. Mar. Biol. Assoc. U.K.*, **56**, 327–344.

Paffenhöfer G.A. & Knowles S.C. (1978) Feeding of marine planktonic copepods in mixed phytoplankton. *Mar. Biol.*, **48**, 143–157.

Paffenhöfer G.A. & Strickland J.D.H. (1970) A note on the feeding of *Calanus helgolandicus* on detritus. *Mar. Biol.*, **5**, 97–99.

Paffenhöfer G.A., Strickler J.R. & Alvaraz M. (1982) Suspension feeding by herbivorous calanoid copepods: a cinematographic study. *Mar. Biol.*, **67**, 193–199.

Paloheimo J.E. (1979) Indices of food preferences by a predator. *J. Fish. Res. Board Can.*, **36**, 470–473.

Pantin C.F.A. (1964) *Notes on Microscopic Techniques for Zoologists.* Cambridge: Cambridge University Press.

Parsons T.R. & Le Brasseur R.J. (1970) The availability of food to different trophic levels in the marine food chain. In J.H.Steele (ed.). *Marine Food Chains.* Berkeley, Calif.: Univ. of California Press.

Parsons T.R., Stephens K. & Strickland J.D.H. (1961) On the chemical composition of eleven species of marine phytoplankton. *J. Fish. Res. Board Can.*, **18**, 1001–1016.

Peters R.H. (1972) *Phosphorus regeneration by zooplankton.* Dissertation. Univ. of Toronto, Toronto, Canada.

Peters R.H. (1975a) Phosphorus excretion and the measurement of feeding and assimilation by zooplankton. *Limnol. Oceanogr.*, **20**, 858–859.

Peters R.H. (1975b) Phosphorus regeneration by natural populations of limnetic zooplankton. *Verh. Internat. Verein. Limnol.*, **19**, 273–279.

Peters R.H. & Lean D.R.S. (1973) The characterization of soluble phosphorus released by limnetic zooplankton. *Limnol. Oceanogr.*, **18**, 270–279.

Peters R.H. & Rigler F.H. (1973) Phosphorus release by *Daphnia*. *Limnol. Oceanogr.*, **18**, 821–839.

Peterson B.J., Hobbie J.E. & Haney J.F. (1978) *Daphnia* grazing on natural bacteria. *Limnol. Oceanogr.*, **23**, 1039–1044.

Pilarska J. (1977) Ecophysiological studies on *Brachionus rubens* Ehrbg. Rotatoria Pol. *Arch. Hydrobiol.*, **24**, 319–354.

Porter K.G. (1973) Selection grazing and differential digestion of algae by zooplankton. *Nature*, **244**, 179–180.

Porter K.G. (1975) Viable gut passage of gelatinous green algae ingested by *Daphnia*. *Verh. Internat. Verein. Limnol.*, **19**, 2840–2850.

Porter K.G. (1976) Enhancement of algal growth and productivity by grazing zooplankton. *Science*, **192**, 1332–1334.

Porter K.G. (1977) The plant animal interface in freshwater ecosystems. *Amer. Sci.*, **65**, 159–170.

Porter K.G. & Feig Y.S. (1980) The use of DAPI for ientification and enumeration of acquatic microflora. *Limnol. Oceanogr.*, **25**, 943–947.

Porter K.G. & Orcutt J.D. (1980) Nutritional adequacy manageability and toxicity as factors that determine the food quality of green and bluegreen algae for *Daphnia*. In W.C.Kerfoot (ed.). *The Evolution and Ecology of Zooplankton Communities.* Hanover, N.H.: University Press of New England.

Porter K.G., Feig Y.S. & Vetter E.F. (in press) Morphology, flow regimes and filtering rates of *Daphnia*, *Ceriodaphnia* and *Bosmina* fed natural bacteria. *Oecologia* (Berl.).

Porter K.G., Gerritsen J. & Orcutt J.D. Jr. (1982) The effect of food concentration on swimming patterns, feeding behaviour, ingestion, assimilation and respiration by *Daphnia. Limnol. Oceanogr.*, **27**, 935–949.

Porter K.G., Pace M.L. & Battey J.F. (1979) Ciliate protozoans as links in freshwater food chains. *Nature*, **277**, 563–565.

Poulet S.A. (1973) Grazing of *Pseudocalanus minutus* in naturally occurring particulate matter. *Limnol. Oceanogr.*, **18**, 564–573.

Poulet S.A. (1974) Seasonal grazing of *Pseudocalanus minutus* on particles. *Mar. Biol.*, **25**, 109–123.

Poulet S.A. (1976) Feeding of *Pseudocalanus minutus* on living and non-living particles. *Mar. Biol.*, **34**, 117–125.

Poulet S.A. (1977) Grazing of marine copepod developmental stages on naturally occurring particles. *J. Fish. Res. Board Can.*, **34**, 2381–2387.

Poulet S.A. & Chanut J.P. (1975) Non-selective feeding of *Pseudocalanus minutus. J. Fish. Res. Board Can.*, **32**, 706–713.

Poulet S.A. & Marsot P. (1978) Chemosensory grazing by marine calanoid copepods (Arthropoda: Crustacea). *Science*, **200**, 1403–1405.

Poulet S.A. & Marsot P. (1980) Chemosensory feeding and food gathering by omnivorous copepods in W.C.Kerfoot (ed.). *Evolution and Ecology of zooplankton communities.* Hanover N.H.: New England University Press.

Pourriot R. (1977) Food and feeding habits of Rotifera. *Arch. Hydrobiol. Beih. Ergebn. Limnol.*, **8**, 243–260.

Prepas E. (1978) Sugar-frosted *Daphnia:* an improved fixation technique for Cladocera. *Limnol. Oceanogr.*, **23**, 557–559.

Rapport D.J., Berger J. & Reid D.B.W. (1972) Determination of food preference of *Stentor coeruleus. Biol. Bull.*, **142**, 103–109.

Rassoulzadegan F. & Etienne M. (1981) Grazing rate of the tintinnid *Stenosemella ventricosa* (Clap. & Lachm). Vorg. on the spectrum of naturally occurring particulate matter from a Mediterranean neritic area. *Limnol. Oceanogr.*, **26**, 258–270.

Richman S. (1958) The transformation of energy by *Daphnia pulex. Ecol. Monogr.*, **28**, 273–291.

Richman S. (1966) The effect of phytoplankton concentrations on the feeding rate of *Diaptomus oregonensis. Verh. Internat. Verein. Limnol.*, **16**, 392–398.

Richman S. & Rogers J.N. (1969) The feeding of *Calanus helgolandicus* on synchronously growing populations of the marine diatom *Ditylum brightwelli. Limnol. Oceanogr.*, **14**, 701–709.

Richman S., Heinle D.R. & Huff R. (1977) Grazing by adult estuarine calanoid copepods of the Chesapeake Bay. *Mar. Biol.*, **42**, 69–84.

Riggs D.S. (1970) *The Mathematical Approach to Physiological Problems.* Cambridge, Mass.: The MIT Press.

Rigler F.H. (1961) The relation between concentration of food and feeding rate of *Daphnia magna* Straus. *Can. J. Zool.*, **39**, 857–868.

Rigler F.H. (1971a) Feeding rates. Zooplankton. In W.T.Edmondson & G.G. Winberg (eds). *A Manual for the Assessment of Secondary Productivity in Freshwaters.* IBP Handbook No. 17. Oxford: Blackwell.

Rigler F.H. (1971b) Methods for measuring the assimilation of food by zooplankton. In W.T.Edmondson & G.G.Winberg (eds.) *A Manual for the Assessment of*

Secondary Productivity in Freshwaters. IBP Handbook No. 17. Oxford: Blackwell.

Ringelberg J. (1969) Spatial orientation of planktonic crustaceans 2. The swimming behaviour in a vertical plane. *Verh. Internat. Verein Limnol.*, **17**, 840–847.

Roman M.R. & Rublee P.A. (1980) Containment effects in copepod grazing experiments. *Limnol. Oceanogr.*, **25**, 982–990.

Rosenberg G.G. (1980) Filmed observations of filter-feeding in the marine planktonic copepod *Acartia clausi. Limnol. Oceanogr.*, **25**, 738–742.

Rubenstein D.I. & Koehl M.A.R. (1977) The mechanisms of filter-feeding: some theoretical considerations. *Amer. Nat.*, **111**, 981–994.

Runge J.A. (1980) Effects of hunger and season on the feeding behaviour of *Calanus pacificus. Limnol. Oceanogr.*, **25**, 134–145.

Runge J.A. & Oman M.D. (1982) Size fractionation of phytoplankton as an estimate of food available to herbivores. *Limnol. Oceanogr.*, **27**, 570–576.

Ryther J.H. (1954) Inhibitory effects of phytoplankton upon the feeding of *Daphnia magna* with reference to growth, reproduction and survival. *Ecology*, **35**, 522–533.

Satomi M. & Pomeroy L.R. (1968) Respiration and phosphorus excretion in some marine populations. *Ecology*, **46**, 877–881.

Saunders J.W. (1972) The transformation of artificial detritus in lake water. In U.Melchiorri-Santolini & J.W.Hopton (eds.). *Detritus and Its Role in Aquatic Environments. Mem. Ist. Ital. Idrobiol. (Suppl.)*, **29**, 261–288.

Schindler D.W. (1968) Feeding assimilation and respiration rates of *D. magna* under various environmental conditions and their relation to production studies. *J. Anim. Ecol.*, **37**, 369–385.

Schröder R. (1961) Über die Schlagfrequenz der 2. Antennen und Mundliednaben bei calanoiden Copepoden. *Arch. Hydrobiol. (Suppl.)*, **25**, 348–349.

Schultz T.W. & Kennedy J.R. (1976) The fine structure of the digestive system of *Daphnia pulex* (Crustacea: Cladocera). *Tissue Cell*, **8**, 479–490.

Sheldon R.W. (1979) Measurement of phytoplankton growth by particle counting. *Limnol. Oceanogr.*, **24**, 760–767.

Sheldon R.W. & Parsons T.R. (1967a) *A practical manual on the use of the Coulter counter in marine science.* Oakville, Ontario: Coulter Electronics of Canada.

Sheldon R.W. & Parsons T.R. (1967b) A continuous size spectrum for particulate matter in the sea. *J. Fish. Res. Board Can.*, **24**, 909–915.

Sheldon R.W., Sutcliffe W.H. Jr. & Prakash A. (1973) The production of particles in the surface waters of the ocean with special reference to the Sargasso Sea. *Limnol. Oceanogr.*, **18**, 719–733.

Singh P.J. (1972) Studies on the food and feeding of the freshwater calanoid *Rhinodiaptomus indicus* Kiefer. 2. Diurnal variations in feeding propensities. *Hydrobiologia*, **39**, 209–215.

Slobodkin L.B. & Richman S. (1956) The effect of removal of fixed percentages of the newborn on size and variability in populations of *Daphnia pulicaria* (Forbes). *Limnol. Oceanogr.*, **1**, 209–237.

Smirnov N.N. (1974) *Fauna of the U.S.S.R. Crustacea. Vol. 1, No. 2*, Veresalus: Acad. Sci. U.S.S.R. Kitir Publ. House.

Smith D.F. & Wiebe W.J. (1977) ^{14}C-labelling of the compounds excreted by phytoplankton for employment as a realistic tracer in secondary productivity measurements. *Microb. Ecol.*, **4**, 1–8.

Smith F.E. & Baylor E.R. (1953) Color response in the cladocerans and their ecological significance. *Amer. Nat.*, **87**, 49–55.

Smyly W.J.P. (1970) Observations of rate of development, longevity and fecundity of *Acanthocyclops viridis* (Jurine) Copepoda: Cyclopoida in relation to type of prey. *Crustaceana*, **18**, 21–36.

Sorokin J.I. (1966) Carbon 14 in the study of the nutrition of aquatic animals. *Int. Revue ges. Hydrobiol.*, **51**, 209–224.

Sorokin J.I. (1968) The use of ^{14}C in the study of nutrition of aquatic animals. *Mitt. Internat. Verein. Limnol.*, **16**, 1–41.

Spomer G.G. (1973) The concept of interaction and operational environment in environmental analyses. *Ecology*, **54**, 200–204.

Starkweather P.L. (1975) Diel patterns of grazing in *Daphnia pulex* Leydig. *Verh. Internat. Verein. Limnol.*, **18**, 2851–2857.

Starkweather P.L. (1978) Diel variations in feeding behaviour of *Daphnia pulex*. Influence of food density and nutritional history of mandibular activity. *Limnol. Oceanogr.*, **23**, 307–317.

Starkweather P.L. (1981) Trophic relationships between rotifer *Brachionus calyciflorus* and the bluegreen alga *Anabaena flos-aquae*. *Verh. Internat. Verein. Limnol.*, **21**, 1507–1514.

Starkweather, P.L. & Gilbert J.J. (1977a) Feeding in the rotifer *Brachionus calyciflorus*. II. Effect of food density on feeding rates using *Euglena gracilis* and *Rhodotorula glutinis*. *Oecologia (Berl.)*, **28**, 133–139.

Starkweather P.L. & Gilbert J.J. (1977b) Radiotracer determination of feeding in *Brachionus calyciflorus:* The importance of gut passage times. *Arch. Hydrobiol. Beih. Ergebn. Limnol.*, **8**, 261–263.

Starkweather P.L. & Gilbert J.J. (1978) Feeding in the rotifer *Brachionus calyciflorus*. IV. Selective feeding on tracer particles as a factor in trophic ecology and on *in situ* techniques. *Verh. Internat. Verein. Limnol.*, **20**, 2389–2394.

Stearns S.C. 1975. Light responses of *Daphnia pulex. Limnol. Oceanogr.*, **20**, 564–570.

Storch O. (1928) Der Nahrungserwerb zweier Copepodennauplien (*Diaptomus gracilis* und *Cyclops strenuus*). *Zool. Jb. (Zool.)*, **45**, 385.

Straškraba M. (1980) The effects of physical variables on freshwater production: analyses based on models. In E.D.LeCren, & R.H.Lowe-McConnell (eds). *The Functioning of Freshwater Ecosystems*. Cambridge: Cambridge University Press.

Strathmann R.R. (1967) Estimating the organic carbon content of phytoplankton from cell volume or plasma volume. *Limnol. Oceanogr.*, **12**, 411–418.

Strickler J.R. (1970) Uber das Schwimmverhalten von Cyclopoiden bie Verminderungen der Bestrahlungsstärke. *Schweiz. Hydrol.*, **32**, 150–179.

Strickler J.R. (1975) Intra- and interspecific information flow among planktonic copepods: receptors. *Verh. Internat. Verein. Limnol.*, **14**, 2951–2958.

Strickler J.R. (1977) Observations of swimming performance of planktonic copepods. *Limnol. Oceanogr.*, **22**, 165–170.

Strickler J.R. & Bal A.K. (1973) Setae of the first antennae of the copepod *Cyclops scutifer* (Garb): their structure and importance. *Proc. Nat. Acad. Sci. U.S.A.*, **70**, 2656–2659.

Sullivan B.K., Miller C.B., Peterson W.T. & Soeldner A.H. (1975) A scanning electron microscope study of the mandibular morphology of boreal copepods. *Mar. Biol.*, **30**, 175–182.

Sushchenya L.M. (1967) Ecological and physiological features of filter feeding in planktonic crustaceans. *Trudy Sev. Biol. St. Akad. Nauk. U.K.U.R.*, **16**, 256–276.

Swift M.C. & Fedorenko A.Y. (1973) A rapid method for the analysis of the crop contents of *Chaoborus* larvae. *Limnol. Oceanogr.*, **18**, 795–798.

Taguchi S. & Fukuchi M. (1975) Filtration rate of zooplankton community during spring bloom in Akeshi Bay. *J. Exp. Mar. Biol. Ecol.*, **19**, 45–164.

Taguchi S. & Ishi H. (1972) Shipboard experiments on respiration, excretion, and grazing of *Calanus cristatus* and *C. plumchrus* (Copepoda) in the northern North Pacific. In A. Takenouti (ed.) *Biological Oceanography of the Northern North Pacific Ocean*. Tokyo: Idemitsu Shoten.

Tappa D.W. (1965) The dynamics of the association of six limnetic species of *Daphnia* in Azycoos Lake, Maine. *Ecol. Monogr.*, **35**, 395–423.

Taub F.B. & Dollar A.M. (1968) The nutritional inadequacy of *Chlorella* and *Chlamydomonas* as food for *Daphnia pulex*. *Limnol. Oceanogr.*, **13**, 607–617.

Tezuka Y. (1971) Feeding of *Daphnia* on planktonic bacteria. *Jap. J. Ecol.*, **21**, 127–134.

Threlkeld S.T. (1976) Starvation and the size structure of zooplankton communities. *Freshwat. Biol.*, **6**, 489–496.

Tonolli V. (1947) Il ritmo cardiaco della *Daphnia pulex* De Geer. *Mem. Ist. Ital. Idrobiol.*, **3**, 415–429.

Turner V.J. (1977) Sinking rates of fecal pellets from the marine copepod *Pontella meadii*. *Mar. Biol.*, **40**, 249–259.

Vanderploeg H.A. (1981) Seasonal particle-size selection by *Diaptomus sicilis* in offshore Lake Michigan. *Can. J. Fish. Aquat. Sci.*, **38**, 504–517.

Vanderploeg H.A. & Scavia D. (1979) Two electivity indices for feeding with special reference to zooplankton grazing. *J. Fish. Res. Board Can.*, **36**, 362–365.

Viaud G. (1951) Le phototropisme chez les cladocères, rotiferes et planaires. *Année Biol.*, **55**, 365–378.

Waite S.W. (1976) Filter feeding dynamics of two Kansas cladocerans. *Emporia State Res. Studies*, **25**, 5–28.

Wallace J.B. & Merritt R.W. (1980) Filter feeding ecology of aquatic insects. *Ann. Rev. Entomol.*, **25**, 103–132.

Wang C.H. & Willis D.L. (1965) *Radiotracer Methodology in Biological Science*. Englewood Cliffs, N.J.: Prentice Hall Inc.

Ward F.J., Wong B. & Robinson G.G.C. (1970) A liquid scintillation procedure for determining the effect of size on self absorption of ^{14}C in *Daphnia pulex*. *Limnol. Oceanogr.*, **15**, 648–652.

Watson S. & Kalff J. (1981) Relationships between nannoplankton and lake trophic status. *Can. J. Fish Aquat. Sci.*, **38**, 960–967.

Webster K.W. & Peters R.H. (1978) Some size dependent inhibitions of larger cladoceran filterers in filamentous suspension. *Limnol. Oceanogr.*, **23**, 1238–1245.

Wightman J.A. (1975) An improved technique for measuring assimilation efficiency by the ^{51}C$_r$-^{14}C twin tracer method. *Oecologia (Berl.)*, **19**, 273–284.

Williamson C.E. (1980) The predatory behaviour of *Mesocyclops edax:* predator preferences, prey defenses, and starvation-induced changes. *Limnol. Oceanogr.*, **25**, 903–909.

Wilson D.S. (1973) Food selection among copepods. *Ecology*, **5**, 909–914.

Young S. (1974) Directional differences in the colour sensitivity of *Daphnia magna*. *J. Exp. Biol.*, **61**, 261–267.

Zankai N.P. & Ponyi J.E. (1974a) On the seasonal fluctuations in the food incorporation of *Eudiaptomus gracilis*. *Annal. Biol. Tihany.*, **41**, 357–362.

Zankai N.P. & Ponyi J.E. (1974b) On the feeding of *Eudiaptomus gracilis* in Lake Balaton. *Annal. Biol. Tihany*, **41**, 363–371.

Zankai N.P. & Ponyi J.E. (1976) Seasonal changes in the filtering rate of *Eudiaptomus gracilis* J.O.Sars in Lake Balaton. *Annal. Biol. Tihany*, **43**, 105–116.

Zaret R.E. (1980) The animal and its viscous environment. In W.C.Kerfoot (ed.). *Evolution and Ecology of Zooplankton Communities*. Hanover, N.H.: University Press of New England.

Zeiss F.R. Jr. (1963) Effect of population densities on zooplankton respiration rates. *Limnol. Oceanogr.*, **8**, 110–116.

Chapter 10. The Measurement of Respiration

WINFRIED LAMPERT

1 Introduction

The aim of estimating secondary production cannot only be to obtain a number for the productivity of a certain lake or river. In order to understand the functioning of a system, one must know which factors limit secondary production and how production changes with changing environmental conditions. The production of different species may respond differently to the change of one factor. Production is the visible result of many physiological processes; it is, therefore, worthwhile to examine closely the processes which contribute to it and the effect of environmental changes. Losses of energy or matter during metabolism are one of the processes important to production.

When production is considered as the sum of accumulated matter in somatic growth and reproduction, it can be determined in long-term experiments without measuring any metabolic losses. However, when the energy or material budget is the center of interest, exact knowledge of the losses and the way in which they vary is essential. It should be mentioned that there is no coupling between the 'metabolic activity' of an animal and its production, *per se* even though animals that exhibit a high metabolic turnover also have a high potential rate of production under optimal conditions, this production rate may not always be realized. Large-scale interspecific comparisons resulted in linear correlations between $\log R$ and $\log P$ (McNeill & Lawton 1970, Humphreys 1979, Lavigne 1982). Different regression lines could be calculated when metabolically similar species were grouped. For a group of short-lived poikilotherms including several freshwater animals, McNeill & Lawton (1970) established the regression line:

$$\log P = 0.8262 \log R - 0.0948 \tag{10.1}$$

(both expressed as $kcal\,m^{-2}\,yr^{-1}$). If reliable measurements of respiration during the season are available, accumulated production can be estimated in this way, even if this can only be a rough approximation due to the considerable scatter of the points obtained. Predictions for individual species under certain environmental conditions should not be made (Lavigne 1982).

When environmental conditions change, the parameters of the balance equation:

$$\text{Production} = \text{Assimilation} - \text{Respiration} - \text{Excretion} \qquad (10.2)$$

may vary independently and may affect production considerably. Availability of food, for example, is a factor which influences assimilation rate and respiration rate differently. Their relationship is illustrated in Fig. 10.1. The assimilation rate is much more dependent on food availability than is the respiration rate. Without any food the assimilation rate is zero, whereas the respiration rate is positive. Because production is the difference between assimilation and metabolic loss, it may be positive or negative, depending on whether assimilation is greater than the losses, or *vice versa*. Negative production may occur under food limitation.

Starving animals lose a considerable amount of body weight per day (Lemcke & Lampert 1975). Of course, this cannot last very long, but how long

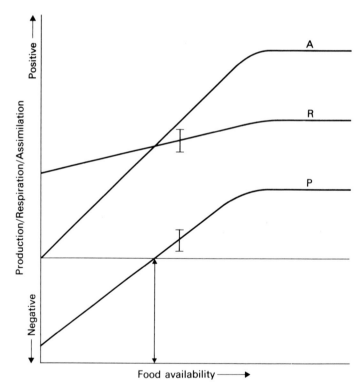

Fig. 10.1 Schematic drawing of the relations between assimilation (A), respiration (R), and production (P) with increasing food availability. The vertical arrows indicate the level of food availability which results in zero production. (see text).

a starving animal will survive depends, besides other factors, on its specific respiration rate. Species-specific or size-specific differences in the respiration rate may, therefore, have consequences for the structure of a community under conditions where food is limited (Threlkeld 1976). Intensity of respiration also influences the food concentration at which production is zero. This is an environmental threshold (Lampert 1977), defining the minimum food availability that allows positive production. In Fig. 10.1, for example, a certain threshold of food availability where positive production is attained can be determined. Since assimilation and respiration rate may respond differently to other environmental changes, this threshold may also vary—for example, when temperature increases above some optimum, the respiration rate will further increase, whereas the assimilation rate will decrease. This results in a dramatic shift of the 'food threshold' to some higher value. From these ideas it becomes clear that under food limiting conditions the production rate is very sensitive to environmental changes. It is evident, therefore, that laboratory measured parameters which are to be applied in field situations must be determined in conditions as close as possible to those in nature.

One more important fact can be seen from Fig. 10.1. The small vertical bars indicate the effect of a 10% error of the measurement of respiration. When the food is limited, the effect of this error on production estimates is much more pronounced. In our case, the 10% respiration measurement error, which is easily introduced by applying only the respiration rates of starving animals to a budget of feeding ones, results in a 50% error in the calculated production. As a consequence, one should measure respiration as exactly as possible. For animals with unlimited food under optimal conditions, this may not be so important. However, we are interested in estimating production in the field where the animals rarely, if ever, live under optimal conditions.

2 Measures of Metabolism

2.1 Choice of the principle method

Because metabolic losses must be measured as exactly as possible, the conditions during the measurement should be as similar to natural conditions as possible. Animals that usually burrow in the sediment will not show the same respiration rates under bright light without any shelter; running water insects need current; a freely swimming zooplankter should not be confined in a very small volume of water. In addition, the energy budget of a feeding animal is different from that of a starving one, so respiration should be measured using fed animals. These conditions will help to ensure that measured rates are similar to natural rates.

Unlike mammals, a 'basal metabolic rate' cannot be defined for poikilotherms, because metabolism is temperature dependent. Therefore, the term 'standard metabolic rate' is used for the minimal respiration rate of a fasting animal at a certain temperature. Total metabolism comprises 'standard metabolism', plus energy costs of motion and increased activity, costs of food gathering (e.g. filtering), and costs of digestion, absorption and transportation of the absorbed food (SDA). For ecologically relevant studies it is not sufficient to know the 'standard metabolic rate' of an animal. A motionless fasting animal will not be able to have a positive production rate. No distinction has to be made between 'resting' and 'active' metabolism, because it should be the aim of the investigator to study respiration at the normal level of activity related to the given environmental conditions.

There are different approaches to measuring metabolic losses. The method chosen depends on the facilities of the researcher and the aim of the study. One might be interested in the flow of energy, or in the flow of matter (e.g. of carbon). Most investigators try to analyze the flow of energy but because energy flow is difficult to measure directly, some uncertain conversions are nearly always included in the calculations. Thus, it might sometimes be better to restrict the conclusions to the mass flow.

True energy output is measured by direct calorimetry. Measuring the heat production is the only method of direct determination of energy losses, and although this method is being developed rapidly it is not yet frequently used.

Measurement of oxygen consumption has a long tradition. Under certain conditions it reflects metabolism and can, therefore, be used as a measure of respiration. However, for use in a budget, oxygen consumption rates must always be converted into some other units and this conversion introduces uncertainties. Nevertheless, it is the mode used most frequently in tackling the problem of respiration.

CO_2 excretion is a true measure of carbon flux. In a budget based on carbon it produces correct figures for the output along with the excretion of organic carbon, but conversion to energy units is still complicated.

A biochemical measure of the potential metabolic activity is provided by a relatively recent method of measuring the activity of the respiratory electron transport system (ETS). It yields integrated measures of respiration which reflect true *in situ* rates, but cannot be used in short-term experiments.

2.2 *Direct calorimetry*

In metabolism, energy is lost as heat. The best method of measuring metabolic losses would be the measurement of heat production by direct calorimetry. During recent years great progress has been made in developing direct calorimetry techniques, even in flow-through systems (see Gnaiger 1979, 1982). With new electronic developments, calorimeters have become very sensitive and stable, so that long-term monitoring of small aquatic animals is possible when a flow-through system is used.

Direct calorimetry is the only method which can be used when anoxic fermentative reactions contribute to the total metabolism. These are not reflected by oxygen consumption, but may sometimes be very important especially for the various aquatic animals, especially benthic organisms, which are able to live, at least partly, under reduced oxygen conditions (Prosser 1973). Direct measurement of heat production is highly recommended, but unfortunately, calorimeters are still expensive and complicated and the method needs some special skill. When the animals are placed in the calorimeter the instrument will be thermally disturbed and re-equilibration requires some hours. Thus, it is not possible to begin the measurements immediately. This might be an advantage because the animals can acclimatize to experimental conditions. To avoid oxygen depletion and accumulation of metabolic products in the chamber, a flow-through system should be used. The flow rate must be low (e.g. $3 \cdot 3$ ml h^{-1}; Gnaiger 1979). As the time constant of the system is dependent on the size of the chamber, the animals must be confined to a small volume of water (e.g. $0 \cdot 5$ ml). Larger chambers may be used, but in this case the time resolution of the system is low, and complicated calculations must be applied. Confinement to a small volume may be a disadvantage for freely swimming animals.

Direct calorimetry is a standard method in biochemistry and physiology but there have been few examples of its application to ecological problems. Nevertheless, this technique is a very valuable tool in ecology, especially when combined with measurements of oxygen consumption.

2.3 Oxygen consumption

2.3.1 General

Measurement of oxygen consumption is the most frequently used method in studies of metabolism. Numerous methods have been developed for a broad range of animal sizes. There are three different modes of experiments in use:

(1) In a closed system the concentration of oxygen or pO_2 is measured at the beginning and at the end of the experiment, or is monitored continuously. Respiration rate is calculated from decreases of oxygen and the volume of the vessel.

(2) Animals are kept in an open-flow system, where water passes slowly through a chamber containing the animals. The concentration of oxygen in the water is measured before and after the chamber. The respiration rate is calculated from the reduction of oxygen concentration and the flow rate of the water.

(3) Animals are kept in water which is equilibrated and in contact with a
     known volume of air. During the experiment the dissolved oxygen
     consumed by the animals is replaced by oxygen from the air and the
     carbon dioxide produced is removed by an absorbant. The volume of air,
     therefore, decreases and this change in volume can be measured
     gasometrically.

The first two methods involve determination of the oxygen in water, which can
be done by measuring the amount of dissolved oxygen by chemical methods or
the partial pressure with a polarographic electrode. The third mode requires
the measurement of the change in gaseous oxygen. This can be done by
holding the pressure constant and measuring the difference in volume, or by
monitoring the pressure changes necessary to keep the volume constant. The
type of experiment selected and the method of oxygen detection used depends
on the sensitivity needed, the size of the animals, and the environmental
conditions to be simulated. The size of the animals is an especially important
factor to be considered when an experiment is designed. Some literature data,
utilizing these methods for animals varying in size by 5 orders of magnitude
are compiled in Fig. 10.2. For the smallest animals (< 1 μg) only the Cartesian
diver principle is used, whereas all the other methods cover a broad range of
sizes. Few measurements have been made using single animals, however. In
the medium size range, most determinations have been made with many
animals per sample. The use of numerous animals in one experiment may be
an advantage, because individual variation is averaged. On the other hand, a
lot of information on individual performance is lost in this way.
    Experiments have to be designed so that the oxygen reduction needed to
measure respiration can be determined with good precision. When dissolved
oxygen is measured with a good system, a 5 % reduction may be sufficient. The
difference should not be greater than absolutely necessary, since the
respiration rate can be proportional to the concentration of oxygen. Reduction
of oxygen in a closed system depends on the total weight of the animals, the
volume of water, the duration of the experiment, and the ambient
temperature. In an open-flow system the difference between the influent and
effluent oxygen concentrations depends mainly on the animals' weight, the
flow rate, and the temperature. The size of the respiration chamber has no
influence on the final concentration but on the response time of the system. If
the ratio of chamber-volume to flow-rate is high, then the final concentration
will be reached very slowly and the response time will be slow. This ratio
cannot be lowered by increasing the flow-rate because in this case, the
reduction of the oxygen concentration might be too small to detect. Thus,
small chambers should be used to improve precision.
    A standard procedure cannot be recommended. Preliminary experiments

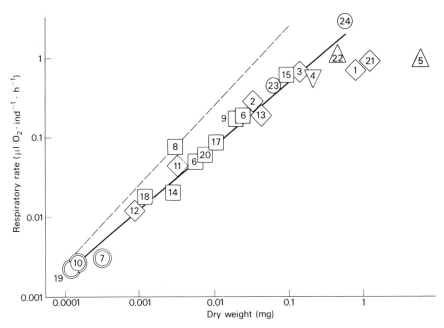

Fig. 10.2 Respiratory rate of different sized aquatic animals at 20 °C. The regression equation for all animals weighing < 0·8 mg (solid line) is log R = 0·794 log W + 0·4828 (r = 0·986; n = 21; 95 % conf. lim. of b: 0·736–0·852). The slope of the dashed line is 1·0. Symbols indicate different methods of measuring respiration:

⊚, Cartesian diver; ◇, gasometric methods; ☐, 'closed bottle', Winkler determination; ○, closed system, membrane electrode; ▽ open-flow system; △ CO_2/IR. Numbers represent different species: 1, *Chaoborus trivittatus* (Swift 1976); 2, *Daphnia pulex* (Goss & Bunting 1980); 3, *Daphnia magna* (Goss & Bunting 1980); 4, *Cloëon dipterum* (Kamler 1969); 5, *Pisidium amnicum* (Holopainen & Ranta 1977); 6, *Daphnia pulex* (Richman 1958); 7, *Brachionus calyciflorus* (Leimeroth 1980); 8, *Diaptomus siciloides* (Comita 1968); 9, *Diaptomus leptopus* (Comita 1968); 10, *Brachionus plicatilis* (Doohan 1973); 11, *Cyclops leuckarti* ♀ (Shcherbakoff 1935); 12, *Cyclops leuckarti* ♂ (Shcherbakoff 1935); 13, *Cyclops strenuus* (Shcherbakoff 1935); 14, 15, *Daphnia magna* (Schindler 1968); 16, *Stenonema pulchellum* (Trama 1972); 17, *Boeckella delicata* (Green & Chapman 1977); 18, *Calamoecia lucasi* (Green & Chapman 1977); 19, *Brachionus rubens* (Pilarska 1977); 20, *Eudiaptomus gracilis* (Kibby 1971); 21, *Chaoborus trivittatus* (Giguère 1980); 22, *Daphnia magna* (Lampert, unpublished); 23, *Daphnia magna* (Kersting & v.d. Leeuw-Leegwater 1976); 24, *Gammarus fossarum* (Franke 1977).

must be performed in all cases. For a rough overview of the literature the conditions in selected experiments of both open and closed types are assembled in Table 10.1.

Methods involving a gas phase are limited by the rate of diffusion of oxygen from air into water; therefore, the volume of water must be small. If a larger volume is needed, the dissolved oxygen concentration must be determined. There is some discussion in the literature comparing the 'closed bottle' to the 'open-flow' method (Kamler 1969; Dries *et al.* 1979; Gnaiger 1982). Kamler (1969) found that the rates of oxygen consumption varied considerably with time, depending on the length of the experimental period. Due to handling of the animals or increased activity, the respiration rates were higher during the first period of an experiment. In an open-flow respirometer, these first measurements can be rejected, but this is impossible in a 'closed bottle' system and the results are, therefore, always too high. This overestimation will increase with decreasing experiment length. Similar results are reported by other authors. Directly after the transfer of *Gammarus fossarum* into a closed chamber with flowing water, the respiration rate was twice as high as it was 4 h later (Franke 1977). Increased output of CO_2 by the mollusc *Pisidium amnicum* during the first hours was observed by Holopainen & Ranta (1977). Larvae of the stonefly *Isoperla buresi* put into a closed bottle showed increased searching and respiratory movements (Kamler 1969).

Rejection of the initial values is possible if the oxygen tension in a closed bottle is continuously recorded by an electrode. In gasometric methods, reading of oxygen consumption may begin some time after the introduction of the animals.

In fact, the interpretation of the initial elevation of the respiratory rate is not easy. Part of the decrease with time may be due to the experimental conditions—the normal activity of the animals may be reduced by the confinement, or the change could be induced by starvation. It is, therefore, not clear whether the initial or the reduced respiratory rate reflects 'normal' conditions. A comparison of the features of both experimental modes adds more arguments to the discussion (Table 10.2). Open-flow respirometry has many advantages and should be used if possible. It is especially useful for continuous long-term monitoring of metabolism and studies on the response of the respiratory rates to changes in environmental factors.

Because respiration is measured with different methods, the results are given in different units, the most frequently used unit being μl O_2 at Standard Temperature and Pressure conditions (STP), i.e. 0 °C and 760 mg Hg. Chemical determinations yield differences in mg O_2. Conversion from microlitres to micrograms can be made by use of the molar volume (1 mol $O_2 = 22 \cdot 3931$). Since these units are not usually used in other fields such as physiology, biochemistry or chemistry there are good reasons for unifying

Table 10.1 Technical features of some published experiments on respiration of aquatic animals of different size.

Species	Ind. weight (mg)	Animals per ml	Approx. weight per ml (mg)	Volume of water (ml)	Period (hrs)	Temp. °C	Method	Author
Closed systems								
Brachionus calyciflorus	0·000 32	?	?	?	2–3	20	Cart. diver	Leimeroth, 1980
Brachionus plicatilis	0·000 18	?	?	?	max. 5	20	Cart. diver	Doohan, 1973
Brachionus plicatilis	0·0002	3000	0·09–0·585	0·0003	2–3	24	Cart. diver	Epp & Lewis, 1979a; personal communication
Chaoborus trivittatus	0·8	0·33	0·26	3	3–30	5–25	volumetric	Swift, 1976
Daphnia pulex	0·025–0·097	1·25	0·031–0·121	4	8	5–30	volumetric	Goss & Bunting, 1980
Daphnia magna	0·141–0·365	1·0	0·141–0·365	4	8	5–25	volumetric	Goss & Bunting, 1980
Simocephalus exspinosus	0·0018–0·112	0·22–2·2	0·004–0·025	9	1	25	volumetric	Obreshkove, 1930
Asellus aquaticus	0·34–4·78	?	?	?	4	23	volumetric	Prus, 1972
Mysis relicta	0·067–13·4	0·04–0·017	0·003–0·22	25–60	20–48	2·4–6·8	Winkler	Ranta & Hakala, 1978
Daphnia pulex	0·006–0·028	0·37–0·74	0·004–0·01	135	24	20	Winkler	Richman, 1958
Diaptomus siciloides	0·0032	1·8	0·006	2·2	2·5–3·4	20	Winkler	Comita, 1968
Diaptomus leptopus	0·0222	0·9	0·02	2·2	6·2–7·4	20	Winkler	Comita, 1968
Daphnia magna	0·003–0·3	0·5–0·1	0·0015–0·03	250	6–12	20	Winkler	Schindler, 1968

(continued)

Table 10.1—(contd)

Species	Ind. weight (mg)	Animals per ml	Approx. weight per ml (mg)	Volume of water (ml)	Period (hrs)	Temp. °C	Method	Author
Stenonema pulchellum	0·5-2	0·04	0·02-0·08	250	24	20	Winkler	Trama, 1972
Boeckella dilatata	0·0045	1-3·3	0·005-0·015	3	4-10	10-25	Winkler	Green & Chapman, 1977
Gammarus pulex	1-14	0·07-0·44	0·44-0·93	45	2-10	2-15	Winkler	Nilsson, 1974
Mysis relicta	0·12-0·7	0·016-0·07	0·008-0·01	150-250	5-8	0-13	Winkler	Lasenby & Langford, 1972
Diaptomus gracilis	0·008	6·7	0·05	100	2-24	5-20	Winkler	Kibby, 1971
Daphnia magna	0·138	0·27	0·038	110	0·5	18	Electrode	Kersting & v.d Leeuw-Leegwater, 1976
Linmocalanus macrurus	0·0001-0·034	0·5-12	0·0012-0·015	6-30	1·8-60	0·2-15	Electrode	Roff, 1973
Gammarus fossarum	0·3-5	1·6	0·5-8	80	0·17	5-23	Electrode	Franke, 1977
Mysis relicta	2-10	0·015	0·03-0·15	667	3	4	Electrode	Foulds & Roff, 1976
Pisidium amnicum	0·2-9·0	1·4-2·9	0·57-12·9	0·35-0·7	10-30	3-20	CO_2/IR	Holopainen & Ranta, 1977
Blackfly larvae	0·025-1·5	0·5-1·1	0·28-0·75	10	0·5-1	15·5	CO_2/IR	Wotton, 1978

Species	Ind. weight (mg)	N	Total weight (mg)	Chamber volume (ml)	Flow rate (ml h^{-1})	Temp. °C	Sensor	Author
Open-flow systems								
Isoperla buresi	5·34	2	10·68	1·2	19·4	8	Dropping mercury electrode	Kamler, 1969
Cloëon dipterum	0·214	30–40	0·63–0·85	7·3	38	20	Dropping mercury electrode	Kamler, 1969
Tubifex barbatus	2	20–40	40–80	?	50–500	16	Dropping mercury electrode	Berg & Jonasson, 1965
Mayfly larvae	?	10–100	?	?	60	8	Dropping mercury electrode	Nagell, 1973
Eurytemora hirundoides	?	11	?	1	1	5–20	Membrane electrode	Gyllenberg, 1973
Cyclops abyssorum	0·036	40	1·42	0·5	5·65	6	Twin flow respirometer	Gnaiger, 1982

Table 10.2 Comparison of 'closed bottle' and 'open-flow' experiments.

'Closed bottle'	'Open-flow'
Disturbance of animals by transfer results in increased respiration rates. Initial values can be rejected, if oxygen is monitored continuously.	Increased rates at the beginning can be ignored.
Oxygen is gradually depleted which can affect animals with oxygen concentration dependent metabolism.	pO_2 constant
Excretory products accumulate.	Excretory products washed out.
Water stagnant, especially harmful for lotic animals.	Water exchange at the body surface of the animal.
No possibility of measurement at constant reduced oxygen tensions.	Low pO_2 conditions can be simulated.
Volume may be large. Calculation simple.	Volume of the chamber must be small, otherwise calculations can be complicated (see Section 2.3.3.).

units and giving all results in terms of molecular volumes. One mole is a relatively large unit so that for freshwater animals μmol (10^{-6} mol) and nmol (10^{-9} mol) are usually the appropriate units. The use of the mole not only makes results more comparable but also allows an easier conversion to energy or carbon units (cf. Table 10.4).

2.3.2 'Closed bottle' methods

This type of technique includes all systems which enclose animals in a fixed volume of water. Ground glass stoppered bottles are often used, but there are other designs which keep the animals in a very small chamber fixed to an electrode tip or in a respiration chamber where water current is produced. The container may be of variable volume (see Table 10.1). The common feature of all these systems is that the oxygen concentration decreases during the experimental period and it is this reduction which is then measured.

A typical example of an experiment using chemical determination of oxygen would be as follows: seven glass bottles of known volume are filled with water from the same well-mixed container. Three bottles receive animals, while two bottles serve as final controls. All bottles are then stoppered and kept under the desired conditions. The remaining 2 bottles are titrated immediately to determine the initial oxygen concentration. The experiment is terminated after some hours. Subsamples are taken from all bottles, avoiding air contamination, and the concentration of oxygen is determined. Animals are removed from the bottles and weighed. Oxygen consumption rates in the bottles with animals have to be corrected for the change in oxygen in the bottles without animals. The true oxygen consumption of the animals is:

$$\text{Oxygen consumption (mg h}^{-1}) = \left(\frac{C_i - C_a}{t_a} - \frac{C_i - C_c}{t_c}\right) \times \frac{V}{1000} \quad (10.3)$$

C_i, C_a, C_c are the oxygen concentrations (mg l^{-1}) of the initial samples, the bottles with animals, and the controls, respectively; t_a and t_c are the incubation periods of the animal bottles and the controls (h), and V is the volume of the bottles containing the animals (ml). If the incubation time is identical for all bottles the formula is reduced to:

$$\text{Oxygen consumption (mg h}^{-1}) = \frac{(C_c - C_a) \cdot V}{t \cdot 1000} \quad (10.4)$$

Multiplication by 31·25 converts mg to μmol. Oxygen consumption may be divided by the number of animals to yield the individual respiration rate (μmol ind^{-1} h^{-1}) or by the total weight of the animals to yield the specific respiration rate (μmol mg^{-1} h^{-1}).

No separate bottles are needed for the initial samples if oxygen is measured by a micro-technique using only a very small amount of water or by an electrode since the initial concentration in each bottle can be measured before it is closed. Alternatively, an electrode may be fixed in the bottle, allowing the oxygen concentration to be recorded continuously. The problem is that the water at the surface of the electrode must be moved. Teal & Halcrow (1962) used a magnetic stirrer, and in order to avoid disturbance of the animals by this stirring, they built a respiration chamber divided into 2 parts by a mesh screen. This mesh allowed mixing of the whole chamber but prevented the animals from coming into contact with the stirrer. Kersting & v.d. Leeuw-Leegwater (1976) used a self-stirring BOD oxygen probe in a similar bottle. Stirring can be omitted when the respiration chamber is very small; Davenport (1976) fixed a very small vial (0·8 ml) at the electrode tip and the water was stirred by the animals themselves.

The results obtained in replicate measurements are always variable. It is, therefore, absolutely necessary to have sufficient replicates. Some of this variability might be introduced by bacterial respiration and some investigators have used antibiotics to reduce the respiration of bacteria incidentally introduced into the vessel (e.g. Kamler 1969; Gyllenberg 1973). They reported that there was no effect on the respiration rate of the animals. Even if this is reasonable in extreme cases, when the oxygen consumption of the controls is very high, one should avoid the additional stress probably introduced by the chemical if possible.

2.3.3 Open-flow systems

Some advantages and disadvantages of open-flow systems have already been discussed. Open-flow apparatus is usually more complicated than closed systems, and this may account for its infrequent use.

In principle, the concentration of oxygen is measured at the inflow and at the outflow of the animal chamber. Respiring animals reduce the oxygen content of the chamber water until a steady state is reached. Under steady state conditions the oxygen consumption is:

Oxygen consumption (mg h^{-1})

$\quad$ = (Concentration at inflow $-$ Concentration at outflow)

$$\times \text{ Flow per hour} \qquad (10.5)$$

Thus, the final difference in oxygen concentration is dependent on the metabolic rate of the animals and the flow rate of water but not on the size of the animal chamber. Flow rate and biomass of the animals have to be adjusted so that a sufficient difference in oxygen concentrations is obtained. The required size of the difference depends on the precision of the oxygen detection system.

The time needed for approaching the steady state depends on the 'system-flushing characteristic time':

$$J(h) = \frac{\omega}{U} \qquad (10.6)$$

where ω is the chamber volume (ml) and U is the velocity of flow (ml h^{-1}). A steady state will be established at a time greater than six times J (Propp *et al.* 1982). Animal size, flow rate, and chamber volume should, therefore, be in an optimal relation. Decreasing the flow rate increases the difference of oxygen concentrations before and after the chamber and the biomass can, therefore, be smaller. At the same time, however, it increases J so that the chamber must be small to prevent too long a 'response time' for the system. This is especially important if the response of the animals to sudden environmental changes shall be measured.

To avoid waiting for the establishment of a steady state, and to allow monitoring of changes of the metabolic activity with sufficient time resolution, equations have been developed which describe the time course of the oxygen concentrations in the chamber (Nimi 1978; Northby 1976; Propp *et al.* 1982). These equations allow the calculation of respiratory rates in a flow-through system for any time after the start of the experiment, but they are, however, much more complicated than equation 10.5, which requires a system in the steady state.

A very simple open-flow system was described by Feldmeth (1971). The respiration chamber is a piece of thick glass tube closed at both ends with rubber stoppers. Glass tubes of smaller diameter pass through the stoppers, so that the chamber is open at both sides. At one side (outflow) the glass tube is formed into a siphon. The animal chamber is submerged in a large tank filled with water, so that the water can run out of the tank and through the animal chamber by means of the siphon. The siphon must be long enough and the tank large enough to assure a constant flow of water for some time. The flow is regulated by a clamp. The end of the siphon is placed at the bottom of a Winkler type oxygen analysis bottle, so the water runs into the bottle. Before oxygen is determined chemically, the bottle should have been flushed with at least twice its volume of water. Overflowing water is collected in a measuring cylinder to determine the flow rate.

Polarographic oxygen sensors allow some improvements to this system. The principle design of such a system is presented in Fig. 10.3a. Water is pumped very slowly from a reservoir through the experimental chamber to the electrodes, where pO^2 is measured. A second path leads directly to the electrode, avoiding the respiration chamber. The electrode can be supplied either with water from the chamber or directly from the reservoir by the use of two 3-way valves. When the system is switched into reference position, water flows through the chamber and the flow rate can be measured at the outlet. Oxygen consumption is calculated as the difference between the oxygen readings in the reservoir and the chamber multiplied by the flow rate.

The first systems of this kind used dropping mercury electrodes for the detection of oxygen (Mann 1958). A very detailed description is given by Klekowski & Kamler (1968) and a condensed description by the same authors (1971) is also available. The system was used successfully by Nagell 1973). Handling of dropping mercury electrodes is not easy, and some authors have replaced them with membrane electrodes. Gyllenberg (1973) used an electrode chamber which has a very small dead volume and does not need to be stirred. Similar systems have been used by Bulnheim (1972), and Scharf *et al.* (1981).

Open-flow systems with one electrode do not provide continuous measurements because recording is necessarily interrupted when the oxygen concentration of the reference water is measured. This disadvantage can be overcome by using two membrane electrodes, one upstream and one downstream from the animal chamber. Dropping mercury cannot be used for this purpose. A system with two electrodes, described by Dries *et al.* (1979), incorporated a valve which enabled the experimental medium to flow through the respiration chamber or to bypass it. Oxygen consumption was calculated automatically from the difference in the oxygen concentrations.

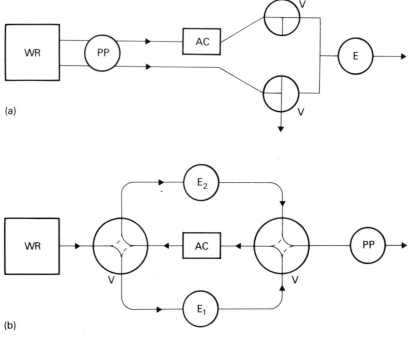

(a)

(b)

Fig. 10.3 Principal of open-flow systems using membrane electrodes as oxygen sensors. (a) System with one electrode. (b) Twin-flow respirometer. WR, water reservoir; AC, animal chamber; E, electrodes; PP, peristaltic pump; V, valve.

A further improvement is the principle of the twin-flow respirometer (Gnaiger 1982), presented in Fig. 10.3b. This system also contains two membrane electrodes, but each electrode can be used alternately before or after the animal chamber, allowing calibration of the electrodes during the experiment. The flow of water is regulated by two 4-way valves which can be switched simultaneously. In the position drawn in Fig. 10.3b, the electrode E_1 is the reference and electrode E_2 measures the oxygen content of the water which passed through the chamber. When the valves are turned by $90°$, E_2 becomes the reference electrode and E_1 measures post-chamber oxygen concentrations, while the direction and magnitude of the water flow through the chamber does not change. Interruptions are reduced to the time taken for new equilibration of the electrode. The valves may be driven by a motor and a timer, so that long-term monitoring of oxygen consumption can be done automatically. The precision of the method is high since the electrodes are frequently recalibrated. To avoid dead space, all of the connecting tubes in a flow-through system should be small in diameter. This often causes problems because tubings are permeable to oxygen, expecially when water with low oxygen content is used. Therefore, gold capillaries are used in the twin-flow respirometer. Comparisons of the open-flow system with other methods have been made by Kamler (1969), Gyllenberg (1973), and Dries *et al.* (1979). Ultimately, however, the sensitivity of open-flow and closed bottle methods depend upon the precision of the oxygen determination method.

2.3.4 Chemical determination of dissolved oxygen

The most wide-spread method of measuring dissolved oxygen is the chemical determination described by Winkler (1888). The procedure is well known, and is described in all collections of water chemistry methods (e.g. Standard Methods 1976; Wetzel & Likens 1979). The reaction is based upon the oxidation of manganous hydroxide by the oxygen dissolved in the water, resulting in the formation of a tetravalent compound. In a second step, the solution is acidified and potassium iodide is oxidized, resulting in the liberation of free iodine. The number of moles of dissolved oxygen is equivalent to the number of moles of iodine liberated. Thus, when the iodine is titrated with a standard solution of sodium thiosulphate, this yields a measure of the oxygen present in the sample.

Carrit & Carpenter (1966) discussed the basic chemistry of the Winkler procedure and carried out intercalibration experiments which showed that there was a great variation in the results of participants from different institutions. The errors resulted mainly from photochemical oxidation of iodide and from loss of iodine through volatilization, but several other possible sources of errors have been pointed out by Carpenter (1965a), e.g. oxygen contributed by reagent solution and a difference between titration end-point and equivalence point.

The Winkler method has been the subject of many modifications which aim to reduce the errors, improve the accuracy by better titration, and to adapt it to very small volumes of water. Fox & Wingfield (1938) carried out reactions in a syringe pipette and used only 1·5 ml of water while obtaining 2 % accuracy even at low concentrations. Several authors have used the micro-Winkler technique as described in Barnes (1959). The method applied by Ranta & Hakala (1978) is similar. By analyzing 3 ml and using an automatic burette (0·005 ml accuracy), they obtained an absolute accuracy of 0·0001 mg O_2 and a coefficient of variation of 2 %.

The precision of the Winkler method is usually considered to be 0·02 mg $O_2 \, l^{-1}$ (Strickland, 1960), i.e. the standard deviation resulting from parallel experiments. There have been some attempts to improve this precision by using different titration techniques: Carpenter (1965b) provides a detailed description of a modification that results in 0·1 % accuracy. Talling (1973) reported a reproducibility of 0.02–0.04 mg $O_2 l^{-1}$ with amperometric end-point titration. Bryan *et al.* (1976) achieved a precision of 0.01 mg $O_2 l^{-1}$ using photometric end-point detection without starch. Tschumi *et al.* (1977) designed a 'phototitrator' consisting of a sensitive photometer and a motor-driven piston burette. After strictly standardizing all manipulations they found a standard deviation of 0.002–0.004 mg $O_2 l^{-1}$ under laboratory conditions. With samples exposed *in situ*, this value was 0.005 mg $O_2 l^{-1}$. A similar photometric system was described in detail by Vargo & Forcé (1981). Variation is always greater in natural waters than in pure laboratory experiments, and it is not always clear how the precision has been determined. The density of phytoplankton present is important, since some iodine may be adsorbed to the algae. In addition, oxidizing and reducing substances may interfere with the reactions.

The error attributed to organic substances is avoided by the iodine difference method developed by Ohle (1953), but this cannot always be used because two subsamples are needed for comparison. Some problems (e.g. volatilization of iodine, interference of dissolved organic carbon) may be overcome by using the ceriometric method (Golterman & Wisselo 1981), which is similar to the Winkler procedure, but is based on the oxidation of $Ce(OH)_3$. Its precision is said to be 1% but this may be improved. It has not yet been used in respiration studies.

2.3.5 *Polarographic sensors*

When a platinum electrode in water is held at a potential of about -1 volt to a silver-silver oxide reference electrode, molecular oxygen is reduced at the platinum surface, causing a current to flow. This current is proportional to the amount of oxygen that comes into contact with the platinum and these electrodes can, therefore, be used to measure the concentration of oxygen present. The current will not be stable for long in a medium which is not completely pure, however, because the platinum surface becomes covered by metals plating out or by other materials that reduce the access of oxygen to the electrode.

There are two ways of overcoming this problem. A dropping mercury electrode (Briggs *et al.* 1956) may be used in which the surface of the electrode is frequently renewed. The second possibility is to cover the platinum electrode with a thin membrane (Clark *et al.* 1953) which is permeable to oxygen but impermeable to impurities. Both systems have advantages and disadvantages. Klekowski (1971a) discusses these and favors the dropping mercury electrode, but 10 years of experience and improved equipment have rendered many of his arguments against the membrane electrode unimportant. Membrane electrodes are much more convenient than the dropping mercury electrode, since safe handling of mercury is not easy, especially when it is distilled or highly purified. Moreover, measurements should be made outside of the animal container in order to avoid possible mercury toxicity. Handling inconvenience may be the reason that the dropping mercury electrode is not used more frequently, whereas a membrane oxygen sensor can be found in most laboratories.

Recently, many good commercial sensors have become available so that there is no need to produce them by hand (see Teal 1971) for routine purposes. The cathode is usually made of platinum, or sometimes of gold, and the anode is silver. Membranes are usually made of polyethylene, teflon or polypropylene. A very small amount of electrolyte solution (e.g. KOH, $KHCO_3$, phosphate-$NaCl$ buffer) is placed between the membrane and the electrode head. In the electrode reaction, oxygen from the buffer is consumed and replaced by diffusion through the membrane. After some period of exposure, a steady-state is reached between consumption and replacement. A strong current of water must be generated to avoid depletion of oxygen in the boundary layer at the surface of the membrane, although this is not necessary if a specially designed electrode chamber with a $70\,\mu l$ sample volume is used. For more technical comments on the functioning of electrodes refer to Carey & Teal (1965), Fatt (1976), Hitchman (1978), or Gnaiger & Forstner (1982).

An electrode for use in respiration experiments should have three special properties:

(1) The oxygen consumption of the electrode should be low. By using very small cathodes, modern sensors have a very low consumption—it can be $<0.1\,\mu g\ O_2\ h^{-1}$ p.p.m. oxygen^{-1}.
(2) The response time should be rapid. This is dependent on the material, the thickness of the membrane and the temperature. When the oxygen concentration is changed, 99% of the new value should usually be reached within 1–2 min.
(3) Precision of measurements should be high. Sensitivity of the respiration measurement depends mainly on the precision of the electrode, i.e. the error obtained by repeatedly measuring the same sample.

As the quantity to be estimated is the difference between oxygen concentrations, the 'accuracy', i.e. the closeness of a measured value to the 'real' oxygen consumption is not as important as the precision. With some skill a precision of 0.01–$0.02\,mg\ O_2\ l^{-1}$ may be reached. One factor determining the precision of measurement is the stability of the system—a good electrode shows a drift of $\ll 1\%$ per day. How long an electrode can be used without renewing the membrane depends on the material and thickness. Precise electrodes have thin membranes (about $20\,\mu m$), which have to be replaced more often. Nevertheless, an electrode should maintain its quality for some weeks.

Polarographic oxygen sensors measure partial pressure of oxygen in water, thus they have to be calibrated frequently. This is usually done by a two-point calibration. For adjustment of the zero-point, solutions of sodium sulfite, sodium dithionate or a commercially available 'zero-solution' can be used. Saturated water is measured for the second reference point. The water must be equilibrated carefully. The partial pressure of oxygen is then calculated according to the barometric pressure.

$$pO_2 = (p_a - p_w) \cdot 0 \cdot 209\ 3 \qquad (10.7)$$

where pO_2 is the desired partial pressure (mmHg), p_a is the barometric pressure (mmHg), and p_w is the partial pressure of steam at the given temperature, which may be taken from tables (e.g. Opitz & Bartels 1955; Chemical Rubber Company 1976). The sensor is then immersed into the saturated water and the display is set to the calculated partial pressure. Calibration of the 'slope' by saturated water has to be done more frequently than zero-point calibration. In experiments at very low oxygen tensions, this type of calibration may not be sufficient. Even at zero oxygen, a sensor shows a small residual current which may be unstable, and under extreme conditions, calibration by a series of measurements on different levels of oxygen is recommended (Gnaiger 1982). Oxygen content can be calculated according to:

$$O_2\,(mg\,l^{-1}) = \frac{S \cdot pO_2}{760} \qquad (10.8)$$

where S is the solubility of oxygen at a certain temperature under standard pressure, and pO_2 is the measured partial pressure (mmHg). Values for the oxygen content of air-saturated water can be taken from commonly used tables (e.g. Hitchman 1978; Wetzel & Likens 1979; Mortimer 1981). The preparation of saturated water often needs more time than expected and may be unsatisfactory. A check of the calibration by Winkler titration can, therefore, be useful.

2.3.6 Volumetric methods

When oxygen is consumed from a given gas volume by respiring animals, and when the CO_2 evolved is trapped simultaneously, the resulting change in gas volume is a direct measure of oxygen consumption. The best known system of this type is the Warburg apparatus, but because shaking of the respirometer flasks may disturb the animals (Wightman 1977), it cannot be recommended. Richman (1958) found the Warburg apparatus unsuitable for *Daphnia* because the animals were caught in the surface film. When the volume of water is small, shaking can be omitted since gas exchange between water and air by diffusion is sufficiently rapid. Two basic types of gasometric respirometers exist: those in which pressure in the system may change and those in which pressure is kept constant.

In the simplest system (Fenn 1927), which has been used for aquatic animals by Obreshkove (1930) and Shcherbakoff (1935), pressure is allowed to change. Two vessels, one containing water with animals, the second containing only water, are connected by a capillary (Fig. 10.4a) in which a

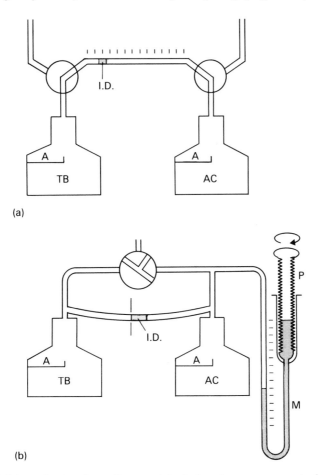

(a)

(b)

Fig. 10.4 Schematic drawings of gasometric devices for measurement of respiration: (a) Constant volume, changing pressure (Obreshkove, 1930). (b) Constant pressure, changing volume (Klekowski 1975). AC, animal chamber; TB, thermobarometer; A, CO_2 absorbant; ID, indicating drop; P, threaded piston; M, mercury.

drop of kerosene is allowed to move. Both vessels contain a spoonlike device to hold a piece of filter paper soaked with NaOH for trapping the CO_2. The system is immersed in a water bath to maintain constant temperature. Two valves allow connection of the chambers to the open air and equilibration. When the valves are closed and the oxygen in one bottle is consumed, the kerosene indicator drop begins to move, and its movement per unit time is recorded. The capillary must be calibrated for the calculation of the volume of oxygen consumed. As the reduction of pressure is shared equally between the two vessels, the volume of oxygen is twice the volume calculated from the distance the drop moved and the cross-sectional area of the capillary.

This system has been improved by holding the pressure constant and changing the volume of the system (Fig. 10.4b) in a micro-respirometer described by Scholander *et al.* (1952). Klekowski (1975) used the same principle. His respirometer, originally designed for terrestrial animals but also used for aquatic ones (e.g. Swift 1976), also consists of two vessels, one containing the animals, the second serving as a thermobarometer. Both vessels contain filter paper saturated with KOH or NaOH, and there are two connections between them, one allowing equilibration, the other, a capillary containing a kerosene drop. The vessel containing the animals is connected to a capillary filled with mercury which is attached to a threaded piston. By turning the piston, the level of mercury in the capillary is moved. At the beginning of an experiment the valve in the equilibration tube is closed. The indicator drop then starts to move and is kept at the original position by gently turning the piston. Thus, the reduction of the volume is compensated by movement of the mercury. The mercury capillary can be calibrated so that the volume of oxygen consumed can be read from the revolutions of the piston.

Scholander *et al.* 1952 demonstrated how CO_2 evolution can be estimated from the difference between experiments with and without absorbant. The absorbant can be removed between two trials or the container holding the filter paper may be closed by a lid without opening the system. However, if the medium is highly buffered the evolution of CO_2 can be confounded, because the gas is directly absorbed into the water. For the same reason an absorbant is not usually necessary if the water is buffered well.

The volumetric respirometers described above are made for oxygen uptake rates of the order of $1\,\mu$mol O_2 h^{-1}. A much more sensitive apparatus, described by Klekowski (1977), uses containers in the shape of a Cartesian diver (see Section 2.3.7) but is modified for shipboard work where a freely floating diver cannot be used. The animal is contained in a drop of water separated from a drop of NaOH solution by a small volume of air. As oxygen from the air is consumed and CO_2 is absorbed, the air volume becomes smaller. The respiration chamber is connected to a thin capillary tube with an indicator bubble of air which moves when oxygen is consumed. The bubble is kept at a fixed position by changing the pressure in the system. This respirometer can be used for measurement of oxygen consumption in the range from 0·005 nmol to 0·02 μmol O_2 h^{-1}, i.e. from single small nauplii to adult copepods.

2.3.7 *Cartesian and gradient divers*

'Divers' are the most sensitive tool for respiration measurement and most studies with very small animals, such as rotifers, have used this type of technique (see Fig. 10.2 and Table 10.1). Even though the use of divers requires some skill, the relatively simple equipment can usually be made by the investigator. The Cartesian diver is a constant volume, variable pressure system in which the animal is enclosed in a small drop of water in a specially designed container (see Fig. 10.5). In addition to water, the container holds an air bubble. The entire 'diver' floats freely in a medium (0·1 NaOH) and is enclosed in a floating vessel which is connected to a manometer filled with Brodie's fluid (Fig. 10.6). The pressure in this closed vessel can be regulated by means of coarse and fine adjusting screws. The diver is equilibrated in the floating medium by adjusting the pressure. Because the bubble enclosed in a

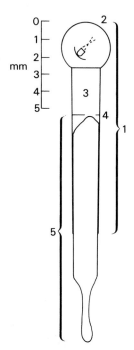

Fig. 10.5 Stoppered diver. 1, diver chamber; 2, chamber head; 3, gas bubble; 4, 0·1 N NaOH solution; 5, stopper. (From Klekowski, 1971b).

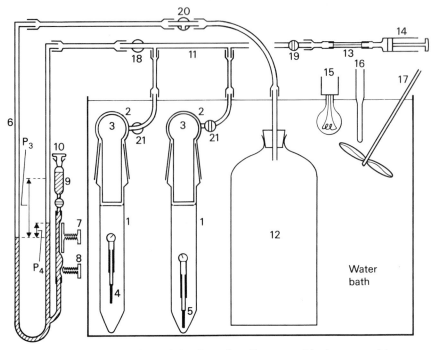

Fig. 10.6 Schematic drawings of the Cartesian diver assembly (not to scale). (From Klekowski, 1971b) 1, Flotation vessel; 2, cap; 3, space occupier; 4, diver floating at the equilibrium mark; 5, diver resting on the bottom between measurements; 6, manometer; 7, 8, coarse and fine screws for pressure regulation; 9, the reservoir with manometric fluid; 10, reservoir stopper; 11, manifold; 12, air bottle; 13, air brake; 14, syringe (100 ml); 15, heating bulb; 16, thermoregulator; 17, stirrer; 18–21, taps.

'stoppered diver' is connected to the surrounding medium, an increase in pressure results in a decrease in the volume of the bubble. Thus, the specific weight of the suspended diver becomes larger and it sinks. If the pressure is decreased, the bubble volume is enlarged and the diver moves upwards. By carefully adjusting the pressure, the diver will stay at its position as long as the volume of the gas is not changed. When an animal inside the diver respires, it consumes oxygen and produces CO_2 which is absorbed by the NaOH solution. The diver sinks and the pressure must be lowered to bring it back to its original position.

Between two measurements the pressure is held at its original level to prevent oxygen moving from the water phase to gas phase, and during this time the diver remains at the bottom of the vessel. From time to time the pressure is lowered until the diver reaches its original position and the changes in pressure are recorded. Eight to ten pressure vessels can be used simultaneously. To calculate the volume of oxygen consumed one must know the volume of the air bubble, which is the so-called 'diver constant'. The oxygen consumption (VO_2; μl O_2 h^{-1}) is calculated according to the formula:

$$VO_2 = \frac{Vg \cdot \Delta P}{P_0 \cdot \Delta t} \cdot \frac{273}{T} \tag{10.9}$$

where Vg = diver constant in μl, ΔP = change of equilibrium pressure (mm Brodie solution), P_0 = normal pressure (10 000 mm Brodie solution), T = water temperature (degrees Kelvin), Δt = time between readings.

Klekowski (1971b) gives a very detailed and useful description of the system, including the preparation, filling, handling, and calibration of the divers, the experimental protocol, and also includes a literature review.

When the divers are operated in a density gradient instead of a homogeneous flotation solution, the system can be open to the atmosphere and need not even be temperature controlled. The theoretical basis and a test of suitability of 'gradient divers', along with practical recommendations are given by Nexø *et al.* (1972). Both closed divers (ampulla) and stoppered divers are in use. The ampulla diver is more sensitive but the stoppered diver can be used repeatedly. A 'control' diver is put into the gradient and finds a steady equilibrium position. If an animal is enclosed, which reduces the gas volume, the diver will sink according to its specific gravity. Control and experimental divers both perform migrations due to changes in barometric pressure and temperature. The oxygen consumption rate is calculated by measuring the difference in position change between control and experimental divers.

Linear gradients are made of H_2O and Na_2SO_4 solutions (density $\sim 1.06 \, g \, ml^{-1}$) and their preparation takes 2–3 h. Density standards (calibrated glass beads) are needed to determine the steepness of the gradient. The sensitivity of the method depends on the precision with which the diver's migration is measured and on the determination of the diver constant. Reading accuracy of the diver's position is ± 0.5 mm with binocular magnification, ± 0.02 mm with photographic recording, and ± 0.005 mm when a cathedometer is used (Nexø *et al.* 1972). Total error in the determination of the diver constant is in the order of 5 % (Hamburger 1981). For animals with a respiratory rate of $< 10^{-3} \, \mu l \, O_2 \, h^{-1}$, ampulla divers are recommended (Hamburger 1981). For these divers, the reading accuracy of the oxygen consumption is in the order of $10^{-4} - 10^{-6} \, \mu l$ (Nexø *et al.* 1972). Technical advice for making ampulla divers, density gradients and glass beads for calibration is given by Klekowski *et al.* (1980).

Reading of the diver's position is tedious, so that there have been several attempts to develop automatic recording techniques. One method involves photographic documentation in a density gradient. Another possibility is the use of an 'electromagnetic' diver which is held in position by the magnetic force generated by a coil located beneath the vessel. This coil starts working when the sinking diver interrupts a light beam, as described by Løvtrup (1973).

2.3.8 Oxycaloric equivalents

When an energy budget is constructed, the energy loss is rarely measured directly as heat production but is usually calculated from oxygen consumption. This is done by use of an energy equivalent, Q_{ox} which, for a given amount of oxygen consumed, depends on the substrate burned, i.e. on the proportion of carbohydrate, fat, and protein. Numerous different values for Q_{ox} can be found in the literature, arising from different substrates. A critical revision of published values and new calculations were made by Elliot & Davison (1975).

Published values of Q_{ox} for carbohydrate agree well with each other, and only a small amount of variation is found among Q_{ox} values determined for fats. In the catabolism of protein, however, oxidation is incomplete and the oxycaloric equivalents will not only depend upon the amino acid composition of the protein, but also upon the nitrogenous compounds excreted. This is not very complicated for aquatic animals because, with rare exceptions, they all excrete ammonia. According to Elliot & Davison (1975), the energy lost in excreta when ammonia is the end product is $82.9 \, kJ \, mol^{-1} \, O_2$. These authors recalculated Q_{ox} values for a 'standard protein'. Their energy equivalents for ammoniotelic animals are assembled in Table 10.3.

There is still some discussion about the correct oxycaloric equivalents for protein, generally due to the questions which surround the amino acid composition of the proteins. Gnaiger (personal communication) assumes that the Q_{ox} for protein should be about 5% higher than the reported value. The main source of error, however, results from the fact that one does not know which substrate is being burned. Table 10.3 shows that the difference

Table 10.3 Oxycaloric equivalents of different substrates according to Elliott & Davison (1975).

Substrate	Oxycaloric equivalent (Q_{ox})		
	cal mg^{-1}	J mg^{-1}	J mmol^{-1}
Carbohydrate	3·53	14·77	472·6
Fat	3·28	13·72	439·0
Protein	3·20	13·39	428·5
General	3·38 (3·29–3·42)	14·14 (13·77–14·31)	452·5 (440·6–457·9)

between the Q_{ox} for pure carbohydrate and pure protein is of the order of 10%. The true Q_{ox} will be between the value for pure protein and that for pure carbohydrate. Some evidence about the substrate can be gained from the RQ (see Section 2.4.5), but a conversion will always include some uncertainty, and this is an argument for the use of direct determination of heat production.

2.4 Excretion of carbon dioxide

2.4.1 General

Very often, parameters of the energy budget are estimated by completely different methods; e.g. energy intake is estimated using ^{14}C-labeled material, growth by increases in dry weight, and metabolic losses by oxygen consumption. All of these measurements must be converted to the same units. To express all parameters of the above example in units of energy one has to know the specific activity and the caloric value of the food, the energy content per dry weight of the animals at the beginning and at the end of the experiment, and the proper oxycaloric equivalent. Since all conversions may introduce specific errors into the budget, it would be better to measure all components of the budget directly in the same units. For example, if ^{14}C is used to measure intake, then it would be logical to measure everything else in terms of carbon, without any conversion factors, i.e. growth as increase of body carbon and respiration as CO_2 losses. There is, therefore, a strong argument for measuring respiration as CO_2 excretion. Moreover, the ratio of CO_2 output to oxygen consumption can provide some insight into the metabolic substrate.

Unfortunately, methods of measuring CO_2 release in water are not as well developed as measurements for oxygen. This is due to the fact that CO_2 is not only dissolved in the water, like oxygen, but is partly bound to the carbonate buffer system. The pool of inorganic carbon is usually rather large, except in waters with very low alkalinity, so that the small difference produced by respiring animals is difficult to measure. Only part of the CO_2 produced by the animals remains free; the pH determines the proportion of the CO_2 that becomes bound chemically (see e.g. Stumm & Morgan 1981).

CO_2 electrodes are available (Jensen *et al.* 1966) but because they measure pCO_2 they cannot be used as a single measure in a buffered system; the pH must be measured simultaneously to calculate the amount of CO_2 that has been converted into bicarbonate. Moreover, pCO_2 electrodes are not as easy to handle as oxygen sensors, are relatively slow, and must be calibrated more frequently. They have, therefore, rarely been used for studies of the respiration of aquatic animals (Gyllenberg 1973). Good precision may be attained using the volumetric methods mentioned above (Section 2.3.6), but CO_2 is only a by-product of measuring the oxygen consumption. Calculation of the respiratory quotient (see Section 2.4.5) is the main aim of CO_2 measurement in most studies; only a few studies use carbon dioxide production as the only measure of animal metabolism. More effort should be put into the measurement of CO_2 excretion.

2.4.2 Change in pH

In a closed system, differences of pCO_2 can be estimated from changes of pH (Verduin 1951; Beyers 1963): the pH of a given water depends on the dissolved CO_2 concentration, so that changes in the CO_2 content result in changes in the pH. The relationship between CO_2 concentration and pH is not linear, however, and a calibration curve must be constructed for each particular water by stepwise titration (Beyers *et al.* 1963). Measurement of pH must be carried out very carefully: a pH meter with a resolution of 0.001 pH should be used (Raymont & Krisnaswamy 1968). This technique has been applied by Richman (1958) and Kibby (1971).

2.4.3 Infra-red analysis

Direct determination of CO_2 is based on extraction and measurement of CO_2 in the water. This has been done by trapping the CO_2 from a stream of air recirculating through the water sample in a closed system (Aldrich 1975), but more often the absorption of infra-red by CO_2 is measured. Holopainen & Ranta (1977) incubated their animals in small cuvettes (0.35–0.7 ml) with sterilized, aerated water for 10–30 h. After the incubation, subsamples of the water were acidified below pH 4 and the CO_2 was extracted by bubbling a carrier gas through the water. CO_2 concentration in the gas was then measured by an infra-red analyser. This method measures total CO_2, and small differences are difficult to detect if the carbonate content of the water is high. In some experiments the authors removed carbonate before the experiment in order to improve the sensitivity: the water was titrated with HCl to pH 5.1, aerated to eliminate CO_2, and titrated back to neutral pH with NaOH. The same system has been used by Wotton (1978) and Ranta & Hakala (1978). The latter authors report an accuracy of 0.01 μg CO_2 and a coefficient of variation of 1 %.

Difficulties in making precise measurements of CO_2 concentration in buffered water may perhaps be overcome by improvements in the method of Teal & Kanwisher (1968). Air is continuously circulated through the water in a closed system; thus an equilibrium of CO_2 is established between water and air. CO_2 concentration in the gas phase is determined by infra-red absorption. If animals in the water produce CO_2 the equilibrium concentration in the air will change, and small differences can be detected since it is not the large quantity of bound CO_2 which is measured but only the change in the gas phase. CO_2 is calculated from the change of equilibrium CO_2 and a previously determined relationship between pCO_2 and total CO_2, unique for each particular water.

2.4.4 Isotope radiotracer method

Respiratory carbon losses can be measured very sensitively by measuring the $^{14}CO_2$ output of animals whose tissues have been homogeneously labeled with ^{14}C (Sorokin 1968). In order to do this, animals are grown for some time with labeled food, which can be prepared by providing algae with ^{14}C-bicarbonate or bacteria with ^{14}C-glucose. The period of feeding with radioactive food must be long enough to ensure that the animals are homogeneously labeled—ideally, they are raised from birth with food of the same specific activity.

To measure the CO_2 release, the animals are rinsed and transferred into clean water. This can be done in an open vessel if the pH of the water is above 8 (Sorokin 1968). After some time, the pH of an aliquot is raised and it is passed through a membrane filter to remove labeled particles produced by the animals. The $^{14}CO_2$ in the water is then measured and the specific activity of the animals is determined. The $^{14}CO_2$ may be precipitated as $Ba^{14}CO_2$ but a more convenient method is to measure the ^{14}C activity directly in a liquid scintillation counter (LSC), using a fluor for aqueous samples.[1] Because excretion of labeled dissolved organic carbon may occur, a second subsample also has to be acidified, bubbled and measured in the LSC. The excreted $^{14}CO_2$ is calculated from the difference in activity between these two types of samples.

The sensitivity of the method depends mainly on the specific activity of the animals. When the water is put directly into the scintillation vial, up to 7 ml can be counted per sample. The sensitivity can be improved if a larger amount of water is acidified, the CO_2 being extracted by bubbling with nitrogen and then caught in a small amount of absorbant (e.g. Phenethylamine). Carbon losses can be calculated:

$$L_c = \frac{DPM_w \cdot V \cdot 100}{DPM_a \cdot \Delta t} \tag{10.10}$$

1. Note: Some of the liquid scintillation cocktails for aqueous samples are acidic; therefore, the CO_2 will escape from the fluor into the overlying air or through the wall of the plastic vial. Significant losses result from this effect. This problem can be eliminated by adding to the sample a small amount of absorbant, which forms a carbamate with the CO_2.

where L_c = carbon loss in % of body carbon h^{-1}, DPM_w = radioactivity of CO_2 ml^{-1} water, DPM_a = radioactivity of the animals, V = container volume, Δt = experimental time period (h).

Carbon dioxide production can be calculated:

$$CO_2 (\text{mmol h}^{-1}) = \frac{DPM_w \cdot C \cdot V \cdot 0.0833}{DPM_a \cdot \Delta t} \qquad (10.11)$$

where C = carbon content of the animals (mg).

The radiotracer method is more sensitive than all of the other methods mentioned and can be recommended, but some comments are necessary, because Sorokin's (1968) description contains errors. After removing the animals from labeled food, he fed them unlabeled food for 3–4 h. He also states that the animals may be fed unlabeled food during the experiment. However, with regard to the CO_2 output, an animal must be considered to be at least a two compartment system (Lampert 1975). These compartments include a 'metabolic pool' that turns over rapidly and a 'structural pool' that turns over more slowly. If a labeled animal eats unlabeled food, its structural pool retains a high specific activity, but the specific activity of the metabolic pool decreases due to dilution by unlabeled food. Thus, the released CO_2 has a much lower specific activity than the animal, and calculated respiration rates are underestimates. For this reason, animals must have no access to unlabeled food. If the gut must be emptied to avoid interference from the gut content, this must be done using inorganic material as a 'food' source rather than with unlabeled metabolizable food. The animal can be fed during an experiment (e.g. to measure the influence of the food on the respiration rate), but the food must have the same specific activity as the animal. Controls must be performed to account for CO_2 release by the food and these controls must be corrected for the amount of food eaten by the animals.

2.4.5 Respiratory quotient

The respiratory quotient (RQ) is needed if oxygen consumption values are to be converted to CO_2 excretion or *vice versa*. It is also needed if one wishes to convert respiration rates to energy equivalents. RQ is defined as the ratio:

$$\frac{\text{vol. } CO_2 \text{ evolved}}{\text{vol. } O_2 \text{ consumed}}$$

Because both oxygen consumption and CO_2 excretion must be measured to calculate RQ, there are not very many measurements available in the literature.

The respiratory quotient depends on the substrate metabolized. When carbohydrate is metabolized, the RQ is 1.0, but because fat oxidation requires more oxygen than carbohydrate, the RQ of fat is lower (about 0·7). Many textbooks give the RQ for protein metabolism as about 0·8 but Elliot & Davison (1975) point out that this is only true for ureotelic animals. Because ammonia is the major excretory product of nearly all aquatic animals, the RQ is 0·949. It may even be a little higher than 1 (Gnaiger personal communication), because the calculation depends on the composition of the 'standard' protein considered. When carbohydrates are transformed into fat, values of RQ > 1·0 can be found. Normally, no pure substrate will be burned, so that the RQ will be somewhere in the range mentioned.

RQ values reported in the literature cover this entire range. Variations within species are very large—for *Mysis relicta*, Ranta & Hakala (1978) found respiratory quotients ranging from 0·61 to 1·17 (mean 0·96 ± 0·13). Moshiri *et al.* (1969) found that the RQ increased from 0·61 to 0·95 with temperature in *Leptodora kindtii*. Part of this variation may be due to the relatively large errors inherent in the CO_2 analysis. Another factor involved may be the nutritional state of the animals. Richman (1958) studied the effect of starvation on the RQ of *Daphnia pulex*. Animals were fed and then starved for 6 days. During this time they showed considerable weight loss. Initially the RQ was 0·92–1·24 (mean 1·03); this dropped to 0·71 after 6 days of starvation. The decrease was due to a reduction of CO_2 excretion, whereas the oxygen consumption on a weight basis did not change.

Little is known about the RQ of actively feeding aquatic animals. From experiments of Bohrer & Lampert (in preparation) it seems that low food concentrations have the same effect as starvation in *Daphnia magna*. RQ increases from 0·7 at very low concentrations of algae to 1·1 at high concentrations.

Differences in the nutritional state may also be responsible for the great seasonal variations in RQ detected by Kibby (1971). During winter, *Diaptomus gracilis* exhibited a respiratory quotient of 0·74 which shifted to 1·25 during summer. Temperature may also contribute to this effect: Grainger (1956) showed that sudden temperature changes caused strong fluctuations in the RQ.

The great variability of reported respiratory quotients may be a problem when comparisons are to be made. Energy budgets are usually constructed for fed animals, however, and all reported values for animals in good nutritional state are rather high. Thus, it may be reasonable to use an RQ near 1 in this case. However, any error inherent to the RQ affects the result of the calculation linearly. If, e.g., carbon or weight losses of an animal under poor food conditions are calculated from oxygen consumption and an RQ of 1 is erroneously applied instead of 0·7, the losses will be overestimated by 42 %. This may have serious consequences for the budget (see Introduction and Fig. 10.1).

2.5 ETS activity

Recently, a completely different method of estimating the metabolic activity of aquatic organisms has been developed (Packard 1971), based on a biochemical determination of the activity of the respiratory electron transport system. Owens & King (1975) have introduced a modification of Packard's method, designed especially for zooplankton.

The idea is that there should be a correlation between the rate of oxygen consumption and the activity of the biochemical structures in the cells which consume the oxygen. These structures are the mitochondrial and microsomal respiratory electron transport system (ETS), a complex chain of cytochromes, flavoproteins, and metallic ions that transports the electrons from catabolized substrate to oxygen. Because the system is complex, the activity of the key enzymes controlling oxygen utilization must be measured in the step that limits the rate of electron transport. This is the oxidation of the coenzyme Q–cytochrome B complex. It can be measured using the artificial electron acceptor 2-(p-iodophenyl)-3-(p-nitrophenyl)-5-phenyl tetrazolium chloride (INT), together with a suitable substrate. The animals are collected from the field, homogenized immediately, centrifuged at 0–4 °C and incubated with

Table 10.4 Conversion factors for use in studies of respiration.

$$1 \text{ mol } O_2 = 32 \text{ g} = 22{\cdot}393 \text{ litres}$$
$$1 \text{ mg } O_2 = 31{\cdot}25 \, \mu\text{mol}$$
$$1 \text{ ml } O_2 = 44{\cdot}66 \, \mu\text{mol}$$
$$1 \text{ mg } O_2 = 0{\cdot}7 \text{ ml}$$

$$1 \text{ mol } CO_2 = 44{\cdot}01 \text{ g} = 22{\cdot}262 \text{ litres}$$
$$1 \text{ mg } CO_2 = 22{\cdot}72 \, \mu\text{mol}$$
$$1 \text{ ml } CO_2 = 44{\cdot}92 \, \mu\text{mol}$$
$$1 \text{ mg } CO_2 = 0{\cdot}506 \text{ ml}$$
$$1 \text{ mg } CO_2 = 0{\cdot}2729 \text{ mg C}$$
$$1 \text{ ml } CO_2 = 0{\cdot}5395 \text{ mg C}$$

$$1 \, \mu\text{mol } O_2 = 1 \, \mu\text{mol C} = 0{\cdot}012 \text{ mg C*}$$
$$1 \text{ ml } O_2 = 0{\cdot}5363 \text{ mg C*}$$
$$1 \text{ mg } O_2 = 0{\cdot}3753 \text{ mg C*}$$

* to be multiplied by RQ

Conversion of a measured gas volume to S.T.P. conditions:

$$V_{(S.T.P.)} = V_a \cdot \frac{P_a \cdot 273}{760 \cdot T}$$

(V_a = actual volume, P_a = actual barometric pressure in mmHg, T = temperature, degrees Kelvin).

INT, NADH, NADPH, buffer and some other chemicals (for details see Packard 1971; Owens & King 1975). The sample is measured photometrically. A refrigerated centrifuge is needed for sample preparation.

ETS activity must be calibrated against some other measure of respiration rate—ratios of ETS activity to oxygen consumption are given by King & Packard (1975). They range from 0·54 to 2·16, depending on the species considered. The ratio is not influenced by temperature and is only slightly affected by the weight of the organisms.

The ETS activity shows a slow response to environmental changes; a new equilibrium of ETS activity is reached 3–4 h after a change in environmental conditions (Båmstedt 1980). It cannot, therefore, be used for the detection of rapid changes in the respiratory rate, but gives an estimate of the upper limit of oxygen consumption under given conditions. When used to measure the *in situ* respiration of a population *in vitro*, this slow response is an advantage because the animals are not handled prior to the experiment, and the results are not affected by short–term changes in factors associated with the sampling procedure. To measure the ETS activity, the animals should be processed immediately and held in the laboratory for as short a time as possible.

2.6 Conversions

As respiration is measured by so many different methods, conversions are necessary for comparisons. Table 10.4 gives the most important conversion factors, and others may be derived from these.

3 Factors Affecting the Respiratory Rate

3.1 Endogenous factors

3.1.1 Body size

Over a wide range of body size, there is a general trend in the respiration rate, both within and among species. Larger individuals consume more oxygen than smaller ones, but the increase of the respiration rate is slower than the increase of the weight. Thus, on a weight basis, the respiration rate (oxygen consumption mg^{-1} weight) decreases with increasing size of the animals (Zeuthen 1953, 1970).

The most common way of expressing the functional relationship between oxygen consumption and body weight is a power function $y = ax^b$ (or in logarithmic form: $\log y = \log a + b \log x$). The coefficients (a) and (b) are easily obtained by plotting the data on a double logarithmic scale and by calculating the appropriate linear regression. Log (a) is given by the intercept of the regression line with the ordinate and (b) by the slope of the regression line (cf. Fig. 9.2). However, some inaccuracy is inherent to this procedure (see Chapter 7) and an iterative method (Glass 1969) may give more precise results. Despite this, the measured relationships for aquatic animals are usually presented as power functions (R = respiratory rate; W = weight): $R = aW^b$; $\log R = \log a + b \log W$, giving the individual respiration rate, or in the weight specific form:

$$R/W = a \cdot W^{(b-1)}; \quad \log \frac{R}{W} = \log a + (b-1) \log W \qquad (10.12)$$

where the respiratory rate is given per unit weight.

Ever since Zeuthen (1953) showed that interspecific comparisons of rates of oxygen consumption yield similar slopes over a wide range of sizes, the exponent (b) has been in the centre of interest. He found $b = 0.95$ for metazoa containing < 1 mg N. Sushchenya (1970) obtained a value of 0.75 for a number of crustaceans. The slope of the regression line calculated for the literature data presented in Fig. 10.1 is about 0.8 and not significantly different from 0.75. A value of 0.75 is generally accepted for large scale interspecific comparisons of 'basal' or 'standard metabolic rate' (Hemmingsen 1960; Lavigne 1982), but the variability of the exponent is greater when a single genus or species is considered. Environmental factors like temperature may affect small and large animals differently and thus change (b) (Newell & Roy 1973; Holopainen & Ranta 1977). To show the possible range, some examples are listed in Table 10.5:

A linear relationship between weight and respiratory rate was found by Trama (1972) for the ephemeropteran *Stenonema pulchellum*.

Table 10.5 Values of b from the literature.

Species	b	Source
Daphnia pulex	0·882	Richman (1958)
Daphnia magna	0·816	Kersting & v.L.L. (1976)
Diaptomus (5 species)	0·626	Comita (1968)
Diaptomus (3 species)	0·517	Siefken & Armitage (1968)
Diaptomus gracilis (average)	0·615	Kibby (1971)
Limnocalanus macrurus	0·698	Roff (1963)
Chaoborus trivittatus	0·598–0·885	Swift (1976)
Mysis relicta	0·957	Ranta & Hakala (1978)
Pisidium amnicum		
3–10 °C	0·795–0·881	Holopainen & Ranta (1977)
20 °C	0·579	
Plectrus palustris	0·71–0·81	Klekowski *et al.* (1979)

Considerable changes may occur in the relationship between size and metabolism during the development of an animal. Epp & Lewis (1980a) found a power function with an exponent (b) near 1 in nauplii of cyclopoid and calanoid copepods. A sudden increase in metabolic rate appeared between the last naupliar stage and the first copepodite stage. For copepodites and adults, b was < 1. The slope of the regression line for all stages of *Macrocyclops albidus* was 0·84, but differences appeared when single stages were considered separately (Klekowski & Shushkina 1966).

Many of the b values listed in Table 10.5 are probably not significantly different but the slope of the regression line is not the only way in which species may differ with respect to their metabolic rate. Schiemer & Duncan (1974) demonstrated that b calculated for the nematode *Tobrilus gracilis* was not significantly different from values of other nematode species, but the elevation of the regression line, a, was. Thus the elevation may be an indication of the species' metabolic intensity.

These few examples show that, when an average 'exponent' is applied to the data instead of measuring animals of different sizes, considerable errors can result. One should keep in mind that the logarithmic relationship obscures the absolute errors on an untransformed scale. For example, the small deviation of point (2) from the regression line in Fig. 10.2 represents a difference of about 40 %.

3.1.2 Activity, diel rhythms

As stated earlier, respiration should be measured at 'normal' rates of activity; however, this 'normal' activity may vary considerably with time. Increased activity means higher energy expenditures, and, therefore, a higher respiration rate. This has been documented by some studies—Berg *et al.* (1962) found a linear increase of oxygen consumption with rate of activity of *Chaoborus flavicans*, but only about 2 % of the metabolic energy was spent in prey attack by *Chaoborus trivittatus* (Giguère 1980). Even the costs of swimming are not easy to evaluate. The cladoceran *Simocephalus vetulus*, which is normally attached to plants, exhibited a 30 % increase in the respiratory rate when swimming (Ivanova & Klekowski 1972), but Vlymen (1970) calculated that the additional costs of vertical migration of continuously swimming copepods were very small.

'Activity' is a complex phenomenon and its components are difficult to separate. It is, therefore, almost impossible to determine the reasons for diurnal rhythms in the metabolic rate, there are a few experiments where these rhythms have been studied. The mayfly nymph, *Isonychia* sp., has been found to exhibit rhythmic diurnal fluctuations with significantly higher night time oxygen utilization. These rates were controlled by both endogenous and exogenous (light) factors (Ulanoski & McDiffett 1972). Duval & Geen (1976) have reported endogenous diurnal rhythms in respiration of mixed zooplankton. The curve of the respiratory rate was bimodal with maxima at dawn and dusk and night respiration rates 2·3 times higher than daytime values. The respiratory rate of *Chaoborus punctipennis* also varied (Sigmon *et al.* 1978), but no predictable diurnal cycles were found, More long-term experiments, best done in flow-through systems, must be performed to find out how frequently aquatic animals exhibit diurnal cycles in metabolism. Using such a flow-through system, Gyllenberg (1981) demonstrated an increase in the respiratory rate of *Eudiaptomus gracilis* after midnight, corresponding to the migratory activity of the animals in the field.

3.2 Exogenous factors

3.2.1 Temperature

Temperature has a striking influence on the rate of metabolism of poikilotherms. Therefore, numerous studies deal with this subject (see review by Ivleva 1980). Response curves are usually similar and the respiratory rate increases more rapidly at higher temperatures (Fig. 10.7). There are some exceptions, however. A pronounced peak was observed at 8 °C for *Cyclops bicuspidatus* (Laybourn-Parry & Strachan 1980). Respiration rate is frequently stable over a portion of the normally encountered thermal range (Obreshkove & Abramowitz 1932; Ranta & Hakala 1977; Epp & Lewis 1980a). This may indicate the ability to maintain a 'preferred' level of metabolism (Epp & Lewis 1980b).

The magnitude of the acceleration of the metabolic rate is generally characterized by the ratio of rates resulting from a temperature increase of $10\,°C\,(Q_{10})$. A Q_{10} value of 2 would mean that a $10\,°C$ increase in temperature caused a doubling of the respiration rate. For the calculation of Q_{10}, it is not necessary to determine two rates exactly $10\,°C$ apart; any two temperatures sufficiently far apart to give reliable information on the temperature effect can be used. Then:

$$Q_{10} = \left(\frac{R_2}{R_1}\right)^{\frac{10}{T_2 - T_1}} \tag{10.13}$$

where R_1 and R_2 are the measured respiratory rates and T_1 and T_2 the corresponding temperatures. With a known Q_{10}, the respiratory rate at a different temperature can be estimated by:

$$R_2 = R_1 \cdot Q_{10}^{\frac{T_2 - T_1}{10}} \tag{10.14}$$

Q_{10} values reported in literature vary remarkably within the same species. For different size classes of *Pisidium amnicum* and over different parts of the temperature range, Holopainen & Ranta (1977) obtained values between 1·5 and 5·6. The same range (1·83–5·3) was measured for *Diaptomus* by Siefken & Armitage (1968). There is evidence that the Q_{10} of a given species varies with the habitat temperature to which it is adapted (Rao & Bullock 1954): in the snail, *Littorina littorina*, the Q_{10} was lower during summer than during winter. Temperature increases elevate the slope of the regression lines relating log metabolism to log dry weight; thus, the Q_{10} differs for animals of different size (Newell & Roy 1973). Distinct changes in Q_{10} during development were also reported for the tropical freshwater copepod *Mesocyclops brasilianus* (Epp & Lewis 1979b).

Conover (1978) reviews the relationship between metabolic rate, activity level and temperature for some marine invertebrates. Different Q_{10} values can be found for 'standard' and 'active' metabolism. The standard respiratory rate is often relatively independent of temperature and shows no acclimatization. The active rate is more temperature dependent and exhibits partial acclimatization to temperature. At very high temperatures, the 'active' rate of oxygen consumption may decrease, because the animals become inactive. Therefore, 'standard' and 'active' metabolism are similar at low and high temperatures, and a great 'scope for activity' (the difference between 'standard' and 'active' rates) is found at some intermediate, and presumably at optimum, temperature conditions.

Acclimatization is important when the temperature dependency of respiration is measured (Ivleva 1980). After a rise of temperature from 16° to 20 °C *Gammarus fossarum* initially showed an overshoot of the acclimatized respiratory rate. A lower final plateau was attained after about two days (Franke 1977). Vollenweider & Ravera (1958) transferred *Daphnia obtusa* from 6·5 °C to 24 °C and *vice versa*. There were significant differences according to whether or not the animals had been adapted to the new temperature for 24 h.

Even though the Q_{10} is often near 2 (e.g. Shcherbakoff 1935; Comita 1968; Trama 1972; Roff 1973), the actual value is dependent on the section of the temperature range over which it is calculated. In order to obtain a single numerical value which describes the whole temperature dependency, a 'temperature characteristic' (μ) can be used. This is analogous to the Vant-Hoff and Arrhenius formula describing the influence of temperature upon the velocity of chemical reactions. The metabolic rate is assumed to follow the equation:

$$R = R_0 \cdot e^{-(\mu/r \cdot T)} \tag{10.15}$$

where R = respiration rate at the given temperature, r = gas constant (8.3 J

mol^{-1} degree^{-1}), T = absolute temperature ($°K$), R_0 = constant reflecting the metabolism when T approaches 0, μ = activation energy (J mol^{-1}).

The numerical value of μ is, therefore, a 'temperature characteristic' which describes the accelerating influence of temperature on the metabolic rate, provided that it agrees with the Vant-Hoff and Arrhenius law. In fact, this has been found to be true in many studies (Obreshkove & Abramovitz 1932; Ivleva 1973). If a graph is plotted with the logarithm of the respiratory rate on the ordinate and the inverse of the absolute temperature on the abscissa, the points very often form a straight line, the slope giving μ. The 'temperature characteristic' can be calculated (Ivleva 1970) from measured values of the respiration rate (R_1, R_2) and the corresponding absolute temperatures (T_1, T_2):

$$\mu = r \cdot \frac{\log R_2 - \log R_1}{1/T_1 - 1/T_2} \tag{10.16}$$

It is usually in the range of 54–67 kJ mol^{-1}. The Q_{10} can be calculated from μ by the equation:

$$\log Q_{10} = 2 \cdot 187 \cdot \frac{\mu}{T_1 \cdot T_2} \tag{10.17}$$

It is evident from this formula that Q_{10} will change depending on the absolute temperature considered in the calculation.

When measurements of the respiratory rate have been made at only one temperature, and μ and Q_{10} are unknown, an estimate of the metabolic activity at a different temperature can be obtained by using Krogh's empirical curve. As can be seen from Fig. 10.7, this curve approximates many measured relationships and it can, therefore, be used for temperature corrections. Factors for correction are tabulated in Winberg (1956 and 1971).

3.2.2 Oxygen tension

Generally speaking, there are two principle ways in which animals can respond to unfavourable oxygen conditions. If oxygen is reduced, some animals (regulators) maintain the consumption rate until a critical pressure is reached; further reduction in oxygen causes a rapid decline. Such animals exhibit a wide range over which their respiration is independent of changes in oxygen pressure. The consumption rate by other animals (conformers) is proportional to the ambient concentration of oxygen (Prosser 1973) and their possibilities of regulating the rate of oxygen consumption are limited. At low oxygen tensions animals have to switch to anaerobic metabolism—many animals do this before their supply of oxygen is exhausted (Mangum & Van Winkle 1973). Oxygen is especially important for profundal and bottom

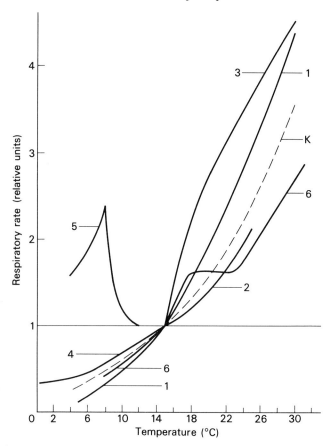

Fig. 10.7 Effect of temperature on the respiratory rate of aquatic animals. 1, *Leptodora kindtii* (Moshiri *et al.* 1969); 2, *Stenonema pulchellum* (Trama 1972); 3, *Chaoborus punctipennis* (Sigmon *et al.* 1978); 4, *Limnocalanus macrurus* (Roff 1973); 5, *Cyclops bicuspidatus* (Laybourn-Parry & Strachan 1980); 6, *Daphnia magna* (Obreshkove & Abramowitz 1932); K. Krogh's normal curve (Winberg 1971).

dwelling animals. Berg *et al.* (1962) described three types of reactions of benthic animals to decreasing oxygen tensions:

(1) A nearly constant oxygen consumption is maintained from saturation to some critical point (7–25 % saturation), below which a marked decrease occurs (*Tubifex barbatus*, *Ilyodrilus hammonensis*, *Chironomus anthracinus*).

(2) Oxygen consumption decreases at a lower rate down to 20–30 % saturation and then more markedly (*Lumbriculus rivalis*, *Procladius*, *Pisidium casertanum*).

(3) Other animals are not able to maintain a constant level. Oxygen consumption is proportional to oxygen concentration over a wide range (*Chaoborus flavicans*).

There are many examples of animals which behave intermediately between true regulators and true conformers (cf. Fig. 10.8). For example, in *Gammarus fossarum* (Franke 1977) the respiratory rate is influenced by temperature and current, but the shape of the dependence of oxygen consumption on oxygen concentration remains similar. Konstantinov (1971) found some chironomid larvae that showed reaction types (2) and (3) to varied oxygen tension. *Leptodora kindtii* maintained the same respiration rate between 14 and 8 mg O_2 l^{-1} (Moshiri *et al.* 1969).

Differences may occur in closely related species. Heisey & Porter (1977) found *Daphnia galeata* to be a conformer, whereas *Daphnia magna* regulated its oxygen consumption rate. They explain this by the different habitats colonized by animals. *Daphnia magna* lives in ponds where it is often exposed to low oxygen tensions whereas the pelagic *Daphnia galeata* does not. Some daphnids contain visibly more haemoglobin when living under reduced oxygen conditions (Fox & Phear 1953); it would be interesting to see whether

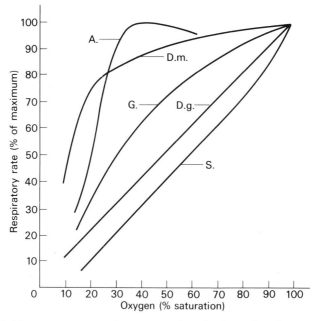

Table 10.8 Alternate response of some aquatic animals to changing oxygen concentrations. A, *Ancylus fluviatilis* (Berg 1952); D.m., *Daphnia magna*, D.g., *Daphnia galeata mendotae* (Heisey & Porter 1977); G, *Gammarus fossarum* (Franke 1977); S, *Simocephalus vetulus* (Hoshi 1957).

the type of response curve is subject to acclimatization in the same species living under different conditions of available oxygen.

Experiments on oxygen utilization at different oxygen concentrations have been made in different ways. Animals have either been put into a container so that the oxygen was reduced by the animals themselves or they have been provided with oxygen deficient water in an open-flow system. The first method is not recommended because there is the possibility that oxygen consumption is influenced by the accumulation of excretory products (e.g. ammonia). This error is avoided in the open-flow method.

3.2.3 Food

The effect of food on the respiratory rate has not yet been studied very extensively. The animals are usually fed or starved prior to the experiment, and only a few studies deal with animals that are actually feeding.

Food may influence the respiration rate in different ways. Activity may change because the searching behavior is changed. For the predaceous cladoceran *Polyphemus pediculus*, visual perception of prey crustacea is enough to increase the respiration rate (Butorina 1979). In filter-feeders, the rate of movement of filtering appendages may decrease with increasing food concentration. When food is ingested, metabolic costs of digestion and biochemical processing of the food (specific dynamic action; SDA) occur. Giguère (1980) estimated the SDA of *Chaoborus trivittatus* to cause an increase of 37 % in oxygen consumption compared to unfed animals.

When the animals are fed before oxygen consumption is measured, respiration rates are usually increased when compared to starved animals. This was found by Comita (1968) for several species of *Diaptomus*. La Row *et al.* (1975) pre-fed *Diaptomus* copepodites and *Daphnia* at different food concentrations and reported an increase of oxygen consumption of about 80 % from the lowest to the highest food level. A 10-fold increase in density of bacterial food resulted in a 14 % increase in the respiration rate of the nematode *Plectrus palustris* (Klekowski *et al.* 1979); on the other hand, Richman (1958) obtained no reduction in the rate of oxygen consumption per unit weight due to starvation of *Daphnia pulex*.

Experiments with feeding animals give controversial results. The presence or absence of natural densities of nannoplankton had no effect on the respiration of *Diaptomus oregonensis* (Richman 1964). Kersting & Van der Leeuw-Leegwater (1976) presented interesting results for *Daphnia magna* fed different concentrations of *Chlorella*—respiration rate was maximum at the incipient limiting level (ILL; see Chapter 8) and decreased at higher concentrations. At a *Chlorella* density of about 6 times the ILL, it amounted only to 46 % of the maximum. These experiments have been repeated with

Daphnia magna with different concentrations of *Scenedesmus* as food (Bohrer & Lampert in preparation) and the outcome of the experiments was completely different. Oxygen consumption increased by 40–50 % from zero-food to the ILL (approximately 0.3 mg C l^{-1}) where a plateau was reached. No reduction was found at high concentrations (up to 3.5 mg C l^{-1}).

With the exception of the findings of Kersting & Van der Leeuw-Leegwater (1976), feeding seems to increase the metabolic rate. Because energy budgets are usually made for growing animals (i.e. those that are fed), while respiration is usually measured using starved animals, respiratory losses are probably underestimated in many budgets, clearly suggesting the need for more reliable studies on the respiration of feeding aquatic animals.

3.2.4 Light

The effect of intensity and quality of light on respiration has been studied for some animals, but the results are again controversial and too scarce. No significant effect of light intensity was found by Bishop (1968) for mixed zooplankton or by Schindler (1968) for *Daphnia magna*. On the other hand, light intensity affected the exponent of the length:respiration regression of *Daphnia pulex*, whereas variation in wavelength produced no significant effect (Buikema 1972). Chironomid larvae also increased their respiratory rates in response to light (Konstantinov 1971); this may have been a result of increased mobility. Because many measurements are performed in the dark, the results of Moshiri *et al.* (1969) are very important. They discovered that the respiration rate of *Leptodora kindtii* in the light was up to twice as high as that in the dark. The effect of light level requires more research, especially since light very often controls activity, and interactions of increased motion and feeding may significantly affect the respiratory rate.

3.2.5 Current

It is obvious that water current is a very important environmental factor to the animals found in running water; they are adapted to their habitat and often have special respiratory organs to utilize the water flow. Ambühl (1959) studied the response of the respiratory rate of stream insect larvae to current and oxygen content of the water. He described different types of dependencies:

(1)   *Ephemerella ignita* responded to oxygen content but not to current.
(2)   *Ecdyonurus venosus* was sensitive to current only at low oxygen concentrations.
(3)   The respiration rates of some species (caseless and case-bearing caddisflies, *Baetis vernus*, *Rhitrogena semicolorata*) were positively dependent on both oxygen content and water velocity.

A good example showing the interacting influence of water flow, temperature, and oxygen partial pressure on the respiratory rate of *Gammarus fossarum* is given by Franke (1977).

When the effect of water velocity is to be studied, a current of several cm sec^{-1} must be produced. The flow rate in an open-flow system (see Section 2.3.3) is much too low to fulfill these requirements, and measurements must, therefore, be performed in a closed system. Recirculating systems containing an animal chamber have usually been used. The animals are prevented from leaving the chamber by mesh screens and the bottom must be roughened to allow the animals to keep their position in the current. A strong current is produced by a propeller (Ambühl 1959), a magnetic stirrer (Zahner 1959; Wotton 1978) or a magnetically impelled centrifugal pump (Eriksen & Feldmeth 1967; Franke 1977).

3.2.6 Crowding and container size

In measurements of respiration, the animals are confined to more or less artificial conditions. Many animals are held in a relatively small volume of water, or single animals are kept in small containers. Several attempts have been made to test the influence of these conditions on the respiratory rate.

No significant crowding effect was detected for *Daphnia magna* and *Daphnia pulex* (0·5–2·0 ind ml^{-1}; Goss & Bunting 1980), or *Limnocalanus macrurus* (0·1–1·8 ind ml^{-1}; Roff 1973). Crowding does not seem to be important at the densities normally used, even though these densities are higher than in nature. Very high densities, on the other hand, necessitate correction (Duval & Geen 1976). The effect should be scrutinized more carefully because the respiration rates of marine zooplankton may increase linearly with density (Satomi & Pomeroy 1965).

Roff (1973) kept *Limnocalanus macrurus* in containers of different sizes (30–330 ml) but at the same density (1 ind ml^{-1}) and discovered no effect on the metabolic activity. Extreme conditions preventing the animals from moving freely should be prevented, however. When Zeiss (1973) enclosed several *Daphnia magna* singly in small mesh covered glass tubes (0·12–0·24 ml) and placed them in a larger vessel, the respiration rate was more than doubled, compared to the same number of animals in a vessel but not confined to the small space.

3.2.7 Other factors

Animals in the field may be exposed to many other factors which may affect the metabolic rate but which have not yet been studied. Such effects may arise from chemical, osmotic or other physical stresses. For example, Ivanova & Klekowski (1972) showed that the pH of the water influenced the respiratory rate of *Simocephalus vetulus*. Hydrostatic pressure was found to suppress the respiration rate of mixed freshwater zooplankton (Bishop 1968) but marine zooplankton were not affected in the range of 16–50 atm (Pearcy & Small 1968).

4 In Situ Studies

Many attempts have been made to measure the respiration rates of aquatic animals or communities under *in situ* conditions (Straškraba 1967; Bishop 1968; Cremer & Duncan 1969; Duncan *et al.* 1970; Roff 1973; Nowak 1975; Ranta & Hakala 1978; Makarewicz & Likens 1979). Except where measurements of the ETS activity are made, however, the methods involved do not measure real *in situ* respiration rates; most are merely laboratory experiments carried out in the field, put into a closed container, and then incubated *in situ*. Usually, animals must be concentrated because no measurement of oxygen consumption can be made at natural densities. This is dangerous because concentration requires that the animals be handled. In addition, the animals are often without sufficient food because they are put into filtered water or the available natural food is exhausted quickly due to the abnormal animal densities.

Glass bottles or disposable syringes (Ranta & Hakala 1978) have been used and experiments have been carried out according to the 'closed bottle' method (Section 2.3.2). Most '*in situ*' studies have been made with zooplankton, because the animals can be concentrated easily using a net. Nowak (1975) tried to minimize handling of the animals before the experiment by attaching a bottle filled with filtered water to the end of a plankton net. After towing the net, he lifted it upwards, leaving the lower part with the bottle in the water. The animals then migrated downwards into the bottle, which could be closed.

When different groups or species must be measured separately, the animals must be sorted by hand, by sieving, or by another technique. Straškraba (1967) developed a narcotization technique to separate rotifers, cladocerans, and copepods. Although this procedure may stress the animals, he still obtained measurements of the respiration rate similar to the results of other investigators. At a temperature of 10–13°C, in April, when copepods dominated the community, he found the respiration rate to be $0.295 \, \mu\text{mol}$ $\text{O}_2 \, \text{mg}^{-1} \, \text{h}^{-1}$, which is in the same range as laboratory data (cf. Table 9.4). The average oxygen consumption of mixed zooplankton at 18–20°C, determined by Makarewicz & Likens (1979), was $0.666 \, \mu\text{mol} \, \text{mg}^{-1} \, \text{h}^{-1}$, which is also in the range to be expected, provided the average size of the zooplankters was relatively small.

There are considerable seasonal changes in the metabolic rate. Nowak

(1975), for example, measured respiration rates for mixed zooplankton of $0.08\,\mu\text{mol O}_2\,\text{mg}^{-1}\text{h}^{-1}$ at 2 °C in January and $0.67\,\mu\text{mol O}_2\,\text{mg}^{-1}\text{h}^{-1}$ at 20 °C in August. A large part of this variation, but not all of it, is explained by the differences in experimental temperature (Cremer & Duncan, 1969).

A comparison of 'field' measurements using the bottle method and laboratory determination of oxygen consumption with the Cartesian diver was carried out by Duncan *et al.* (1970) in London reservoirs. In this case 'field' values were considerably higher, but the reason was not clear. Such comparisons lead one to question whether it is worthwhile to perform field experiments which are not really *in situ* measurements. It might be better to calculate field respiration from pure laboratory results, including the effects of abundances, size structure, and temperature on the populations. Phillipson (1970) is in favour of the latter method proposing a 'best estimate' of respiratory metabolism which is calculated from laboratory data of respiration of all life stages or size classes of a species studied, measured at constant temperature. This yields an average oxygen consumption per unit weight for the species. By correction for the average temperature of the habitat and multiplication by the mean annual biomass, the method provides an estimate of the annual respiration of the population. The author states that the application of the 'best estimate' method gives results with 10 % deviation from more detailed studies.

5 Similarities and Dissimilarities

A collection of measured respiration rates is presented in Table 10.6. This compilation is selective since not all of the available information could be included but it tries to cover a broad range of freshwater invertebrates. In many cases, values for different temperatures and body sizes are contained in the original papers. The reader may refer to them for details. Data are presented as oxygen consumption rates and rates of body carbon loss, because the latter are more relevant to secondary production.

There is a clear partition between planktonic and benthic animals, but this is due to the larger body size of the second group. Despite all of the problems mentioned in the foregoing paragraphs, the values agree astonishingly well in some groups, even though they have been produced by different authors. The three numbers for *Mysis relicta*, for example, are very close to each other. Respiration rates within the calanoid copepods and the daphnids are also very similar. Temperature and body weight seem to produce the main differences.

More variability can be seen in the estimates for large and very small animals. The reason for the greater homogeneity of values for medium sized zooplankton species may be that they have been obtained under more adequate conditions. In addition to body size and temperature, food is the

Table 10.6 Examples of published respiratory rates.

Species	Individual dry weight (mg)	Temp. (°C)	Individual respiration rate (μl O$_2$ ind^{-1} h^{-1})	Specific respiration rate (μmol O$_2$ mg^{-1} h^{-1})	Loss of body carbon (% per day)[#]	Source
Rotatoria						
Brachionus rubens	0.13×10^{-3}	20	2.69×10^{-3}	0.924	60.0	Pilarska, 1977
Brachionus plicatilis	0.16×10^{-3}	20	2.66×10^{-3}	0.752	38.9	Doohan, 1973
Brachionus calyciflorus	0.32×10^{-3}	20	3.04×10^{-3}	0.425	27.6	Leimeroth, 1980
Copepoda						
Calamoecia lucasi	1.23×10^{-3}	15	0.0098	0.356	23.0	Green & Chapman, 1977
*Diaptomus siciloides***	0.0032	20	0.075	1.045	67.7	Comita, 1968
Diaptomus gracilis	0.008	20	0.061	0.341	22.1	Kibby, 1971
Diaptomus oregonensis	0.011	22	0.090	0.365	23.5	Richman, 1964
Diaptomus graciloides ♂	0.0065	20	0.0668	0.459	29.8	Shcherbakoff, 1935
Diaptomus graciloides ♀	0.0123	20	0.0828	0.301	19.4	Shcherbakoff, 1935
*Diaptomus leptopus***	0.0222	20	0.178	0.358	23.2	Comita, 1968
Boeckella delicata	0.0101	15	0.050	0.219	14.2	Green & Chapman, 1977
Limnocalanus macrurus	0.0342	15	0.2286	0.298	15.4	Roff, 1973
Cyclops leuckarti ♀	0.0035	20	0.0432	0.551	35.8	Shcherbakoff, 1935
Cyclops leuckarti ♂	0.9×10^{-3}	20	0.012	0.595	38.4	Shcherbakoff, 1935
Cyclops bicuspidatus	0.008	8	0.0336	0.188	12.2	Laybourn-Parry & Strachan, 1980
Cyclops strenuus	0.0434	20	0.203	0.209	13.4	Shcherbakoff, 1935
Cladocera						
Ceriodaphnia reticulata	0.0041	22	0.050	0.541	35.0	Gophen, 1976
Daphnia longispina	0.0222	20	0.156	0.314	20.4	Shcherbakoff, 1935
Daphnia pulex	0.0346	20	0.2887	0.373	24.0	Goss & Bunting, 1980
Daphnia pulex	0.028	20	0.194	0.309	19.9	Richman, 1958
Daphnia magna	0.1524	20	0.7021	0.206	13.2	Goss & Bunting, 1980
Daphnia magna	0.15	18	0.882	0.263	17.0	Kersting & v.d. Leeuw Leegwater, 1976

Daphnia magna	0·15	20	0·915	0·272	17·6	Schindler, 1968
Simocephalus exspinosus	0·059	25	0·73	0·552	35·8	Obreshkove, 1930
Simocephalus vetulus	0·070	22	0·36	0·230	16·7	Ivanova & Klekowski, 1972
Leptodora kindtii	?	15	—	0·749	52·3	Moshiri et al., 1969
Amphipoda						
Gammarus fossarum	3·0	12	1·92	0·029	1·9	Franke, 1977
Gammarus pulex	8·5	15	14·9	0·078	5·28	Nilsson, 1974
Isopoda						
Asellus aquaticus	3·0	23	4·47	0·066	4·3	Prus, 1972
Mysidacea						
Mysis relicta	5·0	4·6	3·85	0·034	1·9	Ranta & Hakala, 1978
Mysis relicta	5·0	4	3·70	0·033	2·3	Foulds & Roff, 1976
Mysis relicta	5·0	4	4·2	0·0375	2·64	Lasenby & Langford, 1972
Mollusca						
Pisidium amnicum	5·0*	20	0·916	0·0082	0·48	Holopainen & Ranta, 1977
Plecoptera†						
Isoperla buresi	5·34	8	1·506	0·0126	0·82	Kamler, 1969
Ephemeroptera†						
Cloëon dipterum	0·214	20	0·568	0·119	7·7	Kamler, 1969
Stenonema pulchellum	2·0	20	3·48	0·078	5·0	Trama, 1972
Rhithrogena sp.	1·94	18·5	21·86	0·503	31·2	Ambühl, 1959
Ecdyonurus venosus	5·5	18·5	17·3	0·141	9·1	Ambühl, 1959
Diptera†						
Simuliidae**	0·139	15·5	1·04	0·335	24·0	Wotton, 1978
Chaoborus trivittatus	0·8	20	0·751	0·042	2·7	Swift, 1976
Chaoborus flavicans	5·0	18	3·2	0·029	1·9	Berg et al., 1962
Chironomus anthracinus	8·0	15	1·74	0·0097	0·6	Berg et al., 1962

If no other values were given by the author, an RQ of 0·9 and 40% carbon of dry weight was assumed.
* ash free.
** fed.
† larvae.

main factor influencing the respiration rate of these animals, but this factor is excluded from Table 10.6 because, with two exceptions, all of the respiration rates were measured using starved animals. Both *Diaptomus* species, which were fed, in fact showed fairly high values. For larger crustaceans and insect larvae, adequate measurements cannot be made so easily because water movement and substrate may be very important. Thus, greater variations can be expected.

An increasing number of papers on respiration of freshwater animals have been published during recent years, and there are many additional studies on marine animals that have not been considered here. We now seem to have a general overview of the effects of body size and temperature, but information on other topics is missing. Therefore, more effort should be put into simulating environmental conditions as exactly as possible with regard to these other factors. With respect to secondary production, the effect of food on respiration rate seems to be the most important, severely neglected factor. As stated in the introduction of this chapter, respiration losses must be measured with the greatest possible accuracy, when a budget is to be constructed.

When carbon loss values for all non-fed crustacean zooplankters in Table 10.6 are corrected to 20 °C by Krogh's normal curve (see Section 3.2.1) and to 0·04 mg body weight by use of the exponent b = −0·25 (see Section 3.1.1), the average is 19·1 % ± 4·8 % per day (n = 20). This is a rather low standard deviation. Variations due to different feeding conditions seem to be much higher than the species-specific differences. Therefore, new techniques for measuring respiration of feeding animals must be developed. Investigators performing experiments with small, starved animals must be aware that their subject may lose considerable weight during the experimental period. For the zooplankters mentioned above, this was 19 % per day (at 20 °C). Until 'field' experiments allow animals to eat their natural foods, good laboratory experiments may yield results closer to nature than poor field experiments. To estimate the total respiration in the field, it might be better to extrapolate from laboratory respiration rates of feeding animals, while emphasizing improvements in estimates of animal abundance in the field.

6 References

Aldrich J.C. (1975) An improved method for the measurement of CO_2 in marine animals, applied to three species of decapods. *Mar. Biol.*, **29**, 277–282.

Ambühl H. (1959) Die Bedeutung der Strömung als ökologischer Faktor. *Schweiz. Z. Hydrol.*, **21**, 133–264.

Båmstedt V. (1980) ETS activity as an estimator of respiratory rate of zooplankton populations. The significance of variations in environmental factors. *J. Exp. Mar. Biol. Ecol.*, **42**, 267–283.

Barnes H. (1959) *Apparatus and Methods of Oceanography.* New York: Interscience.

Berg K. (1952) On the oxygen consumption of Ancylidae (Gastropoda) from an ecological point of view. *Hydrobiologia*, **4**, 225–267.

Berg K. & Jonasson P.M. (1965) Oxygen consumption of profundal lake animals at low oxygen content of the water. *Hydrobiologia*, **26**, 131–143.

Berg K., Jonasson P.M. & Ockelmann K.W. (1962) The respiration of some animals from the profundal zone of a lake. *Hydrobiologia*, **19**, 1–39.

Beyers R.J. (1963) The metabolism of twelve aquatic laboratory microecosystems. *Ecol. Monogr.*, **33**, 281–306.

Beyers R.J., Larimer J.L., Odum H.T., Parker R.B. & Armstrong N.E. (1963) Directions for the determination of changes in carbon dioxide concentration from changes in pH. *Publ. Inst. Mar. Sci. Texas*, **9**, 454–489.

Bishop J.W. (1968) Respiratory rates of migrating zooplankton in the natural habitat. *Limnol. Oceanogr.*, **13**, 58–62.

Bohrer R.N. & Lampert W. (In preparation) Simultaneous measurement of the effect of food concentration on assimilation and respiration in *Daphnia magna*.

Briggs R., Dyke G.V. & Khoweis G. (1958) Use of wide-bore dropping-mercury electrode for long-period recording of concentration of dissolved oxygen. *Analyst*, **83**, 304–311.

Bryan J.R., Riley J.P. & Williams P.J. Le B. (1976) A Winkler procedure for making precise measurements of oxygen concentration for productivity and related studies. *J. Exp. Mar. Biol. Ecol.*, **21**, 191–197.

Buikema A.L. (1972) Oxygen consumption of the cladoceran *Daphnia pulex*, as a function of body size, light and light acclimation. *Comp. Biochem. Physiol. (Physiol)*, **42**, 877–888.

Bulnheim H.P. (1972) Vergleichende Untersuchungen zur Atmungsphysiologie euryhaliner Gammariden unter besonderer Berücksichtigung der Salzgehaltsanpassung. *Helgoländer Wiss. Meeresuntersuch.*, **23**, 485–534.

Butorina L.G. (1979) Effect of visual perception of environmental conditions on metabolic rate of *Polyphemus pediculus* (L.) (Cladocera). *Sov. J. Ecol.*, **10**, 422–426.

Carey F.G. & Teal J.M. (1965) Responses of oxygen electrodes to variables in construction, assembly and use. *J. Appl. Physiol.*, **20**, 1074–1077.

Carpenter J.H. (1965a) The accuracy of the Winkler method for dissolved oxygen analysis. *Limnol. Oceanogr.*, **10**, 135–140.

Carpenter J.H. (1965b) Chesapeake Bay Institute technique for the Winkler dissolved oxygen method. *Limnol. Oceanogr.*, **10**, 141–143.

Carrit D.E. & Carpenter J.H. (1966) Comparison and evaluation of currently employed modifications of the Winkler method for determining dissolved oxygen in seawater. A NASCO report. *J. Mar. Res.*, **24**, 286–318.

Chemical Rubber Company (1976) *Handbook of Chemistry and Physics.* 57th ed., Cleveland: CRC Press.

Clark L.C., Wolf R., Granger D. & Taylor A. (1953) Continuous recording of blood oxygen tensions by polarography. *J. Appl. Physiol.*, **6**, 189–193.

Comita G.W. (1968) Oxygen consumption in *Diaptomus. Limnol. Oceanogr.*, **13**, 51–57.

Conover R.J. (1978) Transformation of organic matter. In O. Kinne (ed.), *Marine Ecology*, Vol. IV, p. 221–499. Chichester: Wiley & Sons.

Cremer G.A. & Duncan A. (1969) A seasonal study of zooplanktonic respiration under field conditions. *Verh. Int. Ver. Limnol.*, **17**, 181–190.

Davenport J. (1976) A technique for the measurement of oxygen consumption in small aquatic organisms. *Lab. Pract.*, **25**, 693–695.

Doohan M. (1973) An energy budget for adult *Brachionus plicatilis* (Rotatoria). *Oecologia (Berl.)*, **13**, 351–362.

Dries R.R., Eschweiler L. & Theede H. (1979) An improved equipment for continuous measurement of respiration of marine invertebrates. *Kieler Meeresforsch.*, **4**, 310–316.

Duncan A., Cremer G.A. & Andrew T. (1970) The measurement of respiratory rates under field and laboratory conditions during an ecological study on zooplankton. *Pol. Arch. Hydrobiol.*, **17**, 149–160.

Duval W.S. & Geen G.H. (1976) Diel feeding and respiration rhythms in zooplankton. *Limnol. Oceanogr.*, **21**, 823–829.

Elliot J.M. & Davison W. (1975) Energy equivalents of oxygen consumption in animal energetics. *Oecologia (Berl.)*, **19**, 195–201.

Epp R.W. & Lewis W.M. Jr. (1979a) Sexual dimorphism in *Brachionus plicatilis* (Rotifera); Evolutionary and adaptive significance. *Evolution*, **33**, 919–928.

Epp R.W. & Lewis W.M. Jr. (1979b) Metabolic responses to temperature change in a tropical freshwater copepod (*Mesocyclops brasilianus*) and their adaptive significance. *Oecologia (Berl.)*, **42**, 123–138.

Epp R.W. & Lewis W.M. Jr. (1980a) The nature and ecological significance of metabolic changes during the life history of copepods. *Ecology*, **61**, 259–264.

Epp R.W. & Lewis W.M. Jr. (1980b) Metabolic uniformity over the environmental temperature range in *Brachionus plicatilis* (Rotifera). *Hydrobiologia*, **73**, 145–147.

Eriksen C.H. & Feldmeth C.R. (1967) A water-current respirometer. *Hydrobiologia*, **29**, 495–504.

Fatt I. (1976) *Polarographic oxygen sensors*. Cleveland: CRC Press.

Feldmeth C.R. (1971) The effect of current on the respiratory rate of aquatic animals. In W.T.Edmondson & G.G.Winberg (eds.), *A Manual on Methods for the Assessment of Secondary Productivity in Fresh Waters*. IBP Handbook No. 17, 278–280. Oxford: Blackwell.

Fenn W.O. (1927) The gas exchange of nerve during stimulation. *Amer. J. Physiol.*, **80**, 327–346.

Foulds J.B. & Roff J.C. (1976) Oxygen consumption during simulated vertical migration in *Mysis relicta* (Crustacea, Mysidacea). *Can. J. Zool.*, **54**, 377–385.

Fox H.M. & Phear E.A. (1953) Factors influencing hemoglobin synthesis by *Daphnia*. *Proc. R. Soc.*, **141B**, 179–180.

Fox H.M. & Wingfield C.A. (1938) A portable apparatus for the determination of oxygen dissolved in a small volume of water. *J. Anim. Ecol.*, **15**, 437–445.

Franke U. (1977) Experimentelle Untersuchungen zur Respiration von *Gammarus fossarum* Koch 1835 (Crustacea-Amphipoda) in Abhängigkeit von Temperatur, Sauerstoff-Konzentration und Wasserbewegung. *Arch. Hydrobiol. (Suppl.)*, **48**, 369–411.

Giguère L.A. (1980) Metabolic expenditures in *Chaoborus* larvae. *Limnol. Oceanogr.*, **25**, 922–928.

Glass N.R. (1969) Discussion of calculation of power function with special reference to respiratory metabolism in fish. *J. Fish. Res. Board. Can.*, **26**, 2643–2650.

Gnaiger E. (1979) Direct calorimetry in ecological energetics. Long-term monitoring of aquatic animals. *Experientia(Suppl.)*, **37**, 155–165.

Gnaiger E. (1982) The twin-flow microrespirometer and simultaneous calorimetry. In E. Gnaiger & H. Forstner (ed.), *Handbook on Polarographic Oxygen Sensors. Aquatic and Physiological Applications*. Berlin, Heidelberg, New York: Springer.

Gnaiger E. & Forstner H. (1982) *Handbook on Polarographic Oxygen Sensors. Aquatic and Physiological Applications*. Berlin, Heidelberg, New York: Springer.

Golterman H.L. & Wisselo A.G. (1981) Ceriometry, a combined method for chemical oxygen demand and dissolved oxygen (with a discussion on the precision of the Winkler technique). *Hydrobiologia*, **77**, 37–42.

Gophen M. (1976) Temperature dependence of food intake, ammonia excretion and respiration in *Ceriodaphnia reticulata* (Jurine) (Lake Kinneret, Israel). *Freshw. Biol.*, **6**, 451–455.

Goss L.B. & Bunting D.L. (1980) Temperature effects on zooplankton respiration. *Comp. Biochem. Physiol. A.*, **66**, 651–658.

Grainger J.N. (1956) Effects of changes of temperature on the respiration of certain crustacea. *Nature*, **178**, 930–931.

Green J.D. & Chapman M.A. (1977) Temperature effects on oxygen consumption by copepod *Boeckella dilatata*. *N. Z. J. Mar. Freshwat. Res.*, **11**, 375–382.

Gyllenberg G. (1973) Comparison of the Cartesian diver technique and the polarographic method, and open system, for measuring the respiratory rates of three marine copepods. *Commentationes Biologicae*, **60**, 3–13.

Gyllenberg G. (1981) *Eudiaptomus gracilis* (Copepoda, Calanoida): diel vertical migration in the field and diel oxygen consumption rhythm in the laboratory. *Ann. Zool. Fennici*, **18**, 229–232.

Hamburger K. (1981) A gradient diver for measurement of respiration in individual organisms from the micro- and meiofauna. *Mar. Biol.*, **61**, 179–183.

Heisey D. & Porter K.G. (1977) The effect of ambient oxygen concentration on filtering and respiration rates of *Daphnia galeata mendotae* and *Daphnia magna*. *Limnol. Oceanogr.*, **22**, 839–845.

Hemmingsen A.M. (1960) Energy metabolism as related to body size and respiratory surfaces, and its evolution. *Rep. Steno Mem. Hosp. Nordisk Insulin Lab.*, **9**, 7–110.

Hitchman M.L. (1978) Measurement of Dissolved Oxygen. Geneva, New York: Wiley & Sons and Orbishere Co.

Holopainen I.J. & Ranta E. (1977) Respiration of *Pisidium amnicum* (Bivalvia) measured by infrared gas analysis. *Oikos*, **28**, 196–200.

Hoshi T. (1957) Studies on the physiology and ecology of plankton. XII. Changes in O_2-consumption of the daphnid *Simocephalus vetulus*, with the decrease of O_2-concentration. *Sci. Rep. Tohoku Univ.*, *Ser. 5 (Biol.)*, **23**, 27–33.

Humphreys W.F. (1979) Production and respiration in animal populations. *J. Anim. Ecol.*, **48**, 427–453.

Ivanova M.B. & Klekowski R.Z. (1972) Respiratory and filtration rates in *Simocephalus vetulus* (O.F.Müller) at different pH. *Pol. Arch. Hydrobiol.*, **19**, 303–318.

Ivleva I.V. (1970) The influence of temperature on the transformation of matter in marine invertebrates. In J.H.Steele (ed.), *Marine food Chains*, p. 96–112. Berkeley, Los Angeles: University of California Press.

Ivleva I.V. (1973) Quantitative correlation of temperature and respiratory rate in poikilotherm animals. *Pol. Arch. Hydrobiol.*, **20**, 283–300.

Ivleva I.V. (1980) The dependence of crustacean respiration rate on body mass and habitat temperature. *Int. Rev. ges. Hydrobiol.*, **65**, 1–47.

Jensen C.R., van Gundy S.D. & Stolzy L.H. (1966) Diffusion exchange respirometer using the carbon dioxide electrode. *Nature*, **211**, 608–610.

Kamler E. (1969) A comparison of the closed-bottle and flowing water methods for measurement of respiration in aquatic invertebrates. *Pol. Arch. Hydrobiol.*, **16**, 31–49.

Kersting K. & Van der Leeuw-Leegwater C. (1976) Effect of food concentration on the respiration of *Daphnia magna. Hydrobiologia*, **49**, 137–142.

Kibby H.V. (1971) Energetics and population dynamics of *Diaptomus gracilis. Ecol. Monogr.*, **41**, 311–327.

King F.D. & Packard T.T. (1975) Respiration and the activity of the respiratory electron transport system in marine zooplankton. *Limnol. Oceanogr.*, **20**, 849–854.

Klekowski R.Z. (1971a) Remarks on the use of solid or dropping-mercury electrodes for respirometry of water animals. In W.T.Edmondson & G.G.Winberg (eds.), *A Manual on Methods for the Assessment of Secondary Productivity in Fresh Waters.* IBP Handbook No. 17, p. 288–290, Oxford: Blackwell.

Klekowski R.Z. (1971b) Cartesian diver microrespirometry for aquatic animals. *Pol. Arch. Hydrobiol.*, **18**, 93–114.

Klekowski R.Z. (1975) Constant-pressure volumetric microrespirometer for terrestrial invertebrates. In W.Grodzinski, R.Z.Klekowski & A.Duncan (eds.), *Methods for Ecological Bioenergetics.* IBP Handbook No. 24, p. 212–225, Oxford: Blackwell.

Klekowski R.Z. (1977) Microrespirometer for shipboard measurements of metabolic rate of microzooplankton. *Pol Arch. Hydrobiol. Suppl.*, **24**, 455–465.

Klekowski R.Z. & Kamler E. (1968) Flowing water polarographic respirometer for aquatic animals. *Pol. Arch. Hydrobiol.*, **15**, 121–144.

Klekowski R.Z. & Kamler E. (1971) Flowing water polarographic respirometer. In W.T.Edmondson & G.G.Winberg (eds.), *A Manual on Methods for the Assessment of Secondary Productivity in Fresh Waters*, IBP Handbook No. 17, p. 280–287. Oxford: Blackwell.

Klekowski R.Z., Schiemer F. & Duncan A. (1979) A bioenergetic study of a benthic nematode, *Plectus palustris* de Man 1880, through its life cycle. I. The respiratory metabolism at different densities of bacterial food. *Oecologia (Berl.)*, **44**, 119–124.

Klekowski R.Z., Schiemer F. & Duncan A. (1980) Ampulla gradient diver microrespirometry. *Ekol. Pol.*, **28**, 675–683.

Klekowski R.Z. & Shushkina E.A. (1966). The energetic balance of *Macrocyclops albidus* (Jur.) during the period of its development. (in Russian). In *Ekologya vodnikh organismov.* Moscow: Izdat 'Nauka'.

Konstantinov A.S. (1971) Ecological factors affecting respiration in chironomid larvae. *Limnologica*, **8**, 127–134.

Lampert W. (1975) A tracer study on the carbon turnover of *Daphnia pulex. Verh. Int. Ver. Limnol.*, **19**, 2913–2921.

Lampert W. (1977) Studies on the carbon balance of *Daphnia pulex* (de Geer) as related to environmental conditions. IV. Determination of the 'threshold' concentration as a factor controlling the abundance of zooplankton species. *Arch. Hydrobiol. (Suppl.)*, **48**, 361–368.

La Row E.J., Wilkinson J.W. & Kumar K.D. (1975) The effect of food concentration and temperature on respiration and excretion in herbivorous zooplankton. *Verh. Int. Ver. Limnol.*, **19**, 966–973.

Lasenby D.C. & Langford R.R. (1972) Growth, life history and respiration of *Mysis relicta* in an arctic and temperate lake. *J. Fish. Res. Board Can.*, **29**, 1701–1708.

Lavigne D.M. (1982) Similarity in energy budgets of animal populations. *J. Anim. Ecol.*, **51**, 195–206.

Laybourn-Parry J. & Strachan I.M. (1980) Respiratory metabolism of *Cyclops bicuspidatus* (sensu stricta) (Claus) (Copepoda: Cyclopoida) from Esthwaite Water, Cumbria. *Oecologia (Berl.)*, **46**, 386–390.

Leimeroth N. (1980) Respiration of different stages and energy budgets of juvenile *Brachionus calyciflorus*. *Hydrobiologia*, **73**, 195–197.

Lemcke H.W. & Lampert W. (1975) Veränderungen im Gewicht und der chemischen Zusammensetzung von *Daphnia pulex* im Hunger. *Arch. Hydrobiol. (Suppl.)*, **48**, 108–137.

Løvtrup S. (1973) The construction of a micro-respirometer for the determination of respiratory rates of eggs and small embryos. In G.Kerkut (ed.) *Experiments in Physiology and Biochemistry*, Vol. 6, p. 115–152. New York: Academic Press.

Makarewicz J.C. & Likens G.E. (1979) Structure and function of the zooplankton community of Mirror Lake, New Hampshire. *Ecol. Monogr.*, **49**, 109–127.

Mangum C. & van Winkle W. (1973) Response of aquatic invertebrates to declining oxygen conditions. *Am. Zool.*, **13**, 529–541.

Mann K.H. (1958) Seasonal variation in the respiratory acclimatization of the leech *Erpobdella testacea* (Sav.) *J. Exp. Biol.*, **35**, 314–323.

McNeill J. & Lawton J.H. (1970) Annual production and respiration in animal populations. *Nature*, **225**, 472–474.

Mortimer C.H. (1981) The oxygen content of air saturated fresh waters over ranges of temperature and atmospheric pressure of limnological interest. *Mitt. Int. Ver. Limnol.*, **22**, 1–23.

Moshiri G.A., Cummins K.W. & Costa R.R. (1969) Respiratory energy expenditure by the predaceous zooplankter *Leptodora kindtii* (Focke). *Limnol. Oceanogr.*, **14**, 475–484.

Nagell B. (1973) The oxygen consumption of mayfly (Ephemeroptera) and stonefly (Plecoptera) larvae at different oxygen concentrations. *Hydrobiologia*, **42**, 461–489.

Newell R.C. & Roy A. (1973) A statistical model relating the oxygen consumption of a mollusk (*Littorina littorea*) to activity, body size and environmental conditions. *Physiol. Zool.*, **46**, 253–275.

Nexø B.A., Hamburger K. & Zeuthen E. (1972) Simplified microgasometry with gradient divers. *Compt. Rend. Trav. Lab. Carlsberg*, **39**, 33–63.

Nilsson L.M. (1974) Energy budget of a laboratory population of *Gammarus pulex* (Amphipoda). *Oikos*, **25**, 35–42.

Nimi A.J. (1978) Lag adjustment between estimated and actual physiological responses conducted in flow-through systems. *J. Fish. Res. Board Can.*, **35**, 1265–1269.

Northby J.A. (1976) A comment on rate measurements in open systems. *Limnol. Oceanogr.*, **21**, 180–182.

Nowak K.W. (1975). Die Bedeutung des Zooplanktons für den Stoffhaushalt des Schierensees. *Arch. Hydrobiol.*, **75**, 149–224.

Obreshkove V. (1930) Oxygen consumption in the developmental stages of a cladoceran. *Physiol. Zool.*, **3**, 271–282.

Obreshkove V. & Abramowitz A. (1932) Temperature characteristics for the oxygen consumption of a cladoceran. *J. Cellular Comp. Physiol.*, **2**, 133–139.

Ohle W. (1953) Die chemische und die elektrochemische Bestimmung des molekular gelösten Sauerstoffes der Binnengewässer. *Mitt. Int. Ver. Limnol.*, **3**, 1–44.

Opitz E. & Bartels H. (1955) Gasanalyse. In E.F.Hoppe-Seyler & H. Thierfelder (eds.), *Handbuch der physiologisch- und pathologisch-chemischen Analyse*, p. 183–311. Berlin: Springer.

Owens T.G. & King F.D. (1975) The measurement of respiratory electron-transport-system activity in marine zooplankton. *Mar. Biol.*, **30**, 27–3ʊ

Packard, T.T. (1971) The measurement of respiratory electron transport activity in marine phytoplankton. *J. Mar. Res.*, **29**, 235–244.

Pearcy W.G. & Small L.F. (1968) Effects of pressure on the respiration of vertically migrating crustaceans. *J. Fish. Res. Board. Can.*, **25**, 1311–1316.

Phillipson J. (1970) The 'best estimate' of respiratory metabolism: its applicability to field situations. *Pol. Arch. Hydrobiol.*, **17**, 31–41.

Pilarska J. (1977) Eco-physiological studies on *Brachionus rubens* Ehrbg. (Rotatoria). II. Production and respiration. *Pol. Arch. Hydrobiol.*, **24**, 329–343.

Propp M.V., Garber M.R. & Ryabuscko V.I. (1982) Unstable processes in the metabolic rate measurements in flow-through systems. *Mar. Biol.*, **67**, 47–49.

Prosser C.L. (ed.) (1973) *Comparative Animal Physiology*, (3rd Ed.), Philadelphia: Saunders.

Prus T. (1972) Energy requirement, expenditure, and transformation efficiency during development of *Asellus aquaticus* L. (Crustacea, Isopoda). *Pol. Arch. Hydrobiol.*, **19**, 97–112.

Ranta E. & Hakala I. (1978) Respiration of *Mysis relicta*. *Arch. Hydrobiol.*, **83**, 515–523.

Rao K.P. & Bullock T.H. (1954) Q_{10} as a function of size and habitat temperature in poikilotherms. *Am. Nat.*, **88**, 33–44.

Raymont J.E. & Krishnaswamy S. (1968) A method for determining the oxygen uptake and carbon dioxide output of *Neomysis integer*. *Int. Rev. ges. Hydrobiol.*, **53**, 563–572.

Richman S. (1958) The transformation of energy by *Daphnia pulex*. *Ecol. Monogr.*, **28**, 273–291.

Richman S. (1964) Energy transformation studies on *Diaptomus oregonensis*. *Verh. Int. Ver. Limnol.*, **15**, 654–659.

Roff J.C. (1973) Oxygen consumption of *Limnocalanus macrurus Sars*. (Calanoida, Copepoda) in relation to environmental conditions. *Can. J. Zool.*, **51**, 877–885.

Satomi M. & Pomeroy L.R. (1965) Respiration and phosphorus excretion in some marine populations. *Ecology*, **46**, 877–881.

Scharf E.M., v. Oertzen J.A., Scharf W. & Stave A. (1981) A microflow respirometer for measuring the oxygen consumption of small aquatic organisms. *Int. Rev. Ges. Hydrobiol.*, **66**, 895–901.

Schiemer F. & Duncan A. (1974) The oxygen consumption of a freshwater benthic nematode, *Tobrilus gracilis* (Bastian). *Oecologia (Berl.)*, **15**, 121–126.

Schindler D.W. (1968) Feeding, assimilation and respiration rates of *Daphnia magna* under various environmental conditions and their relation to production estimates. *J. Anim. Ecol.*, **37**, 369–385.

Scholander P.F., Claff C.L., Andrews J.R. & Wallach D.F. (1952) Microvolumetric respirometry. *J. gen. Physiol.*, **35**, 375–395.

Shcherbakoff A.P. (1935) Über den Sauerstoffverbrauch von einigen Planktoncrustaceen. *Arb. Limnol. Stat. Kossino*, **19**, 67–89.

Siefken M. & Armitage K.B. (1968) Seasonal variation in metabolism and organic nutrients in three *Diaptomus* (Crustacea, Copepoda) *Comp. Biochem. Physiol.*, **4**, 591–609.

Sigmon C.F., Tombes A.C. & Tilly L. (1978) Diel oxygen uptake in *Chaoborus punctipennis* (Diptera: Culicidae) *Hydrobiologia*, **61**, 69–73.

Sorokin Yu. I. (1968) The use of ^{14}C in the study of nutrition of aquatic animals. *Mitt. Int. Ver. Limnol.*, **16**, 1–41.

Standard Methods for the Examination of Water and Waste-water. (1976) 14th ed., New York: Amer. Public Health Association, Inc.

Straškraba M. (1967) Estimation of respiration in the field of natural populations of Cladocera and Copepoda using the quantitative method of plankton sorting. *Arch. Hydrobiol.*, **63**, 497–511.

Strickland J.D.H. (1960) Measuring the production of marine phytoplankton. *Bull. Fish. Res. Board. Can.*, **122**, 1–172.

Stumm W. & Morgan J.J. (1981) *Aquatic Chemistry*, 2nd Ed., New York: Wiley.

Sushchenya L.M. (1970) Food rations, metabolism and growth of crustaceans. In J.H.Steele (ed.), *Marine Food Chains*, p. 127–141. Berkeley: University of California Press.

Swift M.C. (1976) Energetics of vertical migration in *Chaoborus trivitattus* larvae. *Ecology*, **57**, 900–914.

Talling J.F. (1973) The application of some electrochemical methods to the measurement of photosynthesis and respiration in freshwaters. *Freshw. Biol.*, **3**, 335–362.

Teal J.M. (1971) Respiration and energy flow. In W.T.Edmondson & G.G.Winberg (eds.) *A Manual on Methods for the Assessment of Secondary Productivity in Fresh Waters.* IBP Handbook No. 17, p. 270–276, Oxford: Blackwell.

Teal J.M. & Halcrow K. (1962) A technique for measurement of respiration of single copepods at sea. *J. Cons. Int. Explor. Mer.*, **27**, 125–128.

Teal J. M. & Kanwisher J. (1966) The use of pCO_2 for the calculation of biological production, with examples from waters of Massachusetts. *J. Mar. Res.*, **24**, 4–14.

Threlkeld S. (1976) Starvation and the size structure of zooplankton communities. *Freshw. Biol.*, **6**, 489–496.

Trama F.B. (1972) Transformation of energy by an aquatic herbivore (*Stenonema pulchellum*) Ephemeroptera. *Pol. Arch. Hydrobiol.*, **19**, 113–121.

Tschumi P.A., Zbären D. & Zbären J. (1977) An improved oxygen method for measuring primary production in lakes. *Schweiz. Z. Hydrol.*, **39**, 306–313.

Ulanoski J.T. & McDiffett W.F. (1972) Diurnal variations in respiration of mayfly nymphs (Ephemeroptera). *Physiol. Zool.*, **45**, 97–105.

Vargo S.L. & Forcé R.K. (1981) A simple photometer for precise determination of dissolved oxygen concentration by the Winkler method with recommendations for improving respiration rate measurements in aquatic organisms. *Estuaries*, **4**, 70–74.

Verduin J. (1951) Photoxynthesis in naturally reared aquatic communities. *Plant Physiol.*, **26**, 45–49.

Vlymen W.J. (1970) Energy expenditure of swimming copepods. *Limnol. Oceanogr.*, **15**, 348–356.

Vollenweider R.A. & Ravera O. (1958) Preliminary observations on the oxygen uptake by some freshwater zooplankters. *Verh. Int. Ver. Limnol.*, **13**, 369–380.

Wetzel R.G. & Likens G.E. (1979) *Limnological Analyses*. Philadelphia: Saunders.

Wightman J.A. (1977) Respirometry techniques for terrestrial invertebrates and their application to energetic studies. *N.Z. J. Zool.*, **4**, 453–469.

Winberg G.G. (1956) The metabolic intensity and food requirements of fish. *Fish. Res. Board Can., Transl. Ser.* **194**.

Winberg G.G. (1971) *Methods for the Estimation of Production of Aquatic Animals.* London, New York: Academic Press.

Winkler L.W. (1888) Die Bestimmung des im Wasser gelösten Sauerstoffs. *Ber Dtsch. Chem. Ges.*, **21**, 2843–2854.

Wotton R.S. (1978) Growth, respiration, and assimilation of blackfly larvae (Diptera; Simuliidae) in a lake-outlet in Finland. *Oecologia (Berl.)*, **33**, 279–290.

Zahner R. (1959) Über die Bindung der mitteleuropäischen *Calopteryx-Arten* (Odonata, Zygoptera) an den Lebensraum des strömenden Wassers. *Int. Rev. ges. Hydrobiol.*, **44**, 51–130.

Zeiss F.R. Jr. (1963) Effects of population densities on zooplankton respiration rates. *Limnol. Oceanogr.*, **8**, 110–115.

Zeuthen E. (1953) Oxygen uptake as related to body size in organisms. *Quart. Rev. Biol.*, **28**, 1–12.

Zeuthen E. (1970) Rate of living as related to body size in organisms. *Pol. Arch. Hydrobiol.*, **17**, 21–30.

Author Index

This index lists the page numbers on which authors are cited. Only the first author is listed when the reference was written by more than two authors.

Taxonomic Index

481

Subject Index

485